Handbook of Moral Motivation

MORAL DEVELOPMENT AND CITIZENSHIP EDUCATION

Series Editors: Fritz Oser (fritz.oser@unifr.ch)
University of Fribourg, Switzerland
Wiel Veugelers (W.M.M.H.Veugelers@uva.nl)
University of Amsterdam/University for Humanistics Utrecht, the Netherlands

'*Moral Development and Citizenship Education*' is a book series that focuses on the cultural development of our young people and the pedagogical ideas and educational arrangements to support this development. It includes the social, political and religious domains, as well as cognitive, emotional and action oriented content. The concept of citizenship has extended from being a pure political judgment, to include the social and interpersonal dynamics of people.

Morality has become a multifaceted and highly diversified construct that now includes cultural, developmental, situational and professional aspects. Its theoretical modelling, practical applications and measurements have become central scientific tasks. Citizenship and moral development are connected with the identity constitution of the next generations. A caring and supporting learning environment can help them to participate in society.

Books in this series will be based on different scientific and ideological theories, research methodologies and practical perspectives. The series has an international scope; it will support manuscripts from different parts of the world and it includes authors and practices from various countries and cultures, as well as comparative studies. The series seeks to stimulate a dialogue between different points of view, research traditions and cultures. It contains multi-authored handbooks, focusing on specific issues, and monographs. We invite books that challenge the academic community, bring new perspectives into the community and broaden the horizon of the domain of moral development and citizenship education.

Handbook of Moral Motivation

Theories, Models, Applications

Edited by;

Karin Heinrichs
Goethe-University Frankfurt, Germany

Fritz Oser
University of Fribourg, Switzerland

and

Terence Lovat
University of Newcastle, Australia & University of Oxford, UK

SENSE PUBLISHERS
ROTTERDAM/BOSTON/TAIPEI

A C.I.P. record for this book is available from the Library of Congress.

ISBN: 978-94-6209-273-0 (paperback)
ISBN: 978-94-6209-274-7 (hardback)
ISBN: 978-94-6209-275-4 (e-book)

Published by: Sense Publishers,
P.O. Box 21858,
3001 AW Rotterdam,
The Netherlands
https://www.sensepublishers.com/

Printed on acid-free paper

TABLE OF CONTENTS

PART 7: MORAL MOTIVATION AND MORAL EDUCATION

KARIN HEINRICHS, FRITZ OSER & TERENCE LOVAT

INTRODUCTION

Immoral behaviour is omnipresent: In the daily news, we read about aggressive behaviour, delinquency, sexual abuse, assassinations and racism, sexism and all forms of persistent violence. We hear about banking bonuses, about structural injustice towards immigrants and substantial egocentrism with respect to animals and plants. At the same time, however, we complain about a lack of civility, civil courage, care, responsibility or tolerance in everyday life or we try to find appropriate solutions to ethical problems like immigration or mobbing. What is the force that pushes people to act morally or not? Is there a motor that inhibits morality? Is there a power that – even beyond judgment and rationality - shakes the will to be fully moral? Are there situations or emotional states that make people forget the standards of morality that civilizations have developed over thousands of years?

In spite of all our knowledge and progress, and partly owing to overwhelming problems like pollution, population increase or climate change, and economic injustices, we are still not able to provide sufficient answers to the following questions:

– Why don't people act morally even though they have such great knowledge, so many insights and/or are personally concerned? And what causes them to behave immorally?
– What prevents them from acting consistently, according to their moral judgment, about what should be done?

The editors of this handbook believe that the construct of moral motivation can – at least partly – answer these questions. Even though motivational psychology has achieved many insights into what drives people to behave and to act in general, our knowledge is much less specific about what urges us to cope with and solve *moral* problems appropriately. The drive to do the good is not the same as the drive to win in sport. The need to help another is not the same as the need to perform well in a test. And the external conditions for maintaining a rule of justice or to take responsibility for a socially deprived person is not the same as listening to a well-known musical piece.

The Handbook of Moral Motivation aims to present currently explored approaches and the state of the art in research about what drives, urges and impels humans to moral judging and acting, as well as about the inner and outer conditions preventing us from acting consistently with our judgments or moral norms. In order to understand the basics, it is good to be aware of Kohlberg's, Rest's, Colby & Damon's, or Blasi's

K. Heinrichs, F. Oser & T. Lovat (Eds.), Handbook of Moral Motivation: Theories, Models, Applications, 1–6.

work, but also to understand some philosophical bases like Kant's metaphysik, Arendt's moral philosophy, Rawls' justice, or Habermas' procedural morality concepts. On these bases, we have attempted to collect important results and insights from the fields of moral and motivational psychology, and related fields, in order to elaborate and discuss whether we have already gained answers to the questions above. Moreover, we wanted to point to the lack of adequate research and develop perspectives for further projects in order to get closer to answering the basic questions about why people are willing and manage to do the good or the bad and to act morally or immorally.

What do we already know? Moral psychology has been searching for explanations of immoral behaviour for many decades (see Garz, Oser & Althof, 1999 on the issue of the judgment action gap). As Oser explicates in his paper (this volume), we know at least 12 models are developed in this field that help to explain (or explain partly) why people manage to be good and feel urged to act in ways considered as morally adequate (Kohlberg & Candee, 1984; Rest, 1999; Bebeau & Monson, 2011; Blasi, 1980; Nunner-Winkler & Sodian, 1988; Colby & Damon, 1992; Walker, 2002; Krettenauer, 2011; Haidt, 2001). Though Rest himself admitted in 1999 that moral motivation was the worst elaborated component of his model and lacked appropriate empirical evidence (Rest, 1999, p.109), we notice that there has been much progress in theoretical and empirical research on this issue during the last decade. Approaches to moral motivation (MM) have been more and more elaborated and interlinked with one another. Nonetheless, the current state of the art still points to there being many different perspectives on moral motivation. Comparing the results of related empirical research on moral motivation would be too difficult because different studies refer to varied types of moral problems, moral contexts or psychological preconditions of these, as well as focusing on differences, for example according to age, cultural background, developmental state or personal experience. The scientific landscape on this issue elicits a kind of atomistic topology and the discussion on moral motivation has to be considered as disconnected from fields in other psychological sub-disciplines. So, in line with Lapsley and Narvaez, we would claim that moral psychology is at the crossroads (Lapsley & Narvaez, 2005). There is an unsatisfied demand for enriching research on moral issues and especially on moral motivation and responsibility in the Kohlbergian, Selmanian, Nuccian, and other traditions, for broadening perspectives, thinking 'outside the box' of moral psychology and crossing disciplinary borders.

The concept of MM is unique. Here are three examples: When Arendt (2003) asks who was motivated to resist in World War II, she answers that you find people in each life setting, within poor and rich, within educated and non-educated, the 'holy' and unholy, the naturally heroic and unheroic: people in differing circumstances but all reaching the point where they knew that they couldn't live anymore without acting. Or, when Gibbs (2010) speaks about "the mutual help" approach, asking who were the ones who went forward to challenge those "who regularly victimize others and society" (p. 153). The motive was that the power of such people, for example, alcoholics had to be turned around and thus the drive becomes a different, now positive goal. Or, Damon in "The path to purpose" (2008) states: "Others are involved in civic or political causes, such as lobbying for stronger gun control or environmental regulation, and rallying support for Mideast peace…The clarity of purpose generates in them a prodigious amount of extra positive energy, which not only motivates them to pursue their goal passionately but also to acquire the skills and knowledge they need for this task" (pp. 79-80). All this is motivation, or, in other words, a search for the reason to act. And it is of course not only from one dimension but from a whole cluster of dimensions that a person is driven to fulfill agency.

In the book, we thus intend to induce a sophisticated discussion on moral motivation across disciplines and lines of research - convinced that research on "why be good?" and "how to be driven towards moral action?" is a very important and emerging field of research endeavour.

We encouraged authors from different disciplines to contribute and present their perspectives on how people act morally for the good or bad or how they are driven or impelled to fulfill either the one or the other.

Within our book, we tried to group the chapters into seven parts, referring to different perspectives and models of moral motivation, on the one hand, and two stand alone chapters, on the other hand, providing an umbrella perspective in order to summarize and discuss the presented chapters:

- The book begins with Oser's chapter in order to open the reader's mind to how different currently discussed approaches to moral motivation are. Oser identifies and differentiates 12 different models of moral motivation, summarizing currently discussed concepts of moral motivation. This chapter is followed by seven parts, collecting all the chapters on moral motivation.
- In Part 1, we look for basic foundations on how to conceptualize moral motivation, approaches that are broadly in line with Rest and Kohlberg, as well as other critical and enriching conceptions.
- In Part 2, different concepts of motivation developed in motivational psychology (attribution theory, expectancy-value models, theory of interest, self-determination theory, volitional psychology) are applied specifically to the issue of motivation, as well as motivational deficits in morally relevant situations. Additionally, authors provide a social psychological perspective insofar as they discuss how temporal distance or perceived injustice could contribute to moral motivation.
- Part 3 opens the way to pointing to the personal determinants that are relevant to being driven to act morally by having developed a "moral identity" or a "moral self".
- In Part 4, we raise the question about how moral motivation could develop from early childhood to adulthood, focusing on cognitive, emotional and situational aspects.
- In Part 5, the authors provide approaches to the issue of people who lack moral motivation or conduct themselves immorally, and how they decide between "good" and "bad".

- In Part 6, we followed Rest's advice to study moral motivation in the professions and present different approaches to moral motivation in different professions: dentistry, law, the military as well as teaching and school leadership.
- In Part 7, all chapters concentrate on the field of education and ask how to develop or foster moral motivation.
- As a counterpoint to Oser's chapter at the beginning, Heinrichs provides a chapter at the end that offers a systematic discussion of the presented contributions in parts 1 to 7. She refers to an action-theoretical framework that offers an umbrella-perspective in order to compare the presented approaches on moral issues systematically and to clear the way for an integrative approach about the study of motivational processes and moral action. This chapter could be regarded as an attempt to take a further step forward towards closing the judgment-action gap.

As described, the book offers a contemporary and comprehensive appraisal of an age-old and yet to be fully determined and satisfactorily answered question about motivation to do the good. It utilizes the latest research from a wide range of disciplinary perspectives, wishing to suggest by this that the answer to the question, if to be found at all, will likely not come from one discipline and that the narrowly constructed research approach of the recent past might have contributed to closing off rather than opening up the interdisciplinary lines of research necessary to tackling an issue of such proportions. We commend this research to you, the reader, and we hope it contributes to better understanding of ourselves as a moral species.

REFERENCES

Arendt, H. (2003). Some questions of moral philosophy. In: J. Kohn (ed. of the writings of Arendt), *Responsibility and judgment* (pp. 52–55). New York: Schocken.

Blasi, A. (1980). Bridging moral cognition and moral action: A critical review of the literature. *Psychological Bulletin, 88*, 1–45.

Bebeau, M.J. (2002). The defining issues test and the four component model: Contributions to professional education. *Journal of Moral Education, 31*(3), 271–295.

Bebeau, M.J., & Monson, V.E. (2011). Professional Identity Formation and Transformation Across the Life Span. In A. McKee & M. Eraut (Eds.), *Learning Trajectories, Innovation and Identity for Professional Development: Innovation and Change in Professional Education* (pp. 135–163). Dordrecht et al.: Springer.

Colby, A., & Damon, W. (1992). *Some do care: Contemporary lives of moral commitment.* New York: Free Press.

Damon, W. (2008). *The path to purpose.* New York: Free Press.

Garz D., Oser, F. & Althof, W. (1999). *Moralisches Urteil und Handeln.* Frankfurt: Suhrkamp.

Gibbs, J.C. (2010). *Moral development & reality.* Boston: Allyn & Bacon.

Haidt, J. (2001). The emotional dog and its rational tail: A social intuitionist approach to moral judgment. *Psychological Review, 108*, 814–834.

Heinrichs, K. (2005). *Urteilen und Handeln in moralrelevanten Situationen. Ein Prozessmodell und seine moralpsychologische Spezifizierung.* Frankfurt/Main u.a.: Peter-Lang-Verlag.

Kohlberg, L., & Candee, D. (1984). *Relations of moral judgment to moral action.* In Kohlberg, L. 1984. Essays on Moral Development. Vol. 2: The Psychology of Moral Development. The Nature and Validity of Moral Stages (pp. 373–493). Harper and Row, San Francisco.

Krebs, D.L. & Denton, K. (2005): Toward a more pragmatic approach to morality: A critical evaluation of Kohlberg's model. *Psychological Review, 112* (3), 629–649.

Krettenauer, T. (2011). The dual moral self: Moral centrality and intrinsic moral motivation. *The Journal of Genetic Psychology, 172*, 309–328. doi: 10.1080/00221325.2010.538451

Krettenauer, T. & Eichler, D. (2006). Adolescents' self-attributed emotions following a moral transgression: relations with delinquency, confidence in moral judgment, and age. *British Journal of Developmental Psychology, 24*, 489–506.

Lapsley, D. & Narvaez, D. (Eds.) (2009). *Personality, Identity, and Character: Explorations in Moral Psychology*. New York: Cambridge University Press.

Lapsley, D.K. & Narvaez, D. (2005). Moral psychology at the crossroads. In D.K. Lapsley & F.C. Power (Eds.), *Character psychology and character education* (pp. 18–35). Notre Dame, Louisiana: University of Notre Dame Press.

Malti, T., Gummerum, M., Keller, M., & Buchmann, M. (in press). Children's sympathy and prosocial behavior: The role of moral motivation. *Child Development*.

Minnameier, G. (2010). The problem of moral motivation and the Happy Victimizer Phenomenon – Killing two birds with one stone. *New Directions for Child and Adolescent Development, 129*, 55–75

Narvaez, D. & Lapsley, D. (2005). Psychological foundations of everyday morality and moral expertise. In D.K. Lapsley & Power F. Clark (Eds.), *Character Psychology and Character Education* (pp. 140–165). Notre Dame: Notre Dame University.

Nunner-Winkler, G. (2009). Moral motivation from childhood to early adulthood. In W. Schneider and M. Bullock (Eds.), *Human Development from Early Childhood to Early Adulthood* (pp. 91–118). New York: Psychology Press.

Nunner-Winkler, G. (1999). Moralische Motivation und moralische Itdentität. Zur Kluft zwischen Urteil und Handeln. In D. Garz, F. Oser & W. Althof (Eds.), *Moralisches Urteil und Handeln* (pp. 314–339). Frankfurt/Main: Suhrkamp.

Nunner-Winkler, G. & B. Sodian (1988). Children's understanding of moral emotions. *Child Development, 59*, 1323–1338.

Oser, F. (1999). Die missachtete Freiheit moralischer Alternativen: Urteile über Handeln, Handeln ohne Urteile. In D. Garz, F. Oser & W. Althof (Eds.), *Moralisches Urteil und Handeln* (pp. 168–219). Frankfurt/Main: Suhrkamp

Oser, F., Schmid, E. & Hattersley, L. (2006): The ,unhappy moralist' effect: Emotional conflicts between being good and being successful. In L. Verschaffel (Ed.), *Instructional Psychology: Past, present and future trends* (pp. 149–166). Amsterdam: Elsevier.

Rest, J.R. (1999). Die Rolle des moralischen Urteilens im moralischen Handeln. In D. Garz, F. Oser & W. Althof (Eds.), *Moralisches Urteil und Handeln* (pp. 82–116). Frankfurt/Main: Suhrkamp.

Rest, J.R., Narvaez, D., Thoma, S.J., & Bebeau, M. (2000). A neo-Kohlbergian approach to moral judgment: Overview of the Defining Issues Test Research. *Journal of Moral Education, 29*, 381–397.

Walker, L.J. (2002). Moral exemplarity. In W. Damon (Ed.), *Bringing in a new era in character education* (pp. 65–83). Stanford, CA: Hoover Institution Press.

FRITZ OSER

MODELS OF MORAL MOTIVATION

INTRODUCTION

The issue of Moral Motivation (MM) has, on the one hand, a long and deeply ingrained history but, on the other hand, is possessed by very few clearly defined conceptions. This makes it difficult to declare whether our generation is merely repeating formulas of the past or, as is often claimed, is on the verge of paradigm change or at least the formation of a paradigm shift allowing for an acceptable model of MM that might supersede former models and sub- models. Motivation is a scientific notion with three focusses: a) goal orientation, b) energizing processes and c) perseverance (Rheinberg & Vollmeyer, 2008, 391). Historically, MM starts with the famous "daimonion" of Socrates that tells humans what *not* to do and pulls them away from the wrong things that sometimes develop in their minds. The daimonion does not however indicate what to <u>do</u>, but merely indicates the probable wrongness of the agent.

In the Middle Ages, it was Thomas Aquinas who developed the concept of two consciences, one titled synderesis (inborn force), the other conscientia (learned rule sensibility) both of motivating the person to do the right, but sometimes contradicting each other. A wonderful tractatus on the foundations of morality stems from the philosopher, Schopenhauer, in which he describes "egoism" as the strongest moral motivational force including in its capacity for organizing a life of survival and happiness. This is why he conceives of a moral deed as moral if it is free from any self-centred needs fulfillment. The absence of egoistic motives makes an act in itself moral. In the elimination of self-centric motives, morality begins to develop a face. Freud's notion of the "superego" is another important model for explaining why people act morally or immorally. The superego is a learned or socialized inner force that reacts alarmingly if wrongness supersedes rightness. Furthermore, the motivational concept of Tugendhat (1986) speaks about indignation as the motivating force for fighting for justice, care and truthfulness. If someone suffers indignation, he/she is able to stand up and act morally in a solid and convincing way.

All these models are metaphors of the human search for what moves persons to be just, caring and truthful. Most of these traditional concepts mix moral knowledge, judgment and feelings, and, only in recent decades, have researchers tried to disentangle these capacities, taking into account situational influences and personal differences. Thus, the issue of moral motivation is not the only notion relevant to the question "Why be moral?"; many other moral concepts are essential to explaining this, especially moral reasoning, moral self-efficacy and moral responsibility.

K. Heinrichs, F. Oser & T. Lovat (Eds.), Handbook of Moral Motivation: Theories, Models, Applications, 7–24.

Rather, moral motivation is about "what forces us to act?" after moral deliberation of personal and societal consequences.

There are two ways of seeing and framing MM. The first consists in forming the researched construct from classical motivational theories such as expectancy value theory (Heckhausen, 1987), attributional theories (Weiner, 1988; 2006), self determination theory (Deci & Ryan, 1993), flow concept (Csikszentmihalyi, M., 1990) and interests theories (Schiefele, 2011; Krapp in this volume). Here, as suggested, goal orientation, intentionalities, energizing processes, perseverance, and similar theories constitute general topics. In this case, the moral content is just one application field, such as being motivated to drive a car or to study music, or being motivated to solve a mathematical task or do sport, etc. One of the basic aspects of all these theories is that the general concept can be isolated from different application settings and academic or professional fields. For this first way (see Krapp, and/or Weiner in this volume), we can learn how measurement issues, with respect to general motivational theories, can be solved. Expectancy theories for instance work within the construct "hope for success" versus "fear from failure".

The second way to study moral motivation is different. The framing here starts by analyzing the specific content of a social or moral situation and its intentionalities, such as to be just, not to lie, to help the poor, to invest in supererogative forms of political actions, etc. (see Youniss & Reinders, 2010). The specificity of the moral ought and the situational moral claims offer another picture about why we should act morally and how we are pushed or pulled to keep a rule, a promise, or to balance care, justice and truthfulness, or else to look for excuses and for pretexts not to do so. MM, in this sense, is the drive to fulfill (or prevent from) a basically human demand by the fact that rules of moral conduct (like the ten commandments) are taken as guidelines for realizing a good life, but also connote personal obligation. Thus, the combination of a) inner readiness and willpower, b) outer situational concrete circumstances and conflicts between two goods and, c) a more or less accepted abstract rule system of a society, only makes clear how much MM is also – besides being a personality construct – an educational claim. The distinction between a) MM, b) moral motives and, c) moral claims, as Wren proposes it (in this volume), is pre-conditional for a profound understanding of this tension. The first refers to a psychic power, the second to an external influence, and the third to a good life, in respect of a better world. All three go together, but it makes sense for analytical purposes to disentangle them.

Often forgotten, but central to the issue, is (within or outside of the concept of MM), a moral motive. To assign a motive to someone means to understand the reason for an act, attributionally or predictively; it is a stimulus towards central moral ideas that are guiding humans. Motives to perform well or to be competent (performance motive), to be dominant (power motive), to have new relationships and be part of the group (affiliation motif), and, of course, to be just/ to help others (general moral motif) are more or less strong predictors for moral agency (Haste & Locke, 1983; introduction). Motifs are situation-independent, but are more easily activated in motif related specific situations, such as hope and fear for performance motivation (see Rheinberg & Vollmeyer, 2008, 2012). Many of the chapters in this volume stress moral motifs. A moral motif is a central ethical value that guides a person in a morally relevant situation. A motif can be covered with excuses or hidden or just pseudo accepted, quasi as a pretext for not doing the expected action. Situated stimulation of the motifs, striving to fulfill a motif or struggling to reach a motif, are all referred to as motivation. The motif to keep the Ten Commandments because of religious belief leads to MM in the sense that fulfilling one of these commandments in a critical situation is central to a person's morality. One specific aspect of MM is that the core moral motif is negatively framed. Not to lie, not to steal, not to harm, not to discriminate, etc. are important moral motifs which can be grouped under the guidance of the goal "to realize justice".

In this handbook, different models of MM are proposed. Some go back to the Kohlberg/Candee paradigm, many to Blasi's moral self-concept approach, while others merely propose elements or preconditions of MM. In my own contribution, I try to reconstruct them and, at the end of this chapter, I offer a synopsis that includes other important aspects of what might be classed as MM. In general, we understand by MM three types of meaning, namely, a) to act morally instead of immorally, b) to be forced (pushed or pulled) to consider the moral point of view, even if we do not act on it, and, c) to consider sentiments or feelings of being responsible (for instance, to accept a sense of ethics in a situation of fear, or to keep hope in a contingent situation of danger or to see pro-social necessities as relevant and central (Staub et al., 1984)).

Since we have carefully selected, in this volume, chosen authors who are specialists on research in moral psychology or a related field, our goal was to address the question of whether motivation as the psychological force for taking certain action is a content specific issue (e.g. Selman, or Thoma & Bebeau, in this volume) or merely a generalized driving force pushing or pulling people in a certain direction (e. g. Weiner, or Krapp, in this volume). From the point of view of moral psychology, we have to connect motivation with a specific content, namely moral demands, moral norms, moral values, and, from a domain specific point of view, from social, political, religious or personal values. From the perspective of educational psychology, we have to consider – as suggested before – different types of motivation.

In my contribution, these models will be presented in an attempt to clarify the different concepts by looking at the respective distinguishable criteria.

A STORY TO BEGIN WITH:

In order to circumscribe the phenomenon of MM, Curcio (2008) uses a convincing story: It is Friday evening. The solders want to leave for the weekend. The commander of the company discovers that, after the exercise with live ammunition, three hand grenades are missing. A certain commander stops the weekend leave and orders a search for the missing weapons. Other commanders disagree with this action.

The commander who chooses to retain the 300 soldiers, albeit with all the problems of dissatisfaction and grumbling, has – what we call - responsibility motivation. He is motivated to change the situation and to ensure that children should not be exposed to the danger of an explosion. The other commanders do not have responsibility motivation. As Curcio shows, however, most commanders are at the same stage of the DIT measure (see Rest, 1986), the same intelligence characteristics, similar social contexts, similar status in the military force, and even similar status in the private job carrier (Switzerland has no professional army but only a public militia army), etc. Thus, if the personality constraints are the same, yet the action differs so fundamentally, responsibility motivation, or MM as a general construct is at stake. Interviews elicit that: all people have motives for acting or not acting (cognitive disequilibrium); all have situational knowledge for accepting or denying its seriousness; all reflect about possible consequences (cognitive equilibrium gap); some do not see the action possibilities (seeing the action as impossible); some are denying the sense of necessity (no necessity for acting); some show the will to act against resistance; some try to overcome the fear (very high emotional fear or shame blocking the action); and, some do or do not use their moral identity concept to balance justice, care and truthfulness in this situation. Furthermore, some even show no effort aimed at accomplishing the perceived goals (no volition).

A similar phenomenon was found with regard to small children: (Gasser & Keller, 2009) found that young children do have knowledge about rules, do know about the consequences of bad acting, are at the same stage of moral development, but still differentiate, the one group engaging in mobbing, for instance, the other not.

Thus, in critical situations, political, military and school leaders, but also CEOs of banks and business institutions, might or might not take responsibility for a believed necessary action that is felt under their charge. They are or are not morally motivated. If motivated, they feel accountable; if not, they feel irresponsible. The interesting case is seen where they feel motivated but do not act on it. The question thus is about how these subjects react in a pre-decisional phase, in the decision phase and, afterwards, with respect to their responsibility judgment, and with respect to their felt accountability towards the content, the persons and the methods for solving the respective problematic issue. As Curcio (2008) proposed, we use, on the one hand, aspects of an extended motivation model of Heckhausen (2003) and Rheinberg (2002) and, on the other hand, philosophical elements of a responsibility ethics (Jonas, 1986; Bayertz, 1995) in relation to moral judgment issues of the Kohlbergian and the post-Kohlbergian frame (Kohlberg, 1984; Thoma, 2006) and, finally, central elements of the model of procedural morality. Leaders, similar to children in what are doubtlessly personally concerned critical incident situations, take or do not take responsibility when they refer to the imagined consequences of their action or their non-action and/or to a more or less orthodox rule and principle-orientation. If the consequences are strong, they mostly use a forward strategy of action. If the consequences are low, they often use a rule based strategy, (eg. delegating the responsibility – see Garz, 1999, on week and strong norms in the judgment action context). These facts illustrate the high complexity of MM as a dynamic concept.

Before starting into the models (or the elements of models), we of course know that some of the selected chapters fit with different approaches. For instance, Althof and Berkowitz (in this volume) are relevant certainly for model 1 and model 11, as they rely on a vision, but also deal with content, virtues and moral motifs. This is important because we accept the fact that, the more complex a concept is, the more overlapping models are needed for its causal explanation. The simpler a concept, the more experimentally framed the central determinants can be. If we were to strengthen our investigation into the differentiation between intrinsic and extrinsic MM, many of the chapters would overlap and include both in the same situation.

A MISSING FACTOR: THE GOOD, THE BAD AND THE UGLY

Most of the papers in this volume treat MM as if we know what the good and the bad is in each situation. However, human existence is framed by the fact that often-conflicting values do not restrict the outcome to one clear act. Kohlberg (1981) already stressed this by his simple Heinz-dilemma test, namely, that the outcome itself is often ambiguous. Being motivated to do the right thing means a search for the right thing, accompanied often with doubts and crises. Thus, in this volume, we often do not distinguish between motivation for doing the right thing and motivation for doing the wrong thing. Doing something bad can have at least three motivational dimensions: a) we do it because we are not motivated to do the right thing (e. g. if we do not help because helping will take too much time and it is merely a non-obligatory duty anyway); b) we do it because we are motivated to do the wrong thing (e. g. to sell drugs because of the possibility of an enormous money gain); and, c) we do it because we are the victim of a psychological fallacy, as Zimbardo (2007) infers through his 'Lucifer effect' in which people turn into villainous actors treating others with painful methods and harmful and torturous techniques. This distinction, combined with a theory of domain specificity, would give the concept of MM a new face. In this volume, however, we have merely set out to define and ground the status of the concept in order to generate later a possible new theory of MM.

12 MODELS (OR ELEMENTS OF A RESPECTIVE MODEL)

Model 1: A Vision as MM

Maybe the most simple and most common, but also most powerful moral motivational concept is to build up a vision for the better functioning of a system and then interpret pathways and steps towards the fulfillment of that vision as absolutely necessary. For this model, the following elements are offered:

a) there must be a feeling of insufficiency with respect to moral standards (students in a school steal, cheat, mob, lie, do not clean their study places, do not show helping behaviour, are unfriendly);

b) there must be a general view that we should overcome this state and start a new politick, realizing a (often not very precise) vision;

c) the practical view is "we can have a socio morally better school" that entails more respect, more responsibility, more shared norms (note: the saying is not less cheating, less stealing, less lying, more helping, etc., but it contains a general view of change towards human virtues);

d) there are imagined sources of possible action that, it is believed, can lead to change. These action possibilities are also decided openly and often standardized as rule enforcement.

MM here means a tension between a visionary moral state of a system and the daily struggle for reaching, at least partly, this state. Campbell (in this volume) speaks about a dual expectation, first, exacting ethical standards and, second, a concern the teacher has as an educator and model. Building up such a professional moral sense is an example of a learning process. Teachers' internships can be a place to become morally motivated through practising ethical decision-making (Oja and Craig, in this volume). In a new study, Varghese (2012) investigates the effectiveness of civic education programs, comparing teachers of Karela (in India) with teachers in Switzerland, the former having such a vision, the latter not. Turnaround schools are other good examples for such a motivational concept (Leithwood et al., 2010) in which classroom and school management techniques are believed to lead to moral and pro-social change. "Just community schools" are basically also bound to such a change vision. The title is "How deconstructing the American school system will reconstruct the American school" (Pittella, 2011). In this volume, Lee offers an example of such a basic moral motivational concept, all examples with subtle differentiations. Additional elements like "temporal distance" (see Agerström & Björklund, in this volume) or subcultural norm systems (see Weyers, in this volume) frame this model in the notion of embeddedness in whole correction, school, or work-systems. Measurement is mostly based on a pre- post- follow-up research design.

Model 2: The Moral Act as the Criterion for MM (Kohlberg & Candee)

The presentation of this model is given in Fig. 1 of Minnameier in this volume. In his four steps, Kohlberg thought that moral action depended not only on moral stage /type, but also on the deontic choice (that means yes he/she should or should not do what is at stake), then on a sort of judgment of obligation/responsibility, and finally non moral personality variables like ego controls, IQ, attention, delay of gratification, etc. Kohlberg & Candee presented this model for the first time in 1984 when the criticism in regard to the judgment action gap became central. We have, looking at this model, the possibility to interpret the judgment of responsibility as the moral motivational force. Because when I feel responsible, the probability to act in the desired way is much higher than when I am not obligated. Interestingly, Kohlberg does not speak about MM. So we can see the motivational part either- as mentioned above - as "judgment of responsibility/obligation" - or as one of the ego-controls. If we see it as judgment impelled by obligation, the moral motivational concept would be typically ethics oriented with a special moral feature, namely, precisely to be pushed by one's own personal commitment for being moral. Responsibility/ obligation, in this sense, becomes a moral construct in itself. It is different when we see MM as a personality trait, such as being impelled by ego-controls, self-efficacy or general emotional reaction. In these circumstances, motivation would be outside of the moral realm, namely, as generally being impelled by chance. Even if the model of Kohlberg is plotted as phases, we think that Kohlberg & Candee rather thought of something like factors having simultaneous influences. The measurement of this model is seen in looking at the different factors and comparing or correlating them with the frequencies of an expected moral act. Especially in stage level concepts, measurement of felt obligation and types of moral agency are combined.

Model 3: Deontological and Responsibility Judgment in One as MM

There is an argument that each moral judgment in Kohlberg's stage theory is in itself a moral motivational motor, or, in terms of the Kohlberg/Candee model, each deontic judgment includes or is accompanied necessarily by a responsibility judgment (see Minnameier, in this volume). This position uses a kind of moral internalist argument, suggesting that moral judgments are self-motivating rather than in need of a special force of moral commitment. The logic behind this is that each moral judgment already includes a tendency to act, shown through the concepts of induction, abduction and deduction. One important argument is that all moral motivational concepts include action judgments that are consistent with a serious moral judgment itself. In this model, therefore, the issue is that judgment of morality (ie. what should I do?) and judgment of responsibility (ie. is the act consistent with my moral self?) go together and are separate from phase IV, as Minnameier suggests, namely ego control, delay of gratification, IQ, etc. The phases are: phase I, interpretation and selection of principles; phase II, decision making; phase III, follow through (moral judgment); and, phase IV, follow through (ie. non-moral skills).

Because moral motivation must be possessed of moral grounds, it falls under the command of moral judgment, while "selecting values" (Rest's component III) falls also under the category of judgment. "What Rest calls 'moral motivation' is, in reality a question of moral judgment" (Minnameier, in this volume). In addition, the judgment of responsibility can be seen as a special form of moral judgment itself. This argumentation is related to the hypothesis that any emotional reaction is centrally concerned with content, and that content is part of the judgment structure itself. Thus, according to this model, the three first phases of the Kohlberg/Candee scheme are aspects of moral judgment, and nothing else. Questioning these reflections, we can say that even if so, it is possible to distinguish, not just phases but causal elements of the same judgment. For instance, in terms of multiple regression analysis, we can enquire about how much each of these elements accounts for the explained variance. Then, instead of phases, we can just survey one and the same structure of judgment but this time focusing on deontic, responsibility, value and sincerity (emotional) elements. One problem may be that Rest was turning his components into phases instead of regarding them as terms of causal factors.

Model 4: The Component III (of the Four Component) Model of MM

In this volume, the four-component model of Rest (1983) is often cited and scientists frequently refer to it. The four components are: a) moral judgment, b) moral sensitivity, c) moral motivation, and, d) moral will to act. Originally, the four components resulted from meta- and factor analyses. These components were relatively independent of each other and could be – depending on the situation – more or less adapted and applied.

As Thoma and Bebeau suggest (in this volume), component III is first described as a bridge from a moral situation over the imagined or felt 'ought' to the question of what to do and what decision is the one on which to act. Within the possible alternatives, often conflicting with each other, Rest's component III prioritizes the person's capacity to act under difficult circumstances. Decision making models are substantial parts of component III because, as Rest suggests, the moral action is a precondition for any judgment about others or about societal morality. Additionally, as Thoma and Bebeau (in this volume) stress, Rest developed the four components using a bottom up method, relying on a broad mass of empirical literature.

Component III includes control and competency, but also effective strategies of action planning. If we admit that moral judgments, in the Kohlbergian sense, are prescriptive and that the obligation to act is implicitly given, the moral motivation is something like an inner state, a mechanism leading to act or not to act morally. If the situation is understood as morally necessary and if the action possibilities are coded as worthwhile versus not worthwhile, then moral motivation is the impelling force that determines what has to be seen as good, helpful and appropriate with perseverance. Overcoming resistance and hindering matters are parts of the motivational force. Even if we do not have yet a measure for moral motivation, Rest's model is developmentally framed. This becomes visible if we consult the DIT, which includes at least some moral motivational parts. An excellent application is seen in the work of the Bebeau group, showing precisely this force in professional settings. Related to the clear 'oughts' in the profession, the distinct elements are: …"(1) 'see the ought', a deficiency in moral sensitivity, (2) 'understand the ought', a deficiency in moral reasoning and moral judgment, (3) see the self as responsible 'to do the ought', a deficiency in moral motivation and commitment, or (4) have the will and competence to 'do the ought', a deficiency in moral character and competence". (Bebeau & Monson, 2008, and in this volume). If this is based on the expectations that a society has to the professions and the professions have towards its members, we begin to understand how MM could be framed on the basis of component III and on the basis of what we know from the professional responsibilities. Excellent measurement work in this direction has been done by the Thoma group (Thoma, 2006).

Model 5: The Self as a Regulating Power in MM

"The term 'motivational ability' refers to skills that are important variables in the implementation of personal goals: the skills of motivation regulation (motivating oneself to persevere), decision regulation (quickly coming to a self-congruent decision), activation regulation (readying oneself to act), and self-efficacy (the self being able to bring the intended behaviour to a successful conclusion despite difficulties." (Forstmeier et al., 2012, 353). This is a classical statement of general self-regulation oriented motivation theory. Going a step further, however, is Blasi's concept of the moral self and moral self-management (see in this volume). We discover here that an active guide of the moral functioning of a person's life means monitoring the distance between one's behaviour and the respective goal autonomously. Motivation means an adaptive conscious form of searching for consistency between the situation in which a person has to decide and his/her moral ideal which is part of their ego. Of course, Blasi distinguishes between judgment, the transformation of the judgment into an action and the stability of such actions over days, month and years. Nonetheless, he positions the desire to be moral and to do the moral right thing as firstly intentional and consciously engaging in the realization of one's moral goals. Furthermore, this action must be realized in spite of obstacles, hindering conditions, and any misunderstandings of moral goals and dispositions that a person may have. Interpreting the world through moral criteria means always utilizing moral heuristics, preventing harm and suffering, but striving for reciprocity, care, fairness and justice. The perception of a moral situation, the interpretation through moral criteria, the sensitivity for distortion, errors and self-protecting biases, the transformation into a necessary moral act through moral self-regulation are the elements that comprise moral motivation.

This self-oriented form of moral motivation is interesting because it deals with the fact that "the route from judgment to intention, and from intention to action, can be hesitant, filled with delays, starts-and-stops, fraught by obstacles of different kinds, particularly when the intention has to be realized through a long series of activities" (Blasi, in this volume). Self-monitoring activities thus means consciously ascertaining what is necessary for oneself and how the sense of the self is shaped by moral ideals. Blasi does not speak about the moral personality, because this would be a trait oriented concern; nor does he speak about moral identity which would concern belonging to something or some groups. His moral self is a conscious form of controlled moral identity, of constantly reflected morality and of a rational morality in its emotional expression. Moral motivation is a concept of forced transformation by self-willingness and self-control. That is why the philosopher H. Arendt (2003) speaks about a dialogue with one's self in which we come to a decision whereby the self and the moral demand overlap in a way that I, as the person involved can, after the decision, live with its consequences. Even if no measurement propositions are made, the possible effect of this theoretical top down concept is fruitful because of its validity claim and its existential rootedness.

Krettenauer (in this volume) goes a step further again. For him, the self and morality are one and the same thing. Denying a separation of the two constructs means – at the same time – the suggestion of three layers of this self, the intentional agent, the volitional agent and the identified agent, with each having – even as interweaved elements – a different biographical development and thus stimulating different interacting motivational processes.

Weyers (in this volume) states that there is no remedy for juvenile delinquency but a change of the whole moral self of a young person, not so much a judgment and a remorseful feeling, but a self-transformation through biographical reconstruction. It includes the whole person as a moral subject in a concrete societal context, which is responsible for the possible coming-to-be of a new moral self.

Model 6: Reconciling Agency and Communion as MM

One central characteristic of model 6 (see Walker in this volume) is that it starts with the assumption that MM is always a combination of personality profiles and situational aspects. A further element is that the quest for analyzing moral exemplars is basic for studying motivational aspects of morality which yielded, in earlier work - three clusters of personality types: a) a communal cluster marked by social support and nurturance, b) a deliberative cluster marked by openness for new experiences, and, c) an ordinary cluster marked by normal personality functioning. The two first clusters, expressed through strong topics on a) communion and b) agency or, in other words, on "getting along with" and "getting ahead", produce self-transcendent communal and self-enhancing argentic values. Years ago, both concepts were developed relatively independently of each other, and mostly one stood against the other, but had, if integrated in the one person, a greater potential for predicting MM. The new idea is that the occurrence of both, in a compatible relationship, could produce a greater force being pushed to act because of agency orientation and communion orientation as one moral functioning. Thus, Walker (in this volume) states: "Why be good? Because promoting the interests of others can be fundamentally enhancing to the self" (p. 197). The challenge of this new model is that it is generated from the endpoint of moral development, from an ethical ideal, and it would be worthwhile to investigate the developmental pathway towards its possible growth.

Interesting in Walker's model of reconciliation of agency and communion is that it does not presuppose moral sovereignty. In most of the studies on moral exemplars, the researchers speak about a morally secure and sovereign acting. The moral hero knows what to do and he/she has no doubts about the right thing to do in the situation. To my mind, heroes and models of decision making in concrete moral dilemma situations are models precisely because they contain doubt about which is the right way to go, searching, feeling weaknesses, being insecure, feeling lost, and being internally riven. The moral hero picture is formulated in the following sentence: "Without hesitation or inner conflict and even at high personal cost these persons in their real life decisions gave priority to moral concerns – because morality was constitutive of their identity (happy moralists)" (Nunner-Winkler, in this volume). In our mind, this would be not a moral exemplar, so much as an orthodox morality machine without self-reflection and critical stance and thus become obsolete (see also Thoma & Bebeau in this volume). Of course, moral quality can be conjoined with general happiness, but in general we cannot deny the basic moral core issue, namely, that we need morality only if an immoral situation leads to indignation and a felt disequilibrium.

This also appears in the chapter on moral motivation in the sport setting. As Power (in this volume) suggests, sport is a continuous conflict between a winning tendency and moral duty, team spirit and self-actualization. Models of morality thus do consider what is best for the team, the performance *and* the moral self. The balance of different values is not naturally given, but produces an internal conflict that must be won each and every time. Lovat (in this volume) speaks of MM as a "truly active state of one who is prepared to strike out for moral good, whatever the cost and regardless of expectations" (p. 255). This of course will not eventuate without internal conflict regarding all the costs and consequences.

With respect to measurement, excellent work has been done by the Walker group that developed tested instruments for the communion orientation, the agency orientation and moral centrality.

Model 7: Forming Intentions and Respective Actions as MM

Motivation can be seen as a force compelling action, a veritable package of active elements, by which "individuals formulate beliefs and goals, embrace desires, generate attributions to explain their experiences, and direct their energies as they act" (Thorkildsen, in this volume, p. 85). The most important elements for this model are a) beliefs, b) desires and c) actions. The belief says "I am responsible (or accountable)." The desire says "I want to be a good person/ or rather I want to have a lot of money; I want to be like others/ or I think these laws are lasting." The action says "Let's do this or that (readiness to act)." Instead of relying on moral self and theories of self regulation, this concept is rather intentional; the goal is to understand why people "do what they do and how intentional strategies work to elicit behaviour" (p. 88). The core issue concerns how we form intentions and how we transform these intentions into moral acts. It is important that people produce intentions and relate them to their goals and aspirations. There is a necessity to see how ethical information is used for either producing or supporting what is intended.

The measurement possibilities are given through scales of beliefs and desires, moral aspirations and civil life intentions being correlated with action readiness.

Model 8: Moral Emotion Attributions as Indicators for Individual Moral Motivation

If we take aggressive behaviour as indicative of immoral behaviour, then positive emotion attributions to a perpetrator indicate a strong motivation for one's own aggressive behaviour (see Gasser et al., Krettenauer, and Nunner-Winkler, in this volume). Whereas positive emotions, to oneself as the wrongdoer, are strongly related to one's own negative behaviour; emotional attributions to the perpetrator are less clear. This means that, according to this model, most of how we feel about a perpetrator (or someone who does the good thing) is a causal reason for our own moral (or social) behaviour. Moral emotion ascriptions thus are important indicators even if no financial or material gain is in sight and even if the respective children know the rules and know that the victim feels bad. The schema of multiple sufficient causes is thus overridden by, for example, one's mood, respectively a sufficient feeling with respect to a moral or immoral act. Nunner-Winkler (in this volume) thus concludes that moral motivation is intrinsic (because a norm is transgressed and not because someone will be punished, for example); it is formal (in the sense that subjects do what they feel to be right), and it is a second order desire (if a person does what is right) even if it is in conflict with the first order spontaneous desire. As shown in the same reflections, the transformation of the structure of moral motivation from an external or internal moral motivational authority force to an "ego-syntonic" form with a strong desire to repair makes it clear that emotion attribution is the force for doing what is demanded or for not doing it. As Arendt (1967) states that good persons can have a bad conscience, but that bad persons don't necessarily have a bad conscience. It is indeed very convincing that the emotions attributed to facts elicit the importance that the person ascribes to them. Emotion attribution seems to be an indicator also of moral motivation with respect to actions within relationships, such as friendship, long term relationships in negotiation fields, partnerships, etc. If I consider cheating or hurting a friend in negotiating a conflicting issue, it is a different stance than merely one of winning a bigger part in that negotiation. Friendship thus would make the trading game an intrinsic issue. In this model, the discussion on passion and reasoning becomes central, as Reed (in this volume) illustrates. The different levels of personal functioning are in themselves a navigating moral force.

Measurement issues in the emotion attribution model are illustrated well in experimental work with children, presenting them with stories and material to which to react. Döring (in this volume) offers an outstanding contribution to a highly differentiated measurement process.

Model 9: Justice Motives as Bridges from the Situation to MM

There are two indicators that – according to Baumert et al. (in this volume) – are responsible for the justice motive, namely, belief in a just world and justice sensitivity. These two constructs are central forces for motivating people to act under given circumstances in a specific way, in other words, to be morally motivated. Motives are – in this model – dispositions for striving towards a certain human goal. They are directed against the reductionist model in which every human moral motivation is explained in terms of pure egoism. It includes the justice motive, the injustice experiences with respective feelings of anger, indignation, shame, etc., and then urges the person to restore justice. The more central the justice motive is for the person, the more the overcoming of unjust situations becomes central as a goal. The belief in a just world is related to one's own justice standards, and it is based on an imagined contract defending the positive illusion that everyone gets what he/she deserves, or deserves what she/he gets. Moral sensitivity however is a construct not very much related to this belief, but one nonetheless with high predictive power for acting towards justice. Thus, the individual internalizing principles of deservedness, on the one hand, and justice sensitivity as a central trait, on the other hand, are translated into moral motivation in a self-regulatory process, as further described by Baumert et al. (in this volume). The authors say: "The stronger the justice motive, the more readily justice concerns are activated and the more pronounced the effects on information processing, emotion, and consequently moral motivation are" (p. 173). This process however needs further clarification.

The justice belief is measured by high standardized scales on the "belief in a just world".

Model 10: Informed Social Reflection as MM

Based on the fact that people often do not know their own values, their own systemic embeddedness and their own beliefs (hidden curriculum), Kwok and Selman (in this volume) developed a new theoretical approach; it is based on understanding the past becoming the foundation by which we can fruitfully "navigate our social and cultural environment" (p. 554) in the future. Selman and his group define MM as "occupying a causal role in moral decision-making" (p. 554). When an individual chooses a moral act, he/she uses a catalytic of moral reasoning as an informed justification. Informed understanding means that a person uses his/her whole past to solve a present incident; but not only this; he/she combines what she experienced in an earlier situation with his/her judgment and the respective reflection. The sources of informed social reflections are: a) "Civic orientation", b) "Ethical reflection" and c) "Historical understanding". These elements are mostly effective if MM precedes clearly moral action. In other words, without insight, there is no moral action. Furthermore, this insight is sourced by safety, rules/power, relationships/inclusion and civic incentives. Informed social reflection is the additional gain emanating from any decision-making, in the sense that, with it, we have the guarantee that we can detect egoisms that hinder a positive moral act. Openness thus means that transparency is the moral motivational warranty for choosing the best of the alternatives.

The measurement of informed justification is mostly qualitative in that it opens up the hidden grounding, thought and emotional character of a situation.

Model 11: Motivation by Content: Moral Motifs as MM

A classical motivational concept is interest in a given matter (Schiefele, 2011), content, task, performance or relationship. It is a powerful motor for acting towards such content or within such content. Interest is not justifiable; it is just there. Interest in content is the most intrinsic motivational power that we can understand. For Nucci (2008), it is important to distinguish the so-called domains in the sense that moral, social, personal, religious and political issues do lead to different interests and to different motivational claims. Interests are different in different domains. For Narvaez (in this volume), there are three different contents, namely a safety ethic, an engagement ethic and an imaginative ethic. For Deci & Ryan (1993), it is work fulfilment, relationship (communion) and self determination. For Aristotle, important contents are virtues like justice, courage, loyalty, etc. Situation appropriate compassion (not too much and not too little) and imagination (problem solving capacity) are necessary fundamentals for its realisation. Character education derives from its normative turn: humans shall have such virtues, reflect about their intrinsic necessities and apply them in concrete situations. That is why this movement is targeting a concrete content (knowledge) and a concrete behaviour (competence). The goal is that the content itself makes it worth embarking on. It is motivating within itself, by its very nature. Other than the structural approach, the content motivational approach asks how we can influence people to learn a certain package of important values, to accept them and to apply them at least cognitively to conflicting situations.

Another good example is seen in Klöckner (in this volume). He discusses environmental behaviour, which is directly influenced by, on the one hand, a basic value system and, on the other hand, by norms expressed in expectations and obligations. He speaks about the norm-activation theory in which moral motivation impacts on behaviour. In general, value systems and specific environmental values enter into personal norms and feelings of obligation. Furthermore, the value-belief-norm theory indicates that the real motivation is norm activation, and thus it is moderated by the strength of the knowledge of consequences. Moral motifs in this view can be strong beliefs or weak beliefs (intensity measure); they relate to happiness, to acceptance of oneself, to bounding, to power, or to hope of success/fear of failure; they can be near to or far from one's central value system. They are domain specific. They can also be stage related stimulators of an understood necessary act because they are part of the moral centrality system of a person (see Frimer & Walker, 2009).

This model is a neighbour of the expectation-value motivation theory of Heckhausen (1974), in which the expected outcome and the value of the act itself were said to be influencing directly the respective doing. Also, the approach of Micewski (in this volume) moves – with variations - in the same direction; the value here is the responsibility in the military engagement, thus having concrete motifs that push us to act.

Model 12: Procedural Morality and MM.

Being in a morally relevant conflict situation and anticipating the moral, societal, relational but also financial and status consequences of the respective act, renders the need to form an intention and then to act. This intention is based however on a searched equilibrium between the most important moral duties, namely, justice, care and truthfulness. Often, we experience that being just means not to care, or being caring means not to be truthful. To overcome this conflict, Oser (1998) developed 5 types of dealing with this tension, including a single handed decision making type versus a discourse type based on deliberation and trust in the others' capacity to solve the respective moral problem. In our study, the 5 types of reaction to ethically relevant situations were provided with high external validity attached. The 5 types were: a) avoidance, b) delegating, c) single handed decision making, d) incomplete discourse, and, e) full discourse. These forms are deliberation types. Within the construct of procedural morality, these deliberation forms make a moral problem public and thus distribute the responsibility to act. Part of this model also entails a culture of self-deliberation that is related to an invisible yes-no or neutrality decision in the face of that situation. Anticipating how we act means deliberating the potential consequences of each possible outcome and thus forming an intention. In our first tax cheating study, Oser & Garz (1998) demonstrated that different action scenarios were distinguished by subjects involved in the situation. Dependent on which one of the 5 types of dealing with this tension was enacted, we discovered that the outcome was different. This was the reason that we spoke about procedural morality. As Heinrichs (in this volume) refers to volitional power and energized self-regulation of these action scenarios, they are discourse oriented and thus include also the possible barriers for an action implementation. Thus, the most important elements rest on: a) situational awareness, b) deliberation of all types of consequences, c) the formed and imagined action scenarios, and, d) a "jump" into the act, with all the blind spots with respect to the controllability of what happens. There is in such a process a moment of blind navigating, being typical for what we call a procedural morality, with elements like a moral will that reflects the strength of moral motivation, Another issue concerns exhaustion through a deliberate process and procedural morality in the sense that the outcome is not predetermined (see Apel, 1988). As Krapp (in this volume) clearly states, within any model, the acting (or act or reaction or behaviour) is central to moral relevance. Often, it implicitly includes a loss of financial gain, or a new distribution of goods, or an omission of a habit, or a renouncement of a right, etc. The result of a moral deliberation in the sense of the theory of a realistic discourse thus remains always open. We do not know what the result of a deliberation might be, but we know that the common engagement forces the concerned persons to do afterwards what has been decided. Finally, within this model, we know that the freedom to act (one central condition for morally relevant decision making) can never be fully controlled, and that there is always an unexplained rest, the mentioned jumping into the act, a blind spot which helps us to understand the nature of morality in its special existential frame (see Jaspers, 1956, with his existentialist position on Freedom).

OVERRIDING MORAL MOTIVATIONAL MODEL

In developing the structure and the content of this handbook, we were concerned about having too many different motivational concepts and not enough reality related added value in the sense of one or two new and rather comprehensive models. That is why I have tried to develop: a) an overview of different possible models; but b), also to bring these different elements together in one model. Important elements for such a comprehensive essay on a moral motivational model are seen in Figure 1. Central is the moral self that must be articulated in each new morally relevant situation. The moral judgment and the moral vision are quasi the first and immediate result of this morally activated self. The elements in the second column are additional pre-conditional elements (beliefs, emotion attributions, motifs and interests) for stimulating moral motivational activity characteristics. Depending on the situation and the respective moral maturity and sensibility, these elements receive different values. Column three contains the judgment about my own responsibility and the sense of duty, the former not being the same as the latter. The first would contain a judgment like "I felt responsible for the situation", and the second "I must do it regardless of resistance." Moral deliberation is seen in the fact that the action necessarily becomes public. The topic "free decisional heuristics" means that it is still possible that we cannot act, or decide, or engage if all the elements are given, which was called, in model 12, the blind spot of human liberty in each moral situation. Moral agency finally is the expected outcome, an act that is difficult because it contains the resistance of the context, financial loss, loss of integration into a group, etc.

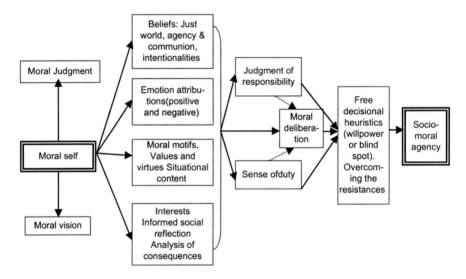

Figure 1: Elements of a global moral motivational model.

This model however is probably not realisable; the task is merely to illustrate how all the dimensions could be brought together, and it represents a synopsis of this handbook. To measure it, we would need many more single relational analyses, for instance, the correlation between the intensity of "deliberation" and the amount of "sense of duty", that is, the relationship between the central moral motive and agency, or the relationship between the moral self and the emotion attribution, or – very importantly – the relationship between judgment of responsibility and sense of duty, or the relationship between the resistance to act and the moral motif power, etc. As it is presented here, the model has a typical differentiation bias; but only in this way does it help us to understand what it means to care about ideas (Noddings, 1992, 2006).

REFERENCES

Apel, K.-O. (1988). *Diskurs und Verantwortung. Das Problem des Übergangs zur post-konventionellen Moral.* (Discourse and responsibility. The problem of the transition into a post-conventional morality). Frankfurt a.M.: Suhrkamp

Arendt, H. (1967, 2006). *Truth and politics* (Wahrheit und Politik). Berlin: Wagenbach

Arendt, H. (2003). *Some questions of moral philosophie* (Über das Böse). München Piper

Bayertz, K. (1995). Eine kurze Geschichte der Verantwortung. (A short history on responsibility.) In. K. Bayertz (Hrsg.). *Verantwortung Prinzip oder Problem?* (pp. 3–71) Darmstadt: Buchgemeinschaft.

Blasi, A. (1984). Moral identiy and its role in moral functioning. In G.L. Gewirtz & W.M. Kurtines (Eds.), *Morality, moral development and behavior* (pp. 128–139). New York: Wiley

Bebeau M.J. & Monson, V. (2008). A way forward for professional ethics education. In: L.P. Nucci & D. Narvaez (Eds.), *Handbook of moral and character education* (pp. 557–582). New York: Routledge.

Csikszentmihalyi, M. & Schiefele, U. (1993): Die Qualität des Erlebens und der Prozess des Lernens. *Zeitschrift für Pädagogik, 39*(2), 207–221

Csikszentmihalyi, M. (1990). *Flow: The psychology of optimal experience.* New York: Harper and Row.

Curcio, G.-P. (2008). *Verantwortungsmotivation zwischen moralität und gerechtigkeit.* (Responsibility motivation between morality and justice). Münster: Waxmann

Deci, E.L. & Ryan, R.M. (1993). Die Selbstbestimmungstheorie der Motivation und ihre Bedeutung für die Pädagogik. *Zeitschrift für Pädagogik, 39,* 223–238.

Forstmeier, S., Maercker, A., van der Bussche, H. and 10 other authors of the AgeCoDe Study Group (2012). Motivational reserve: Motivation-related occupational abilities and risk of mild cocnitve impairment and Alzheimer desease. *Psychology and Aging, 27*(2), 353–363.

Frimer , J.A. & Walker, L.J. (2009). Reconciling the self and morality: An empirical model of moral centrality development. *Developmenal Psychology, 45,* 1669–1681.

Gasser, L., & Keller, M. (2009). Are the competent the morally good? Perspective taking and moral motivation of children involved in bullying. *Social Development,* 18, 798–816.

Garz D. (1999). "Also die Annahme, dass die Wlet gerecht ist, das wäre sehr irrational". Urteil und Handeln und die Moral des Alltagslebens. In Garz, D., Oser, F. & Althof, W. (Eds.), *Moralisches Urteil und Handeln* (Moral judgment and action) (pp. 377–405). Frankfurt a.M.: Suhrkamp.

Garz, D., Oser, F. & Althof, W. (Eds.) (1999). *Moralisches Urteil und Handeln* (Moral judgment and action) Frankfurt a.M.: Suhrkamp.

Haste, H.E. &, Locke, D. (1983). *Morality in the making: Thought, action, and the social context.* New York: John Wiley and Sons Ltd.

Heckhausen, H. (2003). *Motivation und Handeln* (2th ed.). Berlin: Springer,

Heckhausen, H. (1987). Prspektiven einer Psychologie des Wollens. In H. Heckhausen, P.M. Gollwitzer & F.E. Weinert (Eds.), *Jenseits des Rubikon: Der Wille in den Humanwissenschaften* (pp. 143–175). Berlin: Springer.

Heckhausen, H. (1974). *Motivationsforschung.* Volume 2. Leistung und Chancengleichheit. (Hrsg.) Göttingen: Verlag für Psychologie.

Jaspers, K. (1956). *Philosophie* (Volume II). Berlin: Springer.

Jonas, H. (1986). *Das Prinzip der Verantwortung. Versuch einer Ethik für die technische Zivilisation* [The principle of responsibility. Towards an ethics for the technical civilization]. Frankfurt: Insel.

Kohlberg, L. (1981). *Essays on moral development. Vol. I: The philosophy of moral development.* San Fracisco: Harper & Row.

Kohlberg, L. (1984). *Essays on Moral Development.* Vol. 2: The Psychology of Moral Development. The Nature and Validity of Moral Stages. Harper and Row, San Francisco.

Kohlberg, L., & Candee, D. (1984). *Relations of moral judgment to moral action.* In Kohlberg, L. 1984. Essays on Moral Development. Vol. 2: The Psychology of Moral Development. The Nature and Validity of Moral Stages (pp. 373–493). Harper and Row, San Francisco.

Leithwood, K., Harris, A., & Strauss, T. (2010). *Leading school turnaround.* San Francisco: Jossey Bass.

Noddings, N. (1992). *The challenge to care in schools. An alternative approach to education. Advances in Contemporary Educational Thought series, Vol. 8.* New York: Teachers Colleege Press.
Noddings, N. (2006). *Critical lessons: What our school should teach.* Cambridge: Cambridge University Press.
Nucci, L. (2008). Social cognitive domain throry and moral education. In L.P. Nucci & D. Narvaez (Eds.), *Handbook of moral and character education* (pp. 291–309). New York: Routledge.
Oser, F. (1998). *Ethos- die vermenschlichung des erfolgs.* (Ethos-the humanisation of the success)- Opladen: Leske & Budrich.
Oser, F. (1999). Die missachtete Freiheit moralischer Alternativen: Urteile über Handeln, Handeln ohne Urteile. In D. Garz, F. Oser & W. Althof, (Eds. 1999). *Moralisches Urteil und Handeln* (Moral judgment and action) (pp. 168–219). Frankfurt: Suhrkamp.
Pittella, R. (2011). *How deconstructing the American schoolsystem will reconstruct the American dream.* Glenside: Institute for Elemental Ethics and Education
Rheinberg, F. & Vollmeyer, R. (2008; 2012). *Motivation* (8. Aufl.). Stuttgart: Kohlhammer.
Rheinberg, F. (2002). *Motivation.* Stuttgart: Kohlhammer
Reinters, H. & Youniss, J. (2009). School-based required community service and civic development in adolescents. *Applied Developmental Sciences, 10,* 2–12.
Rest, J.R. (1986). *Moral development. Advances in research and theory.* New York: Praeger.
Rest, J.R. (1985). An interdisciplinary approach to moral education. In M. Berkowicz & F. Oser (Eds.), *Moral education: Theory and application* (pp. 9–26). Hillsdale: Earlbaum.
Rest, J.R. (1983). Morality. In: J.H. Flavell & E.M. Markman (Eds.), *Handbook of child psychology* (pp. 556–628). New York: Wiley.
Schiefele, U. (2011). Interests and learning. In N.M. Seel (Eds.), *Encyclopedia of the sciences of learning* (pp. 1623–1626). New York : Springer.
Schopenhauer, A. (1956 ; 2005). Über das Mitleid (On Compassion). München: Beck.
Staub, E., Bar-Tal, D., Karylowski, J., & Reykowskil, J. (1984). *Development and maintenance of prosocial behavior. International perspectives on positive morality.* New York and London: Plenum Press.
Thoma, S.J. (2006). Research on the defining issue test. In M. Killen & J. Smetana (Eds.), *Handbook on moral development* (pp. 67–92). Mahwah: Erlbaum.
Tugendhat, E. (1986). *Probleme der Ethik* (ethical problems). Ditzingen: Reclam.
Turiel, E., & Smetana, J.G. (1986). Soziales Wissen und Handeln: Die Koordination von Bereichen. In F. Oser, W. Althof & D. Garz (Eds.), *Moralische Zugänge zum Menschen - Zugänge zum moralischen Menschen. Beiträge zur Entstehung moralischer Identität* (pp. 108–135). München: Kindt.
Varghese, K.T. (2012). *Ethnographic elements of civic education and civic consciousness: Teachers' concept of civic education in a comparative qualitative research analysis between Kerala (India) and Switzerland.* (Unpublished doctoral dissertation). University of Fribourg, Fribourg.
Weiner, B. 1988. *Motivationspsychologie.* Weinheim: Psychologie Verlags Union
Weiner, B. 2006. *Social motivation, justice, and the moral emotions. An attributional approach.* Mahwah, NJ: Erlbaum.
Youniss, J., & Yates, M. (1997) *Community service and social responsibility in youth.* Chicago: University of Chicago Press.
Youniss, J. & Reinders, H. (2010). Youth and community service: A review of US research, theoretical perspectives, and implications for policy in Germany. *Zeitschrift für Erziehungswissenschaft, 13*(2), 233–248.
Zimbardo, P. (2007). *The Lucifer Effect: How Good People Turn Evil.* London: Rider.

AFFILIATION

Fritz K. Oser,
Department of Education
University of Fribourg
Fribourg, Switzerland

PART 1

FOUNDATIONS OF MORAL MOTIVATION

Foundations consist of fundamental ideas about how to consider, deliberate and study moral motivation (MM). There are philosophical foundations, which basically rely on Kant's metaphysics, general psychological foundations or moral foundations, all synthesizing what influences someone to act or not act morally.

In the first chapter, Wren asks very basically: What drives people to be good? Referring to philosophical traditions, as well as to moral psychological approaches, he shares ideas about how to grasp a person's sources of being driven towards moral acting. His distinction between moral motivation and moral motives seems to contribute meaningfully to a basic understanding of MM.

Thoma and Bebeau refer to Rest's model in which moral motivation is presumed to be the third component relevant for action. They show how this component has been studied in general and in the professions, as suggested by Rest himself, as an appropriate domain for getting to the core of moral motivation.

Minnameier develops a different position in regard to moral motivation by proclaiming the provocative thesis that we do not need Rest's third component to explain moral behaviour. In the tradition of internalism, he delivers theoretically sophisticated ideas about how to conceptualize the motivational impact of moral judgment staying within the classical stage concept of Kohlberg.

Thorkildsen, as a researcher with roots in moral as well as in general motivational psychology, builds a bridge between both schools of thinking. Based on the stance of intentions, she proclaims that moral action is explained best via a dynamic system of moral and non-moral intentions, some of them being developed intuitively, some of them by reflection. To become ready for moral acting is – in the light of this intentional approach – caused by more than motivational and volitional processes, but rather by moral as well as by non-moral needs or motives.

The editors cluster these four chapters together because they represent four classical starting points for thinking about what MM phenomenologically could be.

THOMAS E. WREN

I. "WHY BE MORAL?" A PHILOSOPHICAL
TAXONOMY OF MORAL MOTIVATION[1]

INTRODUCTION

In the following pages I will try to clarify the concept of moral motivation by laying out a "philosophical taxonomy" of the concept that takes into account the classical and contemporary literature of philosophical ethics as well as psychological accounts of human motivation and moral judgment. I say "takes into account" because this chapter is neither a comprehensive review of the diverse literature on moral motivation nor an attempt to construct a new scientific paradigm. I will address the topic of moral motivation from my home discipline, which is moral philosophy, in the hope that what I have to say will be useful to anyone interested in the perennial question "Why be moral?"

This question can be understood in a variety of ways, all of which can be boiled down to two. The first way is to understand the question as asking why people act in accord with their specific moral judgments (or, from the opposite end, why they often fail to act on those judgments). The second way is to understand it as asking why people bother to make moral judgments at all (or, again from the opposite end, why some people feel no need to take any moral point of view whatsoever). Exactly how these two questions are related to each other, as well as whether they are indeed different questions, is a separate issue, which I will discuss at the end of the chapter.

How reasons — moral or otherwise — are related to human action is a long-standing philosophical problem as well as a major issue in contemporary motivational theory. For simplicity's sake I will adopt the usual deontological notion of a *moral principle*, made famous by Immanuel Kant and deployed in cognitive developmental moral psychology, according to which truly moral behaviour is that which is grounded in some sort of normative ought-judgment to the effect that the behaviour in question is consistent with and in some sense or other motivated by a justificatory principle or rule. How cognitive developmentalists such as Jean Piaget and Lawrence Kohlberg have charted the process through which these principles take shape in the minds of children and adolescents is well known, as is the subsequent debate over how and why people who see the social world in terms of moral principles actually act (or fail to act) on them.

Less well known is how these and other moral psychologists have dealt with the second of the two questions mentioned above, namely why people bother to make moral judgments at all. Here social learning theorists have had the most to

K. Heinrichs, F. Oser & T. Lovat (Eds.), Handbook of Moral Motivation: Theories, Models, Applications, 27–48.

say, providing various affect-based accounts of moral motivation that range from early cognitive dissonance theory to later social learning theories of modeling and empathy and cognitive frame theories. However, cognitive developmentalists also have weighed in on this issue, as we will see below.

WHY BE MORAL?

Let us return to the question "Why be moral?", first considering it from a philosophical perspective. As I said above this question can be understood as asking not for an explanation of why people actually act (or think they should act) in accordance with considered moral judgments, but rather for an account of why they even bother to make such judgments. This second version of the question has a rich history in Western philosophy. Its first appearance was in Plato's *Euthyphro*, where Plato answered the question with two alternative accounts of morality, according to which it was either what one must do because the gods command it or what the gods command because it is right. Medieval philosophers explored the first of these two accounts (often under the rubric of *divine law*), enlightenment philosophers developed the second (often under the more secular rubric of *conscience*), and twentieth century existentialists and analytical philosophers chose to question the question itself (usually under the rubrics of *radical choice* or *linguistic implicature*, respectively).

From this potpourri of ways to deal with the question "Why be moral?", I would like to distinguish two that are, in my opinion, the Scylla and Charybdis of attempts to steer through the many conceptions of moral motivation. The first way is what A.N. Whitehead called the fallacy of misplaced concreteness, and the second is unbridled nominalism. I will discuss them in turn.

Misplaced concreteness. The first way is to understand moral experience in causal terms, such that moral judgments are internal states or events that produce the external results that we count as moral behaviour. This approach reflects our general tendency to assume that ordinary language terms such as "conscience" represent something "really out there." Unfortunately, it does not automatically follow from the everyday currency of the term "conscience" that it is useful for scholarly investigations. Still less does it follow that this or similar terms or concepts correspond to some power or property that is "really present" within the moral agent. Admittedly, until now there has been no shortage of philosophers, be they classical or modern, religious or secular, academic or cracker barrel, who have assumed that people really do have *epikeia,* a moral faculty, an inborn sense of right and wrong, or some other sort of wee small voice built in as part of their intrapsychic makeup. Fortunately, today no self-respecting philosopher or psychologist would subscribe to that sort of naïve psychological realism, which is only a small step away from the Jiminy Cricket picture of conscience as a moralizing homunculus. Today the consensus is quite to the contrary, favoring the other extreme, unbridled nominalism, which stands as the Charybdis to the just-mentioned Scylla of misplaced concreteness.

Unbridled nominalism. The problem with this second way is somewhat more complex. Although Anglo-American psychologists are considerably more willing now than they were in the heyday of radical behaviorism to use mentalistic categories, they quite correctly keep their fingers crossed when they use a non-scientific word like "conscience." If pressed, many if not most contemporary psychologists, including those whose specialty is motivation theory, tend to eschew psychological realism in favor of the nominalism of those classically tough-minded theorists of a previous generation typified by the British psychologist H.J. Eysenck (1970, 1976), who fiercely rejected the notion of conscience as an objective fact, phenomenon, power, or unitary process. Combining classical nominalism with reinforcement theory, Eysenck argued that the phenomena collectively denoted by the term "conscience" are a loose array of *conditioned reflexes* for avoiding acts that have been punished by society. He agreed that it may be useful to take a single term like "conscience" as a shorthand designation for a particular group of learned inhibitions, just as labeling a set of actions as "evil" streamlines the moral educator's task by encouraging the child "to react in the future with anxiety to everything thus labeled" (1976, p. 109). However, for Eysenck and those who have followed him in Britain and elsewhere, a term such as "conscience" has no objective reference. In spite of their convenience in everyday discourse, the argument goes, such terms have little or no heuristic value in the sense of helping us discover something about how morality itself really works.

I have called this general approach to psychological matters "nominalistic" because it continues that powerful British tradition by regarding abstract terms as more or less arbitrary designations or "names" rather than as objective categories that carve reality at its joints. To be sure, Eysenck is hardly the first British theorist to take a nominalist line toward conscience. (It goes back to Ockham.) On the contrary: he stands in prestigious philosophical company. Over a century earlier, Jeremy Bentham tried to demythologize moral sense theory by calling conscience "a thing of fictitious existence, supposed to occupy a seat in the mind" (1834/1983, p. 9). The notion of conscience was thereby reduced to what Bertrand Russell would later call a "logical construction,"[2] such that meaningful statements about conscience are supposedly translatable without residue into statements about more fundamental entities or processes of another sort such as the conditioned reflexes mentioned by Eysenck. Unfortunately, that view shares the weakness of all nominalisms, namely its silence about why those and only those fundamental entities (or reflexes or whatever) are gathered under a single name. For these and probably also other reasons, the actual practice of most psychologists who discuss both morality and motivation stops short of the extreme nominalism of Bentham and Russell. As Eysenck's definition of conscience as a socially specified and socially conditioned set of inhibitions illustrates, when psychologists do discuss those topics, the logical-constructionist approach to conscience is usually accompanied by an unspoken but supposedly reality-based consensus regarding the criteria for inclusion in the class "moral." Like most nominalisms actually subscribed to, theirs stops short of the

Humpty-Dumptean conclusion[3] that there is really nothing in common among things bearing the same name other than that they are called by the same name.

The Functions of Conscience

I turn now to the question of whether an intermediate position can be found between these two extremes of reifying conscience as a wee small voice and dismissing it as nothing more than an incidentally useful but basically arbitrary labeling device. The history of moral philosophy suggests that some such middle ground can be found. True, there are enormous substantive differences in the ways philosophers have conceptualized conscience, one of the most crucial being the shift from the Aristotelian notion of an intellectual virtue *(phronesis)* to the 20th century emotivist view that reduced conscience to internal exclamations of "Boo!" or "Hurrah!" By and large, though, the philosophical history of "conscience" has revolved around the *role* conscience is thought to play, from which has arisen a conception of conscience that is not so much substantive as function oriented.[4] Ever since Plato, it has been thought of as an internalized conduct control that commends, blames, and otherwise regulates one's overt and covert behaviour by means of self-monitoring evaluative cognition. This idea is eminently compatible with western theologies, as Augustine's *Confessions* and Joseph Butler's *Sermons* demonstrate. However, it is also quite compatible with naturalistic theories of human behaviour, as Justin Aronfreed tried to show in the opening pages of his watershed theoretical study *Conduct and Conscience* (1968; see also Aronfreed, 1971). This function-oriented notion retains the valid insight of the old moral sense theorists and other philosophers who have reified conscience, namely that there really is something special about moral cognition, and that it is more than just a general feeling tone, a specific kind of behavioral output, or any other empirical feature of conscience.

In the following pages I will try to show how that insight is present in various types of moral psychology. In order to do so I will consider the function of conscience as itself having two aspects or sub-functions. The first can be thought of as the tendency or (better) a set of tendencies to act in conformity with one's moral judgments. These compliance tendencies include other-oriented motives such as love or gratitude and self-oriented ones such as the need for acceptance and approval. In what follows, I will refer to them as *moral motives*. The second role of conscience can be thought of as an underlying sense of conscientiousness or moral care, which in the following pages I will call *moral motivation*. Although its role is really distinct from the first role of conscience, what I have in mind here is a general disposition or metamotivation, cutting across the historical and conceptual manifold of moral situations and their diverse sorts of actions and moral principles, in such a way that the deliverances of moral judgment are understood by the agent as providing *exciting* as well as *discriminating* reasons for action.

The interrelation between these two aspects or roles of conscience is complex, but it can be articulated as a matrix formed by combining the two pairs of contrasting terms already mentioned. The upper part of the matrix is formed by the intersection of two rows, representing moral motives and moral motivation, and two columns, representing the above-mentioned contrast between noncognitivist and cognitivist ways of regarding the subject matter of psychology. The four cells generated by the intersection of these rows and columns refer to the epistemological and metaethical views that can be taken toward each of the two main motivational concepts. In the next few pages I will briefly describe these views under the headings of the *summary* and *constitutive* conceptions (of moral motivation) and the *externalist* and *internalist* perspectives (on moral motives). However, what is especially distinctive about these two rows is their common reference to the *moral domain*. This is hardly a simple concept, and so beneath them I have added a third row, whose two cells refer to alternative ways of conceiving the moral domain. As we will see at the end of this chapter, these ways are not so much theories as definition-generating views, oriented respectively toward either the *contents* or the *core features* of the moral domain. Thus the full picture of our matrix looks like this:

Table 1: Matrix of moral motives and motivation

	NONCOGNITIVISM:	*COGNITIVISM:*
MORAL MOTIVATION:	Summary view	Constitutive view
MORAL MOTIVES:	Externalist view	Internalist view
MORAL DOMAIN:	Contents view	Core features view

There are, of course, many other philosophical categories and distinctions that could be mentioned in connection with morality and motivation. The ones I have singled out here show the general philosophical framework within which the brief psychological audit offered in the following pages will be carried out.

Moral Motives and Moral Motivation

I turn now to the views represented by the six cells of our matrix, with an emphasis on the top row (moral motivation). I will begin with a closer look at the pivotal distinction that structures the top part of the matrix. As already indicated, I am using the first of these two terms of art, "moral motives," to designate a loosely linked set of relatively distinct conative dispositions, many of which bear the same names as the virtuous action patterns they generate, such as kindness, courage, fidelity, and piety. Since they are assumed to function as mediators between thought and action, they are sometimes characterized as dispositions that a moral person "acts out of" (e.g., charity, loyalty, or gratitude). The second term, "moral motivation," refers to their conative foundation or (to borrow a phrase from generative linguistics) a *deep structure* whose function is much like that which Butler and Kant assigned to the so-called "natural faculty," "irresistible impulse," or "instinct" of conscience. I have elsewhere (Wren, 1991) characterized the latter function, whose very existence is indeed disputable, as *moral care*. It can also be characterized as the cross-situational disposition to take a moral point of view, from which specific action tendencies present themselves as moral motives, all charged with moral significance and overriding urgency for the agent as well as for any evaluating onlookers.

I have called the two elements of this distinction "terms of art" because they are ad hoc stipulations and as such are not really subject to debate. However, it remains to be seen just how useful the distinction they portray is to moral psychology — or, more exactly, how relevant it is to what contemporary moral philosophers, moral psychologists, and moral educators are up to. Bearing in mind what was said above about the tendency of psychologists to take a nominalist approach toward folk categories such as "the voice of conscience," one may well ask whether from their perspective the proposed distinction between moral motives and moral motivation could possibly be useful or meaningful. Furthermore, even if it is allowed as meaningful, one may nonetheless ask how sharply the distinction can or should be made, as well as whether the meaning of one of the two terms of the distinction is parasitical on that of the other. Predictably, how one answers such questions will depend on one's other theoretical commitments, sympathies, and orientations. The most important of these probably is the cognitive or noncognitive quality of the orientation from which one theorizes, which for most psychologists is a matter of degree and not fixed by any a priori rule or methodological principle.

I have already suggested that even relatively noncognitive moral psychologists (e.g., Eysenck) assume that there are grounds for grouping certain psychological processes or phenomena under certain labels, and that these grounds amount to something more than merely ad hoc convenience for the theorist. In the present context, this means that, allowing for differences of idiom, among moral psychologists it is generally recognized that to some extent a moral agent "really has" certain dispositions — that is, moral motives — such as a tendency to engage in helping behaviour, a readiness to stand by friends, to tell the truth, and so on.[5]

This is not to deny that psychologists often construe the motivational dimension of morality nominalistically. For instance, in the now-faded controversy over cross-situational personality constructs (which include moral dispositions), what was really under attack was not the idea that people have more or less robust and stable tendencies (moral motives) to comply with moral norms but rather the idea of what the social psychologist Walter Mischel (1976, p. 103) has called "a unitary intrapsychic moral agency like the superego or ... a unitary trait entity of conscience" — which of course corresponds to what I am calling "moral motivation." Social psychologists and social learning theorists like Mischel and (more recently) Martin Hoffman (2000) might argue that my distinction between moral motives and moral motivation is purely linguistic. For them the problem with the latter term is not that it fails to refer but only that what it refers to in the singular is the same set of dispositions that is referred to in the plural by the first term, "moral motives."

MORAL MOTIVATION: ITS SUMMARY AND CONSTITUTIVE CONCEPTIONS

To put it mildly, hard-headed moral psychologists like Mischel and Eysenck, as well as their philosophical forebears such as Bentham and Russell and contemporary philosophers such Michael Slote (2007), would not endorse the distinction I have just made. Nor would they be alone in their reaction. A construct as open-ended as moral motivation is sure to raise eyebrows, if not hackles, among most behavioral scientists, and with good reason. After all, to suppose that a construct is isomorphic or even indirectly correspondent with reality exposes a researcher to the risks of violating the principle of parsimony and, ultimately, of having nothing to show for one's efforts. Hence inquiry into "the" structure of moral motivation might very well turn out to be a snipe hunt, or, to borrow a well-known characterization of metaphysics, a search by a blind man in a dark room for a black cat that isn't there.

One way to avoid these risks without giving up the convenience of using umbrella terms such as "moral motivation" (not to mention more familiar terms such as "conscience" and "conscientiousness") would be to adopt a purely *summary* view according to which moral motivation would be understood as nothing more than a shorthand device, a collective noun that has no content or meaning beyond that of the individual entities to which it refers. In that case the construct of moral motivation could be characterized as verbally but not logically different from that of moral motives. For a motivational account in which the contrast between moral motivation and moral motives is a distinction *with* a difference, we should look to more cognitive forms of moral psychology, of which the most prominent are the cognitive developmental models of Piaget (1932/1965) and Kohlberg (1969/1984). In those accounts the function of what I am calling moral motivation is often (though not always) understood "top-down," by which I mean as a determining factor or regulative disposition that constitutes the stage on which more specific motives provide the transition from moral judgments to moral actions. For this reason I have labeled this view the *constitutive conception* of moral motivation.

Here as in the previous comparison with linguistic theory, we can say that cognitive moral psychologists see moral motivation as a deep structure, without which there would be no determinate, specifically moral inclinations. Their approach stands in sharp contrast to that of noncognitivists, who understand the role of moral motivation "bottom up," which is to say as a purely summary concept, an aggregate of prosocial or other typically moral action tendencies. It is surely no coincidence that as we move toward the cognitive end of the spectrum of moral psychologies, nominalism fades into realism, much as in linguistic theory one finds Chomsky and others working at the mentalistic end of that spectrum arguing for innate structures that in some distinctive sense "are really there."[6]

Another use of the contrast between the summary and constitutive conceptions of motivation can be found in a debate among existentialists that took place in the mid-1900s over the notion of a "fundamental project." Jean-Paul Sartre (1969), who made that term the center of what he called "existential psychoanalysis," believed that day-to-day choices are governed by some sort of super-choice, operating in the wings so to speak and endowing specific projects with value and intelligibility. In contrast, other existentialists of his era such as Maurice Merleau-Ponty (2012) used the term to refer to the aftermath of more specific choices, which is to say as the *resultant* of one's specific, articulated projects rather than their source or cause. Like noncognitive moral psychologists who have a purely summary notion of conscience, they believed that the concept of a life project was simply a matter of convenience, and that the distinction between day-to-day choices and a life project was purely verbal. For them there was no real difference between moral motives and moral motivation.

The Plausibility of a Real Difference

It should be clear from the way I originally introduced the distinction between moral motives and motivation that I regard the top-down or "constitutive" conception of moral motivation as the more useful of the two ideas. However, it should be equally clear that its extreme form is just as untenable as the naive pictures of conscience dismissed above. When drawn along lines analogous to Sartre's picture of a super-choice, the picture of a master motivation holds little promise, though if we regard moral motivation more as a structure (Chomsky's approach) than as a mental act, it may be possible to stay within the limits of plausibility. Here as with so many metatheoretical questions, the proof of the pudding is in the eating. The best way to argue that there really is a difference between the concepts of moral motive and moral motivation, and that this difference is important for psychological theorizing about morality, is to take a look at some moral psychologies and see whether somehow they include these two concepts or their functional equivalents. (For a discussion of the difference between functions and foundational structures in domains other than morality; see van Haaften, Korthals, & Wren, 1997.)

MORAL MOTIVES: INTERNALIST AND EXTERNALIST PERSPECTIVES

The distinction I have drawn between moral motivation and moral motives should not be confused with the distinction between moral judgments and moral actions. Judgments about moral right and wrong or moral good and evil are judgments formed as a result of one's having taken a moral point of view, which is itself not a moral judgment but rather an interpretive tendency, a readiness to process reality in moral terms. Furthermore, from the simple fact that a person is disposed to cognize reality from a moral point of view nothing follows as to whether that person will act morally, either in general or on specific occasions. There is considerable debate among philosophers concerning the logical structure and other formal features of the passage from moral thought to action, just as there is considerable debate among psychologists concerning its more concrete structures. Among philosophers, the debate takes the form of an argument over whether any motivational component is built into the very notion that a given cognition is a moral judgment. Among psychologists, the debate takes the form of an argument over whether moral cognitions are intrinsically motivating. The two sorts of debate do not map perfectly onto each other, but since they share many of the same basic concerns the position a person takes in the first debate usually determines the position he or she takes in the second, and vice versa. Thus, philosophers and psychologists can be of some use to each other, notwithstanding the enormous differences in their jargons, methodologies, and ways of carving up human experience.

The corresponding philosophical (or better, metaethical) debate has been conducted in Anglo-American circles under the billing *Internalism vs. Externalism.* As the second row of our matrix indicates, these terms represent two alternative views of moral motives, or more exactly, two ways of understanding the relationship between moral motives and their cognitive counterparts, moral judgments. The views in question are metaethical, not normative, in that they are views about how ethical thinking itself works. Presumably they have been held implicitly as long as ethical theories have been around, but the distinction between them was not explicitly formulated until the mid-1900s, first in W. D. Falk (1947-48) and a few years later in a well-known article by William Frankena (1958). Externalism, Frankena wrote, is the view that it is not only possible but also commonplace "for an agent to have, or to see that he has, an obligation, even if he has no motivation, actual or dispositional, for doing the action in question" (ibid, p. 40). Internalism, by contrast, is the view that such a radical disconnection between judgment and action would be paradoxical, anomalous, or even logically impossible. This description was subsequently picked up and refined by Thomas Nagel, who defined internalism as the view that in moral action "the necessary motivation is supplied by ethical principles and judgments themselves," and externalism as the view that "an additional psychological sanction is required to motivate our compliance" (1970, p. 7).

The contrast between the internalist and externalist accounts is easily seen by putting the matter schematically as follows. Internalist theories of morality are those which hold that a proposition like

> PI: "Eve believes that abortion is wrong"

entails assertions of the form

> P2: "Eve is at least somewhat motivated to oppose abortion."

Or more simply, the thesis of internalism is: *PI entails P2.* Externalist theories, in turn, are those which implicitly or explicitly deny this entailment, no matter how much importance they otherwise attach to the motivational features of moral living.

Most philosophers who discuss the issue turn out to be internalists, and I am no exception. Some hold what I have elsewhere (Wren, 2010) called the "causal internalist" view, so labeled because they ascribe causal efficacy to the intellectual component of moral judgment (P1). Others take the "expressive internalist" view;

believing that the moral judgment articulates motivational structures (P2) already in place within the agent. Still others, including myself, combine these two versions of internalism in various ways (Wren, 1990, pp. 18-28; see Nagel, 1970, pp. 7-8, and Sytsma, 1990). However, this is not the place to ring the changes on this highly formal and no longer current debate. I mention it only to observe that externalist theories rely on a conception of moral discourse and moral cognition that is proper to *observers,* such as visiting anthropologists trying to catalogue a tribe's mores, whereas internalist theories employ a conception of moral discourse and moral cognition characteristic of the *participants* themselves. The externalist puts mental scare quotes or inverted commas around moral terms, in much the same way that R. M. Hare (1952) did when he allowed that the word "good" could sometimes be used sarcastically or in some other non-commendatory way. Because the scare quotes sense of a term is meaningful only if its straightforward sense is known, externalism is logically parasitical on internalism. This conclusion suggests in turn that the latter is the more suitable metaethical perspective for conducting a study of the motivational dimension of morality — which after all is an inquiry into the psychology of *moral agents,* not cultural anthropologists.

Until now the internalism-externalism issue has remained undiscussed outside the ranks of professional philosophers. I know of no psychological study of morality that has referred to it, even though such studies proceed, usually unwittingly, from one or the other of these metaethical perspectives, as we will see.[7]

THE MORAL DOMAIN: CONTENTS AND CORE FEATURES

Philosophers have written so extensively and differently about the complex referential range of the term "moral" that it can be difficult for them to realize that most people do not regard it as especially ambiguous. In contrast, most psychologists who discuss morality share the general public's confidence that the basic meaning of the term "moral" is self-evident. This confidence has led many psychologists who investigate the moral domain (especially social learning theorists) to ignore its formal properties and instead to understand it only in terms of its *contents.* Not surprisingly, the less cognitive a moral psychology is, the more strictly is its research confined to those moral contents that either are entirely overt behaviours or, in the case of covert behaviours and attitudes can be easily operationalized and measured. In general, these contents are prosocial acts or attitudes such as beneficence or obedience, whose prosociality is itself usually assessed by looking at the objective consequences of such deeds rather than at their subjective intentionality. I say "usually assessed" because as the third row of our matrix suggests, some moral psychologists — usually the more cognitively oriented ones — do look at the intentionality of the behaviours in question, as provided by interviews or self-reports. In doing so, they begin to move from a content orientation toward a more formal understanding of morality. Or, as I prefer to put it, toward an increasingly definite appreciation of the *core features* constituting its conceptual structure. At the far cognitive end of the spectrum stand

Kohlbergian and post-Kohlbergian stage structuralists who are explicitly concerned with the way subjects understand the formal features of morality. That is, they focus their inquiries on other-regarding attitudes and values that, when operationalized as prosocial actions, turn out (not surprisingly) to be the standard contents of the moral domain.

Both approaches have their philosophical problems. As I noted in the last section, philosophers are divided among themselves as to what a consistent and otherwise adequate formal definition of the term "morality" should look like. However, it is impossible for scholars to do without any formal definition at all, since otherwise there would be no way of bringing new cases, actions, or attitudes under the rubric of morality. What usually happens, of course, is that resemblances are noted thanks to which new cases are assigned the same moral labels that older ones already wear. However, sometimes new cases are too novel, or their moral salience too weak, for the case-by-case method of labeling to work. When that happens general, non-nominalistic principles of classification come into play, usually without being formulated very clearly or systematically in the minds of the classifiers. Thus moral worth is conventionally assigned to both virginity and conjugal sexuality, to prudent self-restraint as well as courageous intervention, and so on, not because these practices exhibit a single quality or essence called "morality" but because they are perceived to be members of a domain of human activity that has features that are counted by our linguistic community as more or less necessary conditions for the application of terms such as "moral." I have identified three salient features that seem to be stereotypical or "core" marks of the moral domain (there may also be others), which I will describe here in the briefest possible terms. They are: the *executive* character of morality, the *value* it places on impartial reasoning, and the *seriousness* with which it is taken by those who practice it.[8] These three core features are discernible in observable prosocial behaviours and other standard contents of morality, but they are of a very different conceptual order owing to the implicit reference they have to the "inner" aspects of morality, in particular the reasons for which moral actions are performed.

The first core feature. I have already alluded to the first of these core features, when I noted that morality involves self-regulation. This feature corresponds to the notion of morality as an *executive* function. It falls under the category of what some philosophers have called "higher level motivation" (Alston, 1977) or "second-order desire" (Frankfurt, 1988; Taylor, 1976, 1989). In contrast to the nonreflective desires and aversions we have for things "out there," the objects of reflective desires and aversions are themselves intentional states, namely first-order desires, affections, and other psychic states that influence a person's action in and with the world. Thus I may have envy, anger, and other sorts of hostile attitudes toward you, and at the same time take a disapproving point of view on those attitudes from a higher, second-order perspective. In doing so I evaluate my own conscious life and hence shape or *regulate* it, not mechanically as is the case with homeostatic self-regulating systems such as thermostats but rationally, by means of evaluative cognitions or reasons.

The second core feature. The fruits of these cognitions are moral judgments, formed according to criteria that are themselves parts of our culture's moral heritage. Of these the most important and least culture-specific is probably the criterion that moral judgments must be acceptable from perspectives other than one's own, which in our own time and culture usually means they must be fair, just, other-regarding, etc. This criterion is intertwined with the second core feature of the moral domain, namely its emphasis on *objective reasoning.* It is true that deep personal commitments can have moral weight and even overriding seriousness, but it seems impossible to deny that part of the stereotypical or core meaning of morality is the impersonal perspective from which one recognizes situations in which everyone's claims have equal weight and no one is more important than anyone else. It may well be that, as Nagel claims, "transcendence of one's own point of view in action is the most creative force in ethics" (1986, p. 8). Exactly how this perspective is related to the subjective perspective from which one says "I" and "you" is a complex philosophical matter that we cannot unpack here, though I cannot resist adding two observations to Nagel's comment. The first is that the impulse toward objective thinking originates deep within our subjectivity; the second is that objective thinking is not a bringing of the mind into correspondence with an external reality, as crude moral realists would hold, but rather bringing it into conformity with the demands of its own external view of itself (see Nagel, 1986, p. 148). Some philosophers have chosen to limit the very word "moral" to the impersonal realm of duties and rights, focusing on impartial considerations of justice, fairness, or human rights, and to reserve the term "ethical" for answers to the general question of how one should live. However, that terminology seems not only forced but of little use to the current practice of moral psychology. Suffice it here to note that regardless of what we call the well-lived life, in western moral discourse impartial concepts such as "fair" or "just" are closely associated with such a life as far as most persons and most moral psychologies are concerned.

The third core feature. The final core feature of morality I will discuss is *seriousness.* The philosopher Mary Midgley has captured this point a bit differently but to the same end: "Moral," she tells us, is the superlative of "seriousness," and a serious matter is defined as one "that affects us deeply" (1981, pp. 124-125). Seriousness is what other contemporary philosophers call an agent-relative concept, although it is not an exclusively self-regarding one. (One can also take another person's interests seriously.) That is, a moral issue deals with matters that are perceived as central among our hopes, needs, and so on — which is to say with our web of purposes. Some of these purposes are unique to the individual, but many are common, either because of our shared genetic endowment and overlapping cultures or because (to speak commonsensically, though the same point could be made in the more cumbersome post-Kantian language of "transcendental conditions of possibility") they are just matters that *anyone* would have to take seriously. For example, we may consider how important it is to sustain conditions of fellowship and mobility and, inversely, how drastically serious it would be to find oneself in utter solitude or complete communicative paralysis. The task of discerning what are truly serious matters is, of course, problematic, and requires cognitive skills that are seldom discussed in the literature of moral psychology, e.g., analogical thinking, responsibility judgments, and autobiographical interpretation. Although I will not try to fill this gap myself, at the end of this chapter I will try to show that self-interpretation of this sort is *the* moral dilemma, one that moral agents and moral theorists alike must reckon with if the rest of their moral reasoning is to matter.

This quick tour of the moral domain is just that, a tour, and not a philosophical or empirical argument. It is not meant to advance, much less settle, the ongoing debate among philosophers over where the boundaries of morality should be drawn. The point I have tried to make in this section is essentially negative as well as fairly modest: I have called into question the idea that morality is any single, sharply specified set of behaviours, attitudes, or principles.

TAKING STOCK

In the foregoing pages, I have tried to set forth a number of philosophical claims about moral motivation. Much of what I have said may have seemed to non-philosophers inhospitably arid, and so I will now summarize it by citing a few common-sense reasons for thinking that the "exciting function" of conscience includes a general posture of concern for the moral point of view (moral motivation) as well as compliance tendencies (moral motives).

First of all, it seems very significant that in our everyday discourse about morality we can and often do separate moral agents of all types from those otherwise normal persons who we say "have no conscience." Furthermore, we can speak of the former as having consciences that are weak, strict, tender, and so on, all without regard to the contents or deliverances of those consciences. It is even possible, though often difficult, for us to esteem and commend people for being faithful to consciences that are radically different from our own. Moral tolerance is a special hallmark of today's liberal ethic of living and letting live. However, it is of a piece with the more general expectation, standard throughout the whole history of our western moral tradition, th the truly conscientious person, which is to say anyone with a well-developed conscience, will be solicitous, committed — in a word, *motivated* — not only to pursue whatever he or she determine is a moral course of action, but also to take the trouble to determine it.

This observation echoes the way two great 18th century moral philosophers have described conscience. In his important early work *Lectures on Ethics,* Kant defined conscience as "an involuntary and irresistible impulse in our nature" that makes the continual, often very intrusive demand that we judge not only our actions but also the dispositions leading up to them (1775-1780/1963, p. 69). Butler had made a similar point a few decades earlier in the second of his *Sermons upon Human Nature,* where he called conscience "a superior principle of reflection [that] magisterially exerts itself" (1726/1983, p. 37). Kant and Butler may have gone too far in thinking that conscience is a universally distributed part of human nature as such. However, it seems clear that part of what it means to have a "moral nature" is that one takes one's morality seriously. That idea shows up in various versions. Besides deliberating over issues of right and wrong, one takes morality seriously by undertaking the task of morally educating one's child. One also takes morality seriously when one concedes, however grudgingly, that other persons sincerely following a different moral drummer have moral worth because "it is better to have some principles, even if they sometimes lead to decisions which we regret, than to be morally adrift" (Hare, 1952, p. 73). Each of these versions of the general idea of taking morality seriously is relatively open-textured or content-free, and can be considered as expressions of the general concept "moral motivation." To them we can add those innumerable content-specific instances of moral concern in which an agent takes morality seriously simply by heeding his or her conscience in times of temptation.

To sum up, the question "Why do people care about being moral?" can be focused through a wide-angle lens or a narrow-focused one. In the first case, the question is asked in some broad, open-ended sense. Thus I have represented it as a query about the constitutive conditions of that common experience which Kant called feeling "compelled" to pass moral judgments on ourselves. In the second case, the question is asked in a narrow, content-specific sense involving passages from moral judgments to actions. For instance, it could be asked why someone not usually active in social issues has decided to protest against gender discrimination, or why certain members of Greenpeace take their beliefs in the rights of animals or other environmental considerations so seriously that they are prepared to act on them at great personal cost or risk.

PERSONS IN RELATION

In this final section I will return to the title question of this chapter, "Why be moral?" I have already examined two ways in which it can be understood, namely as asking what motivates us to act on our moral judgments and, more fundamentally, what motivates us to make such judgments in the first place. I will continue to suspend any direct discussion of the hard question of to what extent one can be indifferent to moral issues and still be considered a normally functioning human being. Instead I will ask why it is that most people really care about morality. In other words, I will move from the question "Why [should we] be moral?" to "Why [in fact] *are* we moral?" This is a philosophical question as well as an empirical one, as psychologists and social scientists have often acknowledged, either expressly or, more often, by implication. My own view is that the most promising philosophical approaches to the question are those that regard interpersonal relations as constituent of all forms of evaluation and even of the sense of one's own personhood. The theme of interpersonality has been developed by many important philosophers, several of whom have been explicitly acknowledged by psychologists and sociologists who deal with topics such as moral development or personality theory. For instance Ludwig Binswanger has drawn from Martin Buber's foundational concept of a primordial I-Thou relationship, John Shotter was deeply influenced by John Macmurray's account of persons-in-relation, and Kohlberg frequently acknowledged the influence of George Herbert Mead's interactionism and Jürgen Habermas's model of communicative action.[9]

The idea shared by these otherwise very different authors is that the interrelatedness of human beings is both a matter of fact and a necessary condition of agency. Or better, it is a necessary condition for our *having* anything at all, here using the word "having" in the sense of ownership, where having is a result of specifically human activity. This fundamental conditionality is nicely illustrated by the methodology of archaeological anthropologists, who generally take evidence of culture as one of the criteria for deciding whether skeletal remains are human.

If, as many philosophers, psychologists, and social scientists believe, it would be self-contradictory to speak of action where there is no interaction, then the supposition of a totally isolated agent makes no sense. It is utterly different from, say, the case of Robinson Crusoe, who had interacted with personal others before his shipwreck and then modeled his new solitary life on his previous societal life. In a thought-experiment in which an agent is *totally* isolated — and this means that no interagential considerations of any sort are available, including memories — there could be no proper names or even any sense of gender. This anonymous, genderless creature would live in an otherwise completely impersonal universe, *sans* memories, anticipations, or fancies of the presence of a personal other. Also absent would be any concern about such things as deformities or feebleness, since these are objects of concern only in a society where public standards of beauty, agility, and health evolve as its members make comparisons among themselves.

A similar distinction applies to hermits, who are not truly acultural since the very decision to be a hermit is taken within a social milieu. Such decisions would be positive when made, say, in the hope of achieving certain religious benefits that they know through their society's traditions, and negative when made out of contempt or even fear of society for having rejected its values. Of course, occasional isolation can be attractive, but as William Cowper wrote in his poem "Retirement,"

> I praise the Frenchman; his remark was shrewd,—
> How sweet, how passing sweet, is solitude!
> But grant me still a friend in my retreat,
> Whom I may whisper, Solitude is sweet.

I would add that without a friend, or at least some fellow participant in the institution of language, Cowper's own line "Solitude is sweet" would be a mere flutter of sound. Language, whether it is spoken or thought, is essentially social, and if it is true that all thought is in some sense linguistic (Fodor, 1975), then it follows that thinking is not an interior monologue but rather incipient dialogue. In short, the notion of a totally isolated thinker is chimerical, mainly because such a creature would have no reason to use symbols as well as no conceptual schemes to share with others.[10]

Being rational, like being moral, involves creating formulations which, upon being communicated to other agents, would be recognized and accepted by them. When a formulation or even an entire theory is unacceptable, then the agent who proposed it can only assume that something is *wrong,* with either his rational judgment or that of his forum. This is true of the aesthetic use of rationality as well as its pragmatic exercise, since both activities involve generalizations and representations by means of symbolic forms. And what is symbolic form but a vehicle for communication?

In other words, valuation always presupposes the existence of other agents because totally isolated agents could not know their choices as good or their judgments as true. They could, perhaps, react to their environment with appropriate responses, but there would be nothing in their reaction that could recognize that appropriateness. They would not be able to evaluate what they were doing, because to do so would require stepping outside themselves and into the shoes of an observer. But *ex hypothesi,* no such observer is present, not even imaginatively. The nuclear physicist's counterpart to all this is the ideal case of an isolated particle. It makes no sense to speak of its "motion" in an empty space, since there is no way to fix a point relative to which the particle is moving. It is only with a plurality of particles that distances can be discriminated and motion is possible, and it is only in a field of discourse that happenings become facts and facts become values.

With this we come to a profound truth about the nature of moral agency. The standpoint of the agent includes as a necessary condition the taking of a point of view toward one's self — that is, taking the standpoint of the spectator. A purely subjective being (should there be such a creature) could never perform truly human actions, i.e., be rational and not simply reactive. In other words, if what I am doing is to have meaning for me, I must know my action from the outside as well as from the inside. This is most easily seen in the case of speech: my saying "cat" is meaningful to me the speaker only if I have reason to think that my listeners can know as well as I do what the word refers to or how the saying of it matters. A purely private language is an absurdity, as modern linguistic philosophy has made clear. This general postulate recalls the essentially transitive nature of action, in which whatever change in the world you or I bring about is a change in *the* world, not merely in your or my world — or, even more to the point, it is a change in *our* world.

From this it follows that I know my actions partly through your eyes. This is why we bother to justify our actions and motivations to others as well as to ourselves. Like all linguistic transactions, reason-giving presupposes intersubjective grounds of relevance. There have been extensive epistemological discussions about what makes some cognitive structures count for speaker and hearer alike as truths and, beyond that, as justifications. What is usually only hinted at in these erudite discussions is the possibility of a subject's refusing to play the reason-giving game altogether. Such refusals are neither uncommon nor abnormal when specific games are proposed, such as refusing to justify to others my decision to marry someone I love. The typical way of making such a refusal is to supply a pseudo-answer such as "Because I wanted to" when queried for an account of one's action, though the blunter reply "None of your business" also works on most occasions. Even so, as the philosopher Herbert Fingarette (1967) once observed, there is something ominously odd about such a refusal when it amounts to the refusal to enter into any reason-giving communication whatsoever:

> If an individual will not play a game with us, we can still fall back on the intelligible framework of everyday life outside that game. But what if he will not enter life's fray itself in the spirit in which we enter it? To face such a person, such a reality (and not merely to think it) is to experience a deep anxiety; a queasy helplessness moves in our soul. (Ibid., p. 37)

In the same vein, Gauld and Shotter (1977) have described the anxiety pervading the converse situation: that of an individual who cannot justify (however speciously) his actions:

> The point we are trying to make here is that in ordinary everyday life people have, if they want to do anything, to be able to justify it to others. If they cannot, then … they have lost that attribute which gives them autonomy in relation to others, the ability to reject criticism and to show that their actions do in fact accord with the values and interests agreed to by all in their society. *To be unable to justify oneself is to risk being an outcast, a non-person; it is to lose one's personhood.* (Ibid., pp. 192-3; italics added)

I leave it to that branch of psychology sometimes called personology to delineate the affiliative tendencies and other prosocial dispositions that constitute the conative foundations of what might be called the drive-to-justificatory-discourse. It is enough here to appreciate the great importance we spontaneously assign to interpersonal reason-giving and, by extension, the intrapersonal reason-giving that takes place in the internal forum of an agent's conscience. This importance is a matter of *moral seriousness,* in the sense that failure to give reasons for one's actions can be a moral failure, an irresponsibility that is itself a form of contempt for those who share one's world. As Habermas (1984, 1990) has shown, the fundamental procedures or conditions of human communication are continuous with the moral norms that make interpersonal life possible, especially the norm of respect for persons.[11]

As I have presented the matter here, the antecedent identification of oneself with the ideal of reasonableness and related ideals and values such as fair-mindedness and nonarbitrariness makes it possible for evaluative cognitions (such as the rules of distributive justice) to serve as moral motives. In turn, these rational ideals are rooted in certain primitive tendencies such as a deep-seated aversion to the prospect of being ostracized for refusing to engage in the practice of justifying one's actions. These are perhaps the most important of our identity-constituting tendencies or "basic desires."

However, this is only one of several ways of representing moral motivation. For instance, the personal roots of one's ideal of being a reasonable person might be represented as mastery strivings rather than as desires for affiliation.

Neuropsychologists might prefer to say that people are naturally hardwired to be logotropic, such that they have ingrained propensities of varying strengths to follow the most formally consistent rules of conduct, much as when Hercule Poirot entered a room he felt an urgent need to straighten any pictures that were hanging out of line. However the ideal of reasonableness is packaged, though, it is always understood as an antecedent tendency or basic desire that is relevant and motivationally significant for reasons that go beyond its logical status.

CONCLUSION

Which of these representations is the best hypothesis for studying the moral motivation of the contemporary ethical worlds (including non-Western ones) is a psychological question that can be raised in a philosophical essay, like this one, but it cannot be answered without empirical investigation. Furthermore, similar hypotheses can be proposed for other ideals besides those of reasonableness. Basic desires for the well-being of others may underlie the ideals of benevolence and justice (and their corresponding deontological principles), basic mastery strivings may be the conative deep structures that are displayed as temperance and courage, and so on. The story is undoubtedly extremely complicated, since there is no reason to expect a one-to-one correspondence between basic desires and specific moral ideals or principles. Thus affiliative tendencies (which are probably best thought of in the plural) might be articulated as justice ideals or principles in one context and as loyalty ideals or principles in another context. Furthermore, we may expect that moral actions will often be overdetermined by several complementary ideals, as well as by intermediate tendencies and articulations that should be included in any ethical account: thus one tendency can itself be an expression of another, deeper tendency, and some principles or ideals may be derived from other ones. Finally, we should note that not all moral ideals or principles are authentic self-articulations, even though they might be heavily laden with affect as well as with respectability. Ideals can be cognized (at least by the agent who conforms to them) as general social practices having nothing to do with his or her personality structure. Thus a young person whose socialization has been entirely a matter of external inducements may regard the ideals represented in the Scout Law as correct recipes for social acceptability, but not as integral to his (or her) own self-concept. For a norm to have the urgency of a moral ideal, though, it must be one's "own" in the special sense just described.

NOTES

[1] Portions of this chapter originally appeared elsewhere and are presented here in revised form with the gracious permission of the publishers, namely Routledge/MIT Press (for Wren, 1991) and Transaction Publishing (for Wren 2010).

[2] To illustrate the concept, Russell showed that a national entity such as England was a logical construction out of entities such as its nationals, and hence that facts about England can be expressed

more "ultimately" though often less conveniently by a set of statements about Englishmen, etc. (see Russell, 1905, 1921).

[3] "When *I* use a word, it means just what I choose it to mean — neither more nor less." "The question is," said Alice, "whether you *can* make words mean different things." "The question is," said Humpty Dumpty, "which is to be master — that's all.'"

[4] Note that "function-oriented" is used here without the behavioristic connotations of "functionalism," as the latter term was used earlier in this century in the bitter psychological debates between the partisans of introspection and phenomenology (structuralists) and those who eschewed any such attempts to get inside the black box of the mind (functionalists).

[5] True, such "motivational realism" is often laden with qualifications, and with good reason, given the studies by Hartshorne and May (1928–30) showing the extent to which seemingly established virtues such as honesty wax and wane depending on situational factors. The notion of moral motives as personality variables is still alive and well in the literature of social psychology, in spite of the now largely-spent blasts (e.g., Mischel, 1968) against personality theories about cross-situational dispositions. There may be a lingering wariness among motivation theorists concerning especially broad motivational dispositions such as "obedience" or "reverence," but for the most part their wariness is based not on nominalist suppositions but rather on suspicions that such categories are not so much moral motives as screens behind which people hide in order to rationalize improper and even atrocious behavior.

[6] This is the view that Chomsky made famous in his *Aspects of a Theory of Syntax* (1961). He has since modified his position considerably (see Chomsky, 1995).

[7] The one favored by most moral psychologists is — regrettably, in my view — the externalist perspective.

[8] It may seem a mistake to omit from this list other-regarding features, such as concern for the well-being of others. After all, the Golden Rule is the paradigm of morality for many, perhaps most people (at least in Western cultures). However, if it is the case that human existence is inherently interpersonal, then care, altruism, etc., can be seen as matters of supreme importance or seriousness, and on that last account deemed part of the moral domain. I will make this point below, but only cryptically. The classic discussion of the arguments for and against building other-regardingness into the formal concept of morality is found in Frankena (1958).

[9] See Binswanger (1975), Buber (1923/1958), Macmurray (1961), Shotter (1975), and Kohlberg (1984).

[10] This point has been made by philosophers of many orientations, from Aristotle (1998) to John Dewey (1928) and John Searle (1969).

[11] It is worth noting that Kohlberg claimed Habermas's "discourse ethics" was fully compatible with his own constructivist view of moral autonomy (Kohlberg, Levine, & Hewer, 1984, pp. 375–86; Kohlberg, Boyd, & Levine, 1990).

REFERENCES

Alston, W. (1977). Self-intervention and the structure of motivation. In T. Mischel (Ed.), *The self* (pp. 65–102). New York: Rowman & Littlefield.

Aristotle (1998) *Politics* (C.D.C. Reeve, Ed. and Trans.). Indianapolis: Hackett.

Aronfreed, J. (1968). *Conduct and conscience: The socialization of internalized control over behavior.* New York: Academic Press.

Aronfreed, J. (1971). Some problems for a theory of the acquisition of conscience. In C.M. Beck, B.S. Crittenden, & E.V. Sullivan (Eds.), *Moral education: Interdisciplinary approaches* (pp. 183–199). Toronto: University of Toronto Press.

Bentham, J. (1834/1983). *Deontology* (A. Goldworth, Ed.). Oxford: Oxford University Press.

Buber, M. (1958). *I and thou.* New York: Scribner's. (Original work published 1923)

Binswanger, L. (1975). *Being-in-the-world: Selected papers of Ludwig Binswanger* (Jacob Needleman, Ed. and Trans.). London: Souvenir Press, 1975.

Butler, J. (1983). *Five sermons preached at the Rolls Chapel and a dissertation upon the nature of virtue* (S. Darwall, Ed.). Indianapolis: Hackett. (Original work published 1726)

Chomsky, N. (1961). *Aspects of a theory of syntax*. Cambridge, MA: MIT Press.

Chomsky, N. (1995). *The minimalist program*. Cambridge, MA: MIT Press.

Dewey, J. (1928). *Experience and nature*. LaSalle, IL: Open Court.

Eysenck, H.J. (1970). A dimensional system of psychodiagnostics. In A.R. Mahrer (Ed.), *New approaches to personality classification* (pp. 169–207). New York: Columbia University Press.

Eysenck, H.J. (1976). The biology of morality. In T. Lickona (Ed.), *Moral Development and Behavior: Theory, Research, and Social Issues* (pp. 108–123). New York: Holt, Rinehart & Winston.

Falk, W.D. (1947–1948). 'Ought' and motivation. *Proceedings of the Aristotelian Society, 43*, 111–138.

Fingarette, H. (1967). *On responsibility*. New York: Basic Books.

Fodor, J.A. (1975). *The language of thought*. Cambridge, MA: Harvard University Press.

Frankena, W. (1958). Obligation and motivation in recent moral philosophy. In A.I. Melden (Ed.), *Essays in moral philosophy* (pp. 40–81).Seattle: University of Washington Press.

Frankfurt, H. (1988). Freedom of the will and the concept of a person. In H. Frankfurt (Ed.), *The importance of what we care about: Philosophical essays* (pp. 11–25). Cambridge: Cambridge University Press. (Originally published in *The Journal of Philosophy, 68*(1971), 5–20.)

Gauld, A., & Shotter, J. (1977). *Human action and its psychological investigation*. London: Routledge & Kegan Paul.

Habermas, J. (1984). *The theory of communicative action. Vol. 1: Reason and the rationalization of society* (T. McCarthy, Trans.). Boston: Beacon Press.

Habermas, J. (1990). Justice and solidarity: On the discussion concerning Stage 6. In T. Wren (Ed.), *The moral domain: Essays in the ongoing discussion between philosophy and the social sciences* (pp. 224–251). Cambridge, MA: MIT Press.

Hare, R.M. (1952). *The language of morals*. Oxford: Oxford University Press.

Hartshorne, H., & May, M.A. (1928–1930). *Studies in the nature of character: Vol. 1. Studies in deceit; Vol. 2. Studies in service and self-control; Vol. 3. Studies in organization of character*. New York: Macmillan.

Hoffman, M.L. (2000). *Empathy and moral development: Implications for caring and justice*. New York: Cambridge University Press.

Kant, I. (1963). *Lectures on ethics* (L. Infield, Trans.). New York: Harper & Row. (Original work published 1775–1780)

Kohlberg, L. (1984). Stage and sequence: The cognitive developmental approach to socialization. In L. Kohlberg, *Essays on moral development. Vol. 2. The Psychology of Moral Development*. New York: Harper & Row. (Original work published 1969)

Kohlberg, L., Boyd, D., & Levine, C. (1990). The return of Stage 6: Its principle and moral point of view. In T. Wren (Ed.), *The moral domain: Essays in the ongoing discussion between philosophy and the social sciences* (pp. 151–181).Cambridge, MA: MIT Press.

Kohlberg, L., Levine, C., & Hewer, A. (1983/1984). Moral stages: A current statement and response to critics. In L. Kohlberg (Ed.), *Essays on moral development. Vol. 2. The Psychology of Moral Development*. New York: Harper & Row.

Macmurray, J. (1961). *Persons in relation*. London: Faber & Faber.

Merleau-Ponty, M. (2012). *Phenomenology of perception* (D. Landes, Trans.). London: Routledge.

Midgley, M. (1981). *Heart and mind*. New York: St. Martin's Press.

Mischel, W. (1976). *Introduction to personality*. New York: Holt, Rinehart & Winston.

Mischel, W. (1968). *Personality and assessment*. New York: Wiley.

Nagel, T. (1970). *The possibility of altruism*. Oxford: Clarendon Press.

Nagel, T. (1986). *The view from nowhere*. Oxford: Oxford University Press.

Piaget, J. (1965). *The moral judgment of the child*. (M. Gabain, Trans.). New York: Free Press. (Original work published 1932)

Russell, B. (1905). On denoting. *Mind* (1905) 14:479–493. (Reprinted in R.C. Marsh (Ed.), *Logic and knowledge* (pp. 41–56). London: Allen & Unwin, 1956.)

Russell, B. (1921). *The analysis of mind*. London: Allen & Unwin.

Sartre, J-P. (1969). *Being and nothingness* (H. Barnes, Trans.). London: Methuen.

Searle, J. (1969). *Speech acts: An essay in the philosophy of language*. Cambridge: Cambridge University Press.

Shotter, J. (1975). *Images of man in psychological research*. London: Methuen.

Slote, M. (2007). *The ethics of care and empathy*. New York: Routledge.

Sytsma, S. (1990). Internalism and externalism in ethics (Unpublished doctoral dissertation). Loyola University of Chicago.

Taylor, C. (1976). Responsibility for self. In A. Rorty (Ed.), *The identities of persons* (pp. 281–299). Berkeley: University of California Press.

Taylor, C. (1989). *Sources of the self: The making of the modern identity*. Cambridge, MA: Harvard University Press.

van Haaften, W., Korthals, M., & Wren, T., Eds. (1997). *Philosophy of development: Reconstructing the foundations of human development and education*. Dordrecht & Boston: Kluwer

Wren, T. (1990). The possibility of convergence between moral psychology and metaethics. In T. Wren (Ed.), *The moral domain: Essays in the ongoing discussion between philosophy and the social sciences* (pp. 15–37). Cambridge, MA: MIT Press.

Wren, T. (1991). *Caring about morality*. London: Routledge; Cambridge: MIT Press.

Wren, T. (2010). *Moral obligations: Action, intention, and valuation*. New Brunswick, NJ: Transaction.

AFFILIATION

Thomas E. Wren
Department of Philosophy
Loyola University Chicago
Chicago, USA

STEPHEN J. THOMA & MURIEL J. BEBEAU

II. MORAL MOTIVATION AND THE FOUR COMPONENT MODEL

INTRODUCTION

In the early 1980s, Rest proposed a Four-Component Model of moral functioning in which moral motivation is featured. Although less well articulated than the other three components, Rest suggested that moral motivation influences moral action directly and in interaction with the other components of the moral system. The purpose of this chapter is to describe and summarize the empirical literature generated by Rest's model.

MORAL MOTIVATION AND REST'S FOUR COMPONENT MODEL

Prior to Rest's Four Component model, the cognitive developmental approach to moral motivation was at best a secondary consideration. To Kohlberg and his colleagues, moral motivation could be explained in large part by the moral judgment process (Kohlberg, 1969). In this view, moral judgments were by definition prescriptive—once a situation was understood within a moral framework, the obligation to act was presupposed. The motivation to act, therefore, was associated with the individual's moral understanding of the situation. Kohlberg assumed that the relationship between moral understanding and motivation was not constant across the stage sequence, but that it strengthened with development. Thus the upper stages, by virtue of their alignment with moral ideals, were more closely linked with the motivation to act in concert with moral reasoning (Colby & Kohlberg, 1987). Kohlberg was aware of other factors (e.g., ego strength) that influenced the link between moral reasoning and action, but these processes were viewed as moderators of this relationship and not central to the motivation to act. Furthermore, Kohlberg described the impact of these personal attributes as decreasingly influential across development; this parallels his notion of the how stages and motivation were linked across development (Kohlberg &Candee, 1984). Although Kohlberg later added the importance of living in a just world as a condition for enabling moral motivation and development, he never pulled back from the view that moral stages—especially the higher stages—were inherently prescriptive and the most salient aspect of moral motivation (Colby & Kohlberg, 1987). His view mirrored the Platonic notion—one has to "know the good" in order to "do the good."

During the 1980s, critics (following Kurtines & Grief, 1974) began to question Kohlberg's perspective on the assumed strong ties between the moral reasoning

K. Heinrichs, F. Oser & T. Lovat (Eds.), Handbook of Moral Motivation: Theories, Models, Applications, 49–68.

process and moral motivation. These concerns were often associated with the growing interest in moral action and questions about the ways in which moral judgment measures could be validated. Specifically, Kohlberg and colleagues focused their efforts on demonstrating that their measurement of moral stages conformed to developmental expectations such as sequence invariance (Colby & Kohlberg, 1987). Increasingly, critics questioned the view that moral judgment measures could be judged solely by demonstrating a fit to developmental criteria (Blasi, 1980). For these critics, it was important to supplement information on the developmental properties of the moral judgment measure with information demonstrating that the measure was linked to theoretically meaningful criteria outside of the measurement system— such as moral action. Of particular significance to this debate was Blasi's (1980) review of the judgment and action literature. In this review, Blasi emphasized the importance of testing the Kohlbergian model by focusing on moral action. Indeed, Blasi suggested that moral action was the ultimate criterion for measures of moral judgment. Furthermore, and most significantly, Blasi noted that the evidence for a strong relationship between moral judgments and action had not been established. A gap existed between reasoning and acting and Blasi suggested that the field ought to address it.

Rest's work on developing the four component model was very much in the spirit of Blasi's position. Like Blasi, Rest came to the conclusion that moral judgment processes were necessary but not sufficient for moral action. He noted that reviews of the moral judgment and action research, using his Defining Issues Test (DIT) of moral judgment development, indicated only 11% of the behavioural variance could be accounted for by DIT scores. Like Blasi, Rest recognized the importance of moral action as a primary validating criterion for any measure of moral thinking. Rest often noted (Rest, 1986) that an interest in moral phenomena would quickly erode if the field failed to support a linkage between judgments and actions. However, unlike Blasi's approach to fill the gap between judgment and action, Rest's work took a markedly different direction. During the early 1980s, Rest was commissioned to write the chapter on morality for an upcoming Mussen Handbook of Moral Psychology. His approach to the task was to review the literature from varying theoretical perspectives of the field—broadly defined—with an eye toward information that might be helpful in understanding moral action. By viewing the field from multiple theoretical perspectives and focusing on moral action, he deduced four clusters of findings that represented conceptually independent sources of information that could be claimed to support moral action. These clusters ultimately became the Four Component Model. It is important to note that Rest's approach to filling the judgment and action gap was quite different from other attempts. He developed the model from the bottom up, relying on a broad empirical base to suggest central processes supporting moral actions. Others (e.g., Blasi) approached the task from the top down by focusing at the person level to identify the mechanisms leading to moral action. Some have criticized the Four Component Model as being incomplete or ill-defined (Minnameier, 2010) and often point to the moral motivation component in the model as particularly incomplete. We would agree that moral motivation is probably the least structured of the components but would point out that this lack of specificity was an accurate reflection of the field. It was also a weakness that Rest readily acknowledged (Rest, 1983). In his various descriptions of moral motivation, Rest noted that the field had little to offer in the way of a well-articulated developmental model of moral motivation (Rest, 1986).

A further difference between Rest's approach and more contemporary models of moral motivation is perhaps more limiting. In framing his task to fill in the judgment and action gap, Rest asks us to consider which psychological mechanisms lead to a specific moral action. As mentioned above, his response to this question is the four component model. However, by focusing on the action level, this model does not elaborate on reasons that one might be the type of person for whom moral action is prototypic or why another person characteristically prioritizes other non-moral considerations. That is, by focusing on the events leading to a particular action, Rest did not attend to the person-level factors that are associated with a more generalized moral motivation.

When one compares Rest's model with more contemporary descriptions of motivation that do focus on person level motivational characteristics, the difference in emphasis is apparent (e.g., Schunk & Zimmerman, 2005). In these more general models of motivation, the focus is on the self's evaluation of two main characteristics: Control beliefs—or the individual's perception that the self is able to accomplish desired outcomes given a set of circumstances; and, competency beliefs—defined as whether the individual assumes that he/she has the means and abilities to accomplish desired goals. As Schunk and Zimmerman (2005) make clear, all established motivational models incorporate these two beliefs in some form. Rest's model, by focusing on actions, does not emphasize a direct assessment of the individual's perception of their own moral control and competency beliefs.

By contrast, moral motivation, as defined by research traditions that focus on the person, does provide evidence of the presence of control and competency beliefs. For instance, in the moral exemplar tradition (e.g., Colby & Damon, 1992; Rule & Bebeau, 2005; Frimer & Walker, 2009), one notes the finding that exemplars develop highly effective strategies for implementing action plans. Similarly, these studies note that moral exemplars have a tendency toward optimism in which the individual demonstrates confidence in his or her abilities to bounce back from setbacks and persevere. Indeed, much like the student who is academically oriented and has developed a sense of the abilities and strategies necessary to maintain superior performance, moral exemplars also show a pattern of attitudes and effective strategies that maintain an openness to moral experience, that serve to keep one seeking new knowledge for implementing appropriate actions, and a faith in one's ability to succeed.

These findings, derived from a focus on moral exemplars, suggest that Rest's four components ought to be considered as nested within models that prioritize the role of the person (e.g., Blasi, 1984; Frimer & Walker, 2009; Rule & Bebeau, 2005). In this view, Rest's components represent processes that are evoked to generate a moral response within a specific situation and context but do not address the notion of the centrality of morality. Although each component process that Rest defined has connections to the more general processes captured by models of the moral person (as illustrated by the bedrock moral schema that are at the foundation of Component 2), the particular focus of Rest's model is on specific actions and how these actions are constructed. Few studies have explored how Rest's model is linked to other traditions that focus on the moral person. However, one can speculate on some potential indicators of individual differences in this relationship. As researchers suggest (Rule & Bebeau, 2005; Colby & Damon, 1992), individuals who define themselves by their moral identity ought to be more likely to identify moral issues in their surroundings, engage in identifying the most reasonable actions, feel obligated to act on them and develop reasonable solutions. Overall, it should be evident that an unexplored aspect of Rest's Four Component Model is how the model relates to the psychological mechanisms advanced by research traditions which focus on the centrality of moral action and moral purpose.

Despite the need for further elaboration of the components, as well as their relationship to theories of the moral person, what Rest clearly accomplished with the Four Component model was to promote the transition from a global model of moral action to a multi-process view of moral functioning and, in so doing, pushed the field to look more broadly at how moral action is constructed and specifically how each of the contributing factors develop. Additionally, by transitioning to a multi-process model, Rest was able to propose that moral failings were not simply the result of an individual's weakness but everyone, even well-motivated individuals, could come up short. Each of us, Rest argued, are able to miss the moral problem, fail to effectively reason about how the moral problem ought to be solved, fail to maintain a focus on the moral solution in the face of other considerations, and fail to effectively follow through. Finally, it is important to note that one of Rest's underlying goals was measurement development and the four components were described with an eye toward stimulating the development of measures that capture an expanding view of moral functioning. In this respect, Rest's model has been quite successful (c.f., Thoma, 2006).

Moral Motivation in the Rest Model

The definition of moral motivation provided by Rest highlights the need for a set of processes used to address how one transitions from coding the situation as moral and knowing what one ought to do within moral situations to the decision to act in accordance with the moral perspective. Rest suggested that, within real-life situations, there are always multiple pressures on the individual to act in various ways and often these alternatives are in conflict with the moral ideal. How then does the individual choose? In his descriptions of the Four Component Model, Rest notes two types of studies that help identify how the individual might promote the moral course of action.

The first literature that Rest noted concerned general models of decision making. Focusing on behavioural decision theory (e.g., Rappoport & Wallsten, 1972), Rest proposed that information on how individuals generally confront complex decision making tasks might also help us understand how different claims on the individual are weighted and prioritized within moral contexts. Unfortunately, Rest found more weaknesses than strengths in the literature which, he noted, failed to incorporate affective processes that might be especially salient in moral decision making. For instance, Rest recognized that little attention had be directed towards understanding how emotions evoked by situations altered the individual's appraisal of the situation and action choice. Similarly, Rest noted the possibility of defensive operations being particularly active in moral situations. These defensive operations could have the effect of devaluing the moral basis of the situation and, in so doing, elevate other non-moral considerations (e.g., Bandura, 2002). Finally, Rest identified the obligatory nature of moral decisions which were poorly represented in these cognitive models of decision-making. For example, Rest highlighted the notion that individuals often indicate an overarching claim to: "do the right thing" that does not seem to benefit from a deliberative process. In addition to these concerns, Rest also noted that the developmental properties of the decision-making literature were not particularly clear and very few direct applications to moral phenomena were evident in the literature. He concluded (Rest, 1983, 1986) with the observation that the special nature of moral decisions was unlikely to be easily fitted within more general models of complex decision-making.

The second literature base that Rest used to inform his Component III processes was motivational models that explicitly address moral phenomena. These perspectives on moral motivation were a diverse set of models that ranged from the sociobiological, behavioural, personality and social cognitive ones. Few of the models were supported by extensive empirical work and fewer still had a developmental focus. However, Rest made much of the fact that cognition was involved to a varying degree within these sets of models, and that these cognitions were often influenced by, or were associated with affective processes. That is, for action to occur, Rest argued that one must have some cognitive apparatus to recognize the moral goal and then some affective processes to emphasize the value of pursuing moral goals. Although Rest noted the importance of the affective component of moral functioning, the integration of cognitive and affective components is not fully explored in his writing. However, we would note that more contemporary models that seek to bridge the "gap" between action and judgment are consistent with Rest's overall view of moral functioning. For instance, models which emphasize the self system and suggest that the development of a moral identity is the integrating mechanism which brings together the various cognitive and affective processes involved in moral functioning would be welcomed by Rest—particularly now that there are methodologies in place that can directly assess moral identity (e.g., McAdams, 2001) and empirical support for these claims (Walker & Frimer, 2007; Rule & Bebeau, 2005).

Research Programs Influenced by Rest's Component III

Rest's model has directly influenced three lines of research on moral motivation. Each line explicitly relies on the description of Component III to frame their research questions and methodologies. Two of these approaches focus on moral motivation directly and attempt to identify individual differences in the emphasis placed on moral issues. The other perspective focuses on the decision-making process and the ways in which moral information is either elevated or diminished.

Models of moral motivation. There are two research programs which focus directly on moral motivation. Interestingly, both do so within the context of professional populations. This focus is not a coincidence and much is made about the advantages of working within these populations. The most important advantage is that professionals tend to be more aware that ethical considerations are explicit in their roles and learn early in their training and socialization that one must be ready to provide justifications for their actions (Rest & Narvaez, 1994). This orientation to moral phenomena can be contrasted with general populations that may be more or less experienced in considering moral issues and, thus, influenced by a broader set of considerations—both rational and irrational. Furthermore, minimized in the professional setting is the potential emphasis on self-interest that can be at odds with the moral ideals. Unlike the various roles assumed by individuals in the general population, the role of a professional tends to emphasize actions that benefit others. Of course, professionals vary in the degree to which their decisions are reflective, deliberate and resistant to self interest. However, the point is that within populations that are trained to reflect on the moral basis of their actions and place the interests of the client before the self, the range of idiosyncratic factors influencing action is, if not reduced, at least open to challenge. Thus, the development of measurement systems within professional settings is likely to emphasize the rational and reflective aspects of moral motivation and de-emphasize the irrational, intuitive, and impulsive factors.

An open question is the degree to which findings generated by these measures can generalize to non professional populations unconstrained by a professional identity and training (e.g., Walker, 2002). Clearly, one difference that researchers must address in shifting focus to general populations is the measurement of moral motivation. As described above, the common moral perspective shared by professionals allows the use of proxy measures that piggyback on the link between professional identity and moral identity. The lack of a common moral perspective in the general population shifts the measurement to more ideographic approaches that are sensitive to the individual's moral framework. To this end, projects such as McAdam's narrative approach in assessing a life-story model of human identity, as modified by Frimer and Walker (2009), should be useful in framing general population measures. Of particular interest in this work is the increased focus on the developmental processes that underlie the integration of the self around moral action.

The Professional Role Orientation Inventory (PROI)

The PROI was the first of the measurement systems directly influenced by Rest's conception of component 3 (Bebeau, Born, & Ozar, 1993; Thoma, Bebeau & Born, 1998). Central to the development of the measure was an assumption that professionals differ in how they view their professional role and that these differences also reflect the emphasis placed on moral considerations in their professional interactions. Bebeau and her colleagues note that some professionals focus on the privileged role that society provides for them based on their level of expertise and training. Professionals who emphasize this aspect of the profession may not recognize the moral considerations of their professions as central to their role. Others, by contrast, emphasize the responsibility to society associated with their role. These professionals appear to elevate moral and caring considerations beyond those who orient to other roles. In short, this measurement system is based on the assumption that a professional's role is, in part, a proxy for the relative emphasis on moral criteria in professional decision making.

The PROI[1] is designed around a dimensional conception of profession role identity. With a notion of professional identity borrowed from applied philosophy, researchers argue that different professions can be reliably defined along two dimensions: authority and responsibility. The dimension of Authority contains the view that a profession has, to a varying degree, ownership over profession specific knowledge. This knowledge is obtained through advanced training and is recognized by society as a good that is essential for health and welfare. The second dimension, responsibility, describes the assumption that the profession has an obligation to provide this essential good to society and to monitor its members to assure that expected standards of health and welfare are maintained (Rule & Welie, 2009). Researchers interested in studying professions note that where the profession is located within this two-dimensional space mirrors the relative standing of the field within society. Thus, professions high in authority and responsibility tend to be the most prestigious and learned (e.g., Law, medicine) and those in other quadrants less respected.

These researchers also note that there is within-group variability in the professional orientation. That is, not all professionals agree on the mix of authority and responsibility associated with their field. For instance, some lawyers might emphasize the value of their services and view their profession in more commercial terms (i.e., low on social responsibility but high on authority). Other professionals might view themselves as "hired guns" and are willing to advance their client's or employer's interests at all costs (i.e., low authority and low responsibility). Still others might view themselves as providing a significant service to society, even as they sacrifice the quality of care that is provided (i.e., high on responsibility and low on authority). That is, how one sees his/her role may provide some insight into the individual's motivational set and indirectly how moral criteria are emphasized.

Bebeau and her colleagues used the results of a series of studies to support the claim that the PROI measures an aspect of moral motivation and not simply some general role orientation. The first set of studies focused on a known group validation strategy. This approach focuses on groups of professionals who, by training and clearly identified selection criteria, ought to differ on a measure of moral motivation. Thus, the question asked in these studies was could the PROI reproduce the various groupings? Specifically, these researchers (Bebeau, Born & Ozar, 1993) identified three groups of dentists who differed in their exposure to, and interest in, the moral dimension of the profession. These groups included a convenience sample of upper mid-west dentists, a group of dentists who self-selected into a professional ethics seminar, and a smaller group trained in professional ethics, some of whom were also dentists. Each group was given the PROI. Findings indicated that the sample of upper-Midwest dentists presented a wide range of professional roles as evidenced by roughly equal numbers in each of the four quadrants formed by responses to the responsibility and authority dimension. This broad pattern of roles was shown to be different from the response patterns of the participants in the ethics seminar. Unlike the upper mid-west sample of dentists, the seminar participants were characterized by high ratings on the responsibility dimension with marked variability on the authority dimension. Those trained in dental ethics, by contrast, provided PROI scores that clustered near the midpoint on the authority dimension but were very high on responsibility. However, ethicists who were also dentists tended to score higher on authority—seemingly reflecting the importance of professional expertise. Thus, in support of the view that the PROI reflects a moral motivation component, Bebeau noted that dentists with a varying interest and experience with dental ethics evidenced different professional roles on the PROI in a theoretically consistent way.

The second group of studies used to validate the PROI focused on whether the measure was sensitive to an intervention that was designed to influence students' view of professional ethics, as framed by Rest's Four Component Model. Bebeau compared first year dental students with senior students who had the benefit of an intensive ethics curriculum. As freshmen, the students resembled the mid-west sample of dentists described earlier and produced PROI scores that ranged in all four quadrants defined by authority and responsibility. However, by their senior year, students' PROI scores converged on the responsibility dimension and resembled the previous study's dentists with ethics training. Their education also seemed to develop a greater appreciation for the authority of the profession, as reflected in a general increase on the authority dimension. This important finding shows that roles can be influenced by educational interventions and it is possible to help students develop a professional role that is more aligned with an ethical perspective.

In addition to studies that support the validity of the PROI, researchers have also assessed the relationships between PROI scores and scores derived from the other components in Rest' model. Consistent with Rest's view that the four components represent non-overlapping processes which work together to support moral action, empirical studies linking the PROI to measures of the other components indicate moderate to low correlations. Across components, moral judgment development as measured by the DIT is most often related to PROI scores (Bebeau, 2009a; You & Bebeau, 2012). When the PROI dimensions are treated independently, DIT summary scores are more strongly linked to the responsibility dimension and less so to professional authority. It is perhaps not so surprising that the responsibility dimension is most related to the DIT. As mentioned previously, responsibility in this measure represents the dentist's obligation to society at large. Given that the DIT measures a moral perspective that highlights how individuals understand cooperation as informed by society-wide structures such as the political process, legal systems and social norms, one would expect the responsibility dimension to be conceptually similar (e.g., Thoma, 2006). However, even when focused on this dimension, the magnitude of the relationship between the responsibility dimension and DIT scores is not large and accounts for approximately 10% of the variance (You & Bebeau, 2012). Unfortunately, no studies have linked the PROI individually or in combination with moral action.

Moral identity. A second strategy for exploring moral motivation explicitly derived from Rest's model is Bebeau's and colleagues' (Bebeau & Monson, 2011) work on professional identity. Professional identity differs from the PROI in both methodology and level of assessment. As previously described, the PROI asks participants to reflect on various aspects of their profession, and their perspectives place them along established dimensions generally associated with the professions. Although students and professionals may recognize these dimensions, and reflect on their meaning for the self, there is no guarantee that the individual would spontaneously generate the same dimensions. Furthermore, the PROI does not directly assess professional identity but infers it by locating the individual along the different dimensions. To overcome these limitations, Bebeau and colleagues developed a measurement to assess the individual's own conception of their professional identity. Both strategies are qualitative in nature. The original approach was a written task (The Role Concept Essay) that asked participants to reflect on various aspects of the profession. At its conception, the essay was assessed for the degree to which participants could articulate expectations of a professional and, in particular, address questions of what being a professional means to the participant and what will be expected by society once one becomes a professional. Bebeau (1994) noted that most students, upon entry into professional school, have very little familiarity with concepts of a profession, including moral considerations. However, later in the program and following instruction, these concepts become familiar and part of their understanding of a professional role.

More recently, professional identity has been evaluated using scoring criteria adapted from Kegan's (1982) life-span model of self-development (Bebeau &

Monson, 2011). Kegan's approach is based on constructivist notions that individuals are, by nature, engaged in making sense of the world and, in so doing, form conceptions of various social categories such as the self, the self as a member of society, as a professional, as a parent, and so on. Furthermore, Kegan proposes that there are some commonalities across individuals in how these conceptions of the self unfold, both generally and in specific contexts. Thus, Kegan and his colleagues propose a life-span model in which individuals can be located in terms of prototypic identity formation.

Bebeau and her colleagues reworked Kegan's model to focus on how the professional comes to understand his/her specific professional role (see Bebeau & Thoma, this volume). In short, the modifications made to Kegan's model include a more central focus on the moral self and assess the degree to which moral concerns seem to penetrate the conception of the self. To guide these modifications, Bebeau adopts Blasi's view that individuals differ in the degree to which moral considerations are emphasized in the self system. In this view, an emphasis on the moral dimension within the self system is associated with an increased perspective taking, a responsibility to maintain a focus on the moral dimension within situations and an increased likelihood to act in accordance with moral judgments.

Findings from the professional identity measure suggest that professional school students are varied in their self conceptions with many producing self descriptions at the level where the moral basis for the profession is not clearly recognized. However, assessments on more advanced students drawn from the same population indicatea transition to professional identities which were more in line with a society-wide perspective and a more clearly articulated ethical identity. Although these findings are consistent with PROI findings and the view that professional identity measures are sensitive to educational interventions, the evidence is only suggestive as simple maturation has not been ruled out.

In addition to demonstrating that the professional identity measure can be used to differentiate groups of professionals who reflect different training and exposure to ethical considerations, Rule and Bebeau (2005) applied the modified Kegan scheme to a national group of dentists nominated by their peers as moral exemplars. Consistent with the theoretical model, Rule and Bebeau (2005) found a pattern of highly developed professional identities, complete with a strong sense of responsibility to others. Thus, the model was able to distinguish groups who were different on objective criteria conceptually related to moral functioning.

Using a similar methodology with military cadets, Forsythe and colleagues (Forsythe, Snook, Lewis, & Bartone, 2002) found evidence of growth across the college experience and military training. Furthermore, cadets with higher scores on the Kegan measure were viewed as effective leaders by their subordinates, their peers and superiors. These findings suggest a link between professional identity and cadet behaviour over time. The authors attributed this cadet success to a self identity that enabled these cadets to attend better to the interests of others, while keeping a focus on the overall goal or mission. Interestingly, Forsythe found that officers who had achieved significant promotions, such as made them eligible for advanced education and career development that precedes appointment to senior leadership positions, had achieved key transitions in self identity. Thus, a professional identity which emphasizes both the personal and professional dimension, while maintaining a sense of responsibility to others, is a clear advantage for professional development—both short and long-term (Lewis, Forsythe, Sweeney, Bartone & Bullis, 2005).

Taken together, the application of the Kegan model has been helpful in indicating how identity formation helps place moral motivation within the person's moral self. This work is more conceptually rich than the PROI studies but, interestingly, provides some complementary data. In general, professionals who are identified through objective criteria as moral exemplars emphasize the responsibility one has to the larger community and society. Furthermore, both measures indicate that moral exemplars have a clear sense of professional authority and do not back off from their responsibility to the field. Finally, on both measures, individuals who emphasize moral action have an explicit sense of obligation to act and, in the case of the interview measure, take the position that their actions are not special but simply required. Additionally, on both measures, there is evidence of growth across a student's professional development. The latter further suggests that there is a developmental aspect to professional identity which can be influenced by educational interventions.

Influences on moral decision-making.   As mentioned previously, Rest also focused on a second cluster of processes to provide insight into Component III functioning. This sub cluster included various decision-making models and individual characteristics that influence the relative weighting given to moral information in determining an appropriate action. Surprisingly, only one empirical study has directly assessed this aspect of Rest's model. Focusing on rape supportive perspectives, Carroll (2009) designed a study that assessed the role of moral thinking, setting conditions, and moral disengagement processes on college students' decisions about a date rape incident.

Moral disengagement is a model that describes the systematic downgrading of moral considerations in formulating a course of action (e.g., Bandura, 2002). In Bandura's view, moral functioning is a joint process of moral thinking and environmental factors that are mutually supportive. Through experiences and direct instruction, the individual learns acceptable behaviours as well as the rationale for appropriate actions. These knowledge systems become the ethical standards that one follows in order to maintain a consistent moral self and avoid negative consequences. How one maintains a focus on these moral standards is explained through affective self-regulatory mechanisms that motivate and maintain moral action. Moral weakness or transgressions occasion a negative self-appraisal and affective arousal that produces self sanctions and ultimately a behavioural correction (see Bandura, 2002).

Bandura also suggests that there are social mechanisms that can alter the moral system by disengaging one's moral standards from action. That is, in Bandura's model, motivational processes are not fixed but must be activated to promote actions based on internalized moral standards. However, if not activated, other non-moral considerations take precedence and may fail to serve appropriate moral goals. Factors that lead to a failure to engage moral standards and the self-regulatory systems that promote moral action, have in common the effect of distorting the situation to avoid a moral obligation. These disengaging factors diminish the moral worth of the other individuals involved in the situation or by denying that a moral action is required. For example, Bandura makes much of how war-time propaganda tends to remove the moral worth of the enemy or competitors such that the moral standards one would otherwise evoke to constrain violence against others are never engaged. The horrific behaviour of combatants on civilians during the time of war can be modeled by noting the process of moral disengagement. Similarly, euphemistic labeling of actions can deflect moral activation by sanitizing the situation to avoid the moral component (e.g., using the term "taking out" the enemy rather than killing). In short, Bandura makes much of the setting conditions that can lead to an alteration of the moral decision making process and the subsequent disengagement of moral standards from moral action.

Noting the higher incidence of violence toward women in college students who are associated with college social fraternities, Carroll wondered whether the fraternity context might be linked to an increased likelihood of moral disengagement. Following Rest's (1983) view that moral components interact with, and influence each other, she also speculated that moral judgment development—a component II process—might buffer the influence of the fraternity setting on moral disengagement processes. To test these hypotheses, Carroll devised a measure of rape supportive attitudes that would be less susceptible to social desirability effects. Specifically, she asked male college student participants to take the role of a student judiciary member who has been asked to consider a date rape case. The specifics of the case are described as well as statements from the aggrieved and the accused parties. The study participant was then asked to assign the degree of fault to the male and female protagonists and then make a determination about whether the case should be forwarded to the court for full consideration or terminated for lack of merit. Of interest to Carroll's study were the decisions to terminate the case and the rating of relative fault given to the female protagonist. Rape supportive attitudes were indicated by a decision to terminate the case and assign a higher degree of blame to the female—both decisions that were at odds with expert appraisal of the case. An equal number of fraternity and non-fraternity members were assessed.

Carroll found that, compared to their non-fraternity peers, fraternity members were more likely to favour the male's side in the case, were higher in moral disengagement scores and lower in their moral judgment scores as measured by the Defining Issues Test of moral judgment development (the DIT). Using structural equation modeling, Carroll found that DIT and moral disengagement scores uniquely predicted rape supportive attitudes. Importantly, moral judgment development buffered moral disengagement in the fraternity context. That is, fraternity members with higher moral judgment scores were less likely to display rape supportive attitudes and had lower disengagement scores. Interestingly, the Carroll study clearly demonstrates the effect of Rest's Component 2 processes as assessed by the DIT as a constraint on the moral disengagement relationship with an outcome variable. That is, the study demonstrates component 2 effects on the link between component 3 and the choice variable.

More generally, the Carroll study is important in demonstrating the role of setting on moral motivation processes and suggests that social groupings and the climate they create can have both positive (i.e., the just community environment) and negative effects (e.g., fraternities, athletic teams) on the moral motivational process. Additionally, this study is one of the few that assesses relationships between components and outcome variables using statistical techniques that more closely resemble the theoretical linkages between components suggested by Rest (1983). Using these statistical techniques, Carroll finds differences by group (fraternity vs. non-fraternity) on the relationship between components, as well as direct and indirect effects of the moral judgment and disengagement variables on an outcome variable. These findings support the notion that the moral components that Rest identified are highly interactive and can be expected to support action directly and indirectly through other related processes. Furthermore, Carroll 's use of two different theoretical models—Bandura's Cognitive Social Learning approach and Rest's Cognitive Developmental perspective—is in the spirit of Rest's model building and his position that there is utility in attending to theoretically distinct research traditions.

SUMMARY

Rest's description of Component III is informed by two types of research questions, both of which focus on the relative emphasis on moral considerations in comparison with other claims on the individual. The first question focuses on the ways in which individuals weigh information in complex decision-making and the various defensive operations that can influence these choices. The second include more general models that specifically address moral motivation. To date, there are three lines of research directly influenced by Rest's description of Component III. Although the empirical research is not extensive there are some patterns and emphasizes that stand out.

A Focus on Development

Following Rest's description of Component III, all of the studies which reference his model attend in some way to the developmental properties of moral motivation. As described above the focus of this work is primarily on what develops, what influences change, and how developmental processes promote moral functioning. These emphases can be clearly seen in Bebeau and colleagues' work in adapting Kegan's model to explore professional identity. Development is also evident in the

PROI literature in both the descriptions of professional roles as sensitive to change and the use of the PROI measure to evaluate ethics intervention programs. Carroll's work attends to development through the assumption that the distortions associated with moral disengagement are minimized as moral judgment development proceeds.

This focus on development can be contrasted to other research traditions, which have placed an emphasis on personality characteristics that inform moral motivation. For instance, Walker and his colleague's (e.g., Frimer & Walker, 2009) research program on moral exemplars has produced data suggesting that exemplars differ from comparison group participants on the ability to integrate the personality traits of communion and agency. Thus moral motivation is furthered when individuals have a sense of connection between the self and others as well as a confidence in one's ability to affect change. The reconciliation model suggested by Frimer and Walker (2009), describe development as the shift from the person's conscious recognition of a tension between agency and communion to an active integration of the two.

It is interesting to note the similarities and differences between the developmental and personality approaches to exemplarity. Common to both models is the emphasis on a connection between the self and others captured by the communion personality type in the Walker approach and professional responsibility in the Rule and Bebeau model. Similarly, both models highlight the sense of active engagement and confidence in one's ability to achieve their goals. Walker's notion of agency and Rule and Bebeau's description of the committed professional are very similar as both address an active engagement in life events. Both the Walker and Rule/Bebeau approach highlight the path to leadership roles and to a consistent focus on serving others. Particularly evident in the dental exemplars was the ability to critically evaluate their profession while being clearly identified with it.

These similarities in outcomes notwithstanding there are clear differences in the explanations given for how individuals arrive at exemplarity. For personality models of moral functioning the operating assumption is that different personality characteristics guide the self toward moral phenomena in characteristic ways. These personality characteristics cover a wide terrain and influence the ways we present ourselves to others, react to information, motivate ourselves toward goals—moral or otherwise, and express our inner states. Additionally, personality characteristics can affect moral functioning through the ways we orient ourselves to knowledge and experience. These orientations can promote the development of moral processes through personality constructs such as those that foster openness to new experiences and promote (or hinder) the integration of moral functioning within the self system. Thus, personality operates in the background creating the conditions that influence the ways in which we function in the social world including moral functioning.

The research questions generated by personality approaches are also quite different from those framed within Rest's approach. In short, personality studies lead to the identification of clusters of characteristic that are implicated in moral functioning with the goal of describing how the implicated personality characteristics interact to promote various moral types. These moral types may be associated with an emphasis on moral phenomena or a devaluation of the moral. However the expectation is that researchers will find multiple sets of intermediate types that promote some aspect of moral functioning and not others (e.g., Walker 2004).

Developmental models of moral motivation on the other hand, locate individuals by the degree of integration, self reflection and recognition one presents in the assessment process. Personality characteristics are acknowledged in this system but often they are presented as impediments that needed to be addressed, acknowledged or overcome across the participant's life. The focus is on the characteristic ways the individual describes the self as a window into current functioning or professional/self development. Further, groups of participants who share some common status such as entering professional students can be described by their location on the developmental scheme and this location can provide a starting point for educational interventions. A developmental description of moral motivation is clearly more aligned with Rest's (1983) attention to developmental processes in his description of Component III and addresses his lament over the then near absence of a developmental focus in the research programs which informed this component.

A Focus on Education

Across all of the studies associated with Component III there is a sustained attention to educational applications. This focus is consistent with the longstanding applied interests that have been traditionally associated with the cognitive developmental approach to morality research dating back to Kohlberg's early work. Clearly, Bebeau's research program has as its goal an understanding of development and the processes that are most central in promoting growth. The goal of this line of research is that with an understanding of development processes one can then design appropriate and empirically supported educational interventions. These interventions should result in an effective way to promote in young professionals a well-established professional self system that features ethical behaviour. Although less central to its purpose, Carroll's study also emphasizes educational interventions. She notes the need for higher education institutions to intervene in groups of students associated with a particular setting that may be expected to foster the development of a culture that is disrespectful to others. As she highlights in her study, such environments are associated with the propensity to disengage moral motivation, leading to an increased likelihood of inappropriate actions and the devaluing of other students. Further, in identifying moral processes that are associated with these settings, Carroll suggests specific types of interventions designed for all undergraduate students early in their college careers.

An Acknowledgment of Settings

Throughout this work there is a consistent finding that settings matter. Carroll's work discusses this notion explicitly in interpreting her findings. She notes that the fraternity lifestyle is associated with attitudes and experiences that increase the likelihood of disengaging moral processes when interacting with women across a variety of social and educational settings. Bebeau and her colleagues also highlight that the development of young professionals requires educational environments that actively engage moral phenomena. She also finds that in the absence of a sustained attention to professional ethics, the traditional educational environment is associated with moral and professional development that is much more haphazard and diffuse. Continuing to monitor interactions between social settings on moral motivation seems particularly warranted given the current findings on development and professional growth that characterizes these studies.

CONCLUSION

Rest began his work that resulted in his four component model with an assumption that much could be learned about moral functioning by noting patterns in the empirical literature across different research traditions and theoretical models. This bottom up approach was clearly helpful in organizing the field but the resulting model was only as good as the existing data. Component III and moral motivation in particular, suffered from a broad and theoretically diverse literature base that varied greatly in quality and precision. Some researchers have noted this weakness and suggest independent processes such as the four components are incomplete models of moral functioning and one must look to broader constructs such as the individual's personality system (e.g., Blasi, 1984). In our view, the two approaches are not incompatible. Regardless of the theoretical model and level of assessment one should expect that moral sensitivity, judgment, motivation, and perseverance represent aspects of morality that need to be addressed and measured. To that end, Rest's model offers some guidance in framing these measurements and his description of moral motivation has stimulated research programs that have improved the state of knowledge about the conditions under which moral information is prioritized.

The issue now becomes how we integrate Rest's model and proposed measurements within a larger motivation system presupposed by traditional models of motivation and supported by researchers who study the moral self. As we noted earlier, by contrasting the Rest model with these alternative research traditions, we see the emergence of a second gap between social cognitive processes and moral action. If Blasi helped us identify the judgment and action gap (Blasi, 1980), then Rest's model suggests that we must also attend to the gap between the more context driven processes he described by the components and the personality and developmental processes identified as contributing to the moral self (e.g., Frimer & Walker, 2009). To move forward on this agenda we suggest two basic approaches. First, we can build up from the components. That is, we can move forward by noting patterns across components in order to identify profiles that convey a coordinated approach to moral phenomena that is reminiscent of the findings derived from the work on moral exemplars. For example and using Frimer and Walker's (2009) reconciliation model mentioned earlier, individuals who emphasize either agency or communion ought to present a pattern across Rest's components that highlights the lack of coordination between these two competing claims on one's motivation. We note Walker and Frimer's (2007) finding that statistical interactions between agency and communion do not out predict the individual main effects. Nevertheless we suggest that a lack of coordination between these themes would be evidenced not by statistical interactions, but through the identification of profiles across the components as defined by mean differences and the strength of paths between components. It is interesting to note that Bebeau (2009a; 2009b) found that dentists who were disciplined by their governing bodies did not show evidence of a failing on a particular component in Rest's system. Instead most noticeable was a lack of coordination across components and a particular weakness in one of them. It is interesting to speculate whether professionals who fail to uphold standards of the profession do so in characteristic ways based on an uncoordinated emphasis on agency or communion.

An alternative approach to reconcile the four components with personality and self-systems models is to focus on moderators and mediators of the component assessments. For instance Seligman, (1991) defines an affective/motivational dimension labeled "learned optimism" that has been independently noted in the moral exemplar literature (e.g., Colby & Damon, 1992; Rule & Bebeau, 2005). It seems reasonable to expect that measures that capture learned optimism may moderate the link between processes and moral action. Secondly, we suggest further exploring Kegan's model within a broader range of populations. Bebeau and her colleagues have demonstrated how measures of identity development have clear implications for understanding how moral motivation becomes integrated into the moral self (Bebeau & Monson, 2011; Rule & Bebeau, 2005). Although this work has focused on professional populations, the consistent findings supporting a link between the development of identity and moral motivation indicates that a more representative test of these claims is warranted. Taken together we see the development of a second generation of research that helps to connect the moral self literature with the key insights from Rest's model.

NOTE

[1] The full version of the PROI has two additional dimensions: Agency and Autonomy. These dimensions have not been emphasized in the literature and are not described here.

REFERENCES

Bandura, A. (2002). Selective moral disengagement in the exercise of moral agency. *Journal of Moral Education, 31*(2), 101–119.

Bebeau, M.J. (2009a). Enhancing professionalism using ethics education as part of a dental licensing board's disciplinary action: Part 1 An evidence-based process. *Journal of the American College of Dentists, 76*(2), 38–50.

Bebeau, M.J. (1994). Influencing the moral dimensions of dental practice. In J. Rest, & D. Narvaez, (Eds.), *Moral development in the professions: Psychology and applied ethics* (pp. 121–146). New York: Erlbaum Associates.

Bebeau, M.J. (2009b). Enhancing professionalism using ethics education as part of a dental licensing board's disciplinary action: Part 2 Evidence the process works. *Journal of the American College of Dentists, 76*(3), 32–45.

Bebeau, M.J., Born, D.O., & Ozar, D.T. (1993). The development of a professional role orientation inventory. *Journal of the American College of Dentists, 60*(2), 27–33.

Bebeau, M.J., & Monson, V.E. (2011) Professional identity formation and transformation across the life span. In A. McKee & M. Eraut (Eds.), *Learning trajectories, innovation and identity for professional development* (pp. 135–163). Springer: New York.

Blasi, A. (1980). Bridging moral cognition and moral action: A critical review of the literature. *Psychological Bulletin, 88*, 593–637.

Blasi, A. (1984). Moral identity: Its role in moral functioning. In W. Kurtines & Gewirtz (Eds.), *Morality, moral behavior, and moral development* (pp. 128–139). New York: Academic Press.

Carroll, J.A. (2009). Impact of Moral Judgment and Moral Disengagement on Rape Supportive Attitudes in College Males (Unpublished doctoral dissertation), University of Alabama.

Colby, A., & Damon, W. (1992). *Some do care: Contemporary lives of moral commitment.* New York: Free Press.

Colby, A., & Kohlberg, L. (1987). *The measurement of moral judgement.* Cambridge: Cambridge University Press.

Frimer, J.A., & Walker, L.J. (2009). Reconciling the self and morality: An empirical model of moral centrality development. *Developmental Psychology, 45*, 1669–1681.

Forsythe, G.B., Snook, S., Lewis, P., & Bartone, P. (2002). Making sense of officership: Developing a professional identity for 21st century army officers. In D. Snider and G. Watkins (Eds.), *The future of the Army Profession* (pp. 357–378). New York; McGraw Hill.

Kegan, R. (1982). *The evolving self.* Cambridge: Harvard University Press.

Kurtines, W., & Grief, E. (1974). The development of moral thought: Review and evaluation of Kohlberg's approach. *Psychological Bulletin, 81*, 453–470.

Kohlberg, L. (1969). Stage and sequence.The cognitive- developmental approach to socialization. In Goslin (Ed.), *Handbook of socialization theory and research.* Chicago: Rand McNally.

Kohlberg, L., & Candee, D. (1984).The relation of moral judgment to moral action.In W. Kurtines & Gewirtz (Eds.), *Morality, moral behavior, and moral development* (pp. 52–73). New York: Academic Press.

Lewis, P., Forsythe, G., Sweeney, P., Bartone, P.T., & Bullis, C. (2005). Identity development during the College years: Findings from the West Point Longitudinal Study. *Journal of College Student Development, 46*, 357–373.

McAdams, D.P. (2001). Coding autobiographical episodes for themes of agencyand communion. Unpublished manuscript, Northwestern University, Evanston, IL.

Minnameier, G. (2010). The problem of moral motivation and the happy victimizer phenomenon - Killing two birds with one stone. *Journal of New Directions for Child and Adolescent Development.*

Rappoport, A., & Wallsten, T.S. (1972). Individual decision behavior. *Annual Review of Psychology, 23*, 131–175.

Rest, J.R. (1983). Morality. In P.H. Mussen (Ed.), *Manual of child psychology* (pp. 495–555). 4th ed., Vol.3. New York: Wiley.

Rest, J.R. (1986). *Moral development: advances in research and theory.* New York: Praeger.

Rest J.R., & Narvaez, D. (1994). *Moral development in the professions: Psychology and applied ethics.* Lawrence Erlbaum Associates.

Rule, J.T., & Bebeau, M.J. (2005). *Dentists who care: Inspiring stories of professional commitment.* Carol Stream, IL: Quintessence Publishing Co, Inc.

Rule, J.T., & Welie, J.V.M. (2009). The access to care dilemma: Symptom of a systemic condition. *Dental Clinics of North America.*

Schunk, D.H., & Zimmerman, B. (2005). Competence and control beliefs: Distinguishing the means and ends. In P.A. Alexander & P.H. Winne (Eds.), *Handbook of educational psychology* (2nd ed., pp. 349–367). Mahwah, NJ: Erlbaum.

Seligman, M.E.P. (1991). *Learned optimism: How to change your mind and your life*. New York: Knopf.

Thoma, S.J. (2006). Research using the Defining Issues Test. In M. Killen & J. Smetana (Eds.), *Handbook of moral development* (pp. 67–91). L. Earlbaum: Mawah, NJ.

Thoma, S.J., Bebeau, M.J., & Born, D.O. (1998). Further analysis of the Professional Role Orientation Inventory. *Journal of Dental Research, 77,* Special Issues, Abstract, 116–120.

Walker, L.J. (2002). The model and the measure: An appraisal of the Minnesota approach to moral development. *Journal of Moral Education, 31*, 353–367.

Walker, L.J. (2004). Gus in the gap: Bridging the judgment-action gap in moral functioning. In D.K. Lapsley & D. Narvaez (Eds.), *Moral development, self, and identity* (pp. 1–20). Mahwah, NJ: Erlbaum.

Walker, L.J., & Frimer, J. (2007). Moral personality of brave and caring exemplars. *Journal of Personality and Social Psychology, 93*, 845–860.

You, D., & Bebeau, M.J. (2012). Gender difference in ethical abilities of dental students. *Journal of Dental Education, 76*, 1137–1149.

AFFILIATIONS

Stephen J. Thoma
Educational Psychology
College of Education
University of Alabama
Tuscaloosa, USA

Muriel J. Bebeau
Department of Primary Dental Care
School of Dentistry
University of Minnesota
Minneapolis, USA

GERHARD MINNAMEIER

III. DEONTIC AND RESPONSIBILITY JUDGMENTS

An Inferential Analysis

INTRODUCTION

Judgments of responsibility are considered a key component of moral functioning beyond mere deontic judgments. Contrary to most of those concerned with moral "responsibility", "motivation", "identity" and the like, the present paper argues that these commitment-yielding processes are part and parcel of moral judgment as such, rather than an obscure additional moral component. Apart from conceptual problems in particular with the notion of "moral motivation", moral responsibility can be shown to be an essential part of the overall process of moral reasoning proper. This is done on the basis of the Peircean inferential triad of abduction, deduction, and induction.

The "moral personality" has been a key topic in recent years (see e.g. Narvaez & Lapsley, 2009; Koops, Brugman, Ferguson, & Sanders, 2010), including research on moral exemplars (e.g. Walker & Frimer, 2007; 2009), moral character (e.g. Lapsley & Narvaez, 2006; Nucci & Narvaez, 2007), moral identity (see e.g. Blasi, 1983; 2004; Schlenker, Miller& Johnson, 2009) and responsibility (see Kohlberg & Candee, 1984). An important foil for these analyses has been the four component model which was originally put forth by Rest (1983) and taken over and adapted by Kohlberg and Candee (1984). A - if not *the*- key question in this overall framework is "Why be moral?" (see also Bergman, 2002; Nunner-Winkler, 2007), because it is held that moral judgment alone would not bring about personal commitment. "Deontic judgments" (to use Kohlberg's terminology) would have to be supported by or transformed into "judgments of responsibility", or "moral motivation" in Rest's terms. Apart from conceptual problems, in particular with the notion of "moral motivation", moral responsibility can be shown to be part and parcel of the overall process of moral reasoning, if it is analyzed in terms of the Peircean inferential triad of abduction, deduction, and induction.

As for the critique, moral motivation has proved to be a paradoxical concept and should therefore be rejected in the form originally suggested by Rest (see Minnameier, 2010a - see also the section on "The true problem of moral responsibility and the paradox of moral motivation"). It is argued that the processes that are typically subsumed under"judgments of responsibility" or "moral motivation" all belong to moral judgment as such and should not be divorced from it.[1]

K. Heinrichs, F. Oser & T. Lovat (Eds.), Handbook of Moral Motivation: Theories, Models, Applications, 69–82.

As a consequence, it is necessary to spell out how moral responsibility is addressed or brought about in the context of moral judgment itself. The present paper focuses on this question, relying on an inferential theory of reasoning that goes back to C.S. Peirce (see Minnameier, 2004; 2010b; 2010c), and where the overall process of reasoning and decision taking is divided into three specific inferences: abduction, deduction, and induction. This inferential framework allows us to reconstruct the process of moral judgment in a differentiated and highly coherent way. It comes out very clearly how deontic and responsibility judgments are (inter)related, what cognitive processes are involved in judgments of responsibility and what makes them valid or invalid.

The point to be made is that in the moral domain, abduction denotes the process of activating (or inventing) a moral principle with respect to a given situated moral problem, deduction refers to applying this principle to the case and inferring what follows or would follow for the agents involved, while induction concerns weighing the pros and cons of these consequences to decide whether to accept the judgment or not (that is whether the principle can be induced for situations like the one at hand). In other words, judgments of responsibility are held to be truly inductive inferences, whereas deontic judgments are deductive inferences (and questions of moral sensitivity fall into the scope of abductive inferences). It will also be demonstrated how the inferential approach can be tested in the moral domain.

In 1984, and drawing on a similar approach by Rest, Kohlberg and Candee proposed a model of moral functioning consisting of four phases (see Figure 1): (1) interpretation and selection of principles; (2) deontic choice; (3) judgment of responsibility or obligation; and, (4) non-moral skills/ego controls. Ever since, however, it has not been clear how much or how little especially judgments of responsibility have to do with moral judgment as such. In particular, byRest's account, they appear to be strictly divorced from moral judgment, while Kohlberg and Candee seem to see all the first three phases as components of a broader context of moral decision-making.

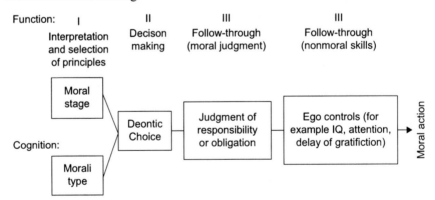

Figure 1. Model of the relationship of moral judgment to moral action (Kohlberg & Candee, 1984, p. 71).

The idea behind this sequence is that not every situation which is morally relevant, in principle, is also perceived as such by the agent, that not every moral (or deontic) judgment is complemented by the necessary will to put the moral decision into practice (especially committing oneself to what is generally thought to be morally right), and that not every moral commitment results in moral action owing to weakness of the will or other internal obstacles that prevent action.

THE RECEIVED VIEW(S) OF MORAL FUNCTIONING: AGREEMENT ON THE SURFACE, INCONSISTENCIES ON THE GROUND

As a general model, this approach seems to be widely accepted in moral psychology. It has been developed and advocated by Rest and his co-workers (see especially Rest, Narvaez, Bebeau, & Thoma, 1999) and, to my knowledge, has never been seriously questioned (apart from my own critique and the philosophical controversy on this very notion of moral motivation; see Minnameier, 2010a). Differences seem to exist only with respect to the details of moral functioning within this framework and to the question of independence or interdependence of the four components (see Bergman, 2002).

The Rest model consists of four so-called components: moral sensitivity, moral judgment, moral motivation, and moral character. In Rest et al., they are defined as follows:

"Moral *sensitivity* (interpreting the situation, role taking how various actions would affect the parties concerned, imagining cause-effect chains of events, and being aware that there is a moral problem when it exists)

Moral *judgment* (judging which action would be most justifiable in a moral sense ...)

Moral *motivation* (the degree of commitment to taking the moral course of action, valuing moral values over other values, and taking personal responsibility for moral outcomes)

Moral *character* (persisting in a moral task, having courage, overcoming fatigue and temptations, and implementing subroutines that serve a moral goal)" (Rest et al., 1999, p. 101).

While the model looks similar to that of Kohlberg and Candee, there are marked (and remarkable) differences between them. In particular, Rest clearly divorces moral judgment from moral motivation (see also Rest, 1983, p. 564; 1984, pp. 27, 32), whereas Kohlberg and Candee "hypothesize that there are two distinguishable but related modes or kinds of moral judgment" (1984, p. 56). In their view, moral judgment as a whole is divided up into two parts, a deontic judgment and a judgment of responsibility (see ibid, p. 57).

However, Kohlberg and Candee obviously agree with Rest (and Blasi) that "moral responsibility" (or "moral motivation" for that matter) is all about consistency between judgment and action. They expressly follow Blasi in identifying the idea of "moral responsibility" with the idea of "action consistent with the content of moral judgment" (1984, p. 56) and claim that subjects at higher stages are more likely to act responsibly, that is "to act in accord with choices about situations that they judged to be right when they were somewhat removed from the situation itself" (1984, p. 56).

Now, it may be asked whether Kohlberg and Candee's notion of moral responsibility is, after all, more in line with Rest's notion of moral motivation than stated above. As a matter of fact this seems to be true, but by the same token it also implies that Kohlberg and Candee's approach is inconsistent.

The inconsistency here is that responsibility judgments are meant to serve two quite different purposes: securing consistency between moral judgment and moral action, while at the same time playing a distinctive role within the overall process of moral judgment as such. In the terms of the first account, judgments of responsibility *follow* moral judgments, on the second judgments of responsibility are an integral *part of* moral judgment. By this account, moral judgment as a whole, consists of the interpretation of the situation and selection of a suitable moral principle (I), the deontic judgment (II) and the judgment of responsibility (III). These two views clearly contradict each other.

Consequently, there can hardly be a true understanding of Kohlberg and Candee's approach, but it has to be decided which way of conceptualizing moral functioning is most suitable from a psychological point of view. In this respect, most scholars seem to have tended toward the understanding that judgments of responsibility are logically independent from moral judgment, just in the sense of Rest's notion of "moral motivation" (cf. Bergman, 2002; Hardy & Carlo, 2005; Hardy, 2006; Nunner-Winkler, 1999; 2007; Malti, Gummerum, Keller, & Buchmann, 2009). However, the other option seems tenable, too, if not necessary, and I will argue for it on three different grounds.

First, the main dividing line that Kohlberg and Candee draw with respect to the gap between moral judgment and action seems to cut between Phases III and IV rather than between Phases II and III. Second, the whole idea of moral motivation seems utterly flawed. Third, the three different aspects of moral judgment as a whole, running across Phases I through III, can be perfectly accommodated by an inferential theory of reasoning applied to the domain of moral judgment.

THE TRUE PROBLEM OF MORAL RESPONSIBILITY AND THE PARADOX OF MORAL MOTIVATION

When discussing deontic and responsibility judgments, Kohlberg and Candee refer to philosophical analyses, and point out that "a deontic judgment may be seen as a first-order judgment of rightness, and responsibility as a second-order affirmation of the will to act in terms of that judgment" (1984, p. 56). This obviously concerns the move from Phase II to Phase III. And quite in line with that they move on quoting Blasi (1983) who argues that "(t)he function of a responsibility judgment is to determine to what extent that which is morally good or right is also strictly necessary for the self" (Kohlberg & Candee, 1984, p. 57). However, the quotation goes on to a point where Blasi says the following: "The transition from a judgment of responsibility to action is supported by a tendency toward self consistency" and "Following an action inconsistent with one's judgment of responsibility, guilt is experienced as an emotional response" (ibid.).

To be sure, the latter argument on inconsistency and the corresponding emotional reaction concerns the transition *from*- not to (!) - judgments of responsibility to action, which is mediated by *Phase IV*. The problems addressed here are down to weakness of will and all the related aspects mentioned by Kohlberg and Candee as well as by Rest in the context of their fourth phase or component. Hence the following passage, with which Kohlberg and Candee end their discussion, is at least unclear:

> To clarify the suggestions we take from Galon and Blasi, we might say that moral judgments of real situations go through two phases. The first phase is a judgment of rightness. The second phase is a judgment of responsibility, of the self's accountability to perform the right action, to "follow through." (Kohlberg & Candee, 1984, p. 57).

So much can be said: if the gap between judgment and action results from inconsistencies between judgments of responsibility and action, then it is located between phases III and IV rather than phases II and III. This is not to say that the move from Phase II to III is irrelevant or even not existent. It is only argued that phase III completes moral judgment (see the following section), so that any gap between judgment and action would consequently have to be located after that. But before turning to this point let us briefly consider the idea of "moral motivation".

Just recently a substantial critique of "moral motivation" was published which I would like to refer to for a detailed analysis (Minnameier, 2010a). Here, I will only summarize two connected points that, at least to my mind, reveal flaws of this concept. *First of all*, moral motivation must have its grounds or causes, if it is to be regarded as a source of the will that is independent from moral judgment (this is what so-called moral externalists argue for)[2]. However, moral motivation can be reduced neither to moral nor to non-moral grounds. In the former case it would have to be reduced to - at least implicit - moral reasons and would therefore fall into the realm of moral judgment. In the latter case (non-moral grounds) moral motivation would degenerate to something like mere inclination, bare of any specific moral character. It comes out that any emotion or motivation we might call "moral" has to relate to some kind of moral understanding, i.e. to moral cognition, or else it simply isn't "moral". Blasi (2004) has made this point very clear, and "moral motivation" in the Restian sense therefore remains as an unexplained, and in fact unexplainable, moral concept. For the larger philosophical context, see Minnameier (2010a; see also Birnbacher, 2003).

The *second point* focuses on the relationship between moral judgment and moral motivation. Moral motivation according to Rest is about selecting among competing values and deciding whether or not to fulfill one's moral ideal (1983, p. 564; 1984, pp. 27, 32). Now, if I ask myself whether I should follow some moral precinct in a certain situation or whether I should not, is this not a moral question itself, requiring a moral judgment? Indeed, the classic question whether Heinz should break into the druggist's to get himself the wanted drug is exactly of this kind. Whether he needs the drug for himself or for his wife and how serious the situation is, is another matter. The question as such poses a downright moral problem par excellence. What Rest calls "moral motivation" is, in reality, a question of moral judgment.

As a result, the notion of "moral motivation" reduces to an aspect of moral judgment, and trying to uphold the conceptual separation, in the way Rest and his followers tries it, ends up in self-contradiction. According to my first argument, the contradiction is that "moral motivation" fails to meet the criterion of morality; via the second argument, it is that what is thought to be distinguished from moral judgment is proved to be indistinguishable from it. Therefore, Rest's concept of moral motivation is clearly refuted.

The good news is that this does not force us to deny the relevance and substance of *judgments of responsibility* and to through the baby out with the bath water. It suffices to reject the externalist interpretation of moral motivation, particularly in the way that the Rest group has suggested it. However, we can still accommodate judgments of responsibility as a specific class of *judgments* within the overall context of moral reasoning. This can be done within an inferential approach that differentiates between abduction, deduction and induction (see below). What's more, this approach also allows us to integrate the first phase (interpretation of the situation) in this overall context and thus to explicate how these processes really hang together. In the following two sections we shall first discuss the inferential approach as such and then apply it in the sense of an inferential reconstruction of Kohlberg and Candee's model (at least the first three phases of it).

THE INFERENTIAL APPROACH

It remains to be shown what role judgments of responsibility play in the overall context of moral judgment. In order to explicate this, let us consider an inferential theory of reasoning that was originally developed by C. S. Peirce and that is being discussed, today, in many contexts and disciplines (see e. g. Aliseda, 2006; Campos, 2011; Gabbay & Woods, 2005; Magnani, 2009; Minnameier, 2004; 2005; 2010b; 2010c; Schurz, 2008).

On the Peircean account, reasoning is divided into three distinct inferences that cover the whole process from perceiving the original situation until the final judgment on the truth of an explanatory theory or the appropriateness of a practical approach or technology[3] (see Minnameier, 2004; 2010b; 2010c). Moral judgments fall into the second category, because they refer to principles that allow us to solve a practical problem, i.e. balancing different people's claims. In Peirce's original words, the inferences are described as follows:

Abduction is the process of forming an explanatory hypothesis. It is the only logical operation which introduces any new idea; for induction does nothing but determine a value, and deduction merely evolves the necessary consequences of a pure hypothesis. Deduction proves that something *must* be; Induction shows that something *actually is* operative; Abduction merely suggests that something *may be*. Its only justification is that from its suggestion deduction can draw a prediction which can be tested by induction, and that, if we are ever to learn anything or to understand phenomena at all, it must be by abduction that this is to be brought about. (Peirce, 1903/1934, p. 106 [CP 5.171][4])

Taken together, the three inferences constitute a dynamic and recursive structure, which is illustrated in Figure 2. *Abduction*[5] starts from a certain problematic situation that needs to be addressed by some theory. These can be surprising facts that demand in explanation or, in the practical context, a technical, a strategic or a moral problem. In the latter case, conflicting claims have to be balanced in a unifying approach (just as inconsistent phenomena have to be unified by a suitable explanatory theory). In particular, abduction marks the creative process that leads to new concepts. The validity of deduction depends on the capacity of the inferred concept to accommodate those facts in principle. Therefore, abduction produces one, or several, *possible* solutions to the initial problem.

Deduction allows us to draw necessary consequences from the suggested hypotheses or principles and the situational premises. In the cases of explanatory problems this yields testable empirical hypotheses, in the case of moral principles it yields action plans. To be sure, deduction can only result in logical truths, not empirical truths. Therefore its results have to be evaluated inductively.

In the context of inductive reasoning experimental results or past experiences are observed and considered until the epistemic subject is convinced that the theory must be true or that the chosen moral principle best fits the problem at hand. If the evidence sanctions such a judgment, the theory of principle is projected onto all relevant cases, i. e. all cases that share the relevant features, which comprises the original problematic situation, the other empirical examples that have been considered in induction and all other past and future cases that are of the same kind (as for the validity of inductive judgments see Minnameier, 2010c).

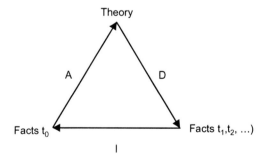

Figure 2. The dynamical interaction of abduction, deduction, and induction.

Anytime when such a new case is encountered the theory or principle ought to be applied accordingly. However, every new situation also functions as a new test case that can either reinforce or challenge the theory. This underpins the recursive nature of the inferential approach.

What is important in the context of moral functioning, i. e. the activation of moral-cognitive structures and the further processes in the models described above is that the inferential triad is passed through in the recognition and consideration of every newly encountered case. Therefore, and in this sense, the phases in Kohlberg and Candee's model can, at least to some extent, be reconstructed in terms of the inferential approach.

INFERENTIAL RECONSTRUCTION OF PHASES OF MORAL FUNCTIONING

The inferential theory can be applied rather straightforwardly to the field of moral functioning, and apart from a detailed and systematic reconstruction two more aspects become salient: First, it turns out that the phases suggested in the received models are much more closely linked to moral judgment as such than it was originally believed, and second, it can also been shown how ordinary moral reasoning at some point lead into cognitive conflicts and subsequent developmental progress. We try to reveal and illustrate both in this section.[6]

As can be easily derived from the above description of the three inferences, *abduction* relates to Phase 1, that is, to the interpretation of the situation and activation of a suitable stage principle. For instance, in the famous Heinz dilemma the situation has as its central features: (1) that Heinz is desperate, because his wife is about to die and because there is a drug that could save here, which he, however, cannot afford; and, (2) that the druggist could sell the drug at an affordable price, but tries to maximize his profit as a monopolist and therefore charges an amount that Heinz cannot possibly pay. In this situation, the moral question arises about whether Heinz has to accept this or whether he should burgle the druggist's shop in order to procure the drug for himself.

In terms of Kohlberg's stages[7], a suitable moral principle would be that of Stage 3. We have to consider two incompatible interests of persons that are in no close relationship. These can be compared by the Golden Rule. On top of this, Heinz's responsibility for his wife might also be a criterion. Both aspects clearly belong to Kohlberg's concept of Stage 3.[8] And both fit the present situation.

These principles can now be *deductively* applied to the situation. According to the Golden Rule, one could argue (in favor of Heinz's stealing the drug) that if the druggist were in Heinz's shoes he would also wish to be helped and therefore has no valid moral claim. He should give the drug away at a cheaper price that Heinz can afford and, more generally, he should help Heinz and his wife. Given the further premises that the druggist is not willing to compromise and that stealing is the only way out for Heinz, it follows that he ought to steal in order to save his wife and to counter the druggist's injustice.

Finally, it has to be evaluated *inductively* whether this result is acceptable. Note that the abductive choice of a principle does not force one to accept the resulting consequences. In particular it has to be judged, whether stealing would not create further problems, so that Heinz should ultimately refrain from it. Some of these points may be strategically relevant. For instance, it may be argued that Heinz could have to go to jail, which would mean extra hardship for him, but also for his wife (who would be alone and would have no one to care for her). Although morally justified in principle it might therefore be strategically wrong for Heinz to steal, where "strategically" means that stealing in this case would in the end not serve the pursued moral goal, which is helping his wife.

However, inductive evaluation may also reveal aspects that challenge the moral principle itself, not just affect its putting into practice. One might think of all the other people with wives and husbands suffering from cancer who are in need of medical treatment that they cannot afford. This is a pity, of course, but it is certainly not morally acceptable that all those people provide themselves with the wanted drugs using illegal methods, let alone the fact that the drugs in stock or that can be produced might not suffice for all. Thus, the observation that many others are in the same position as Heinz could cause a disequilibrationwithinKohlberg Stage 3 thinking and lead on to Stage 4 in a process of creative abduction.

COGNITION AND AFFECTIVITY

What does all that mean for the relationship of moral cognition and emotion, and what role would there remain, if any, for a "moral self"? Only a few sketchy points can and shall be addressed here, and it should be said in advance that, first, I assume a parallelism and mutual dependence of moral cognition and affectivity, and, second, that the moral self plays an important role despite the extended view of moral judgment expressed in this paper.

As for cognition and affectivity in general it has to be clear that no subject would undergo a process of moral reasoning if s/he were not motivated by a moral concern for others that constitutes the moral problem as such. For instance, somebody grabs an old lady's handbag. We would perceive it, be indignant and grumble about this lout. Robbing is a basic form of violating others' rights or property, and therefore considered wrong if there is no other justification. We see what happens and are sensitive to the violation; then we (in this case immediately) judge that it is a violation. It might be more difficult, if a poor boy lifts something in a shop. Again, someone is harmed which activates moral judgment and, in this case, might trigger a process of reflecting on whether the boy is just mean or whether he is desperate because he lives on the street and hasn't got anything to eat. This would perhaps justify his stealing. Whatever is the case and whatever we really think, here we can very well distinguish moral sensitivity, deontic judgment, and even the responsibility judgments, because different deontic judgments depend on certain assumptions, and responsibility judgment would have to qualify the boy's real situation or the one we think most likely. However, neither abduction, nor deduction, nor induction would have come about without the emotional arousal based on a basic moral marker such as, in this case, the robbery itself.

In other words, emotions mark both the beginning (arousal) and the end (satisfaction with the result) and guide the whole process of moral judgment. At the same time, reacting to a situational moral marker requires the moral understanding of this marker and hence necessarily involves moral cognition as well. What we learn from this is that moral functioning always has at least a cognitive and affective aspect and that therefore Piaget's original idea of a cognitive and affective parallelism seems to be adequate (Piaget, 1954/1981). Moreover, research on the emotional aspect tells us the same story, since *empathy* as the basis of and precondition for the feeling of sympathy has a strong cognitive aspect in terms of a perspective-taking capacity (see e.g. Eisenberg, Spinrad&Sadovsky, 2006, p. 518). And also Haidt acknowledges that cognition is always involved, to some extent, in any kind of intuitive moral responding (see Haidt & Kesebir, 2010, pp. 801-808). If we assume - as many do today - that different forms of moral cognition are activated depending on the situation rather than being driven top-down as Kohlberg believed, there seems to be little controversy.

Consequently, the inferential analysis of moral reasoning does not prevent us from assigning a proper role to the "moral self" in moral functioning, even one that is at least twofold. On the one hand, a strong moral self may be associated with moral sensitivity, that is, the individual's sensitivity to respond to morally relevant aspects of a given situation and also the strength (or the degree of emotional heat) of such an arousal. On the other hand, some people may identify more with certain moral practices than others. As a consequence, these people would be more likely to stick to a certain principle, even in situations in which others do not (even though they may all evaluate the situation on the same moral cognitive background in terms of moral stage).

It should be noted thatthis kind of steadiness may also be detrimental. We not only know people who allegedly lack this kind of "moral motivation" (the so-called "happy victimizers")[9], but we also know those who seem to have too much of it (the so-called "unhappy moralists"). Unhappy moralists uphold their principles, they pay their taxes, never cheat, and so on, but they realize that this may be a mistake, because real life often does not function this way (see Oser & Reichenbach, 2005; Oser, Schmid & Hattersley, 2006). It seems obvious, then, that the moral emotions involved have to be in line with the inductive evaluation discussed in the inferential context. And we may, in this respect, recall Aristotle's view of moral virtue as the mean between the extremes of deficiency and excess. One can certainly be too complacent (lack of moral responsibility) or too rigid (with an exaggerated sense of moral responsibility), and the mean would be measured by sound inductive moral judgment.

Therefore, I do not wish either deny or to downplay the role of moral emotions and the moral self. I only wish to make a point for the threepartitestructure of moral reasoning, the integral unity of abduction, deduction, and induction in this respect, and that this includes *judgments* of responsibility as *inductive judgments* in the moral domain.

CONCLUSION

Analyzed within the context of the inferential triad, the first three phases of Kohlberg and Candee's model of moral functioning can be reconstructed as three distinct phases of the overall process of moral judgment. This is an important result, because it reveals that the two phases, preceding and succeeding deontic choice, are not to be divorced from moral judgment. In particular, this account refutes the idea of moral motivation with which Rest substantiated his concept of "component 3" in his model and which was taken up by many scholars since, especially in order to explain the happy victimizer phenomenon.

Whereas the very idea of moral motivation is to be rejected on this account (see also Minnameier, 2010a), we need not throw out the baby with the bathwater and reject the general four phase model. We can rather put more and deeper meaning to it and understand the processes better.

Further research questions would arise and have to be dealt with in the context of this reconstruction. In particular, it should be determined how cognition and emotion interact in the overall inferential process. In the light of our reconstruction, a simple opposition or sequential separation, where cognition and emotion are regarded as more or less independent "modules" of moral functioning, appears as far too simple (see also Gibbs, 2010).

NOTES

[1] To be sure, this does not apply to those aspects that the remaining two components ("moral sensitivity" and "moral character") refer to.

[2] Their philosophical counterparts are the moral internalists who believe that moral judgments are motivating in themselves. Internalists argue that it would be practically irrational for a subject S to hold that A would be the proper course of action and still decide not to do A, absent distorting influences of weakness of the will (see e.g. Smith 1994/2005, p. 61).

[3] It is well established that abduction is not restricted to explanatory problems. Some abductions do not aim at truths, but merely at suitable strategies to achieve practical goals. Magnani (2009), e. g., refers to it as "instrumental abduction".

[4] This is the common way of referring to the "Collected Papers of Charles Sanders Peirce", where the first number indicates the volume and the volume and the second the paragraph in that volume.

[5] As for abduction there is quite some confusion around this notion (see Hintikka, 1998;Flach, 2000; Minnameier, 2004;Paavola, 2006; Schurz, 2008). To a large part this is due to Peirce himself, who first developed an inferential approach (1878/1931, esp. p. 374 [CP 2.623]) that he later turned around completely. And his main insight in this respect was that "in almost everything I printed before the beginning of this century (the 20th, G. M.) I more or less mixed up hypothesis (which was later called 'abduction', G. M.) and Induction" (c. 1910/1958, p.176 [CP 8.227]). Another problem is that Peirce largely squared abduction with a kind "guessing instinct" which by modern standards misses the point and conceals the deeper inferential aspect of abduction (see Paavola, 2005; Minnameier, 2010c).

[6] It has to be acknowledged that we will not reconstruct these phases in all possible detail. In particular, we cannot, for reasons of brevity, address the fact that each inference can be analytically split up into three subprocesses which Peirce calls "colligation", "observation", and "judgment" (c. 1893/1931, pp.267-269 [CP 2.442-444]). *Colligation* refers to the collection and representation of premises, *observation* to reflecting upon those premises and the initial generation of a solution, and *judgment* to probing whether the obtained result fits the validity criterion of the respective inference. It has to be left to the reader to analyze the examples given below in terms of these subprocesses.

[7] Kohlberg's stages are used as a common ground in the present context. However, they clearly do not suffice to address all relevant forms of moral reasoning. Therefore an alternative taxonomy that is both more differentiated and based on clear structural developmental principles has been suggested by the author (see e. g. Minnameier, 2000; 2001; 2005; 2009).

[8] Although these two aspects both belong to Kohlberg's Stage 3, it has to be noticed that they are entirely different forms of moral reasoning. Within the framework of the author's own taxonomy the first principle belongs to Stage 2C while the second refers to Stage 3A (see note vii).

[9] It should be noted that a stage-theoretical interpretation that evades moral motivation as the explanatory concept for the happy victimizer phenomenon is possible and has been proposed in Minnameier (2010a; submitted).

REFERENCES

Aliseda, A. (2006). *Abductive reasoning: Logical investigations into discovery and explanation.* Dordrecht: Springer.

Bergman, R. (2002). Why be moral? A conceptual model from developmental psychology. *Human Development, 45,* 104–124.

Birnbacher, D. (2003). *Analytische Einführung in die Ethik.* Berlin: de Gruyter.

Blasi, A. (1983). Moral cognition and moral action: A theoretical perspective. *Developmental Review, 3,* 178–210.

Blasi, A. (2004). Moral functioning: Moral understanding and personality. In D.K. Lapsley & D. Narvaez (Eds.), *Moral development, self, and identity* (pp. 335–347). Mahwah, NJ: Lawrence Erlbaum Associates.

Campos, D.G. (2011).On the distinction between Peirce's abduction and Lipton's inference to the best explanation.*Synthese, 180,* 419–442.

Eisenberg, N., Spinrad, T.L., & Sadovsky, A. (2006). Empathy-related responding in children. In M. Killen & J.G. Smetana (Eds.), *Handbook of moral development* (pp. 517–549). Mahwah, NJ: Lawrence Erlbaum Associates.

Flach, P.A. (2000). *Abduction and induction. Essays on their relation and integration.* Dordrecht: Kluwer Academic.

Gabbay, D.M., & Woods, J. (2005). *A practical logic of cognitive systems, Vol. 2: The reach of abduction - insight and trial.* Amsterdam: Elsevier.

Gibbs, J.C. (2010). *Moral development and reality: Beyond the theories of Kohlberg and Hoffman* (2nd ed.). Boston, MA: Allyn & Bacon

Haidt, J., & Kesebir, S. (2010). Morality. In S. Fiske, D. Gilbert, & G. Lindzey (Eds.), *Handbook of Social Psychology,* 5th ed. (pp. 797–832). Hobeken, NJ: Wiley.

Hardy, S.A. & Carlo, G. (2005). Identity as a source of moral motivation. *Human Development, 48,* 232–256.

Hardy, S.A. (2006). Identity, reasoning, and emotion: An empirical comparison of three sources of moral motivation. *Motivation and Emotion, 30,* 2007–2015.

Hintikka, J. (1998). What is abduction? The fundamental problem of contemporary epistemology. *Transactions of the Charles S. Peirce Society, 34,* 503–533.

Kohlberg, L., & Candee, D. (1984). The relationship of moral judgment to moral action. In W.M. Kurtines & J.L. Gewirtz (Eds.), *Morality, moral behavior, and moral development* (pp. 52–73). New York: Wiley & Sons.

Koops, W., Brugman, D., Ferguson, T., & Sanders, A.F. (Eds.) (2010). *The development and structure of conscience.* Hove: Psychology Press.

Lapsley, D.K., & Narvaez, D. (2006). Character education. In K.A. Renninger& I.E. Sigel (Eds.). *Handbook of Child Psychology, Vol. 4: Child Psychology in practice* (6th ed., pp. 248–296). New York: Wiley.

Magnani, L. (2009). *Abductive cognition: The epistemological and eco-cognitive dimensions of hypothetical reasoning.* Berlin: Springer.

Malti, T., Gummerum, M., Keller, M. & Buchmann, M. (2009). Children's moral motivation, sympathy, and prosocial behavior. *Child Development, 80,* 442–460.

Minnameier, G. (2000). *Strukturgenese moralischen Denkens: Eine Rekonstruktion der Piagetschen Entwicklungslogik und ihre moraltheoretischen Folgen.*Münster: Waxmann.

Minnameier, G. (2001). A new "stairway to moral heaven"? A systematic reconstruction of stages of moral thinking based on a Piagetian "logic" of cognitive development. Journal *of Moral Education, 30,* 317–337.

Minnameier, G. (2004). Peirce-suit of truth: Why inference to the best explanation and abduction ought not to be confused. *Erkenntnis, 60,* 75–105.

Minnameier, G. (2005). Developmental progress in ancient Greek ethics. *European Journal of Developmental Psychology, 2,* 71–99.

Minnameier, G. (2009). Measuring moral progress: A neo-Kohlbergian approach and two case studies. *Journal of Adult Development, 16,* 131–143.

Minnameier, G. (2010a). The problem of moral otivation and the happy victimizer phenomenon: Killing two birds with one stone. *New Directions for Child and Adolescent Development, 129,* 55–75.

Minnameier, G. (2010b). Abduction, induction, and analogy: On the compound character of analogical inferences. In W. Carnielli, L. Magnani & C. Pizzi (Eds.), *Model-based reasoning in science and technology: Abduction, logic, and computational discovery* (pp. 107–119). Heidelberg: Springer.

Minnameier, G. (2010c). The logicality of abduction, deduction, and induction. In M. Bergman, S. Paavola, A.-V. Pietarinen & H. Rydenfelt (Eds.), *Ideas in action: Procedures of the Applying Peirce conference*(pp. 239–251). Helsinki: Nordic Pragmatism Network.

Minnameier, G. (submitted). A cognitive approach to the "happy victimiser" and its educational implications, *Journal of Moral Education.*

Narvaez, D., & Lapsley, D.K. (Eds.) (2009).*Personality, identity and character: Explorations in moral psychology.* New York: Cambridge University Press.

Nucci, L., & Narvaez, D. (Eds.), (2007). *Handbook of moral and character education.* Mahwah, NJ: Lawrence Erlbaum Associates.

Nunner-Winkler, G. (1999). Development of moral understanding and moral motivation. In F.E. Weinert & W. Schneider (Eds.), *Individual development from 3 to 12: Findings from the Munich longitudinal study* (pp. 253–290). New York: Cambridge University Press.

Nunner-Winkler, G. (2007). Development of moral motivation from childhood to early adulthood. *Journal of Moral Education, 36,* 399–414.

Oser, F. &Reichenbach, R. (2005).Moral resilience: The unhappy moralist. In W. Edelstein & G. Nunner-Winkler (Eds.), *Morality in context* (pp. 203–224). Amsterdam: Elsevier.

Oser, F., Schmid, E. & Hattersley, L. (2006). The "unhappy moralist" effect: Emotional conflicts between being good and being successful. In L Verschaffel, F. Dochy, M Boekaerts& S. Vosniadou (Eds.), *Instructional psychology: Past, present and future trends* (pp. 149–168). Amsterdam: Elsevier.

Paavola, S. (2005).Peircean abduction: instinct or inference? *Semiotica153,* 131–154.

Paavola, S. (2006): Hansonian and Harmanian abduction as models of discovery. *International Studies in the Philosophy of Science, 20,* 93–108.

Peirce, C.S. (1878/1931). Deduction, induction, and hypothesis. In C. Hartshorne & P. Weiss (Eds.), *Collected papers of Charles Sanders Peirce, Vol. 2* (pp. 372–388). Cambridge, MA: Harvard University Press.

Peirce, C.S. (1903/1934). Lectures on pragmatism. In C. Hartshorne & P. Weiss (Eds.), *Collected papers of Charles Sanders Peirce, Vol. 5* (pp. 11–131). Cambridge, MA: Harvard University Press.

Peirce, C.S. (c. 1893/1931). The grammatical theory of judgment and inference. In C. Hartshorne & P. Weiss (Eds.), *Collected papers of Charles Sanders Peirce, Vol. 2* (pp. 265–269). Cambridge, MA: Harvard University Press.

Peirce, C.S. (c. 1910/1958). To Paul Carus, on "illustrations of the logic of science". In A.W. Burks (Ed.), *Collected papers of Charles Sanders Peirce, Vol. 8* (pp. 171–179). Cambridge, MA: Harvard University Press.

Piaget, J. (1954/1981). *Intelligence and affectivity: Their relationship during child development.* Palo Alto, CA: Annual Reviews.

Rest, J.R. (1983). Morality. In J.H. Flavell & E.M. Markman (Volume Eds.), *Handbook of child psychology (ed. by P.H. Mussen), Vol. III: Cognitive development* (4th ed.)(pp. 556–629). New York: Wiley.

Rest, J.R. (1984). The major components of morality. In W.M. Kurtinez & J.L. Gewirtz (Eds.), *Morality, moral behavior, and moral development* (pp. 24–38). New York: Wiley.

Rest, J., Narvaez, D., Bebeau, M.J., & Thoma, S.J. (1999). *Postconventional moral thinking: A neo-Kohlbergian approach.* Mahwah, NJ: Lawrence Erlbaum Associates.

Schlenker, B.R., Miller, M.L., & Johnson, R.M. (2009). Moral identity, integrity, and personal responsibility. In D. Narvaez & D.K. Lapsley (Eds.), *Personality, identity and character: Explorations in moral psychology* (pp. 316–340). New York: Cambridge University Press.

Schurz, G. (2008). Patterns of abduction. *Synthese, 164,* 201–324.

Smith, M. (1994/2005). *The moral problem.* Oxford: Blackwell

Walker, L.J., & Frimer, J.A. (2007). Moral personality of brave and caring exemplars. *Journal of Personality and Social Psychology, 93,* 845–860.

Walker, L.J., & Frimer, J. A. (2009). Moral personality exemplified. In D. Narvaez & D. K. Lapsley (Eds.), *Personality, identity and character: Explorations in moral psychology* (pp. 232–255). New York: Cambridge University Press.

AFFILIATION

Gerhard Minnameier
Department of Business Education
Goethe University
Frankfurt, Germany

THERESA A. THORKILDSEN

IV. MOTIVATION AS THE READINESS TO ACT ON MORAL COMMITMENTS

INTRODUCTION

A famous musician was walking through a park. A busker recognized him and immediately begged him to play. The musician initially refused, but a crowd began to grow and chant with the anticipation of witnessing a concert. Sighing, the musician took the busker's instrument and played so badly that everyone covered their ears. Upon finishing the piece, the musician took a brief bow and politely excused himself.

Those of us who work with intentional perspectives on motivation find it fascinating to imagine the motivation of actors in these types of situations (Dennett, 1987; Nicholls, 1989). Was the musician's reputation based on "studio magic"? Did the spontaneity of the crowd prove to be too intimidating? Or, did the musician operate with another intention in mind? What moral implications are embedded in this range of activities? In this chapter, I will describe how researchers use intentional frameworks to explain the process of motivation and extend that logic to questions of moral motivation. By applying the tenets of one intentional perspective to moral problems, I will illustrate why it may not be surprising to find weak relations between individuals' moral judgment and their moral action. Moral judgments, in this view, can easily reflect reasoning that is detached from opportunities to act, yet moral motivation requires action.

Motivation, according to this framework, is the force that compels action. In many models of motivation, intentional perspectives among them, action is part of motivation rather than a force that is independent of motivation (Atkinson & Raynor, 1974; Lewin, 1926; Weiner, 1972). Motivation is the means by which individuals formulate beliefs and goals, embrace desires, generate attributions to explain their experiences, and direct their energies as they act. Intentional theorists take this assumption one step further and explore how we predict our own and others' actions. An intentional stance toward explaining motivation typically involves a third person perspective whereby individuals' beliefs and desires are used to predict their behaviour (Dennett, 1987). Similarly, intentional action reflects a chain of steps that begins with a protracted, vigorous struggle of motives followed by an act of choice that terminates the struggle, and culminates with observable behaviour (Lewin, 1926). Figure 1 offers a diagram of one process by which predictions about action are defended.

K. Heinrichs, F. Oser & T. Lovat (Eds.), Handbook of Moral Motivation: Theories, Models, Applications, 83–96.

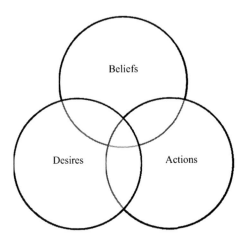

Figure 1. The intentional stance.

Researchers have asked a number of questions about each phase of the process, most notably about the formation of motives that are part of an individual's intentional struggle. Theories are grounded in a variety of assumptions ranging from the idea that individuals are guided by a collection of basic psychological needs (Atkinson & Raynor, 1974) to the idea that individuals are lay scientists who use the results of one set of actions to inform choices about subsequent actions (Kukla, 1972; Weiner, 1972). Some attributions that guide decision-making involve beliefs about how external forces affect individuals' choices whereas others focus on internal processes.

Applying an intentional stance to the question of how individuals decide to act morally raises the concept of personal responsibility. Individuals who accept personal responsibility for their actions make internal, controllable attributions to explain their previous actions, using those results to inform later goals and actions (Weiner, 1995). Put another way, personal responsibility reflects intentional behaviour that involves a conscious awareness of goals, needs, and outside expectations in decision-making, and action is part of this cycle rather than tangential to it.

Moral psychologists have explored issues of responsibility by focusing on identity and character as often as intentions. Without fully elaborating how individuals accept moral responsibility, they have noted that individuals' moral reasoning or understanding is likely to be translated into moral action if they accept personal responsibility for their behaviour (Blasi, 1980). This sort of moral responsibility has been defined as an individual's integration of morality into their identity or sense of self. While this work led to a body of research focused on moral identity and character, it has not been able to fully explain differences in moral action and dismisses the viability of children's ability to act morally (Blasi, 1993). Intentional perspectives, in contrast, are not dependent on externally imposed judgments of identity and character, but do involve third-person representations of individuals' reasons for their actions.

Comparing individuals' moral aspirations and goals, I will introduce and offer preliminary data on two models of moral responsibility grounded in an intentional stance. This choice of models is selected as a reminder of the well-established human frailty known as the actor-observer bias (Jones & Nisbett, 1971; Malle, 2006). While individuals generally evaluate their own behaviour by considering situational contingencies, they readily evaluate the behaviour of others in dispositional terms. Furthermore, individuals are usually quite poor at generating accurate representations of their own dispositions. When intentions are interpreted without the awareness of actor-observer bias, misrepresentations are as likely as accurate predictions of behaviour.

The comparisons reported in this chapter include three general elements, each of which were assessed at a single point in time. First, individuals' reports of their moral aspirations were used to represent their self-awareness and claims about their moral self. Second, individuals' reported local and global life goals as well as their belief in a just world were assessed to represent their sense of responsibility for participating in civil discourse. Finally, individuals' readiness to act on their intentions was assessed using indicators of their readiness to work hard, to cheat or take shortcuts, and to address justice.

A stronger test of the actor-observer bias would involve a direct assessment of participants' behaviour, but measuring these self-representations illustrates why a focus on identity and the self or on simple beliefs about the world might fail to foster accurate predictions of behaviour. When individuals formulate beliefs and desires about the tasks at hand, they are more likely to act than when they focus on their identity or self (Nicholls, 1989). Nevertheless, individuals who report complex representations of their motives reveal the type of Aristotelian balance that is sometimes seen as central to optimal and sustained moral functioning (Aquinas, 1964). Before using assessments from a sample of adults to evaluate predictions of an actor-observer bias, it is helpful to have additional information on the intentional stance.

INTENTIONAL STRUCTURES

Intentional theorists differ notably from self or identity theorists in a number of ways, most notably in how much emphasis is placed on the self (Nicholls, 1989). Like many identity theorists, intentional theorists view motivation as a dialogical process rather than simply as a mechanism that explains behaviour (Dennett, 1987). Nevertheless, intentions are most easily understood by embracing a third-person perspective while acknowledging informational factors that change over time. Investigators who adopt an intentional stance identify individuals' beliefs and desires. Grounded in information deemed factual or knowable, beliefs refer to the physical world and how it operates, conceptions of the self, or representations about the behaviour of others. Beliefs are detectable if they can be evaluated for their relative truth, include a theme or purpose, and are narrow enough to be graspable in someone's mind. Desires are comprised of goals, interests, aspirations, and preferences that emerge from what individuals want.

Researchers who adopt a physical stance may endeavour to explain behaviour by measuring its observable, material properties (e.g., handing a toy to someone).

Researchers who adopt a design stance may endeavour to build explanations of how parts of a behavioural system function in a broader context (e.g., the process of sharing). In contrast to these, researchers who adopt the intentional stance try to reliably understand *why* people do what they do and *how* intentional strategies work to elicit behaviour.

Understanding Why

Reliable predictions about why people do what they do can emerge from at least three systems of thought (Dennett, 1987). They can emerge from folk psychology, intentional systems theory, and sub-personal cognitive psychology.

Folk psychology is the least rigorous means of predicting behaviour, yet it is the most practical and parsimonious approach. Individuals, in that mode, generate highly reliable predictions of their own and others' behaviour by relying on their intuitions and ability to reflect on their experiences. Research grounded in personal narratives reflects this style of functioning (Pratt, Arnold, Pratt & Diessner, 1999).

Intentional systems theories, on the other hand, require recursive-reflective thought and the ability to generate third-person accounts of why people do what they do. As noted earlier, many theories of motivation reflect these assumptions, but individuals can consider multiple recursive orders depending on the number of perspectives they acknowledge.

Finally, micro-level, sub-personal cognitive psychology focuses on the interactions of individuals' physiological functioning and their folk psychologies. Research on brain functioning, for example, highlights ways in which the temporoparietal junction and the medial prefrontal cortex work together when individuals form intentions, but the two junctions undergo development in infants and young children (Van Overwalle, 2009).

Bridging conversations between moral and motivational theorists, it is important to note that distinctions between moral and non-moral functioning or conscious and unconscious forms of mental functioning add nothing to the explanatory power of intentional theories. The same can also be said for claims about the relative explicitness of intentions. All intentional acts and states are assumed to embody moral content, and questions about where intentions exist reflect a level of tangibility that is devoid of semantic meaning. By representing the gist of someone's experiences, accurate predictions can be generated just as easily as would be possible if the nuanced complexity of a person's perspective were fully documented.

Understanding How

Intentional systems theorists explore how intentional strategies offer accurate predictions of behaviour. They use concepts of adaptation and mentalism to explain how individuals organize data, explain interrelations between levels of functioning, and evaluate why behaviour occurs. Developmental psychologists embracing such theories have explored how intentional belief systems and desires evolve and are expressed over time. Social psychologists often explore how situational factors influence the informational assumptions individuals construct.

At least two developmental questions need answers if we are to determine whether actor-observer bias places constraints on individuals' representations of their intentions. First, it is important to establish that individuals' self-understanding and awareness of others gains complexity over time. Second, it is important to understand which sorts of intentional functioning are being tapped by the design of particular research tools.

Even in the earliest stages of life individuals seem to understand their own intentions and visible intentions of others (Karniol, 2003). Furthermore, individuals acquire these abilities before they can make stable inferences about their own and others' personality traits or about more enduring social scripts (Apperly, Samson & Humphreys, 2009; deVignemont, 2009). Put another way, the intentional stance can be detected at very early ages, even though individuals seem to rely on the actor perspective more easily than on the observer perspective.

Debates about the abilities needed to consider both actor and observer perspectives continue to flourish as more is learned about the physiological limitations of people at different ages (Hughes, 1998). Nevertheless, it is clear that intentions can be assessed when individuals engage in three types of executive functioning; intuitive, reflective, and recursive-reflective means of detecting and organizing information. It is not always easy to determine which type of functioning is called forth by different measurement procedures, yet the adult participants in this project are likely to be able to use all three.

Participants who rely on intuitive functioning are sometimes thought of as pre-intentional, yet adults as well as infants use such largely non-verbal abilities whenforming intentions. Intuition reflects an ability to act without formally constructing goals. Individuals obtain information directly from facial expressions, gestures, vocal tones, and other nonverbal movements and use that awareness in action. In moral terms, intuitive functioning largely involves imitation or joint attention between the self and others without requiring the spoken word. A moral course of action just feels right (Hallie, 1979).

Participants who rely on reflective functioning hold information in their minds, set goals, and otherwise behave in 'planful' ways (Hughes, 1998). This method of forming intentions is explored in many of the most rudimentary form of intention in theories that assess how individuals evaluate their experiences (Lewin, 1926; Weiner, 1972). As language becomes a means of representing information, individuals are better able to combine planning, working memory, attentional flexibility, and inhibitory control abilities when forming goals. Individuals' moral functioning can be improved by offering instruction to assist them in gathering new information and advice on how to think about such knowledge.

Participants who rely on the most complex form of functioning realize that two people may make legitimate but different interpretations of the same external stimuli and form goals with an awareness of these differences. Such recursive-reflective functioning requires the full range of executive and language functions as well as a willingness to direct these abilities toward acting in a particular situation. Changes in an individual's recursive-reflective functioning becomes likely during collaborative learning and other activities in which individuals can construct a dialogue between their own intentional states and acts, and the consequences of such decisions (Tomasello, Kruger & Ratner, 1993). Such activities allow individuals to witness others' reflective abilities or consider more perspectives on a situation than their own.

Motivational studies of individuals' ability to distinguish a wide range of achievement attributions reveal just how young children struggle to understand concepts such as task difficulty, ability, effort, luck, and skill as they endeavor to build intentions and represent their goals and aspirations (Nicholls, 1989). Similarly, work on students' conceptions of the fairness and effectiveness of educational practices offer additional information on how learners struggle to understand what is expected of them and of others in educational settings (Thorkildsen, 2000). And, studies of moral judgment exploring how individuals use information to generate assumptions about what people ought to do require recursive-reflective functioning (Kohlberg, 1969). These studies were designed to elicit participants' most sophisticated levels of reasoning while testing specific predictions about individuals' abilities. More commonly, and the approach that is used in this chapter, individuals' intentions are recorded using less demanding forms of executive functioning.

Social psychologists offer a reminder that research settings reflect an environment that may differentially influence participants' functioning. Although investigators have relatively little control over how individuals use their intentional system to report on their intentions, a study's design and measurement procedures play a role in how participants respond. Distorted representations of individuals' daily functioning emerge when such limitations remain unacknowledged. Individuals' ability to formulate beliefs, for example, have been distinguished from the content of their beliefs in studies of moral reasoning, yet findings from these studies have been used as evidence of someone's intentions. Participants in these interview studies and the experiments that include such tools have been judged more and less able or willing to act. Claims about action remain invalid when measurement instruments rely exclusively on verbal expressions of beliefs that require recursive-reflective forms of executive functioning; a form of reasoning that is rarely used in everyday settings. Another level of distortion is introduced when studies conducted in the tradition of behaviourism require only that individuals use their most primitive executive functioning abilities. Studies of behaviour alone fail to include verbal measures of intentions. In all these cases, researchers' own biases are embedded in the design and measurement of variables. It is also difficult to ensure an adequate alignment of researchers' goals and participants' intentions in a study.

INTENTIONAL MODELS OF MORAL MOTIVATION

The survey methods used for this project emphasized individuals reactions to ideas extracted from more demanding interviews. Although I could not control which form of executive functioning individuals chose to use, surveys of this nature largely required reflective forms of executive functioning. Instruments assessing the gist of how participating adults represented their moral dispositions elicited an observer perspective whereas those assessing adults' belief in a just world and life goals required an actor perspective. Comparing these assessments of adults' dispositions and goals with measures of their action readiness served to document their intentions.

Participants (n = 238) in this study included undergraduate and graduate students attending one of four introductory courses in human development. Because women outnumber men in these courses to a very large degree, I created a comparison group of female volunteers (119; M(age) = 27.50, sd = 8.75) that matched the ethnicity and age of the sample of male volunteers (119; M(age) = 27.71, sd = 8.47). The sample ranged in age from 19 to 61 years and included multiple ethnic groups (14 Asian/Asian American, 20 Black/African American, 50 Latino/Hispanic, 148 White/ Caucasian, 6 Biracial/Dual ethnic).

Everyone completed the battery of measures noted in Tables 1 and 2. As was predicted for the observer role, there was a restricted range of responses to the moral aspirations scales (Table 3), suggesting that most participants did not offer a nuanced representation of their dispositional habits. Many participants endorsed all the moral aspirations even when these choices called for contradictory actions. Individuals' reports of their civil commitments showed the type of variance that might be expected when they embrace an actor role. Consistent with the tenets of intentional systems theory, adults' life goals were moderately associated with all of their moral aspirations, but their belief in a just world was not associated with assessments of their moral desires (Table 4).

Table 1: Alignment of moral virtues with the big five personality dimensions

Big Five personality dimensions	Moral virtues
	I feel most successful when I am...
Agreeableness (α = .91)	accepting, empathic, fair, forgiving, generous, honest, loving, thoughtful.
Conscientiousness (α = .86)	conscientious, hard-working, honorable, intelligent, loyal, realistic, responsible, self-disciplined, virtuous.
Extraversion (α = .83)	brave, confident, friendly, helpful, independent, respectable, strong., wise
Neuroticism (α=.80)	cautious, critical, faithful, opinionated, principled, proud, religious, rigid, self-sacrificing, serious, stubborn.
Openness (α=.86)	aware, caring, friendly, helpful, open-minded, sincere, trustworthy, unselfish.

Note. Respondents used a scale ranging from 5=very important to 1=very unimportant when rating their commitments to each virtue. Virtues were obtained from Walker & Pitts (1998), and factor analysis, item analysis, and internal consistency evaluations were used to align moral attributes with the Big Five dimensions. Although these virtues can be used in a variety of ways, for the purpose of this exercise, the resulting classifications were compared with sample survey items from a Big Five Inventory (Costa & McCrae, 2008).

Table 2: Descriptions of civil life goals and action readiness instruments

Instrument name	Sample items
Civil life goals	
Local life goals (19 items, α=.85)	I will feel most satisfied if I can I earn enough money to live comfortably; do what my family expects of me; figure out how to take care of myself; discover more about my abilities.
Global life goals (19 items, α=.90)	I will feel most satisfied if I can help solve global problems; make sure everyone's rights are protected; learn how democracy works; study different cultures.
Belief in a just world (13 items, α=.86)	When thinking about the world, I assume that I am treated fairly; believe that I typically get what I deserve; believe that most things happening in my life are fair.
Action readiness	
Readiness to work hard (36 items, α=.89)	I work hard when I see how I might use the ideas; people care about me; I can figure out problems on my own; rules for behaviour are fair; the material fascinates me.
Readiness to cheat or take shortcuts (40 items, α=.98)	I take shortcuts or cheat when I am not sure how to do the work; the work won't help me in the future; everyone else is cheating; no one will notice; the task feels like busywork; I want to add fun into my day.
Readiness to address justice (13 items, α=.86)	I think I am more affected by justice than most people. Nothing angers me more than seeing injustice. I am especially tormented when I cause injustice.

Note. Respondents used a Likert scale ranging from 5=strongly agree to 1=strongly disagree. These measures reflect improved versions of the instruments used in Thorkildsen, Golant, & Cambray-Engstrom (2008). Local and global life goal instruments include references to proximal and distal life goals. Instruments assessing the readiness to work hard and to cheat or take shortcut include a balance of items reflecting individuals' basic psychological needs and situational interest. Justice measures were adapted from Dalbert (1999) and Dalbert & Umlauft (2003).

Table 3: Means and Standard deviations for moral intentions by gender

	Male		Female	
Beliefs and desires	*Mean*	*sd*	*Mean*	*sd*
Agreeableness	4.27	.59	4.60	.41
Conscientiousness	4.34	.49	4.51	.41
Extraversion	4.30	.48	4.48	.44
Neuroticism	3.51	.58	3.50	.61
Openness	4.36	.44	4.63	.41
Local life goals	3.87	.50	4.05	.45
Global life goals	3.76	.48	3.85	.57
Belief in a just world	3.23	.61	3.30	.56
Readiness to work hard	3.90	.42	4.04	.39

	Male		Female	
Readiness to cheat/take shortcuts	2.26	.81	2.26	.79
Readiness to address justice	3.40	.60	3.41	.54

Note. Only the agreeableness measure showed skewness and kurtosis scores that feel beyond the +/- 1.00 criterion for distortion. Simple comparison of means indicated that gender differences were apparent only for agreeableness and openness scales when the Bonferroni correction for the number of tests was used. These and possible age differences were not apparent in any of the more complex analyses.

Table 4: Correlations between individuals' moral aspirations and civil life goals

Moral aspirations	Civil life goals		
	Local goals	Global goals	Belief in a just world
Agreeableness	.29**	.20*	.09
Conscientiousness	.41**	.24**	.12
Extraversion	.51**	.29**	.14
Neuroticism	.53**	.31**	.16
Openness	.35*	.24**	.09

Note. * p<.05, ** p<.01 when the Bonferonni corrections for the number of tests is applied

To test for a possible actor-observer bias in how adults represent their moral intentions, I measured individuals' readiness to act on their beliefs. This causal-comparative design is parallel work on how individuals align their emotions with their action readiness (Frijda, Kuipers & ter Schure, 1989). The readiness to work hard and to cheat or take shortcuts included items reflecting individuals' basic psychological needs for self-determination, competence, and belongingness (Atkinson & Raynor, 1974), yet these needs were represented in different ways. Readiness to work hard assessed individuals' commitment to putting forth the effort or deep learning needed to meet their needs. Readiness to cheat or take shortcuts focused on whether expedience was central to individuals' action readiness. Additionally, the readiness to address justice instrument assessed the centrality of justice in individuals' action readiness. Responses to each of these measures were standardized and then used in cluster analysis to identify profiles of action readiness, allowing for a nuanced comparison that is not possible when each set of measures is used in isolation.

As was the case for other measurement steps, the resulting clusters were validated by comparing findings obtained with samples from other studies (e.g., Thorkildsen, Golant & Cambray-Engstrom, 2008). In each sample, an alienated profile reflected a strong willingness to cheat or take shortcuts without a comparable readiness to work hard or address justice. An apathetic profile reflected a resistance to action of all sorts. The profile labelled here as a perfectionist profile was consistent with the concept of the unhappy moralist (Oser, 2010) wherein individuals are ready to work hard and address justice, but never to cheat or take shortcuts. The final resourceful profile was consistent with what might be expected for individuals who endeavour to achieve an Aristotelian balance in their life; these individuals reported a readiness to act in all three ways as detected by particular situational constraints.

To test for a possible actor-observer bias in adults' self-reported intentions, I compared two models. Using action readiness classification as an independent variable and moral aspirations as within-subjects variables, there was no significant interaction between adults' moral aspirations and their action readiness profile (Table 5). Nevertheless, there was a significant interaction when comparable analyses were completed using civil life commitments as within-subjects variables (Table 6). Together, these findings suggest that adults are better at representing their intentions when taking an actor stance than when embracing an observer stance.

Table 5: Means and standard errors for moral aspirations by action readiness

| | Action readiness | | | | | | | |
| | Alienated | | Apathetic | | Perfectionist | | Resourceful | |
Moral aspirations	M	SE	M	SE	M	SE	M	SE
Agreeableness	4.11	.10	4.31	.06	4.52	.05	4.75	.05
Conscientiousness	4.15	.07	4.32	.06	4.50	.04	4.72	.05
Extraversion	4.13	.07	4.35	.05	4.39	.05	4.71	.05
Neuroticism	3.19	.06	3.41	.07	3.56	.07	3.84	.09
Openness	4.26	.07	4.40	.05	4.53	.05	4.78	.05
Sample (n=238)	47		63		78		50	

Note. When within-subjects ANOVA was used to compare respondents' action readiness profiles with their moral aspirations, there were main effects for action readiness, $F_{(3, 234)}=21.13$, $p<.001$, partial $\eta^2=.21$ and moral aspirations $F_{(4, 936)}= 461.46$, $p<.001$, partial $\eta^2=.66$, but no interaction.

Table 6: Means and standard errors for civil life goals by action readiness

| | Action readiness | | | | | | | |
| | Alienated | | Apathetic | | Perfectionist | | Resourceful | |
Civil life goals	M	SE	M	SE	M	SE	M	SE
Local life goals	3.72[a]	.07	3.95[b]	.06	3.93[ab]	.05	4.24	.07
Global life goals	3.63[a]	.08	3.72[a]	.06	3.83[a]	.06	4.05	.07
Belief in a just world	3.18[a]	.08	3.31[a]	.06	3.27[a]	.07	3.30[a]	.10
Sample (n=238)	47		63		78		50	

Note. When within-subjects ANOVA was used to compare respondents' action readiness profiles with their civil life goals, there were significant main effects for action readiness, $F_{(3, 234)}=7.15$, $p<.001$, $\eta^2=.08$, and civil life goals, $F_{(1, 234)}= 30.32$, $p<.001$, $\eta^2=.12$, as well as an interaction, $F_{(3, 234)}=4.08$, $p<.01$, $\eta^2=.05$. Matching superscripts indicate no differences in post hoc tests.

CONCLUSION

This small-scale study confirms the value of recognizing the multifaceted nature of individuals' intentions. It is consistent with the tenets of dynamic systems theory wherein human functioning is represented as a complex, nonlinear array of systems that show predictable forms of internal consistency while remaining dynamic in someone's overall functioning (Thelen & Smith, 1998). If intentions are comprised of intuitive, reflective, and recursive reflective forms of executive functioning, they are likely to hold a number of features that are free to change when those intentions compel action. When considering moral dilemmas, it might be fair to assume that judgments requiring recursive reflective decision-making may be more remote from action than those based on intuitive decision-making, yet adults have more control than children over how to allow these types of intentions to direct their actions.

As is the case for most representations of human functioning, I have only identified part of adults' intentional system. Relying on measures that can be completed using reflective functioning allowed for the detection of a number of differences in how respondents thought about their moral aspirations, goals for civil discourse, and action readiness. By isolating part of adults' intentional system, it is possible to detect distortions in why adults act as they do. Taken in conjunction with direct measures of behaviour, intentional systems theory can be used to assist those who endeavour to offer policy decisions that might govern civil society. Nevertheless, a few caveats are worth bearing in mind.

First, relying on folk psychology is perhaps the most parsimonious means of predicting everyday behaviour because such personal representations of intentions allow for the straightforward crafting of explanations that include real-world dialogue (Thorkildsen & Nicholls, 2002). Intentional systems theory, as it was used in this chapter, makes it possible to detect distortions and regularities in why and how behaviour occurs. Identifying various intentional systems allows for the systematic measurement of intentional behaviour and the testing of important predictions needed to generate policies and interventions for groups of people (Thorkildsen & Walberg, 2004). Exploring intentions using sub-personal cognitive psychology strengthens knowledge of how intentions are formed and the types of perceptual abilities needed to learn and draw inferences from experience.

Second, when recognizing intentions as a dynamic system, moral action can be explained without declaring some people moral and others immoral or amoral. This removes the burden of demonstrating that individuals' moral action as consistent over time. It seems problematic to assume that once a person is capable of morally elegant action, they will always exhibit moral behaviour. Moral responsibility, in an intentional framework, is placed in dynamic competition with other forms of responsible decision-making as intentions compel action.

A third caveat flows from the question of who is capable of moral action. In many studies related to moral identity and the self, children and individuals with limited intellectual capacity are judged incapable of responsible moral action (Blasi, 1980,

1993). Yet, intentional systems theory suggests that anyone can be a responsible moral agent, even if some may be capable of more complex forms of moral functioning than others. As anyone who watches an infant develop across the first 3 months of life can discern, individuals need only be capable of intuitive functioning to form the most rudimentary forms of intention. With this approach, the establishment of moral habits of mind can begin as soon as individuals can receive feedback on their efforts.

If intentions are multifaceted, moral education can become a constantly evolving process that takes place anywhere and anytime. Individuals can learn through imitation, direct instruction, and collaborative activities. They can learn new ways to think about moral problems and act on their understanding immediately rather than wait until they are old enough to fully imagine how others judge them. Moral habits are formed well before individuals are ready to use reflective-recursive reasoning.

Returning to the possible intentions evident in the musician's dilemma, it is easy to see multiple opportunities to appraise the situation using intuitive, reflective, and recursive reflective executive functions. Folk psychology can help us draw inferences about why individuals acted as they did, although this would be less clear if we focused only on the dispositional characteristics of the individuals involved. An actor perspective tells us that the busker could have monitored the musician's gestures, eye contact, or other nonverbal actions to be more sensitive to the needs of the musician. The musician could have been more honest with the crowd about his disinterest in playing. Crowd members could have put less pressure on the musician to play. Perhaps the musician was exhibiting his true abilities and his reputation was based on an intentional misrepresentation of his skills.

Discerning why the activities unfolded as they did would require information from multiple actors. Generating behavioural policies would require a more systematic approach to the study of intentions. Sub-cognitive approaches to evaluating the situation might offer stronger explanations for how specific intentions were formed. Taken as a whole, these characteristics of the intentional stance allow us to draw solid inferences about whether each of the individuals in the musical story reflected on the moral implications of their decisions and took responsibility for their actions.

REFERENCES

Apperly, I., Samson, D., & Humphreys, G. (2009). Studies of adults can inform accounts of theory of mind development. *Developmental Psychology, 45*, 190–201. doi: 10.1037/a0014098

Aquinas, T. (1964). *Commentary on Aristotle's Nicomachean Ethics*. Notre Dame, IN: Dumb Ox Books.

Atkinson, J.W., & Raynor, J.O. (1974). *Motivation and achievement*. Washington, DC: Winston.

Blasi, A. (1980). Bridging moral cognition and moral action: A critical review of the literature. *Psychological Bulletin, 88*, 1–45.

Blasi, A. (1993). The development of identity: Some implications for moral functioning. In G.G. Noam, & T.E. Wren (Eds.), *The moral self* (pp.99–122). Cambridge, MA: MIT Press.

Costa, P.T., & McCrae, R.R. (2008). The NEO inventories. In R.P. Archer, & S.R. Smith (Eds.), *Personality assessment* (pp. 213–245). New York, NY: Routledge/Taylor & Francis Group.

Dalbert, C. (1999). The world is more just for me than generally: About the personal belief in a Just World Scale's validity. *Social Justice Research, 12*, 79–98. doi:10.1023/A:1022091609047

Dalbert, C. & Umlauft, S. (2003). *Justice centrality scale.* Unpublished scale, Martin Luther University of Halle Wittenberg, Germany.

Dennett, D.C. (1987). *The intentional stance.* Cambridge, MA: MIT Press.

deVingemont, F. (2009). Drawing the boundary between low-level and high-level mindreading. *Philosophical Studies, 144*, 457–466.

Frijda, N.H., Kuipers, P., & ter Schure, E. (1989). Relations among emotion, appraisal, and emotional action readiness. *Journal of Personality and Social Psychology, 57*, 212–228.

Hallie, P. (1979). *Lest innocent blood be shed: The story of the village of LeChambon and how goodness happened there.* New York: Harper Perennial.

Hughes, C. (1998). Executive function in preschoolers: Links with theory of mind and verbal ability. *British Journal of Developmental Psychology, 16*, 233–253.

Jones, E.E., & Nisbett, R.E. (1971). *The actor and the observer: Divergent perceptions of the causes of behavior.* Morristown, NJ: General Learning Press.

Karniol, R. (2003). Egocentrism versus protocentrism: The status of self in social prediction. *Psychological Review, 110*, 564–580. doi: 10.1037/0033-295X.110.3.564

Kohlberg, L. (1969). Stage and sequence: The cognitive developmental approach to socialization. In D.A. Goslin (Ed.), *Handbook of socialization theory and research* (pp. 347–480). Chicago: Rand McNally

Kukla, A. (1972). Foundations of attribution theory. *Psychological Review, 79*, 454–470.

Lewin, K. (1926). Vorsatz, Wille, und Bedürfnis. *Psychologische Forschung, 7*, 330–385. [Translated by D. Rapaport (1951) in *Organization and pathology of thought.* (pp. 95–153) New York: Columbia University Press. Reprinted in M. Gold (1999), *The complete social scientist: A Kurt Lewin reader.* (pp. 83–115). Washington, DC: American Psychological Association.]

Malle, B.F. (2006). The actor-observer asymmetry in attribution: A (surprising) meta-analysis, *Psychological Bulletin, 132*, 895–919.

Nicholls, J.G. (1989). *The competitive ethos and democratic education.* Cambridge, MA: Harvard University Press.

Oser, F. (2010). The unhappy moralist effect: A story of hybrid moral dynamics. In T. Lovat, R. Toomey & N. Clement (Eds.), *International research handbook on values education and student wellbeing* (pp. 605–614). Dordrecht, Netherlands: Springer.

Pratt, M.W., Arnold, M.L., Pratt, A.T., & Diessner, R. (1999). Predicting adolescent moral reasoning from family climate: A longitudinal study. *Journal of Early Adolescence, 19*, 148–175. doi: 10.1177/0272431699019002002

Thelen, E., & Smith, L.B. (1998). Dynamic systems theories. In W. Damon & R.M. Lerner (Eds.), *Handbook of child psychology, Vol. 1: Theoretical models of human development* (5th ed., pp. 563–634). New York: John Wiley & Sons.

Thorkildsen, T.A. (2000). Children's coordination of procedural and commutative justice in school. In W. van Haaften, T. Wren & A. Tellings (Eds.), *Moral sensibilities and education II: The schoolchild* (pp. 61–88). Bemmel, Netherlands: Concorde Publishing House.

Thorkildsen, T.A., Golant, C.J., & Cambray-Engstrom, E. (2008). Essential solidarities for understanding Latino adolescents' moral and academic engagement. In C. Hudley & A.E. Gottfried (Eds.), *Academic motivation and the culture of schooling in childhood and adolescence* (pp. 73–98). Oxford: Oxford University Press.

Thorkildsen, T.A., & Nicholls, J.G. (with Bates, A., Brankis, N., & DeBolt, T.). (2002). *Motivation and the struggle to learn: Responding to fractured experience.* Boston, MA: Allyn & Bacon.

Thorkildsen, T.A., & Walberg, H.J. (Eds.). (2004). *Nurturing morality.* New York, NY: Kluwer.

Tomasello, M., Kruger, A., & Ratner, H. (1993). Cultural learning. *Behavioral and Brain Sciences, 16*, 495–552.

Van Overwalle, F. (2009). Social cognition and the brain: A meta-analysis. *Human Brain Mapping, 30*, 829–858.

Walker, L.J., & Pitts, R.C. (1998). Naturalistic conceptions of moral maturity. *Developmental Psychology, 34*, 403–419. doi: 10.1037/0012-1649.34.3.403

Weiner, B. (1972). *Theories of motivation: From mechanism to cognition*. Chicago: Markham.
Weiner, B. (1995). *Judgments of responsibility: A foundation for a theory of social conduct*. New York, NY: Guilford Press.

AFFILIATION

Theresa A. Thorkildsen
Department of Educational Psychology
University of Illinois
Chicago, USA

PART 2

MOTIVATIONAL THEORY AND MORAL MOTIVATION

Exploring the issues that characterize moral psychology, we have to admit that this school of thinking has not really been overly concerned with motivational psychology. In this part, motivational and social psychologists present their knowledge about motivation in general and attempt to apply their preferred concept of motivation to moral issues.

Weiner's attribution theory proposes distal and proximal determinants of the motivation to help. In his paper, Weiner concentrates on proximal determinants. He shows that attributions of personal control or lack of control by the person in need have important impact on whether the bystander feels responsible, on what kind of emotions emerge and to what extent the agent is urged to help.

Krapp assumes that moral motivation should be conceptualized as a kind of intrinsic motivation. He discusses the self-determination theory as well as the theory of personal interest as a fruitful way to grasp a personal determinant driving towards moral acting.

Vollmeyer, Jenderek and Tozman point to how different concepts of motivation could contribute to explaining moral behaviour as well as immoral behaviour. They focus especially on what would happen if there were different types of motivational as well as volitional deficits.

Baumert, Rothmund, Thomas, Gollwitzer and Schmitt study the justice motive as one morally relevant driver of moral behaviour. They investigate how this justice motive and injustice-sensitivity interact and influence moral emotions and behaviour.

Agerström and Björklund take a social psychological perspective. They identify temporal distance as one special situational determinant and argue, based on empirical studies, that temporal distance affects the motivational impulsion towards moral action. Incidents in the near future reduce the individual's motivational power to act morally, in contrast incidents at a greater temporal distance.

In all these models, motivation is more important than morality. The idea is that these models have impact on any content, on sport, leisure, work, and, similarly, on morality. This is of course a shortcoming, and we see that Baumert et al. try to bridge the gap and to think of moral motivation as something other than just an application to a motivational model to morality.

BERNARD WEINER

I. ULTIMATE AND PROXIMAL (ATTRIBUTION-RELATED) MOTIVATIONAL DETERMINANTS OF MORAL BEHAVIOUR

INTRODUCTION

A distinction is made between distal (ultimate) and proximal (immediate) determinants of moral behaviour (here confined to altruism). The distal determinants, reviewed in the first part of this chapter, are primarily based on evolution but also include hedonism. They are not subject to proof or disproof but do add to our understanding of moral actions. Proximal determinants of altruism can be experimentally manipulated and thus are subject to empirical verification or disconfirmation. In the second part of the chapter an attributional approach to altruism that focuses on proximal determinants is examined. The immediate determinants of help-giving are claimed to be observer attributions of personal control or lack of control by the person in need. These produce inferences of responsibility or lack of responsibility, which in turn give rise to the respective moral emotions of anger and sympathy. Emotions then arouse anti- or pro-social actions. Thus, attribution theory proposes a thinking-feeling-acting motivational sequence in which the initiating determinants of help-giving reside not in the giver but in the potential recipient of aid, who is judged as deserving or not deserving of help. This proximal analysis is then linked to a possible distal behavioural determinant. Likely objections or questions about this theory are posed and answers are offered.

To address the motivational basis of moral behaviour, a known distinction between distal (ultimate) versus proximal (immediate) determinants of motivation is introduced. Ultimate determinants of action are first examined and applied to the understanding of moral behaviours. Then I turn from distal goals and consider immediate influences on moral behaviour. Among these proximal determinants, causal beliefs and the emotions they generate are the focus of the second part of the chapter. I restrict my consideration to help giving (altruism) versus neglect of others, ignoring other moral and ethical behaviours such as picking up trash from the sidewalk or refraining from cheating on an exam. The general position I hold is that, in a manner similar to other motivational domains including achievement striving, affiliation, aggression, and so on, there are multiple sufficient causes of moral and ethical behaviours, none of which are necessary.

K. Heinrichs, F. Oser & T. Lovat (Eds.), Handbook of Moral Motivation: Theories, Models, Applications, 99–112.

DISTAL (ULTIMATE) VERSUS PROXIMAL (IMMEDIATE) MOTIVATORS

Distal or ultimate determinants of behaviour refer to the underlying, basic, or fundamental causes of all behaviour. On the other hand, proximal or immediate motivators encompass those personal characteristics and environmental factors influencing behaviour at a moment in time (Scott-Phillips et al.). For example, it has been contended that the ultimate motivator of eating behaviour is the desire to survive. However, the immediate determinants of food consumption (the amount one eats, the persistence and intensity of this activity) include how deprived the person is, what food incentives are available, whether others are also eating, momentary emotional states, and on and on.

Ultimate goals, in contrast to immediate determinants, are not subject to experimental proof or disconfirmation. Rather, an array of evidence is examined to infer the existence of these desired end states. For example, the facts that hours of deprivation influence eating behaviour, and that individuals desperate for food engage in desperate acts to attain this goal, might be considered sources of evidence to confirm the distal goal of survival. On the other hand, people postpone food-related activities to engage in behaviours that apparently do not promote survival, such as book writing. In addition, the food ingested often is not most beneficial for survival. In sum, the distal goals postulated by motivation psychologists, which are soon to be examined, often have an evolutionary component and are accompanied by both confirmatory and disconfirmatory evidence.

In contrast to ultimate goals, one can experimentally manipulate the proximal factors hypothesized to influence eating behaviour, such as the type and amount of food available. In so doing, their status as motivational determinants can be verified or discarded. Thus, distal and proximal determinants of behaviour differ in a number of respects and this distinction is worth maintaining when asking motivational questions.

What are the Ultimate (Real) Determinants of Behaviour?

What, then, are the underlying behaviour motivators of moral actions? To my knowledge, four have been postulated by motivational psychologists, although there are likely to be others that could be added to this list. As already mentioned, ultimate goals frequently have appeal to evolutionary principles.

Personal survival. Classical (Darwinian) evolutionary psychologists presume that behaviour is functional and promotes personal survival (Confer et al., 2010). We undertake those behaviours that have "worked" in the past and increase the likelihood of remaining alive. Given this position, altruism and related moral behaviours might be anticipated to extinguish over time because they often decrease personal survival fitness. After all, helping others is accompanied by personal costs. Yet altruistic behaviours have persisted (Trivers, 1971). How can they then be subject to an evolutionary analysis?

Concepts such as reciprocal altruism ("If you help me, I will help you.") and observations of cooperation intimate that personal survival can be aided by implicit contracts with others that include mutual aid. Therefore, it has been argued that moral behaviours promote self-survival, rendering "true" altruism nonexistent but providing an evolutionary determinant for some moral (and immoral) actions.

Nevertheless, this seems to be a relatively weak argument and not a very compelling explanation for the vast majority of moral behaviour. If appears difficult to fathom how many types of self-sacrifice (e.g., sending money to poor children in a distant land) might help personal survival. However, this certainly does not rule out the possibility that some moral and ethical acts have positive survival consequences for the actor, although the "ultimate" purpose of these acts is not necessarily part of the conscious understanding of the help-provider or of observers (Hamilton, 1963).

Genetic Survival

For many, classical (Darwinian) fitness theory has given way to inclusive fitness theory as the dominant approach to evolution (Buss, 2008). Instead of personal survival, inclusive fitness theorists postulate that maintenance of the genetic pool, rather than the self, is paramount. Hence, saving our two children from death is (roughly) equivalent to saving oneself inasmuch as they each carry 50% of our genes (Hamilton, 1964). This approach helps account for moral actions because any supposedly altruistic action helping a relative can be embraced within the evolutionary rubric of genetic survival. Since most helping is toward family rather than strangers, an inclusive fitness perspective aids in explaining a number of observations of "altruism" (Buss, 2008). Of course, this account fails in the interpretation of any moral act that is not self-directed or relative-directed without the inclusion of concepts such as reciprocal altruism. It certainly falls short as a full explanation of moral and ethical behaviour but serves well in accounting for some activity that decreases personal fitness and provides a more coherent explanation for certain moral actions than can be supplied by classical evolutionary theory.

Survival of the Social System

As members of a hunter-gatherer society, the self and/or genetic survival is linked to community survival. This expansion of the "ego-sphere," or sources of social identification, could have resulted in behaviours such as cooperation, self-sacrifice, and contributions to the common (Wilson, 1975). Altruistic or moral actions are applauded by group members, who adopt the role of judges, declaring others as "good or bad," "moral or immoral," or "innocent or guilty." In addition, mechanisms may have developed including emotional reactions of guilt, anger and gratitude that motivate others to engage in actions that serve the common good or withdraw from behaviour that harms others. Moral behaviours thus serve a function and again true "altruism," given this perspective, is a mirage because personal survival is facilitated through the survival of the social system. This view of evolution is certainly more compatible with the observation of moral behaviours than are the relatively individualistic conceptions of classical and inclusive fitness theory.

Maximizing pleasure (happiness, benefits) and minimizing pain (unhappiness, costs). For many motivational psychologists, the pleasure-pain principle, with advocates ranging from Freud to current decision theorists, dominates as the ultimate source of all behaviour (Weiner, 1992). Individuals are proposed to engage in actions that maximize their pleasures (happiness) and minimize their pains. All behaviour therefore involves the calculation of costs and benefits, with the individual engaging in the most "selfish" behaviour. Paradoxically, this calculation does not eliminate the possibility of moral actions and altruism providing, of course, that such actions also result in more positive than negative affect and greater benefit than cost.

Yet it seems tautological (circular?) to state that: "All behaviour makes us happy; we help (or harm) others; therefore, it makes us happy." What is needed is specification of the mechanisms or the sources of these positive feelings. For example, it may be that help-giving reduces guilt or perhaps the feelings of distress at the sight of needy others - negative, self-directed emotions that cry for elimination. It also may be that helping others raises one's personal esteem or self-view since such acts are favored and rewarded by others (Hamilton, 1963). Hence, it is certainly possible to invoke personal happiness as the source of some altruistic actions and not appeal to evolutionary principles as the only "ultimate" source of behaviour.

Summary of the distal determinants. Altruistic and moral behaviours have been addressed from an ultimate perspective. At times this linkage is evident and appropriate, as when examining the sacrificing behaviour of a mother toward her child (genetic survival) or husband (self and group survival). Yet it also is apparent that many moral and ethical behaviours are only vaguely incorporated by distal goals and that this approach is not subject to definitive experimental proof or disproof. One somehow feels unfulfilled or disappointed when moral actions are traced to some "ultimate" source, with the mediators rather murky. Therefore, the vast majority of psychologists have focused on proximal determinants of moral and ethical behaviour, manipulating or varying their magnitude and examining their immediate influence on choice or other indicators of motivated action.

PROXIMAL (IMMEDIATE) DETERMINANTS OF MORAL BEHAVIOUR

Moral and ethical actions often are traced to moral properties or states of the help-giver (Rushton, Fulker, Neale, Nias & Eysenck, 1986). The person may be a "Good Samaritan," perhaps assessed with concepts such as conscientiousness, or hold ideals or values fostered by religious beliefs that include help-giving. Or, as already intimated, the person may be attempting to reduce negative affects including guilt, regret, distress, and so forth. Altruistic actions also may be traced to the desire to increase positive affects, including pride, self-esteem, and so on.

Alternately, the determinants of altruistic and moral actions may be located in the environment. These influencing factors also range widely and include the observation or lack of moral models, social norms, the number of individuals available to help (diffusion of responsibility), and even the presence or absence of materials that enhance feelings of disgust or "cleanliness." For example, one is more likely to help another fix a flat tire if such behaviour has been recently witnessed, but less likely to help another in distress if many others are available to help. As I voiced previously, the totality of these determinants is so great that it is not possible, in my mind, to have a "complete" theory of altruism or help-giving unless stated at such a molar and abstract level as to be meaningless in terms of predictive value (e.g., behaviour is a function of the person and the environment).

Rather, a more feasible approach may be to find a law or principle or rule that can explain some altruistic actions and then apply or generalize this law to other motivational domains such as achievement and affiliation. What would then emerge is a general principle, or perhaps a mini-theory, of motivated actions that has domain generality (Weiner, 2006). With this caveat in mind I turn to causal attributions and their role in moral action. I hope to demonstrate that an attributional perspective provides insights into some aspects of help-giving and functions similarly across other motivational domains.

ATTRIBUTIONS AND MORAL ACTIONS

Rather than locating the source of altruism within the giver or doer, labeling the individual a Good Samaritan or an amoral or immoral person who helps or neglects needy others, attribution theory designates the potential receiver of aid as moral or immoral (Weiner, 2006). That is, the potential aid recipient is judged as deserving or not deserving and this perception or belief in part gives rise to help or neglect. Consistent with this shift in the locus or location of moral judgments, the emotional determinants of aid shift from self-directed feelings such as pride, guilt and distress to other-directed emotions including sympathy, pity, and anger (Weiner, Graham & Chandler, 1982). Given this perspective, morality lies in the eyes of the giver, who responds to the moral pulls and pushes in the environment.

The general theoretical contention is as follows. Negative, unexpected, and/or important events and outcomes generate attributional search. One desires to know why he or she failed an exam, was rejected when applying for a job or a club, or performed poorly during a sporting event, and so on. This desire for knowledge concerns not only the self but also regarding others. One wonders why another's marriage ended in failure, why a star athlete lost a match, why a particular person is impoverished and in need of aid, and on and on. At times, a cause is readily available and a search is not necessary. For example, it may be that the sight of a distraught person immediately calls forth mental illness or alcoholism as the cause of this plight.

Some causal inferences tend to be more prevalent than others, although these beliefs vary between motivational contexts (Weiner, 1985). For example, the most dominant perceived causes of success and failure in achievement tasks are ability and effort: one succeeds because of high ability and/or hard work, and fails due to lack of ability and/or not trying (Weiner, 1985). But the main causes of affiliative rejection are quite different and include personality characteristics and attractiveness, while the causes of poverty include laziness and lack of available jobs. However, in spite of these qualitative differences between causes both within and across motivational domains, causal ascriptions share certain characteristics and can be compared quantitatively. This is accomplished by placing the causes within a taxonomic structure.

The Structure of Phenomenal Causality

Causes have three underlying properties, or dimensions, on which they may be compared and contrasted. One characteristic is causal location, which is regarded as within or outside the skin of the actor. For example, four causes mentioned previously that pertain to achievement and affiliative success and failure (ability, effort, personality, attractiveness) are similar in that they refer to (are internal to) the person under consideration. On the other hand, achievement failure because of chance or an unfair teacher, or affiliative rejection because the club has no space for new members or the desired partner already has a plans for that evening, are considered causes external to the actor.

All causes may be classified on an internal-external continuum or dimension. Hence, it might be contended that low ability as a cause of achievement failure is similar to a boring personality as a cause of affiliative failure and laziness as a cause of poverty (they are internal to the actor) but differ from the desired partner having to study as a cause of rejection (which is considered an external cause).

It was previously indicated that one might engage in moral actions because they make one "feel good" about oneself. Beliefs about causal locus play a role here in that pride and self-esteem increments require perceptions of internal causality. If, for example, a mother says "Help your sister or you will not get supper," then any subsequent helping behaviour will not give rise to pride because the cause is external to the help-giver. But this is a phenomenological system, so if the brother believes he imparted special assistance or that the mother's threat did not influence him, then he might perceive the help-giving as personally caused and experience increments in self-esteem (Weiner, 1985).

A second causal property, particularly important in the moral domain, is causal control or the extent to which the cause is subject to volitional change. This causal construal relates to the concept of free will (Weiner, 1995). Some internal causes are regarded as controllable by the actor whereas others are not. For example, exam failure ascribed to lack of aptitude is perceived as uncontrollable, whereas failure because of party-going will be considered a controllable cause by both the failing actor and observers. In a similar manner and moving to an area more closely associated with altruism, stigmas may be regarded as due to controllable versus uncontrollable internal causes (e.g., heart disease due to not exercising versus genetic characteristics; homosexuality as a lifestyle choice versus biological givens; poverty ascribed to lack of planning versus illness (Weiner, Perry & Magnusson, 1988)). Controllable versus uncontrollable causes of stigmas, which are linked to inferences of responsibility and nonresponsibility, are closely related to the respective labels of sin versus sickness.

It might be contended that all controllable causes are internal to the actor so that locus and control are not orthogonal causal dimensions. On the other hand, it also is possible to consider external causes as controllable by others rather than the self. For example, exam failure because the teacher is biased might be regarded by the failing student as external to the self yet controllable by others. If this is acceptable, then causes of achievement failure, stigmas, or poverty, for example, can be regarded as internal and uncontrollable (aptitude, illness); internal and controllable (lack of effort, lifestyle choice); external and uncontrollable by anyone (bad luck, economic conditions); or external and controllable by the other (unfair teacher, discrimination). Remember, however, that this is phenomenological causality so that, for example, luck may be regarded as internal ("an unlucky person") and other causes also may vary in their dimensional placement.

To summarize, a negative or unexpected event or state (e.g., a person asking for help, the perception of a stigma) gives rise to a causal search and a causal ascription (e.g., low effort, lifestyle choice), with the cause classified on two causal dimensions (locus and control). A third identified causal property is stability or relative endurance (e.g., compare aptitude to a temporary lack of skill) but this property is ignored here because it is of lesser importance in the moral domain than, for example, achievement strivings inasmuch as causal stability is linked with success expectations.

Relating Causal Structure to Moral Responsibility and Moral Emotions

A designation of personal causality is necessary in determining if an individual is responsible or not responsible for his or her plight (Weiner, 1995). For example, one is responsible for failure due to not studying or for obesity because of over-eating, as opposed to being nonresponsible for failure due to low ability or obesity because of a thyroid problem. But other factors enter into this decision, particularly the presence or absence of mitigating circumstances. For example, considering the student regarded as responsible for failure due to lack of studying, information that the failure to study was because the student had to take a sick parent to the hospital mitigates that inference. In a similar manner, the mentally ill and young children may not be regarded as responsible for a personally controllable transgression because they cannot distinguish right from wrong or understand the consequences of their actions. However, assuming the lack of mitigating factors, an internal and controllable cause of an event or need gives rise to an inference of moral responsibility.

Responsibility beliefs, in turn, are sufficient for the arousal of the moral emotions of sympathy and anger (Weiner, 2006). Imagine your reactions to the failure of a child in school or on the athletic field when that negative outcome is due to lack of aptitude (or motor co-ordination) versus not studying (or missing practice). In a similar manner, the reactions to lung cancer of another who unknowingly lives in a polluted area versus smoking, to homelessness because of low wages versus drinking, to poverty because of illness versus not willing to work, and on and on, produce reactions of sympathy and pity versus anger and annoyance. All these examples can be subsumed within the same conceptual framework, which is as follows (and assumes no mitigating circumstances):

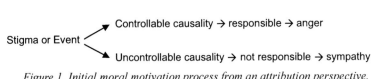

Stigma or Event
Controllable causality → responsible → anger
Uncontrollable causality → not responsible → sympathy

Figure 1. Initial moral motivation process from an attribution perspective.

Altruistic Actions

Thus far, a process has been outlined that goes from outcomes (e.g., exam failure, stigma) to thinking (causes and responsibility inferences) to feeling. Emotions then give rise to classes of actions that are goaded by these experiential states. Anger calls forth anti-social behaviour, whereas the motivational message of sympathy is a pro-social reaction. Thus, we neglect those who can help themselves and help those who are not responsible for their plights. Four motivational episodes illustrating these associations are:

1. Jim needs money and asks for help. He is not working because he prefers to spend his time at the beach. This controllable cause of the need results in an inference of personal responsibility, anger, and neglect.
2. Jim is obese. He refuses to exercise, spending his time playing video games, and while playing eats unhealthy foods. These controllable causes of a need produce inferences of personal responsibility, anger, and neglect.
3. Jim needs money and asks for help. He is not working because he was ill and hospitalized, which resulted in a job loss. He has been trying to find a new job but economic conditions are severe. These uncontrollable causes of need give rise to an inference of nonresponsibility, sympathy, and help giving.
4. Jim is obese. He has a thyroid problem and has been trying different medical treatments to help him lose weight. He eats little and often works out at the gym. The uncontrollable causes of need produce inferences of nonresponsibility, sympathy and help.

Given this line of reasoning, moral behaviour is dependent upon the deservedness of the potential help-receiver. That is, morality is a product of social perception, an end-result of a thinking-feeling-action sequence in which motivated behaviour is pushed by social emotions (Weiner, 2006).

It might be contended that the ultimate goal or end-result of this sequence is the maintenance of the social system in that sympathy rebalances the scales of social justice and anger conveys to the recipient not to engage in socially unacceptable behaviour. These communications and behaviours thus function to help the survival of society. Hence, the attribution perspective is compatible with a distal, evolutionary analysis. However, as previously indicated, this "ultimate" speculation is neither subject to experimental proof nor disproof. On the other hand, the moral sequences outlined above have been documented many times and verified in meta-analytic reviews (see Weiner, 1995, 2006). The confirming research investigations typically manipulate the cause of a need and then assess emotions (anger, sympathy, and/or their variants) as well as altruistic actions (help-giving). The strength of the findings leaves no doubt as to the existence of the postulated thinking-feeling-action associations.

As indicated earlier, it is not anticipated that this process underlies all moral and ethical behaviours. Obviously, another individual (rather than a material object) is targeted in this analysis and moral determinants such as social norms, availability or absence of moral models, the number of others available to help, and on and on, are not part of this conception. Thus, attribution theory accounts for only a portion of moral behaviour. Yet this should not minimize its value inasmuch as this statement or conclusion about this field of study can be extended to virtually any account of moral action.

Theoretical Generality

It was previously contended that one positive feature of this approach is that the proposed conceptual sequence also may be applicable to actions not in the moral domain. Consider, for example, achievement strivings. It has been documented that self-attribution of failure to lack of aptitude produces subsequent performance decrements, as opposed to ascriptions of failure to lack of effort, which results in later performance enhancement (Weiner, 1985). These attribution-action relations are mediated by perceptions of causal control (ignoring here the third causal dimension of stability) and their linked emotions in the following manner:

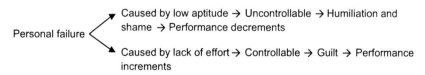

Figure 2. Achievement motivation process from an attribution perspective (self-perception).

In a similar manner, the reactions of others who witness this failure are captured by the following sequences:

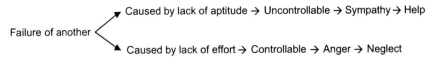

Figure 3. Achievement motivation process from an attribution perspective (other-perception).

Still other motivation domains, including social aggression (analyzed by contrasting perceived intentional versus unintentional harm) and social power (contrasting controllable reward-seeking actions versus behaviours driven by uncontrollable anticipated punishment) have been subject to the same conceptual analysis (Rudolph, Roesch, Greitemeyer & Weiner, 2004). For example, assume your toes have been stepped upon while riding in the subway. If this is interpreted as an intentional act, then anger is aroused and there is a tendency to retaliate. On the other hand, if it is inferred that this was an accident, then such aggressive actions are not activated. Similarly, even if one engaged in a morally reprehensible action such as stealing an art object, considerations of responsibility are paramount. If the object was taken because another promised a financial reward, then responsibility is inferred, anger aroused, and punishment desired. But say the object was stolen because a powerful other threatened you or a family member personal harm if this was not done. In that case, responsibility, anger, and punishment are lessened. Hence, a general principle of motivated behaviour has been put forth that captures some behaviours across domains.

QUESTIONS AND ANSWERS; DOUBTS AND UNCERTAINTIES

A number of issues and questions can be raised about an attributional analysis of help-giving. What follows are some of the anticipated questions and attempts at answers, when they are available.

Must the Sight of a Person in Need Give Rise to an Attribution Process? Isn't Help Giving an Immediate Reaction without Complex Cognitive and Affective Mediators?

It certainly may be the case that help-giving is an immediate reaction to a perception of need. We react instantly to protect someone from falling, or to prevent a child from running into the street. As was indicated previously, there are many sufficient causes of altruistic actions, none of which are necessary. Many times attributions are not part of the motivational process. On the other hand, often help-giving is a calculated reaction. To what charity will we allocate money? Which of our children might inherit more than an equal share? What is our opinion about the government's welfare program? Answers to these questions do engage attributional thoughts and impact altruistic actions. In addition, attributional thinking need not be conscious and deliberate and on occasion is automatic and does not involve conscious awareness.

Given an Attribution for a Need, must that Ascription be Classified According to Controllability? Isn't it the Case that Consequences may be Linked to the Cause Itself?

The meaning of a cause – its definition, essence and significance, is supplied by placement within a three dimensional taxonomic space. Thus, for example, aptitude "is" something internal to the person, stable, and not controllable. Nonetheless, in some situations certain causal properties are more central than others and thus are prominent. For example, following exam failure a student may be most interested in predicting what will happen on the next exam and thus especially seek information or reach some decisions about causal stability. In moral situations, where inferences of intention are of prime importance, it is likely that perceived controllability of the need will be especially salient. For example, it has been reported that reactions to stigmas and mental illness are primarily determined by perceptions of personal responsibility that are elicited by these states and conditions (Feldman & Crandall, 2007). Thus, I believe part of the causal analysis in situations of help-giving will include placement on the control dimension of causality.

Must Perceptions of Control Give Rise to Affects? Must Control be Linked to Anger and Lack of Control to Sympathy? Can't One be Sympathetic at the Plight of Another Regardless of the Cause and its Controllability?

What has been outlined here is a psychology of the ordinary person. This analysis may not extend to saints, who do not experience anger when the other intentionally perform an immoral act, and it may not extend to psychopaths or hardened criminals, who may not feel sympathy in spite of the uncontrollability of the plight of another. The position of most emotional appraisal theorists is that, in a majority of instances, particular thoughts give rise to particular emotions. More specifically, ascriptions regarding the responsibility of a person for his or her plight are linked with feeling sorry for that individual (given no responsibility) or anger (assuming responsibility; Roseman, 1991). Of course, there are complexities that seem to violate these laws. For example, we might feel sympathy toward a dieing person who was responsible for this state (e.g., lung cancer because of smoking; HIV/AIDS due to promiscuous sexual behaviour). In these situations, the offset of death may be regarded as uncontrollable so that sympathy is also aroused, or the end-result so negative that some pro-social emotion is engaged.

I consider the control-emotion link spontaneous, with the affect automatically following the attribution. This is not true for all people at all times, but nonetheless is a highly predictable linkage (Weiner, 2006). In addition, the association may be masked because of competing thought-feeling linkages.

Must Anger Give Rise to Anti-Social Reactions (e.g., Neglect) and Sympathy to Pro-Social Behaviour (Altruism and Help-Giving)? Can't One Help Another Even Though Angry or Ignore Another Even Though Sympathetic?

Of all the associations within this theory, the ones between affect and action are weakest and the behaviour most likely to violate theoretical predictions. This is because help-giving and altruism often require the presence of facilitating factors and are over-determined behaviours. To help another, want or desire is not sufficient; "can" or ability often is also necessary. For example, I may desire to help a drowning victim but cannot swim; I may want to help someone who is living in poverty but have no money; I may be motivated to help a blind person to cross the street but my leg is in a cast. In these situations, sympathy may not give rise to the predicted pro-social reaction, as opposed to the desire to act without its expression in action. Of course, actions differ in a number of essential characteristics so instead of jumping in the water perhaps I can call a lifeguard or instead of giving the impoverished money perhaps I can at some time bring my supper. But often one is helpless to fulfill altruistic desires in spite of the presence of pro-social emotions.

A similar logic regarding over-determination applies in situations of anger. I may be angry at my unfair boss but not engage in anti-social behaviour for fear of losing my job. Or, one may be angry at a spouse for coming late for an appointment but not want to initiate an argument and thus not reprimand his or her tardiness. And I may be angry at another for teasing me but do not respond for fear of further aggressive action.

In short, given an emotion, the action prompted by that affect may not be exhibited in action. As already indicated, the affect-behaviour pairing is the weakest link in the theory in terms of prediction. On the other hand, it also is the case that anger and sympathy often do elicit their behavioural goals. Because of the obstacles to expressing emotions in action, I have often favored simulation studies where these barriers are removed.

Can't Parts within this Sequence be Reversed so that, for Example, Affects Produce Attributions? If One is Angry, for Example, Might That Give Rise to Attributions of Responsibility Rather than Vice-Versa?

I do believe that free-floating anger (one wonders what causes this anger if not some prior responsibility antecedent) can bias perceptions that increase responsibility inferences. That is, there are quite likely to be right-to-left or bi-directional linkages within the theory. However, it is my belief that the left-to-right associations, that is, the sequence going thinking-feeling-acting, predominates motivational life.

Aren't Individual and Cultural Differences Being Neglected? Some People Help more than Others, and in Some Cultures Altruism is More Evident than in Others.

It is the case that this theory focuses on main effects due to environmental factors and relatively ignores effects traced to the person (actor) and person X environment interactions. When effects are ascribed to the person, the theory specifies that they are likely to be traced to differences in ascriptions of causality, particularly regarding the perceived controllability of the causes of a need. In support of this position, it has been documented that liberals, or those on the left of the political spectrum, are more likely than conservatives, or those politically to the right, to ascribe poverty to environmental factors such as low wages or lack of educational opportunities. On the other hand, conservatives tend to see poverty as caused by laziness, lack of planning, or drug and alcoholic use, which are perceived as controllable by the person (Weiner, Osborne, & Rudolph, 2011). That is, poverty is perceived as a moral failure. These attributions are in accord with the desire of liberals to alter society and conservatives' beliefs in maintenance of the status quo. Consistent with these causal ascriptions, democrats more endorse governmental welfare and other forms of help giving than do conservatives.

The general implication of these findings is that the theory does not reject individual or cultural differences. Rather, these differences are traced to the mediators postulated between the event or state and the final behaviour- perceptions of causality, placement of the cause in dimensional space, and affective experience.

CONCLUSION

Moral and ethical actions have many explanations -for example, they may be mere habits, interpreted with a machine metaphor of motivation; or they may be calculated actions, guided by anticipated punishments and understood with hedonistic principles. On the other hand, it is contended in this chapter that moral actions are determined by perceptions of responsibility, interpreted with the metaphor that persons are judges and that life is a courtroom where decisions about intent and fairness are dominant. Attribution theory is consistent with this metaphorical view and altruism is observed when the other is construed as not responsible for a personal plight, that is, the individual is a deserving member of the social system. This metaphor and the proximal behavioural determinants of causal beliefs and elicited emotions are not capable to capturing all moral and ethical actions, such as picking up trash from the street. But an attributional analysis deserves representation among the most viable explanations of moral conduct.

REFERENCES

Buss, D.M. (2008). *Evolutionary psychology: The new science of the mind* (3rd ed.). Boston: Allyn & Bacon.

Confer, J.C., Easton, J.A., Fleischman, D.S., Goetz, C.D., Lewis, D.M.G., Perilloux, C., & Buss, D.M. (2010). Evolutionary psychology. *American Psychologist, 65,* 110–126.

Feldman, D.B., & Crandall, C.S. (2007). Dimensions of mental illness stigma: What about mental illness causes social rejection? *Journal of Social & Clinical Psychology, 26,* 137–154.

Hamilton, W.D. (1963). The evolution of altruistic behavior. *The American Naturalist, 97,* 354–356.

Hamilton, W.D. (1964). The general evolution of social behavior. *Journal of Theoretical Biology, 7,* 1–52.

Roseman, I. (1991). Appraisal determinants of discrete emotions. *Cognition and Emotion, 5,* 161–200.

Rudolph, U., Roesch, S.C., Greitemeyer, T., & Weiner, B. (2004). A meta-analytic review of help giving and aggression from an attributional perspective. *Cognition and Emotion, 18,* 815–848.

Rushton, J.P., Fulker, D.W., Neale, M.C., Nias, D.K.B., & Eysenck, H.J. (1986). Altruism and aggression: The heritability of individual differences. *Journal of Personality and Social Psychology, 50,* 1192–1198.

Trivers, R.L. (1971). The evolution of reciprocal altruism. *The Quarterly Review of Biology, 46,* 35–57.

Weiner, B. (1985). An attributional theory of achievement-related emotion and motivation. *Psychological Review, 29,* 548–573.

Weiner, B. (1992). *Human motivation: Metaphors, theories, and research.* Newbury Park, CA: Sage.

Weiner, B. (1995). *Judgments of responsibility: A foundation for a theory of social conduct.* New York: Guilford.

Weiner, B. (2006). *Social motivation, justice, and the moral emotions.* Mahway, N.J.:Erlbaum.

Weiner, B., Graham, S., & Chandler, C.C. (1982). Pity, anger, and guilt: An attributional analysis. *Personality and Social Psychology Bulletin, 8,* 226–232,

Weiner, B., Osborne, D., & Rudolph, U. (2011). An attributional analysis of reactions to poverty: The political ideology of the giver and the perceived morality of the   receiver. *Personality and Social Psychology Review, 15,* 199–213.

Weiner, B., Perry, R.P., & Magnusson, J. (1988). An attributional analysis of reactions tostigmas. *Journal of Personality and Social Psychology, 55,* 738–748.

Wilson, E.O. (1975). *Sociobiology.* Cambridge, MA: Harvard University Press.

AFFILIATION

Bernard Weiner
Department of Psychology
University of California
Los Angeles, USA

ANDREAS KRAPP

II. MORAL MOTIVATION FROM THE PERSPECTIVE OF THE SELF-DETERMINATION THEORY AND THE PERSON-OBJECT THEORY OF INTEREST

INTRODUCTION

Many researchers working in the tradition of Kohlberg's theoretical approach to morality have shared his central hypothesis that moral judgment and moral behaviour are closely related. (cf. Kohlberg & Candee, 1984). The higher the level of moral development, the more one can expect a person to act in accordance with his/her moral judgment. Empirical studies, however, have shown that this thesis cannot claim general validity (Nunner-Winkler, 1999; Noam, 1999). There are many well-documented examples of a striking discrepancy between an individual's moral judgment and his/her observed behaviour (Garz, Oser & Althof, 1999; Oser & Näpflin, 2010).

Since these findings were published, researchers from different scientific disciplines have been concerned with the question of how this fact can be explained. One explanatory variable which is often recognized is *"moral motivation"*. In Rest's (1986/1999) *"four-component model"*, this variable is interpreted as one of the most important conditions of moral behaviour. This model serves primarily as a general basis for discussing the presumed influence of motivation but does not describe in detail the way in which motivational factors govern the occurrence and realization of moral behaviour in a specific situation. From a psychological point of view, this is a rather complex process which includes a variety of different cognitive and affective factors (Heinrichs, 2005).

I agree with the position of Oser, Heinrichs and Lovat outlined in the introductory chapter of this book that a thorough scientific debate about (the many facets of) moral motivation should take different theoretical concepts and models into account - including those developed recently in the domain of motivational psychology (see Vollmeyer, Jenderek & Tozman, this volume).

The explicit consideration of psychological theories in the discussion about moral motivation can be based on two different strategies. The *first* strategy represents the usual procedure employed in moral psychology and other neighboring disciplines. Its primary goal is to use psychological concepts congruent with one's own theoretical considerations to support or further develop these considerations. Sometimes, this happens without regarding the critical evaluation of these concepts

K. Heinrichs, F. Oser & T. Lovat (Eds.), Handbook of Moral Motivation: Theories, Models, Applications, 113–140.

in modern psychology. Typical examples are psychoanalytic or trait-oriented interpretations of human motivation which have turned out to be incompatible with the results from empirical research. The *second* strategy goes in the opposite direction and implicates a change to the dominant theoretical perspective. The starting point is not a specific approach within moral psychology; rather, it is the selection of certain theoretical and empirical approaches within the domain of motivational psychology which are then discussed with regard to the question of whether or not these concepts (and results) can be used to theoretically reconstruct and to explore certain facets of the global construct *moral motivation* in an innovative way.

This is the strategy I will try to pursue in my paper by referring to two theories of human motivation that have received growing recognition in the last two decades - especially in different fields of applied psychology (e.g., education), namely the *self-determination theory (*SDT) and the *person-object theory of interest (*POI). Both theories are characterized by a specific combination of meta-theoretical beliefs, including the conviction that it is not sufficient to reconstruct human motivation on the basis of action-theoretical models which represent the dominant research paradigm in modern psychology. A further equally important aspect of both theories is the discussion of the role of motivation in human development from the perspective of a dynamic theory of personality.

Before starting with this outline, I think it is necessary to clarify my concept of moral motivation and to highlight how my psychological approach differs from the ways of thinking used in influential theories of moral psychology. A central aspect of my approach is based on the conviction that moral motivation has to be interpreted as a multifaceted phenomenon which can only be reconstructed in a sufficiently comprehensive way when the complex theoretical construct is broken down into separate aspects that can be empirically explored on the basis of specific theories and research approaches. Here, motivational psychology can offer various models and concepts which have already been able to demonstrate their usefulness in other contexts. For our purpose, I think it is of special importance to develop a frame model of the content structure of the global concept of moral motivation which also contains a description of the theoretically relevant relationship between different components of this construct. In order to provide a basis for the discussion of this (in some way meta-theoretical) problem, I will present an outline of such a model in the second section of this paper. It also provides a general theoretical background for my considerations in section three about how certain basic ideas and selected concepts from the SDT and POI could be used to explore and theoretically reconstruct certain important aspects of moral motivation.

A PSYCHOLOGICAL APPROACH TO INTERPRETING
THE CONCEPT OF MORAL MOTIVATION

In my opinion, moral motivation is not a unique area of human motivation that requires specific methods of theoretical reconstruction. Rather, it is a specific domain which – at at least to some degree – can be described and explained on the basis of existing general theories of human motivation. The distinctive feature of moral motivation lies in the fact that morally relevant circumstances exist in a given situation and the person in the given situation recognizes this as a problem that must be considered. These circumstances thus have an influence on that person's behaviour. This interpretation corresponds with empirically based models of the regular course of moral behaviour (e.g. von Esser, 1996; Heinrichs, 2005) which accordingly assume that the starting point of any action-episode is characterized by the specific makeup of the situation. Under certain circumstances, this can lead to the insight (or belief) that a morally relevant problem exists which prompts the person in the given situation to take moral considerations or principles into account. In this case, a morally relevant action is set into operation.

In moral psychology, the concept of moral motivation is usually conceptualized in a much narrower way, namely as the "...desire to act in a morally correct way, or to be a moral person" (Nunner-Winkler, 1993, p. 300). Moral motivation is defined as the "readiness to do the right thing, not only when one would do it spontaneously anyway, but also when it implies disregarding one's own needs and their fulfilment" (Nunner-Winkler, 1993, p. 297). According to Blasi (1999, p. 59), this moral-theoretical position is based on a philosophically derived dualistic concept about the structure of human motivation which is characterized by the speculative idea of the existence of irresolvable conflicting motivational forces, which necessarily lead to conflicts in morally relevant situations. With this in mind, Nunner-Winkler (1999) and Blasi (1983/1999; 2005) refer to the distinction between *"first-order desires"* and *"second-order desires"* made in Harry Frankfurt's philosophy of the will (Frankfurt, 1988) for a more specific description of the postulated dualistic structure of moral motivation. In the first case, an individual follows his/her spontaneous desires and needs - regardless of whether or not the related actions meet morally relevant criteria. In the second case, it is postulated that human beings normally develop a moral "meta-need" (*Metabedürfnis*). This becomes obvious when an individual evaluates spontaneously occurring desires according to moral criteria, which now operate as a kind of gatekeeper in everyday behaviour. From this point of view, moral motivation represents a "second-order desire" which can have the effect that a person only acquires and maintains personal goals which have passed through the filter of moral judgment (Nunner-Winkler, 1999, p. 327).

From the viewpoint of modern psychology, this concept of moral motivation is based on questionable theoretical assumptions (see also Krettenauer's chapter in this book). First, it seems highly unlikely that the philosophical idea of the existence of an innate motivational dualism can be empirically proven. There is a long tradition of empirical research that has aimed at the identification of a universal classification system of human instincts or motives that could be used as a general diagnostic tool for describing and comparing the motivational structure of individuals. However, all of these research endeavors have failed to reach this aim. Rather, it has become clear that the system of human motivation is much more complex and cannot simply be understood as a specific pattern or combination of motivational dispositions. (Heckhausen, 1989/1991). None of the many hypotheses about the existence of an innate basic structure of human motives that were in vogue in earlier decades of the last century could be empirically validated.

Another critical point refers to the concept of a specified moral motive that is responsible for the kind of behaviour shown in a morally relevant situation. According to this concept, the extent to which this motive is pronounced in individuals should differ. Furthermore, it is postulated that the realization of morally adequate action depends first of all on the "motivational power" derived from this motive (e.g. Blasi, 1983/1999, p. 51). This kind of thinking is typical for the way in which the influence of motivation on human behaviour is interpreted in naïve psychological theories in everyday life, and it also played an important role in previous periods of psychological research. Results from a vast amount of empirical studies, however, have changed our knowledge about the manifold interrelationships between stable structures of human personality, the occurrence of specific forms of motivation, and their influence on planning and realizing an activity in a particular situation.

The seemingly plausible idea that an individual acquires increasingly stable personality traits that, to a large degree, govern his/her actual behaviour in a certain type of situation (e.g., morally relevant situations) has too often turned out to be wrong and, therefore, can no longer be accepted as a valid approach to explaining human behaviour. All acknowledged theories in the domain of modern personality and motivation psychology would agree that an adequate explanation of behaviour has to take a variety of different factors into account. Besides relatively stable dispositional factors, the situation-specific conditions of the actual environment also play an important role. Psychological researchers, therefore, mistrust trait-oriented explanations of human behaviour and rely on action-oriented approaches in which human behaviour is interpreted as the result of both cognitive-rational and emotional evaluations that are not only based on an individual's relatively stable goals, interests, attitudes and other trait-like dispositions but also on earlier experiences in similar situations and the perceived challenges at the moment (see Baumert et al., this volume).

This also holds true for theoretical reconstructions of human motivation. Action-theoretical models, such as the "rubicon model of action phases" (Heckhausen & Gollwitzer, 1987; Achziger & Gollwitzer, 2007; see below) interpret motivation as a dynamic system of action control, including cognitive, emotional and volitional factors (cf. Heckhausen & Heckhausen, 2006/2008).

Thus, from a psychological perspective, it seems to be problematic to reconstruct the narrower meaning of moral motivation, namely, the readiness to do the "right" or "good" thing even under difficult conditions, primarily on the basis of a kind of trait-concept of morality. Independent of reasonable doubts about the empirical validity of this common explanatory approach, I think one should, in principle, not restrict the area of possible explanations before even reaching the scientific discussion stage.

Instead, I would suggest starting with a rather broad concept of moral motivation and exploring different aspects of this concept while considering existing empirically validated theories and concepts. An important step in this direction is to develop ideas about how the general construct of moral motivation could be subdivided into theoretically meaningful structural components and empirically testable relationships. In the following section, I want to present a preliminary frame model, the basic ideas of which have been developed in educational-psychological fields of motivation research (Krapp, 1993; Krapp & Hascher, in press).

A GENERAL MODEL FOR DIFFERENTIATING BETWEEN THEORETICALLY IMPORTANT ASPECTS OF MORAL MOTIVATION

The theoretical background is provided by psychological concepts and research approaches which aim to offer an answer to the general question about the "why" or "whereto" of human behaviour. Looking back at the history of science concerned with motivation, a broad variety of descriptive and explanatory concepts have been developed and have been taken up in partly heterogeneous theories, many of which have been excluded from the scientific discussion because they could not sustain the accumulated empirical knowledge in their domain (Cofer & Appley, 1964; Heckhausen, 2006; Weiner, 1992).

At a rather general level of inspection, two different kinds of motivation theories can be distinguished: (1) Theories that deal primarily with motivational dispositions, such as the trait- or need-theories already mentioned (e.g. Murray, 1938). Some of these theories also refer to the very important question about how motivational dispositions develop and change over the course of an individual's life. (2) Theories which are primarily concerned with motivational processes on the basis of an action-theoretical framework. The following model tries to incorporate both ways of thinking in an adequate way. Its central aim is to provide a rather general description of motivational conditions and effects that are of relevance for a comprehensive theoretical reconstruction of moral behaviour.

Acting in Morally Relevant Situations

From a psychological point of view, the terms action, acting or behaviour denote different issues (see Heinrichs, 2005; this volume). An action comprises the whole actual genetic process of initiating, realizing and evaluating the outcome of a whole action episode, whereas an activity refers to the actual concrete behaviour exhibited in a certain situation. Although, in everyday life, people mostly interact with their environment automatically, that is, by habit, spontaneously, and without detailed cognitive-reflexive control, one can assume that most of these behaviour routines have been established in the past on the basis of deliberate considerations, about which the person can often provide information (see also Blasi, this volume). Types of behaviour which cannot be characterized in this way (for example spontaneous affective reactions such as the angry outburst of a child) do not belong to the category of motivated actions. Deci and Ryan (1985, 2002) have coined the term 'amotivation' for a general description of this kind of behaviour (see below: Figure 2). For our discussion, it is important to recognize that the psychological concept of action or human activity only represents a subset of people's observable behaviour. A central characteristic is the existence of an intention that is based on consciously selected action goals. This also holds true for the domain of moral behaviour which can be characterized at a rather general level of examination as "*action in morally relevant situations*" (Heinrichs, 2005, p.116).

Such a relatively broad conceptualization of moral behaviour would also embrace situations in which only outsiders recognize a moral problem but not the acting person him/herself - for example, when somebody has occupied a seat for disabled people and remains seated although a seemingly disabled person has entered the train. A more circumscribed meaning of this concept is limited to situations in which a person has noticed a moral problem and tries to act in an adequate manner while considering the moral criteria. In Heinrich's (2005) model, this kind of behaviour is characterized as "*moral-thematic activity*".

The question of how the concept of motivation can be used to explain this kind of behaviour has been discussed in many different ways. From my point of view, it is neither desirable nor possible to look for the best or the only correct explanatory concept. Rather, I think moral motivation should be understood as a complex theoretical construct which refers to a variety of theoretically separable aspects of motivation in morally relevant situations. From this point of view, a promising approach would be to differentiate between motivational conditions and effects on the basis of a frame model that, on the one hand, provides an overview of the important structural and dynamic components of the general construct and, on the other hand, can be used to describe and evaluate empirical research approaches used in this domain. In the following section, I want to outline a frame model which is based on theoretical considerations about the role of motivation in learning and human development (Krapp, 1993; Krapp & Hascher, in press).

The Main Features of a Theoretical Frame Model

A sufficiently comprehensive theoretical reconstruction of moral motivation has to recognize action-theoretical interpretations as well as concepts and ideas derived from theories of personality and human development. Figure 1 depicts the important aspects of motivation in morally relevant situations on the basis of an action-theoretical frame model. It categorizes the conditions, processes and effects of moral motivation on a hypothetical time axis and describes six motivationally relevant aspects whose interrelationships can be scientifically explored in more detail.

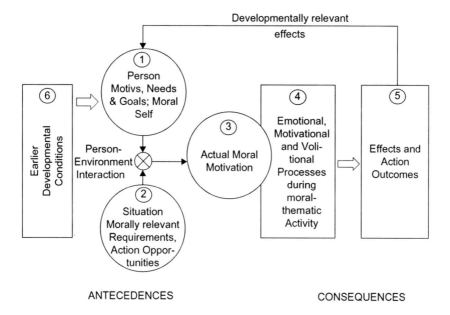

Figure 1. A frame model for describing theoretically important aspects of moral motivation.

The *actual moral motivation exhibited* is put in the center of this model (see field 3). This motivational state results from preceding conditions (antecedents) which can be ascribed either to the acting *person* (1), or the actually given *situation* (2). Among the conditions anchored in the person are morally relevant motives and attitudes, volitional competences, or memories of previous attempts to cope with moral problems in certain situations. From a (dynamic) personality perspective, all of these components differ with respect to the degree of personal or "ego" relevance. The most important components are those which the person would consider to represent the central area of his/her personality, and thus represent an individual's *identity* or *"self" (see below)*. The model postulates a substructure that is directly related to moral-thematic activities and is labeled as a *"moral self"*.

The term *situation* (2) denotes the sections of reality that are perceived by the acting person and could be of relevance for planning and realizing the next steps of person-environment-interactions: for example, the actually effective demands and possibilities for action, the presence of other persons and the kinds of social relationships experienced, or the recognition of morally relevant expectations and problems. The motivational state which determines the kind of moral-thematic activity undertaken does not occur automatically, i.e. by activating a related moral motive or any other personality trait that is relevant for moral behaviour. Rather, it is the result of a complicated internal negotiation process which is influenced by both personal and environmental conditions. This idea is indicated by the label *person-environment-interaction.*

The existing motivational dispositions of an individual must be interpreted as the result of previous experiences and learning processes which have been determined by *earlier developmental conditions* (6). Despite the fact that dispositions or traits tend to become more and more stabilized over the course of a lifetime, one has to take into account that they also can be changed and undergo developmental modifications. Besides formal educational programs which aim at fostering moral judgment and behaviour, the general socialization conditions of an individual's lifespace ("Lebensraum") and his/her experiences in previous moral situations often have an unobserved influence on the development of the person's morally relevant characteristics.

The *actual moral motivation exhibited* (3) has a decisive influence on the cognitive and emotional processes which take place during a moral-thematic activity (4). Its specific manifestation determines, for example, whether or not the acting person is ready to adopt moral standards in his/her decisions and activities and how an action is realized in order to meet accepted moral norms to a sufficient degree. An important aspect is the consistency and persistence of behaviour under difficult circumstances, such as the occurrence of unexpected problems or attractive alternatives of action. Let's imagine, for example, the situation of an adolescent who is a voluntary member of a social organization and has declared his readiness to organize and undertake a day trip with a wheelchair user. All the necessary preparations have been made, and the wheelchair user is looking forward to taking this trip, which has been firmly promised. Shortly before departure, the adolescent gets a message from his girlfriend who lives in another town, and whom he has not met for quite a long time, telling him that she has got a lift and would like to spend the day with him. The adolescent experiences this situation as a moral conflict because he feels morally obliged to keep a promise, and at the same time he wants to be perceived from both sides as a reliable partner. What will he do? Will he try to cancel the trip, or will he abandon the meeting with his girlfriend, although he expects her to be very disappointed? And which effect will any of these alternative actions have on his subjective experience during the day or on future decisions in similar situations? Related (scientific) questions belong to the fields (4) and (5) in the frame model.

Field (4) points to the many motivationally relevant *psychic processes* that take place during the course of a moral-thematic activity. I only want to mention two issues that can demonstrate the important role of these processes in an exemplary way. First, one has to recognize that motivation is closely connected to emotional processes which provide feedback about the adequacy of the actual person-environment-interactions, often not consciously noticed. Positive emotional experiences such as joy, happiness or pride may indicate a high level of agreement between an individual's intention to act in an appropriately moral way and what he/she has really undertaken until now. Negatively connoted emotional reactions, such as anger or shame may, on the other hand, result from the impression that the individual has not been able to realize his/her moral goals and intentions. Second, it is important to notice that any goal-oriented action requires regulatory measures to make sure that the action plan is actually carried out consistently. This is especially necessary in situations that are already conflict-laden at the beginning, or when unexpected problems occur during the course of a moral-thematic activity, such as the one described in the previous example.

In modern action-oriented theories of human motivation, forms of action control which are used deliberately are denoted as *volition*. The well-known "rubicon model of action phases" (Heckhausen & Gollwitzer, 1987; Achziger & Gollwitzer, 2007) makes an explicit theoretical distinction between volitional and motivational processes in a narrower sense. According to this model, motivation primarily refers to the (cognitive) processes of intention-formation, that is, the selection and clarification of action goals and situation-specific intentions. All the regulatory processes which take place during an action and make sure that the person consistently tries to reach the selected action goal are ascribed to the concept of volition. This theoretical differentiation corresponds with Kuhl's (1983) distinction between selection motivation and realization motivation. Heinrichs (2005) also suggests differentiating between motivational and volitional aspects in a comprehensive theoretical model of moral behaviour. Another scientific concept that deals with the question of how individuals succeed in reaching a selected action goal is *self-regulation*. According to Blasi (this volume), the discussion about moral motivation should concentrate its considerations on existing theories and empirical research concerned with the motivational basis of self-regulation.

Like any other action, a moral-thematic action leads to particular effects (*action outcomes*; see field 5) which are evaluated at the end of the activity at a more or less subconscious level. An important aspect of retrospective evaluation refers to the question of whether or not the intended action goals have been achieved; this may also include critical considerations about the fulfillment of moral standards and possible reasons for an unsatisfactory result. One can assume that reflective evaluations of the outcome of moral-thematic activities will have an effect on an individual's morally relevant attitudes and motives and, thus, will contribute to an individual's moral development. This general hypothesis is indicated by the arrow pointing backwards from field (5) to field (1). It also documents the fact that there are close interrelationships between moral behaviour and moral development which require thorough scientific exploration.

Not all of the effects of a moral-thematic activity that have a long-lasting (ontogenetic) influence are based on cognitive-reflexive evaluations of the final outcome. I think it is important to take emotional factors into account as well. One could, for example, imagine specific deep emotional experiences, such as shame or anger, which only occur occasionally during a long action-episode without having an obvious effect on the final result. Nevertheless, it is possible that these experiences are stored in the long-term memory and enforce existing mental representations which may in future become more and more dominant in similar morally relevant situations.

Different Perspectives of Analysis in Psychological Research Approaches

On the basis of this frame model, it is possible to identify typical problem areas and empirically meaningful research directions for analyzing the psychological structures and processes related to the concept of moral motivation. Whereas many (older) psychological theories and research approaches deal with the question of which characteristics of the person (e.g. motives, attitudes, level of moral reasoning) are responsible for a desirable level of moral judgment and behaviour, there is now a growing number of research approaches that primarily aim at an empirically founded reconstruction of the psychic processes which take place during the whole course of a moral-thematic action. The first research direction is based on hypotheses and theoretical concepts about the "moral personality" or specific structural components of the personality (e.g., traits, attitudes etc.) that are assumed to be responsible for moral behaviour (field 1 in the frame model; see also Edelstein, Nunner-Winkler & Noam, 2003; Narvaez & Lapsley, 2009). The second research direction refers primarily to the process-oriented aspects of moral motivation, addressed in field 3 and 4 of the model). Here, action-theories and concepts derived from dynamic theories of personality and human behaviour are used as theoretical background (Heinrichs, 2005; see also Döring in this volume; Krettenauer in this volume).

An important aim of empirical research is to analyze theoretically postulated relationships, for example, whether or not the behaviour shown in a morally relevant situation can be predicted by particular personality characteristics. In this case, empirical studies would refer to variables located in field 1, on the one hand, and field 3 or 4, on the other hand. An important precondition for this kind of research is the availability of diagnostic instruments (e.g., tests) for measuring morally relevant personality variables (e.g., altruism vs. egocentrism, honesty, sense of justice, pro-social attitude, etc.). Furthermore, empirical indicators for describing and evaluating moral behaviour are required. The relationships between these two groups of variables are mostly explored on the basis of larger data-sets and quite sophisticated statistical analysis procedures. These kinds of empirical studies comply with the classical research paradigm of differential psychology (Anastasi, 1958; Tyler, 1965) which is broadly used in psychological research, although it has limitations and shortcomings that are often ignored. Blasi (1983/1999, p. 48) has, with good reason, pointed to the danger that the functional psychological relationships between personality factors and the actual moral behaviour exhibited get lost or are not recognized in an adequate manner.

Another theoretical approach that can be used for analyzing these relationships comes from dynamic theories of personality that also take developmental aspects into account. A central concern of these theories is to reconstruct the emergence and the effects of motivational dispositions at the level of functional processes - including those related to ontogenetic developmental changes inmotivational dispositions.

Summary

Our considerations up until now make it clear that, from a psychological viewpoint, *moral motivation* is a multilayered and multifaceted phenomenon. Therefore, there can be no simple answer to the question which comprises the central theme of this book – "What makes people act morally right?" A serious scientific discussion calls for fundamental theoretical considerations about how broadly or narrowly the construct of moral motivation should be defined and also how the questions related to this construct can be broken down more clearly. Furthermore, it must be assumed that specific theoretical explanatory approaches are necessary for the clarification of specific questions and that empirical research approaches which are tailored towards these theoretical approaches are therefore also required.

In the following section, I will introduce some of the basic ideas and concepts of the SDT and the POI which seem to me to be relevant for any further discussions about the diverse questions relating to moral motivation. They refer to various fields in Figure 1. With regard to the conditions anchored in the person (Field 1), the SDT and POI provide information about the structure and function of the self as a central component of the human personality which, for example, could possibly be applied to the concept of the moral self. Another important point concerns the question of the differentiation of human motivation according to the qualitative criteria of the subjectively perceived self-determination (Field 3). Furthermore, the SDT and POI provide information about the emergence of and change in motivational dispositions which not only concern previous developmental conditions (Field 6) but also the direct emotional experience gained over the course of morally-related actions (Field 4 and 5 in the diagram).

THE THEORETICAL CONCEPTS OF THE SDT AND THE POI WHICH SEEM TO BE RELEVANT FOR A PSYCHOLOGICAL RECONSTRUCTION OF THE CONCEPT OF MORAL MOTIVATION

The SDT is a comparably comprehensive theoretical system which is empirically well-founded and comprises several sub-theories (mini-theories) (cf. Deci & Ryan 2002). Its central concern is to describe and explain a form of motivation which is based on self-determination. The SDT began with considerations and examinations of intrinsic motivation which was originally considered to be a prototype of self-determined motivation and interpreted as a counter pole to extrinsic motivation which was widely construed as being externally determined (Deci, 1975). In the 1980s, this dichotomous concept was replaced by a multi-leveled model of motivational regulation which placed extrinsic motivation in an entirely new light (see below).

Over the last decades, the SDT has been used in many psychological and educational research fields and fields of application, including those which have a connection to moral behaviour, e.g., in studies on the motivational conditions of pro-social behaviour (Assor, 2012; Weinstein & Ryan, 2010).

The central topic of *interest theories* is the emergence and mode of operation of content-specific motivational dispositions which are presumed to have a lasting effect on learning and human development (Renninger, Hidi & Krapp, 1992; Silvia, 2006). One interest theory which was developed specifically for the field of education is the *POI* (Prenzel, Krapp & Schiefele, 1986; Krapp, 2002a, b).

I am convinced that the theoretical concepts developed in both theories can provide important suggestions and ideas for a continued theoretical discussion of the central topics of moral motivation. Their specific importance lies, amongst other things, in the fact that they not only consider moral motivation from the perspective of the cognitive-action theoretical research paradigm which dominates current research – they also discuss personality and developmental issues. Furthermore, they provide innovative explanations for the emergence of a form of motivation which is based on self-determination and personal interests. These explanations can, amongst other things, be used when considering the development of important components of moral motivation.

In the following section, I would like to explain this evaluation in more detail on the basis of the following ideas and concepts which I have chosen as examples for this purpose:

1. A dynamic approach to personality and the concept of self;
2. Types of autonomous motivation;
3. Interest-based acquisition of moral knowledge;
4. The hypothesis of a dual regulation system; and,
5. The concept of basic needs.

(1) A Dynamic Approach to Personality and the Concept of Self

The SDT and POI use a dynamic approach to personality that reconstructs motivational aspects of the developing person not only with respect to structural components (dispositions, traits, etc.) but also with respect to functional relations. Of special importance for our discussion is the *concept of self*. It is based on the assumption that an individual's personality structure consists of different areas that are more or less experienced as personally important or relevant for the recognition of one's identity.

In theoretical conceptions which played an important role in older theories of the human personality (e.g., Lewin, 1936), it is postulated that the human personality has a core structure which has a significant importance for self-determined action and the further development of the human personality.

According to this theoretical position, an individual's self is manifested not only in the way in which the person perceives himself or herself (self-concept), but also in the way the person evaluates his or her capacities, goals, and attitudes (self-esteem), and in the way he/she assesses the potential for coping with actual and forthcoming life-tasks. It is characterized by a hierarchical organization of processes and structures that include cognitive, motivational, and affective components, some of which may more or less obviously be related to moral motivation, such as knowledge of moral rules and norms, the value orientations which the person accepts, or attitudes which are based on moral judgments. The components of the self important for moral action can be summarized by using the term *moral self*. According to this theoretical conception, they form a substructure of the individual self (cf. Figure 1, Field 1).

This relatively general definition leaves the following questions open: what concretely belongs to the moral self and what does not? And, what is the relationship between the different cognitive, affective or motivational components? The basic standpoint of the SDT and the POI is consistent with the *self-model of moral behaviour* developed by Blasi (1983/1999). In this model, moral knowledge and the willingness to act morally can be perceived as central components of the individual self and are described by Blasi with the term "essential self". Furthermore, it can be assumed that different people attach high individual importance to different aspects of morality. In accordance with considerations in the theoretical tradition of Kohlberg, it seems plausible that some people, for example, are quite strongly interested in the topic of social justice and are thus particularly sensitive to moral problems related to this, while others concentrate more on problem areas which deal with caring for and helping fellow citizens who are in need. The example which we sketched above can be assigned to the second category.

The development of the moral self must be understood as a lifelong process which is not limited to the stages of childhood and adolescence. Over the course of development, morally important convictions are repeatedly questioned and are, if necessary, revised. In this context, Noam (1999, p. 350) refers to an ongoing "process of importance structuring *(Bedeutungsstrukturierung)* with regard to the individual him/herself, other people and the whole world". This can be expressed both in a differentiation of the existing structures of the moral self and in a change in moral values and principles. The levels of moral judgment described in the Kohlberg tradition also refer to this.

The changes which the self-system undergoes over the course of human development, some of which can be quite profound, lead not infrequently to tension and breaks between the different subsystems. In serious cases, this can lead to mental-health problems and long lasting illness (cf. Noam, 1999). Nevertheless, in normal cases, over the course of a lifetime, a person sees him/herself as somebody who has a stable core and perceives this stable core as determining his or her personality.

The Concept of Organismic Integration

A mentally healthy person lives in relative harmony with his or her attitudes, goals, accumulated capacities, and knowledge structures. According to the SDT, there is an inborn propensity towards *organismic integration*.

This concept helps to explain how two general development tendencies of the person-environment system which are principally at war with each other can be held in a functional balance. The *first* general development tendency concerns the "personal growth" of the individual which is, for example, documented in the continual facilitation of that individual's personal skills and capacities. The *second* development tendency concerns the securing of social systems in which the person is embedded and on whose further existence he or she is reliant as a social entity. The structures and functional patterns of social systems are maintained and further developed by the members of this system. Despite these permanent changes, under normal conditions, social life environments possess a measure of stability. The concept of the SDT states that this fact can only be explained by a regulation mechanism which is part of human nature and which adapts individual development processes to the requirements of a sufficiently stable social system. This development principle makes sure that, amongst other things, all members of a social group develop a commonly shared pool of knowledge, skills, attitudes and behaviourally regulative norms and that these are permanently anchored in the psychic structure. This also includes people's social norms and moral principles.

While cognitive theories of moral development (e.g. Kohlberg & Candee, 1984; Blasi, 1983/1999) essentially make cognitive-rational decision processes or volitional mechanisms of conscious action regulation responsible for this, the SDT and POI, in accordance with neurobiological theories (see Narvaez, this volume), assume that affectively regulated processes play an equally important role, such as the satisfaction of fundamental psychological needs (see below).

A further important point concerns the initially posed question as to why a person's moral judgment does not generate sufficient motivation for morally appropriate behaviour. Blasi (1983/1999) and other authors (see Walker in this volume) believe that moral convictions have a "motivational strength" and that the absence or an inadequate level of this is considered to be responsible for such insufficient motivation. From the viewpoint of the SDT, the concept of motivational strength is, however, unsatisfactory. The consideration of *qualitative* differences, e.g., with regard to the question of whether the actual motivation exhibited is perceived as being heteronomous or self-determined, is at least as important. According to the SDT, such qualitative differences occur due to the fact that motivational dispositions are deeply anchored in the person's self-system.

As already mentioned above, Blasi (1983/1999, p. 59) assumes that the discrepancy between moral thinking and acting which can frequently be observed stems from a dualistic motivation structure which is part of human nature. It is unchangeable and thus inevitably leads to motivational conflicts. The SDT and POI would not agree with this interpretation. True, the fact that people often struggle with motivational conflicts in everyday life cannot be dismissed (e.g., Hofer, 2007) but this in no way excludes the fact that people set up motivational structures which largely hinder the occurrence of a serious motivational conflict – either in general, or in specific fields of action. Whether this is successful or not is, according to the SDT, primarily a question of the inner structure of the self-system. The stronger the individual motivational components of the self (e.g., aims, personal values, attitudes) are harmonized with each other and thus keep opposed efforts in a generally conflict-free balance, the more seldom insolvable tension and serious motivational conflicts have to be reckoned with. The decisive psychological mechanism is the *identification* with the aims, value orientations and interests perceived to be of particular importance on a personal level, as well as the willingness to make a decision in favor of these central aim categories in the case of conflict.

In this case, people experience themselves as being autonomous or self-determined, if they have to forego certain aims which seem very attractive at the time because they believe that they are doing this voluntarily. Under particularly favorable developmental conditions, a person succeeds to harmonize his or her subjectively important aims and value orientations, to such an extent that conflicts can hardly be expected in the first place or can be resolved relatively easily with appropriate strategies. This represents a kind of motivational regulation that is called *integration* in the SDT (see below).

(2) Types of Autonomous Motivation

The SDT has proposed a taxonomy of types of motivation which differ in the degree to which they represent autonomy, i.e. the degree to which regulations or their underlying values have been integrated.

This theoretical conception is important for our purpose because, according to several moral philosophers and psychologists (e.g. Kohlberg), one can only speak of moral motivation if it is based on an autonomously made decision to do the morally right thing. A clear line is thereby drawn between autonomous and non-autonomous motivation. The SDT takes a different stance on this.

From the viewpoint of the SDT, all intentional behaviours can vary in terms of the degree to which they are experienced as autonomous or controlled (Ryan & Deci, 2000, 2002). *Autonomous motivation* concerns actions that are experienced as congruent with one's self, and, thus, reflect one's central values or interests. In contrast, *controlled motivation* is experienced as emanating either from self-imposed or external pressures. In attributional terms, autonomous and controlled motivation are characterized by a perceived internal vs. external locus of causality (deCharms, 1968; Ryan & Connell, 1989).

Figure 2 presents a taxonomy of types of motivational regulation that can be placed along a continuum of perceived autonomy - ranging from totally non-self-determined (or controlled) behaviour to fully self-determined behaviour.

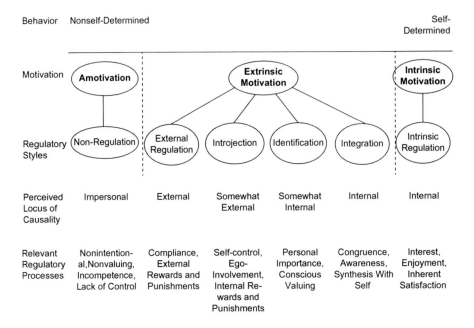

Behavior   Nonself-Determined

Self-Determined

Figure 2. The self-determination continuum showing types of motivation with their regulation style, loci of causality, and corresponding processes (Ryan & Deci, 2000, p. 72).

In the discussion about a theoretically suitable reconstruction of moral motivation, we must first remember that only those actions which fulfill the previously mentioned criterion of intentionality (see above) fall into the category of "motivated action". For our purpose, a further conceptual difference is also important; namely, the difference between *extrinsic* and *intrinsic motivation*. Extrinsically motivated actions are characterized by the fact that they are directed towards an aim outside the current action. All instrumental actions can thus, by definition, be classified as extrinsic. In contrast to this, with intrinsically motivated actions, the motivational incentive lies in the current action itself. Classical examples for this are a child's play or an action based solely on personal interests.

An intrinsically motivated person perceives him/herself as absolutely autonomous. In contrast, in the case of extrinsic motivation, the question of whether and to what extent the action is perceived as being self-determined depends on the specific type of motivation being exhibited in the particular situation. According to the SDT, at a quick glance, four types of extrinsic motivation can be differentiated which basically represent a continuum from complete heteronomy to absolute autonomy.

A first type of extrinsic motivation is characterized by *external regulation*. Behaviour at this level includes the classical instance of being motivated to obtain rewards or avoid punishment. In general, it is experienced as originating from external contingencies involving physical threats or the offering or withdrawal of material rewards. The behaviours are experienced as clearly non-autonomous and they persist only when the contingencies are present.

A consideration of moral norms brought about by this motivational basis corresponds to the first level of the pre-conventional stage in Kohlberg's theory.

A second type of motivation is based on *introjected regulation.* This is the case when external demands have been internalized, but not truly accepted by the individual's sense of self. Under the influence of this kind of motivation, behaviour is controlled by an attempt to avoid feeling guilty, ashamed, or unworthy. In such a situation, people feel they are acting because they must, not because they want to. The source of the coercion that was once external has been introjected and now resides inside. According to Assor (2012), introjection is a process in which people feel as if values or goals were inserted into them by a person of reference whose appreciation they needed, without having the option of modifying or even evaluating these normative expectations or regulations (see also Assor, Roth & Deci, 2004).

The first two types of motivation do not fulfill the criterion of self-determined (moral) action. The criterion of autonomous action regulation is only fulfilled in the other two types of motivation which are based on identified and integrated regulation. A person acting at the level of *identified regulation* has accepted the values of the activity as his or her own.

This person orientates his/her action towards moral standards because he/she considers them to be important at a personal level and he/she also identifies with them at this level. The key to understanding identified action regulation is the personal reference to the values and normative aspects which may be connected to this action or could result from the action. Theoretically, this can be explained by the fact that the person assumes these aspects into his/her self-system. A young person who perceives him/herself to be a reliable, helpful person will, for example, willingly help a sick neighbor and do shopping for the neighbor even if he/she has to sacrifice his/her own time and a meeting with friends because of this. Furthermore, he/she will perceive his/her willingness to help as an autonomous decision made in favor of his/her own moral principles.

Of course, one cannot expect people to always act in all circumstances in accordance with the moral convictions with which they identify themselves. This is mainly due to the fact that a person generally pursues many different and partially heterogeneous aims which are sometimes not fully aligned with their moral values and principles. Therefore, in eryday activities, moral conflicts and value dilemmas repeatedly occur (cf. Nunner-Winkler, 1999). It is thus in no way unusual for people who have a high level of moral judgment to make a completely conscious decision and to have subjectively plausible grounds for an action alternative which contradicts their own moral convictions and beliefs (e.g. Nisan, 1993).

However, there is also empirical evidence for a high consistency between moral conviction, moral motivation and actual action. A classical example can be found in the results of Colby & Damon (1982) on *"moral exemplars"*. From the viewpoint of the SDT, these people represent examples for the fourth type of motivation, which is characterized as *integrated regulation.*

This most autonomous form of extrinsically motivated behaviour occurs "... when identifications have been evaluated and brought into coherence with the personally endorsed values, goals, and needs that are already part of the self" (Ryan & Deci, 2002, p. 18). It is called integrated because the goals and behaviours that are enacted are not only experienced as reflecting central aspects of one's authentic self or identity but also because, to a large extent, they are consistently anchored in the overall system of personal values and aims.

The theoretical position expressed in the concept of integrated regulation corresponds in principal with the concept of *integrity* discussed by Blasi (this volume) and other authors (e.g. Nucci & Lee, 1993). This concept of integrity is considered to be an important prerequisite for moral behaviour. Blasi understands this to be "the need to maintain the unity, the wholeness, of one's subjective sense of self, as manifested in consistency with one's chosen commitments" (Blasi, this volume, p. 237).

Ryan and Deci (2002, p. 18) emphasize that their model of a relative autonomy continuum is intended to provide a model about typical levels of regulation that can be used to describe types of motivation in an exemplary way. The SDT does not suggest that it is a developmental continuum, nor does it claim that one must progress through each stage of internalization in order to reach a higher level of self-determination.

The taxonomy of different types of motivation suggested by Deci and Ryan provides an innovative approach for both a new description and a new theoretical specification of the concepts of the *moral self* which have been discussed until now. This is particularly true for the idea that two conditions must be fulfilled before a person can perceive a decision to act in accordance with moral criteria to be self-determined, despite the "costs" related to this decision and while simultaneously defending the decision against both internal and external resistance. These two conditions are (1) a strong identification with the moral values and norms considered to be relevant in this situation and (2) a coherent structure of harmonized personal goals, interests and morally relevant beliefs which belong to the core constituents of the human personality and the individual self. These components of the individual self which constitute the moral self provide a decisive basis for moral motivation.

Further Questions

Against the background of these theoretical considerations, many further questions arise, which can be allocated to Field 1 in our model. One important question concerns, for example, the content of the structural components of the moral self. Alongside the concept of the level of moral judgment, which has been discussed in detail in moral psychology, numerous other factors probably play an important role; for example, knowledge of and the subjective evaluation of the normative behavioural rules prevalent in the society or the relevant reference groups, as well as the ideas about justice, assumptions about the background and cause of typical moral conflicts, or the availability of strategies for solving conflicts in problem situations of a moral nature. I believe an important aim of future research should be the empirical analysis of the structural components of the moral self and its relationship to other components of the individual self. The results of this research will form an important foundation for the understanding of moral development and how it can be supported by educational measures (Oser & Althof, 1997; Oser & Näpflin, 2010).

Another important question focuses specifically on the acquisition of moral knowledge and moral beliefs and the integration of these into the moral self. In our frame model, this question is shown in Field 6 which refers to the conditions behind the emergence and development of moral motivation.

The SDT and POI have offered theoretical concepts that can be used for a deeper understanding of these processes, such as interest-based learning of morally relevant knowledge, the hypothesis of a dual regulation system, or the fulfillment of basic needs as an important condition of reliable moral behaviour.

(3) Interest-Based Acquisition of Moral Knowledge

Both moral judgment and the moral motivation exhibited in a certain situation are based on cognitive structures (e.g. knowledge and skills) whose basis is mostly formed incidentally over the course of a child's socialization, i.e. without an explicit intention to learn (Nunner-Winkler, 1999). The older people become, the more important are the intentional learning processes which have been initiated by explicit educational measures. Without such external impulses, young people could hardly be expected to reach higher levels of moral judgment. The targeted relaying of moral knowledge or moral ideas within the context of educational programs which promote morals (Oser & Althof, 1997; Oser & Näpflin, 2010) often causes great problems because the students only acquire "inert knowledge". In educational psychology, this type of knowledge is characterized as only being used to pass school and academic examinations but not to deal with the practical problems of everyday life. Theories and results on inert knowledge (cf. Renkl, 1996) draw our attention to the fact that the way in which knowledge is imparted and the quality of the learning motivation activated in the learning process play an important role.

From the viewpoint of the POI, this is also true for the acquisition of moral knowledge. The more successfully a learning situation can be constructed in such a way that the students perceive it to be subjectively important and authentic, and the more interest can be stimulated in the morally important issues and problems, which in turn induces effective learning, the more it can be expected that the knowledge acquired will be permanently integrated into the structure of the actively used knowledge (Krapp, 1999; Schiefele, 2009). It is not necessary for the learners to develop a lasting individual interest in moral topics; rather, it is sufficient if the intentional learning which takes place in the context of moral education occurs on the basis of a time-limited interest in the specific situation. Interest theory considerations provide indications for how educational concepts for moral promotion can be further developed (Oser & Näpflin, 2010). One important aspect is the consideration of the relevant age and gender-specific interests of the students as a motivational link for dealing with morally related questions.

The acquisition of moral knowledge, including the moral beliefs relevant to moral action, is one prerequisite but not the only condition necessary for the realization of behaviour which conforms to the norm. As already mentioned, what is decisive is that the knowledge and the rules and norms are internalized and integrated into the person's self-system. Which "psychological mechanisms" regulate these developmental processes? In the following section, I would like to refer to two theoretical conceptions which open up a new theoretical perspective for the discussion of the questions which have arisen here; namely, the hypothesis of a dual regulation system for the regulation of motivated action, and the concept of basic needs which is integrated within this system.

(4) The Hypothesis of a Dual Regulation System and the Concept of Basic Needs

In accordance with theoretical paradigms discussed in other fields of psychological research (Efklides, Kuhl & Sorrentino, 2001; Evans, 2010; Heckhausen, 2000; Sun, 2002), the POI postulates a psychological control system which operates at different levels of human experience. It is assumed to be responsible for the internalization and integration of motivational dispositions into the existing structure of an individual's self-system (cf. Krapp, 2000, 2002a, 2005). The different components of this system can be analyzed (and theoretically reconstructed) at different levels of specification. From a general point of view, two interrelated subsystems have to be taken into account. The first subsystem is mainly represented by conscious-cognitive factors. In addition to other functions, these factors are responsible for the process of rational-analytic intention formation. The function of this system becomes evident when a person has to control his or her actions in a conscious effortful way in order to overcome obstacles during a goal-oriented activity or to accomplish an uninteresting but important task. Similar problems arise in situations that are characterized by a moral or value conflict (Nunner-Winkler, 1999). The second subsystem has a strong biological component. It is primarily based on emotional experiences that provide an immediate feedback about the organism's state of functioning with respect to the actual requirements of the situation. Following the ideas developed in process-oriented concepts of motivational action control (e.g., Boekaerts, 1996; Nuttin, 1984; Epstein, 1990), it is assumed that the emotional part of this regulation system works partly beside or "beneath" the system of conscious-cognitive control. Informational processes on this level occur mostly without conscious-reflexive control. Instead we experience the mechanisms and feedback processes as specific emotional qualities of experience accompanying an action.

Basically, this hypothesis of a dual regulation system says that, alongside the cognitive-volitional control processes, a primarily emotion-controlled feedback and gratification system which continually provides the organism with information about the functional quality of actual life is involved in the regulation of human behaviour and ontogenetic development.

This idea is consistent with arguments presented in recent publications on the role of moral emotions (e.g. Latzko & Malti, 2010) and is supported by empirical results gained in neurobiological research approaches to moral behaviour (see Narvaez, this volume). From the perspective of the SDT and POI, emotional experiences related to the hypothetical system of basic needs play an important role.

(5) The Concept of Basic Needs

According to Nuttin's (1984) relational theory of behavioural dynamics and the theory of self-determination (SDT; Deci & Ryan, 1991, 2000, 2002; Ryan, 1995), it is assumed that living organisms are naturally endowed with a system of primary, or innate, basic psychological needs. During ontogenesis, these needs become more and more integrated into increasingly complex systems of behaviour and motivation control. Their basic efficacy, however, remains unaffected by this process.

The system of needs is hypothesized to be universal. Just as the fulfillment of biological needs is a natural necessity, sufficient fulfillment of psychological needs is a necessary requirement for the optimal functioning of the entire psychological system and a person's ongoing person-object engagements (Nuttin, 1984; Ryan, 1995). There is, however, an important difference between biological needs and psychological needs: whereas biological drives tend to operate cyclically (in that once satisfied they do not reemerge for some time), basic psychological needs are persistent.

A basic need does not describe a motive that is directed to a specific cognitively represented future goal; rather, the term need is used to designate "the fundamental dynamism inherent in the behavioural functioning of living beings" (Nuttin, 1984, p. 14). It depicts a general functional principle that controls both action and development (Ryan, 1995). It is assumed that there are three essential needs that are important with respect to a variety of developmental processes, including the development of higher levels of self-determined motivation and individual interests: autonomy, relatedness and competence.

Autonomy refers to the "desire to be self-initiating and to have a sense of acting in accord with one's own sense of self" (Deci, 1998, p. 152). When somebody is able to satisfy this basic need in a certain situation he/she experiences release and has the feeling of being independent from undesired external and internal pressure. The need for self-determination must not be confused with the pursuit of total freedom or complete independence from the influences of other people. Freedom of action is only desired when the individual believes that he/she is capable of successfully mastering impending tasks (Assor, Kaplan, & Roth, 2002). The pursuit of an optimal level of autonomy is, at the same time, an important prerequisite for fulfilling the need of competence since the successful mastering of a task can only be experienced when it has been solved to some degree without the support and detailed instructions of others.

Relatedness refers to the desire to feel connected to and to be accepted by significant others. The fact that human beings have a strong need for social contacts and the belief that the fulfillment of this need is a necessary prerequisite for well-being and for physical and mental health is one of the most commonly-known and generally discussed phenomena about the nature of mankind. Not only philosophical and psychological, but also neurobiological theories (see Narvaez, this volume) have discussed the role of social relations in human behaviour and development. There is broad agreement with respect to the fact that human beings cannot live and develop in a healthy way when their desire for satisfactory social contacts and relations is frustrated to a certain degree. On the other hand, results from many empirical studies clearly show that the quality of social relations is a significant predictor for positively evaluated aspects of motivation and development (Ryan & Deci, 2000).

Finally, *competence* refers to the desire to feel efficacious, to have an effect on one's environment, and to be able to attain valued outcomes (Deci, 1998, p. 152). This basic need is closely related to the inherent satisfaction that results from exercising and extending one's own capabilities, and the central corresponding effect is the feeling of efficacy (Bandura, 1997; White 1959).

With regard to moral action and the development of morally important dispositions, the following general thesis is now of central importance. A person will only deal with moral questions in a lasting way and with an inner conviction if he/she assesses them to be important enough and if, over the course of dealing with the topic, an overall positive balance is gained in the quality of the emotional experience, with regard to the three basic needs. For a more enduring orientation of action towards specific content aims (e.g. interests) or values, what is decisive is that the basic needs can be satisfied sufficiently. Numerous empirical research findings from the area of educational psychology on the conditions necessary for the emergence of an optimal learning and performance motivation confirm the validity of this thesis (Deci & Ryan, 2000; Kunter, Baumert & Köller, 2007; Ryan, 1995, 2008; Tsai, Kunter, Lüdtke, Trautwein & Ryan, 2008). Therefore, it seems to make sense to transfer the theoretical considerations which form the basis of this thesis to other subject areas of human motivation.

In my opinion, differences in moral motivation can be explained in a much more detailed and realistic way with the theoretical concepts discussed in the SDT and POI than with classical trait or need theories. This is the case both for the explanation of differences in behaviour in certain morally relevant action episodes and for the explanation of differences in developmental processes which lead to different moral types of personality or "moral characters" (Rest, 1984/1999).

In order to illustrate the explanatory potential in concrete moral action episodes in more detail, I would like once again to return to the example of the young person mentioned above, who despite the temptation of his girlfriend is not put off from taking the promised trip with the disabled wheelchair user. The decision in favor of or against keeping the promise is in no way based only on cognitive-rational considerations. If asked about the reasons for his behaviour, the young person would probably refer primarily to these. However, in actual fact, it must be recognized that emotional factors play at least as important a role. However, the person acting in the situation is often not aware of them in the same way as he/she is aware of the cognitive-rational considerations because their influence is not consciously recognized. Nevertheless, the results of psychological and neuroscientific research have convincingly proven that cognitions such as memories of previous events are always emotionally coded and, therefore, when they are activated, subjective judgments almost automatically become operational (Baumeister, Vohs, DeWall & Zhang, 2007). How this affects the generation of intention and the decision in favor of a certain action alternative, and whether and in what way moral criteria, for example, are taken into consideration, are questions that are not easy to answer and that require more fundamental empirical analyses. In general, the selection of arguments and their subjective weighting is thereby already affected. Against the background of the considerations about the structure of the moral self sketched above, it can be assumed that the more the person personally identifies with the values and norms related to a decision, the more probable it is that a pro and contra argument is considered when making the decision. In our example, it is plausible that the young person would like to be a completely reliable person who tries to keep a promise at all costs.

In addition, saved memories from past action episodes which have an emotional slant, concern comparable topics and provide the possibility to satisfy basic needs over the course of the current action also have a strong influence. The more often our protagonist from the example mentioned above has, in previous morally relevant conflict situations, experienced that he was in a position to make a decision recognized by others as being autonomous, despite the conflicting expectations of his social environment, and that he was able to implement this decision while also taking his own moral standards into consideration, the better the accumulated need-related "emotional balance" is and the higher the probability that he will decide in favor of the morally "challenging" action alternative in future morally-relevant conflict situations.

CONCLUSION

A major aim of the present book is to enrich the moral psychological discussion by adding contributions in line with different approaches of motivational psychology. In this chapter, I have presented basic considerations about the meaning of the theoretical construct of moral motivation from a selection of theoretical ideas and concepts from the *self-determination theory (*SDT) and the *person-object theory of interest* (POI) that might be relevant for this discussion.

In this final section, I would like to summarize my considerations about the meaning of the theoretical construct of moral motivation made at the beginning of this chapter and the outline of some important aspects of the two presented theories in form of statements, that also contain suggestions about how the presented ideas probably can be used in forthcoming attempts to develop a psychologically founded theory of moral motivation.

(1) From the viewpoint of psychology, moral motivation is a multifaceted phenomenon which can be examined and interpreted from different theoretical perspectives. The apparently plausible conjecture that the typical subject areas of action, such as performance, aesthetics or morals, each has its own motif (or need) and that the reliability and persistence of the action in each of the fields of action depends on the strength of this motif has not been proven to be sustainable by empirical research. Instead, the motivation decisive for the regulation of action must be interpreted as a phenomenon which is constantly reforming itself and is determined by influential factors which are both personal and situational.

(2) In order to break down the global theoretical construct of moral motivation, a theoretical frame model is suggested which identifies the many conditional factors and processes of motivational action in morally relevant situations in more detail and puts them in relation to each other. Furthermore, it provides a basis for the discussion of the classification and the scientific evaluation of research approaches relevant for moral motivation.

(3) An important differentiation results from the fact that moral motivation can be empirically examined and theoretically reconstructed at two different levels of analysis; namely, at the level of dispositional personal characteristics (Field 1 in Figure 1) and at the level of action regulation processes (Fields 3 and 4). Furthermore, the model draws attention to the fact that the accumulated effects and results of individual morally relevant action episodes (Field 5) can have a strong influence on morally important personality traits and therefore, from an ontogenetic viewpoint, represent an important developmental condition (Field 6).

(4) According to the SDT and the POI, the concept of the individual self plays an important role in any further discussion of the personal conditions of moral behaviour. This is based on the assumption that a person identifies more strongly with certain aims, motives and other motivationally relevant attitudes and beliefs than with others and perceives these to be an important aspect of his/her own personality (or individual identity). The sum total of these identity relevant components assumes a central role in the overall system of the organization of the personality and in the process of action regulation. Following the style of previous dynamic personality theories, this central area of the human personality is termed the individual self. The components of the individual self that are relevant for moral action can be regarded as a substructure of this system. For this reason, the concept of the moral self has established itself in moral psychological literature.

(5) Whether a person takes moral criteria into consideration in concrete action episodes and if so, under which conditions, primarily depends on how the cognitive, motivational and affective components relevant for moral action are anchored in the self-system. A decisive factor is the degree to which the moral principles are

integrated into the overall structure of individual value orientations and interests. For example, one can imagine that people with a stronger materialistic attitude are less sensitive towards morally relevant problem situations that involve supporting socially disadvantaged population groups than people who have a pro-social attitude or whose aims in life are strongly influenced by religious beliefs.

(6) In normal everyday understanding, self-determination (autonomy) is an important characteristic of moral action (cf. the contributions of Althof and Berkowitz in this volume). According to the SDT, however, a clear line cannot be drawn between heteronomous and autonomous action. Rather, a continuum of different levels of subjectively perceived autonomy is postulated. On the basis of this concept, Deci and Ryan suggested a classification model for describing different types of self-determined motivation which could possibly also be drawn on for a differential description of moral motivation.

(7) From the point of view of education, what needs to be clarified is how the personal characteristics (e.g. moral knowledge, level of moral judgment, moral sensitivity, action pattern when dealing with morally relevant conflict situations) relevant for moral action emerge, i.e. how they can be learned and under what conditions a person identifies at a personal level with this knowledge and these principles. The theoretical concepts and research approaches developed within the context of the SDT and the POI can possibly provide ideas or suggestions for research in the area of moral psychology. This also includes considerations on the interest-based relaying of moral knowledge and moral norms, and the hypothesis of a dual regulation system which is involved both in the regulation of actual-genetic and ontogenetic developmental processes.

(8) Within this context, the so-called basic needs play a central role. It is presumed that both the reliability and the persistence of moral action, as well as the development of a moral self decisively depend on whether a sufficient chance to satisfy the three basic needs of autonomy, social relatedness and experience of competency exists in the individual action episodes and the developments within these episodes.

(9) The theoretical concepts developed within the framework of the SDT and the POI, up until now, have not been systematically transferred to the research area of moral motivation. The way I see it, future empirical research in this area could profit not only from the theoretical ideas but also from the methodology and findings in other research areas (c.f., Deci & Ryan, 2002; Silvia, 2006; U. Schiefele, 2009).

REFERENCES

Achtziger, A., & Gollwitzer, P.M (2007). Rubicon model of action phases. In: R.F. Baumeister & K .D. Vohs (Eds.), *Encyclopedia of social psychology* (pp. 769–770). Los Angeles: Sage.

Anastasi, A. (1958). *Differential psychology*. New York: Macmillan.

Assor, A. (2012). Autonomous moral motivation: consequences, socializing antecedents, and the unique role of integrated moral principles. In M. Mikulincer & P.R. Shaver (Eds.), *The social psychology of morality. Exploring the causes of good and evil* (pp. 239–255). Washington, DC: American Psychological Association.

Assor, A., Kaplan H., & Roth G. (2002). Choice is good, but relevance is excellent: Autonomy-enhancing and suppressing teacher behaviours predicting students' engagement in schoolwork. *British Journal of Educational Psychology, 72*, 261–278.

Assor, A., Roth, G., & Deci, E.L. (2004). The emotional costs of parents' conditional regard: A self determination theory analysis. *Journal of Personality, 72*(1), 47–88.

Bandura, A. (1997). *Self-efficacy: The exercise of control*. New York: Freeman.

Baumeister, R.F., Vohs, K.D., DeWall, C.N., & Zhang, L. (2007). How emotion shapes behavior: Feedback, anticipation, and reflection, rather than direct causation. *Personality and Social Psychology Review, 11*, 167–203.

Boekaerts, M. (1996). Personality and the psychology of learning. *European Journal of Personality, 10*, 377–404.

Blasi, A. (1983/1999). Moral cognition and moral action: A theoretical perspective. *Developmental Review, 3*, 178–210. [German Translation: Moralische Kognition und moralisches Handeln. Eine theoretische Perspektive. In D. Garz, F. Oser, & W. Althof (Eds.), Beiträge zur Soziogenese der Handlungsfähigkeit. Moralisches Urteil und Handeln (pp. 47–81). Frankfurt a.M.: Suhrkamp, 1999]

Blasi, A. (2005). Moral character: A psychological approach. In D.K. Lapsley & F.C. Power (Eds.), *Character psychology and character education* (pp. 67–100). Notre Dame, Ind: University of Notre Dame Press.

Blasi, A. (1999). Moralische Kognition und moralisches Handeln. Eine theoretische Perspektive. In D. Garz, F. Oser, & W. Althof (Eds.), *Beiträge zur Soziogenese der Handlungsfähigkeit. Moralisches Urteil und Handeln* (pp. 47–81). Frankfurt a.M.: Suhrkamp

Colby, A., & Damon, W. (1992). *Some do care: Contemporary lives of moral commitment*. New York: Free Press

Cofer, C.N. & Appley, M.H. (1964). *Motivation: Theory and research*. New York: Wiley.

DeCharms, R. (1968). *Personal causation*. New York: Academic Press.

Deci, E.L. (1975). *Intrinsic motivation*. New York: Plenum Press.

Deci, E.L. (1998). The relation of interest to motivation and human needs - the self-determination theory viewpoint. In L. Hoffmann, A. Krapp, K.A. Renninger & J. Baumert (Eds.), *Interest and learning. Proceedings of the Seeon-Conference on interest and gender* (pp. 146–162). Kiel: IPN.

Deci, E.L., & Ryan, R.M. (1985). *Intrinsic motivation and self-determination in human behavior*. New York: Plenum Press.

Deci, E.L., & Ryan, R.M. (1991). A motivational approach to self: Integration in personality. In R. Dienstbier (Ed.), *Nebraska Symposium on Motivation: Vol. 38: Perspectives on Motivation* (pp. 237–288). Lincoln, NE: University of Nebraska Press.

Deci, E.L. & Ryan, R.M. (2000). The "what" and "why" of goal pursuits: Human needs and the self-determination of behavior. *Psychological Inquiry, 11*, 227–-268.

Deci, E.L. & Ryan, R.M. (2002). *Handbook of self-determination research*. Rochester: University of Rochester Press.

Edelstein, W., Nunner-Winkler, G., & Noam, G.G. (Eds.). (1993). *Moral und Person*. Frankfurt a.M.: Suhrkamp.

Efklides, A., Kuhl, J., & Sorrentino, R.M. (2001). *Trends and prospects in motivation research*. Dordrecht, Boston, London: Kluwer.

Epstein, S. (1990). Cognitive-experiential self-theory. In L. Pervin (Ed.), *Handbook of personality: Theory and research* (pp. 165–192). New York: Guilford.

Evans, J.B.T. (2010). *Thinking twice: Two minds in one brain*. New York: Oxford University Press.

Esser, H. (1996). Die Definition der Situation. *Kölner Zeitschrift für Soziologie und Sozialpsychologie, 48*, 1–34.

Heckhausen, H. (1989/1991). *Motivation und Handeln*. Berlin: Springer. [English Version: Motivation and action. Berlin: Springer, 1991].

Heckhausen. H. (2006). Entwicklungslinien der Motivationsforschung. In J. Heckhausen & H. Heckhausen (Eds.), *Motivation und Handeln* (pp. 235–253). Berlin: Springer.

Heckhausen, H., & Gollwitzer, P.M. (1987). Thought contents and cognitive functioning in motivational versus volitional states of mind. *Motivation and Emotion, 11*(2), 101–120.

Heckhausen, J. (Ed.). (2000). *Motivational psychology of human development*. Amsterdam: Elsevier.

Heckhausen, J., & Heckhausen, H. (2006/2008). *Motivation und Handeln*. Berlin: Springer. [English Version: Motivation and action. Cambridge: Cambridge University Press, 2008].

Heinrichs, K. (2005). *Urteilen und Handeln: Ein Prozessmodell und seine moralpsychologische Spezifizierung*. New York u.a.: Lang.

Hofer, M. (2007). Goal conflicts and self-regulation: A new look at pupils' off-task behaviour in the classroom. *Educational Research Review, 2*, 28–38.

Kohlberg, L., & Candee, D. (1984). The relationship of moral judgment to moral action. In W.M. Kurtines & J.L. Gewirtz (Eds.), *Morality, moral behavior, and moral development* (pp. 52–73). New York: John Wiley & Sons

Krapp, A. (1993). Psychologie der Lernmotivation - Perspektiven der Forschung und Probleme ihrer pädagogischen Rezeption. *Zeitschrift für Pädagogik, 39*, 187–206.

Krapp, A. (1999). Interest, motivation and learning: An educational-psychological perspective. *European Journal of Psychology in Education, 14*, 23–40.

Krapp, A. (2000). Interest and human development during adolescence: An educational-psychological approach. In J. Heckhausen (Ed.), *Motivational psychology of human development* (pp. 109–128). London: Elsevier.

Krapp, A. (2002a). An educational-psychological theory of interest and its relation to self-determination theory. In E. Deci & R. Ryan (Eds.), *The handbook of self-determination research* (pp. 405–427). Rochester: University of Rochester Press.

Krapp, A. (2002b). Structural and dynamic aspects of interest development: Theoretical considerations from an ontogenetic perspective. *Learning and Instruction, 12*, 383–409.

Krapp, A. (2005). Basic needs and the development of interest. *Learning and Instruction, 14*, 381–395.

Krapp, A. & Hascher, T. (in press). Theorien der Lern- und Leistungsmotivation. In L. Ahnert (Eds.), *Theorien der Entwicklungspsychologie*. Heidelberg: Spektrum Akademischer Verlag

Kuhl, J. (1983). *Motivation, Konflikt und Handlungskontrolle*. Berlin: Springer.

Kunter, M., Baumert, J., & Köller, O. (2007). Effective classroom management and the development of subject-related interest. *Learning and Instruction, 17* (5), 494–509.

Latzko, B. & Malti, T. (2010). Children's moral emotions and moral cognition: Towards an integrative perspective. *New Directions for Child and Adolescent Development, 129*, 1–10.

Lewin, K. (1936). *A dynamic theory of personality*. New York: McGraw-Hill.

Murray, H.A. (1938). *Explorations in personality*. New York: Oxford University Press.

Narvaez, D., & Lapsley, D.K. (Eds.) (2009). *Personality, identity, and character: Explorations in moral psychology*. New York: Cambridge University Press.

Nisan, M. (1993). Nisan, M., Bilanzierte Identität. Moralität und andere Identitätswerte. In W. Edelstein, G. Nunner-Winkler, & G.G. Noam (Eds.), *Moral und Person* (pp. 232–258). Frankfurt a.M.: Suhrkamp.

Noam, G.G. (1999). Moralisches Verhalten: Brauchen wir ein ‚Selbst'? In D. Garz, F. Oser, & W. Althof (Eds.), *Beiträge zur Soziogenese der Handlungsfähigkeit. Moralisches Urteil und Handeln* (pp. 340–376). Frankfurt a.M.: Suhrkamp.

Nucci, L., & Lee, J. (1993). Moral und personale Autonomie. In W. Edelstein, G. Nunner-Winkler & G.G. Noam (Eds.), *Moral und Person* (pp. 69–103). Frankfurt a.M.: Suhrkamp

Nunner-Winkler, G. (1999). *Moralische Motivation und moralische Identität. Zur Kluft zwischen Urteil und Handeln. In D. Garz, F. Oser, & W. Althof (Eds.), Beiträge zur Soziogenese der Handlungsfähigkeit. Moralisches Urteil und Handeln* (pp. 314–339). Frankfurt am Main: Suhrkamp.

Nunner-Winkler, G. (1993). Die Entwicklung moralischer Motivation. In W. Edelstein, G. Nunner-Winkler, & G.G. Noam (Eds.), *Moral und Person* (pp. 278–303). Frankfurt a.M.: Suhrkamp.

Nuttin, J. (1984). *Motivation, planning, and action*. Leuven/Louvain (Belgium): Leuven University Press.

Oser, F., & Althof, W. (1997). *Moralische Selbstbestimmung: Modelle der Entwicklung und Erziehung im Wertebereich*. Stuttgart: Klett-Cotta.

Oser, F., & Näpflin, C. (2010). Moralentwicklung und Moralförderung. In D.H. Rost (Ed.), *Handwörterbuch Pädagogische Psychologie* (pp. 566–577). Weinheim: Beltz.

Prenzel, M., Krapp, A. & Schiefele, H. (1986). Grundzüge einer pädagogischen Interessentheorie. *Zeitschrift für Pädagogik, 32*, 163–173.

Renkl, A. (1996). Träges Wissen: Wenn Erlerntes nicht genutzt wird. *Psychologische Rundschau, 47,* 78–92.

Renninger, K.A., Hidi, S.,& Krapp, A. (Eds.). (1992). *The role of interest in learning and development.* Hillsdale, NY: Erlbaum.

Rest, J.R. (1986). *Moral development: Advances in research and theory.* New York: Praeger.

Rest, J.R. (1999). Die Rolle des moralischen Urteilens im moralischen Handeln. In D. Garz, F. Oser& W. Althof (Eds.), *Beiträge zur Soziogenese der Handlungsfähigkeit. Moralisches Urteil und Handeln* (pp. 82–116). Frankfurt a.M.: Suhrkamp.

Ryan, R.M. (1995). Psychological needs and the facilitation of integrative process. *Journal of Personality, 63*(3), 397–427.

Ryan, R.M., & Connell, J.P. (1989). Perceived locus of causality an internalization: Examining reasons for acting in two domains. *Journal of Personality an Social Psychology, 57,* 749–761.

Ryan, R.M., & Deci, E.L. (2000). Self-Determination theory and the facilitation of intrinsic motivation, social development, and well-being. *American Psychologist, 55* (1), 68–78.

Ryan, R.M., & Deci, E.L. (2002). An overview of self-determination theory: An organismic-dialectice perspective. In E.L. Deci & R.M. Ryan (Eds.), *Handbook of self-determination research* (pp. 3–33). Rochester: University of Rochester Press.

Schiefele, U. (2009). Situational and individual interest. In K.R. Wentzel & A. Wigfield (Eds.), *Handbook of motivation at school* (pp. 197–222). Mahwah, NJ: Erlbaum.

Silvia, P.J. (2006). *Exploring the psychology of interest.* New York: Oxford University Press.

Sun, R. (2002). *Duality of the mind.* Mahwah, NJ: Erlbaum.

Tsai, Y., Kunter, M., Lüdtke, O.,Trautwein, U. & Ryan, R. (2008). What makes lessons interesting? The role of situational and individual factors in three school subjects. *Journal of Educational Psychology, 100,* 460–472.

Tyler, L.E. (1965). *The psychology of human differences.* New York: Appleton-Century-Crofts.

Weiner, B. (1992). *Human motivation.* London: Sage.

Weinstein, N., & Ryan, R.M. (2010). When helping helps: Autonomous motivation for prosocial behavior and its influence on well-being for the helper and recipient. *Journal of Personality and Social Psychology, 98,* 222–244.

White, R.W. (1959). Motivation reconsidered: The concept of competence. *Psychological Review, 66,* 297–333.

AFFILIATION

Andreas Krapp
Psychologie und Erziehungswissenschaften
University of the Bundeswehr München
Munich, Germany

REGINA VOLLMEYER, KONSTANZE JENDEREK &
TAHMINE TOZMAN

III. HOW DIFFERENT MOTIVATIONAL ASPECTS CAN AFFECT MORAL BEHAVIOUR

INTRODUCTION

Whenever we see people helping other people without receiving any benefits, we assume that these helpers are highly motivated to support others and that this motivation is due to a high level of morality. For example, people who hid Jews from Germans during World War II are judged as having high moral standards because they risked their lives to save others. Especially after the Eichmann trial in the 1960s, researchers tried to find explanations for these brave actions (London, 1970).

An initial explanation was that this action might have been triggered by a single motive. Motives are defined as stable personality traits (Rheinberg, 2008) and Murray (1938) described a candidate's motive as *need nurturance*. Need nurturance causes a person:

> ... to give sympathy and gratify the needs of a helpless O(ther); an infant or any O that is weak, disabled, tired, inexperienced, infirm, defeated, humiliated, lonely, rejected, sick, mentally confused. To assist an O in danger. To feed, help, support, console, protect, comfort, nurse, heal (p. 184).

However, such an explanation is circular: People who help others possess high need nurturance, and people with high need nurturance help others. Perhaps for this reason researchers did not pursue this construct and, in addition, there was some criticism about using a single motive to explain moral behaviour. Hill and Roberts (2010) developed this criticism in arguing that the study of moral personality development should start with the assumption that a singular moral personality does not exist.

The assumption that people have a *need nurturance* motive entails another problem: It would be very difficult to differentiate between need nurturance and the well-documented *need for power*. McClelland (1975) defined the need for power:

> ...as the need primarily to feel strong, and secondarily to act powerfully. Influencing others is just one of several ways of satisfying the need to feel strong (p. 77).

K. Heinrichs, F. Oser & T. Lovat (Eds.), Handbook of Moral Motivation: Theories, Models, Applications, 141–158.

WHY DO PEOPLE HELP?

According to McClelland, the need for power takes two forms: personal and social power. People high on personal power want to direct others. As leaders in an organization, Yukl (1989) described people who are high on personal power as having little inhibition or self control, and thus they may exercise power impulsively. When they give advice or support, they do not want to help the other person; instead, they want to further bolster their own status. Their actions may not conform to moral standards. People high on social power want to help other people, but also organizations. As leaders, they organize the efforts of others to further larger goals, such as those of their organizations. Of course, such leaders have high moral standards. In summary, need for power is used to explain moral as well as immoral behaviour. However, as we have already suggested, one single motive cannot explain all moral behaviour. Further aspects need to be taken into account.

Lewin (1946) emphasized that not only do a person's characteristics trigger their behaviour but also the situation or environment. This assumption is captured in Lewin's equation, Behaviour = f(Person, Environment), and is the basis for Rheinberg, Vollmeyer and Rollett's (2000) model that motivation results from personal characteristics and situational variables. This model will help us to introduce aspects of motivation beyond a single motive and allow us to differentiate aspects of motivation that explain moral behaviour. Especially in the field of social psychology, researchers have studied situational variables such as time pressure (Heckhausen, 1980) and not only personal variables.

Up to now, we have treated the terms prosocial behaviour and moral behaviour as interchangeable. In the following, we will separately define each construct. Prosocial behaviour refers to the phenomenon of people helping each other with no thought of reward or compensation (Heckhausen, 1980). According to Gibbs (2003), prosocial behaviour has a genuine moral quality. Whereas prosocial behaviour is intrinsically motivated (i. e., the helpers help for the sake of helping), moral behaviour is also guided by norms and values. People understand what is good and bad and decide intentionally and consciously how to act (Blasi, 1999). Tangney, Stuewig and Mashek (2007) differentiate between *moral standards* and *moral behaviour* andassume that moral emotions are the link between intention (i. e., moral standard) and behaviour. In this chapter, we will favor the term 'moral behaviour' in order to emphasize that it is behaviour that should reflect whether a person has consciously decided to do something good or something bad.

This definition is in line with Rest, Narvaez, Bebeau, & Thoma's (1999) ideas of moral motivation as far as moral behaviour is concerned. Rest defines moral motivation as the "...degree of commitment to taking the moral course of action, valuing moral values over other values and taking personal responsibility for moral outcomes". (p. 101) However, we go beyond moral standards in including, for example, expectancies and volition which are necessary variables to explain why, in spite of having moral standards, people do not perform morally although they might reflect moral standards on a high level (Kohlberg, 1981). Maybe such a broadening will trigger an exchange between motivational psychology and moral psychology, two research areas that coexist without benefiting from each other sufficiently.

Motivational psychology offers many theories which explain behaviour in general. Beside motives, especially the power motive, expectations and values come into play. Schwartz (1977) was one of the few researchers who used motivational concepts to explain prosocial behaviour. He described prosocial behaviour in terms of norms and expectations in a nine step process for how people decide to act morally. This theory can be classified as an expectancy-value model (for a review, see Eccles & Wigfield, 2002). Expectancy-value models have in common that people act only if their expectancies and values are positive. If either of them is zero, people do not act. For moral behaviour, this means if the values respective standards are high, but people do not expect that they are able to behave as required (i.e., low expectancy), they do not act. In the famous Heinz-dilemma (Kohlberg, 1969), a person could argue that Heinz should steal the drug to save his wife's life ("If Heinz does not do everything he can to save his wife, than he is putting some value higher than the value of life. It doesn't make sense to put respect for property above respect for life itself." Stage 6). Although this is the highest moral stage, according to expectancy-value models, Heinz would not steal the drug if he believed he was unable to break into the druggist's home. To predict Heinz' behaviour, it is important to know his self-efficacy beliefs (Bandura, 1986): Does he believe he is able to open a closed door or a safe? From an expectancy-value perspective, it would be useless to discuss moral motivation only in terms of standards if such expectancies are low.

However, motivational psychology developed even more concepts than values and expectancies. Rheinberg (2004) developed a model to integrate and schematize these many and varied concepts. This model might expand moral motivation sensu Rest (1999) in terms of values, expectancies, self-regulation, and volition. To demonstrate the advantage of such a broad understanding of moral motivation leading to moral behaviour, we will use Rheinberg's schema which includes many motivational aspects, and not only values respective standards.

MOTIVATIONAL ASPECTS FOR MORAL BEHAVIOUR

A single behaviour may be explained by several motivational aspects. In order to explain people's moral or immoral behaviour through motivation, we will follow Rheinberg's (2004) schema which is constructed as a flowchart (see Figure 1) but not as a determined sequence. By saying that it is not a determined sequence, we assume that the questions can be asked in a flexible order that means it is not necessary to start at the first question; it can be started at an arbitrary question. The main point is that as soon as there is a motivational deficit a person does not act. Therefore, to predict the lack of moral behaviour several motivational aspects can be responsible. In total, there are seven questions that can be answered with "yes" or "no". Each answer leads to a new question, resulting in a classification into one of four forms of motivation or of four motivational deficits. We will go through the flowchart by giving examples, describing first moral behaviour. In the next part, we will then apply the schema to the topic of *bullying* as an example of immoral behaviour.

Self-Initiated, Spontaneous Activity

If people are in a situation in which they can decide what to do without external obligations, then they tend to choose activities that they like (Rheinberg, Iser, & Pfauser, 1997). So, the first question is: "Does the activity promise to be fun?" (see Figure 1). Answering "yes" to this question leads to the form of motivation called "self-initiated, spontaneous activity". This form is what we normally mean when we talk about motivation in everyday life: a person is completely absorbed in an activity and experiences positive emotions.

Motivational theories that describe this phenomenon are the theory of interest (Krapp, Hidi & Renninger, 1992), the theory of flow (Csikszentmihalyi, 1975), and self-determination theory (Deci & Ryan, 1985). They have in common that, during the activity, people experience positive emotions. Interest theory emphasizes that the activity is highly valued, flow theory that the activity must be challenging, and self-determination theory stresses that the person has chosen the activity autonomously without any external incentive; thus, it is a case of intrinsic motivation.

There has been a debate over whether helping a person could be intrinsically (i.e., altruistically) motivated (Batson, Duncan, Ackerman, Buckley & Birch, 1981) instead of extrinsically (i. e., egoistically) motivated. For example, helping would be extrinsically motivated when a person helps another person only because he or she might expect to be helped as well (i. e., receive equity). Helping that is intrinsically motivated is well described by the Good Samaritan parable in the Bible (Luke 10: 30-35), in which only the Samaritan took care of the robbed and unconscious man. The Samaritan helped because he felt empathy with the man and he did not think about the consequences. If he valued helping per se, then interest theory could describe the Samaritan's behaviour. As the Samaritan chose helping autonomously, self-determination theory could also explain his behaviour. To explain it in terms of flow theory, we have to add more details to the parable. According to the components of flow, there should be a balance between challenge and ability (Csikszentmihalyi, 1975). Focusing on the Samaritan, flow theory might suggest that he felt optimally challenged by saving someone's life. In addition, the Samaritan must feel competent to coordinate and organize this situation so that he is able to transport the unconscious man to a safe place where he can receive care and support. Compared to moral motivation sensu Rest et al. (1999), the activity itself must be enjoyable and not only a reflection of standards.

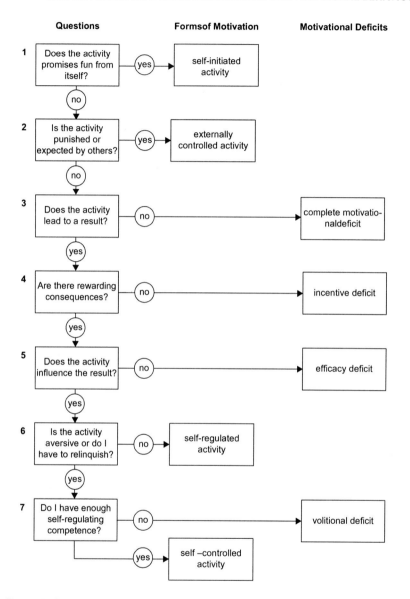

Figure 1. Question and answer sequence to define forms of motivation and motivational deficits (Rheinberg, 2004).

Externally Controlled Activity

The second question in the schema is whether the activity was punished or expected by other people. Expectations can be norms, laws, cultural traditions and moral standards. If this question is answered with "yes", then the form of motivation is externally controlled activity. According to Rest et al. (1999), this form of motivation is not 'moral motivation'; Kohlberg (1969) would claim that it represents a low stage of moral development.

For example, in Germany, by law, road users must help in a road accident. Therefore, helping in an accident is a moral behaviour but it is extrinsically motivated if people help only because it is their duty. However, according to Deci and Ryan's (1985) self-determination theory, people spend more time with an intrinsically motivating activity than with an externally guided activity. Extrinsic reward such as money or presents may even reduce intrinsic motivation. Kunda and Schwartz (1983) showed that external rewards, like payment for help, undermined the sense of moral obligation. Unpaid helpers showed more intrinsic motivation than paid helpers.

Activity Without Result

If the first two questions have been answered with "no", then the third question is: "Does the activity have a result?" If this question is answered: "No, there is no result," then we have a *complete motivational deficit*.

A good example is again illustrated by the parable of the Good Samaritan. A priest and a Levite passed by without helping. Given that nobody was around, it was not controlled activity (Question 2) and they had no particular empathy with the half dead man (Question 1). Helping this man would have no result for the priest or for the Levite; therefore, they had a complete motivational deficit.

Activity Without Incentives

If a person expects a result (Question 3 in Figure 1), then the question that follows concerns whether this result has rewarding consequences (Question 4). Such a rewarding consequence can take many forms, for example, a confirmation of one's self-concept or a positive emotion. This definition corresponds to Blasi's (1999) definition of moral behaviour: people understand what is good and bad and decide intentionally and consciously how to act.

People faced with a situation in which they either act or leave the situation without any action first reflect on values and norms. If helping or in general acting morally is an important value in one's life, he or she will act. The action's result is a positive outcome because the person's self-concept is confirmed.

Another positive consequence is a positive emotion which follows the activity. At the beginning of this chapter, we described the power motive. The positive emotion following a powerful action is the feeling to be strong. People who have a high power motive enjoy this feeling, which is accompanied by an increase in testosterone (e. g., Schultheiss & Rohde, 2002). For example, a person who organized a concert to help people in a crises zone may feel powerful after giving the money to people in need.

However, what happens if there is no chance of a reward, no positive feeling, no confirmation of one's self-concept? According to Rheinberg's (2004) model in Figure 1, people experience an incentive deficit. Why should they help if there are better things to do?

As an example, let's think about people who are asked to donate money for victims of an earthquake. There is no law to donate money (Question 2), so even if people understand that the money will reduce the victims' distress (Question 3), if they do not anticipate a rewarding consequence (Question 4), they do not donate money. Especially if they doubt that donating money is the right way to help the victims because the government is not trustworthy, they might expect mixed emotions and their reflections of standards may not match their self-concept. All in all there might be an incentive deficit, a lack of being driven towards helping.

Activity does not Influence Result

People who agree that there are rewarding results from helping (Question 4 in Figure 1) could ask themselves: does their help lead to the result they want to achieve? Are they really able to help? Do they have the competence? If they come to the view that they are not competent enough, then they experience an efficacy deficit which is another motivational aspect. When faced with such an efficacy deficit, people do not help. Such an efficacy deficit may be temporary as a state, however, if such an expectation occurs in many situations, it can be generalized as a trait.

It was Bandura (1986) who first described this phenomenon in terms of self-efficacy. Self-efficacy is a subjective feeling of how certain people are that they will reach the goal they want. Whenever a person experiences the absence of self-efficacy, he or she will avoid the action.

Consider a woman who arrives at an accident. Even if she expects rewarding consequences (Question 4), she may feel uncertain whether she could help (Question 5). She might be too weak to open the doors of the car or too ignorant to provide first aid. Therefore, she leaves without helping although she had accepted the moral standard that she should help (Question 2).

Self-Regulated Activity

If people have high self-efficacy beliefs (Question 5 in Figure 1), the next question they reflect on is whether the activity is aversive or whether they have to relinquish a plan (Question 6). If they answer this question with "no", then the motivational form is *self-regulated activity*. A self-regulated activity is an activity during which a person does not experience fun, however, it is chosen voluntarily because he or she expects positive rewards.

A positive reward could be that one's sad emotion improves. Baumann, Cialdini, and Kenrick (1981) studied this phenomenon with the help of their *negative state relief* model. This model describes how people regulate their negative mood. The assumption is that people do not want to keep their negative mood and therefore they help people in order to receive a smile or a "thank you". These little rewards can improve their mood.

Self-Directed Activity

However, if people have to admit that the activity is aversive and/or they have to relinquish their plans (Question 6), then this will increase the cost of taking action. Therefore, they have to check whether they can force themselves to act volitionally (Question 7), especially if they reflect consciously on the cost of their behaviour. Cost-benefit models in social psychology (e. g., Latané & Darley, 1970) tried to explain whether people help or not. Berkowitz and Daniels (1964) found that people help less if the costs are high. This is also true for aversive activities that need volitional control (e. g., in case of an accident people have to see blood).

If people lack the competence to force themselves to take action, then they encounter a volitional deficit. With self-regulating competencies, we call the activity self-directed. For example, imagine the situation in which a woman drives to an appointment and suddenly witnesses a road accident in which people are injured and need help. As she does not know the injured persons, she does not experience positive feelings (Question 1), and nobody saw her arriving at the accident, thus, no one can sue her for not helping (Question 2). However, if she helped the injured people, she would arrive too late to her appointment and miss signing an important contract (Question 6). For her, there would be a very high cost for helping. On the other hand, she accepts the norm that in our society people should help others in distress (Question 4). If she has enough self-regulating competencies to force herself to help, she will stop and help the injured people (i. e., self-controlled activity). Techniques for how to volitionally use self-control are described by Kuhl (1983).

To summarize, Rheinberg's (2004) model can help us to explore pro-social behaviour and its motivational aspects, and to predict whether a person helps or not. Now the question is whether it also can explain immoral behaviour?

BULLYING - MOTIVATIONAL ASPECTS FOR IMMORAL BEHAVIOUR

Up to now, we have discussed only moral behaviour: Which motivational aspects can explain whether people help each other? However, in real life, immoral behaviour is more obvious than moral behaviour. Day after day, the news reports more illegal and criminal activities than moral activities. Therefore, we will apply Rheinberg's (2004) model in Figure 1 to bullying which is an immoral behaviour. A further specification is that we look at bullying only in work environments, leaving other contexts unconsidered. We use Brodsky's (1976) definition, who describes bullying as:

> (a)…gradually evolving process, whereby an individual ends up in an inferior position and becomes the target of systematic negative social acts by one or more perpetrators (as cited in Hauge, Skogstad and Einarsen, 2009, p. 350).

Bullying is an especially interesting topic for immoral behaviour as the perpetrator decides intentionally to harm a person in an inferior position which is against moral standards. In the following, we start with Question 1 in Figure 1 and go through the flowchart.

An example will help the reader to imagine the bullying scenario in a work environment. Two banker colleagues in manager positions are in competition over whose work is more effective. That competition leads to conflicts. First, there are official conflicts, which later turned into personal conflicts, and in the end no third person can mediate the conflict situation. In this case, we are talking about an escalated conflict, in which both parties are in a 'lose-lose' situation. That means that both are trying to harm each other on purpose. Meanwhile, Colleague A climbed into a psychological superior position, so he became the perpetrator. While Colleague B got into a mental inferior position, so he became the target. From this point, we call the negative behaviour "bullying", and if it continues, we consider it immoral behaviour. In this example, the perpetrator may act immorally by (1) distorting the target's work results with the aim of damaging the target, (2) giving purposfully wrong information to the target, (3) holding back important information which the target needs to fulfill his or her tasks with the aim of damaging the target.

Bullying is not Self-Initiated, Spontaneous Activity

First of all, we want to explore Question 1, namely: "Is bullying a self-initiated, spontaneous activity?" (see Figure 1). Do the perpetrators have fun when they bully the target? Djurkovic, McCormack, and Casimir (2006) and other researchers have found repeatedly that bullying is an extreme social stressor for all participants, even for the perpetrators. It is not only a stressor but an escalated conflict with the goal of eliminating the target (Keashly & Nowell, 2010). Although the perpetrators are in the superior position, they are damaged after the conflict escalates. Therefore, by definition and by research results, we conclude that the perpetrators have no fun in the activity. So, for bullying, the motivational form of spontaneous activity or self-initiation is not accurate. The perpetrators do not start bullying because it is fun. However, bullying could be included within a broader definition of this form of motivation; for example, if bullying is defined when a person is exposed, repeatedly and over time, to negative actions on the part of one or more other persons. This definition is often used in the media. For this chapter, we are focusing on a longer history of bullying.

Bullying is no Externally Controlled Activity

After we concluded that bullying is no self-initiated activity, we proceed to Question 2 in Figure 1. Question 2 asks whether bullying is punished on the one hand or whether it is expected on the other hand.

Usually, bullying in the workplace is quite subtle which makes it hard to be noticed at all. Several case studies, as well as large bullying investigations, found that bullying takes place largely subliminally, not noticeable by a third person. Bullying avoids leaving obvious or objective evidence (Zapf, 1999) and, if it is not noticed, it cannot be punished.

Einarsen, Hoel, and Notelaers (2009) described several bullying strategies which should not be expected in a performance-oriented work environment. Organizational bullying strategies usually concern the task as well as the deprivation of the authority to decide. Other bullying strategies include spreading rumors and backbiting directed at the target. These bullying strategies show a high correlation with negative work content, a bad social environment as well as psychological disorders. Thus, we conclude that bullying does not accord with any moral norms and expectations, but still it is not punished. To illustrate our analysis, we will consider three examples in business meetings.

1. First, consider a perpetrator who manipulates the target's depot taking away the target's printed agenda for a meeting that takes place in ten minutes. The target will not be able to print and edit the whole presentation before the meeting starts. Alternatively, the perpetrator hides the target's USB-stick so he or she will not be able to show his or her work and agenda to the committee during the meeting.
2. An example of giving wrong information is when the perpetrator tells the target, that the very important meeting is going to take place on the 1st floor in Room 12 although it takes place on the 11th floor in Room 21. If the target then comes late or does not come at all, then the perpetrator has achieved his or her goal by making the target look like a fool.
3. A good example of holding back information with the intention to damage the target is when the perpetrator does not tell the target that there is any meeting at all.

None of these actions would be immoral if they were not done on purpose. However, they are immoral if they are done with the intention of damaging the other party. Furthermore, we emphasize again that bullying is not externally obvious because it is subtle and there is often no proof to be had. To put it in a nutshell, this is not the form of motivation we would describe as "externally controlled activity."

Bullying as an Activity Leading to a Result

We could not apply the first two questions to Brodsky's (1976) narrow definition of bullying, so we continue with Question 3 (see Figure 1): "Does the bullying activity lead to a result?" Yes, it does! According to the definition, successful bullying always ends up with the result that the target is left in an inferior position.

Furthermore, the examples show that there are several subordinated results for the perpetrator. In Example 1, the result of the bullying activity is that the target's work is damaged. Another result is that the target will not be able to show his or her work in the meeting. A third result is that the target may look foolish at the meeting.

In Examples 2 and 3, the result of the bullying activity is that the target will not participate in the business meeting. There is another result, namely that the target will look like a fool. A third result is that the target will not be able to give any opposition to the perpetrator's plans.

Therefore, Question 3 cannot be answered with "no" (see Figure 1) so a complete motivational deficit will not occur. If potential perpetrators could not anticipate a result (maybe the target transferring to another work domain), then they would give up bullying.

Bullying as an Activity with Rewarding Consequences

By affirming Question 3, namely, that the bullying activity leads to the result of getting the target into an inferior position, the fourth question (see Figure 1) then becomes: "Are there rewarding consequences?" Again, for bullying, we cannot say "no" (i.e., there is no incentive deficit) because the reason for bullying, and hence the most important consequence, is that the perpetrators receive more resources (Salin, 2005).

In our discussion of moral behaviour, we introduced McClelland's (1975) power motive. Using this concept (especially personal power), leads to the research question whether perpetrators are high on need for power. People with such a motive enjoy being strong and powerful and therefore perpetrators will use bullying strategies to reach their goals.

In Example 1, the perpetrator gets the reward, namely, that the target looks like a fool and falls deeper into the inferior position. One reward may be to gloat over the target's damage, and another one may be the feeling of a superior mental position for the perpetrator. In Examples 2 and 3, the perpetrator receives a reward, namely, that the target will not attend the meeting and so he or she will not be able to support any opposition against the perpetrator's agenda.

Bullying as an Activity Influencing Results

Even if perpetrators expect a rewarding consequence (Question 4), they must expect that their bullying activity produces results and that their self-efficacy is high. Do they have the competence to use bullying strategies, for example, taking away the target's authority to make decisions? If they do not believe in their efficacy (i. e., have an efficacy deficit), then they give up bullying. Therefore, a research question is whether only self-efficacious people will show bullying behaviour. The three examples show the perpetrator's self-efficacy in fooling and eliminating the target.

Bullying as a Self-Regulated Activity and More

Next, we want to explore Question 6 (see Figure 1), whether bullying is aversive or whether the perpetrator has to give up something. There are good reasons to answer this question either with "no" or with "yes". There is not only one possible answer to this question because there is not only one kind of perpetrator.

In Salin's (2005) research, we see illustrated an answer to this question that: "No, bullying is not aversive and the perpetrators do not have to give up something." Salin concludes that potential perpetrators try to eliminate perceived competitors as well as other colleagues who are threatening their personal interest. There are no hints of any ambivalence concerning the perpetrators; it seems as if their bullying behaviour does not meet moral standards. Given that our answer to Question 6 is "no", we have to call this form of motivation a self-regulated activity.

In Hauge, Skogstad, and Einarsen's (2009) research, we see perpetrators answering Question 6 by saying: "Yes, bullying is aversive and I have to give up something, for example moral standards." They found that one third of the perpetrator population is a target of bullying itself, so there is a reasonable overlap between both targets and perpetrators (Glomb & Liao, 2003). This phenomenon contradicts Kant's (2004) imperative and, as a result of this, it shows that it must be ambivalent for the perpetrators because they have to give up something. Kant's imperative would demand that the target should not bully others merely because they had suffered from bullying themselves. So, in the case of consciously hurting Kant's imperative, the perpetrators consider bullying as aversive because they experience conflict with moral standards. Bullying must imply denial of Kant's imperative. As our answer to Question 6 is "yes", we are going to highlight Question 7.

Bullying as a Self-Directed Activity

Taking into account that perpetrators experience bullying activity as aversive or that they have to give up something, we proceed to Question 7 (see Figure 1): "Do the perpetrators have enough self-regulation competence?"

Kacmar and Baron (1999) found that perpetrators have sufficient self-regulation competence. They describe perpetrators as having attributes like social cleverness, interpersonal influence, and networking abilities (Ferris, Treadway, Kolodinsky, Hochwarter, Kacmar, Douglas & Frink, 2005; Mintzberg, 1983; Pfeffer, 1981; Snyder, 1987). Perrewé, Zellars, Ferris, Rossi, Kacmar, and Ralston (2004) interpret this complex of attributions as a kind of coping strategy, in reference to Lazarus (1991). In fact, some researchers argue that bullying results from self-regulatory processes that protect one's self-esteem. That is why situational factors, like work-related and organizational factors, also have to be taken into account (Zapf & Einarsen, 2003). Spector and Fox (2005) suggest that aggression is related to whether the individual perceives himself or herself to not be in control of the situation, which induces the experience of stress and negative emotions. This is the case for the chosen example of perpetrators in a bullying situation, so there is a volitional deficit. At the same time, we may call this form of motivation a self-controlled activity.

CONCLUSION

The aim of our chapter has been to explain moral behaviour from a motivational perspective. As there are innumerable motivational constructs and theories, it was necessary to find a schema to classify motivational forms. Therefore, we used Rheinberg's (2004) schema to differentiate motivational forms and deficits. In addition, we applied the schema to moral as well as to immoral behaviour.

As an example for moral behaviour, we chose helping and for immoral behaviour bullying. The concept of motivational deficits helps to reveal why people do not help or why they stop bullying. This schema not only demonstrates how personality, personal variables and situational variables interacted, but it also provides some insight into understanding the complexity of moral behaviour.

Significance for Research

When comparing the definition of moral motivation and motivation in general, we noticed that moral motivation is restricted to values, that is, people are morally motivated if they prefer moral standards to their own needs and wishes. However, motivation is more than only values. What happens if people want to act morally, but they think that they are not competent for the action (i. e., efficacy-deficit), or they know that they have no will to do something aversive (i. e., volitional deficit)? Following a broader definition of motivation, we would predict low motivation. This difference between definitions has consequences for research.

First, a broader definition needs another operationalization of moral motivation. Often, participants are presented with stories after which they have to decide how they would react in such a situation (e. g., Heinz-dilemma; Kohlberg, 1969) or they receive a questionnaire on moral standards. With a broader definition of moral motivation, it is necessary not only to ask for values, but also expectancies and volition. Therefore, researchers have to develop methods that measure, for example, self-efficacy as a state for certain situations or generalized self-efficacy as a trait.

Second, a broader definition may also lead to a better prediction of moral behaviour, and hence, a better validation of the construct. Similarly, Fishbein and Ajzen (1975) had to extend their theory of reasoned action by several variables to predict more accurately how attitudes lead to actual behaviour. To do so, Fishbein and Ajzen also included aspects from expectancy-values models.

One aspect of motivation has been completely neglected by moral motivation sensu Rest et al. (1999), that is, the form of motivation described as "self-initiated activity" in Figure 1. Under this form of motivation, we can subsume concepts like Deci and Ryan's (1985) intrinsic motivation or Csikszentmihalyi's (1975) flow. Self-initiated activity means that people look forward to this activity and they enjoy the activity. How does this motivational form fit with the idea that moral motivation results from a reflection, in which a person prefers moral standards to his or her own wishes or even accepting personal losses? Such a definition of moral motivation seems to contradict a self-initiated activity promising fun. Whenever personal values must be suppressed, we believe that volition is necessary to realize the planned activity. Furthermore, as Sokolowski (1997) described, a volitionally controlled activity needs much more effort compared to a self-initiated activity. A volitionally controlled activity needs effort to get started and it needs effort that no other intentions capture the person's attention. Therefore, using a broader definition of moral motivation would be desirable to shed light on moral activities promising enjoyment. As a consequence, empirical research has to demonstrate whether indeed self-initiated moral activities are preferred to volitionally-controlled moral activities.

Significance for Intervention

Research should aim to help increase moral behaviour and to decrease immoral behaviour. The motivational schema is a helpful instrument to give practitioners some advice. For example, behaviour which is a self-initiated activity promises to be performed often and persistently. However, especially with helping behaviour, this is difficult to arrange because it is often accompanied by costs (e. g., time, money). It would be necessary to arouse positive feelings in order for a person to repeat the activity.

If a self-initiated activity is an immoral behaviour that we want to reduce, it may be quite difficult. For example, graffiti spraying is an immoral behaviour, but Rheinberg and Manig (2003) found that young perpetrators take many costs upon themselves. Even if they risk being caught by police, they enjoy spraying in the middle of the night. Maybe teaching moral standards or punishment might reduce their activity. However, there are no studies testing such interventions concerning graffiti.

In summary, looking at moral behaviour through a motivational psychologist's eyes suggests new questions about why some people help and others hurt people.

REFERENCES

Bandura, A. (1986). *Social foundations of thought and action: A social cognitive theory.* Englewood Cliffs, NJ: Prentice Hall.
Batson, C.D., Duncan, B.D., Ackerman, P., Buckley, T., & Birch, K. (1981). Is empathic emotion a source of altruistic motivation? *Journal of Personality & Social Psychology, 40,* 290–302.
Baumann, D.J., Cialdini, R.B., & Kenrick, D.T. (1981). Altruism as hedonism: Helping and self-gratification as equivalent responses. *Journal of Personality and Social Psychology, 40,* 1039–1046.
Berkowitz, L., & Daniels, L.R. (1964). Responsibility and dependency. *Journal of Abnormal and Social Psychology, 66,* 429–436.
Blasi, A. (1999). Emotions and moral motivation. *Journal for the Theory of Social Behavior, 29,* 1–19.
Brodsky, C.M. (1976). *The harassed worker.* Toronto, ON: Lexington Books.
Csikszentmihalyi, M. (1975). *Beyond boredom and anxiety.* San Francisco: Jossey-Bass.

Deci, E.L., & Ryan, R.M. (1985). *Intrinsic motivation and self-determination in human behavior*. New York: Plenum.

Djurkovic, N., McCormack, D., & Casimir, G. (2006). Neuroticism and the psychosomatic model of workplace bullying. *Journal of Managerial Psychology, 21*, 73–88.

Eccles, J.S., & Wigfield, A. (2002). Motivational beliefs, values, and goals. *Annual Review of Psychology, 53*, 109–132.

Einarsen, S., Hoel, H., & Notelaers, G. (2009). Measuring exposure to bullying and harassment at work: Validity, factor structure and psychometric properties of the Negative Acts Questionnaire-Revised. *Work & Stress, 23*, 24–44.

Ferris, R.G., Treadway, D.C., Kolodinsky, R.W., Hochwarter, W.A., Kacmar, C.J., Douglas, C., & Frink, D.D. (2005). Development and validation of the Political Skill Inventory. *Journal of Management, 31*, 126–152.

Fishbein, M., & Ajzen, I. (1975). *Belief, attitude, intention, and behavior: An introduction to theory and research*. Reading, MA: Addison-Wesley.

Gibbs, J.C. (2003). *Moral development and reality. Beyond the theories of Kohlberg and Hoffman*. Thousand Oaks, CA: Sage.

Glomb, T.M., & Liao, H. (2003). Interpersonal aggression in work groups: Social influence, reciprocal, and individual effects. *Academy of Management Journal, 46*, 486–496.

Hauge, L.J., Skogstad, A., & Einarsen, S. (2009). Individual and situational predictors of workplace bullying: Why do perpetrators engage in the bullying of others. *Work & Stress, 23*, 349–358.

Heckhausen, H. (1980). *Motivation und Handeln*. Berlin: Springer.

Hill, P.L., & Roberts, B.W. (2010). Propositions for the study of moral personality development. *Current Directions in Psychological Science, 19*, 380–383.

Kacmar, K.M., & Baron, R.A. (1999). Organizational politics: The state of the field, links to related processes, and an agenda for future research. In G.R. Ferris (Ed.), *Research in personnel and human resources management* (pp. 1–39). Greenwich: JAI Press.

Kant, I. (2004). *Kritik der praktischen Vernunft. Grundlegung zur Metaphysik der Sitten [Critique of Practical Reason. Groundwork of the Metaphysics of Morals]. In W. Weischedel (Ed.)*. Frankfurt a.M.: Suhrkamp Verlag.

Keashly, L., & Nowell, B.L. (2010). Workplace bullying, conflict and conflict resolution. In S. Einarsen, H. Hoel & D. Zapf (Eds.). *Workplace bullying and harassment: Developments in theory, research and practice* (pp. 423–455). LondonUK: Taylor Francis.

Kohlberg, L. (1969). Stage and sequence: The cognitive-developmental approach to socialization. In D.A. Goslin (Ed.), *Handbook of socialization theory and research* (pp. 347–480). Chicago: Rand McNally.

Kohlberg, L. (1981). *Essays on moral development. The philosophy of moral development*. San Francisco, CA: Harper & Row.

Krapp, A., Hidi, S., & Renninger, K.A. (1992). Interest, learning and development. In K.A. Renninger, S. Hidi & A. Krapp (Eds.), *The role of interest in learning and development* (pp. 3–25). Hillsdale, NJ: Erlbaum.

Kuhl, J. (1983). *Motivation, konflikt und handlungskontrolle* [Motivation, conflict, and action control]. Berlin: Springer.

Kunda, Z., & Schwartz, S.H. (1983). Undermining intrinsic moral motivation: External reward and self-presentation. *Journal of Personality and Social Psychology, 45*, 763–771.

Latané, B., & Darley, J.M. (1970). *The unresponsive bystander: Why doesn't he help?* New York: Appleton-Century-Crofts.

Lazarus, R.S. (1991). Progress on a cognitive-motivational-relational theory of emotions. *American Psychologist, 46*, 819–834.

Lewin, K. (1946). Action research and minority problems. *Journal of Social Issues, 2*, 4–46.

London, P. (1970): The rescuers: Motivational hypotheses about Christians who saved Jews from the Nazis. In J.R. Macaulay, & L. Berkowitz (Eds.), *Altruism and helping behavior* (p. 241–250). New York: Academic Press.

Mintzberg, H. (1983). *Power in and around organizations.* Englewood Cliffs: Prentice-Hall.

McClelland, D.C. (1975). *Power: The inner experience*. New York: Irvington.

Murray, H.A. (1938). *Explorations in personality.*New York: Oxford University Press.
Perrewé, P.L., Zellars, K.L., Ferris, G.R., Rossi, A.M., Kacmar, C.J., & Ralston, D.A. (2004). Neutralizing job stressors: Political skill as an antidote to the dysfunctional consequences of role conflict stressors. *Academy of Management Journal, 47,* 141–152.
Pfeffer, J. (1981). *Power in organizations.* Boston: Pitman.
Rest, J., Narvaez, D. Bebeau, M.J. & Thoma, S.J. (1999). *Postconventional moral thinking: A Neo Kohlbergian approach.* Mahwah, NJ: Lawrence Erlbaum Associates.
Rheinberg, F. (2004). *Motivationsdiagnostik* [Motivational assessment]. Göttingen: Hogrefe.
Rheinberg, F. (2008). *Motivation* (Vol. 7). Stuttgart: Kohlhammer.
Rheinberg, F., Iser, I., & Pfauser, S. (1997). Freude am Tun und/oder zweckorientiertes Schaffen? Zur transsituativen Konsistenz und konvergenten Validitäten der AF-Skala [Doing something for fun and/or for gain? Transsituational consistency and convergent validity of the Incentive-Focus-Scale]. *Diagnostica, 43,* 174–191.
Rheinberg, F., & Manig, Y. (2003). Was macht Spaß am Graffiti-Sprayen? Eine induktive Anreizanalyse [Why is graffiti spraying fun?]. *Report Psychologie, 4,* 222–234.
Rheinberg, F., Vollmeyer, R., & Rollett, W. (2000). Motivation and action in self-regulated learning. In M. Boekaerts, P. Pintrich& M. Zeidner (Eds.), *Handbook of self-regulation* (pp. 503–529). San Diego: Academic Press.
Salin, D. (2005). Workplace bullying among business professionals: Differences and the role of organizational politics. *Pistes, 7,* 1–11.
Schultheis, O.C., & Robde, W. (2002). Implicit power motivation predicts men's testosterone changes and implicit learning in a contest situation. *Hormones and Behavior, 36,* 195–202.
Schwartz, S.H. (1977). Normative influences on altruism. In L. Berkowitz (Ed.), *Advances in Experimental Social Psychology* (Vol. 10, pp. 221–279). New York: Academic Press.
Snyder, M. (1987). *Public appearances, private realities: The psychology of self-monitoring.*New York: Freeman.
Sokolowski, K. (1997). Sequentielle und imperative Konzepte des Willens. *Psychologische Beiträge, 39,* 339–369.
Spector, P.E., & Fox, S. (2005). The stressor-emotion model of counterproductive work behavior. In S. Fox & P.E. Spector (Eds.), *Counterproductive behavior. Investigations of actors and targets* (pp. 151–174). Washington, DC: American Psychological Association.
Tangney, J.P., Stuewig, J., & Mashek, D.J. (2007). Moral emotions and moral behavior. *Annual Review of Psychology, 58,* 345–372.
Yukl, G. (1989). Managerial leadership: A review of theory and research. *Journal of Management, 15,* 251–289.
Zapf, D. (1999). Mobbing in Organisationen. Ein Überblick zum Stand der Forschung [Bullying at work. An overview of current research]. *Zeitschrift für Arbeits- und Organisationspsychologie, 43,* 1–25.
Zapf, D., & Einarsen, S. (2003). Individual antecedents of bullying: victims and perpetrators. In S. Einarsen, H. Hoel, D. Zapf & C.L. Cooper (Eds.). *Bullying and emotional abuse in the workplace. International perspectives in research and practice* (pp. 165–184). London: Taylor & Francis.

AFFILIATIONS

Regina Vollmeyer
Institute for Psychology
Goethe-University Frankfurt
Frankfurt/Main, Germany

Konstanze Jenderek
Institute for Psychology

Goethe-University Frankfurt
Frankfurt/Main, Germany

Tahmine Tozman
Institute for Psychology
Goethe-University Frankfurt
Frankfurt/Main, Germany

ANNA BAUMERT, TOBIAS ROTHMUND, NADINE THOMAS,
MARIO GOLLWITZER & MANFRED SCHMITT

IV. JUSTICE AS A MORAL MOTIVE

*Belief in a Just World and Justice Sensitivity as Potential
Indicators of the Justice Motive*

INTRODUCTION

As theoretical considerations and empirical research suggest, human behaviour is guided by a fundamental justice motive. In the present chapter, we discuss two theoretical constructs that have been proposed to capture inter-individual differences in the strength of the justice motive: belief in a just world and justice sensitivity. We review research that is important with regard to the relationship of each of these constructs to the justice motive. Specifically, we focus on how measures of belief in a just world and justice sensitivity predict justice-related emotion and behaviour and how they are linked with systematic individual differences in the processing of justice-related information. Subsequently, we focus on the striking issue that measures of belief in a just world and justice sensitivity do not overlap empirically despite the conceptualization of both as indicators of the justice motive. Three potential responses to this issue are presented and discussed.

JUSTICE AND MORALITY

Justice is considered to be a fundamental concern in human social life. Within moral philosophy, Aristotle (1998) proposed two notions of justice. According to a broad conceptualization, justice embraces all moral virtues because it predisposes the individual to be guided by virtuous goals and reasons, with regard to not only one's own affairs but to other people as well (Aristotle, 1998). In this sense, justice is considered to be a super-ordinate moral virtue. Thus, it seems indispensable to consider the domain of justice when seeking a full understanding of moral motivation.

In a more narrow sense, Aristotle counted justice as one of four cardinal virtues (along with prudence, temperance, and courage). In this sense, justice refers to the proportionality of exchanges, of allocations of goods and burdens, as well as of the retribution of rule violations. Moreover, justice serves also as a standard by which to evaluate decision procedures independent of the resulting (distributive or retributive) decision. Beginning with the concept that equals ought to receive equally and be treated equally, a central question related to justice judgments is

*K. Heinrichs, F. Oser & T. Lovat (Eds.), Handbook of Moral Motivation: Theories,
Models, Applications, 159–180.*

whether achievements, deeds, or attributes distinguish a person and make him or her more or less *deserving* of a specific outcome or treatment.

Since the second half of the last century, the empirical social sciences have begun to focus on justice issues. Researchers in the fields of psychology, economy, and sociology are specifically interested in when and why people feel unfairly treated and which cognitive, emotional, and behavioural reactions are related to the experience of injustice. Going beyond a character-oriented perspective in virtue ethics, where it is of main importance whether a person's feelings and strivings are in accordance with moral principles, in psychological justice research, justice is investigated also as a standard of evaluation that people employ for events that are not caused by a human being. This means that misfortunes may be perceived as undeserved and, thus, unjust without someone (other than fate or God) who is able to be blamed for deliberately violating justice standards. As an example, parents may have to deal with feelings of injustice if their child dies of a very rare disease. Hence, in social justice research, the realm of justice and the realm of morality are suggested as domains of substantial but not full overlap (Folger, Cropanzano, & Goldman, 2005). Within this overlap, research on justice and on the justice motive in particular enriches our understanding of the moral processes that guide behaviour.

In the present chapter, we discuss justice as a fundamental human motive that differs inter-individually in strength. We review research on two constructs aimed at capturing these differences in the individual concern for justice: belief in a just world and justice sensitivity. As empirical results show, these constructs shape justice-related information processing, emotions, motivation and behaviour. However, both constructs have been found to be only weakly correlated. Hence, we discuss potential distinctions between these constructs. We propose that both constructs tap into distinct facets of the justice motive: The belief in a just world may reflect the need for justice as a principle of order in the world, whereas justice sensitivity may reflect a concern for justice as a moral principle. Finally, we discuss how these two facets of a fundamental human justice motive are linked to processes of moral self-regulation, to moral identity and moral motivation.

THE JUSTICE MOTIVE

Refuting Reductionism

In psychology and recently also in economy, justice has been identified as a fundamental human motive (Montada, 2007). Motives are defined as "dispositions to be concerned with and to strive for a certain class of incentives or goals" (Emmons, 1989, p. 32). According to the assumption of a fundamental justice motive, humans are generally motivated to strive for justice and to avoid injustice: People want to get what they deserve and deserve what they get (Lerner, 1980). Moreover, they also want other people to be treated fairly, and they are motivated to adhere to principles of justice themselves.

The assumption of a justice motive stands in conflict with a reductionist account that aims to explain human motivation by egoistic strivings alone. According to this reductionist view, justice is not an end in itself but rather a means that serves to protect the self-interests of individuals. Several scholars have rejected this view with theoretical arguments (e.g., Lerner, 2003; Miller & Ratner, 1996; Montada, 1998). In addition, empirical evidence supports the existence of a justice motive that cannot be equated with self-interest. Perhaps the most intriguing evidence for this assertion comes from studies in which justice-oriented behaviour is in conflict with self-interest. For example, extensive research employing the so-called dictator game has shown that people will share considerable amounts of money with anonymous others without any pressure to do so (Güth & Tietz, 1990). Moreover, social dilemma research as well as research on bystander intervention in real-life settings (civil courage) has demonstrated that people are disposed to invest their own resources and to take risks to punish rule violations even when a direct self-interest is not involved (*altruistic punishment*; Fehr & Fischbacher, 2004; Fehr & Gächter, 2002; Fischer, Greitemeyer, Pollozek, & Frey, 2006).

Perceptions of Injustice as Moral Motivation

As we know from general conceptions of motives, motives represent recurrent concerns (McClelland, 1985). They describe typical motivational patterns occurring in relevant situations. Motives are activated by situational incentives or cues that indicate relevance for the respective motive. They guide cognitive processes, such that attention is directed toward relevant cues, and situations are interpreted in terms of their potential to achieve motive-related goals (e.g., McClelland, 1985; Schultheiss & Hale, 2007). Most importantly, motives provide the drive for goal-directed behaviour. Thus, motives are also closely linked with affective reactions that signal whether relevant goals have been attained or not (Schmitt & Brunstein, 2005).

Assuming that justice is a fundamental motive for individuals means that the perception of a potential injustice triggers emotional reactions (e.g., anger, moral outrage, compassion, guilt) and urges the individual to act in order to restore justice or to avoid the injustice. Hence, the concept of a human justice motive implies the assumption of a psychological link between the perception of (potential) injustice and affective and behavioural reactions. This is exactly what is stressed by Aristotle's term *practical reasoning*. In contrast to theoretical reasoning, practical reasoning provides reasons to act in a certain way (von Wright, 1963).

Of course, we know that this link between perceptions of (potential) injustice, affect, and behaviour is not deterministic. A prominent example is provided by a psychopath who is able to correctly identify unjust incidents, but for whom no motivational consequences follow from this perception (Damasio, Tranel & Damasio, 1990; Gini, Pozzoli & Hauser, 2011; Hare, 1993). Also, in healthy people, psychological mechanisms exist that allow them to disengage situationally from justice standards that they consider being crucial in other situations (Bandura, 1991). Nevertheless, despite exceptions, the notion of a justice motive suggests that, in general, perceptions of injustice provide a motivation to redress the injustice. Moreover, stable individual differences in the strength of the justice motive may help to explain variance in justice-related emotion and behaviour.

Individual Differences in the Justice Motive

People are assumed to differ systematically in how central justice concerns are for them personally (e.g., Schmitt, Gollwitzer, Maes & Arbach, 2005). Following these assumptions, the more important justice principles are for an individual, the more readily situations are perceived as justice-related, and the more often justice concerns are situationally activated and guide behaviour. Furthermore, emotions resulting from the perception of injustice are more pronounced and motivate action in accordance with justice principles the more the stronger the individual's justice concerns. Of particular importance to the present chapter are constructs that may capture differential strengths of the justice motive. Most prominently, the belief in a just world is considered to be an indicator of this strength (Lerner, 1980; Rubin & Peplau, 1973). A further potential candidate is justice sensitivity (Schmitt, Baumert, Gollwitzer & Maes, 2010; Schmitt et al., 2005). Whereas there is a clear consensus in the literature about a psychological link between the justice motive and belief in a just world, there is a need for discussion regarding whether and how justice sensitivity relates to the justice motive.

In the next sections, we will outline the theoretical backgrounds of both constructs—the belief in a just world and justice sensitivity. We will provide examples for their predictive power regarding justice-related emotion and behaviour, and we briefly present differentiations within these constructs that have been introduced through empirical results and theoretical considerations. Both constructs have been investigated within a social-cognitive perspective. Thus, we will review results on how differential information processing may explain consequences of the belief in a just world and justice sensitivity, respectively. However, rather than providing complete reviews of research on these individual difference constructs, we aim to focus on results that (a) highlight the relation of the respective construct to the justice motive, (b) provide insight into the processes by which the justice motive guides behaviour, and (c) allow for comparing and contrasting the constructs, which we will elaborate on in the discussion section.

BELIEF IN A JUST WORLD

According to Lerner's just world theory (Lerner, 1980), people have a need to believe that the world is a just place. They want to be sure to live in a world where people get what they deserve and deserve what they get. This belief is assumed to develop during childhood and to serve important psychological functions as it forms the basis for any goal seeking and delay of gratification. As Lerner (1977) states, the just world belief is at the core of the *personal contract* consisting of the implicit agreement that abiding by rules and norms will in return guarantee the entitlement to a deserved outcome.

> If the child—and later the adult—becomes persuaded that he lives in a world where these procedures and rules of entitlement or deserving do not apply, he will give up living by his personal contract and act as if he lives in a jungle with all the attendant psychological consequences. (Lerner, 1977, p. 6)

According to the just world theory, it is the commitment to this personal contract that motivates individuals to observe standards of justice in their own lives and to take action in order to restore justice if standards are violated by others. Injustice poses a threat to the personal contract and, thus, to the stability of the individual.

Notably, consequences of the motivation to defend the belief in a just world may take paradoxical forms, as Lerner and Simmons (1966) demonstrated in a compelling experiment. Participants witnessed the suffering of an ostensible other participant. If participants received the opportunity to end the suffering and compensate the victim, most of them did so. However, if participants were powerless, they tended to derogate the victim in a subsequent evaluation compared to participants who had the opportunity to compensate. In terms of just world theory, this means that if continued injustice cannot be redressed, people tend to distort reality and reinterpret the situation in order to avoid a threat to their belief in a just world. Victim derogation and victim blame are well-documented reactions that can be understood as efforts to perceive the world as a just place (Montada & Lerner, 1998).

Following, we outline the development of measures for individual differences in the belief in a just world and findings on their predictive validity for paradoxical effects of the justice motive, on the one hand, and adherence to justice principles, on the other hand. In order to gain insight into how the belief in a just world shapes behaviour, we review social-cognitive approaches to individual differences in the processing of justice-related information. Taken together, we summarize arguments that the belief in a just world can be assumed to capture the individual need for justice.

Individual Differences in the Belief in a Just World

Building on Lerner's just world theory, Rubin and Peplau (1973) were the first to consider systematic inter-individual differences in the belief in a just world as a person variable indicating the strength of an individual's justice motive. They developed a self-report scale that assesses how strongly persons endorse statements like "Basically, the world is a just place." To test this scale's predictive power regarding victim derogation, they employed it in a real-life field experiment realized during the national draft lottery in 1971 in the USA. This draft lottery was established to assign priorities to young men for induction into the armed forces and, thus, for being sent to fight in Vietnam. Consequently, this lottery could be seen as assigning people at random to a bad fate. Assuming that this situation could threaten the belief in a just world, Rubin and Peplau (1973) expected their participants to devalue other participants who received a bad outcome in the lottery. Moreover, they expected stronger devaluation among participants who strongly endorsed the belief in a just world. Results partly confirmed their predictions. Most important, young men with a bad outcome in the lottery were evaluated less favourably by participants with a strong belief in a just world than by persons with a weak belief in a just world.

Following this seminal study, much research has been conducted on individual differences in the belief in a just world, its measurement, and its consequences. Most work has been dedicated to understanding the paradoxical effect that unjust reactions—meaning the denial of observed injustice—are motivated by a need to believe in a just world (for reviews, see e.g., Furnham & Procter, 1989; Hafer & Bègue, 2005; Hafer & Gosse, 2010). Additionally, there is also evidence supporting the basic assumption that the belief in a just world is related to a person's own adherence to justice standards, such as helping innocent victims (e.g., Bierhoff, Klein & Kramp, 1991; DePalma, Madey, Tillman & Wheeler, 1999; Miller, 1977). Dalbert and Umlauft (2009) found that, in a dictator game, persons with a strong belief in a just world made more monetary offers to anonymous others that were in accordance with the equality principle compared to persons with a weak belief in a just world. Moreover, Dalbert (1999) showed that being reminded of one's own unfair behaviour was associated with a decrease in self-esteem for persons with a strong rather than a weak belief in a just world.

Research on the consequences of individual differences in the belief in a just world eventually led to the introduction into the literature of several differentiations on this construct (Maes, 1998a). For instance, differentiating the individual strength of a belief in a *general* just world and of a belief in a *personal* just world (Dalbert, 1999) has provided a host of evidence on positive psychological correlates of a strong personal just world belief (Dalbert, 2001). Importantly, empirical results suggest that specifically the strength of a belief in a personal just world is predictive of renouncing delinquent intentions (Sutton & Winnard, 2007), refraining from bullying at school (Correia & Dalbert, 2008), and provoking fewer disciplinary problems during imprisonment (Otto & Dalbert, 2005). Thus, specifically, the individual belief in a just personal world appears to be linked to the commitment to justice principles.

Belief in a Just World and Information Processing

How does the belief in a just world guide behaviour? Generally, motives are assumed to guide information processing through the activation of concerns of a specific type that thus provide the motivation to act. Regarding the mechanisms underlying the observed behavioural effects of the belief in a just world, research taking a social-cognitive approach provides important insights (Hafer & Bègue, 2005). In a series of studies, Hafer (2000, 2002) adopted a modified Stroop procedure to show that witnessing the suffering of an innocent victim automatically directs attention toward justice-related stimuli. In these experiments, participants watched a film clip displaying an unjust episode in which the injustice was either redressed later (just condition) or not (unjust condition). A modified Stroop task that was administered right after the justice episode revealed that participants had longer color naming latencies for justice-related words than for any other word category (i.e., words related to features of the story, to physical harm, or to social harm, or completely neutral words). This effect was stronger in the unjust condition than in the just condition and mediated the extent to which the victim was derogated by participants (Hafer, 2000).

Importantly, the Stroop interference for justice-related words was found to be more pronounced among participants with a strong belief in a just world than among participants with a weak just world belief, as measured with a self-report scale (Hafer, 2002). Callan, Ellard, and Nicol (2006) replicated Hafer's (2000) results by showing that, in general, knowing about the prolonged suffering of an innocent victim resulted in selective attention for justice-related stimuli. These studies provide more direct evidence that innocent victims pose a threat to the belief in a just world—as indicated by the attention-grabbing potential of justice-related cues—and that this process is responsible for victim derogation.

Aside from attentional processes as captured by the modified Stroop procedure, research has also investigated how the belief in a just world affects memory processes. Specifically, research revealed systematically biased recollection of (one's own and others') past deeds in accordance with the valence of current outcomes (e.g., winning or losing a lottery)—a memory distortion that served specifically to portray chance outcomes as more fair (Callan, Kay, Davidenko & Ellard, 2009). Other than research on attentional processes, memory research has not been linked to individual differences in the belief in a just world yet. However, it can be speculated that memory effects should be more pronounced among persons who endorse a belief in a just world more strongly, and that distorted recollection may be one type of process driving the paradoxical effects of a need for justice.

Belief in a Just World and the Justice Motive

Taken together, according to Lerner's just world theory (1977, 1980), the human justice motive is reflected in a need to believe in a just world. This need is grounded in the crucial psychological functions of the so-called personal contract. The commitment to this contract motivates people to sustain and defend the *positive delusion* that they live in a world in which everyone gets what he or she deserves and, vice versa, deserves what he or she gets.

Following this conception, the belief in a just world has been interpreted as an indirect indicator of the strength of the justice motive (Dalbert, 2001; Schmitt, 1998). Consistent with this interpretation, empirical research has shown that individual differences in the belief in a just world are linked to (a) adherence to justice rules, (b) trust in the fairness of others (e.g., Maes, 1998), (c) engagement in redressing rule violations (by means of punishment or compensation), and, if restoring justice is not possible, (d) systematic distortion of reality.

Theoretically, linking the belief in a just world with the *need* to believe in a just world is in accordance with the notion that motives are closely related to and shape convictions or beliefs (e.g., Kunda, 1990). In other words, the need for justice may delude the person's justice belief. It is important to note, however, that self-report measures of the belief in a just world most probably confound knowledge components with consequences of the justice motive (Schmitt, 1998).

JUSTICE SENSITIVITY

Besides the belief in a just world, justice sensitivity has been proposed as an indicator of the individual concern for justice. Parallel to the previous section, in the current section we will present research on the emotional and behavioural consequences of justice sensitivity. Different from the belief in a just world, justice sensitivity has been decomposed into four facets that reflect the different perspectives that can be adopted toward a potential injustice. We outline emotional and behavioural effects for each justice sensitivity perspective as well as the social-cognitive processes that are assumed to mediate these effects.

People differ systematically in their *readiness* to perceive injustice and in the *strength* of their cognitive, emotional, and behavioural reactions to injustice. These differences have been shown to be stable across time and consistent across situations (Dar & Resh, 2001; Lovas & Wolt, 2002; Schmitt, 1996; Schmitt et al., 2005; van den Bos, Maas, Waldring & Semin, 2003). Thus, justice sensitivity is considered a trait variable that reflects the importance of justice issues in people's everyday lives.

To measure justice sensitivity, Schmitt, Neumann, and Montada (1995; Schmitt, 1996) proposed four components of the construct, one relating to the perception of injustice and three to reactions toward this perception. First, regarding its perceptual component, justice sensitivity is assumed to involve the activation threshold and activation potential of concepts related to injustice. Inter-individual differences in this threshold and activation potential should cause persons high in justice sensitivity to perceive injustice more frequently than persons low in justice sensitivity.

Second, the strength of emotional reactions should indicate the subjective significance of a perceived injustice and should, thus, be indicative of an individual's level of justice sensitivity. Third, incidents of high personal importance tend to result in repetitive and intrusive thoughts (Rime, Philippot, Boca, & Mesquita, 1992). Therefore, rumination about injustice has been suggested as a cognitive component of justice sensitivity. Fourth, according to the notion of a close link between the perception of injustice and motivation resulting from this perception, it is assumed that justice sensitivity involves a motivational component. Persons high in justice sensitivity should feel an urge to restore justice and avoid injustice and should display a willingness to act accordingly.

Studies employing self-report scales of justice sensitivity have revealed a substantial convergence of the proposed components (Schmitt, 1996; Schmitt et al., 1995). However, because convergence of emotional and ruminative reactions was strongest, only these components were employed as indicators of the construct on a subsequent short form of the scale (10 items). Nevertheless, perceptual and motivational processes are assumed to be at the core of the construct (e.g., Schmitt et al., 2005, 2010).

Four Perspectives on Injustice

In the case of an unjust incident, cognitive, emotional and behavioural reactions differ largely depending on the perspective from which injustice is perceived (Mikula, 1994; Mikula, Petri, & Tanzer, 1990). Victims of injustice typically experience anger as their emotional reaction, neutral observers may be morally outraged, and perpetrators and beneficiaries tend to feel guilty (e.g., Montada, Dalbert, Reichle, & Schmitt, 1986; Weiss, Suckow, & Cropanzano, 1999). According to these different perspectives, justice sensitivity has been decomposed into the sensitivity to become a victim of injustice and the sensitivities of a neutral observer, a passive beneficiary, or an active perpetrator (Schmitt et al., 2005, 2010). Several studies have addressed the specificity of the perspectives of justice sensitivity (for an overview, see Thomas, Baumert & Schmitt, 2012) and have demonstrated that the four assumed perspectives—victim, observer, beneficiary, and perpetrator sensitivity—can be empirically distinguished and measured reliably by short and valid scales (Schmitt et al., 2010).

Moreover, empirical research has demonstrated the predictive power of the perspectives of justice sensitivity for justice-related emotion and behaviour, over and above potentially competing predictors. For example, *victim sensitivity* has been shown to predict anger and protest as reactions to one's own disadvantages in resource allocations in the laboratory and in the field, even when constructs such as trait anger or self-assertiveness were controlled for (Mohiyeddini & Schmitt, 1997; Schmitt & Mohiyeddini, 1996). In the work context, Schmitt and Dörfel (1999) found victim sensitivity to amplify the impact of perceived procedural unfairness on a reduction of organizational citizenship behaviour (i.e., work satisfaction, turn-over intentions, number of sick days). Moreover, after being laid-off, persons high in victim sensitivity perceived the decision process as more unfair and reacted with intentions of revenge compared to persons low in victim sensitivity (Schmitt, Rebele, Bennecke, & Förster, 2008).

Further studies have demonstrated that *beneficiary sensitivity* is predictive of solidarity with disadvantaged others. Persons high in beneficiary sensitivity were found to experience existential guilt toward persons defaced by an accident or disease and were willing to support historically disadvantaged groups (Gollwitzer,

Schmitt, Schalke, Maes & Baer, 2005). Moreover, a recent study on bystander intervention (*civil courage*) found that justice-sensitive persons, specifically from the beneficiary's perspective, were more likely to intervene against a norm violation (a theft in the laboratory) compared to persons low in beneficiary sensitivity, despite not being personally affected by the theft, and despite risking negative reactions by the thief (Baumert, Halmburger, & Schmitt, in preparation).

Research employing experimental games additionally revealed the behavioural relevance of *observer sensitivity*. In several studies, persons high in observer sensitivity were particularly prone to reject unequal monetary offers in the ultimatum game as well as unequal offers to third persons in an extension of this game (Fetchenhauer & Huang, 2004). In the ultimatum game (Camerer, 2003; Camerer & Thaler, 1995; Güth, 1995), a person A is endowed with an amount of money that he or she may share with an anonymous other person B. Person B is informed about A's decision and can either accept it or reject it; if Person B rejects it, the money is lost and both A and B receive nothing. From a self-interested point of view, any amount of money should be accepted by B as a financial gain. In contrast to this prediction, there is great variance in how much deviance from an equal split is accepted (e.g., Pruitt & Kimmel, 1977). In a variation of this game (*third-person punishment game*; Brandstätter, Güth, Himmelbauer & Kriz, 1999), person A decides how to share the money with person B, who, in this case, is powerless. In addition, a third person C is introduced who is informed about A's decision, but is unaffected by it because he or she receives a fixed amount of money. However, person C can decide to reject the offer of person A in which case none of the three receives any money. In both variations of the game, observer-sensitive persons were less willing to accept an unequal offer from A than persons low in observer sensitivity, and, thus, tolerated a financial loss in order to avoid a resource allocation that violated a justice principle (Fetchenhauer & Huang, 2004).

For *perpetrator sensitivity*, which is the sensitivity for actively committed injustices, only recently has a scale been developed for its assessment (Schmitt et al., 2010). Therefore, its predictive power remains to be investigated by future studies.

In sum, justice sensitivity is an important predictor of justice-related emotion and behaviour. Correlations among the perspectives suggest that they all share a common element, which is assumed to consist of the individual *concern for justice*. However, observer, beneficiary, and perpetrator sensitivity are more closely related, whereas victim sensitivity is rather distinct from the other sensitivities. Moreover, correlational patterns of the perspectives with other constructs and criteria indicate that observer, beneficiary, and perpetrator sensitivity may reflect a *genuine* justice concern, whereas victim sensitivity appears to capture a rather egoistic concern for justice for the *self* (Gollwitzer et al., 2005; Schmitt et al., 2005). Novel developments propose that victim sensitivity indicates the sensitivity to the mean intentions of others (Gollwitzer & Rothmund, 2009). Persons high in victim sensitivity seem to fear exploitation and victimization and are, thus, reluctant to cooperate in situations in which they have to trust in the benevolence of interaction partners (Gollwitzer, Rothmund, Pfeiffer & Ensenbach, 2009; Rothmund, Gollwitzer & Klimmt, 2011).

Justice Sensitivity and Information Processing

In order to understand the processes underlying the reported effects, attentional, interpretational, and memory processes linked with justice sensitivity have been investigated (Baumert, Gollwitzer, Staubach & Schmitt, 2011; Baumert, Otto, Thomas, Bobocel & Schmitt, 2012; Baumert & Schmitt, 2009; Bell & Buchner, 2010).

These studies consistently indicate that justice sensitivity involves the *activation potential* of justice-related concepts. In situations in which these concepts become activated, they guide information processing more strongly for persons high in justice sensitivity than for persons low in justice sensitivity. Specifically, after witnessing unjust incidents, persons high in justice sensitivity were found to attend more strongly to unjust cues, and they interpreted ambiguous situations as justice-related compared to persons low in justice sensitivity. Importantly, results showed that these effects are domain-specific: Justice sensitivity shaped only the processing of justice-related information but not the processing of justice-unrelated, negatively or positively valenced information (Baumert et al., 2011, 2012; Baumert & Schmitt, 2009).

Additionally, further studies have suggested that justice sensitivity involves also the *degree of elaboration* of justice-related concepts that enable persons high in justice sensitivity to encode and later remember pertinent information more accurately (Baumert et al., 2011, 2012; Bell & Buchner, 2010). For example, persons high in justice sensitivity have been found to remember more unjust information correctly than persons low in justice sensitivity, both after a short retention interval bridged by a distracter task and after a longer interval of 1 week. Taken together, research regarding how justice sensitivity involves differential information processing allows detailed insight into the processes that explain individual differences in justice-related emotion and behaviour.

Justice Sensitivity and the Justice Motive

The reported findings concerning justice sensitivity indicate a psychological link between this concept and a latent justice motive. Justice sensitivity is proposed to reflect the individual's concern for justice, meaning the personal importance of justice principles (e.g., Schmitt et al., 2005). As the studies cited above suggest, justice sensitivity involves several characteristics that are crucial for defining motives (McClelland, 1985): Justice sensitivity guides information processing once justice concepts become activated by relevant situational cues. Attentional and interpretational tendencies predispose persons high in justice sensitivity to perceive injustice more readily compared to persons low in justice sensitivity. Importantly, evidence for the predictive value of justice sensitivity for individual differences in justice-related behaviour indicates that this construct involves a close link between perceived injustice and moral motivation. Apparently, for persons high in justice sensitivity, perceiving (potential) injustice provides a strong motivation to act in order to avoid injustice or restore justice. Finally, affective processes are one component of justice sensitivity and shape strong emotional responses to perceptions of violations of justice principles.

DISCUSSION

Belief in a Just World and Justice Sensitivity as Indicators of the Justice Motive?

In the present chapter, we presented two constructs that capture justice-related inter-individual differences: the strength of the belief in a just world and justice sensitivity. These constructs stem from somewhat distinct theoretical backgrounds, but are both considered to be indicative of the justice motive and to explain justice-related perception, emotion, and behaviour. The question to be discussed here is whether both constructs indeed capture a concern for justice as a source of moral motivation.

If both constructs are considered to be indicators for individual differences in the justice motive, their measures should substantially overlap. However, empirical results have shown that (a) their correlation is very low (e.g., between -.04 and .18 depending on the specific measure of belief in a just world and on the perspective of justice sensitivity; Schmitt et al., 2005), and (b) they explain distinct parts of the variance in justice-related outcomes (e.g., Baumert et al., 2011; Dalbert & Umlauft, 2009). How then can these findings be reconciled with the notion that both constructs indicate a common justice motive?

One possible answer could be that reconciliation is not possible and that justice sensitivity should be viewed as a personality *trait* and not indicative of the justice *motive*. Literature on the distinction between traits and motives defines traits as "stylistic and habitual patterns of cognition, affect, and behaviour" (Emmons, 1989, p. 32), whereas motives are defined as "dispositions to be concerned with and to strive for a certain class of incentives or goals" (Emmons, 1989, p. 32; Winter, John, Stewart, Klohnen, & Duncan, 1998). From a social-cognitive approach (e.g., Caprara, Steca, Cervone & Artistico, 2003), justice sensitivity could be understood as a *trait* involving several parameters of cognitive and affective processes (such as the activation potential of justice concepts; Baumert & Schmitt, 2009; or in the case of victim sensitivity, the accessibility of suspicious schemata; Gollwitzer & Rothmund, 2009) that cause differential patterns of perception and reactions toward injustice across situations. Following this account, these patterns are habitual and not motive-guided. However, this account neglects the motivational component of justice sensitivity and thus contradicts the original conception of the construct (Schmitt et al., 1995).

Furthermore, there is also a more general argument against this account of justice sensitivity as a satisfying response for why belief in a just world and justice sensitivity do not overlap empirically: If conceptualized as a trait variable, justice sensitivity has to be located at the level of personality facets rather than broad factors (Schmitt et al., 2010). At this level, traits capture highly domain-specific "patterns of cognition, affect, and behaviour" (Emmons, 1989, p. 32). This makes the distinction between trait and motive "a matter of degree" (Allport, 1937, p. 324) rather than a categorical one. In the case of justice sensitivity, patterns of cognition, affect, and behaviour specifically concern information relevant for the attainment of justice-related goals. Thus, the distinction from a justice motive as involving a recurrent concern for justice is not a sharp one, and further explanations are necessary regarding the lack of overlap between belief in a just world and justice sensitivity.

An alternative answer has been proposed by Dalbert and Umlauft (2009). Drawing on the distinction between implicit and explicit motives (McClelland, Koestner, & Weinberger, 1989), they construe the belief in a just world as an indirect indicator of the justice motive, capturing distinct representations of this motive compared to justice sensitivity as a direct indicator of the justice motive. Following this argument, belief in a just world captures a rather experiential and unconscious representation (Epstein, 1994) of the justice motive consisting of associations of relevant stimuli with emotional-motivational states (Schultheiss, 2001). By contrast, justice sensitivity is seen to reflect a self-attributed justice motive (Dalbert & Umlauft, 2009) represented in a conscious, propositional format. According to dual-process theories of information processing and behaviour (e.g., Smith & DeCostner, 2000; Strack & Deutsch, 2004), this notion implies that belief in a just world should be predictive of automatic, intuitive reactions, whereas justice sensitivity should predict rather controlled responses to injustice. However, as the research reviewed above shows, this distinction does not consistently apply to the effects of both constructs. Specifically, it seems difficult to label all outcomes of belief in a just world as uncontrolled and intuitive (see also, van den Bos & Maas, 2009): Whereas the derogation of innocent victims may be a rather uncontrolled process (Lerner, 2003; Simons & Piliavin, 1972), reports of delinquent intentions (Sutton & Winnard, 2007), for instance, appear to be (mainly) guided by controlled processes. Additionally, there is evidence that justice sensitivity also guides automatic information processing (automatic attention allocation), even when belief in a just world is controlled for (Baumert et al., 2011).

How else then can it be understood that justice sensitivity and belief in a just world do not overlap, despite both being considered to be indicators of the justice motive? A third potential answer also assumes that both constructs tap into different facets of the justice motive. However, this account does not distinguish these facets according to representational forms and automaticity of consequences. Rather, the distinction is based on considerations regarding a psychological need for justice as a principle of order in the world, on the one hand, and the commitment to justice as a moral principle, on the other hand.

As Lerner (1980) proposed, the need for justice is grounded in the *functional value* of justice for goal seeking and the delay of gratification of the individual.

According to this assertion, people are committed to justice principles *because* they want others to act justly in return and *as long as* they maintain the belief in a just world. Different from Lerner's view, however, it could be argued that, across the lifespan, justice principles may gain *moral authority,* which is not conditional on the perception of the world as just anymore. In line with this reasoning, it is plausible to assume that the personal commitment to justice as a moral principle can become (at least partially) independent of a person's need to believe that the world is a just place. Thus, the justice motive may consist of two partially independent facets: First, the psychological need for justice as a general principle of order in the world and, second, the motivation to adhere to justice as a moral principle.

How can this argument explain the unrelatedness of justice sensitivity and the individual belief in a just world? The belief in a just world may primarily capture the need for justice as a general principle of order in the world. For this reason, individual differences in the belief in a just world reflect the motivated tendency to distort reality in order to satisfy a need for justice (Lerner, 1980). Moreover, for persons with a strong belief in a just world, the need for justice provides the foundation for justice motivation, meaning that, dependent on the trust that everyone gets what he or she deserves, the person stays committed to justice principles. Thus, the belief in a just world reflects a conditional concern for justice. By contrast, a rather unconditional concern for justice may be captured by justice sensitivity (particularly by observer, beneficiary, and perpetrator sensitivity). In this sense, justice sensitivity can be understood as a more direct indicator of the motivation to adhere to justice as a universal moral principle. A similar distinction between belief in a just world and justice sensitivity has been proposed previously (Montada, 1998).

Of course, this third answer is highly speculative. In order to corroborate it, it may be informative to investigate whether justice sensitivity (but not belief in a just world) is unrelated to attentional or interpretational disengagement from injustice. If justice sensitivity captures an unconditional concern for justice, this should be the case. Furthermore, whereas paradoxical effects of the belief in a just world are a well established finding, evidence is still lacking regarding the effect of justice sensitivity in situations in which the (functional) need for justice and justice as a moral principle dictate different reactions. Following the speculative account proposed above, justice sensitivity should predict the unconditional adherence to justice principles independent of different kinds of temptations. Finally, developmental factors of belief in a just world and justice sensitivity might be (partially) distinct. Unfortunately, longitudinal studies on these constructs are extremely scarce (for exceptions see Dalbert & Stoeber, 2006; Reichle & Schmitt, 2002). Consistent with our proposition, belief in a just world has been considered a premature coping strategy that is eventually replaced by more sophisticated self regulation that allow handling the world as neither orderly nor just (Oppenheimer, 2005, 2006). Research is needed to reveal patterns and determinants of development, particularly regarding justice sensitivity and belief in a just world in direct comparison. It could be expected that frequent confrontation with injustices over time leads to a decrease in belief in a just world but to an increase in justice sensitivity because justice concerns become activated repeatedly, thus lowering their activation threshold and increasing their activation potential.

The Justice Motive and Moral Motivation

Justice and morality are domains of fundamental overlap (Aristotle, 1998; Folger et al., 2005). In order to reach a broader understanding of moral motivation, it seems crucial to integrate research on the human justice motive into moral psychology. How does the justice motive shape moral motivation? Following the notion of a fundamental human justice motive, it is assumed that individuals internalize principles of deservingness that become integrated into a self-regulatory process by which they are translated into moral motivation and ultimately behaviour (e.g., Bandura, 1991). In a specific situation, the concern for justice is assumed to be activated by relevant cues, to guide information processing, including the monitoring of one's own behaviour, and to trigger moral emotions that fuel the motivation to adhere to or to restore justice principles (Blasi, 1999). Affective self-directed reactions following goal-attainment (versus failure) can be assumed to reinforce and further strengthen the concern for justice. This self-regulatory process is shaped by the individual strength of the justice motive: The stronger the justice motive, the more readily justice concerns are activated and the more pronounced their effects on information processing, emotion, and consequently moral motivation. In addition, among persons with a strong individual justice motive, tendencies to situationally disengage from one's internalized justice standards should be weak (Bandura, 1991; Blasi, 1984) so that the described self-regulatory process guides behaviour in accordance with justice principles.

In sum, the concept of justice as a motive that varies inter-individually in strength is consistent with approaches to moral motivation that posit the centrality of moral principles within the self-concept as crucial for their emotional and motivational relevance (Aquino & Reed, 2002; Blasi, 1984; Monin & Jordan, 2009; Narvaez, Lapsley, Hagele & Lasky, 2006; Perugini & Leone, 2009). Following the assumptions outlined above, for persons with a strong justice motive principles of justice are closely tied to self identity in that they are crucial in the process of moral self regulation and, thus, for the integrity of the person (Blasi, 1984).

Importantly, regarding the consequences of the justice motive for moral motivation and moral action, it is necessary to distinguish (1) the degree to which the adherence to justice principles forms an ultimate and unconditional goal for an individual (in the sense of the justice motive presumably captured by justice sensitivity) from (2) the degree to which justice serves for the attainment of further goals (in the sense of the psychological need for justice as a principle of order as proposed to be captured by the belief in a just world). This distinction is important because only in the first sense, the justice motive can be assumed to guide genuinely moral motivation by the described self regulatory process, whereas in the second sense, paradoxical effects have to be expected in situations where goals of controllability and structure are at conflict with principles of justice. Following this line of arguments, it seems highly interesting to investigate how belief in a just world and justice sensitivity are empirically related to individual differences in moral self-regulation, such as the self-importance of moral identity (Aquino & Reed, 2002; Narvaez et al., 2006; Perugini & Leone, 2009) or dispositional tendencies toward moral disengagement (Bandura, Barbaranelli, Caprara & Pastorelli, 1996).

CONCLUSION

In conclusion, based on empirical research and theoretical arguments, justice is considered to be a fundamental motive in human life. We have reviewed research on two individual difference constructs, belief in a just world and justice sensitivity, which are assumed to indicate the individual strength of the justice motive. We have focused on results that are informative with regard to the psychological links between the presented constructs and the justice motive. Because self-report measures of these construct do not overlap empirically, we have discussed how the constructs could relate to distinct facets of the justice motive. One distinction that has been proposed in the literature construes the belief in a just world to indicate an experiential, associative representation of the justice motive; and justice sensitivity to indicate a self-attributed, deliberative justice motive. In the present chapter, we have suggested an alternative distinction with belief in a just world reflecting the need for justice as a principle of order and a conditional adherence to justice principles; and justice sensitivity reflecting a commitment to justice as a moral principle that is (at least partially) independent from a psychological need for justice. We hope that this speculative account of justice sensitivity and belief in a just world will stimulate further theoretical discussions and empirical research in the future that promise to yield highly interesting insights into the nature of the human justice motive.

REFERENCES

Allport, G.W. (1937). *Personality: A psychological interpretation*. New York: Holt.

Aquino, K.,& Reed II, A. (2002). The self-importance of moral identity. *Journal of Personality and Social Psychology, 83*, 1423–1440.

Aristoteles (1998). *Die Nikomachische Ethik*. [Nicomachean Ethics]. München, Germany: DTV.

Bandura, A. (1991). Social cognitive theory of self-regulation. *Organizational Behavior and Human Decision Processes, 50*, 248–287.

Bandura, A., Barbaranelli, C., Caprara, G.V., & Pastorelli, C. (1996). Mechanisms of moral disengagement in the excercise of moral agency. *Journal of Personality and Social Psychology, 71*, 364–374.

Baumert, A., Gollwitzer, M., Staubach, M., & Schmitt, M. (2011). Justice sensitivity and the processing of justice-related information. *European Journal of Personality, 25*, 386–397.

Baumert, A., Halmburger, A., & Schmitt, M. (in preparation). *Bystander intervention against norm violations: Personality determinants of self-reported and real civil courage*.

Baumert, A., Otto, K., Thomas, N., Bobocel, D.R., & Schmitt, M. (2012). Processing of unjust and just information: Interpretation and memory performance related to dispositional victim sensitivity. *European Journal of Personality, 26*, 99–110.

Baumert, A. & Schmitt, M. (2009). Justice sensitive interpretations of ambiguous situations. *Australian Journal of Psychology, 61(1)*, 6–12.

Bell, R. & Buchner, A. (2010). Justice sensitivity and source memory for cheaters. *Journal of Research in Personality, 44*, 677–683.

Bierhoff, H.W., Klein, R., & Kramp, P. (1991). Evidence for the altruistic personality from data on accident research. *Journal of Personality, 59*, 263 - 280.

Blasi, A. (1984). Moral identity: Its role in moral functioning. In: W.M. Kurtines & J.L. Gewirtz (Eds.),*Morality, moral behavior and moral development* (pp.128–139). New York: Wiley.

Blasi, A. (1999). Emotions and moral motivation. *Journal for the Theory of Social Behavior, 29*, 1–19.

Brandstätter, H., Güth, W., Himmelbauer, J., & Kriz, W. (1999). Prior dispositions and actual behavior in dictator and ultimatum games. In: *Proceedings of the 24th Annual Colloquium of the International Association for Research in Economic Psychology*. Belgirate, Italy.

Callan, M.J., Ellard, J.H., & Nicol, J.E. (2006). The belief in a just world and immanent justice reasoning in adults. *Personality and Social Psychology Bulletin, 32*, 1646.

Callan, M.J., Kay, A.C., Davidenko, N., & Ellard, J.H. (2009). The effects of justice motivation on memory for self- and other-relevant events. *Journal of Experimental Social Psychology, 45*, 614–623.

Camerer, C. (2003). *Behavioral game theory: experiments on strategic interaction*. Princeton NJ: University Press.

Camerer, C., & Thaler, R. (1995). Ultimatums, dictators and manners. *Journal of Economic Perspectives, 9*, 209–219.

Caprara, G.V., Steca, P., Cervone, D., & Artistico, D. (2003). The contribution of self-efficacy beliefs to dispositional shyness: On social-cognitive systems and the development of personality dispositions. *Journal of Personality, 71*, 943–970.

Correia, I., & Dalbert, C. (2008). School bullying: Belief in a personal just world of bullies, victims, and defenders. *European Psychologist, 13*, 249–254. .

Dalbert, C. (1999). The world is more just for me than generally: About the personal belief in a just world scale's validity. *Social Justice Research, 12*, 79–98.

Dalbert, C. (2001*). The justice motive as a personal resource*. New York: Kluwer.

Dalbert, C., & Stoeber, J. (2006). The personal belief in a just world and domain-specific beliefs about justice at school and in the family: A longitudinal study with adolescents. *International Journal of Behavioral Development, 20*, 200–207.

Dalbert, C. & Umlauft, S. (2009). The role of the justice motive in economic decision making. *Journal of Economic Psychology, 30*, 172–180.

Damasio, A.R., Tranel, D., & Damasio, H. (1990). Individuals with sociopathic behavior caused by frontal damage fail to respond autonomically to social stimuli. *Behavioral Brain Research, 41*, 81–94.

Dar, Y.,& Resh, N. (2001). Exploring the multifaceted structure of sense of deprivation. *European Journal of Social Psychology, 31*, 63–81.

DePalma, M.T., Madey, S.F., Tillman, T.C., & Wheeler, J. (1999). Perceived patient responsibility and belief in a just world affect helping. *Basic and Applied Social Psychology, 21*, 131–137.

Emmons, R.A. (1989). Exploring the relations between motives and traits: The case of narcissism. In D. Buss & N. Cantor (Eds.), *Personality psychology: Recent trends and emerging directions* (pp. 32–44). New York: Springer.

Epstein, S. (1994). Integration of the cognitive and psychodynamic unconscious. *American Psychologist, 49*, 709–724.

Fehr, E., & Fischbacher, U. (2004). Third-party punishment and social norms. *Evolution and Human Behavior, 25*, 63–87.

Fehr, E., & Gächter, S. (2002). Altruistic punishment in humans. *Nature, 415*, 137–140.

Fetchenhauer, D. & Huang, X. (2004). Justice sensitivity and distributive decisions in experimental games. *Personality and Individual Differences, 36*, 1015–1029.

Fischer, P., Greitemeyer, T., Pollozek, F., & Frey, D. (2006). The unresponsive bystander: Are bystanders more responsive in dangerous emergencies? *European Journal of Social Psychology, 36*, 267–278.

Folger, R., Cropanzano, R., & Goldman, B. (2005). What is the relationship between justice and morality? In J. Greenberg & J.A. Colquitt (Eds.), *Handbook of organizational justice* (pp. 215–245). Mahwah, NJ: Erlbaum.

Furnham, A. & Procter, E. (1989). Belief in a just world: Review and critique of the individual difference literature. *British Journal of Social Psychology, 28,* 365–384.

Gini, G., Pozzoli, T., & Hauser, M. (2011). Bullies have enhanced moral competence to judge relative to victims, but lack moral compassion. *Personality and Individual Differences, 50,* 603–608.

Gollwitzer, M., Schmitt, M., Schalke, R., Maes, J.,& Baer, A. (2005). Asymmetrical effects of justice sensitivity perspectives on prosocial and antisocial behavior. *Social Justice Research, 18,* 183–201.

Gollwitzer, M., & Rothmund, T. (2009). When the need to trust results in unethical behavior: The sensitivity to mean intentions (SeMI) model. In D. De Cremer (Ed.), *Psychological perspectives on ethical behavior and decision making* (pp. 135–152).Charlotte, NC: Information Age.

Gollwitzer, M., Rothmund, T., Pfeiffer, A.,& Ensenbach, C. (2009). Why and when Justice Sensitivity leads to pro- and antisocial behavior. *Journal of Research in Personality, 43,* 999–1005.

Güth, W. (1995). On ultimatum bargaining experiments: a personal review. *Journal of Economic Behavior and Organization, 27,* 329 – 344.

Güth, W., & Tietz, R. (1990). Ultimatum bargaining behavior: A survey and comparison of experimental results. *Journal of Economic Psychology, 11,* 417–449.

Hafer, C.L. (2000). Do innocent victims threaten the belief in a just world? Evidence from a modified Stroop task. *Journal of Personality and Social Psychology, 79,* 165–173.

Hafer, C.L. (2002).Why we reject innocent victims. In M. Ross & D.T. Miller (Eds.), *The justice motive in everyday life* (pp. 109–126). Cambridge, UK: Cambridge University Press.

Hafer, C.L., & Begue, L. (2005). Experimental research on just world theory: Problems, developments, and future challenges. *Psychological Bulletin, 131,* 128–166.

Hafer, C.L., & Gosse, L. (2010). Preserving the belief in a just world: When and for whom are different strategies preferred?. In D.R. Bobocel, A.C. Kay, M.P. Zanna & J.M. Olson (Eds.), *The psychology of justice and legitimacy: The Ontario symposium* (Vol. 11, pp. 79–102). New York: Psychology Press.

Hare, R.D. (1993). *Without conscience.* New York: Pocket Books.

Kunda, Z. (1990). The case for motivated reasoning. *Psychological Bulletin, 108,* 480–498.

Lerner, M.J. (1977). The justice motive in social behavior. Some hypotheses as to its origins and forms. *Journal of Personality, 45,* 1–52.

Lerner, M.J. (1980). *The belief in a just world. A fundamental delusion.* New York: Plenum.

Lerner, M. (2003). The justice motive: Where social psychologists found it, how they lost it, and why they may not find it again. *Personality and Social Psychology Review, 7,* 388–399.

Lerner, M.J., & Simmons, C.H. (1966). The observer's reaction to the "innocent victim": Compassion or rejection? *Journal of Personality and Social Psychology, 4,* 203–210.

Lovas, L., &Wolt, R. (2002). Sensitivity to injustice in the context of some personality traits. *Studia Psychologica, 44,* 125–131.

Maes, J. (1998). Eight stages in the development of research on the construct of belief in a just world. In M.J. Lerner & L. Montada (Eds.), *Responses to ictimizations and belief in a just world* (pp. 163–186). New York: Plenum.

McClelland, D.C. (1985). *Human motivation.* Glenview, IL: Scott-Foresman.

McClelland, D.C., Koestner, R., & Weinberger, J. (1989). How do self-attributed and implicit motives differ? *Psychological Review, 96,* 690–702.

Mikula, G. (1994). Perspective-related differences in interpretations of injustice by victims and victimizers: A test with close relationships. In M.J. Lerner & G. Mikula (Eds.), *Entitlement and the affectional bond* (pp. 175–203). New York: Plenum.

Mikula, G., Petri, B. & Tanzer, N. (1990). What people regard as unjust: Types and structures of everyday experiences of injustice. *European Journal of Social Psychology, 20,* 133–149.

Miller, D.T. (1977). Altruism and threat to a belief in a just world. *Journal of Experimental Social Psychology, 13,* 113–124.

Miller, D.T. & Ratner, R.K. (1996). The power of the myth of self-interest. In L. Montada & M.J. Lerner (Eds.), *Current societal concerns about justice* (p. 25–48). New York: Plenum Press.

Mohiyeddini, C.,& Schmitt, M. (1997). Sensitivity to befallen injustice and reactions to unfair treatment in a laboratory situation. *Social Justice Research, 10*, 333–353.

Monin, B., & Jordan, A.H. (2009). The dynamic moral self: A social psychological perspective. In D. Narvaez & D.K. Lapsley (Eds.), *Personality, identity, and character: Explorations in moral psychology* (pp. 341–354). New York, NY: Cambridge University Press.

Montada, L. (1998). Belief in a just world: A hybrid of justice motive and self-interest? In L. Montada & M.J. Lerner (Eds.), *Responses to victimizations and belief in a just world* (pp. 217–246). New York: Plenum.

Montada, L. (2007). Justice conflicts and the justice of conflict resolution. In K. Törnblom & R. Vermunt (Eds.), *Distributive and procedural justice. Research and applications* (pp. 255–268). Burlington: Ashgate/Glower.

Montada, L., Dalbert, C., Reichle, B., & Schmitt, M. (1986). Urteile über Gerechtigkeit, „existentielle Schuld" und Strategien der Schuldabwehr [Judgments on justice, existential guilt, and defense mechanisms against guilt]. In F. Oser, W. Althof & D. Garz (Eds.), *Moralische Zugänge zum Menschen - Zugänge zum moralischen Menschen. Beiträge zur Entstehung moralischer Identität* (pp. 205–225). München: Kindt.

Montada, L. & Lerner, M.J. (1998). *Responses to victimizations and belief in a just world*. New York: Plenum.

Narvaez, D., Lapsley, D.K., Hagele, S., & Lasky, B. (2006). Moral chronicity and social information processing: Tests of a social cognitive approach to the moral personality. *Journal of Research in Personality 40*, 966–985.

Oppenheimer, L. (2005). Justice and the belief in a just world: A developmental perspective. *Personality and Individual Differences, 38*, 1793–1803.

Oppenheimer, L. (2006). The belief in a just world and subjective perceptions of society: A developmental perspective. *Journal of Adolescence, 29*, 655–669.

Otto, K., & Dalbert, C. (2005). Belief in a just world and its functions for young prisoners. *Journal of Research in Personality, 39*, 559–573.

Perugini, M., & Leone, L. (2009). Implicit self-concept and moral action. *Journal of Research in Personality, 43*, 747–754.

Pruitt, D.G., & Kimmel, M.J. (1977). Twenty years of experimental gaming: Critique, synthesis, and suggestions for the future. *Annual Review of Psychology, 28*, 363–392.

Reichle, B., & Schmitt, M. (2002). Helping and rationalization as alternative strategies for restoring the belief in a just world: Evidence from longitudinal change analyses. In M. Ross & D.T. Miller (Eds.), *The justice motive in everyday life* (pp.127–148). New York, NY: Cambridge University Press.

Rime, B., Philippot, P., Boca, S.,& Mesquita, B. (1992). Longlasting cognitive and social consequences of emotion: Social sharing and rumination. In W. Stroebe & M. Hewstone (Eds.), *European review of social psychology* (Vol. 3., pp. 225–258). Chichester: Wiley.

Rothmund, T., Gollwitzer, M. & Klimmt, C. (2011). Of virtual victims and victimized virtues: Differential effects of experienced aggression in video games on social cooperation. *Personality and Social Psychology Bulletin, 37*(1), 107–119.

Rubin, Z. & Peplau, L.A. (1973). Belief in a just world and reactions to another's lot: A study of participants in the National Draft Lottery. *Journal of Social Issues, 29*(4), 73–93.

Schmitt, C.H., & Brunstein, J.C. (2005). Motive [Motives]. In H. Weber & T. Rammsayer (Eds.), *Handbuch der Persönlichkeitspsychologie und Differentiellen Psychologie* (pp. 288–297). Göttingen: Hogrefe.

Schmitt, M. (1996). Individual differences in Sensitivity to Befallen Injustice (SBI). *Personality and Individual Differences, 21* (1), 3–20.

Schmitt, M. (1998). Methodological strategies in research to validate measures of belief in a just world. In L. Montada & M.J. Lerner (Eds.), *Responses to victimization and belief in a just world* (pp. 187–215). New York, NY: Plenum Press.

Schmitt, M., Baumert, A., Gollwitzer, M., & Maes, J. (2010). The Justice Sensitivity Inventory: Factorial validity, location in the personality facet space, demographic pattern, and normative data. *Social Justice Research, 23*, 211–238.

Schmitt, M.,& Dörfel, M. (1999). Procedural injustice at work, justice sensitivity, job satisfaction and psychosomatic wellbeing. *European Journal of Social Psychology, 29*, 443–453.

Schmitt, M., Gollwitzer, M., Maes, J.,& Arbach, D. (2005). Justice sensitivity: Assessment and location in the personality space. *European Journal of Psychological Assessment, 21*, 202–211.

Schmitt, M.,& Mohiyeddini, C. (1996). Sensitivity to befallen injustice and reactions to a real life disadvantage. *Social Justice Research, 9*, 223–238.

Schmitt, M., Neumann, R.,& Montada, L. (1995). Dispositional sensitivity to befallen injustice. *Social Justice Research, 8*, 385–407.

Schmitt, M., Rebele, J., Bennecke, J.,& Förster, N. (2008). Ungerechtigkeitssensibilität, Kündigungsgerechtigkeit und Verantwortlichkeitszuschreibungen als Korrelate von Einstellungen und Verhalten Gekündigter gegenüber ihrem früheren Arbeitgeber (Post Citizenship Behavior). *Wirtschaftspsychologie 10*, 101–110.

Schultheiss, O.C. (2001). An information processing account of implicit motive arousal. In M.L. Maehr & P. Pintrich (Eds.), *Advances in motivation and achievement* (Vol. 12: New directions in measures and methods, pp. 1–41). Greenwich, CT: JAI Press.

Schultheiss, O.C., & Hale, J.A. (2007). Implicit motives modulate attentional orienting to perceived facial expressions of emotion. *Motivation and Emotion, 31*, 13–24.

Simons, C., & Piliavin, J. (1972). The effect of deception on reactions to a victim. *Journal of Personality and Social Psychology,21*, 56–60.

Smith, E.R., & DeCoster, J. (2000). Dual-process models in social and cognitive psychology: Conceptual integration and links to underlying memory systems. *Personality and Social Psychology Review, 4*(2) 108–131.

Sutton, R.M., & Winnard, E.J. (2007). Looking ahead through lenses of justice: The relevance of just-world beliefs to intentions and confidence in the future. *British Journal of Social Psychology, 46*, 649–666.

Strack, F., & Deutsch, R. (2004). Reflective and impulsive determinants of social behavior. *Personality and Social Psychology Review, 8*, 220–247.

Thomas, N., Baumert, A., & Schmitt, M. (2012). Justice sensitivity as a risk and protective factor in social conflicts. In E. Kals & J. Maes (Eds.), *Justice and Conflicts* (pp. 107–120). Berlin: Springer-Verlag.

van den Bos, K., & Maas, M. (2009). On the psychology of the belief in a just world: Exploring experiential and rationalistic paths to victim blaming. *Personality and Social Psychology Bulletin, 35*, 1567–1578.

van den Bos, K., Maas, M., Waldring, I., & Semin, G.P. (2003). Toward understanding the psychology of reactions to perceived fairness: The role of affect intensity. *Social Justice Research, 16*, 151–168.

Von Wright, G.H. (1963). Practical inference. *Philosophical Review, 72*, 159–179.

Weiss, H.M., Suckow, K., & Cropanzano, R. (1999). Effects of justice conditions on discrete emotions. *Journal of Applied Psychology, 84*(5), 786–794.

Winter, D.G., John, O.P., Stewart, A.J., Klohnen, E.C., & Duncan, L.E. (1998). Traits and motives: Toward and integration of two traditions in personality research. *Psychological Review, 105*, 230–250.

AFFILIATION

Anna Baumert
Department of Psychology
University of Koblenz-Landau
Landau, Germany

Tobias Rothmund
Department of Psychology
University of Koblenz-Landau
Landau, Germany

Nadine Thomas
Department of Psychology
University of Koblenz-Landau
Landau, Germany

Mario Gollwitzer
Department of Psychology
Philipps-University Marburg
Marburg, Germany
Manfred Schmitt
Department of PsychologyUniversity of Koblenz-Landau
Landau, Germany

JENS AGERSTRÖM & FREDRIK BJÖRKLUND

V. TEMPORAL CONSTRUAL AND MORAL MOTIVATION

INTRODUCTION

Since time is an integral part of human existence, people not only have to make judgments and decisions with moral implications in response to events that occur in the here and now. They also have to do so in response to events that are temporally remote. In referendums, for example, people are asked to vote for or against environmentally friendly reforms that, if gaining approval, would not go into effect until a time in the distant future. In daily life, people may be asked to schedule a blood donation appointment, for instance, or to sign up for charity work for some future time rather than the same day. In the judicial domain, jurors may have to make decisions about the guilt or innocence of a defendant who is being charged with a crime that took place several years ago.

Surprisingly, although temporal distance has been implicated in everyday psychological phenomena such as preference inconsistencies (see e.g., Ainslie & Haslam, 1992) and planning errors (see e.g., Buehler, Griffin, & Ross, 1994), until recently temporal distance has been overlooked in the study of morality. In the present chapter, we argue that the temporal distance of an event is a significant factor that influences people's willingness to endorse and act in accordance with moral ideals and values (moral motivation; Van Lange, 1999). It should be noted that, although we describe the same basic phenomenon, our conceptualization of moral motivation may differ somewhat from others in this volume. Our conceptualization is representative for the social cognitive theoretical approach that we adopt here. In this approach, values are typically viewed as motivational constructs that guide behaviour across a broad range of situations and contexts (e.g., Feather, 1990). Furthermore, we primarily describe experimental social psychological studies performed on an adult population. The measures of moral motivation related to this research may differ from those used in studies on children and adolescents, or in studies focusing on individual differences.

The chapter is organized as follows: First, we present Construal Level Theory (Trope & Liberman, 2003; 2010), which is the theoretical framework adopted in this chapter, along with research showing that temporally distant events are represented abstractly. Next, we discuss moral values as abstract motivational constructs and present the link between temporal distance and moral motivation. We continue by

K. Heinrichs, F. Oser & T. Lovat (Eds.), Handbook of Moral Motivation: Theories, Models, Applications, 181–194.

reviewing substantial research evidence, showing that temporal distance affects the extent to which people (1) construe an event as being morally relevant in the first place, (2) endorse morality by condemning moral transgressors and praising moral acts, and (3) are motivated to act morally and resist "moral temptations". Moreover, we discuss the role of mental construal and how moral values and temporal distance interplay to affect moral concerns. Before we conclude, we discuss important practical implications.

CONSTRUAL LEVEL THEORY

We propose that temporal inconsistencies in moral motivation can be understood in terms of Construal Level Theory (Trope & Liberman, 2003; 2010). Construal Level Theory (CLT) is a general theory of different kinds of psychological distance, including temporal (e.g., present vs. future), spatial (nearby vs. far away), social (e.g., self vs. others), and hypothetical distance (e.g., real vs. hypothetical events). The basic assumption of CLT is that psychologically distal objects and events are represented at a higher and more abstract level (high-level construals) than psychologically near objects and events, which are represented at a lower and more concrete level (low-level construals). High-level construals are perceptually poor and undifferentiated, whereas low-level construals are more immediate, and rich in contextual detail. When high-level construals are employed, superordinate, primary, and goal relevant concerns become more salient. In contrast, when low-level construals are adopted, subordinate, secondary, goal-irrelevant concerns become more prominent. In other words, the employment of high-level construals enables us to abstract the general meaning of an event and to perceive the essence of things, while the employment of low-level construals makes us focus on the incidental, peripheral details. As an analogy, Trope and Liberman (2003, p. 416) refer to visual objects. When they are further away, the main features are more prominent, but as they get nearer, the details are more prominent. From a distant perspective, we see the forest, but from a near perspective, we see the trees.

As touched upon above, we propose that temporal distance exerts its effect on moral motivation through level of mental construal. Thus, it seems appropriate to briefly review some research confirming that people indeed think more abstractly about distant-future than near-future objects and events.

EFFECTS OF TEMPORAL DISTANCE ON LEVEL OF ABSTRACTION

Actions can be identified at multiple levels of abstraction. For instance, "writing a book chapter" can be construed concretely as "pressing keys on a computer keyboard" or, alternatively, it can be represented in more abstract terms as "sharing ideas". The former is a low-level description of the activity in that it refers to *how* it is performed whereas the latter is a high-level description because it refers to *why* the activity is performed; that is, it conveys the overall meaning of the activity.

In order to examine the CLT prediction that greater temporal distance elicits more abstract mental processing, Liberman and Trope (1998) presented undergraduate students with a list of various activities and asked them to imagine themselves performing these activities either tomorrow or next year. The participants were then asked to choose which of two restatements best described these activities. As expected, they chose significantly more abstract (why) restatements than concrete (how) restatements when the activities were described as taking place in the distant as compared to the near future. In a related study objects (e.g., tent, toothbrush) intended for use in conjunction with a distant-future event (camping trip) were classified into a few broad (i.e., abstract) categories, whereas the same objects were classified into a greater number of narrower (i.e., concrete) categories when intended for use in conjunction with a near-future event (Liberman, Sagristano & Trope, 2002).

The aforementioned studies are only two examples from a larger research program demonstrating the impact of psychological distance on level of mental construal. Psychological distance has been found to affect other construal-level related outcomes, such as person perception (Nussbaum, Trope & Liberman, 2003), and complex behaviours such as problem solving (Förster, Friedman & Liberman, 2004), negotiation (Henderson, Trope & Carnevale, 2006), and persuasion (Fujita, Eyal, Chaiken, Trope & Liberman, 2008). Specifically, greater temporal distance leads to better solutions to abstract (vs. concrete) insight problems, negotiators to reach more integrative (vs. piecemeal) agreements and make fewer concessions on high-priority (vs. low-priority) issues, and people to attend to arguments that highlight primary (high-level) rather than incidental (low-level) features. With these findings in mind, let us now turn to the link between construal level and moral values.

MORAL VALUES AS ABSTRACT MOTIVATIONAL CONSTRUCTS

Moral values are typically viewed as higher-order constructs that guide behaviour across a broad range of situations and contexts (e.g., Trope & Liberman, 2003). Values are abstract representations about desired end states and are hierarchically organized according to their significance to the self (Feather, 1990; Torelli & Kaikati, 2009). In addition, they are motivational constructs which incorporate the beliefs that people have about desirable goals (Schwartz, 1990). Moral values differ with respect to their motivational content and the types of abstract goals that they are linked with (Torelli & Kaikati, 2009). For example, justice values (see e.g., Kohlberg, 1981) are associated with the abstract goal of treating other people impartially, whereas care values (see e.g., Gilligan, 1982) are connected to the abstract goal of looking out for the welfare of close others. According to Torelli and Kaikati (2009), moral values are motivational constructs that help define a situation (e.g., one where altruism is involved), activate goals (e.g., increase the welfare of other people), and guide action (e.g., donate blood at the hospital).

When an event is construed at a high rather than low level, moral values are more likely to be invoked insofar as they relate to the central meaning of the event in question. In contrast, a low-level construal of an action, which focuses on contextual details and concrete experiences, is likely to direct attention away from the values that may be relevant in the situation. For instance, when construed at a high level, a blood donation situation may be represented in terms of altruistic values as an opportunity to help other people. When construed at a low-level, however, the same event may be represented in terms of a painful needle stick. In other words, whether high- or low-level construals are employed in a given situation will influence how the situation is defined; that is, whether it is perceived as being value-relevant. If a person, akin to what has been called "moral sensitivity", perceives a situation as being morally relevant rather than devoid of moral implications, moral action is more likely to ensue.

THE LINK BETWEEN TEMPORAL DISTANCE AND MORAL MOTIVATION

Since it is widely established that people think more abstractly about temporally distant objects and events, and since moral values and principles constitute abstract, superordinate constructs that apply to a broad range of behaviours and situations, we propose that people will be more likely to express moral motivation in response to distant-future than near-future events. We specifically propose that in the initial chain of events people are more likely to construe distant-future versus near-future events and behaviours in high-level terms, i.e., as being morally relevant, rather than in terms of low-level contextual information. Defining the situations as having moral implications, in turn, should increase the likelihood that people become motivated to endorse moral values by, for instance, condemning those who break moral principles and praising those who uphold them. Moreover, because moral values and principles are more salient when high-level construals are employed, people should be more motivated to act in accordance with their moral ideals themselves when they consider temporally distant events.

Moral motivation is closely related to emotion. Moral emotions provide us with feedback as to whether our actions bring us closer to attaining our value-related goals or not. Moral emotions thus have an important action guiding role, and arguably constitute part of the thrust of moral motivation. As the current chapter concerns moral motivation in a temporal construal perspective, we have to ask ourselves what impact the moral emotions that we experience when contemplating future situations have on our motivation to act morally in the here and now. Our answer may appear counter intuitive; contemplation of temporally remote events should elicit *stronger* moral emotions than temporally closer events. In other words, to the extent that a person's current behaviour is guided by moral emotions related to future scenarios, the relative impact of moral motivation (as compared to other kinds of motivation) on our decisions should be stronger when we imagine distant as compared to close morally relevant situations. We next review and discuss the available research examining each of these propositions, respectively.

TEMPORAL DISTANCE AND CONSTRUAL OF MORAL EVENTS

Are temporally distant events more readily represented in moral terms than temporally near events? This question was addressed in a study where participants were presented with scenarios depicting a violation of a moral rule (Eyal, Liberman & Trope, 2008; Study 1). For example, one scenario depicted sexual intercourse between siblings, another depicted a family cooking and eating their own dead dog, and yet another described a person cleaning the toilet with the national flag. Each scenario also contained contextual details that mitigated the severity of the "taboo behaviour" (e.g., the fact that the siblings used contraceptives). As a manipulation of temporal distance, the participants imagined that the scenarios were to occur either in the near future (tomorrow) or in the distant future (next year). As a measure of construal level, participants were asked to choose which of two restatements that best described the action depicted in each scenario. One restatement pertained to an abstract moral principle (high-level construal) whereas the other referred to the concrete means of carrying out the action (low-level construal). For example, the restatements for the sibling scenario were "incest" (high-level) and "sexual intercourse between siblings" (low-level), and for the dog scenario they were "dishonoring a dead pet" (high-level) and "eating the meat of a dead dog" (low-level). Consistent with CLT, it was found that more high-level restatements were chosen when the participants envisioned that the events happened in the distant as compared to the near future. Put differently, distant-future situations were, to a larger extent, construed in terms of moral principles than near-future situations, which were more likely to be construed in concrete incidental terms. To the extent that level of abstraction is a factor behind the propensity to categorize events in terms of moral concerns, values that are relatively more abstract should be more influential with greater temporal distance. As these differences are relatively small the effects may be marginal and difficult to study, but preliminary evidence indicates that justice is affected more than care (Agerström, Björklund & Allwood, 2010).

The extent to which people attribute morally questionable actions to abstract personal dispositions rather than concrete situational factors is another indicator of level of mental construal (Nussbaum et al., 2003). When individuals attribute morally questionable actions to factors that have to do with the personality of the "moral transgressor" rather than situational forces and constraints, they are likely to perceive these actions as more immoral, and thus as being more morally charged. Agerström and Björklund (2009a) examined the prediction that temporally distant actions would be perceived as being more dispositionally caused than situationally caused by presenting Swedish undergraduates with ambiguous scenarios that were left to interpretation with respect to whether the protagonist had acted immorally. In one scenario, participants learned that a specific individual did not give to charity but not the reason for this. They were asked to indicate to what extent they believed that the protagonist's behaviour could be attributed to personal dispositions (e.g., selfishness) and situational factors (e.g., circumstance), respectively. Consistent with the assumption that temporally distant actions are construed as more morally relevant is the fact that people made more dispositional attributions of morally questionable behaviour when they adopted a distant-future as compared to a near-future time perspective. In other words, people perceived distant-future actions as being increasingly caused by a selfish personality, but perceived near-future actions as being increasingly caused by situational influences that were beyond the protagonist's control.

In another domain, Rogers and Bazerman (2008) examined whether public policy programs are represented more in terms of their abstract, superordinate purpose or more in terms of their concrete specific consequences when they are temporally distant versus temporally near. In one of their experiments, participants were presented with a "gas tax program" that would increase the price of gas. The program was said to be implemented either as soon as possible or in four years. Construal level was assessed by asking participants to list the consequences of the program. As would be expected by CLT, more high-level consequences (e.g., "impact on environment/ pollution") relative to low-level concrete consequences (e.g., "a change in dollars at the pump or in one's wallet") of the tax increase program were listed when it was to be implemented in the distant future.

Apparently, morally charged events are increasingly construed as being morally relevant when they are temporally distant as compared to close. As noted above, defining a situation as being a moral one is assumed to be important since it would seem more likely to motivate moral action.

TEMPORAL DISTANCE AND THE MOTIVATION TO BLAME MORAL TRANSGRESSORS

How individuals judge the moral status of other people's actions has been a major theme within moral psychology (Monin, Pizarro, & Beer, 2007). What influences people's motivation to condemn and punish moral misdeeds? Again, we argue that temporal distance matters. Given that moral values and principles are abstract psychological constructs that are more salient with greater temporal distance from an event, people should be more condemning of and more motivated to punish a moral transgressor when they imagine that these values or principles are being violated in the future.

This proposition has recently received empirical support in different moral domains. Eyal et al. (2008) examined whether widely recognized taboo behaviours are judged more harshly when they are temporally distant. The scenarios included contextual details that made the moral transgressions harmless. For instance, in the "incest scenario", the siblings used contraceptives and never told anyone about their sexual relationship. Participants imagined that the same taboo behaviours were either performed tomorrow or one year into the future, and as expected, taboo transgressions were evaluated more harshly when they were temporally distant.

Temporal distance influences the extent of blame in situations that are more commonplace too (Agerström, 2008; Agerström & Björklund, 2009a). In one scenario, participants read about a healthy Swedish citizen who did not bother to donate blood to the hospital during a blood shortage crisis. In another, they encountered a person who out of convenience and without any concern for the environment dumped household waste without recycling it. Asked to evaluate these morally questionable acts, participants attributed greater moral blame to the protagonist when they were imagined from a temporally distant perspective. Interestingly, individuals not only increasingly condemn other people's distant-future morally questionable behaviour, but they also judge their own questionable actions as being more immoral when these actions are temporally distant (Agerström & Björklund, 2009b). Notably, the same happens when people imagine their own actions from a distant (third-person) visual perspective as opposed to a proximal (first-person) perspective (Agerström, Björklund & Carlsson, in press).

Besides eliciting judgments of blame, distant-future morally questionable actions also invoke more anger than near-future morally questionable actions (Agerström & Björklund, 2009a). This is interesting, since emotions are typically seen as motivational processes that guide action.

In sum, temporal distance affects the endorsement of moral principles and how people judge the moral status of others' actions, across different moral domains. We now turn to the question of whether the effect holds for moral behaviour too.

TEMPORAL DISTANCE AND THE MOTIVATION TO ACT MORALLY

Some recent studies have examined whether temporal distance influences people's motivation to act in accordance with moral values and ideals. Agerström and Björklund (2009b) examined whether the temporal distance of an event would affect people's behavioural intentions in response to everyday "moral temptations" where subordinate selfish motives (low-level concerns) clashed with more superordinate altruistic motives (high-level concerns). In the "recycling dilemma", the participants were asked to envision themselves standing in the garbage disposal hovel (with no roof) outside his/her new apartment in the cold rain. They were told that they had forgotten to sort out their household garbage in a way that allowed for its contents to be easily thrown into their respective garbage bins, and that not bothering to sort the garbage into their appropriate bins would be extremely convenient. In other words, this situation consisted of highly concrete contextual features that served as lures (i.e., escaping from the cold rain) that conflicted with a more abstract moral motive (i.e., saving the environment for future generations). In another scenario, participants were asked to contemplate whether they would help a friend who was in desperate need of help to move out of his apartment (high-level concern), instead of spending the day outside in the wonderful weather relaxing (low-level concern). The participants were asked to indicate how they would have acted, and were found to be more willing to choose moral over selfish behaviour when the target event was temporally distant. The effects were interpreted as being related to the mental construal of the situation at hand. When a situation is construed abstractly, morally relevant constructs such as values are accessible and thus exert more influence on one's decisions and behaviour. When a situation is construed less abstractly, moral values tend to fade out of the picture. Other concerns may prevail, and result in weaker moral motivation.

Related research shows that people are more prone to make choices that serve the deliberate "should self" rather than the affective "want self" when these choices would be implemented in the distant versus near future (Rogers & Bazerman, 2008). For instance, participants were asked to complete a survey and specifically to indicate whether they would support (should decision) or oppose (want decision) a policy which, on the one hand would increase the price on fish for all consumers (low-level concern), but which, on the other, would protect the fish stocks in the oceans, as well as sustain the survival of the fishing industry (high-level concern). Consistent with our CLT-derived proposition, the policy was increasingly supported when it would be implemented in the distant as compared to the near future. This suggests that people would be more willing to commit to accept inconvenient laws (e.g., conservation laws that serve the "greater good") when these laws are pushed to distant dates.

People may experience emotional reactions to future events. If these events are to take place in the distant future, people can be expected to anticipate stronger moral emotions. This is the case since emotions that demand taking a socially distant perspective (e.g. guilt) are represented at a higher level of abstractness. Characteristics which are distal on both the temporal and social dimension fit with respect to level of abstractness, and when level of abstractness fits, anticipated emotional intensity should be higher (consistent with the regulatory fit perspective; Freitas & Higgins, 2002). Some recent experiments (Agerström, Björklund & Carlsson, 2012) corroborate that anticipated high-level and low-level emotions are affected differently by a temporal distance manipulation. For example, when imagining failing to sort the garbage in a distant-future version of the recycling dilemma mentioned above, the participants reported expecting stronger guilt but weaker pleasure than when imagining a near-future version of the same situation. Emotions are often assumed to guide behaviour, and there is no reason to believe that expected emotional experiences don't. Anticipated emotional reactions, particularly to distant future events, can be expected to involve moral emotions, and trigger the motivation to behave morally.

Arguably, the most convincing indicator of moral motivation is moral action. However, because we cannot measure behaviour that will happen in the future, research on temporal distance and moral "behaviour" typically has to rely on people's behavioural commitments. Consistent with the idea that people are more committed to act morally in response to distant-future events, Pronin, Olivola and Kennedy (2008) found that students are increasingly willing to commit to altruistic behaviour, sacrificing their own spare-time to help a student with academic difficulties, with greater temporal distance from the event. Similarly, people are more inclined to sign up for a short interview with a moral purpose (sustainability) when it is scheduled to take place in nine months as compared to next week (Agerström & Björklund, 2009b; Experiment 5).

The research reviewed in this section relies on research paradigms in which people encounter "moral temptations" and have to make decisions about whether to succumb to the motivation implied by the low-level value, which would provide short-term gratification, or to act in accordance with the motivation implied by the high-level value, which would be more appealing in the long term (e.g., keeping the atmosphere clean for future generations). This bears resemblance to the notion of self-control. The crucial distinction is that when people exercise "moral self-control" rather than "prototypical self-control", they act in accordance with higher-order goals that are other-oriented (e.g., helping others), and not self-oriented (e.g., resisting cookies in order to avoid becoming overweight).

THE MODERATING ROLE OF VALUE STRENGTH

It might be tempting to conclude that temporal distance increases moral concerns across the board. However, on the basis of CLT, moral aspects of behaviour should weigh more heavily in the distant future only if they are perceived as being superordinate in nature and linked to one's core values. Indeed, the boundaries of the temporal distance effect have been established in several studies. One such boundary is that people only make increasingly moral judgments and decisions insofar as they embrace the moral values implicated in the moral dilemma (Agerström & Björklund, 2009b; Experiment 2 & 3). Participants who saw environmental values as central and hedonistic values as more peripheral to their identity invested more money in a hypothetical environmental fund, despite low guaranteed money returns, when the decision was framed in the distant versus near future. In contrast, those individuals who did not regard the environmental values to be more important than the hedonistic values did not show this effect. In a similar vein, priming people with a future time perspective increases cooperative behaviour among individuals whose values reflect a pro-social but not pro-self motivational orientation (Giacomantonio, De Dreu, Shalvi, Sligte & Leder, 2010).

THE ROLE OF ABSTRACTION IN MORAL MOTIVATION

Thus far, we have looked at research that has manipulated abstraction indirectly by changing the temporal distance of the target event. However, more direct manipulations yield analogous effects on moral motivation. Furthermore, thinking about the abstract goals of a situation facilitates construing an action in terms of its relevant values, which subsequently facilitates the expression of these values through value-congruent behaviour. Indeed, central values predict corresponding behaviour better when people are induced with an abstract mindset (Torelli & Kaikati, 2009).

Thus, it appears that central values are more likely to guide intentions and behaviours when there is a large temporal distance to the target event, or when our thinking operates in an abstract mode. When no salient external constraints or opportunities are present, such as when people contemplate choices with distant future consequences, they should be increasingly likely to think schematically and ignore the context of the choice situation by focusing on core values and overarching goals. For example, the decision to accept a higher price on gas in the distant future is likely to reflect one's environmental values while the decision to do this in the near future is more likely to reflect specific situational factors, such as the financial situation one is in at the time of the decision. In other words, higher-order moral values may become primary guides for responding to distant-future situations, whereas low-level specifics of the situation are likely to be salient and guide near-future actions.

Given the experimental evidence above that abstract construal (paired with moral values) leads to stronger moral motivation, one would suspect that people who are inclined to think abstractly would also be more motivated to do the right thing. The role of individual differences in level of mental construal is currently understudied in moral psychology. Although the well known developmental work of Kohlberg is clearly related, it differs in that it regards level of justice related reasoning rather than level of abstraction. Tentative evidence that the propensity to construe objects and events in an abstract way matters for moral motivation comes from a study by Levy, Freitas & Salovey (2002), showing that people who tend to construe abstractly also are more willing to help the needy. To the extent that men and women represent moral values at different levels of abstraction, there may be individual differences related to gender too, not least regarding justice and care (Agerström, Björklund & Allwood, 2010).

PRACTICAL IMPLICATIONS

The findings discussed in this chapter have clear practical implications. The facilitating effect of temporal distance on moral concerns suggests that one way in which motivation to perform moral actions can be enhanced is by having people in advance commit to moral courses of action that will not be performed until some later point in time. As seems to have been noticed by charity organizations, money donations to people in need could probably be increased by using a direct debit system. People's decisions whether or not to commit to this type of behaviour should be more influenced by moral values and less influenced by practical considerations and selfish temptations when the monetary consequences will not be felt until later. Similarly, governments may also be more successful in getting their citizens to make "painful" concessions in the name of the greater good if they will not be materialized until the distant future. For instance, they may be more likely to reduce carbon monoxide emissions in the long run if people can be convinced to accept today a substantial tax increase on gas that will not take effect until let's say two years into the future. Convincing people to accept an immediate tax increase would arguably be a more difficult endeavor.

Although only touched upon briefly in this chapter, recent research shows that abstract high-level moral emotions (e.g., guilt, shame) are experienced with greater intensity than are concrete low-level visceral drives (e.g., pleasure) and emotions (e.g., sadness) when people anticipate their reactions to temporally distant events (Agerström, Björklund & Carlsson, 2012). It is possible then that anticipated emotions are an important mediator between values and decision making, especially for events that differ in temporal distance. Future research could test whether manipulation of anticipated pride, shame and guilt is a useful tool for influencing pro-social behavioural decisions (e.g. in charity drives). Both the anticipated pride of contributing and the anticipated guilt of not contributing should loom larger for charitable activities that take place in the future. Emphasizing the high-level emotional benefits of doing the right thing may increase the inclination to commit to future donations and pro-social behaviour since such decisions are based not only on what we currently believe and feel, but also on what we anticipate feeling. It might also be useful as a tool to increase self-control, where higher-level construals have been shown to increase the adoption of both immediate (Magen & Gross, 2007; Schmeichel & Vohs, 2009) and prospective (Fujita & Roberts, 2010) self-control strategies.

The finding that people are more condemning of others' moral infractions when they adopt a distant-future time perspective may have implications for the justice system. Judges, for instance, may mete out sentences that are less stringent than the laws actually prescribe (see Carlsmith, 2008 for related research). After all, when laws are written by legislators they are, along with the punishment prescribed by them, abstractly construed. Furthermore, because laws tend to be abstract and general in nature, judges may not follow the law completely when deciding on real cases in which a great deal of specific contextual information that may be mitigating in nature suddenly enters the picture. Insofar as mitigating contextual information is given more weight when the future becomes 'now', which the research reviewed in this section clearly suggests, actual sentences may be less severe than the law prescribes. Moreover, it has been found that the greater the perceived retrospective distance from an event, the greater is the propensity to blame parties (e.g., a company) for negative events (Kyung, Menon & Trope, 2010). Hence, it is possible that the temporal distance between when a crime was committed and the time of the jury's deliberation could affect the severity of the verdict, with crimes committed in the distant past resulting in more severe verdicts. To demonstrate that temporal distance plays a significant role in applied settings is an important topic for future research.

CONCLUSION

The research reviewed in this chapter shows that temporal distance influences various aspects of moral motivation and that temporal inconsistencies in moral motivation can be understood in terms of Construal Level Theory. Not only does this research confirm a theoretical assumption, it may also have significant applied value in contexts ranging from fundraising to the court. If people move beyond their immediate experiences by doing a little bit of mental time travelling, moral behaviour may ensue.

ACKNOWLEDGEMENT

We are grateful to the Crafoord Foundation for supporting the writing of this chapter (grant no. 20091016).

REFERENCES

Agerström, J. (2008). *Temporal distance and morality: Moral concerns loom larger for temporally distant events* (Unpublished doctoral dissertation). Lund University, Sweden.

Agerström, J., & Björklund, F. (2009a). Temporal distance and moral concerns: Future morally questionable behavior is perceived as more wrong and evokes stronger prosocial intentions. *Basic and Applied Social Psychology, 31*, 49–59.

Agerström, J., & Björklund, F. (2009b). Moral concerns are greater for temporally distant events and are moderated by value strength. *Social Cognition, 27*, 261–282.

Agerström, J., Björklund, F., & Allwood, C.M. (2010). The influence of temporal distance on justice and care morality. *Scandinavian Journal of Psychology, 51*, 46–55.

Agerström, J., Björklund, F., & Carlsson, R. (in press). Look at yourself!: Visual perspective influences moral judgment through level of mental construal. *Social Psychology.*

Agerström, J., Björklund, F., & Carlsson, R. (2012). Emotions in time: Moral emotions appear more intense with temporal distance. *Social Cognition, 30*, 181–198.

Ainslie, G., & Haslam, N. (1992). Hyperbolic discounting.In G. Loewenstein & J. Elster (Eds.), *Choice over time* (pp. 57–92). New York: Russell Sage Foundation.

Buehler, R., Griffin, D., & Ross, M. (1994). Exploring the "planning fallacy": Why people underestimate their task completion times. *Journal of Personality and Social Psychology, 67*, 366–381.

Carlsmith, K.M. (2008). On justifying punishment: The discrepancy between words and actions. *Social Justice Research, 21*, 119–137.

Eyal, T., Liberman, N., & Trope, Y. (2008). Judging near and distant virtue and vice. *Journal of Experimental Social Psychology, 44*, 1204–1209.

Feather, N.T. (1990). Bridging the gap between values and actions: Recent applications of the expectancy-value model. In T.E. Higgins & R.M. Sorrentino (Eds.), *Handbook of motivation and cognition: Foundations of social behavior* (Vol. 2, pp. 151–192). New York: Guilford Press.

Freitas, A.L. & Higgins, E.T. (2002). Enjoying goal-directed action: The role of regulatory fit. *Psychological Science, 13*, 1–6.

Fujita, K., & Roberts, J.C. (2010). Promoting prospective self-control through abstraction. *Journal of Experimental Social Psychology, 46*, 1049–1054.

Fujita, K., Eyal, T., Chaiken, S., Trope, Y., &Liberman, N. (2008). Influencing attitudes toward near and distant objects. *Journal of Experimental Social Psychology, 44*, 562–572.

Förster, J., Friedman, R.S., & Liberman, N. (2004). Temporal construal effects on abstract and concrete thinking: Consequences for insight and creative cognition. *Journal of Personality and Social Psychology, 87*, 177–189.

Giacomantonio, M., De Dreu, K.W., Shalvi, S., Sligte, D., & Leder, S. (2010). Psychological distance boosts value-behavior correspondence in ultimatum bargaining and integrative negotiation. *Journal of Experimental Social Psychology, 46*, 824–830.

Gilligan, C. (1982). *In a different voice.* Cambridge, MA.: Harvard University Press.

Henderson, M.D., Trope, Y., & Carnevale, P.J. (2006). Negotiation from a near and distant time perspective. *Journal of Personality and Social Psychology, 91*, 712–729.

Kohlberg, L. (1981). *The philosophy of moral development: Moral stages and the idea of justice.* San Francisco: Harper & Row.

Kyung, E.J., Menon, G., & Trope, Y. (2010). Reconstruction of things past: Why do some memories feel so close and others so far away. *Journal of Experimental Social Psychology, 46*, 217–220.

Levy, S.R., Freitas, A.L., & Salovey, P. (2002). Construing action abstractly and blurring social distinctions: Implications for perceiving homogeneity among, but also empathizing with and helping, others. *Journal of Personality and Social Psychology, 83*, 1224–1238.

Liberman, N., Sagristano, M., & Trope, Y. (2002). The effect of temporal distance on level of construal. *Journal of Experimental Social Psychology, 38*, 523–535.

Liberman, N., & Trope, Y. (1998). The role of feasibility and desirability considerations in near and distant future decisions: A test of temporal construal theory. *Journal of Personality and Social Psychology, 75*, 5–18.

Magen, E., & Gross, J.J. (2007). Harnessing the need for immediate gratification: Cognitive reconstrual modulates the reward value of temptations. *Emotion, 7*, 415–428.

Monin, B., Pizarro, D., & Beer, J. (2007). Deciding vs. reacting: Conceptions of moral judgment and the reason-affect debate. *Review of General Psychology, 11*, 99–111.

Nussbaum, S., Trope, Y., & Liberman, N. (2003). Creeping dispositionism: The temporal dynamics of behavior prediction. *Journal of Personality and Social Psychology, 84*, 485–497.

Pronin, E., Olivola, C.Y., & Kennedy, K.A. (2008). Doing unto future selves as you would unto others: Psychological distance and decision making. *Personality and Social Psychology Bulletin, 34*, 224–236.

Rogers, T. & Bazerman, M.H. (2008). Future lock-in: Future implementation increases selection of 'should' choices. *Organizational Behavior and Human Decision Processes, 106*, 1–20.

Schmeichel, B.J., & Vohs, K. (2009). Self-affirmation and self-control: Affirming core values counteracts ego depletion. *Journal of Personality and Social Psychology, 96*, 770–782.

Schwartz, S.H. (1990). Individualism-collectivism: Critique and proposed refinements. *Journal of Cross-Cultural Psychology, 21*, 139–157.

Torelli, C.J. & Kaikati, A.M. (2009). Values as predictors of judgments and behaviors: The role of abstract and concrete mindsets. *Journal of Personality and Social Psychology, 96*, 231–247.

Trope, Y., & Liberman, N. (2003). Temporal construal. *Psychological Review, 110*, 403–421.

Trope, Y., & Liberman, N. (2010). Construal-level theory of psychological distance. *Psychological Review, 117*, 440–463.

Van Lange, P.A.M. (1999). The pursuit of joint outcomes and equality in outcomes: An integrative model of social value orientation. *Journal of Personality and Social Psychology, 77*, 337–349.

AFFILIATIONS

Jens Agerström
Department of Psychology
Lund University
Lund, Sweden

Fredrik Björklund
Department of Psychology
Lund University
Lund, Sweden

PART 3

MORAL SELF, IDENTITY AND MORAL MOTIVATION

The moral self is more than a moral judgment; that is why a prime issue that MM deals with concerns the compliance of self and external demands. Well-known approaches try to point to personal determinants which are considered helpful in explaining why people become intrinsically motivated to act in line with their own moral judgment often against moral norms and values. Encouraged by Blasi's publications (1983), many authors assume that indeed the self has to be brought into equilibrium with the felt necessity to act or to be committed to act morally. Exploring how the moral self can be conceptualized, many authors refer to exemplars conceptualized and studied from a developmental as well as in an action-oriented perspective.

Walker's studies on moral exemplars provide empirical evidence that the moral maturity of outstanding people indicates that promoting the interests of others can be fundamentally enhancing the self as well. Walker claims that communion and agency can be brought together precisely within the concept of moral motivation,

Krettenauer is studying the development of the moral self as an integration of self and morality quite early in development. This early integration gives rise to a minimal moral self that later is extended into more comprehensive forms. The moral self claims explicate differentiation and integration of specific motivational processes relevant for moral behaviour.

Blasi, in this paper, does not extend his conception of the moral self as being fruitful for bridging the judgment-action-gap in, encouraging rather the exploration of individual strategies by which to manage one's own moral life and functioning. He proclaims self-regulation abilities to be helpful for becoming an individual who is autonomous in moral issues.

Lovat presents theological and philosophical literature, as well as human sciences, in explicating how self-knowing and self-reflection, including in the context of spirituality and mysticism, can become a source of moral motivation that is stable over time.

LAWRENCE J. WALKER

I. MORAL MOTIVATION THROUGH THE PERSPECTIVE OF EXEMPLARITY

INTRODUCTION

Why be good? This simple question, so profoundly important for human existence, has befuddled thinkers across the ages (Richter, 2007). It remains an enigma for the field of moral psychology, as evidenced by the mere existence of the present volume and the diversity of perspectives proffered herein. What engenders and sustains morally appropriate behaviour? What is the nature and source of moral motivation? Answers to these sorts of questions reflect our conceptualization of the moral domain, our understanding of the psychological processes that explain moral functioning, and the efficacy of our endeavors to foster moral development through socialization and education. So much hinges on this issue of moral motivation.

Many scholars in the field of moral psychology have attempted to address this issue of moral motivation, but, in my view, have come up short on a viable resolution. The cognitive-developmental perspective, long regnant in the field, is illustrative in this regard. The cognitive revolution in psychology, beginning in the 1960s, trumpeted the significance and salience of cognition in human functioning. Thus, in moral psychology, the focus was on moral judgment (Kohlberg, 1969; Piaget, 1932/1977; Rest, 1979; Turiel, 1983), which was assumed to be auto-motivating, reflecting the Platonic adage that to know the good is to do the good. Moral development entailed ideally transitioning from an egocentric self-interested orientation to more conventional understandings and then to a principled orientation, one which required that we universalize our judgments and blind ourselves to our interests. However, this claim of the auto-motivating power of moral judgment fell on empirical hard times with the accumulating evidence demonstrating that moral cognition only weakly predicts moral action (Blasi, 1980; Walker, 2004; Walker & Frimer, 2007), what would become known as the judgment-action gap.

The cognitive-developmental perspective was hardly the sole contender. Other theories of moral motivation have also been put forth. Noteworthy among them are the explanatory constructs of prosociality and empathy (for example, as advanced by de Waal, 2009; Eisenberg, 2005; Hoffman, 2000). These notions imply that promoting the interests of others and responding to their needs are prior to one's own interests which, somehow, should be set aside.

K. Heinrichs, F. Oser & T. Lovat (Eds.), Handbook of Moral Motivation: Theories, Models, Applications, 197–214.

Bluntly put, the problem with all of these approaches to moral motivation is that they require one to act out of drear duty, onerous obligation, and selfless sacrifice – and against one's natural inclinations and personal interests. So wherein, in these approaches, is the motivation to act morally? It seems to be vacuous and inert. The fundamental failure inherent in these approaches is their presumption that morality should not be self-regarding, that there is no moral credit in promoting the self's interests. This does not seem to be a psychologically realistic conception.

Flanagan (1991, 2009) has a couple of helpful insights on this issue. First, he notes that people are indeed partial to their own interests, projects, and commitments, all of which impart meaning to life, and that such meaning is integral to morality (perhaps referencing a more eudaimonic, Aristotelian view of the moral domain). And second, Flanagan holds that, for any moral theory to be viable, it must explain the motivational functioning for the actualization of its posited ideals and that such functioning must be psychologically feasible "for creatures like us" (1991, p. 48). If Flanagan's arguments prevail, then we need to provide an account of moral functioning that is based on a psychologically realistic motivational mechanism. In contradistinction to many extant notions, the argument I proffer in this chapter is that morality can, and indeed should be, self-regarding. And I will provide empirical evidence, through a series of studies, that such a motivational mechanism is clearly evident in moral maturity, in the functioning of moral exemplars.

This argument heralds a turn to notions of personality and motivation in moral psychology, explanatory concepts that have long been eschewed (as indicated, for example, by Kohlberg's, 1981, dismissive comments regarding the "bag of virtues" and by Turiel's, 1983, hiving off of the personal from the moral domain). The psychological maneuver explored in this chapter is the appropriation of morality into one's identity and personality. This maneuver is such that one's (self-enhancing) personal interests and fulfillment are accomplished through the (self-transcending) promotion of the interests and needs of others. This notion flies in the face of the conventional understandings of motivation and of relationships which imply that self-advancement is typically enacted at the expense of others and that other-promotion is, in significant ways, costly to the self. The psychological maneuvre I propose transforms this duality.

THE PERSPECTIVE OF EXEMPLARITY

This examination of moral motivation has been largely undertaken in our program of research through the perspective of moral exemplarity – through an analysis of the lives of exceptional people who have demonstrated some noteworthy measure of moral excellence.

There are several reasons to focus on exemplars (Walker, 2002). One is that the research involves an examination of the psychological functioning of people who have engaged in extraordinary moral action that has real-world significance (in contrast to inconsequential experimental manipulations of moral behaviour in the lab). Another is that the use of "extreme" groups (such as contrasting extraordinary moral exemplars with ordinary folk) magnifies processes of moral functioning, allowing them to be more clearly identified. A third justification is that conducting person-level analyses of the lives of exemplars may yield more holistic understandings of the complexities and interrelationships among aspects of moral functioning (Dunlop, Walker & Matsuba, 2012). Fourth, this focus facilitates a more meaningful examination of the psychological functioning that characterizes the endpoint of moral development and whether such functioning can take different forms – which, of course, informs the ethical ideals that are assumed in our models of moral motivation. Fifth, the psychological maneuver I propose here should be most clearly evident in moral maturity, so a focus on exemplars would seem to be the optimal launching-point. And, finally, this represents a "reverse-engineering" enterprise wherein the initial phase is analyzing, in detail, the workings of the "finished product," and then working backwards to figure out the processes operative in its development.

ALIGNMENT OF MORALITY WITH THE SELF

Perhaps the central theme of this emerging interest in moral motivation has been the alignment of morality with the self. Both Blasi (1983, 1984) and Damon (1984) posited the self as the central explanatory concept in moral functioning. Among other notions they advanced (including self-consistency, personal responsibility, and willpower), the one sparking the most empirical attention (Walker, in press) is *moral centrality* – the extent to which morality is central to one's sense of self. In contrast to Erikson's (1968) view that identity is constructed primarily around issues of occupational choice and political ideology, Blasi and Damon contended that self-identity could also be framed by moral considerations and awareness, and that the extent to which morality was central to the self would help to explain moral motivation. If morality has been, to a considerable extent, appropriated to the self, then acting on such concerns would be self-enhancing, whereas failing to do so would be self-denying.

The now-classic study of moral exemplars was conducted by Colby and Damon (1992). Their first, and not inconsequential, challenge was in identifying moral exemplars (no easy task given the adage that one person's saint is often another's scoundrel). So they had a diverse group of ethical experts formulate a set of explicit criteria defining moral exemplarity and then nominate people who met these criteria. Colby and Damon's case-study analysis of a small sample of these nominated exemplars indicated several features of mature moral development including: considerable certainty about moral values and principles which was tempered by openness to new insights and adherence to truth; a continual process of, and capacity for, change; and a personality embodying positivity, humility, unremitting love, and an underlying faith. However, the feature of mature moral development that most impressed Colby and Damon was that these moral exemplars had a coherent identity that meaningfully fused the personal and the moral aspects of their lives. Exemplars had appropriated morality into their identity such that they garnered personal fulfillment from pursuing their extraordinarily prosocial concerns, while rejecting any implication that their actions arose from a sense of duty, obligation, or sacrifice.

Other notable qualitative research has similarly, at least in some respects, intimated the integration of personal and moral concerns in the lives of different types of moral exemplars, including Holocaust rescuers, Carnegie and military heroes, philanthropists, hospice volunteers, and so on (Monroe, 2002; Oliner, 2003; Oliner & Oliner, 1988). The rarity of such exemplars (by definition) has contributed to the reliance on qualitative research methodology. Although many heuristic insights have been generated by such research, the lack of objective methodology, broadband assessments of psychological functioning, and appropriate comparison groups makes valid and reliable inferences about processes of moral development rather tenuous. The methods of psychological science have much to commend themselves in this regard. It is to our recent program of research on these issues, backed by these methods,– that we now turn.

DISPOSITIONS VERSUS SITUATIONS

A fundamental assumption underlying our program of research (as well as much of that contained in this volume) is that dispositional motivations – aspects of character – are causally operative in moral action. But this assumption has not gone unchallenged. Indeed, within social psychology (Doris, 2002; Harman, 2009; Zimbardo, 2007), a contrary perspective has been advanced which contends that it is primarily situational forces in the environment, operating on otherwise ordinary people, that instigate moral behaviour. In this *situational perspective*, contextual factors potently function to induce action and then, in a post hoc fashion, individuals may script accounts of their motivation to bring them into alignment with their behaviour. As a consequence, the situational perspective denies any causal significance for dispositional factors in moral action.

In contrast, in the *dispositional perspective*, motivational factors, reflecting aspects of individuals' developing character, are responsible for initiating and sustaining moral behaviour (Flanagan, 2009; McAdams, 2009). It should be apparent that the situational perspective represents a full-frontal challenge to the framing of this chapter and so warrants some consideration.

Walker, Frimer, and Dunlop (2010) examined the viability of the construct of causally operative moral motivation. To do this, they conducted a cluster analysis (a statistical grouping procedure that identifies similar cases), based on a comprehensive set of personality variables, of a sample of Canadian award recipients who had been recognized for some kind of exemplary moral action (specifically, long-term caring service or exceptional bravery in rescuing another), and then compared the resultant clusters to matched comparison participants.

The situational perspective makes the straightforward prediction that the moral exemplars will not meaningfully differ from comparison participants in their motivational and personality functioning given its presumption that it is contextual factors that are causally operative.

The dispositional perspective, in contrast, contends that exemplars will differ from comparison participants in their personality – that the construct of moral motivation is a viable one – but there are variations in the predictions regarding both the number and nature of such personality dispositions. One variant is Aristotle's (trans. 1962; Watson, 1984) notion of the unity-of-the-virtues, which implies a functional, psychological interdependence among various aspects of personality such that a single cluster of exemplars should materialize with its cases being exemplary on the full array of morally relevant variables (which should hang together). Another variant is Kohlberg's (1981) notion of the primacy of principles of justice, which also implies a single cluster of exemplars but its cases should be exemplary on the one variable of moral reasoning. And, a final variant is Flanagan's (1991) notion of varieties of moral personality – that moral excellence can take qualitatively different forms – which implies that multiple clusters will emerge, each distinctive and partial in its personality composition.

The analysis of the personalities of moral exemplars undertaken by Walker et al. (2010) indicated that a three-cluster solution best fit the data, with these clusters characterized as follows: (a) a *communal* cluster (marked by dispositional traits of nurturance, relational and generative goal motivation, and themes of communion in life stories – all reflective of prosocial emotionality and interrelatedness); (b) a *deliberative* cluster (marked by dispositional traits of openness to experience, goal motivation for personal growth, and advanced epistemic and moral reasoning. reflective of a broad worldview and thoughtfulness); and (c) an *ordinary* cluster (marked by banal personality functioning in contrast to other exemplars and indistinguishable from matched comparison participants – uniformly unremarkable in personality).

So what does this pattern of findings imply? That multiple clusters emerged from the analysis substantiates Flanagan's (1991) notion that there are different types of moral excellence – themes of social interdependence versus themes of thoughtful meaning-making and personal growth – and undermines Aristotle's (trans. 1962) and Kohlberg's (1981) notions that moral excellence must take a singular form.

Regarding the competing explanations of the dispositional and situational perspectives, the distinctive personality profiles of the communal and deliberative clusters accord with the dispositional perspective, but the commonplace personality profile of the ordinary cluster better fits the situational perspective. A closer examination of the membership of these clusters offers a clue to appropriate interpretation. The ordinary cluster was predominantly comprised of bravery award recipients who had risked their lives in rescuing another. The other two clusters were predominantly comprised of caring award recipients who had engaged in long-term volunteer service. The differing composition of these clusters suggests that one-off heroic action may often be instigated by the powerful contextual factors operating in emergency (or strong) situations, whereas a career of moral engagement may reflect sustained dispositional factors of moral motivation. Astutely, Fleeson (2004) contends that both of these competing positions on the person × situation issue have merit: The situational perspective may better account for single, momentary behaviours but the dispositional account may better explain long-term behavioural trends.

FOUNDATIONAL CORE OF MORAL FUNCTIONING

Our interest in this chapter is on the motivational aspects of the moral personality, so the question presents itself: What are the foundational core variables to which we should primarily attend? This issue of the "psychological essentia" of moral functioning was the focus of Walker and Frimer's (2007) study of moral exemplarity.

To provide a fair test of what constitutes this foundational core, the research enterprise needed to start with a comprehensive and broadband assessment of psychological functioning. The study employed multiple measures (including several personality inventories and an extensive life-review interview which could be coded for a variety of psychological themes), tapping all three levels of personality description (McAdams, 1995, 2009): (a) *dispositional traits* (broad and decontextualized dimensions of personality); (b) *characteristic adaptations* (motivational, strategic, and developmental aspects of personality that are more particular to contexts and social roles), and (c) *integrative life narratives* (the psychosocial construction of a personal identity that imparts unity, purpose, and meaning in life). As will become evident in what follows, assessing moral motivation in terms of characteristic adaptations and integrative life narratives, in particular, has been especially informative, speaking to the heuristic value of a multi-level typology of personality functioning.

Walker and Frimer (2007) assessed the personality functioning of two quite different types of moral exemplars (brave vs. caring, as mentioned earlier). These exemplars were national award recipients who were demographically matched with comparison participants drawn from the general community. Analyses focused on the aspects of personality that were shared by the brave and caring exemplar groups and that also distinguished them from the comparison participants – the "psychological essentia" of moral functioning. The same pattern of exceptional personality functioning was found for several personality variables: both agentic and communal motivation, themes of redemption (the tendency to construe life events such that some benefit is discerned out of adversity), and formative relationships in childhood as evidenced by the spontaneous recall of secure attachments and the involvement of "helpers" who fostered development. These aspects of personality, common to disparate types of moral exemplarity, suggest their centrality in mature moral functioning and its development.

The early life experiences identified in this research speak to the developmental roots of prosocial moral concern (Walker & Frimer, 2011), particularly the significance of secure relationships and influential mentors. Redemptive themes identified by Walker and Frimer's (2007) research reflect the tendency to positively reframe ("redeem") negative life events and to exude pervasive (albeit not delusional) optimism. McAdams (2006) has demonstrated that the redemptive framing of life events represents a particularly adaptive coping strategy. But perhaps the most intriguing finding is that both types of exemplars expressed strong themes of *both* agency and communion in their life stories (and not simply that brave exemplars primarily evidenced agentic motivation and caring exemplars, communal motivation). Agency and communion are typically conceptualized as competing motives. That these disparate types of moral exemplars evidenced pronounced levels of *both* agency and communion – the fundamental duality of human existence (Bakan, 1966) – may be particularly informative of the motivation that underlies exemplary moral action. Have moral exemplars somehow reconciled the antagonism in motivational functioning between self-interested agency and other-promoting communion? So perhaps these are the core variables to which our attention should be focused.

AGENCY AND COMMUNION RECONCILED?

The dominant themes that pervade the study of motivation are agency and communion (Bakan, 1966; McAdams, 1988) – "getting ahead" and "getting along," respectively (Hogan, 1982). Agency represents the self-enhancing aspects of motivation, dispositions that individuate and advance the self, whereas communion represents the other-enhancing aspects, dispositions that contribute to social cohesion. Therefore, it is not surprising that these motivations are typically conceptualized as mutually interfering and oppositional.

This conceptualization is illustrated by Schwartz's (1992) values paradigm which places the agentic values of power and achievement in conceptual and empirical opposition to the communal values of benevolence and universalism. Power motivation focuses on control or status over people and the attainment of material wealth, whereas achievement focuses on personal success through demonstrating competence. Power and achievement are self-enhancing values. In contrast, benevolence focuses on concern for the welfare of others in everyday interactions, whereas universalism focuses on understanding, appreciating, and promoting the welfare of people beyond the primary reference group and for nature. Benevolence and universalism are self-transcending values that advance the interests of others. Thus, Schwartz (1992) argues that the "acceptance of others as equals and concern for their welfare *interferes* with the pursuit of one's own relative success and dominance over others" (p. 15, emphasis added). And, indeed, Schwartz's evidence is that endorsement of one set of values comes at the "expense" of the opposing set.

The view that these dual motives are mutually interfering has had widespread acceptance as evidenced, for example, by Horney's (1937) and Angyal's (1941) now-classic theorizing, by Bellah, Madsen, Sullivan, Swidler, and Tipton's (1985) social commentary, and by Oser, Schmid, and Hattersley's (2006) findings regarding the "unhappy moralist" who pits morality against success. And, certainly, in naturalistic conceptions of morality (Hardy, Walker, Olsen, Skalski & Basinger, 2011; Walker & Hennig, 2004; Walker & Pitts, 1998), the primary dimension capturing ordinary understandings has self-focused concerns at one pole and other-focused concerns at the other pole, representing the apparent antagonism between agency and communion.

However, recent theorizing has begun to explore the adaptive qualities of conceptualizing the relationship between agency and communion as in some sense synergistic, rather than interfering (Blasi, 2004; Colby & Damon, 1992; McAdams, 1993; Wiggins, 1995). Particularly relevant is Frimer and Walker's (2009) reconciliation model that provides a developmental reframing of the relationship between agency and communion in moral functioning – that is, it proposes that the relationship between agency and communion changes dramatically over the course of development. In this model, each of these competing motivations is held to develop in relative segregation throughout childhood and adolescence until their evolving strength and salience provokes a head-butting dis-equilibrating crisis, typically in early adulthood.

This tension can be reduced, and often is, by abandoning one motivation in favour of the other. The attenuation of communion results in *unmitigated agency* – the unbridled pursuit of power and achievement for its own sake. Unmitigated agency is often viewed as a problematic life orientation ("the villain," according to Bakan, 1966, p. 14). Another resolution is the attenuation of agency (much rarer in contemporary societies), resulting in *unmitigated communion*. Unmitigated communion entails relatively enervated personality functioning and is seemingly rather benign. Thus, it is typical early in the lifespan and indeed later among many adults for these motives to function dualistically – segregated initially and then unfettered later (with one motive dominating in behaviour and the other atrophied). These unmitigated forms of resolution represent stagnations in the developmental process.

However, the reconciliation model proposes another resolution of the evolving tension between these two motives wherein the psychological maneuver is their meaningful *integration*. Thus, the model points to a developmental transformation of the relationship between these two fundamental motives; from an early state of independence to a mature state of synergistic interdependence wherein, for example, the motivation for self-enhancement and fulfillment is readily accomplished by advancing the welfare of others. This maneuver represents the appropriation of prosocial moral concerns to the self. The notion of an integrated personality that reconciles agency and communion has greater potential to explain the developmental roots of moral motivation than those conceptual frameworks that regard them as irredeemably at loggerheads because it imparts realistic motivational oomph to moral action. The self has a meaningful stake in morality.

Thus, the reconciliation model predicts that moral exemplars will evidence the synergistic integration of agency and communion – of reconciling the interests of self and others in some variant of enlightened self-interest. This prediction resonates with Blasi's (1983, 1984) and Damon's (1984) theorizing regarding the appropriation of morality to the self and with Colby and Damon's (1992) impression that their moral exemplars had come to fuse their moral concerns with their personal ambitions. However, solid empirical evidence of such a synergistic integration of agency and communion has, until recently, not been available. A synergistic interaction generates a total effect that is greater than the sum of its constituent parts. It is to an examination of such research that we now turn.

THE QUEST FOR THE HOLY GRAIL OF INTEGRATION

Recall the finding in Walker and Frimer's (2007) study that moral exemplars evidenced clearly accentuated themes of both agency and of communion relative to comparison participants, suggesting that both motives are strongly operative. While exemplars are considerably more motivated in general than ordinary folk (they are both more agentic and more communal), the question remains: Is there evidence of some synergistic interaction between these two motives, as predicted by the reconciliation model?

To examine this question, Walker and Frimer (2007) conducted a logistic regression analysis, predicting group status (exemplar vs. comparison) on the basis of these two motives. In the first step of the analysis, both agency and communion were entered as baseline control variables; and then, in the second step, their (statistical) interaction was entered to determine whether or not it would improve predictability of group classification. Contrary to expectations, the interaction term did not significantly add to the predictive ability of the regression equation. That is, although both agency and communion made strong, independent contributions to moral exemplarity, there was no evidence of a synergistic interactive effect between them.

Puzzled by this null finding, Frimer, Walker, Dunlop, Lee, and Riches (2011) revisited the issue, searching for evidence of some synergistic integration between agency and communion among exemplars. Their focus was on the caring exemplars from Walker and Frimer's (2007) study, given the evidence that those exemplars were more distinguished in their moral personality than the brave exemplars.

First, they reconsidered the analytic approach for assessing interactions. Walker and Frimer (2007) had examined the statistical interaction between agency and communion using the traditional variable-level approach. But this approach cannot distinguish between qualitatively different patterns of motivation (even though the overall amount of agency and communion may be equal): in one pattern, the individual vacillates between one motive and the other, keeping them compartmentalized and far from integrated in self-understanding; the other pattern, in comparison, reflects a meaningful integration with the two motives coordinated and woven together in thought. In contrast to the variable-level analytic strategy, the person-level approach (Magnusson, 1999) is sensitive to this distinction as it is able to assess integration within each individual by quantifying the phenomenologically real co-occurrence of agency and communion within the same thought structure.

In Frimer et al.'s (2011) study, agency and communion were assessed in the context of a life-review interview which had several sections (including chapters of the life story and critical life events). In the within-person analytic strategy, the interaction between agency and communion is reflected by the co-occurrence of these motives within sections of the interview that deal with the same topic (rather than being based on the overall strength of each variable, as in the variable-level approach). However, Frimer et al.'s re-analysis indicated that, even when using the person-level analytic approach, there was no evidence of greater integration of agency and communion among exemplars than comparisons.

Not to be thwarted, however, Frimer et al. (2011) revisited the integration issue by considering the conceptualization of agency and communion. In Walker and Frimer's (2007) original analysis, agency and communion had been coded based on McAdams's (1993, 2001; McAdams, Hoffman, Mansfield & Day, 1996) definitions and coding system. There is considerable variability within the field of personality in how these fundamental motives are construed and defined (Paulhus & Trapnell, 2008; Wiggins, 1991). McAdams operationalizes agency in terms of four themes (self-mastery, status/victory, achievement/responsibility, and empowerment) and communion by four themes (love/friendship, dialog, caring/help, and unity/togetherness).

McAdams's (1993, 2001) conceptualization seems to mix several aspects, particularly when considering our framing of the issue as the appropriation of morality to the self in which the tension is between self-enhancing and other-enhancing motivation. To focus on these more pertinent aspects of motivation, Frimer et al. operationalized agency as only the explicitly self-promoting themes of status/victory and achievement/responsibility (and not self-mastery and empowerment), and communion as only the explicitly other-promoting theme of caring/help (and not love/friendship, dialog, and unity/togetherness). Relying on this more precise conceptualization of agency and communion, they re-ran the variable-level analysis, only to again fail to find a statistical interaction between these two motives in predicting moral exemplarity.

It was not until Frimer et al. (2011) simultaneously implemented the person-level analytic approach and the more precise conceptualization of agency and communion in their analysis that they found the first empirical evidence of integration, with both motivational themes frequently co-occurring within sections of the interview for caring exemplars whereas comparison participants did not deviate from chance co-occurrence. Thus, both precise definitions and a person-level analytic strategy are necessary to detect the adaptive integration of agency and communion.

This evidence, while promising, is, less than satisfactory in a couple of respects: First, the McAdams (2001) macro-analytic coding system is not particularly sensitive because it permits only a simple assessment of the presence/absence of a motivational theme in oftentimes lengthy and rich narrative passages. Second, integration is tapped only by the co-occurrence of themes of agency and communion in such passages where they may not be functionally related at all.

In order to obtain a more fine-grained and precise assessment of agency and communion as well as to assess their functional relationships in narrative text, Frimer et al. (2011) introduced a micro-analytic coding system derived from the conceptual and empirical foundation of Schwartz's (1992) typology of values. In this coding system (Frimer, Walker & Dunlop, 2009), the self-enhancing values of power and achievement reflect agentic motivation and the self-transcending (other-promoting) values of benevolence and universalism reflect communal motivation. In this system, phrases (and sometimes even single words) are first coded as reflecting agency or communion and then, subsequently, coded for functionally compatible relationships (meaningful linkages) between them. An example of such a relationship would be: "I've been working diligently to raise funds for UNICEF humanitarian relief projects." The agentic motivation of working diligently is functionally directed in support of a communal cause.

Frimer et al.'s (2011) analyses, based on this micro-analytic coding of agency and communion, revealed convincing evidence of the adaptive integration of these motives. Exemplars evidenced levels of meaningfully integrated relationships between agency and communion that both exceeded the comparison group and chance levels of co-occurrence. Frimer et al. then replicated the analyses with a different measure of goal motivation elicited in a different context, the personal strivings list (Emmons, 1999), and found the same pattern, indicating that the basic phenomenon is robust. Finally, they tested whether the accentuated integration of agency and communion among exemplars was particular to these motivational themes or merely reflective of exemplars' greater level of general integration or complexity. These analyses ruled out a generalized integration mechanism, confirming the significance of agency-communion integration in moral functioning.

THE HIERARCHICAL INTEGRATION OF AGENCY AND COMMUNION

Although Frimer et al.'s (2011) study provided initial evidence of the integration of agency and communion in moral maturity, the search is far from over. One of the limitations of this study was that the interaction between agency and communion was tapped by the mere *co-occurrence* of these motives (a compatible relationship) within a thought structure, but that does not indicate the directionality between them. These motives could co-occur in the form of agency promoting communion (e.g., "I'm working hard to earn money to help the poor") or in the form of communion promoting agency ("I'm helping the poor in order to make money"). These two different forms carry vastly different moral weight.

To directly address this ambiguity, Frimer, Walker, Lee, Riches, and Dunlop (in press) revised their coding procedures to assess the directionality between motives in an instrumental-terminal relationship. Rokeach (1973) introduced the distinction between instrumental and terminal values: an instrumental value is a means to, or in service to, something else; a terminal value represents an end in itself. In the example above ("I'm working hard to earn money to help the poor"), the expressed value of working hard is instrumental to the terminal or ultimate goal of helping the poor.

In some of our previous research discussed earlier, we examined the psychological functioning of moral exemplars that were identified, through the Canadian honors system, as national awardees for extraordinary moral action. Frimer et al. (in press) took a different tack in identifying exemplars. Subjects in this study were influential people of the past century as identified by TIME magazine ("TIME 100," 1998, 1999). These are the world's 105 most influential leaders, revolutionaries, heroes, and icons of recent times – of both positive and negative renown. A large sample of social-science experts rated these target figures in terms of their moral exemplarity, using the five criteria for moral excellence, derived by Colby and Damon's (1992) panel, as evaluative dimensions: principled/virtuous, consistent, brave, inspiring, and humble (see their Appendix A). An overall index of moral exemplarity was derived by summing the ratings of these five dimensions.

The top-ranking of these target figures were classified as moral exemplars and the bottom-ranking as comparison figures of similar influence. The top-ranking "moral dream team" of the century includes familiar exemplars (including several Nobel Peace Prize laureates): Rosa Parks, Shirin Ebadi, Nelson Mandela, Mohandas Gandhi, Aung San Suu Kyi, the Dalai Lama, Martin Luther King, Jr., Andrei Sakharov, Emmeline Pankhurst, Eleanor Roosevelt, Mother Teresa, Harvey Milk, Helen Keller, Margaret Sanger, and Lech Walesa.

The bottom-ranking comparison figures were Kim Jong Il, Eliot Spitzer, Vladmir Putin, Donald Rumsfeld, Mel Gibson, George W. Bush, Adolf Hitler, David Beckham, Bill Belichick, Hu Jintao, Arnold Schwarzenegger, Marilyn Monroe, Mao Zedong, Condoleezza Rice, and Ariel Sharon. Note that while a bottom-ranking score does imply that the figure is un-prototypic of moral exemplarity, it does not necessarily indicate that this person exudes a particular negative quality (such as villainry). There are various ways in which one might lack moral exemplarity. Thus, it is not surprising that the comparison figures comprise a somewhat motley group of political leaders of various ilk, actors, athletes, celebrity icons, and so on. Nevertheless, these influential people in the comparison group were all adjudged to be un-prototypic of moral excellence.

Granted that these influential figures were either deceased or otherwise not available for participation in research, their personality functioning could only be studied "at a distance" via the content analysis of archival materials, an approach which has considerable validity (Suedfeld, 2010). The 15 top-ranking and the 15 bottom-ranking figures comprised the exemplar and comparison groups, respectively.

Excerpts from four speeches and interviews for each figure were first coded for agency (power and achievement) and communion (benevolence and universalism), using Frimer et al.'s (2009) coding manual, and then a second iteration of coding assessed the relationship between these motives by determining which concepts were instrumental to (as a means to) each terminal concept (an end in itself) within the text. This coding procedure allowed for the assessment of the hierarchical directionality between motivational themes.

Analyses revealed a readily interpretable pattern of findings: Comparison subjects had considerably more agency than communion at both the instrumental and terminal levels of motivation – the embodiment of unmitigated agency. Their value motivation was pervasively steeped in agency. Exemplars also had considerably more agency than communion at the instrumental level – which would be entirely expected of highly influential people – however, at the terminal level, communion reigned supreme. This is where the groups diverged. Simply put, both groups had the same equipment in their arsenal (instrumental agency), but were advancing vastly different projects (agency vs. communion). Exemplars expressed their agency as a means toward the end of communion, an integrated moral motivational pattern that reflects enlightened self-interest: personal fulfillment, achievement, and influence realized primarily through advancing the interests of others.

CONCLUSION

Why be good? I opened this chapter with that fundamental question. Extant theories do not have a ready answer to this question because they ignore or denigrate the role of the self in moral motivation. In contrast, my position is that morality can, and fundamentally should be, self-regarding. In other words, moral credit does accrue in promoting the self's interests, fulfillment, and actualization when they are accomplished through promoting the interests of others (either individuals or broader society). This psychological mechanism involves appropriating prosocial moral concerns into one's identity and motivational structure. This integrated personality formation can be profoundly motivating "for creatures like us" (Flanagan, 1991, p. 48).

We investigated this source of moral motivation through the perspective of moral exemplarity by examining the personality functioning of individuals who had engaged in extraordinary moral action. This approach allows us to better understand the endpoint of moral development, both as a normative ethical ideal and as an explanation of a psychological phenomenon. Our intent is that this is but the initial step in a process of "reverse engineering" – first finding evidence of integrated motivation and then later deconstructing it to explore its developmental roots, trajectories, and processes.

There are many issues to explore in the development of moral motivation and our current research is focused in that regard. For example, what are the early aspects of socialization that foster the development of both agentic and communal motivation? How best to encourage the adaptive forms of such motivation and inhibit the maladaptive forms? Is there typically a motivational crisis in late adolescence or early adulthood when each mode of motivation vies for supremacy? What stokes this crisis and how is it resolved? What contextual and psychological factors explain the various possible trajectories of moral motivation into adulthood: integration, unmitigated agency, unmitigated communion, continued segregation, or the diminishment of any form of motivation?

In this chapter, we sought evidence of the hierarchical integration of personal and moral concerns in mature moral functioning. In our program of research, we first found evidence that both agency and communion are at the foundational core of mature moral functioning. Typically, these dual modes of motivation are conceptualized as in opposition.

However, our reconciliation model posits that this tension can be resolved through a process of integration in moral maturity. Our program of research yielded clear evidence of such integration, but the enterprise required a precise conceptualization of agency and communion (as self- and other-promoting, respectively) and a within-person analytic strategy (in contrast to a variable-level approach). Moral exemplars preferentially integrated agency and communion, but this integration was evidenced in a particular hierarchical relationship, with their instrumental agency serving their terminal values of communion. So why be good? Because promoting the interests of others can be fundamentally enhancing to the self.

REFERENCES

Angyal, A. (1941). *Foundations for a science of personality*. New York: The Commonwealth Fund.

Aristotle (trans. 1962). *Nicomachean ethics* (M. Ostwald, Trans.). Indianapolis, IN: Bobbs-Merrill.

Bakan, D. (1966). *The duality of human existence: An essay on psychology and religion*. Chicago: Rand McNally.

Bellah, R.N., Madsen, R., Sullivan, W.M., Swidler, A., & Tipton, S.M. (1985). *Habits of the heart: Individualism and commitment in American life*. Berkeley, CA: University of California Press.

Blasi, A. (1980). Bridging moral cognition and moral action: A critical review of the literature. *Psychological Bulletin, 88*, 1–45. doi:10.1037/0033-2909.88.1.1

Blasi, A. (1983). Moral cognition and moral action: A theoretical perspective. *Developmental Review, 3*, 178–210. doi:10.1016/0273-2297(83)90029-1

Blasi, A. (1984). Moral identity: Its role in moral functioning. In W.M. Kurtines & J.L. Gewirtz (Eds.), *Morality, moral behavior, and moral development* (pp. 128–139). New York: Wiley.

Blasi, A. (2004). Moral functioning: Moral understanding and personality. In D.K. Lapsley & D. Narvaez (Eds.), *Moral development, self, and identity* (pp. 335–347). Mahwah, NJ: Erlbaum.

Colby, A., & Damon, W. (1992). *Some do care: Contemporary lives of moral commitment*. New York: Free Press.

Damon, W. (1984). Self-understanding and moral development from childhood to adolescence. In W.M. Kurtines & J.L. Gewirtz (Eds.), *Morality, moral behavior, and moral development* (pp. 109–127). New York: Wiley.

de Waal, F. (2009). *The age of empathy: Nature's lessons for a kinder society*. New York: Three Rivers Press.

Doris, J.M. (2002). *Lack of character: Personality and moral behavior*. Cambridge, England: Cambridge University Press.

Dunlop, W.L., Walker, L.J., & Matsuba, M.K. (2012). The distinctive moral personality of care exemplars. *Journal of Positive Psychology*, 7, 131–143. doi:10.1080/17439760.2012.662994

Eisenberg, N. (2005). The development of empathy-related responding. In G. Carlo & C.P. Edwards (Eds.), *Nebraska Symposium on Motivation: Vol. 51. Moral motivation through the life span* (pp. 73–117). Lincoln, NE: University of Nebraska Press.

Emmons, R.A. (1999). *The psychology of ultimate concerns: Motivation and spirituality in personality.* New York: Guilford Press.

Erikson, E.H. (1968). *Identity, youth, and crisis.* New York: Norton.

Flanagan, O. (1991). *Varieties of moral personality: Ethics and psychological realism.* Cambridge, MA: Harvard University Press.

Flanagan, O. (2009). Moral science? Still metaphysical after all these years. In D. Narvaez & D.K. Lapsley (Eds.), *Personality, identity, and character: Explorations in moral psychology* (pp. 52–78). New York: Cambridge University Press.

Fleeson, W. (2004). Moving personality beyond the person-situation debate: The challenge and the opportunity of within-person variability. *Current Directions in Psychological Science*, 13, 83–87. doi:10.1111/j.0963-7214.2004.00280.x

Frimer, J.A., & Walker, L.J. (2009). Reconciling the self and morality: An empirical model of moral centrality development. *Developmental Psychology*, 45, 1669–1681. doi:10.1037/a0017418

Frimer, J.A., Walker, L.J., & Dunlop, W.L. (2009). *Values embedded in narrative (VEiN) coding manual.* Unpublished manuscript, University of British Columbia, Vancouver.

Frimer, J.A., Walker, L.J., Dunlop, W.L., Lee, B.H., & Riches, A. (2011). The integration of agency and communion in moral personality: Evidence of enlightened self-interest. *Journal of Personality and Social Psychology*, 101, 149–163. doi:10.1037/a0023780

Frimer, J.A., Walker, L.J., Lee, B.H., Riches, A., & Dunlop, W.L. (in press). Hierarchical integration of agency and communion: A study of influential moral figures. *Journal of Personality.* doi:10.1111/j.1467-6494.2012.00764.x

Hardy, S.A., Walker, L.J., Olsen, J.A., Skalski, J.E., & Basinger, J.C. (2011). Adolescent naturalistic conceptions of moral maturity. *Social Development*, 20, 562–586. doi:10.1111/j.1467-9507.2010.00590.x

Harman, G. (2009). Skepticism about character traits. *Journal of Ethics*, 13, 235–242. doi:10.1007/s10892-009-9050-6

Hoffman, M.L. (2000). *Empathy and moral development: Implications for caring and justice.* Cambridge, England: Cambridge University Press.

Hogan, R. (1982). A socioanalytic theory of personality. In M.M. Page (Ed.), *Nebraska Symposium on Motivation: Vol. 30. Personality: Current theory and research* (pp. 55–89). Lincoln, NE: University of Nebraska Press.

Horney, K. (1937). *The neurotic personality of our time.* New York: Norton.

Kohlberg, L. (1969). Stage and sequence: The cognitive-developmental approach to socialization. In D.A. Goslin (Ed.), *Handbook of socialization theory and research* (pp. 347–480). Chicago: Rand McNally.

Kohlberg, L. (1981). *Essays on moral development: Vol. 1. The philosophy of moral development.* San Francisco: Harper & Row.

Magnusson, D. (1999). Holistic interactionism: A perspective for research on personality development. In L.A. Pervin & O.P. John (Eds.), *Handbook of personality: Theory and research* (2nd ed., pp. 219–247). New York: Guilford Press.

McAdams, D.P. (1988). *Power, intimacy, and the life story: Personological inquiries into identity.* New York: Guilford Press.

McAdams, D.P. (1993). *The stories we live by: Personal myths and the making of the self.* New York: Guilford Press.

McAdams, D.P. (1995). What do we know when we know a person? *Journal of Personality*, 63, 365–396. doi:10.1111/j.1467-6494.1995.tb00500.x

McAdams, D.P. (2001). *Coding autobiographical episodes for themes of agency and communion.* Unpublished manuscript, Northwestern University, Evanston, IL.

McAdams, D.P. (2006). *The redemptive self: Stories Americans live by*. New York: Oxford University Press.

McAdams, D.P. (2009). The moral personality. In D. Narvaez & D.K. Lapsley (Eds.), *Personality, identity, and character: Explorations in moral psychology* (pp. 11–29). New York: Cambridge University Press.

McAdams, D.P., Hoffman, B.J., Mansfield, E.D., & Day, R. (1996). Themes of agency and communion in significant autobiographical scenes. *Journal of Personality, 64*, 339–377. doi:10.1111/j.1467-6494.1996.tb00514.x

Monroe, K.R. (2002). Explicating altruism. In S.G. Post, L.G. Underwood, J.P. Schloss, & W.B. Hurlbut (Eds.), *Altruism and altruistic love: Science, philosophy, and religion in dialogue* (pp. 106–122). New York: Oxford University Press.

Oliner, S.P. (2003). *Do unto others: Extraordinary acts of ordinary people*. Boulder, CO: Westview.

Oliner, S.P., & Oliner, P.M. (1988). *The altruistic personality: Rescuers of Jews in Nazi Europe*. New York: Free Press.

Oser, F., Schmid, E., & Hattersley, L. (2006). The "unhappy moralist" effect: Emotional conflicts between being good and being successful. In L. Verschaffel, F. Dochy, M. Boekaerts, & S. Vosniadou (Eds.), *Instructional psychology: Past, present and future trends: Sixteen essays in honour of Erik De Corte* (pp. 149–166). Amsterdam: Elsevier.

Paulhus, D.L., & Trapnell, P.D. (2008). Self-presentation of personality: An agency-communion framework. In O.P. John, R.W. Robins, & L.A. Pervin (Eds.), *Handbook of personality psychology* (pp. 492–517). New York: Guilford Press.

Piaget, J. (1977). *The moral judgment of the child* (M. Gabain, Trans.). Harmondsworth, England: Penguin Books. (Original work published 1932)

Rest, J.R. (1979). *Development in judging moral issues*. Minneapolis: University of Minnesota Press.

Richter, D. (2007). *Why be good? A historical introduction to ethics*. New York: Oxford University Press.

Rokeach, M. (1973). *The nature of human values*. New York: Free Press.

Suedfeld, P. (2010). The cognitive processing of politics and politicians: Archival studies of conceptual and integrative complexity. *Journal of Personality, 78*, 1669–1702. doi:10.111/j.1467-6494.2010.00666.x

TIME 100: Heroes and icons. (1999, June 14). *TIME, 153*(23).

TIME 100: Leaders and revolutionaries. (1998, April 13). *TIME, 151*(14).

Turiel, E. (1983). *The development of social knowledge: Morality and convention*. Cambridge, England: Cambridge University Press.

Walker, L.J. (2002). Moral exemplarity. In W. Damon (Ed.), *Bringing in a new era in character education* (pp. 65–83). Stanford, CA: Hoover Institution Press.

Walker, L.J. (2004). Gus in the gap: Bridging the judgment-action gap in moral functioning. In D.K. Lapsley & D. Narvaez (Eds.), *Moral development, self, and identity* (pp. 1–20). Mahwah, NJ: Erlbaum.

Walker, L.J. (in press). Moral personality, motivation, and identity. In M. Killen & J.G. Smetana (Eds.), *Handbook of moral development* (2nd ed.). New York: Taylor & Francis.

Walker, L.J., & Frimer, J.A. (2007). Moral personality of brave and caring exemplars. *Journal of Personality and Social Psychology, 93*, 845–860. doi:10.1037/0022-3514.93.5.845

Walker, L.J., & Frimer, J.A. (2011). The science of moral development. In M.K. Underwood & L.H. Rosen (Eds.), *Social development: Relationships in infancy, childhood, and adolescence* (pp. 235–262). New York: Guilford Press.

Walker, L.J., Frimer, J.A., & Dunlop, W.L. (2010). Varieties of moral personality: Beyond the banality of heroism. *Journal of Personality, 78*, 907–942. doi:10.1111/j.1467-6494.2010.00637.x

Walker, L.J., & Hennig, K.H. (2004). Differing conceptions of moral exemplarity: Just, brave, and caring. *Journal of Personality and Social Psychology, 86*, 629–647. doi:10.1037/0022-3514.86.4.629

Walker, L.J., & Pitts, R.C. (1998). Naturalistic conceptions of moral maturity. *Developmental Psychology, 34*, 403–419. doi:10.1037/0012-1649.34.3.403

Watson, G. (1984). Virtues in excess. *Philosophical Studies, 46*, 57–74.

Wiggins, J.S. (1991). Agency and communion as conceptual coordinates for the understanding and measurement of interpersonal behavior. In D. Cicchetti & W.M. Grove (Eds.), *Thinking clearly about psychology: Essays in honor of Paul E. Meehl* (Vol. 2, pp. 89–113). Minneapolis: University of Minnesota Press.

Wiggins, J.S. (1995). *Interpersonal Adjective Scales: Professional manual.* Odessa, FL: Psychological Assessment Resources.

Zimbardo, P.G. (2007). The banality of evil, the banality of heroism. In J. Brockman (Ed.), *What is your dangerous idea? Today's leading thinkers on the unthinkable* (pp. 275–276). New York: Harper Perennial.

AFFILIATION

Lawrence J. Walker
Department of Psychology
University of British Columbia
Vancouver, Canada

TOBIAS KRETTENAUER

II. MORAL MOTIVATION, RESPONSIBILITY AND THE DEVELOPMENT OF THE MORAL SELF

INTRODUCTION

The concept of the moral self is essentially a motivational construct. Blasi (1983) introduced the self-model into moral psychology as an attempt to bridge the gap over the divide that separates moral judgment from moral action. The moral self has been demonstrated to account for moral action, pro-social engagement and sustained moral commitment (Hardy & Carlo, 2005). Although the empirical connection between the moral self/moral identity and actual behaviour has been documented many times, the processes by which an individual's moral self or moral identity leads to action is far from understood (Hardy & Carlo, 2011).

Blasi, in many of his writings, stressed the importance of responsibility (see also Blasi in this volume). As individuals develop a moral self, they increasingly feel responsible for their moral actions. Responsibility in this context is not confined to a judgment, as in Kohlberg and Candee's model (1984). Responsibility involves emotions and desires. It is also not limited to liability and accountability (i.e., whether individuals accept to be held accountable for their past (im)moral actions). Moral responsibility, in the broader sense, is proactive, as individuals feel responsible for the choices they make, the moral actions they take and the lives they live. The philosopher, Ronald Dworkin, describes this notion of responsibility as a virtue and differentiates it from responsibility as a relational concept that connects people with events (Dworkin, 2011). Much of the psychological research on responsibility focuses on denial of responsibility in the latter sense (e.g. Bandura et al., 1996). Strikingly, the more fundamental question, what factors constitute a sense of moral responsibility from which individuals may actively disengage, is largely left out.

Why do individuals feel morally responsible for the decisions they make and actions they take? Any meaningful psychological account of moral motivation needs to be able to provide an answer to this question. Research on the moral self came forward with a compellingly simple and straightforward answer: responsibility results from an integration of self and morality. As self and morality become integrated in the course of development, individuals start to profoundly care about matters of morality and ethical conduct which, in turn, leads to a heightened sense of moral responsibility. The idea of an integration of self and morality rests on the assumption that self and morality are largely separated at the onset of development (cf. Damon 1984, 1996). However, there is evidence to suggest that children at a very young

K. Heinrichs, F. Oser & T. Lovat (Eds.), Handbook of Moral Motivation: Theories, Models, Applications, 215–228.

age are able to spontaneously engage in pro-social actions of helping, sharing and consoling others. Young children are genuinely concerned about others' well-being. Thus, on the level of singular actions, self and morality are well-integrated quite early in development.

Ultimately, the problem we face is: If moral self-integration is already present in young children, how can we make sense of the notion of an integration of self and morality in the course of development? What exactly is integrated in the course of moral self development that accounts for the development of moral responsibility, if it is not self and morality in totality? These are the leading questions of the present chapter.

This chapter presents a model of moral self development that starts from a different premise than most models on the development of the moral self. As these models are based on the assumption that self and morality are separated at the onset of development, moral self development is construed as an integration of self and morality that typically takes place in adolescence (cf. Bergman, 2002). Contrary to this perspective, in this chapter, it is argued that an integration of self and morality is present quite early in development. This early integration gives rise to a minimal moral self that later is extended into more comprehensive forms. Following this view, moral self development is a differentiation and integration of specific motivational processes that are all pertinent for moral responsibility and, *a fortiori*, for moral action.

The argument is developed in four consecutive steps. First, I review the common assumption upheld in most of the research on the moral self that self and morality are separated in childhood and become integrated in adolescence. This view is contrasted with the empirical evidence showing that young children spontaneously engage in acts of helping others. In the second step, a model of moral self development is presented that responds to this conceptual challenge. This model distinguishes three different conceptions of the moral self that capture different meanings of moral agency: the moral self as intentional, volitional and identified agent. It is argued that these different conceptions of moral selfhood form three layers of moral self development. In the final step, commonalities and differences between the model presented in this chapter and other concepts of moral self development are discussed. Although the main focus of this chapter is on the moral self, it clearly has implications for moral motivation. As the rest of the chapter will demonstrate, the moral self is constituted by important motivational processes and, in turn, orchestrates these processes. Thus, the moral self essentially is both product and producer of the development of moral motivation.

INTEGRATING SELF AND MORALITY: THE CHALLENGE

Many advocates of the self-model in moral psychology maintain that self and morality are two developmental systems that are largely unconnected in childhood but become gradually integrated in the course of adolescent development (Bergman,

2002). It is, thus, the integration of moral values into the adolescent self-concept that gives rise to a moral self (i.e., a self that profoundly cares about matters of morality and ethical conduct). This process of moral self-integration in adolescence was first proposed by Damon (1984; see also Damon & Hart, 1988, Damon 1996) and received some empirical support by research on moral exemplars (Hart & Fegley, 1995; for an overview, see Hardy & Carlo, 2005). It was recently reconfirmed by Frimer and Walker (2009) who proposed the Reconciliation Model of moral development. According to this model, there is a fundamental motivational duality between agency and communion. Individuals either work towards achieving their own goals and projects (agency) or towards advancing those of others (communion). This duality is proposed to be strongest in childhood. However, with development, individuals experience a growing tension between agency and communion, which eventually leads to an acute phase of disequilibrium. This disequilibrium is solved by either prioritizing one motivational system over the other, or by reconciling the two. According to Frimer and Walker, the successful reconciliation of agency and communion lays the foundation for the extraordinary moral achievements that become evident in the lives of moral exemplars.

The assumption that self and morality are separated in childhood is questionable. Following Heinz Werner's Orthogenetic Principle, one might argue that development typically does not begin with fully differentiated systems but with a lack of differentiation. Development proceeds through differentiation to hierarchical integration. While this argument undermines the plausibility of the idea of an initial separation of self and morality, it by no means refutes it. However, once we take into account the many observations of toddlers' spontaneous acts of helping and sharing that were amassed in the literature on children's pro-social behaviour (for an overview see Eisenberg, 2000), the principal assumption becomes questionable. If young children have the spontaneous desire to help, to share, and to console, the basic tenet of a separation of self of morality in childhood – on which much of the research on the development of a moral self rests – becomes highly implausible. If young children are able to carry genuine pro-social intentions, self and morality are well integrated at the onset of the development. At this point, the moral self appears to be one of the many developmental constructs in the history of developmental psychology that initially were meant to mark an important end-point of development but were later described as an early developmental achievement (similar to e.g. principled moral reasoning, perspective taking, formal operational thinking).

Yet, we should not throw out the baby with the bathwater. Pointing out early developmental achievements is not to deny development of more mature forms later on. Thus, even if there are indicators of an early integration of self and morality, this by no means implies that more mature forms of moral self-integration do not emerge later in the course of development. Rather than pitting accounts of early and late developmental achievements against each, both approaches should form a cooperative relationship: a more accurate grasp of the starting point of moral self development helps to better understand what exactly develops later. Following this guideline, we need to distinguish various forms of moral self-integration, where some forms may be present early and others may emerge later in the course of development.

THE MORAL SELF AS INTENTIONAL, VOLITIONAL AND IDENTIFIED AGENT

As described at the beginning of this chapter, the concept of the moral self has motivational meaning through responsibility-taking. Any account of responsibility, in turn, requires an agentic view of the self. If morality were the outcome of purely impersonal systems (e.g., cognitive, evolutionary, neurological) without the involvement of an agentic self, responsibility would not exist. Thus, responsibility is imbued with selfhood and agency. Various conceptions of agency differ on a continuum from 'thick' to 'thin' (Sokol & Huerta, 2010). In a 'thin' sense, the term refers to overt goal-directed behaviour. A thin view of agency offers a minimalist account of behaviour as guided by mental states such as beliefs and desires. In a 'thick' sense, agency refers to the self-conscious person who is able to reflect upon his/her own actions, put them in broader perspective, and imbue them with meaning derived from a sense of personal identity.

The Moral Self as Intentional Agent

Starting from a thin or minimalist account of agency, the definition of selfhood in infancy and childhood appears to be straightforward: the self is present once a child is capable of intentional actions. Typically, an intention is considered a combination of desire and belief. There is no question that children around the age of 2.5 years (i.e., well before they develop of a theory of mind), understand subjective desires and the emotional implications of fulfilling a desire or frustrating it (Wellman & Phillips, 2001). The understanding that individuals hold subjective beliefs that are independent from external reality develops along with a theory of mind (see Astington, 2001). Thus, the self as intentional agent is surely present between the ages of 3 to 5 years. What does this imply for the self as moral agent?

Research on children's early understanding of desires and intentions has been almost exclusively focused on instrumental actions, where desires are about action outcomes and beliefs about means-ends. Moral actions are inherently different from instrumental actions. Their success is not defined by attaining a goal but by conforming to a collectively shared standard or norm. Despite this difference, Wellman and Miller (2008) argued that the understanding of intentional actions and deontological reasoning are not only connected but, in fact, inseparable as they mutually constitute each other. Deontological reasoning (i.e., reasoning about obligatory and permissive acts) regulates when belief-desire reasoning is in place. Permissions allow the actor to 'engage in an action if I desire'; whereas obligations require the actor to 'engage in an action regardless of my desires' (Wellman & Miller, 2008, p. 111). The idea that moral obligations require an action 'regardless of my desires' keeps instrumental actions that follow a belief-desire theory of mind fully separated from moral actions. Thus, moral desires by definition cannot exist. As a consequence, chances that young children carry genuine moral intentions (or are able to develop them) are slim.

However, this conclusion is in stark contrast with research on young children's capabilities to feel sympathy with others and the many observations of spontaneous acts of helping and sharing that were amassed in the literature on children's pro-social behaviour (for an overview see Eisenberg, 2000). Children around the age of 18 months have a desire to help others in need. They help consistently and frequently without expecting a favor in return as was more recently shown in a series of experiments by Warneken and Tomasello (2009).

Pro-social behaviour is about socially desirable acts rather than strict obligations and permissions. However, even actions that are morally obligated may be based on a spontaneous desire, namely the desire NOT to inflict physical or psychological harm on others. Such a desire might be an outgrowth of spontaneous feelings of empathy or sympathy. It might be further informed by children's general understanding of moral rules that prohibits actions that are harmful to others (cf. Smetana, 2006). From this perspective, young children can clearly desire moral actions. As desired action, they can be said to be intentional and, thus, meet a minimal or 'thin' requirement for moral selfhood.

The Moral Self as Volitional Agent

Young children around the age of 2 years have moral desires. Still, at that young age, children regularly fail to act morally. Quite frequently, they are overpowered by emotions of anger or envy leading to acts of instrumental or retaliatory aggression. Very often, egoistic desires prevail. Moral actions involve more than a spontaneous desire to help others or not to inflict harm on them. Moral actions require the ability to regulate egoistic desires and to resist anti-social impulses. In other words, moral actions need a volitional self. It is important to note that in the context of moral action, the notion of a "volitional self" refers to two different processes (see Blasi, 2005). Volition may reflect will-power, that is, the ability to perform an action even when facing unanticipated obstacles, backlashes, or other adverse side-effects. Will-power is required after an intention has been formed. It is an essential ingredient in all goal-directed behaviour, including moral actions. In the context of moral actions, however, the volitional self is present not only when carrying out an action but also when forming an intention in the face of conflicting desires. The child may have the spontaneous desire to share his/her treats with other children, and at the same time, experience an equally strong desire to keep all for him/herself. In this case, choosing between one of the two opposing desires requires an act of volition.

A well-established empirical paradigm in developmental psychology that addresses the notion of the volitional self in the latter sense is research on children's delay of gratification (for an overview see Tobin & Graziano, 2010). The ability to delay gratification (i.e., to choose a later more distant goal at the expense of an immediate goal), gradually increases with the child's age (Mischel, 1974). Children need to be able to conceive of the self as extended over time in order to understand that the present desire will be better served in the future by waiting for the superior reward (see Barresi, 1999; Lemmon & Moore, 2001). This concern for the future self requires that the desire for the smaller reward be contained. Strikingly, the understanding of a temporally extended self does not only account for choosing future self-rewards, but also for the ability to make future choices that benefit others (Thompson, Barresi, & Moore, 1997). Thus, the understanding of the self as extended over time has implications for social behaviour, as well.

Still, it is obvious that the delay choice paradigm does not fully capture all requirements of the volitional self that are pertinent for moral actions. In the context of moral action, the child needs to understand that the currently dominant desire (e.g., the desire for a toy another child is playing with) might be less important in a future situation than the opposite moral desire (e.g., not to hurt the other child by taking away the toy). By contrast, in the delay choice paradigm, the child needs to project just one dominant desire into the future. It is, thus, the ability to prioritize a moral desire over another temporarily stronger desire that constitutes the moral self as a volitional agent. Piaget (1954/1995), in his lectures on "Intelligence and Affectivity", described this ability as a "conservation of values" that makes it possible to subject a temporarily stronger impulse to a normative feeling (see Sokol & Hammond, 2009). According to Piaget (1954/1995), this conservation of values is tied to the development of concrete operations around the age of 7 to 8 years. Krettenauer, Malti & Sokol (2008) noted a striking parallel between Piaget's notion and research on children's moral emotion expectancies, which demonstrates that children typically do not anticipate negative self-evaluative emotions when transgressing a moral rule to achieve a desired goal before the age of 7 to 8 years. The anticipation of moral emotions in such situations indicates the child's ability to uphold a moral desire even when an opposing immoral desire is currently dominant.

The Moral Self as Identified Agent

Once children have developed a volitional self, they are able to regulate egoistic desires and resist anti-social impulses by giving priority to moral desires. However, at this point in development, they still lack an integration of moral values in the self-system that makes moral actions a form of self-expression, as stressed in research on moral exemplars. In fact, at younger ages, children's volitional acts might be fully based on considerations external to the self (e.g., fear of punishment). In the context of moral action, a fully integrated (and autonomous) sense of self requires that the individual experiences the act of prioritizing a moral desire over an immoral desire as a volition that emanates from the self rather than as a decision that is imposed by external factors.

In the context of moral action, this process has often been described as rule internalization (Kochanska & Thompson, 1997). When rules are internalized they are experienced as binding, regardless of others' reactions. Thus, evaluations of significant others are transformed into self-evaluative reactions (e.g., feelings of guilt). However, as pointed out by Self-Determination Theory, rule internalization is just one step towards higher levels of internal motivation (see Ryan &Deci, 2000, Grolnick, Deci& Ryan, 1997). Rule internalization leads to an introjected mode of self-regulation, where rule compliance becomes independent of explicit demands of others. Still, on the introjected level, norms are subjectively experienced as rules one has to follow rather than as standards one wants to meet. The transformation of "shoulds" into "wants" takes place once individuals develop identified and integrated modes of self-regulation. On the identified level, individuals express a basic personal agreement with a norm or societal expectations; whereas on the integrated level, norms are experienced as self-ideals the person does not want to betray. Various models of self, ego, and identity development propose a general developmental trend towards higher levels of self-integration. These models generally assume that individuals' commitments to life-goals, values, and ideals are increasingly experienced as self-chosen (e.g., Blasi & Glodis, 1995; Loevinger, 1976; Marcia, Waterman, Matteson, Archer & Orlofsky, 1993).

Once a child or teenager prioritizes moral desires over egoistic desires and s/he feels that this prioritization reflects the way s/he wants to be, the volitional self has turned into an identified agent. Note that this form of prioritization can be specific to particular contexts and situations and need not be generalized across various life domains. Thus, the self as identified agent does not imply a moral identity.

THREE LAYERS IN THE DEVELOPMENTOF MORAL SELFHOOD

In the previous paragraphs, three different notions of moral selfhood were outlined. It was argued that a comprehensive conception of moral selfhood requires a self as intentional, volitional, and identified agent. However, one question still remains: how do the various notions of moral selfhood relate to each other? This question is addressed in the following.

The various notions of moral selfhood are hierarchical. Thus, the self as intentional agent is foundational for developing a volitional self, and the volitional self is foundational for the self as identified agent. However, this hierarchical relationship does not imply stages. The self as intentional agent is not replaced by the volitional self, nor is the volitional self superseded by the self as identified agent. All three forms of moral selfhood coexist and each form is subject to further change after first emerging in the course of development. It therefore is more appropriate to view the three notions of moral selfhood as layers, where each layer adds an important quality to the moral self (for a pictorial illustration see Figure 1). Layer I is defined by the self as intentional agent. Layer II constitutes the moral self as a volitional agent, and Layer III equips the moral self with a rudimentary sense of identity. As these layers are not stages, higher layers do not overturn lower ones. Moreover, there is no developmental continuity implied between the layers. The developmental factors that constitute Layer I are different from those that constitute Layers II and III. Having stressed the foundational nature of the lower layers, it is important to note that higher layers influence lower ones. Thus, value identifications inform volitional processes. Volitional processes, in turn, likely form and transform moral desires (i.e., impact the self as intentional agent).

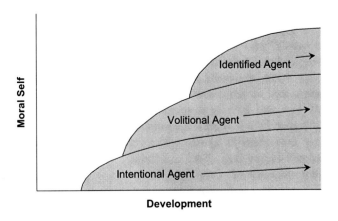

Figure 1. Three layers in the development of moral selfhood.

Although the relationship between chronological age and development is complicated, and age is not necessarily a good indicator of development (see Moshman, 2009; Krettenauer, in press), a legitimate question to be asked at this point is: when in the course of development do the three proposed layers of moral selfhood typically emerge? When discussing various developmental achievements in the cognitive, emotional, as well as motivational domain and relating them to the three different conceptions of the moral self, we have alluded to the answer. Summarizing this information, the following abstract relations between moral self development and age can be assumed. It was argued that children's early moral desires are an outgrowth of their first sympathetic reactions that typically occur in the second half of the second year and are associated with children's mirror self-recognition (Bischof-Köhler, 1988). Thus, the moral self as intentional agent can be assumed to emerge around the age of 2 years. In the delay of gratification choice paradigm, the emergence of a volitional self was related to children's understanding of the temporally extended self around the age of 4 years (Lemmon & Moore, 2001). However, as noted above, in the context of moral action, the volitional self requires more than extending just one desire into the future. The development of the volitional moral self is more demanding. If we take the ability to anticipate negatively charged self-evaluative emotions in the context of moral transgressions as an indicator of a "conservation of values", and hence a volitional moral self, we may assume that the volitional moral self normally develops between 6 and 8 years of age. Finally, the association between age and the development of the moral self as identified agent might be more varied. As noted at the beginning of this chapter, it is the age period of mid to late adolescence that typically is considered crucial for the formation of a moral identity. However, the moral self as identified agent does not require a full moral identity that is generalized across contexts and domains. The self as identified agent therefore might emerge well before middle adolescence.

MORAL RESPONSIBILITY AND THE INTEGRATION OF SELF AND MORALITY: COMPARING DIFFERENT MODELS

This chapter started with a simple but fundamental question: what makes individuals feel morally responsible for the choices they make, the actions they take and the lives they live? It is commonly assumed that the integration of self and morality in adolescence (or the reconciliation of agency and communion as Frimer and Walker (2009) would put it) gives rise to a moral self that constitutes a strong sense of moral responsibility. The present chapter questions this view. It is argued that the integration of self and morality is not limited to a specific developmental period. A minimal sense of moral responsibility is already present in young children around the age of 2 years who act on the basis of spontaneous pro-social desires and intentions. Children at this age want to help others and are genuinely concerned about their well-being. However, the moral self in this minimal sense falters when spontaneous moral desires conflict with egoistic desires or antisocial impulses. Taking responsibility in the face of conflicting desires requires the development of a volitional moral self that prioritizes moral over amoral and immoral concerns. This volitional moral self may first operate on concerns external to the self (e.g., fear of punishment or other negative consequences). Once, children have developed value identifications that allow them to prioritize moral concerns over conflicting desires, even if these desires are temporarily stronger, a new quality of taking moral responsibility is achieved: children are able to act morally based on the understanding that moral values take priority for them under varying circumstances as well as in future situations. Thus, forming an intention, investing will-power, and adopting moral values as personal values are different forms of taking moral responsibility. Together, these processes constitute the moral self.

From this perspective, the integration of self and morality, as described by Damon and others, is not an integration of self and morality in totality, but a differentiation and hierarchical integration of motivational processes that are all pertinent for responsibility-taking and for moral action. What Colby and Damon (1992) describe as a unity of self and morality that is achieved in moral exemplars may be more adequately conceptualized as a seamless coordination of value identifications with volitional processes leading to moral intentions.

The proposed model of the development of moral self and responsibility bears important similarities but also differences with the 7 steps in the development of moral will as outlined in Blasi (2005). Here, the "moral will" is defined in contradistinction to mere will-power as a person's desire toward the moral good. Step 1 in Blasi's sequence marks the absence of a moral will ("The child experiences desires, frequently in conflict with each other; however he is not capable of distancing himself from them, of choosing among them. His intentional action follows the more immediate or pressing desire. There is no volition", Blasi, 2005, p. 82). Step 2 in this sequence denotes an important transition, namely the early formation of a moral will ("... In making his preferred desire effective, the child begins to form volitions: he appropriates existing desires and brings them under the domain of his agency", Blasi, 2005, p. 82). Critical for the transition from Step 1 to Step 2 is the emergence of "second-order-desires" (i.e., the child's ability to form desires about desires). According to Blasi (2005), second-order desires establish an order of preferences, while second-order volitions are supposed to effectively translate these preferences into action. The following Steps 3 to 5 in the development of the moral will are characterized by extension (the child appropriates more and more desires by developing second-order volitions) and by reflective abstraction (the child develops an appreciation for general values that are abstracted from concrete desires). In Step 6, moral centrality becomes an important aspect of an individual's self-definition, and at the same time, a dimension of individual differences. The final Step 7 is marked by an acute sense of moral self-integration. Similar to Colby and Damon's (1992) description of moral exemplars, moral action becomes an important mode of self-expression ("In some people, specific virtues or a general moral desire become the basic concerns around which the will is structured. Their "wholehearted commitment" to the moral good produces, at the same time the core identity and an undivided will", Blasi, 2005, p. 82).

An important difference between Blasi's 7 steps in the development of the moral will and the proposed three layers in the development of the moral self lies in the idea of "second-order-desires". For Blasi, the moral self essentially requires the ability to form second-order desires, whereas the model presented here does not make this assumption. Children can act out of spontaneous moral desires which provide the foundation for a minimal moral self as intentional agent. Blasi denies the moral significance of these spontaneous desires (see Blasi, 2000). This difference between the two models has important ramification for the second layer (or Step 2 in Blasi's model): the development of the volitional self. For Blasi, this step is tied to the child's ability to form second-order-desires. Second-order desires reflect upon first-order desires, and thus operate on a meta-level. By contrast, in the proposed model, the development of the volitional self simply requires an ability to prioritize a moral desire that it is temporarily dominated by non-moral desires. This process is better described as "conservation of values" rather than as a "second-order desire". Thus, children do not need to develop second order desires to establish a volitional moral self as they have spontaneous moral desires on the level of intentional actions.

Blasi (2005) chooses the notion of moral centrality to account for later steps in the development of the moral will; individuals extend their sense of responsibility by appropriating more and more first-order desires. In this way, moral values become central to individual's sense of self or identity. It is important to note, however, that moral centrality does not necessarily imply value identification and internal moral motivation. Even if morality is experienced as central to the self, individuals still may be motivated by external factors (e.g., other's disapproval). In fact, moral centrality and internal moral motivation reflect two different aspects of the moral self (for details see Krettenauer, 2011).

As outlined above, value identifications can be highly context specific and rather segmented across different life domains. Thus, they do not imply a moral identity. Children and adolescents might feel it is important to be honest with their friends but still not apply any importance to honesty in an academic context where cheating is common. If this context-specificity and segmentation prevails in the course of development, the likelihood of experiencing value conflicts within specific areas of life (e.g., work, family) and across domains (e.g., private versus public) prevails. Value conflicts foster the compartmentalization of moral life where moral values that govern one area are disconnected from those that govern others. As noted by Dworkin (2011), value conflicts undermine individuals' sense of responsibility, as moral values partly endorse and partly condemn a certain way of action. In this situation, responsibility is restricted to the volitional self (i.e., the second level outlined in the proposed model); we may choose a certain way of action but we could easily decide the opposite. If value identifications foster individuals' sense of responsibility in the long term, they need to form a moral identity (i.e., a value structure that provides a sense of coherence, unity, and continuity over time). This is a major reason why Blasi considers "wholehearted commitment" and an "undivided will" in his model as the endpoint and final step in the development of the moral self. The model presented in this chapter does not propose such an endpoint. It considers the organization and coordination of value identifications as a never-ending process that begins once individuals have reached the third layer. That is, once they have developed a moral self as identified agent. Some individuals may achieve an "undivided moral will", however others may not.

CONCLUSION

The present chapter argued for a conceptual differentiation of three different notions of moral selfhood: the moral self as intentional, volitional, and identified agent. At the same time, it introduced a model that outlines how the three different conceptions of moral selfhood relate to each other from a developmental point of view. This model is certainly no less speculative than other models on the development of the moral self discussed in this chapter, and awaits future empirical validation. However, regardless of whether it may turn out to be too simplistic and in need of revisions, this by no means disqualifies the conceptual distinction between the different notions of moral selfhood. These notions, on different levels and scales, describe what it means to take ownership for a moral action (or conversely to deny it). It is this sense of ownership that implies responsibility. Ownership of moral actions, in turn, is not black or white, nor a matter of "Yes" or "No". Ownership varies with regard to type and degree. In this contribution, three sources of ownership or responsibility were discussed that correspond with three layers in the development of moral selfhood. To form an intention, invest will-power and adopt moral values as personal values means to take responsibility in different ways and on different scales.

At this point, it is important to note that the moral self, as conceived in this model, does not simply unfold as part of nature's grand plan. It does not develop in social isolation. The moral self crystallizes where different motivational processes intersect. Development of these processes requires different social support systems at different ages. If support is limited, the moral self and, *a fortiori*, individual's sense of moral responsibility may become impoverished and restricted. Even if adequate social support is provided, the readiness to take full responsibility in the various arenas of social, moral, and political life is not guaranteed. This is because moral responsibility, as it emanates from the self, is intimately tied to autonomy. No child can be forced to feel responsible. Responsibility can only be suggested. Ultimately, it needs to be chosen. This is why teaching responsibility is one of the most complicated tasks that parents and teachers face. Yet, it is a task of tremendous importance, as no one would want to live in a world without responsibility.

REFERENCES

Astington, J.W. (2001). The paradox of intention: Assessing children's metarepresentational understandings. In B.F. Malle, L.J. Moses & D.A. Baldwin (Eds.), *Intentions and intentionality* (pp. 85–104). Cambridge: MIT Press.

Baressi, J. (1999). On becoming a person. *Philosophical Psychology, 12*, 79–98.

Bandura, A., Barbaranelli, C., Caprara, G.V., & Pastorelli, C. (1996). Mechanisms of moral disengagement and the exercise of moral agency. *Journal of Personality and Social Psychology,* (71), 364–374.

Bergman, R. (2002). Why be moral? A conceptual model from developmental psychology. *Human Development, 45*, 104–124.

Bischof-Köhler, D. (1988). Über den Zusammenhang von Empathie und der Fähigkeit, sich im Spiegel zu erkennen. *Schweizerische Zeitschrift für Psychologie, 47*, 147–159.

Blasi, A. (1983). Moral cognition and moral action: A theoretical perspective. *Developmental Review* (3), 178–210.

Blasi, A. (2000). Was sollte als moralisches Verhalten gelten? Das Wesen der ‚frühen Moral' in der kindlichen Entwicklung. In W. Edelstein & G. Nunner-Winkler (Eds.), *Moral im sozialen Kontext* (pp. 116–145). Frankfurt a.M.: Suhrkamp.

Blasi, A. (2005). Moral character: A psychological approach. In D.K. Lapsley& F.C. Power (Eds.), *Character psychology and character education* (pp. 67–100). Notre Dame: University of Notre Dame Press.

Blasi, A., & Glodis, K. (1995). The development of identity. A critical analysis from the perspective of the self as subject. *Developmental Review, 15*, 404–433.

Colby, A., & Damon, W. (1992). *Some do care*. New York: Free Press.

Damon, W. (1984). Self-understanding and moral development from childhood to adolescence. In W.M. Kurtines & J.L. Gewirtz (Eds.), *Morality, moral behavior, and moral development* (pp. 109–127). New York: Wiley.

Damon, W. (1996). The lifelong transformation of moral goals through social influence. In P.B. Baltes & U.M. Staudinger (Eds.), *Interactive minds* (pp. 198–220). Cambridge: Cambridge University Press.

Damon, W. & Hart, D. (1988). *Self-understanding in childhood and adolescence*. Newe York: Cambridge University Press.

Dworkin, R. (2011). *Justice for Hedgehogs*. Cambridge: Harvard University Press.

Eisenberg, N. (2000). Emotion, regulation, and moral development. *Annual Review of Psychology, 51,* 665–697.

Frimer, J.A., & Walker, L.J. (2009). Reconciling the self and morality: An empirical model of moral centrality development. *Developmental Psychology, 45,* 1669–1681.

Grolnick, W.S., Deci, E.L., & Ryan, R.M. (1997). Internalization within the family: The Self-Determination Theory perspective. In J.E. Grusec& L. Kuczynski (Eds.), *Parenting and children's internalization of values* (pp. 135–161). New York: Wiley & Sons.

Hardy, S., & Carlo, G. (2005). Identity as a source of moral motivation. *Human Development, 48,* 232–256.

Hardy, S., & Carlo, G. (2011). Moral identity. In S.J. Schwartz (Ed.), *Handbook of identity theory and research* (pp. 495–513). New York: Springer Science+Business Media.

Hart, D., & Fegley, S. (1995). Prosocial behavior and caring in adolescence: Relations to self-understanding and social judgment. *Child Development, 66,* 1346–1359.

Hoffman, M.L. (2000). *Empathy and moral development*. Cambridge: Cambridge University Press.

Kochanska, G., & Thompson, R.A. (1997). The emergence and development of conscience in toddlerhood and early childhood. In J.E. Grusec& L. Kuczynski (Eds.), *Parenting and children's internalization of values* (pp. 53–77). New York: Wiley & Sons.

Kohlberg, L., & Candee, D. (1984). The relationship of moral judgment to moral action. In L. Kohlberg (Ed.), *The psychology of moral development* (pp. 499–581). San Francisco: Harper & Row.

Krettenauer, T. (in press). Konzepte, Theorien, Paradigmen: Betrachtungen zum Entwicklungsbegriff in der Psychologie. In L. Ahnert (Ed.),*Theorien in der Entwicklungspsychologie*. Heidelberg: Spektrum.

Krettenauer, T. (2011). The dual moral self: Moral centrality and intrinsic moral motivation. *The Journal of Genetic Psychology, 172,* 309–328. doi: 10.1080/00221325.2010.538451

Krettenauer, T., Malti, T., & Sokol, B.W. (2008). Development of moral emotions and the happy-victimizer phenomenon: A critical review of theory and application. *European Journal of Developmental Science, 2,* 221–235.

Lemmon, K., & Moore, C. (2001). Binding the self in time. In C. Moore & K. Lemmon (Eds.), *The self in time* (pp. 163–179). Mahwah: Erlbaum.

Loevinger, J. (1976). *Ego development*. San Francisco: Jossey-Bass.

Marcia, J.E., Waterman, A.S., Matteson, D.R., Archer, S.L., & Orlofsky, J.L. (1993). *Ego identity.* New York: Springer-Verlag.

Mischel, W. (1974). Processes in delay of gratification. In L. Berkowitz (Ed.), *Advances in experimental social psychology* (Vol. 7, pp. 249–292). New York: Academic Press.

Moshman, D. (2009). Identity, morality, and adolescent development. *Human Development, 52,* 287–290.

Piaget, J. (1954/1995). *Intelligenz und Affektivität in der Entwicklung des Kindes*. Frankfurt a.M..: Suhrkamp.

Ryan, R.M., & Deci, E.L. (2000). Self-determination theory and the facilitation of intrinsic motivation, social development and well-being. *American Psychologist, 55,* 68–78.

Smetana, J.G. (2006). Social-cognitive domain theory: Consistencies and variations in children's moral and social judgments. In M. Killen & J.G. Smetana (Eds.), *Handbook of moral development* (pp. 119–153). Mahwah, NJ: Erlbaum.

Sokol, B.W., & Hammond, S.I. (2009). Piaget and affectivity. In U. Müller, J.I.M. Carpendale & L. Smith (Eds.), *The Cambridge companion to Piaget* (pp. 309–323). Cambridge: Cambridge University Press.

Sokol, B.W., & Huerta, S. (2010). Through thick and thin: Agency as 'taking' perspectives. *Human Development, 53,* 46–52.

Thompson, C., Barresi, J., & Moore, C. (1997). The development of future-oriented prudence and altruism in preschoolers. *Cognitive Development, 12,* 199–212.

Tobin, R.M., & Graziano, W.G. (2010). Delay of gratification: A review of fifty years of regulation research. In R.H. Hoyle (Ed.), *Handbook of personality and self-regulation* (pp. 47–63). New York: Wiley-Blackwell.

Warneken, F. & Tomasello, M. (209). The roots of human altruism. *British Jounal of Psychology* (100), 455–471. doi: 10. 1348/000712608X379061

Wellman, H.M., & Miller, J.G. (2008). Including deontic reasoning as fundamental to theory of mind. *Human Development, 51,* 105–135.

Wellman, H.M., & Phillips, A.T. (2001). Developing intentional understandings. In B.F. Malle, L.J. Moses & D.A. Baldwin (Eds.), *Intentions and intentionality* (pp. 125–148). Cambridge: MIT Press.

AFFILIATION

Tobias Krettenauer
Department of Psychology
Wilfrid Laurier University
Waterloo, Canada

AUGUSTO BLASI

III. THE SELF AND THE MANAGEMENT OF THE MORAL LIFE

INTRODUCTION

If an intelligent Martian, naturally unable to grasp the tacit assumptions that underlie everyday language among humans, tried to understand what it is that we call morality by reading extensively the literature of scientific psychology, he or she or it would conclude that moral behaviour is something that just happens to people, brought about by factors that are either internal in the individual or from his or her environment. This conclusion is almost inevitable, when one goes through the explanations given by Freudian and other psychoanalytic schools, biological-evolutionary theories, the different versions of behaviourism and learning theories, sociological and social psychological treatments, and so on. This conclusion would seem to be even more convincing, as these theories also tell us how people's beliefs that they are free and responsible agents of their moral actions are in fact a result of distorting and self-deceptive strategies.

THE NOTION OF SELF-MANAGEMENT

Many psychologists may not subscribe, at least explicitly, to the theories mentioned above. However, they too, in explaining behaviour, including moral behaviour, use a language that conveys the idea of impersonality and of causal determination: behaviour, they claim, is a result of this or that emotion, this or that trait or combination of traits, this or that environmental condition, etc. The impression of impersonality does not change when explanations rely on structural concepts – personality systems; stages, or even moral structures; the ego (in the psychoanalytic meaning), and so on. Most confusing is that those authors, who rely on these structural or systemic concepts, frequently believe that, in doing so, they succeed in salvaging the role of free agency.

They lightly mix the language of impersonal causation with that of personal agency, without bothering to explain the relations between the two sets of expressions, seemingly unaware that such relations are far from obvious and ought to be justified; in particular, they do not explain how intentions – that's where moral agency begins – are linked to a person's system, structure, or stage. In other words, in all these approaches the focus is on the impersonal tools – traits, emotions, structures, stages – by which behaviour is produced, and not on the person agent using the tools.

K. Heinrichs, F. Oser & T. Lovat (Eds.), Handbook of Moral Motivation: Theories, Models, Applications, 229–248.

However, if instead of asking the Martian, we ask lay people how they see the relations they have with their action and their lives, we arrive at very different conclusions. In general, people seem to believe that, of course, there are impersonal forces, but their actions frequently are a result of choices, decisions, and even planning. Interestingly, they stick to these beliefs, even when they emphasize social constrictions, educational determinants, biological factors, the role of stars and planets, or of the powerful fate. These assumptions are so strong that many of us have a hard time accepting the loss of responsibility in those cases where such a conclusion ought to be rationally accepted.

These common beliefs cannot be a simple result of invincible illusions and self-deceptive processes. In fact people do distinguish between those who actually do manage their lives and those who don't ("get your act together," they say); and they note the different consequences of succeeding or failing in managing one's life. One example with which most of us are familiar is the protracted intellectual and personal transformations that, starting with the early school experience, lead us to professional competencies and commitments. In spite of the crucial role of cultural and educational institutions, of parents and teachers, of internalised standards of competence, etc., there is a point for many young people when they take over the management of their school and professional preparation; then they guide themselves in the pursuit of their goals, remind themselves of previous failures and of what produced them; observe those who do well, and try to learn from them; ask for advice and help; repeatedly renew their motivation and their desire for accomplishments and success. Some may even question school expectations and professional standards, may modify them, and finally appropriate them, so as to be personally responsible for pursuing them successfully. In their essence, the strategies for managing one's moral life are not that different.

There is a field of study in psychology that mirrors our common experience of managing our life, the field of self-regulation. In general, self-regulation refers to the attempts within the personality system to modulate, modify, and organize its own processes in order to produce behaviour that is more adaptive and better suited to one's goals. Already Freud understood the necessity of an agency within the human organism that could control one's powerful impulses and transform them into adaptive and acceptable expressions; he called this agency the ego, assigning to it a series of regulating processes and functions. Eventually the ego grew in importance within psychoanalysis, and was given motivational autonomy; this new perspective produced important empirical work under the labels, ego controls and cognitive controls (cf. Gardner, Holzman, Klein, Linton & Spence, 1959). Closer to us, within experimental and personality psychology, the work of Bandura (e.g., 1986), Mischel (e.g., 1981), and others can be considered the starting points of the spectacular growth that the field of self-regulation underwent in the past 20 years.[1]

Self-regulation was studied in various applied fields: health and illness, including such clinical disorders as anxiety and depression; antisocial behaviour, delinquency, and psychopathy; the domain of work and organizational settings; learning in academic and other settings. Disappointingly, moral functioning, let alone moral self-management, is almost entirely absent. Much work was done on general processes of self-regulation; e.g., attentional control; action monitoring and self-monitoring; goal setting; affect regulation, and hierarchical planning. These processes are sometimes structured into explanatory models, e.g., Carver & Scheier's (1998) feedback-loop model; Cervone's (2006) Knowledge-and-Appraisal Personality Architecture; Mischel & Shoda's (1995) Cognitive-Affective Personality Systems model. There seems to be general agreement that the essential elements of self-regulation are: a goal with its motivational pull; hierarchical planning; attention in the form of monitoring the distance between one's behaviour and the goal; and between one's behaviour change and the same goal. Interestingly, when these many concepts and models are stripped of their jargon quality, one realizes that all this scientific armamentarium is very similar to our everyday language and our commonsense understanding of self-control and self-management.

In what follows, I will be using the findings about self-regulation, but only sparingly. There are two reasons for my approach. The first is that, as I mentioned earlier, the work on self-regulation was not applied yet with any consistency or depth to problems of moral functioning. The second reason is of a theoretical, or meta-theoretical, nature, and goes back to the discussion at the beginning of this chapter. Psychologists working on self-regulation, both as a group and individually, are uncertain, or ambivalent whether the processes that they study are agentic in nature and can therefore be viewed as falling under the domain of personal responsibility. Descriptively, practically everyone recognizes that self-regulation processes are, at times, automatic and unconscious, and, at other times, conscious and intentional or wilful. However, when it comes to the process as a whole, important differences appear: at one extreme, there are those like Bargh (e.g., 2005), who, impressed by the extensive automaticity not only of perceptual processes, but also of affective and motivational processes, believe that "even complex social behaviour can unfold without an act of will or awareness of its sources" (ib., p. 54). At the other extreme there are those "humanistically oriented writers" (the label is Bargh & Chartrand's, 1999), who insist that the subject of self-regulation is the whole person, intentionally and effortfully engaged at managing oneself (e.g., Cervone, 2006, and Mischel & Shoda, 1996). The words appear to be reassuring. The context is less so: the molar process, in fact, is fragmented into many sub-functions, which then need to be coherently organized. In describing how such an organization is achieved, these authors rely on the language of triggers and activation, with its clear impersonal connotations. In other words, these models are presented in such a way as if they were guided by a sort of mechanical rationality. As a result, when the mechanism breaks down, then, theoretically, the models too seem to break down.

THE MANY TASKS OF MANAGING ONE'S MORAL LIFE

In what follows I attempt to provide a description of what is involved in the process of deciding how to live morally. The purpose is to give a general idea of potential problems and possible obstacles, but also of the desirability to take an active approach to one's moral life as a whole. This description relies on common experience and on commonly shared concepts and language; therefore, managing is understood to be a basically conscious intentional pursuit. As the psychological literature on self-regulation repeatedly points out, many regulatory and control processes are automatic rather than intentional, operating below the level of consciousness. This fact is taken into account, here, in discussing the problems people encounter in living their morality, when "automatic controls" may lead to morally negative intentions and decisions. The theoretical, philosophical, issues that arise from the mixture of conscious intentions and unconscious processes will be briefly discussed in a later section.

The story of moral self-management is schematically divided in three main steps: the formulation of a moral judgment; the transformation of the judgment into a moral intention and a moral action; the extension of this process from action to action, day after day, in a project that lasts as long as life does. Of course, nothing is so linear and clean, certainly not morality. But this scheme should allow me to discuss the various issues in some orderly way. The first section, on moral judgment, is more detailed than the others, because of the importance of this first step, and also because the issues that are raised in that context can be transferred imaginatively to the other steps of the process.

At the starting point there must be a reasonable level of moral motivation, a desire to be moral and to do what is morally right. The presence of such a desire is simply assumed here; without it, without moral goals, one cannot expect that a person will intentionally and consciously engage in guiding his or her moral life. But moral desires may be limited – by other desires; by one's understanding of morality and of what really matters morally; by one's capacities for self-regulation, and also by one's grasp of what is involved in actively realizing one's moral goals. I also assume that living one's life well does not come spontaneously or easily; that the process, extended in time, is difficult and requires the use of all one's mental and social resources; that at every step there may be obstacles and problems, even when one is not aware of them. There are two general questions that ought to interest psychologists: First, how, using which strategies, do people manage their moral situations in order to arrive where they wish to go, without being deceived by appearances, or being seduced by a simplistic criterion of sincerity? Second, do people approach these tasks, and to what extent, from the perspective of the agentic self – that is, not only consciously and intentionally, but also taking responsibility for each step? Here, by responsibility I mean appropriating the various processes, feeling that each is one's very own. I will come back to this idea in a later section.

I wish I could present a review of the literature on this topic, but there is no psychological literature on managing a moral life. This is surprising, considering that the topic (though not the term) of self-regulation has been with us almost from the beginning of empirical psychology, and considering that Piaget's seminal work on moral development is 80 years old, while Kohlberg's earlier publications are almost

50. But the field of self-regulation, with rare exceptions, has not been interested in morality, while moral psychology and moral developmental psychology have been occupied with other issues. What I am presenting here, then, is a result of common reflection on everyday experience, of repeated observations, and also of what we have been learning from psychology concerning human actions and projects, the pursuit of goals and its failures, and the widespread influence of biases and distortions.

Formulating Moral Judgments

Many in and out of psychology, when they think of morality, naturally put the emphasis on action, and then explain moral action by stressing such non-cognitive processes as emotions, social influence, and conformity to social standards and models. I think, however, that the formulation of appropriate, unbiased, moral judgments is arguably the most important step in moral functioning. There are two main reasons for my belief: first, a judgment that is guided by a perhaps vague idea of the moral good provides moral meaning to every successive step, framing the whole process, from intention to action, in moral terms. No other factor can replace moral judgment for this role.

The second reason is that formulating moral judgments is a seriously problematic process. Not infrequently decisions that have negative, even disastrous consequences are a result of unreflected, hasty, poorly grounded, or biased judgments. It could be argued that these faulty judgments produce more damage to society than moral hypocrisy. At times one is surprised and dismayed in hearing how people justify their disastrous actions. Their judgments may not be self-serving, and may express a sincere commitment to personal values, that are neither reflected on nor justified. In these instances, being confronted with sincerity can be terribly frustrating, because, even when it hides shallowness and laziness, sincerity is practically unassailable.

A judgment that is a morally adequate response to a situation is the outcome of two elements: an undistorted, and, in moral terms, relatively complete perception of its factual characteristics, and an interpretation of it through appropriate moral criteria. A moral judgment will be faulty, with more or less serious consequences, when either one of these sources is flawed or compromised. For example, conflicts among siblings marked by a deep sense of injustice and a desire for revenge, may arise from a misperception of the way the parents distribute rewards, affection, and tasks. Much more complex and serious, the judgment that one should support the war in Iraq for many was the result, in part, of erroneous beliefs concerning the arms of mass destruction, and probably a miscalculation about the consequences that a war would have for hundreds of thousands of people, American and Iraqi.

As is well known, our perception of people and events is frequently partial and distorted. Sometimes we are distracted, too tired and lazy, or not sufficiently interested to make the effort that is required to carefully look at what is happening and to analyse the circumstances. More fundamentally, however, our perception is frequently shaped automatically by the objects we encounter, not only in the obvious sense that the world determines what we perceive, but also in another sense: external events are associated with certain internal orientations and biases in such a way as to produce, spontaneously and outside our awareness, perceptions that in some ways do not correspond to reality. Being completely spontaneous, these perceptions carry the illusion of truth. Bargh and his colleagues, in their decades-long research program (e.g., Bargh & Morsella, 2008), studied many aspects of such automaticity: e.g., the coding of events, objects, and people into ready-made categories; the spontaneous, unintentional, stereotyping of a person as soon as certain distinguishing group characteristics are perceived; the interpretation of an event through contextual priming, etc. According to Bargh, frequently these perceptions are associated with simple emotional reactions, preferential orientations, motivations and goals, together leading the perceiver to a strong interpretive orientation of people and events.

To these phenomena one should add the automatic, unintentional effect of other cognitive biases that are reported in social psychological research: the tendency to "anchor" one's perception on one aspect of the event, and to rely heavily on one trait or piece of information; the tendency to spontaneously search for what confirms one's preconceptions; the excessive attention to either negative or positive aspects; the "halo effect"; the "in-group bias"; the "just world" expectation, spontaneously suggesting that what a victim suffers is deserved, and many others.

In order to arrive at a moral judgment concerning a concrete situation – I should or should not behave in such a way; the way so and so acted is completely wrong, etc. – the situation has to be interpreted through moral criteria, whose function is to give such expressions as "should," "wrong," "good," "unforgivable" a specifically moral meaning. In this context, I take "moral criteria" to refer to ideas, frequently simple, and perhaps unverbalized, concerning the aspects, the reasons, according to which the contemplated action-in-context is right or wrong, good or bad. If verbalized, these ideas could be expressed by a "because" followed by a statement that at least implicitly contains a rule sounding phrase: because – it is good to help, – he needs help, – he is my friend, – it's my family, – it is your duty, – cheating is dishonest, etc. Thus understood, these common criteria are at a rather low, concrete level in the logical hierarchy of moral criteria.

Excepting those relatively infrequent instances when the process of arriving at a moral judgment is complex, difficult, or conflicted, the criteria by which we determine the morality of an action are not, at least immediately, the result of reasoning through the situation; rather, frequently they seem to arise spontaneously, almost embedded in the situation itself; they feel intuitive and obvious. Of course, some of these criteria, at least for some people, in times past were either derived from a process of reasoning, or analysed through thoughtful reflection, and then, by repeated use, had acquired the characteristics of habitual intuitions – intuitions, however, whose origin could be easily recaptured, thus providing these criteria with the force of rational conviction.

In other instances, perhaps the large majority, the moral criteria are expressions of internalised norms and social expectations, of a commonsense crystallized in proverbs, maxims, and the like; they were never seriously reflected upon, but simply accepted as matters of course. Among these criteria I would include the "moral heuristics" proposed by some cognitive scientists (e.g., Gigerenzer, 2008; Cosmides & Tooby, 2004) and Haidt's (e.g., Haidt & Bjorklund, 2008) basic moral intuitions. The former are presented as rules of thumb operating rapidly and economically, at a non-conscious level, in response to environmental cues to produce judgments and decisions; they would cover such various issues as sexuality and inbreeding, cooperation and sharing, fairness, obedience and conformity, responsibility and punishment. Similarly, Haidt presents his intuitions as the source of moral judgments and the basic elements of moral functioning. In his theory, they would derive from five moral categories inscripted in the brain, and generating five sets of moral sensitivities concerning harm, suffering, and care; reciprocity, fairness, and justice; in-group affiliation and loyalty; authority and obedience; and the purity and sanctity of the human body. What matters for my present purposes are not the specific theories of moral heuristics or of social intuitionism, but the fact that these rules and sensitivities are seen as immediate, unreflected, intuitive sources of moral judgment.

Unfortunately, these low level, concrete criteria are also those that are more readily exposed to the distorting influence of self-serving and other biases, and that more directly affect action. For instance, many of the strategies that Bandura (e.g., 1990; 2002) describes as facilitating moral disengagement can also be used as genuine moral criteria. There are no criteria, no reasons, on which we rely to justify our behaviour, that unequivocally indicate either truthful or self-protective and distorted intentions. The same concrete reasons may serve both purposes: the interests of one's family or loyalty to one's group, obedience to the legitimate authorities, concern for social justice and equality can be used to justify moral, even heroic, actions, or, vice-versa, as unconscious masks to excuse one's immoral and cruel intentions (cf. Blasi, 1982).

In addition, intuitive moral criteria, particularly when they seem obvious, even when they are not used for defensive or self-interested purposes, may lead to moral judgments that are faulty under the circumstances, or lead to destructive consequences for oneself and other people. Several cognitive scientists pointed to unfortunate, and on occasion morally repulsive, consequences of actions that were regulated by heuristics and intuitions (Gigerenzer, 2008; Cosmides & Tooby, 2006; Sunstein, 2008); two examples are a vindictive and useless approach to punishment, and a restricted, tribal, attitude toward sharing the resources. I would like to emphasize, in particular, the natural tendency to obey the authority and to be loyal to one's group, even when one knows, at some level, that what is being demanded is harmful and unjust. The emotional and motivational force of the obedience criterion, internalised when we were children, continues to produce its effects also in our adulthood, at times overwhelming our more mature criteria.

To summarize, moral judgment, central to moral functioning, depends on the perception of a morally relevant situation and on its interpretation through moral criteria; however, both of these elements are easily open to distortion and error, as well as to self-serving and self-protective biases, processes that frequently operate outside our awareness. Thus, they may engage us in actions of which we would be deeply ashamed, if we could see them as they really are from an objectively moral perspective.

This is the situation that a person who cares about morality must confront. How can this person protect himself or herself? How can he or she remedy the fragility of moral judgment? One cannot find much in academic psychology that would be helpful in trying to answer these questions. There is now a small but growing field of research that is working on techniques to modify cognitive biases, particularly as they affect emotional disorders (for a review, cf. the special issue of the Journal of Abnormal Psychology, 2009, vol. 118, No. 1). The important lesson for moral psychology of this work is that cognitive and social biases, also when they operate automatically and unconsciously, can be controlled and regulated; in formulating moral judgments we don't need to be passive victims of their influence. Once again, however, with few exceptions (Greenberg, 1983; Ford, Gambino, Lee, Mayo & Ferguson, 2004; Demuijnck, 2009; Sherman, Gawronski, Gonsalkorale, Hugenberg, Allen & Groom, 2008), this work was not concerned with moral judgments and decisions.[2]

Therefore, a person's effort to manage his or her moral life can only rely on commonsense ideas, on what one knows about oneself, and also on what is known about the general ways of operating of distorting processes. One essential prerequisite, in addition to reawakening one's moral motivation,[3] is a degree of humility, that is, the realization of the difficulty of formulating unbiased judgments, and the acceptance of one's personal vulnerability to the effects of self-deceptive processes (in this context, Zimbardo, 2007, and Pratkanis & Aronson, 2001, write about the "illusion of invulnerability"). When one is willing to entertain doubts about one's perceptions and moral criteria, only then can one raise the necessary questions about one's moral judgments.

The central strategy in working through one's moral judgments is to ask oneself questions, to sharpen one's awareness. Those psychologists who advise people on how to protect themselves from the negative effects of social influence and propaganda, most frequently speak of awareness, mindfulness, and critical thinking (Pratkanis & Aronson, 2001; Zimbardo, 2007). The morally motivated person can raise questions about oneself both concerning one's typical tendencies, needs, vulnerabilities, and specifically about the present situation – one's possible personal interests, what one would gain or lose in acting in one or another way, or the possible effects of one's ideology and prejudices. One can also ask questions about the people who are involved in the situation: whether one understood the predicament of each of them and their perspective, how the decision of one would affect each of them; whether one can trust the sources of information, for instance, the accounts and explanations of events provided by the authorities or the media. One can think through the criteria used to arrive at the judgment: Are they appropriate? Would one use the same criteria, if one were to occupy a different role in the same situation? Are one's present criteria coherent with one's moral ideas and ideals, with the kind of person one wants to be; or, vice-versa, are the criteria one is using inappropriately sensitive to social pressure, family demands, or one's concern for reputation and image? In particular, are they reflecting the rigid influence of childish, or in any way less mature moral concerns?

The morally motivated person can finally raise questions about cognitive and social biases, and the way these may affect one's judgment in the present situation. Since many of these biases operate unconsciously, raising this question may seem useless. The facts, however, are more complex. It is indeed the case that those cognitive biases that automatically lead to erroneous judgments are not open to direct conscious realization; but one could have discovered that certain perceptual patterns depart systematically from the way other people see things. As for the self-serving and self-protective tendencies leading to self-deceptive judgments, their inaccessibility to conscious analysis is rarely total. There are probabilistic indicators of self-deceptive processes: for instance, inconsistencies with one's general beliefs; contradictions between what a person allows for oneself or one's friends and what he or she allows for other people; the avoidance of discrepant information, and resistance to engage in discussion about one's conclusions; the use of "forced," specious arguments; emotionality, anxiety in particular, when one is constrained to confront the issues. Moreover it is not unusual for some people to recognize their self-deception, to experience a vague discomfort, even a sense that something is missing, at the very moment of formulating the judgment or making a moral decision. It is this vague sense that something is not quite right that the morally motivated person can explore.

If the morally motivated person feels responsible for the consequences of his or her actions and not only for his or her sincere intentions, there are other ways to achieve that goal in addition to becoming aware of how he or she arrived at the moral judgment. One would be to carefully consider what the consequences of different decisions would be. Another would be to learn the effective strategies to neutralize the influence of biases. For instance, psychologists have been finding: that self-awareness (through the mirror technique) tends to control the egocentric bias (Greenberg, 1983); that introducing a condition of accountability to others tends to control racial bias among managers engaged in hiring employees (Ford, et al., 2004); that training oneself to negate biased associations – a strategy that attempts to replace certain automatisms with other equally mindless but preferable automatisms – is also effective in controlling racial bias (Sherman, 2008). Even instructions and self-instructions may work to regulate automatic biases under certain conditions.

Finally one may want to compare his or her moral judgment with the judgments formulated by other people for the same situation, discuss the differences, inquire about the reasons for their different judgments, and try to find a resolution. Haidt (e.g., with Bjorklund, 2008), who is generally sceptical about the role of reflection and reasoning, recognizes that good, unbiased, reasoning could emerge in a social context, in discussion, when the participants are open to the reasons of their partners. I should add a point that Haidt seems to miss, namely, that relying on social exchanges to critically examine one's moral judgments does not eliminate the person's responsibility to decide which of several possible reasons and judgments is actually right and should be followed. From this perspective, the resort to dialogue and discussion still is an attempt to manage one's moral life.

From Moral Judgment to Moral Action

Not all moral judgments call for action, but some do. A moral action may consist in refraining from acting, and can be as simple as voicing one's indignation, signing a petition, or voting on political elections; simple is not the same as unimportant or inconsequential. In some instances the distance between moral judgment and action is practically nonexistent, as the former is embedded in, and undistinguishable from the spontaneous decision. In other instances the judgment leads to an intention to be actualised at a future time. Sometimes, finally, moral judgments do not inform a single action, but rather project-like activities that have to be pursued through an extended period of time.

The central task of moral self-management, now, is to see that one's responsible judgment give form to a decision to act, and then shape one's moral activity. But rarely things are so linear. The situation may change; or one's perception of it may change (perhaps as a result of new or more accurately considered information); or one may have a different moral insight about the same situation. In sum, one may realize that what was a responsible judgment is no longer accurate and acceptable, and it would not be responsible to stick with it for the sake of consistency. A judgment, as responsibly as it was originally formulated, is never fixed; there frequently are reconsiderations, second and third thoughts, before it is translated into action, and also afterwards in the form of regret. From the perspective of moral management, it should be understood that the same biases, distorting and self-deceptive processes that threatened the original judgment are also at work in its successive reconsiderations.

Even when the judgment that one ought to behave in a certain way is clear and firm, the route from judgment to intention, and from intention to action, can be hesitant, filled with delays, start-and-stops, fraught by obstacles of different kinds, particularly when the intention has to be realized at a later time or through a long series of activities. At times the problem is simply a result of inertia, entrenched habits, the necessity to change comfortable roles, or the embarrassment of being different from one's usual self. There may be practical, logistical, bureaucratic difficulties in carrying out one's intentions. There may be disagreements and misunderstandings with family and friends, oppositions from other people; there may be teasing and mocking, and a variety of strategies aimed at obtaining conformity and obedience, when one's moral intentions are perceived as going against the group's expectations or the authorities' decisions. Of course, these social pressures are powerful to the extent that they find internal collusions in the person, in his or her need to be liked and accepted, to impress others, or to be at the center of social attention. There is, then, the work of those self-deceptive excusing strategies that are described in psychoanalytic work and in social psychological research on attribution and accounts, and on moral disengagement (Bandura, 1990; Scott & Lyman, 1968; Semin & Manstead, 1983).

Here too, if the morally motivated person is convinced that his or her judgment was formulated responsibly, the effective strategy is what self-regulation experts emphasize, namely, self-monitoring. This person needs to maintain one's attention focused on one's goal as expressed in his or her intention; to keep track of the distance between one's behaviour at the moment and where one should be according to one's intention; to become aware of the precise obstacles that are preventing him or her from reaching the goal, and of the strategies one can use to overcome them. In attempting to manage one's moral life, attention has to be directed to several aspects of the task. Some are practical in nature, concerning the obstacles and the strategies to bypass them. I suspect, however, that the aspects that matter most, the most effective to reach the goal, are motivational. These include one's moral ideals and desires in their most general and abstract form, and also in the specific ways these ideals are translated in the present intention; they include the specific concerns that led the person to judge the contemplated action as morally necessary for oneself, and the consequences of acting in one or another way for other people and for society. It should not be easy to withstand the tension created by repeatedly shifting one's attention back and forth, between the detailed consequences of one's action and the generalities of what one deeply cares about.

A second motivational aspect has to do with the sense of oneself, of who one is, as it was shaped by one's most central values and ideals. Here I am referring to integrity, namely, the need to maintain the unity, the wholeness, of one's subjective sense of self, as manifested in consistency with one's chosen commitments (cf. Blasi, 2005). In this case, the person's desires are not only oriented to the object of one's moral concerns, namely, the welfare of other people and of humanity as a whole, but are also directed at the intactness of the subjective self that was constructed around the same concerns. When the sense of self is shaped by moral ideals, certain actions are felt to be unthinkable (Frankfurt, 1988); engaging, then, in contradictory action would be experienced as the collapse of one's essential being.

The Moral Life

A moral life can be understood as a life punctuated, now and then, by responses to morally relevant situations. But there is a different, more active, way of approaching a life, when living morally becomes a project that one pursues, day after day, as long as one is capable of managing one's existence. Also for those who are not, nor wish to be, moral heroes, for whom daily events revolve around a normal family and work life, and whose lives are taken up with many interests and pursuits, there can be an active continuity in living morally. It seems to me that this project involves three aspects: the intention to fulfil one's moral obligations, to accomplish one's duties and responsibilities, and to avoid all that is unjust and hurtful to others; the attempt to find an appropriate balance between one's interests and concerns for others' well-being; and finally the cultivation of what I call "moral sensibility." Here, I mostly limit myself to a discussion of this third aspect, which can significantly affect also the other two.

We know of people – we have encountered them – who are very attentive to the moral aspects of situations and events, who seem to always be ready to raise moral questions and to take a moral stance also when they are not directly involved or required to act; who respond with moral indignation at glaring immorality, and seem to experience sadness and depression at the vastness of moral problems, particularly when they feel powerless to prevent wrongdoings and injustices. Not infrequently these people are labelled "moralists," and are accused of being rigid, narrow-minded, judgmental, given to boring preaching in their wish to regulate the morality of other people; their behaviour and attitudes are interpreted as unconscious expressions of a deep-seated fear of their impulses, of a suspicion of anything that is pleasurable and sensual, or as an unconscious desire to prove their superiority, at least in the moral domain. That this disturbing portrait is sometimes observed; that these characteristics are real risks of a moral life is undeniable. However, the fact that moral values, like any value, can be abused, and can be corrupted and exploited by other needs does not disprove the possibility of their being genuine. There is moral hypocrisy; but there is also genuine moral sensibility; its foundations are a real conviction of the importance of morality not only in one's life, but also in the affairs of the world; and, related to it, the lived presence of moral desires.

By moral sensibility I am not referring to some hypothetical natural attunement, a sort of spontaneous empathic orientation that people may have to moral situations and events. I mean, rather, a developed, intentionally or unintentionally constructed, facility to perceive the morally relevant aspects of what surrounds us, and a readiness to respond to these aspects with judgments and emotions. Such a sensibility may have a starting point in spontaneous emotions and intuitions (however these may come about), and a basis in those moral judgments concerning one's obligations and altruistic responses that have become habitual. These habits of judgment, emotion, and action become a sensibility through repetition, and particularly through their progressive extension to include domains of reality that earlier were outside the horizon of one's moral attention. One way to cultivate one's moral sensibility, the way I would like to emphasize here, would consist precisely in extending one's attention and one's moral capacities to areas that do not yet evoke a moral response. Then not only more and more of one's world would come under the influence of one's moral concerns, providing the continuity that makes a moral life, but, in confronting new situations and problems, one's mental and emotional capacities would, in turn, become more secure and highly developed.

I think that a person's moral sensibility could be extended at least in three directions. The first one concerns those duties and obligations in which one is already engaged, but frequently are not immediately perceived as moral. There are many routine obligations – for example, duties at work, commitments within one's family, relationships of reciprocity with one's friends – that, though clearly moral, are not looked at as formally moral, especially if they are approached with genuine interest and pleasure. Their moral nature would immediately appear as soon as one separates one's idea of morality from some of its frequent but erroneous connotations: as being externally imposed, burdensome, disagreeable, effortful, and calculated. At first sight, the attempt to view as moral what one already does with ease and pleasure may appear to be somewhat perverse. And yet, in addition to freeing oneself from the above connotations, what one gains in so extending one's moral sight is the immediate realization of the role and importance of morality in one's daily life, and also the experienced presence of moral motivation.

Moral sensibility could be extended in a second direction, namely, toward that infinite and complex world of human needs and of one's responsibility in it. Considering the immensity of people's necessities and miseries, the limitations of one's material and emotional resources, and one's legitimate desire to pursue personal interests and the interests of family and friends, it is clear that one's moral responsibilities in this area are also limited; as many would agree, people do have a general obligation to contribute to human welfare, but not a specific obligation in each and every instance of need. In each case judgment is required to decide whether and how one should help. One potential problem, here, is that one feels overwhelmed emotionally and morally, and thus trains one's eyes and mind not to see. It is here that moral sensibility plays an important role, to slowly bring the person to formulate a set of fair and perhaps generous altruism rules for oneself to apply flexibly and yet firmly in one's life. Once formulated, these rules may free the person of some of his or her guilt, and would open his or her mind and emotions to the extension and enormity of human suffering.

In addition, and this is the third direction, there is a world of situations that present morally relevant aspects, but in which one is not directly involved, nor is one called to act upon in any specific way; behaviours that one observes in others, or that one hears or reads about in the media and books, including fictional stories. In some instances the moral aspect is readily seen; many other situations, however, even important ones, frequently are not classified as moral, nor are they perceived as such by many of us. Among these, there is that vast domain of issues that concern what can be called "public morality." We live and participate in organizations and institutions – the companies we work for, our communities and neighborhoods, our cities and countries; the industrial and the business world; the world of sports and religious institutions, and so on – where moral issues frequently arise, and about which adults, whether they are participants or observers, are called to take a stance, to behave as moral judges, and, when appropriate, to act accordingly. To use only a few examples, many issues arise in the context of work – the conditions in which work takes place, decisions about hiring and firing, the adequacy and justice of salaries; the nature of the products that are created and the ways they are marketed.

Other issues concern the political world and social policies at every level of our societies: for instance, decisions concerning health and medical care; or the ways poverty and migration are dealt with, and the adequacy of the adopted solutions from a moral perspective, and not only from the perspective of public opinion or the electoral vote. One particularly important chapter concerns war, with all its casualties, destructions, social and psychological consequences.

It is not difficult to multiply these examples, and to realize then the space and the importance that morality could occupy in the minds of morally motivated people. And yet, as I discussed elsewhere (Blasi 2009), these issues not only have been neglected in moral psychology, but frequently are not reached by our moral sensibility. One reason is that we tend to rely on different categories to interpret them and make sense of them – business or commerce, labour relations, politics and law, arts and aesthetics, etc. –, as if morality were one specific domain in life, operating next to the other life domains and in contrast with them, rather than being a special perspective that cuts across all areas of life. We may have opinions about, and also critical responses to, what happens in the public domain; but too rarely does our response proceed from a moral perspective, or is it driven by a personal moral commitment.

Briefly, the task that was emphasized here is the cultivation of an attitude of continuous attention to and interest for the moral aspects of the world that surrounds us; such an attitude would maintain one's moral desires present in one's consciousness, and would be an affirmation of the moral perspective. At the same time one would want to be aware of the risks that attend any moral sensibility, watchful that it not be corrupted by needs of which one is not fully conscious, and that would transform it into a caricature of itself – a spirit of complacency, righteousness, contempt for other people, and moral superiority.

Now, at the end of my descriptive excursus, it may be useful to step back and discuss the picture of morality that was presented here, namely, a morality that is controlled, constantly reflected on, striving to be rational also in its emotional aspects. There are two general objections to this view. For many morality is essentially a matter of spontaneous emotions; the idea of a moral life that is coldly rational and controlled, the very term, management, are felt to be calculating and repugnant. The other objection comes from contemporary cognitive science: for many of its authors (e.g., Gazzaniga, 2005; Gigerenzer, 2008; Haidt & Bjorklund, 2008; Hauser, 2006) moral judgments are essentially intuitive, whether or not the intuitions are emotional in nature; reflection and reasoning, instead, overall are seen to have a corruptive influence, introducing distortions and self-serving biases. These two views share a similar attitude: when it comes to morality, the truth is in what is natural; corruption lies in cultivated rationality.

The issue is important, and can be considered both from the perspective of society and of humanity as a whole, and from the perspective of the individual moral agent. There is no doubt that the institution of morality was created primarily to serve the welfare of individuals and societies, to control aggressive and destructive impulses, and to facilitate social participation, reciprocity, and altruism. If moral judgments and intentions are indeed vulnerable to distorting processes; if natural impulses and intuitions may themselves be corrupted and produce harmful consequences, in what way can human beings protect the intrinsic purposes of morality, except by reflecting on intuitions, impulses, and judgments, and by carefully monitoring whether they are serving the aims of morality, or rather are working against them?

From the perspective of the individual agent, it would seem to be highly desirable that each one of us learned to be responsible for one's life – one's health, one's social relationships, one's work and profession, and also one's moral life. To be responsible for one's moral functioning means to be responsible for one's moral judgments (an idea that is rarely considered in the social sciences) and for carrying these judgments through the intention and the action. To be responsible for this process means to be in charge and own it, by owning, as much as possible, its components and the processes by which they were carried out, from the perception of the situation to the resistance to biasing factors and self-deception. In doing so, one has to be ready to reject what one finds, ready-made, within oneself (intuitions, impulses, habits, crystallized criteria, and also emotions), as well as external influences and pressures, but one has to do so responsibly, everything considered. Spontaneity may be desirable in morality, however, not a natural spontaneity, but one that is arrived at, like for the professional musician, through reflection and long practice.

THE ROLE OF THE SELF IN MANAGING ONE'S MORAL LIFE

Post-Kohlbergian moral developmental psychology, with its shift from the almost exclusive emphasis on judgment and reasoning to a study of the personality context in which moral cognition operates, in addition to opening new perspectives, has already produced interesting findings. And yet it is disappointing at least in one respect. The new investigations (for examples see the various chapters in Narvaez & Lapsley, 2009) are frequently located either under the label "moral personality" or under "moral self." On close inspection, however, one finds that "self" almost always is taken as being equivalent to personality, and personality is understood as the structure of traits or other dimensions of individual differences, to be studied by correlational and factorial methods. Here the general question is: when we consider temperamental characteristics, emotional and motivational tendencies, and other personality traits, and add them to cognitive variables, which variables or combinations of variables contribute most to the variance in one or another aspect of moral behaviour?

This approach to the moral personality is limited in two important ways. First, traits and similar personality concepts are static, that is, as Cervone et al. (2006), among many others, forcefully emphasized, conceptually traits do not imply causation; they do not refer to processes, do not produce effects, and do not lend themselves to functional analyses. Second, when it comes to human action and morality in particular, the various functional processes and personality characteristics do not behave like independent entities but as tools used by an agent. In other words, moral functioning is the work of a subject self, that attempts to reach its goals and satisfy its desires (in this case, moral desires) by bringing together all its resources – memory and judgment, emotional and motivational tendencies, temperamental characteristics and traits, and so on. This is what it means for moral behaviour to be personal and not impersonal in nature. The various resources available to the subject self, as well as the strategies of using them to produce moral functioning, change through development; therefore the study of the moral self is open to developmental analyses. I tend to think that the study of the moral self, understood in these terms, did not yet begin. While we already know a great deal about several moral aspects, from judgment and reasoning to motivation and emotions, we still know very little about the ways all these resources are brought together to generate moral decisions and actions.

By self (or self as subject, to differentiate this concept from other very different meanings of the term) I (e.g., Blasi, 2004) am referring to that component of the human personality, irreducible to either the cognitive or the affective dimension, on which our sense of subjectivity and agency depend. Its foundation lies in the immediate, unreflected experience of being the source and the owner of one's actions that originates with the child's first intentional action and characterizes all successive actions and experiences. This experience of self involves several related, though distinguishable, aspects: that I act, that the action is mine, that the desire that I feel and guides the action is mine, and so is my intention, that there is a mine and a not-mine, and so on. In other words, in the early development of the subjective self, and forever after, there is the convergence of two central aspect characterizing the self: the experience of agency, and the experience of 'mineness' in agency and in desire; both the experience of desiring and of acting are shot through with the characteristic of ownership and possession.

The subject self develops and grows; it does so by expanding the domain of what is mine, by bringing more and more of the world that one experiences and also of oneself under its possession, that is, under the sense that it is mine. Thus, as one grasps the various features of the external world – concepts and ideas, customs and rules, models, values, etc. –, as one increasingly masters and possesses these "objects," these are experienced as one's own, as elements of who one is, and as components of one's desires and will. Similarly, the self progressively brings under the domain of the mine various internal aspects that objectively already were one's own, but were not really controlled, possessed, really felt as "mine": for example, one's emotions and desires, habits and other processes, temperamental and other personality characteristics, ideas that were blindly internalised, including certain views of morality, reasons and judgments. In fact, there are different degrees in the experience of mineness: there is the mine of what simply happens to be there, in my mind and body; there is the mine of what is there, but I wish were not there; there is the mine of what is wanted at the moment, and the mine of what is wanted also for the rest of one's life, for example, a moral ideal that one desires to have and cares about to the point of making oneself responsible for its realization; and there is the mine that is placed at the core of one's sense of self, a component of one's essential self (for a presentation of these ideas, see Frankfurt, 1988).

While the self, the experience of being a subject and an agent, is present in every action through the unreflected consciousness of acting, there are actions and processes that are accompanied by a clearer and more intense sense of agency and of being a separate, individual self: examples would be the experiences of attentive reflection on oneself, of a search for one's real feelings and motives; of effortful control and self-control, of self-contradiction and the search for self-consistency. The conscious attempt to manage one's life belongs in this network of processes and relies on them to achieve its goals.

In applying the notion of self-management to one's moral life, there are three aspects of the subject self that are particularly central and should be emphasized. The first concerns the appropriation of moral rules, principles, and ideals, to the point of feeling that they are one's very own, the objects of one's desires. Then, one wishes not only to do the morally right thing when the opportunity arrives, but also would want to control one's way of thinking and one's motives, and to organize one's life so as to make it difficult, if not impossible, to do what is unfair or hurtful, even when such behaviours were the result of unintentional errors and distortions. The second orientation, the accountability side of personal responsibility, concerns the conscious appropriation and ownership of the actions that one has already performed. One would then recognize as one's own not only the action itself, but also the entire sequence that led the person to act as he or she did; one would feel responsible for accurately perceiving the situation, for the moral criteria that one followed to arrive at a moral judgment; for controlling conflicting needs and desires, temptations and social pressures. The third orientation has to do with the need, and personal obligation, to consciously bring coherence and unity in one's moral life, including the need to resolve possible contradictions – among one's beliefs, beliefs and action, actions and the accounts one gives of them. One important aspect here is the construction of, and reliance on, strategies to protect oneself from self-deception, a major source of splits and fractures in the moral self. What is common to these three aspects and unifies them is an attitude of responsibility, once again understood as personal ownership and possession. Incidentally, to those among us who explain that the self as subject cannot be studied because it cannot be directly observed, one could reply that responsibility can be considered as the royal road to the self, and responsibility – the way people understand it, and how it develops – certainly can be investigated.

Am I not extending responsibility too far, beyond the limits of what a human will can possibly control? As discussed earlier, many processes automatically and non-consciously influence our perception and, through it, our motives and decisions. Are we responsible for what they do? The simple answer is that we are not. Kuhl and Koole (e.g., 2004), wishing to maintain the reality of the phenomenal will, and also wanting to study empirically the way it functions in self-management, argued that we ought to distinguish two wills, one corresponding to the wilfulness of experience, and the other that includes also "volitional processes" that are inaccessible to conscious experience. Many important choices, in their view, are not consciously experienced as choices, but can only be inferred after the fact. I think this language is unnecessarily confusing. The will begins with an intentional act and, conceptually, implies consciousness. There are no completely unconscious decisions and choices, and it is not clear what unconscious volitional processes could be. The act of willing might have been influenced by automatic unconscious processes, but the act itself must be conscious by definition, even though we may not be aware of all its antecedents. As long as the automatic unconscious processes do not strictly determine the action and its consequences, we are responsible for willing the action and for the intention that subtends it; we are responsible for managing the processes that lead to our judgment and intention, if we can be directly or indirectly aware of them; whether or not we are aware of their antecedent influences, we are responsible for monitoring and correcting intention and action, whenever their consequences are unacceptable from the perspective of our moral standards. I believe that Kuhl and Koole would agree.

CONCLUSION

It is not among the tasks and competencies of psychology to take a moral stance about the way people manage their moral life. But it should be of interest to psychologists that some people actively guide their moral functioning and others do not; that some adults try and succeed in managing, for example, their health and career, but are completely casual about morality; it would be psychologically interesting to find out which strategies people use to guide their moral functioning, and which of these strategies are effective and which are not. It is interesting that self-management, under the label, self-regulation, is such a lively field of research both basic and applied, but that, so far, it has not extended in any consistent way to the area of morality. One particular consequence is that the huge area of human functioning that includes self-deception, concern with self-deception, and resistance to it, still is for psychology a largely unexplored territory.

NOTES

[1]   This growth is testified by a special issue of the <u>Applied Psychology: An International Review</u> (2006, vol. 55, No. 3) and by two recent handbooks (Boekarts et al., 2005; Baumeister and Vohs, 2007).

[2]   It is interesting and puzzling that psychological research devoted a great deal of effort to provide us with long lists of distortions, systematically categorizing defence mechanisms and biases, and to demonstrate how vulnerable people are to their negative effects; but very little was done to study the resistance to bias and self-deception. One possible explanation of this collective orientation is that we psychologists, as a group, tend to believe that bias and self-deception are normal and ordinary; we also tend to share the assumption that cognitive processes are automatic and impersonal, and not guided by intention and responsibility. The idea that one may attempt to counteract, if not the processes,

at least the effects, of distortions did not yet acquire, also in moral psychology, the salience that it should have.

[3] Several studies found that motivation is effective also in controlling non-conscious biases: for instance, people who are personally motivated to control their racial prejudices perform better than those who are not so motivated on a stereotype-inhibition task (Sherman, 2008).

REFERENCES

Bandura, A. (1986). *Social foundations of thoughts and action.* Englewood Cliffs, NJ: Prentice Hall.

Bandura, A. (1990) Mechanisms of moral disengagement. In W. Reich (Ed.), *Origins of terrorism: psychologies, ideologies, theologies, states of mind* (pp. 161–191). Cambridge, Cambridge University Press.

Bandura, A. (2002). Selective moral disengagement in the exercise of moral agency. *Journal of moral education, 31,* 101–119.

Bargh, J.A. (2005). Bypassing the will: Towards demystifying behavioral priming effects. In R. Hassin, J. Uleman & J. Bargh (Eds.), *The new unconscious* (pp. 37–58). Oxford, UK: Oxford University Press.

Bargh, J.A., & Chartrand, T.L. (1999). The unbearable automaticity of being. *American psychologist, 44,* 462–479.

Bargh, J.A., & Morsella, E. (2008). The unconscious mind. *Perspectives on psychological science, 3,* 73–79.

Baumeister, R.F., & Vohs, K.D. (Eds.). (2007). *Handbook of self-regulation. Research, theory, and applications.* New York: The Guilford Press.

Blasi, A. (1982). Kognition, Erkenntnis und das Selbst [Knowledge in social cognition]. In W. Edelstein, & M. Keller (Eds.), *Perspektivität und Interpretation* (pp. 289–319). Frankfurt a.M..: Suhrkamp Verlag.

Blasi, A. (2004). Neither personality nor cognition: An alternative approach to the nature of the self. In C. Lightfoot, C. Lalonde, and M.J. Chandler (Eds.), *Changing conceptions of psychological life* (pp. 3–25). Mahwah, NJ: Erlbaum.

Blasi, A. (2005). Moral character: A psychological approach. In D.K. Lapsley and F.C. Power (Eds.), *Character psychology and character education* (pp. 67–100). Notre Dame, IN: University of Notre Dame Press.

Blasi, A. (2009). The moral functioning of mature adults and the possibility of fair moral reasoning. In D. Narvaez and D.K. Lapsley (Eds.), *Personality, identity and character. Explorations in moral psychology* (pp. 396–440). New York: Cambridge University Press.

Boekaerts, M., Pintrich, P.R., & Zeidner, M. (Eds.). (2005). *Handbook of self-regulation.* San Diego, CA: Academic Press.

Carver, C.S., & Scheier, M.F. (1998). *On the self-regulation of behavior.* New York: Cambridge University Press.

Cervone, D., Shadel, W.G., Smith, R.E., & Fiori, M. (2006). Self-regulation: Reminders and suggestions from personality science. *Applied Psychology: An International Review, 55,* 333–385.

Cosmides, L., and Tooby, J. (2004). Knowing thyself: The evolutionary psychology of moral reasoning and moral sentiments. In R.E. Freeman and P. Werhane (Eds.), *Business, Science, and Ethics. The Ruffin Series in Business Ethics* (Vol. 4, pp. 93–128). Charlottesville, VA: Society for Business Ethics.

Cosmides, L, & Tooby, J. (2006). Evolutionary psychology, moral heuristics and the law. In G. Gigerenzer, and C. Engel (Eds.), *Heuristics and the law* (pp. 181–211). Cambridge, MA: MIT Press.

Demuijnck, G. (2009). Non-discrimination in human resources management as moral obligation. *Journal of Business Ethics, 88,* 83–101.

Ford, T.A., Gambino, F., Lee, H., Mayo, E., & Ferguson, M.A. (2004). The role of accountability in suppressing managers' preinterview bias against African-American sales job applicants. *Journal of Personal Selling & Sales Management, 24,* 113–124.

Frankfurt, H. (1988). *The importance of what we care about.* New York: Cambridge University Press.

Gardner, R.W., Holzman, P.S., Klein, G.S., Linton, H.B., & Spence, D.P. (1959). Cognitive control: A study of individual consistencies in cognitive behavior. *Psychological Issues, 1* No. 4.

Gazzaniga, M.S. (2005). *The ethical brain*. New York: The Dana Press.

Gigerenzer, G. (2008). Moral intuition = Fast and frugal heuristics? In W. Sinnott-Armstrong (Ed.), *Moral psychology. Vol. 2: The cognitive science of morality: Intuition and diversity* (pp. 1–26). Cambridge, MA: MIT Press.

Greenberg, J. (1983). Overcoming egocentric bias in perceived fairness through self-awareness. *Social Psychology Quarterly, 46*, 152–156.

Haidt, J., & Bjorklund, F. (2008). Social intuitionists answer six questions about moral psychology. In W. Sinnott-Armstrong (Ed.), *Moral psychology. Vol. 2: The cognitive science of morality: Intuition and diversity* (pp. 181–218). Cambridge, MA: MIT Press.

Hauser, M.D. (2006). *Moral minds: How nature designed our universal sense of right and wrong*. New York: Ecco Press.

Kuhl, J., & Koole, S.L. (2004). Workings of the will: A functional approach. In J. Greenberg, S.L. Koole, & T. Pyszczynski (Eds.), *Handbook of experimental existential psychology* (pp. 411–430). New York: Guilford Press.

Mischel, W. (1981). Metacognition and the rules of delay. In J.H. Flavell and L. Ross (Eds.), *Social cognitive development: Frontiers and possible futures* (pp. 240–271). New York: Cambridge University Press.

Mischel, W., & Shoda, Y. (1995). A cognitive-affective system theory of personality: Reconceptualizing situations, dispositions, dynamics, and invariance in personality structure. *Psychological Review, 102*, 246–268.

Narvaez, D., & Lapsley, D.K. (2009). *Personality, identity, and character. Explorations in moral psychology*. New York: Cambridge University Press.

Pratkanis, A.R. & Aronson, E. (2001). *Age of propaganda: The everyday use and abuse of persuasion*. New York: W.H. Freeman/Holt.

Scott, M.B., & Lyman, S.M. (1968). Accounts. *American Sociological Review, 23*, 46–62.

Semin, G.R., & Manstead, A.S.R. (1983). *The accountability of conduct. A social psychological perspective*. London: Academic Press.

Sherman, J.W., Gawronski, B., Gonsalkorale, K., Hugenberg, K., Allen, T.J., & Groom, C.J. (2008). The self-regulation of automatic associations and behavioral impulses. *Psychological Review, 115*, 113–124.

Sunstein, C.R. (2008). Fast, frugal, and (sometimes) wrong. In W. Sinnott-Armstrong (Ed.), *Moral Psychology. Vol. 2: The cognitive science of morality: Intuition and diversity* (pp. 27–30). Cambridge, MA: MIT Press.

Zimbardo, P. (2007). *The Lucifer effect*. New York: Random House.

AFFILIATION

Augusto Blasi
Department of Psychology
University of Massachusetts Boston
Boston, MA, USA

TERENCE LOVAT

IV. PRACTICAL MYSTICISM, SELF-KNOWING AND MORAL MOTIVATION

INTRODUCTION

The chapter addresses the issue of moral motivation through creating a conversation between the ancient tradition of practical mysticism and current human sciences research. The focus in both cases is on the intensity of a knowing of self that impels acceding to the good in ways that exceed the norm. Through case study analysis and exploration of ancient and modern texts, both religious and social scientific, the argument is proffered that there is a form of knowing self that has potential to motivate superlative moral action. Furthermore, this knowing of self seems to be the common feature of moral motivation across the very different traditions under analysis. It is argued that this is an important insight for a generation that sits between religious and non-religious influences.

CASE STUDIES: MORE AND BONHOEFFER

Thomas More, Lord High Chancellor of England under King Henry VIII, paid the ultimate price for refusing to sign the Succession Act that would grant the rights to inherit the throne to any children resulting from Henry's marriage to Anne Boleyn. Henry had married Queen Anne 'outside the church of Rome' after divorcing Queen Catherine, a decision with which Thomas could not agree on conscientious grounds. Apart from the testimony around his personal reputation for integrity and his own personal religious faith, More's (1989) academic writings labour the point about the need for all people to achieve personal integrity and conform their actions to what is for the common good. This was the central task of any education, in his view, a truly moral education with potential to transform the individual towards enduring moral motivation, a persistent commitment to do the good. In Robert Bolt's (1990) play, *A Man for all Seasons*, the struggle that More endured in coming to the decision that would ultimately cost him his life is found in the verse: "'But what matters to me is not whether it's true or not but that I believe it to be true, or rather not that I *believe* it but that *I* believe it." (p. 53) Bolt has captured here the profound sense of self that sat at the heart of More's integrity. Again, in arguably the most heartrending scene in the play, when his favourite daughter, Meg, has been sent to the prison to convince Thomas that all the King wants is for him to sign the document, not necessarily to believe it, and that this tiny compromise would mean he could come home to the

K. Heinrichs, F. Oser & T. Lovat (Eds.), Handbook of Moral Motivation: Theories, Models, Applications, 249–264.

family he loves so much and for which he is grieving, he says: "When a man takes an oath, Meg, he is holding his own self in his own hands." (p. 83) In Bolt's caricature, at least, this profoundly religious man, who was no doubt morally motivated in part by his faith, nonetheless did not refer to his religious faith, so much as his knowing of self and attached personal integrity, in justifying the stance that would cost him his life.

In similar vein, in the Nazi prison for his actions against Hitler and abandoned by the church of his childhood, Dietrich Bonhoeffer (1998) struggled to answer the question 'Who is Christ for us today?' Who is Christ for a church that had surrendered its credibility in the face of such vile opposition? What could it mean to be Christian anymore? In seeking to answer the question, this erstwhile conservative Christian engaged in exploration quite beyond his own tradition and its beliefs. Part of this exploration involved his fraternity with the 'non-faithed', with those with whom he found himself sharing commitment and the conditions of prison but who were not at all motivated by a religious faith. As Bonhoeffer perceived it, their sole motivation was a profoundly moral one, underpinned by a deep and comfortable sense of self that impelled commitment to standing for what they knew was right, just and good. Bonhoeffer could not help but contrast these 'non-faithed', sometimes self-professed 'atheists' and 'agnostics', with so many of his 'enfaithed' colleagues whom he saw justifying piously their own inaction. He also could not but compare the sense of inner peace that he saw resulting from those who followed their own sense of integrity, regardless of the cost, with the inauthentic sense of self that he saw resulting from inaction and complicity with an unjust regime. In the end, Bonhoeffer (1959) posited the notion of 'religionless Christianity' as the only Christian form that could credibly survive the times in which he was living. The knowing that would underpin this 'religionless' faith for individual Christians was what he described as 'the arcane discipline', a deeply personal knowing of self that would emanate from complete conformity between one's understanding, one's dispositions and one's actions. It was arcane in the sense that it was part of one's private spirituality, remaining a secret between the individual and her or his God. The sign of its authenticity would not be in the 'cheap grace' of faith attachment but in what he described as the 'costly grace' of conforming one's life and actions to one's beliefs, a profound moral motivation. Again, like More, Bonhoeffer was clearly morally motivated by his religious faith but does not rely on it in the end to take the stand that would cost him his life. Indeed, he juxtaposes the cosmetics of faith with the true moral goodness he sees in those people of non-faith with whom he shares resistance to Hitler.

More and Bonhoeffer have it in common that the key to moral motivation lies in a profound self-knowing, one that, in their own cases, was impelled at least in part by religious faith. In a day and age that has seen religion displaced in large measure from the public square and in which there has been an attached discomfort with ascribing morality to spiritual impulsions, least of all to mystical experience, it is easy enough to dismiss the moral motivation implicit in More and Bonhoeffer as one belonging exclusively to those of religious faith. However, the very public engagement with the troubles of their day renders it an inadequate response to say of either More or Bonhoeffer that their moral motivation can simply be ascribed to religious faith, as one might say of the ascetic or enclosed monk. It should be noted that neither More nor Bonhoeffer finally justified their own moral actions in purely religious terms, choosing rather to make reference variously to noble action, integrity and self-knowing in ways that implied these were motivations available to all, religious and non-religious. This is especially important at a time in history, largely regarded as non-religious or post-religious, wherein prominent architects of moral thinking, epistemic and social philosophers (cf. Habermas, 1972, 1990) and moral psychologists (cf. Blasi, 1999, 2005) speak of the centrality to morality of self-knowing.

There are two areas of scholarship, one new and one old, that I wish to explore in reference to the above. First, there is renewed interest in the secular human sciences in notions such as spiritual intelligence, spiritual consciousness and even mysticism that seem persistently to include reference to moral motivation of the high order witnessed to in the case instances of More and Bonhoeffer. At the heart of this moral motivation is the notion of self-knowing. Second, and perhaps more intriguingly, we find at the heart of some of the most sophisticated mystical theologies available to us a persistent theme that suggests a non-religious if not anti-religious option for mystics that is deeply about moral engagement regardless of the cost. Again, the concept of self-knowing is central to moral motivation of this kind. I wish to explore each of these two scholarships below.

SPIRITUALITY, MYSTICISM AND MORAL MOTIVATION IN THE HUMAN SCIENCES

Notions of moral intention and moral motivation are mainly constructed in contemporary research within and around the terms set by the human sciences and by moral psychology in particular. In this context, spirituality and mysticism have largely been ignored if not discredited as traditions irrelevant to such research, at least in the public domain. However, the advent of new insights in psychology and the neurosciences that highlight the greater complexity of human cognition and intelligence than had obtained in most twentieth century thought include explicit reference to the notions of spirituality and mysticism and, moreover, these human facets are seen to have persistent bearing on the issue of moral motivation. Such updated insights impel one to think it might be helpful to recover and explore again some of the far older spiritual and mystical traditions and their perspective on what it is that impels moral motivation. Indeed, it could be that they help not only in recovering a moral motivation perspective for those who function in a religious world but, moreover, for the non-religious as well.

The modern neurosciences (Damasio, 2003; Immordino-Yang & Damasio, 2007; Northoff, 2010) represent a set of research findings concerned with the brain, its constitution and functioning, and hence a range of related issues around cognition, learning and human development. In contrast with many of their forebears, these neurosciences have established contingent relationships between cognition, affect, sociality and other developmental factors, including morality. In other words, the view that development is driven principally by a separable form of cognition has yielded to the realization that all developmental factors are in a synergistic relationship with each other. Arguably, it was Gardner (1983, 1999) who most imaginatively captured and grounded this understanding in his work on multiple intelligences. Gardner's original theory posited seven intelligences, namely, linguistic, logical, spatial, musical, bodily, interpersonal and intrapersonal. In acknowledging the debt owed to Gardner, Sternberg refers to two other forms of intelligence about which Gardner mused:

> Gardner has also suggested that there may be two other 'candidate' intelligences: spiritual intelligence and existential intelligence. Spiritual intelligence involves a concern with cosmic or existential issues and the recognition of the spiritual as the achievement of a state of being. (Sternberg, 2004, p. 426)

While Sternberg agrees with Gardner that these other candidates have not been subject to the same empirical tests as can be drawn on to demonstrate the original seven intelligences, he nonetheless argues that, such is the multivariate complexity of intelligence as now being understood, finding the 'balance' required of what he terms 'successful intelligence' demands we both keep an open mind about these other candidates and attempt to subject them to the same intensity (if not identical methods of) empirical scrutiny as have been applied to the rest.

Since this time, there has been no shortage of effort, albeit taking a variety of forms, to do precisely as Sternberg recommended (Beauregard & O'Leary, 2007; Walach, 2007; Beauregard & Paquette, 2008; Han et al., 2008; Barrett, 2010; Han et al., 2010; Heelas, 2011; Spezio, 2011). Emmons (2000) reviews evidence for spiritual intelligence against a number of empirical measures. His research proposes that spiritual intelligence consists of the following:

> (a) the capacity for transcendence; (b) the ability to enter into heightened spiritual states of consciousness; (c) the ability to invest everyday activities, events, and relationships with a sense of the sacred; (d) the ability to utilize spiritual resources to solve problems in living; and (e) the capacity to engage in virtuous behaviour (to show forgiveness, to express gratitude, to be humble, to display compassion). (p. 3)

In Emmons' definition, we see immediately the progressive linkages between the form of intelligence described as 'spiritual', the heightened consciousness (knowing) that ensues, the newfound resources one then brings to solving day to day problems and, especially under (e), these new resources taking the form of a fortified capacity (and presumably will) to engage in moral behaviour that is beyond the human norm and which has potential to transform the day to day situation (to forgive, show compassion, etc.). In Emmons' work, the capacity to engage in virtuous behaviour is underpinned by a moral motivation that centres on self-knowing, an abiding comfort with who one is, 'at peace in one's own skin'. Of the capacity for profound humility, as a case in point, Emmons proffers:

> It is the ability to … have a sense of self-acceptance, an understanding of one's imperfections, and to be free from arrogance and low self esteem. (Emmons, 2003, p. 171)

In such a conception, rendered from the modern human sciences, I would argue we see reflections of the link between spirituality and morality, such as was a common perspective in the ancient and medieval mystical traditions.

Mayer (2000) proffers that 'spiritual consciousness' is a better phrase than 'spiritual intelligence' for a human artefact that he nonetheless takes seriously and infers he has also perceived in his long-term empirical work in and around intelligence research. In reference to Emmons' categories, he contends that they are more convincingly referred to under the heading of 'spiritual consciousness' because intelligence implies abstract reasoning, whereas the phenomena classified as 'spiritual' are better understood as experiential, personalized and connoting heightened awareness of the Ultimate in relation to awareness of self and others (Elkins et al., 1988). Hence, he modifies Emmons' notion to speak of spirituality as 'directed consciousness', better understood as 'altered states of mind', and so more aptly framed in the following way:

1. *Attending* to the unity of the world and transcending one's existence.
2. *Consciously entering* into heightened spiritual states.
3. *Attending* to the sacred in everyday activities, events, and relationships.
4. *Structuring consciousness* so that problems in living are seen in the context of life's ultimate concerns.
5. *Desiring* to act, and consequently, acting in virtuous ways (to show forgiveness, to express gratitude, to be humble, to display compassion). (Mayer, 2000, p. 48)

In Mayer's (2000) modification, the role of spiritual consciousness as an 'altered state of mind' in impelling virtuous acts is made even more explicit and the imputed link with moral motivation made even clearer with the addition of the notion of 'desire'. This heightened spiritual state plays a direct role in motivating one to engage in moral goodness that is beyond the norm. Moreover, 'consciously entering' into this heightened spiritual state allows one to structure consciousness in a way that enhances and sharpens one's sense of knowing and understanding: "… such structuring guides a person's attention to certain mental phenomena … until the conscious state is altered." (p. 51) It is in this context that Mayer utilizes the language of mysticism:

> Mysticism involves entering spiritual states of consciousness in which … one may become especially contemplative, have flashes of insight, or even see

visions. Thus, both transcendence and mysticism appear primarily to involve highly structured conscious processes, with cognition providing a supporting role by representing the things that must be transcended or contemplated, but with little requirement for abstract reasoning. (pp. 51–52)

In the link between 1–4 and 5 above, it seems it is the apparently richer and more integrated knowing (including the ramifying effects that one's context in life has for one's self, or 'self-knowing') implied by the mystical experience that drives the desire to engage in moral goodness of such inordinate proportions. Again, one sees the ancient and medieval link being made between mysticism and moral motivation. It is to this tradition that I now wish to turn, especially through consideration of the notion of 'practical mysticism', a form of mysticism with particularly enviable credentials for impelling moral behaviour of a superlative kind.

PRACTICAL MYSTICISM AND MORAL MOTIVATION

Plotinus (1964), the Egyptian philosopher of the third century CE, is the ancient with the strongest credentials in appraising the strengths and weaknesses of various forms of spirituality and mysticism. As recorded in history (Armstrong, 1996), he is characterized principally as a pragmatic teacher whose main interest was in communicating to his students ways in which they could succeed in the world. Part of this success was in and around their spiritual life, no doubt an essential facet of anyone wishing for career success in the societies he knew but also essential to personal integrity and happiness. Hence, he proposed a balance of spiritualities that could work for people in their day to day settings while also guaranteeing a constructive relationship with their god. At the heart of Plotinus's discourses on mysticism, therefore, we find a distinction between what might be termed a public versus private spirituality.

Public spirituality and its various manifestations were for the world to see and behold, constituted of outer expressions of religiousness. Private spirituality, on the other hand, concerned what passed between individuals and their god. While public spirituality had a role to play in social order and personal achievement, Plotinus seems clearly to be of the view that it is only through private spirituality that higher consciousness about god and understanding the implications of the mystical relationship that ensued from such consciousness could be achieved. As a commentator on spirituality, Plotinus was considered to be elitist in his inference that while many might master the displays of outer religiousness, only a few would achieve the deeper religiousness denoted by private spirituality. This deeper religiousness is referred to by Idel and McGinn (1999) as "… Plotinus's … favoring of love over understanding." (p. 22) 'Favoring of love over understanding' lies at the heart of Plotinus's reflections on 'practical mysticism' as the deepest and most authentic expression of private spirituality. It also lies at the heart of the connection with moral motivation being argued herein.

Underhill (1915) testifies that it is Plotinus's name that is most associated with the notion of practical mysticism, the counter-intuitive conception that mysticism is not best defined via the connotation of inactivity, retreat or disengagement, but rather through its opposite, namely active moral engagement: "The active man is a mystic when he knows his actions to be a part of a greater activity," says Underhill (1915) in reference to Plotinus's understanding. Underhill also proffers that "mysticism is the art of union with reality." The mystic, in other words, is not one who indulges in outward displays of religiousness, no matter how effusive and seemingly holy, but rather the one who, in Plotinus's terms, favours and effects love, practical action for good, as the essential outpouring derived from one's loving relationship with god. Mysticism is seen as an impulsion of moral motivation and, in turn, in the acting out of moral good, one's mystical experience is enhanced, indeed realized:

> Action always has some good or other in view – a good for oneself, to be possessed. Possessed where? In the soul. The circuit is complete: through action, the soul comes back to contemplation. (Plotinus, 1964, pp. 167–168)

Plotinus's dichotomy between public and private spirituality, one about understanding versus one about love, may well provide the substance of an ancient philosophical and theological distinction being made between moral intention and moral motivation. In this context, moral intention is to be understood as the relatively passive state that results from conformity to a code or set of expectations, perhaps according with Kohlberg's (1963) lower levels of moral development. It is what is 'expected' of someone who belongs or is associated with an ideology or any movement with a moral attachment. In moral terms, it has the effect of constraining overtly immoral action and, furthermore, directing moral good in a generalized fashion and in accord with expectations. Moral motivation, on the other hand, is best understood as the truly active state of one who is prepared to strike out for moral good, whatever the cost and regardless of expectations. In this sense, it seems to accord, at least in principle, with Kohlberg's thinking about the higher stages of moral development. It also fits well with updated work on the mystical intersections to be found between Jewish, Christian and Islamic mystical traditions. Idel and McGinn (1999) state:

> (Christian) mystics constantly break through existing theological theories in order to stress the unity of love and cognition ... Gregory the Great's *amor ipse notitia* ('love itself is knowledge') provided Western contemplatives with a basis for affirming again and again that the highest love includes supreme knowledge ... We detect a similar favouring of love among Muslim mystics. (p. 22)

Idel and McGinn go on to make the same claims around Jewish mysticism, confirming the thesis and point of their work that, in terms of the nature of mysticism, there is more in common within these three religions than separates them and that the common core is to be found around Plotinus' favouring of love over understanding, the most authentic religious expression for the Jewish, Christian and Islamic traditions, an authenticity that is replete with a sense of ethical mission:

> The division of the mind postulated here enables the mystic to combine a contemplative life with one of active service. Yet by describing the two attitudes as juxtaposed, one risks missing their real nature. For one is not superimposed to the other: the two intimately collaborate and reinforce each other … the mystical state, far from diminishing this unique ability to integrate, enhances the powers from a single dynamic source of concentration.

> Generally speaking, for each of the three religions, the mystical union enhances a person's capacity to fulfil his or her given or assumed task … All genuine mysticism results in spiritual fecundity … Having come to partake in God's life, the contemplative also feels called to share in God's life-giving love. (Idel & McGinn, 1999, pp. 13–14)

For Plotinus, the authentic mystical experience that rendered love over understanding as the supreme moral motivation was to be found in an equally authentic self-knowing. Just as the morally charged practical mysticism rested on a private spirituality, so the form of self-knowing that underpinned it was a radically private form. Citing from the Enneads, Rappe (2000) offers the following:

> Plotinus demands a kind of ultimate privacy from the person who wishes to gain self-knowledge. He demands an activity of the mind that is entirely self-directed. "We have no perception of what is our own, and since we are like this we understand ourselves best when we have made our self-knowledge one with ourselves." (p. 64)

Plotinus's fine detailing around mysticism is important because he is regarded not only as having captured the best of what went before him in Greek philosophy but was also most instrumental in the development of higher forms of mysticism in the later developments to be found in Judaism, Christianity and Islam. In terms of what went before, he represents the finest of balances between the thought of Plato and Aristotle. Indeed, such is the rare syncretism to be found between the two that Armstrong (1996) ponders on the extent to which Plotinus's Plato is really an Aristotelian Plato, that the Plato that Plotinus promoted was really Plato as seen through the eyes of Aristotle. This idea is of interest to the thesis behind this chapter because Aristotle is rightly regarded as a giant in the development of both the forms of spirituality that developed in Judaism, Christianity and Islam and of moral thought generally in the Western tradition (cf. Janz, 2005).

Eudaemonia was Aristotle's (1985) supreme good, but it was not a good that could be pursued merely by being known. It was a good that required living out in practice. It was the veritable key to human integrity and happiness, to being humanly complete, that one would live out the practical moral life. The kind of judgment essential to the pursuit of *eudaemonia* was what Aristotle finally described as a 'practical' judgment, based on intellect and sense experience and, most essentially, leading to practical action. At the heart of the concept of *eudaemonia* lay the notion that it was only in the conjunction of knowing and doing that one could achieve the completeness of wellbeing. This supreme form of wellbeing (happiness) arose from the integrity of having one's intentions and actions in alignment. Implicit in this scheme of thinking was that one could only achieve happiness by knowing one's self and, hence, knowing that one's practical actions were aligned with this self.

Aristotle was the major influence on the thought of Abu al-Ghazali, Muslim scholar and Sufi mystic of the eleventh century. Ghazali speaks much about knowing and the importance of acquiring knowledge yet the pointlessness of not then using it for the good of others. Knowledge is a gift from God that religious leaders, in particular, must use to foster the knowledge of those in their care. Above all, for Ghazali, knowledge was given only so that its necessary concomitant, action, could be informed and well-directed. Knowing's only usefulness was in impelling benevolent action. So, in his *Book of Religious Learnings,* we read:

> The learned are the heirs of the prophets …the best of people is a believing learned man who does good. (al-Ghazali, 1991, p. 15)

Ghazali's perspective would seem to be reflective of Plotinus's notion of practical mysticism. This is the kind of mysticism that conjoins knowing, including self-knowing, and practical action. It is not the path of the showy mystic, the pietistic or the sanctimonious. It is the path of the one who, in the vein of More and Bonhoeffer, aligns religious faith with the kind of personal integrity that issues in practical action for the moral good. For Ghazali, only the person who knows one's self could be trusted to act in accordance with one's stated beliefs and apparent intentions. In terms of moral motivation, one might say the motivation to act for the good rests on the kind of personal integrity that can only result from intense knowing of self and the attached sense of duty to be true to one's self in the actions one takes. In modern scholarship, it accords with Blasi's (1983) notion of 'moral self', of moral motivation resting finally not merely on moral prescriptions, as Kohlberg would have it, but on one's sense of self in relation to those prescriptions. In other words, doing the good is more than understanding what is good but, in a more holistic and integrated sense, conforming oneself, one's integrity, to the good (Blasi, 2004).

Ghazali's was a particularly important influence in reforming Islam's own mystical tradition, Sufism, away from pietism towards the kind of practical mysticism that he saw as more befitting of Islam. Resulting directly from his access to the writings of Ghazali, Thomas Aquinas (thirteenth century scholar and friar) played a similar role in Christianity in freeing it from conceptions that the holy life was about withdrawal into isolationist and highly cognitive spiritualities divorced from the practicalities of action for good. The result was in Aquinas's importing from Aristotelianism a new elicitation of moral knowing in the concept of *synderesis*, described in the Summa (cf. Aquinas, 1948) as an inborn facility that urged us not only to seek truth but to put it into practice. As with Ghazali, so with Aquinas, knowing truth was above all knowing what it meant for one's self and then possessing the commitment to act accordingly.

In Moses ben Jacob Cordovero, the sixteenth century Spanish Jewish mystic, we find one of the firmest expressions of the practical mysticism of Plotinus. Cordovero (1974), a seminal figure in the later medieval revival of Jewish mysticism, is painstaking in emphasizing that there can ultimately be no true mystical experience without emulating God in his *sephiroth*, in a word, in his total immersion in the practical matters of life. Likewise, the true mystic must engage in practical action which conforms to godly practice. Cordovero teased this practice out in the form of thirteen attributes which captured the essence of God's *sephiroth*. These attributes included complete identification with one's neighbour, mercy beyond the letter of the law, forgiveness to the point of eradicating the evil done and eliminating all traces of vengefulness. Like the moral good alluded to by Emmons and Mayer, these attributes were clearly beyond the norms of human virtue. For Cordovero, that was precisely the point, namely, that such levels of virtue could only be achieved through mystical experience but, in turn, the mystical experience was identifiable and confirmed only by their having been achieved (cf. Epstein, 1988). The motivation to do the good was embedded in a profound sense of one's own integrity (in this case, in relationship with God) and the consequent requirement (desire) to act for the moral good.

In similar vein, Moshe Idel, one of contemporary Judaism's major scholars of mysticism, is at pains to correct common misapprehensions that the Jewish mystical tradition known as *Kabbalah* is essentially an austere and reclusive entity divorced from the practicalities of life. Idel makes use of the writings of the thirteenth century mystic, Abraham ben Samuel Abulafia, in emphasizing the circularity of the genuine mystical experience, that is, that the noblest forms of human behaviour play a role both as cause and effect of authentic mystical experience:

> ... in the profundities of human thought there is no one more profound and more excellent than it (= the product of mystical union) and it alone unites human thought with the divine (thought) to the extent of the human capability and according to human nature. And it is known that human thought is the cause of his wisdom, and his wisdom is the cause of his understanding, and his understanding is the cause of his mercy, and his mercy is the cause of his reverence of his Creator. (Idel, 1988, p. 147)

So wisdom causes understanding which, in turn, causes mercy but, in a circular move, it is mercy that causes knowledge and submission to one's God. There can be no authentic claim to have achieved mystical union without the practical expression of doing the good. Hence, we perceive what might be seen as an ancient and medieval spelling out in detail of moral motivation in the terms of practical mysticism. What is it that motivates the purported mystic to do good, rather than merely intend it or postulate on it? The motivation is in a knowing and understanding of one's self, of what it is that constitutes one's coherent and sustainable 'self' and that union of this self with one's God necessitates exalted moral action. Hence, one desires to do good because one's self cannot be complete without it. For the mystics of old, the final constitution of this self was wrapped in a relationship with one's creator whereby one came to know and understand that practical action for good is not merely the effect but also the cause of that relationship. For the practical mystic, cause and effect merge to become one action. There can be no relationship or even claim of a relationship with God without the outpouring of mercy.

The challenge in drawing out an implication of this scheme of thought for the contemporary search for the grounds of moral motivation for all, mystics and non-mystics, religious believers and otherwise, is in unpicking the extent to which the twin notions of 'knowing one's self' and 'knowing one's self in relationship with God' are separable. At this point, I wish to re-introduce Aristotle and introduce Jurgen Habermas, twentieth century epistemologist and, broadly, neo-Marxist. While Habermas has written much of late about religion and its place in the polity, his disposition is one of critique. He takes no refuge at all in religious faith, experience or motivations.

KNOWING SELF AND MORAL MOTIVATION IN HABERMAS

As suggested above, the idea that Plotinus's notion of practical mysticism is inspired by Aristotle is of interest because Aristotle is implicated in both the forms of spirituality that developed in the religions in question, especially after the advent of Islam and the latter's influence on later mysticisms in Judaism and Christianity, and on moral thought generally in the three intertwined traditions (cf. Janz, 2005). Much of the purely philosophical Aristotelian underpinnings that Plotinus employed in his notion of practical mysticism are to be found, I would suggest, in the contemporary epistemological scholarship of Habermas (1972, 1974, 1984, 1987, 1990, 2001). The proposition is, in part, that Habermas is defining, for a secularized generation, foundational moral postulations that have been in our mystical traditions for millennia, albeit partly on the basis of more explicitly religious formulae. Habermas's great contribution to the contemporary moral debate is in its two fold capacity both to take us back to the foundations of Western philosophy by its radical re-formulations around the phenomenon of knowing and, at the same time, to translate these foundations into a concept that lies at the heart of mysticism of all kinds but that has particular ramifications for practical mysticism. It is also useful in that, in similar vein to the work of Mayer, it makes some of the thought of mysticism, and especially practical mysticism, available to an era that is not naturally disposed to such things.

In these postulations, I would suggest that Habermas has provided an updated and highly credible epistemological justification and elaboration of the kind of mysticism deemed to be most authentic in the Abrahamic religious traditions, namely, practical mysticism in the way defined by Plotinus. Furthermore, just as practical mysticism as an impulse for moral motivation rested, in the minds of Ghazali, Aquinas, Cordovero and Abulafia, on the kind of profound knowing of self that came (for them) from the deepest form of relationship with and experience of God, so Habermas's impulsion for moral motivation (in this case, *praxis*) rests on a similar knowing of self that does not allow for deviation from following through on practical action for good.

In Habermas, I would suggest, we find the case for a practical mysticism that does not rely so much on the notion of a God but renders in the same life-changing self-knowing and the form of radical, unswerving action for the common good that one finds at the heart of the mystical tradition in the notion of practical mysticism. Moral motivation, being moved to do the good rather than merely postulate on it, results from a self-knowing that demands one's practical actions conform to one's beliefs and intentions. Hence, we find this form of moral motivation in both religious and non-religious people and the burning question remains around the extent to which there is a fundamental difference. Does Habermasian self-knowing serve as a key to bridging understandings about moral motivation between those of explicit religious persuasion and those without such persuasion? Let us return to the instances with which this exploration began.

More's moral motivation took the form of an intense allying of his knowledge of what represented integrity with the action he finally took, even against the pressure from those he loved most. The action for good was the result of a deep knowing of self and the concomitant need to act only in accord with the beliefs of that self. As former Lord High Chancellor, responsible for the *mores* of England, he was clearly also acting for the common good, as he perceived it, prepared to give his life to preserve both his own integrity and the ultimate good of the polity. In More's case, his religious faith and its disciplines were instrumental in his moral action and, in that sense, he provides a case instance of Plotinus's practical mysticism in action. His is also an interesting case study for the forms of spiritual consciousness and mysticism of which Mayer (2000) speaks, forms that underline the links between such states of mind and the desire to act for the moral good in ways that surpass the norm for human activity. In both Emmons' (2000, 2003) and Mayer's (2000) estimation, it is the state of mind itself (and the self-knowing implied) that is most instrumental in impelling the desire to act in such elevated forms of human virtue, rather than the belief in an objective religious force (eg. God) that might, or might not, underpin the state of mind. The imponderable question regarding More's case study is then whether he might have displayed exactly the same moral motivation had he not been a religious believer but merely acting for his own integrity and the good of England. According to the vital words in his play cited above, Robert Bolt (1990) at least leaves us pondering on the question.

In the Bonhoeffer case instance, the imponderable question becomes a little more ponderable because, even though he is personally a man of religious faith, he makes explicit reference to its relative, rather than absolute, role in the moral motivation he witnessed in his fellow prisoners. He originally proposed the dyad of 'cheap versus costly grace' to explain the differences between what he saw as inauthentic and authentic options for people of religious faith. The more challenging musings came after some time in prison when he admitted to feeling more in common with those who professed no religious faith but who shared his essential commitment than with those of faith who did not. His intrigue was with those who were motivated to the good through deeply held personal convictions, whether motivated by faith in God or merely by their sense of who they were and for what their practical actions must stand (cf. Bonhoeffer, 1959). Again, Bonhoeffer can be classed as a case instance of practical mysticism (Lovat, 2006) in that his profound sense of conformity with God's immersion in the trials of his time impelled him to immerse himself in moral action, for the sake of preserving his own integrity and for the common good of the German people, such as would cost him his life. He is also however, an interesting case instance of the kind of modern mystic presaged by Emmons and Mayer, wherein the altered state of mind brought on by spiritual consciousness and the resultant ramifying effects on one's self of one's context in life impel the desire to act in radical fashion for the moral good. It could be argued that, like Habermas, in his 'religionless Christianity' and his ponderings on the extent to which religiousness is essential (or not) to the most heroic of actions for good, Bonhoeffer was heralding an era in which the essentials of practical mysticism and the moral motivation that is impelled by it could be preserved in a profound self-knowing that renders their religious foundations dispensable.

One cannot but see a further connection in all the above with Blasi's (2005) understanding of integrity as that which impels in an individual "...the need to maintain the unity, the wholeness, of one's subjective sense of self, as manifested in consistency with one's chosen commitments," and that without which one risks "...the collapse of one's essential being." (Blasi, this volume, p. 239) It is this fundamental self-knowing that finally underpins moral motivation. It is also important for educationists to place this thinking in the context not only of moral development but religious development as well. Just as Fowler (1995) distinguished between religious conformity and the autonomy of faith, and Oser (1980, 1991) between more basic stages of religious development and the point at which one is truly grappling with the Ultimate (in whatever form), so we see in More and Bonhoeffer the clear distinction between religious and moral conformity, on the one hand, and the moral motivation that comes from the sense of dealing with the Ultimate, in terms of both/either a transcendent other and/or one's ultimate self.

CONCLUSION

The distinctive contribution of this chapter is argued to be the perspective on self-knowing, and its inherent impact on moral motivation, that is derived from exploring both contemporary research in the human sciences and ancient mystical traditions. In Plotinus' 'practical mysticism', we find the notion of a profound knowing of self such that one is impelled by it to act for the good, regardless of the cost. Typically, within the traditions of mysticism, this impulsion is assumed to result ultimately from belief in, relationship with and a transforming experience of God. However, through tempering consideration of the nature of mysticism provided by the modern human sciences, Habermasian epistemology and, furthermore, the witness provided by the supreme moral acts of Thomas More and Dietrich Bonhoeffer, one senses that the moral motivation impelled by self-knowing might well be a human artefact with enduring power beyond religious belief.

REFERENCES

al-Ghazali, A. (1991). *The book of religious learnings*. New Delhi: Islamic Book Services.

Aquinas, T. (1948). *Summa theologica*(Fathers of the English Dominican Province, Trans.). New York: Benziger Bros.

Aristotle, (1985). *Nicomachean ethics* (T. Irwin, Trans.). Indianapolis: Hackett.

Armstrong, A. tr. (1996). *Plotinus, Ennead II*. Loeb Classical Library. Cambridge, MA: Harvard University Press.

Barrett, J. (Ed.), (2010). *Psychology of religion*. London: Routledge.

Beauregard, M., & O'Leary, D. (2007). *The spiritual brain: A neuroscientist's case for the existence of the soul* (1st ed.). New York: HarperOne.

Beauregard, M., & Paquette, V. (2008). EEG activity in Carmelite nuns during a mystical experience. *Neuroscience Letters,444*(1), 1–4.

Blasi, A. (1983). Moral cognition and moral action: A theoretical perspective. *Developmental Review, 3,* 178–210.

Blasi, A. (1999). Emotions and moral motivation. *Journal for the Theory of Social Behavior, 29,* 1–19.

Blasi, A. (2004). Neither personality nor cognition: An alternative approach to the nature of the self. In C. Lightfoot, C. Lalonde & M. Chandler (Eds.), *Changing conceptions of psychological life* (pp. 3–26) Mahwah, NJ: Erlbaum.

Blasi, A. (2005). Moral character: A psychological approach. In D.K. Lapsley and F.C. Power (Eds.), *Character psychology and character education* (pp. 67–100). Notre Dame, IN: University of Notre Dame Press.

Bolt, R. (1990). *A man for all seasons*. New York: Vintage Books.

Bonhoeffer, D. (1959). *The cost of discipleship*. London: SCM.

Bonhoeffer, D. (1998). *Letters and papers from prison*. London: SCM.

Cordovero, M. (1974). *The palm tree of Deborah*(L. Jacobs, Trans.) New York: Hermon Press.

Damasio, A.R. (2003). *Looking for Spinoza: Joy, sorrow, and the feeling brain* (1st ed.). New York: Harcourt.

Elkins, D.N., Hedstrom, L.J., Hughes, L.L., Leaf, J.A., & Saunders, C.L. (1988). Toward a humanistic-phenomenological spirituality: Definition, description, and measurement. *Journal of Humanistic Psychology, 28,* 5–18.

Emmons, R. (2000). Is spirituality an intelligence? Motivation, cognition and the psychology of ultimate concern. *International Journal for the Psychology of Religion, 10*(1), 3–26.

Emmons, R. (2003). *The psychology of ultimate concerns: Motivation and spirituality in personality.* New York: The Guilford Press.

Epstein, P. (1988). *Kabbalah: The way of the Jewish mystic*. Boston: Shambhala.

Fowler, J. (1995). *Stages of faith: The psychology of human development and the quest for meaning.* New York: Harper Collins.

Gardner, H. (1983). *Frames of mind: The theory of multiple intelligences*. New York: Basic Books.

Gardner, H. (1999). Are there additional intelligences? The case for naturalist, spiritual and existential intelligences. In J. Kane (Ed.), *Education, information and transformation* (pp. 111–131). New York: Prentice-Hall.

Habermas, J. (1972). *Knowledge and human interests* (J. Shapiro, Trans.). London: Heinemann.

Habermas, J. (1974). *Theory and practice*(J. Viertal, Trans.). London: Heinemann.

Habermas, J (1984). *Theory of communicative action* (vol. I) (T. McCarthy, Trans.). Boston: Beacon Press.

Habermas, J (1987). *Theory of communicative action* (vol. II) (T. McCarthy, Trans.). Boston: Beacon Press.

Habermas, J. (1990). *Moral consciousness and communicative action* (C. Lenhardt & S. Nicholson, trans.). Cambridge, MASS: Massachusetts Institute of Technology Press.

Habermas, J. (2001). *The liberating power of symbols: Philosophical essays.* Cambridge: Polity Press.

Han, S., Gu, X., Mao, L., Ge, J., Wang, G., & Ma, Y. (2010). Neural substrates of self-referential processing in Chinese Buddhists. *Social Cognitive and Affective Neuroscience, 5*(2–3), 332–339.

Han, S., Mao, L., Gu, X., Zhu, Y., Ge, J., & Ma, Y. (2008). Neural consequences of religious belief on self-referential processing. *Social Neuroscience,3*(1), 1–15.

Heelas, P. (Ed.), (2011). *Spirituality in the modern world: Within religious tradition and beyond.* London: Routledge.

Idel, M. (1988). *Kabbalah: New perspectives.* New Haven, Conn: Yale University Press.

Idel, M. & McGinn, B. (eds.). (1999). *Mystical union in Judaism, Christianity, and Islam: An ecumenical dialogue.* New York: Continuum.

Immordino-Yang, M.H., & Damasio, A.R. (2007). We feel, therefore we learn: The relevance of affect and social neuroscience to education. *Mind, Brain, and Education, 1,* 3–10.

Janz, B. (2005). *Pre-Christian mystics and influences on mysticism.* Available at: http://www.clas.ufl.edu/users/gthursby/mys/whoswho.htm

Kohlberg, L. (1963). The development of children's orientations toward a moral order: I. Sequence in the development of moral thought. *Vita Humana, 6,* 11–33.

Lovat, T. (2006). Practical mysticism as authentic religiousness: A Bonhoeffer case study. *Australian E-Journal of Theology, 6.* Available at: http://dlibrary.acu.edu.au/research/theology/ejournal/aejt_6/lovat.htm

Mayer, J. (2000). Spiritual intelligence or spiritual consciousness? *International Journal for the Psychology of Religion, 10*(1), 47–56.

More, T. (1989). *Utopia* (R. Logan & G. Adams, Trans.).Cambridge: Cambridge University Press.

Northoff, G. (2010). Humans, brains, and their environment: Marriage between neuroscience and anthropology? *Neuron, 65,* 748–751.

Oser, F. (1980). Stages of religious judgement. In C. Brusselmans, (Ed.), *Toward moral and religious maturity* (pp. 277–315). Morristown, NJ: Silver Burdett.

Oser, F. (1991). A logic of religious development. In J.W. Fowler, K.E. Nipkow, & E Schweitzer (Eds.), *Stages of faith and religious development: Implications for church, education, and society* (pp. 37–64). New York: Crossroad.

Plotinus (1964). *The essential Plotinus* (E. O'Brien, Trans.). Indiana, Ind: Hackett Publishing co.

Rappe, S. (2000). *Reading Neo-Platonism: Non-discursive thinking in the texts of Plotinus, Proclus, and Damascius.* Cambridge: Cambridge University Press.

Spezio, M.L. (2011). The neuroscience of emotion and reasoning in social contexts: Implications for moral theology. *Modern Theology, 27*(2), 339–356.

Sternberg, R. (2004). North American approaches to intelligence. In R. Sternberg (Ed.), *International handbook of intelligence* (pp. 411–444). Cambridge: Cambridge University Press.

Underhill, E. (1915). *Practical mysticism.* New York: E.P. Dutton & co. Available at: http://isom.vnsalvation.com/Resources%20English/Christian%20Ebooks/Evelyn%20Underhill%20Practical%20Mysticism.pdf

Walach, H. (2007). Mind, body, spirituality. *Mind and Matter, 5*(2), 215–240.

AFFILIATION

Terence Lovat
Faculty of Education and Arts
University of Newcastle
Newcastle, Australia
Senior Research Fellow
University of Oxford, UK

PART 4

DEVELOPMENTAL EFFECTS, EMOTIONS AND MORAL MOTIVATION

One central form of MM is related to emotion attributions. Here it becomes clear that the assumption that moral motivation is innate and that humans are born to be good is not supportable. Furthermore, we find approaches studying moral motivation as emotional elements, sometimes stable over time and across situations, sometimes not, as well as other conceptions stressing how moral motivation depends on personal as well as situational determinants. Interesting also is the question about neurobiolological foundations with respect to being morally motivated in a particular situation on the way to action, as well as with respect to a developmental perspective. The chapters presented in this part vary in their ideas of how MM develops and how personal and situational contexts determine the state that impels acting morally.

Nunner-Winkler argues that the happy victimizer phenomenon that she has investigated in a longitudinal study could be explained best by a position of externalism towards motivation. This means that positive emotions attributed to a transgressor though knowing the moral rule which was broken points to the relevance of sources driving moral behaviour in spite of moral judgments.

Döring questions the idea that moral motivation increases during adolescence. The results here indicate regressions in moral motivation from childhood to adolescence. These results point to challenges that are typical for identity development at that age.

Gasser, Gutzwiller-Helfenfinger, Latzko and Malti argue that moral emotions serve as a central source of moral motivation. In their view, moral emotions lie at the core of explaining the link between moral motivation and (im)moral behaviour. They try to confirm this hypothesis by referring especially to investigations on the happy victimizer phenomenon.

Narvaez reveals that moral motivation is not only influenced by personal determinants. Moreover, she postulates "moral mindsets" which might be activated in particular situations. This approach enriches the discussion on the moral personality by arguing based on neurobiological approaches and by discussing the interaction between situational as well as personal determinants.

Reed develops a bi-level-approach to moral motivation. Referring to a mixture of theories, Hume and Kant, as well as to Haidt and Blasi, he argues that both contribute to complementary facets of moral motivation.

GERTRUD NUNNER-WINKLER

I. MORAL MOTIVATION AND THE HAPPY VICTIMIZER PHENOMENON

INTRODUCTION

Kohlberg's (1981, 1984) description of moral development is based on the assumption of cognitive-affective parallelism: At the pre-conventional level, children up to about 10 years of age believe norms hold because they are set by authorities and backed by sanctions and are followed to avoid punishment or win rewards. At the conventional level, typical of most adults, norms are seen to hold because they are prevailing in one's group or society and are followed to win social acceptance or avoid pangs of conscience. At the post-conventional level reached by only a few, norms are derived from universal moral principles such as equality and respect for the dignity of the individual and are followed from insight into their intrinsic validity. The structural core of this development is an increase in role-taking ability: the egotistic perspective of 4-year olds roughly by age 6 comes to be replaced by subjective, by age 8, self-reflexive perspective taking and, from age 10 onwards, children begin to grasp the third-person-perspective (Selman & Byrne, 1974; Perner & Wimmer, 1985). During adolescence, the system perspective is acquired, namely, an understanding of the inherent autonomy of systems that is irreducible to the laws of face-to-face interactions. Some adults will reach the highest level, the prior-to-society perspective whereby one is in accord with the perspective of all rational beings.

REVISING KOHLBERG

Recent research suggests a revision of Kohlberg's theory. It amalgamates three dimensions: understanding of the categorical nature of moral commands; growth of moral motivation; and, development of formal socio-cognitive thinking structures. It neglects however a fourth dimension, namely, substantive knowledge systems. Proficiency in these four dimensions is acquired by different learning processes – universal and differential ones, early and delayed ones.

In this chapter, I will focus on the independent development of a cognitive understanding of the constitutive aspect of morality, the 'categorical ought', on the one hand, and the growth of moral motivation, on the other hand. I will start with a critique of Kohlberg's depiction of children's moral understanding; then describe measuring moral motivation by emotion ascriptions to wrongdoers and present first

K. Heinrichs, F. Oser & T. Lovat (Eds.), Handbook of Moral Motivation: Theories, Models, Applications, 267–288.

results. Next, an excursus on the happy victimizer debate will follow: After briefly discussing the influence of variations in assessment procedures and various cognitive interpretations, I will argue for a motivational interpretation of emotion attributions. This interpretation will allow a more detailed reconstruction of dimensions of moral motivation – its strength, type and structure. The paper will conclude with a brief dispute about internalists' dismissal of the theoretical construct of moral motivation.

Critique of the Pre-Conventional Stage

Kohlberg's description of children's instrumentalist moral understanding was critiqued from two sides. Concerning the *cognitive dimension*, domain theory showed that even young children adequately differentiate between moral, conventional and religious rules: Moral rules, pertaining to harm avoidance, rights and duties, are seen as universally, unalterably and authority-independently valid. Conventional rules, pertaining to issues of organization and order in social groups and societies, are valid only for members, can be altered by authorities or consensus, and are independent of God's commands. Religious rules, regulating man's relationship to the transcendental, are unalterable, only valid for members and depend on God's commands (Turiel, 1983, Nucci & Turiel, 1993). Thus, already children understand that moral rules enjoy intrinsic validity. Later development mainly involves changes in socio-cognitive structures and growth of knowledge systems. Empirically, the claims of domain theory are widely supported (Smetana, 2006). Concerning the *motivational dimension*, research on altruism demonstrated that even young children unselfishly share with others, console and help them (Hoffmann, 2000).

Measuring Children's Moral Understanding – First Results

These contradictions in the empirical findings might be due to differences in the measurement procedures used. Kohlberg asked for action recommendations in moral dilemmas, that is, in situations in which valid norms stand in contradiction. Turiel (1983) explored children's understanding of the validity of norms. Research on altruism observed spontaneously displayed behaviour. Possibly, children – in accord with Turiel – do understand the intrinsic validity of moral norms yet, if they lack moral motivation, will interpret Kohlberg's test question in prudential terms, that is, they will advise as best what actually serves their own interests. Also – in accord with studies on altruism – children might unselfishly help and share – but only if they feel like it. For clarification, moral knowledge and moral motivation have to be measured independently in situations in which spontaneous (first order) desires contradict moral norms.

We followed these considerations in a first exploratory study by presenting 4-, 6-, and 8-year olds with moral conflicts, that is, situations in which personal desire and moral norms are contradictory. For example, the protagonist considers taking another child's sweets. In the temptation situation, moral knowledge is explored: 'May (protagonist) I take the sweets? Why? / Why not?' Next, the protagonist is shown to take the sweets. After the transgression, moral motivation is measured: 'How does (the protagonist) feel? Why does s/he feel that way?' The idea of operationalizing moral motivation by emotion attributions to wrongdoers is derived from a cognitivist understanding of emotions according to which emotions are – albeit rash and global – cognitive judgments about the subjective importance of objective facts (Solomon, 1976). By ascribing an emotion to the wrongdoer, children indicate which of the two facts are simultaneously true of the protagonist – s/he transgressed a norm and satisfied a desire – they see as more important.

We found that most 4-year-olds and still many of the 6-year olds expected the protagonist to feel good even though they know the moral rules in question and understand their intrinsic validity. Since this was a surprising finding – older children and adults expect wrongdoers to feel bad (Barden et al., 1989) – we tested for its robustness. It turned out: Children expect the wrongdoer to feel good even though they know that the victim of a transgression will feel bad and that a repentant sinner is better than a gleeful one. The amoral emotion ascriptions are not due to younger children's tendency to generally expect people to feel good: They expect a 'moral hero', namely, a protagonist who overcomes a temptation, to feel bad because s/he forwent fulfilling his/her own desires. Neither are they due to their tendency to be swayed by concrete material gains: They expect the wrongdoer to feel good, even if the profit gained is non-tangible, for example, consisting only in satisfying the wish to annoy another child. Nor are they due to lack of emotional knowledge. They understand moral emotions such as regret and empathy, for example, they expect even an ill-motivated actor to feel bad after having unintentionally harmed another child and expect a bystander who witnessed a harmful event to experience concern for the victim. Thus, children expect a person to feel good when s/he does what s/he wants to do (e.g. harms the child s/he wants to annoy) and to feel bad when s/he does not do what s/he wants to do (e.g. resists the temptation to take the desired sweets) or does what she does not want to do (e.g. unintentionally harms another child). In view of this close connection between emotions and action tendencies, we interpreted the amoral emotion attributions of younger children as indicating a delay in growth of moral motivation (Nunner-Winkler & Sodian, 1988).

EXCURSUS: THE HAPPY VICTIMIZER PHENOMENON

Meanwhile, younger children's amoral emotion ascriptions, labelled 'happy victimizer phenomenon', have stood up to many tests and frequently been replicated. There is, however, considerable disagreement concerning the size of the phenomenon. Thus, the percentage of 'happy victimizers' ranges from 93% (Arsenio & Lover, 1995, Lourenco, 1997) to 42% (Keller et al., 2003) among the 4–5 year olds, from 90% (Youill et al., 1996) to 33% (Murgatroyd & Robinson, 1993) among the 5 year olds, from 93% (Arsenio & Lover, 1995) to 55% (Nunner-Winkler, 2008b) among the 6–7 year olds, and from 67% (Lourenco, 1997) to 35% (Nunner-Winkler, 2008) among the 8–9 year olds. Even though there may be idiosyncratic and/or systematic, e.g. cultural or socio-economic, differences between samples, the large discrepancies reported are more likely to result from variations in assessment procedures. Some will briefly be discussed (for comprehensive reviews see Arsenio et al. 2006; Krettenauer et al., 2008).

Variations in Assessment Procedures

By intensive probing and offering *opposite valence emotions* the frequency of negative emotion attributions among 6- and 8-year olds is increased. Most 4-year-olds, however, persisted in expecting the victimizer to feel happy (Arsenio & Kramer, 1992). Positive emotion attributions decrease as the *gravity of the transgression* increases.

Salience is an important factor. In the original theft story the protagonist's strong desire was explicitly pointed out ('Protagonist has a special craving for this kind of sweets.'), understanding was controlled ('Does protagonist want to have the sweets?'), moral knowledge was explored before and emotion attributions were requested after the transgression. Keller et al. (2003; cf. Malti et al., 2009) did not highlight the protagonist's strong desire. They explored moral understanding after the transgression and directly afterwards asked for emotion attributions ('Is it right, what protagonist did? Why / why not? How does protagonist feel?'). Among the 4–5 year olds, the original version drew considerably more happy responses (60%) than the version used by Keller et al. (42%). Yuill et al. (1996), explicitly testing the influence of saliency, found that significantly more positive emotions were given when the control question focused on the protagonist's intentions ('Was that what the protagonist wanted/did not want to happen?') (81%) than when it focused on moral evaluation ('Was that a good/bad thing to do?') (50%).

The exact *specification of intentions* also matters. Thus, for the same story (harming another child in order to get to play on the swing), Murgatroyd & Robinson (1993) found 63% and Lourenco (1997) 93% positive emotion attributions among 5-year-olds. Lourenco had unmistakably specified the goal (protagonist pushes child off the swing because he wants to swing and there is only one swing). Murgatroyd & Robinson inserted a further reason: '(Protagonist) is in a bad mood and hits the other child in order to get on the swing'. On this basis, attribution theory offers the following evidence: If one cause suffices for producing an effect, any further causes will be devalued ('schema of multiple sufficient causes'). Accepting that a bad mood may be a sufficient reason for hitting children might have ignored the protagonist's proper intention (to get to the swing), mentioned only as a second thought. Those who presume that aggressive acting out will not really improve one's mood might then expect the protagonist to still feel bad.

A very important factor is *type of conflict*. In a strong conflict, personal desire and moral norm are strictly opposed, thus no benefit can be attained without transgressing the norm; in a weak conflict, moral or immoral action decisions entail some other benefit or additional costs. Lourenco's depiction of the swing story and the original theft story are both strong conflict stories. In contrast, the stories that Keller et al. (2003) used describe weak conflicts: in the promise story, the protagonist had agreed to play table tennis with another child, yet watched TV instead. In the friendship dilemma, the protagonist accepted a new classmate's attractive invitation for a time s/he had an appointment with a longstanding friend. In both stories, the authors find more negative emotion attributions than did Lourenco and Nunner-Winkler & Sodian. These, however, might in part be founded in non-moral concerns. Thus, some children might regret the broken promise because they prefer table tennis to TV, enjoy being with another child, hope to make a new friend or fear their old friend might terminate their friendship.

Keller et al. (2003) introduced an interesting procedural variation. They requested *emotion attributions to self* in the role of a hypothetical wrongdoer as well. The self-condition drew considerably more negative responses than the protagonist-condition: at age 5–6, the difference amounts to about 20%, and at age 8–9, about 30%. This finding has been replicated in two studies which added the responses of 4–6-year-olds (Malti, 2007) and 8–10- year-olds to two strong and two weak conflicts (Malti & Keller, 2010). Two other studies, however, which presented only strong conflicts, found no noteworthy differences between the two conditions among 6 year old Swiss children (Malti et al., 2007) and among 6 and 8 year old Icelandic children (Malti & Keller, 2010), although, for whatever reason, differences were found among 4, 6, and 9-year old Chinese children.

To sum up: Procedural variations impact on the percentage of positive emotion attributions. They decrease if opposite valence emotions are offered, if grave transgressions or weak conflicts are presented, if the wrongdoer's intention stays unstressed and if emotions are to be attributed to self rather than to a protagonist. These variations, however, do not cancel the happy victimizer phenomenon: in every experimental condition, a considerable number of (especially younger) children expected the victimizer to feel good. Thus, the happy victimizer is a robust phenomenon rather than a methodological artefact. Its interpretation, nonetheless, remains controversial.

Cognitive Interpretations

Keller et al. (2003) explain the self-other split in terms of different stances taken. Positive emotion attributions reflect a *cognitive-predictive stance,* for example, the awareness that transgressors are likely not to feel bad about hurting others. Negative emotion attributions reflect a *moral stance*, for example, an understanding that wrongdoers should feel bad. Younger children are assumed to take the cognitive-predictive stance. Owing to their higher role-taking abilities, older children are better able to distinguish and coordinate self-other-perspectives and thus are expected to favour the moral stance. Hence, children's positive emotion attributions would not necessarily indicate "emotional and moral immaturity or their moral motivation"

(p. 14). Rather, their moral knowledge – all knew that the wrongdoer is a bad person and that feeling happy after transgressing is bad – is taken to document their "moral awareness" (p. 15).

This reasoning, however, is not conclusive. From about 5 years on, children can flexibly take either stance towards moral conflicts (Yuill et al., 1966). Thus, higher role taking abilities do not explain why younger children should prefer the cognitive-predictive stance and older ones the moral stance. Moreover, the fact that negative emotion attributions to self may reflect social desirability concerns is not adequately taken into account: having reached the level of reflexive role-taking, 7–8 year olds realize that others may judge them by their responses. Since they know that a repentant sinner is better than a happy one, their negative self-attributions need not imply that they "are more advanced in their sensitivity to others' needs and plight" (Keller et al., 2003, p. 15) but might reflect their concern with a positive self-presentation. Keller et al. mention the problem. Yet, rather than acknowledging that it might invalidate their interpretation, they take it as confirming their data: "Our findings are also consonant with previous findings in social psychology which show that, when making judgements about self or others, participants tend to present themselves in a positive manner (i.e. self-serving bias)" (p. 16). In any case, age dependent changes in stance taken would not explain why, in the theft story, so many children (in their study 50% of the 5–6-year olds and 20% of the 8–9-year olds) nevertheless attribute positive emotions to self in the role of the wrongdoer.

Following up on Piaget, Sokol (2004; Sokol & Chandler, 2003) ascribes the shift in emotion attributions to children's growing *understanding of agency*. Initially, the child's will is determined by arbitrary desires and spontaneous impulses. Gradually, there emerges an autonomous will enabling the child to subordinate impulses to "a permanent scale of values" (Piaget, 1954/1981, p. 65, quoted from Krettenauer et al., 2008, p. 226). Understanding the rootedness of individual agency in an autonomous locus of control – so Sokol claims – goes along with acknowledging the relevance of interpersonal or social constraints.

The shift from positive to negative emotion attributions in middle to late childhood does indeed reflect socio-cognitive growth inasmuch as it presupposes the ability of distancing oneself from immediate impulses in view of other values or interests. Yet, this new competence describes a necessary condition only. It is required for pursuing any higher order goal (e. g. for achieving in sports or science, for accumulating wealth or power). Thus, the willingness to subordinate spontaneous impulses or other values to moral concerns is not determined by cognitive development.

Krettenauer & Eichler (2006) studied *meta-ethical understanding*. In early adolescence, young people advance an intuitionist understanding of morality: The rightness or wrongness of an act is self-evident – it is simply 'seen'. During middle adolescence, they develop a subjectivist understanding: moral judgements are considered a matter of personal preference and subjective feeling. On that level, emotional expectations become an important source of moral knowledge and moral emotional expectations increase confidence in moral judgement.

Thus, "...adolescents' understanding of moral emotions helped to consolidate their moral beliefs" (Krettenauer et al., 2008, p. 228).

The causal interpretation of this relationship, however, is open to debate. From a motivational perspective, moral emotional expectations indicate the importance ascribed to morality and those who care about morality more likely will assume that their moral beliefs are justifiable, whereas the assumption that they merely reflect subjective (e.g. arbitrary) preferences is more likely to be a correlate of moral indifference.

Motivational Interpretation

Cognitive interpretations assume that the happy victimizer pattern recedes with socio-cognitive development. From a motivational perspective, specific cognitive competences are seen as necessary but not sufficient conditions for moral emotional attributions. Once children have acquired these prerequisites, emotional ascriptions to wrongdoers are taken to indicate the importance they ascribe to morality. The motivational interpretation differs from the cognitive interpretation in two respects: It focuses on individual differences and it assumes the independence of the cognitive and the affective dimension of moral development.

Theories of cognitive development following Piaget pursue a universalistic perspective: (Almost) everybody reaches the basic levels of cognitive, socio-cognitive and moral thinking; differences pertain only to speed of development and the highest levels reached. The motivational perspective, in contrast, focuses on *individual differences* with respect to the importance allotted to morality as compared to non-moral interests or values.

Contrary to Kohlberg's cognitive-affective parallelism, moral judgement ('what is right?') and moral motivation ('why do what is right?') are considered as partially independent dimensions (for theoretical considerations in support of this assumption see Blasi, 1980, 1983; Rest, 1986, 1999, for empirical findings see Colby & Damon, 1992; Walker, 1999; Walker et al., 1987). Children's moral development provides two arguments in support: the underlying learning processes take *different courses* and they involve *different learning mechanisms*. Moral knowledge is an early universal acquisition, whereas moral motivation is built up in a delayed differential learning process. Young children read moral knowledge from everyday practices (e.g. their interaction experiences with educators, Nucci & Weber, 1995 or peers, Weyers et al., 2007) and from the collectively shared moral language game (Wittgenstein, 1984; Putnam 1994). With socio-cognitive development and the acquisition of specific knowledge systems they become able to apply rules to more complex situations, e.g. to problems on the societal level or to issues involving intricate and long-term empirical consequences. In contrast, the willingness to act in accordance with moral norms is influenced by the importance morality is allotted in the contexts in which the child grows (e.g. family, school, Higgins, 1991; Nunner-Winkler et al., 2006, local community, Damon, 1997; society at large, Putnam et al., 1993). Moreover, it is a question of self-socialisation given that, in pluralistic societies, individuals are granted greater leeway for deciding which values to pursue.

In the following, I will argue for a motivational interpretation of the happy victimizer phenomenon. First, I will present theoretical arguments concerning the function of emotions, then specify cognitive prerequisites for moral emotion attributions and, finally, cite empirical data in support of the motivational interpretation.

The main *theoretical argument* is derived from a cognitive understanding of emotions according to which emotions indicate the subjective importance a participant attributes to objectively given facts (see above). This understanding agrees with the appraisal function ascribed to emotions in psychology (Montada, 1993). In the happy victimizer paradigm, negative emotion attributions are taken to indicate that the child cares more about fulfilling the norm than about getting the desired benefit.

This motivational interpretation is warranted only inasmuch as children fulfil specific *cognitive prerequisites*. As shown above, their *moral knowledge* is adequate. Yet, before they can attribute moral emotions, children need to fully understand the *concept of desire* (Yuill et al., 1996). Although even 2–3-year-olds see others as intentional agents executing goal-directed actions, a full understanding requires an appreciation of the consequences of the fulfilment or denial of desires. Thus, 3- year-olds can attribute appropriate emotions to actors who did or did not achieve a desired end, but only in stories involving value neutral desires (e.g. wanting one of two potential recipients to catch the ball). However, if an immoral desire was satisfied (e.g. protagonist wanted to hit another child with a ball and succeeded), they expected the protagonist to feel bad. They still view desirability as an objective property of objects and situations. Only later do they come to understand desire as a subjective property relating a person to a situation. Therefore, young children have difficulty in judging emotions when an outcome has a predetermined value independent of the desire. By age 4–5, children can judge an actor's emotion in relation to intentions even in a negative context – now they understand that actors may feel pleased at achieving something objectively bad if that was what they wanted (Perner, 1991; Yuill et al., 1996).

Most authors explain the shift from predominantly positive to negative emotion attributions to a wrongdoer normally occurring between ages 4 to 8 by higher levels of *coordinating abilities*, although they specify what needs to be coordinated in somewhat different terms. Nunner-Winkler & Sodian (1988) argue that younger children focus solely on the relation between personal desires and action outcome, whereas older children become capable of integrating a third dimension – moral standards. Sokol speaks of children becoming able to coordinate own actions in relation to those of others. Yuill et al. (1996) refer to increasing role-taking abilities: they see children's awareness that one person can have two different desires toward the same object as a correlate of their growing understanding that two people can have different desires towards the same object. Both achievements result from 5–6 year-olds making the transition from the objective to the subjective role-taking stage which now enables them – as noted above – to flexibly take either a moral or a personal stance towards moral conflicts. Arsenio & Kramer (1992) interpret the shift in terms of an increased ability to coordinate emotions experienced by the different parties to the conflict.

Overall, different strands of cognitive development interplay in allowing the shift in emotional attributions. At first, children acquire a purely informational (cold) knowledge of moral rules. As socio-cognitive competencies develop, a full understanding of the subjective nature of desires is achieved, coordinating abilities increase and the ability of distancing oneself from the immediately given is acquired. Finally, reflexive role-taking abilities allow viewing oneself from a third person perspective. Now, children realize that, from positive emotional attributions to self as a wrongdoer, the experimenter might infer that they are bad persons. These various cognitive prerequisites entail a diagnostic problem. As a function of an individual child's socio-cognitive development, the same response may have quite different meanings. Expecting a wrongdoer to feel bad might reflect a deficient understanding of the subjective nature of desires; it might reflect the inability to integrate moral concerns with intentions, or victim's and victimizer's emotions, or it might reflect the self-reflexive ability to guide one's responses by social desirability concerns. This diagnostic problem could, in principle, be solved by carefully controlling socio-cognitive competencies. However, even among adults who clearly satisfy the cognitive prerequisites for making moral emotional attributions, there are still quite a few who expect to feel good about having unethically fulfilled personal desires or values (e.g. Murgatroyd & Robinson, 1993, found 35% among 18–25 year olds, Nunner-Winkler, 2008, 18% among 22-year-olds) or do in fact feel good after having unethically achieved professional success (as did more than half of 110 adult participants in courses on negotiating, Oser & Reichenbach, 2005). Thus, socio-cognitive competencies do not warrant moral emotion attributions. What is decisive is caring about morality, that is, moral motivation. The true test for this interpretation is information about real life behaviour.

The *empirical evidence* on behaviour supports the motivational interpretation. Some results may briefly be listed (Krettenauer et al., 2008; Arsenio et al., 2006). Beginning from about 5–6 years of age, attribution patterns make a difference in morally relevant behaviour: children who consistently ascribe amoral emotions were found to be much more likely to cheat and to ruthlessly push through their own interests (Asendorpf & Nunner-Winkler, 1992), to show disruptive behaviour (Hughes & Dunn, 2000; Dunn & Hughes, 2001; Arsenio & Fleiss, 1996), to display bullying (Gasser & Keller, 2009) or aggressive behaviour (Malti, 2007). Adolescents who expect wrongdoers to feel good show higher rates of disruptive behaviour (Arsenio et al., 2004) and of delinquent acts (Krettenauer & Eichler, 2006; Nunner-Winkler, 2008; Krettenauer et al., in print).

To sum up: The happy victimizer is a robust phenomenon despite disagreements concerning its size. The differences reported arise from two factors – variations in assessment procedures and individual differences in speed of socio-cognitive development. Nevertheless, across all procedures the happy victimizer pattern –

although every so often downsized – persisted and is found even in older age groups. A motivational interpretation is warranted if cognitive prerequisites for moral attributions are fulfilled and social desirability concerns controlled for. Under these conditions, it is valid for theoretical and empirical reasons: emotions indicate the subjective importance accorded to objective facts, and amoral emotion attributions correlate with antisocial behaviour.

THE THEORETICAL CONSTRUCT OF MORAL MOTIVATION

Provided the motivational interpretation proves cogent, emotion attributions allow a more detailed analysis of different aspects of moral motivation: strength of moral motivation refers to the relative importance attributed to moral issues as compared to other values or personal interests. Type of motive refers to the concerns that motivate norm conformity. Structure of moral motivation refers to the way in which the disposition to abide by moral norms is anchored in the personality. Direction and justifications of emotion attributions and emotion terms used provide evidence for each of these aspects.

Strength of Moral Motivation

Once the cognitive prerequisites are fulfilled, the shift from amoral to moral emotion ascriptions is a question of moral commitment. One pole of this dimension is exemplified by 'moral exemplars' (Colby & Damon, 1992). Without hesitation or inner conflict and even at high personal cost, these persons in their real life decisions gave priority to moral concerns – because morality was constitutive of their identity (happy moralists). Persons who do not care for morality at all represent the anti-pole. People in the middle position do care for morality, but other interests and values are also important to them. Depending on the costs incurred, they may disclaim conflicting interests or betray their moral beliefs – in either case they may suffer. Moral betrayal is illustrated by some 'informal collaborators' of the DDR intelligence service who, from fear of endangering their children's educational opportunities, cooperated and felt bitter remorse afterwards (unhappy victimizer). Renouncement of personal aspirations is illustrated by subjects who, as divorce lawyers, put the wellbeing of the children involved above the interests of those clients who claimed the right to custody. These subjects felt bad in view of their professional failure (unhappy moralists, Oser & Reichenbach, 2005).

In the context of LOGIC, a longitudinal study of a representative sample of originally 200 subjects (Weinert & Schneider, 1999; Schneider & Bullock, 2008), I studied the development of moral motivation from age 4 to 22 (Nunner-Winkler, 1999, 2008). At ages 4, 6, and 8, strength of moral motivation was measured by number of moral emotions attributed to wrongdoers in 4 moral conflicts. At ages 17 (n=176) and 22 (n=152), we used ratings based on the direction and justification of action decisions and emotion attributions to self as actor and as hypothetical victim of another's like transgression in 3 moral conflicts and emotion expectancies after a hypothetical transgression. At age 22, 47% of the participants were rated as high in moral motivation: they consistently had chosen a moral course of action (although many of them expected to feel bad about the loss incurred, exemplifying Oser & Reichenbach's type of unhappy moralist) and anticipated to feel bad had they committed the transgression presented. About 18% were rated as low: They justified their action decisions and emotion attributions (almost) exclusively in pragmatic terms, that is, by an interest in avoiding negative consequences to self or in securing personal benefits (evidencing the existence of happy victimizers among adults). The remaining 35% were rated in the middle: depending on story context and type of cost, they would make a moral or non-moral action decision.

These findings approximately correspond to results reported by Malti & Buchmann (2010) for a representative Swiss sample of 15- and 21-year-olds. They presented subjects with two of the LOGIC vignettes and used the same questioning procedure. For the analysis, they devised a simple yet valid 3-point indicator (e.g. they assigned the lowest value 1 if participants in both stories justified action decisions on pragmatic terms and for pragmatic reasons felt good or neutral about these decisions). The mean value for the 21-year olds was 2.19. This is only slightly below the mean of 2.29 that can be calculated from the distribution of the LOGIC subjects. The difference might be due to a morally relevant differential attrition rate in the longitudinal study: Subjects who (against the agreement) failed to inform the researchers of changes in address dropped out of the sample.

Both studies measured strength of moral motivation by responses to hypothetical moral conflicts. All the more, it is interesting that an analysis of real life behaviour agrees on the uneven distribution of moral motivation: a study of 300 cases of enforced Aryanisation of Jewish firms under the Nazi regime differentiated three types of buyers: unscrupulous buyers (about 40%) unhesitatingly used threats and blackmailing to even further cut down the price already underestimated by party officials; formally correct buyers (about 40%) paid the estimated price; fair buyers (20%) remunerated the real value (Bajohr 2000). Roughly, these types can be said to display low, medium or high moral motivation. The fact that low moral motivation shows more frequently in real life behaviour than in hypothetical discussions bespeaks the importance of actual consequences and the possibility that social desirability concerns might 'sugar-coat' hypothetical responses.

Type of Motive

Whereas direction and intensity of the emotion attributions (feels very good, good, bad, very bad) indicate strength of moral motivation, the justifications provided for negative emotions ascribed to wrongdoers offer insight into children's understanding of moral motivation. Three features were found – moral motivation is intrinsic, formal and a second order desire.

Moral motivation is *intrinsic*: Across all stories most of the 4-, 6-, and 8-year olds who expected the protagonist to feel bad referred to the fact that a valid norm had been transgressed, a wrong committed. Mention of consequences (positive or negative) ensuing to the wrongdoer never exceeded 18% of the responses.

Moral motivation is *formal:* In LOGIC, this aspect elucidated from responses to two stories dealing with sharing. In one story, the protagonist had undeservedly been awarded a prize; was s/he to share it with the disadvantaged competitor? In the other story, a thirsty child asked the protagonist for a sip of his drink. Justifications for the obligation to share varied with story content: In the prize story, almost all children referred to justice concerns (e.g. "Both did equally well", "The prize was unfairly assigned"), in the drink story many (especially of the younger subjects) referred to altruistic concerns (e.g. "Otherwise he'll die from thirst"). However, these differences were not reflected in the reasons given for the negative emotions attributed to the protagonist who refused to share. In both stories, children explained that the protagonist feels bad, because s/he knows s/he did wrong, s/he should have shared, s/he considers making up. These explanations reflect a formal readiness to do what one judges to be right. What is right in a given situation is determined by concretely contextualized moral judgements (e.g. in the prize story fairness, in the drink story compassion bids to share). Thus, moral motivation is intrinsically tied to moral judgement.

Moral motivation is a *second order desire.* It requires taking a stance towards one's spontaneous (first-order) desires (Frankfurt, 1988) and acting only upon morally compatible ones. To illustrate: In one story children had to attribute emotions to two protagonists who were involved in a competitive task (making many cookies) – one had refused to help a third child, the other did help. Among the 6-year olds some (19%) gave a moral attribution pattern (helper feels good for having helped, non-helper feels bad for not having helped), others (26%) gave an amoral pattern (helper feels bad for having made only few cookies, non-helper feels good for having made many cookies). One third, however, produced a kind of 'ideal world' pattern expecting both protagonists to feel good – the helper because s/he helped, and the non-helper, because s/he did well on the task. In other words, both were expected to feel good upon following their spontaneous inclinations. Now, undoubtedly, acting on altruistic inclinations (like the helper) is good, yet does not evidence moral motivation. Moral motivation is warranted only when a person does what is right, even when this conflicts with his/her spontaneous (first-order) desires.

To sum up: Even at an early age, all children cognitively grasp the intrinsic nature of moral rules. Moral motivation is built up in a delayed differential learning process. Persons caring for morality want to follow norms not in order to maximize benefits but from respect for their binding character. Moral motivation requires the ability to take a stance towards spontaneous impulses and implies the willingness to guide one's actions by contextualized moral judgements.

Structure of Moral Motivation

Each generation of new-borns is an invasion of barbarians. Different socialization theories discuss different mechanisms for getting them to abide by societal norms.

In *behaviourism,* conformity is produced by conditioning. If deviations are immediately sanctioned the very idea of transgressing soon will trigger fear of punishment (classical conditioning). If behaviour is rewarded as it gradually approximates culturally prescribed conduct it can be shaped (instrumental conditioning). In the first case, deviant impulses remain conscious and are suppressed only to avoid negative consequences. In the second case, subjects – eagerly pursuing rewards – may believe to do what they want to do and remain unaware of the external manipulation. *Psychoanalytic theories* provide generalized and internalized variants of these two learning mechanisms. From fear of castration the young boy internalizes the norms set by his father (identification with the aggressor) and henceforth follows them to avoid harsh super-ego sanctions (pangs of conscience). In order to secure her affection recognized as contingent on own behaviour, children from early on seek to fulfil their mother's expectations (anaclitic identification). Again, in the first case deviant impulses and societal constraints remain conscious. In the second case the need for conformity has become 'second nature'. *Cognitive theories* recognize non-instrumental concerns: Human behaviour is (at least in part) motivated by an intrinsic interest in truth (Piaget) and in moral rightness (Kohlberg's post-conventional level).

In the following I want to claim that formerly moral motivation largely corresponded to the psychoanalytic model, whereas today children develop an intrinsic motivation. As noted above, children rarely justified negative emotion ascriptions by fear of physical (e.g. punishment by authorities), social (e.g. disdain by peers), or inner sanctions (e.g. guilt or shame which are mentioned by less than 10% even of the 8-year olds). Most describe feelings of sorrow and regret, with the younger ones quite frequently even using the adjective 'sad' (Hascher, 1994). Given that regret is felt in case personal strivings fail, this indicates that they want to act in agreement with their moral persuasions. This ego-syntonic second-order desire to do what is judged to be right is a modern type of moral motivation. In previous generations, moral motivation entailed strict super-ego controls or a deeply ingrained conformity disposition.

Evidence for this claim comes from a study comparing moral understanding of 100 subjects of each of 4 generations: 65–75-, 40–50-, 20–30 year olds and 17-year old LOGIC participants (Nunner-Winkler, 2008; Nunner-Winkler & Nikele, 2001). For assessing the structure of moral motivation, subjects were asked how they would feel had they committed a grave transgression (cheating their father's last will resp. for the 17-year-olds keeping a wallet some needy old woman had lost). Then they had to offer a rating, employing emotional reactions that described fear of religious, legal, social and super-ego sanctions, a deeply ingrained conformity disposition and openly amoral reactions. A factor analysis of these ratings was performed. The oldest generation scored highest on the factors representing religious sanctions (e.g. 'God might punish me') and a deeply ingrained conformity disposition (e.g. 'The very idea is repulsive', 'This is against nature'). Both middle generations display a higher affinity to the super-ego language (e.g. 'I'd forever be conscience stricken') with the 20–30-year-olds explicitly distancing themselves from items expressing an almost automatic conformity disposition. The 17-year olds most decidedly rejected religious sanctions and super-ego controls; instead they most clearly affirmed (openly amoral as well as moral) ego-syntonic reactions (e.g. 'I'd soon get over it', 'I'd feel very sorry', 'I would consider how to make up for it'). Thus, across the generations ego-alien reactions gradually wane: the deeply ingrained need disposition for conformity of the oldest subjects gives way to a conscious awareness of superego dictates in the middle cohorts and finally is replaced by ego-syntonic responses in the youngest generation. The spontaneous answers to the open-ended question illustrate the change. First, an older subject is quoted who rejected the transgression in view of anticipated vindictive super-ego reactions: "I would never have done something like this. If, however, I had...I'd feel very miserable as if everybody could tell from my face...very horrible, guilty in any case and shame and simply fear to live on, fear of having done something bad, ... I don't know whether I could ever really laugh again or be happy." In contrast, younger subjects reason about the wrongness of the act which for them entails a binding obligation to refrain from doing it. Should they nevertheless have transgressed they do not refer to consequences imposed on the wrongdoer by some external or internal audience or authority (shame or guilt) but instead think about making up to the victim. To illustrate: "As far as I am concerned – normally I could not muster the ability. I would not have the will power to do something like that. For me this is a double breach of confidence...I can't really picture myself doing something like that. I can imagine that had I done it, I think I wouldn't feel good at all and sooner or later I'd probably..." These spontaneous reactions reflect cross-generational changes in the way morality is anchored in the personality. In the traditional model conformity to preordained norms is secured by super ego controls threatening lifelong retributions in case of deviance or by a total blockage of the very thought of transgressing from conscious awareness. In the ego-syntonic model the individual identifies with norms s/he understands to be justified and in case of transgression expects to feel regret and a desire for repair. This indicates that s/he experiences the lapse as a betrayal of self-chosen and willingly affirmed aspirations.

The change in the structure of moral motivation is related to changes in the *foundation of morality*. With secularisation and enlightenment moral norms are no longer understood as commands set by God, religious authorities, time-honoured traditions or by natural law. Rather, they are derived from 'our common will' (Tugendhat, 2006) for which Rawls' (1972) model of consensus under the veil of ignorance – operationalizing the basic moral principles of impartiality, equality, harm avoidance – provides a good reconstruction. This new focus on minimizing harm rather than on punctually obeying divine powers decreases the size of the moral domain and allows for exceptions from moral rules if by transgressing greater harm can be avoided than by conforming (Gert, 1988). Both changes can be observed across the generations studied. With respect to the *justifiability of exceptions* older subjects largely agree with Kant's (1797/1959) claim that negative duties enjoy strict validity. For, as Kant argues, any harm ensuing from rule following is caused not by the agent, but by fate – a kind of mundane proxy for God. For 5 vignettes presented (e.g. neglect to sort waste) subjects condemning this behaviour were asked whether they could imagine circumstances in which they might judge differently. Two thirds of the 65–75-year olds – versus one third of the 20–30-year olds – denied that (e.g. "Order must be. If there are containers you should use them. Even if they throw it together afterwards" versus: "If the containers are so far away that you burn up more gas than it is worth"/"If people are old or sick"). Children growing up today clearly allow for justifiable exceptions (Nunner-Winkler, 1999, Weyers et al., 2007). With respect to the *delimitation of morality*, younger subjects will reckon behaviour considered as morally relevant by the older ones under the personal domain as long as it does not harm others. To illustrate: Older subjects would strictly condemn homosexual behaviour even among consenting adults (e.g. "This is sinful/unnatural/pathological/ disgusting"). Younger subjects, in contrast, would freely accept it (e.g. "That's their decision – as long as it is a good relationship"). These changes in the cognitive moral understanding fit with the changes described in the structure of moral motivation. Allowing for exceptions requires a formal motive structure tied to moral judgement. For if clear cut concrete rules are inserted in a strictly controlling super-ego or the disposition to conform is experienced as a spontaneous, natural need, exceptions are unthinkable. At the same time, the delimitation of morality to those rules that all could freely agree upon facilitates an ego-syntonic motive structure.

Socialization styles have changed correspondingly. Increasingly, the former educational goals of order, cleanliness and obedience have receded to an emphasis on autonomy and independence. Also, children have been granted more of a say in family decisions (Reuband, 1988, 1997). Children today grow up in a more open democratic atmosphere in which early conditioning and power threats give way to negotiations and reasoning. To the extent children understand that moral rules are to ensure fair cooperation and nonviolent conflict regulation they may willingly follow them from insight.

To sum up: Emotions indicate the importance persons ascribe to facts. Emotion attributions to a decision maker in a moral conflict indicate the relative weight subjects give to moral as compared to non-moral values or interests. Direction and justifications of such attributions allow inferences concerning the strength of moral commitment, the motives guiding norm conformity and the way morality is anchored in the person. Modern moral motivation is an intrinsic formal second-order desire to do what is judged to be right even at personal costs. This ego-syntonic structure corresponds to a secularized morality which clearly demarcates a minimal set of rationally justifiable, universally valid norms from social conventions, religious commands and the personal domain. More comprehensive traditional moralities more likely are fixed in form of a controlling super-ego structure or a deeply ingrained conformity disposition.

AN INTERNALIST CRITIQUE OF THE CONCEPT OF MORAL MOTIVATION

In the Kohlberg tradition, the concept of moral motivation has been introduced in order to bridge the gap between moral judgement and action (Blasi, 1980, 1983;

Rest, 1984; Colby & Damon, 1992). This notion is rejected by moral internalists who hold that moral judgements are self-motivating and hence take relapses as evidence of "practical irrationality" or weakness of will: "If an agent judges it is right for her to □ in circumstances C, then either she is motivated to □ in C or she is practically irrational" (Smith, 1994, p. 61, quoted from Minnameier, 2011, p. 59). In this statement, knowledge of prevalent rules is distinguished from individual moral judgments examining the question "of whether common moral precincts should be binding for me in circumstances C" (Minnameier, 2011, p. 62). From this internalist perspective, Minnameier reconstructs the happy victimizer phenomenon as a correlate of younger children's "special form of moral reasoning and understanding" (p. 65) according to which they "accept moral rules out of empathy and insight into others' needs and desires" (p. 69). Only later do they acquire a "superior perspective" that allows them to "weigh individual interests independently and disinterestedly" (p. 70). Now they link moral emotions "with a sense of moral obligation", i.e. "understand and accept moral duties above and beyond their sympathy with others" (p. 71).

There are several objections to this argumentation. To start with a theoretical consideration: If a person does not care about morality, the judgement that "it is right for her to □ in circumstances C" most likely is a prudential one advocating following one's own interests in moral conflicts. In motivational terms, such a judgement would indicate lack of moral motivation. Minnameier, instead, treats the question of what to do in a moral conflict "as a downright moral one and therefore fully covered by the process of moral reflection and judgment" (p. 64), explicitly accepting that this "relativizes moral obligation to circumstances C and to the agent's believing in her obligation" (p. 60). This coincides with his treating happy victimizer thinking as a special form of moral reasoning. In consequence, however, the term 'moral' becomes equivocal – decisions to fulfil other-regarding moral obligations as well as those serving conflicting own interests both accrue from moral reflection. Kohlberg avoided such ambiguities by calling self-centred reasoning 'pre-conventional' thus clearly distinguishing it from conventional and principled moral thinking. In contrast, Minnameier's conceptual decision obscures the fact that moral obligations are not reducible to individual beliefs but constitute a system of collectively accepted commands backed by (formal and/or informal) sanctions.

From an empirical point of view, the problem is that Minnameier's reconstruction of the happy victimizer phenomenon does not fit with relevant data. First, it is not true that younger children accept moral rules "out of empathy and insight into other's needs and desires" (p. 69). Instead, from early on, most children adequately differentiate between situations. Thus, in justifying the wrongness of stealing, only 10% of the 4-year-olds in LOGIC mentioned the victim's needs or desires, whereas 80% gave deontological reasons, that is, referred to the fact that a rule exists (e.g. "One may not steal") or gave a negative evaluation of the deed or the wrongdoer (e.g. "This is mean" or "S/he is a thief"). In contrast, a large majority pointed to victim's needs when sharing one's drink with a thirsty playmate was at issue (e.g. "Otherwise s/he'll die from thirst"). Apparently, children have an early (implicit) understanding that negative duties hold at all places, all times and towards everybody whereas the positive duty to help arises only from needs of the person concerned. This finding weakens Minnameier's argument that – in contrast to common moral knowledge – moral judgements deal with the "peculiarities of the situation" and derive their binding force therefrom. In moral conflicts involving negative duties situational specifics are irrelevant. They need to be considered only in moral dilemmas, when the justifiability of exceptions from rules is at stake.

Secondly, by linking happy victimizer reactions to undeveloped role-taking abilities Minnameier disregards the fact that such reactions are also found among older children and adults. In fact, role-taking is neither a necessary nor a sufficient condition for moral behaviour. It is not necessary – other mechanisms may be at work. For example, in a large study on rescuers of Jews during Nazi times Oliner&Oliner (1988) found that indeed some were motivated by compassion. Yet, others were motivated by their religious faith or by their moral convictions, i.e. acted from obedience to divine commands or from respect for the moral law neither of which requires concretely situated interpersonal role-taking. Role-taking also is not sufficient – it runs the risk of particularism. The spontaneous tendency to identify with and then favour those close to or similar to oneself is hard to overcome. This is convincingly evidenced in studies on organ transplant showing that white middle class married males, i.e. patients doctors in charge could most easily identify with, received considerably more than their fair share of scarce organs (Elster, 1992).

Minnameier raises the question of "how motivation is motivated" (p. 61). Different socialization theories present different models for instilling in children a disposition to conform to prevalent social rules (see above). In light of a secularized minimal morality and egalitarian socialization styles, self-socialization plays an increasingly larger role. Pluralistic modern societies grant people quite some leeway for selecting interests and values. Contexts influence but do not determine their choices. In this respect truly caring for morality (rather than merely conforming in view of sanctions) may not differ too much from caring for truth, beauty, power, money. By actively identifying with values individuals generate self-imposed volitional necessities that constitute their essential nature as persons (Frankfurt, 1988, 1992). In these terms, moral motivation is tantamount neither to a cognitive judgement nor to emotions but to a volitional characteristic of personhood. Cognitive judgements lack motivational power. Emotions no longer motivate behaviour as described in behaviourist or psychoanalytic paradigms (e.g. by fear of punishment, shame or pangs of conscience), but indicate values a person cares for. Caring for values implies being invested in them, being unable to muster the will to betray them.

A final argument concerns the costs entailed by waiving the concept of moral motivation, that is, the questions left unanswered. There is a counterpart to Minnameier's sceptic question 'how is motivation motivated?': 'What determines the agent's judgement that it is right for her to □ in circumstances C?' Inasmuch as undeveloped role-taking abilities no longer affect older children's or adults' moral reflection – what does explain whether an agent judges it right for her to follow moral obligations under any circumstances or only at reasonable costs or not at all if there are any costs? What types of reasons underlie these judgements? To what extent are they autonomous? Internalism remains silent on such questions which can be tackled in a motivational frame of reference and which are an important part of moral psychology. In any case, in the long run the controversy between internalism and externalism will not be decided on the level of terminology or philosophical assumptions but by empirical research clarifying the relative explanatory and predictive power of either position.

REFERENCES

Arsenio, W.,& Fleiss, K. (1996). Typical and behaviourally disruptive children's understanding of the emotional consequences of sociomoral events. *British Journal of Developmental Psychology, 14*, 173–186

Arsenio, W., J. Gold, & Adams, E. (2004). Adolescents' emotion expectancies regarding aggressive and nonaggresive events: Connetons with behaviour problems. *Journal of Experimental Child Psychology, 8*, 338–355.

Arsenio, W., Gold, J., & Adams, E. (2006) Children's conceptions of moral emotions. In M. Killen & J. Smetana (Eds.), *Handbook of moral development* (pp. 581–610). Matwah: Lawrence Erlbaum.

Arsenio, W., & R. Kramer (1992). Victimizers and their victims. *Child Development, 63*, 915–927

Arsenio, W., & A. Lover (1995). Children's conceptions of sociomoral affect: Happy victimizers, mixed emotions, and other expectancies. In M. Killen and D. Hart (Eds.), *Morality in everyday life* (pp. 87–128). New York: Cambridge University Press.

Asendorpf, J.B.,&. Nunner-Winkler, G. (1992). Children's moral motive strength and temperamental inhibition reduce their immoral tendencies in real moral conflicts. *Child Development, 63*, 1223–1235.

Bajohr, F. (2000). Verfolgung aus gesellschaftsgeschichtlicher Perspektive. Die wirtschaftliche Existenzvernichtung der Juden und die deutsche Gesellschaft. *Geschichte und Gesellschaft, 26*, 629–652.

Barden, R.G., F.A. Zelko et al (1980). Children's consensual knowledge about the experiential determinants of emotion. *Journal of Personality and Social Psychology, 39*, 968–976.

Blasi, A. (1980). Bridging moral cognition and moral action: A critical review of the literature. *American Psychological Association, 88*, 1–45.

Blasi, A. (1983). Bridging moral cognition and moral action: A theoretical perspective. *Development Review, 3*, 178–210.

Colby, A. Damon, W. (1992). *Some do care: Contemporary lives of moral commitment*. New York: Free Press.

Damon, W. (1997). *The youth charter: How communities can work together to raise standards for all our children*. New York: Free Press.

Dunn, J.,&Hughes, C. (2001). I got some swords and you are dead!: Violent fantasy, antisocial behaviour, friendship and moral sensibility in young children. *Child Development, 77*(2), 491–505.

Elster, J. (1992). *Local justice. How institutions allocate scarce goods and necessary burdens*. New York: Russell Sage Foundation.

Frankfurt, H.G. (1988). *The importance of what we care about. Philosophical Essays*. Cambridge: Cambridge University Press.

Frankfurt, H.G. (1992). On the necessity of ideals. In G. Noam & T.E. Wren (Eds.), *The moral self* (pp. 292–309). Cambridge, MA: MIT Press.

Gasser, L.,& Keller, M. (2009). Are the competent the morally good? Social-cognitive competencies and moral motivation of children involved in bullying. *Social Development, 18*, 798–816.

Gert, B. (1988). *Morality. A new justification of the moral rules*. New York, Oxford: Oxford University Press.

Hascher, T. (1994). *Emotionsbeschreibung und Emotionsverstehen. Zur Entwicklung des Emotionsvokabulars und des Ambivalenzverstehens im Kindesalter*. Münster: Waxmann.

Higgins, A. (1991). The Just Community approach to moral education: Evolution of the idea and recent findings. In W.M. Kurtines & J.L. Gewirtz (Eds.), *Handbook of moral behavior and development. Vol 3: Application* (pp. 111–141). Hillsdale, NJ: Erlbaum.

Hoffman, M.L. (2000). *Empathy and moral development: Implications for caring and justice*. Cambridge, UK: Cambridge UP.

Hughes, C.,& Dunn, J. (2000). Hedonism or empathy? Hard-to-manage children's moral awareness and links with cognitive and and maternal characteristics. *British Journal of Developmental Psychology, 18*, 227–245.

Kant, I. (1797/1959). Über ein vermeintliches Recht, aus Menschenliebe zu lügen. In: I. Kant *Metaphysik der Sitten* (pp. *637–643)*. Frankfurt a.M.: Suhrkamp.

Keller, M., O. Lourenco, et al. (2003). The multifaceted phenomenon of 'happy victimizers': A cross-cultural comparison of moral emotions. *British Journal of Developmental Psychology, 21*, 1–18.

Kohlberg, L. (1981). *Essays on moral development: Vol.1. The philosophy of moral development. Moral stages and the idea of justice*. San Francisco: Harper & Row.

Kohlberg, L. (1984). *Essays on moral development: Vol.2. The psychology of moral development. The nature and validity of moral stages*. San Francisco: Harper&Row

Krettenauer, T., Asendorpf, J. & Nuner-Winkler, G. (in print). Moral Emotion Attribution and Personality Traits as Long Term Predictors of Antisocial Conduct in Earliy Adulthood. Findings from a 20 Year Longitudinal Study, *International Journal of Behavioral Development*

Krettenauer, T. and D. Eichler (2006). "Adolescents' self-attributed moral emotions followig a moral transgression: relations with delinquency, confidence in moral judgement, and age." *British Journal of Developmental Psychology, 24*(3), 489–506.

Krettenauer, T., T. Malti, Sokol, B.W.et al. (2008). The development of moral emotion expectancies and the happy victimizer phenomenon: A critical review and application. *European Journal of Developmental Science, 2*(3), 221–235.

Lourenco, O. (1997). Children's attributions of moral emotions to victimizers: Some data, doubts and suggestions. *British Journal of Developmental Psychology, 15*, 425–438.

Malti, T. (2007). Moral emotions and aggressive behaviour. In G. Steffgen and M. Gollwitzer (Eds). *Emotions and aggressive behaviour* (pp. 185–200). Göttingen: Hogrefe.

Malti, T., M. Gummerum, Buchmann, M. (2007). Contemporaneous and one-year longitudinal prediction of children's prosocial behaviour from sympathy and moral motivation. *Journal of Genetic Psychology, 168*, 277–299.

Malti, T., M. Gummerum, et al. (2009). Children's moral motivation, sympathy, and prosocial behaviour. *Child Development 80*, 442–460.

Malti, T., M. Keller, et al. (2010). Moral emotions in cross-cultural context. Emotions, aggression, and moral development. In W. Arsenio and E. Lemrise (Eds.), *Emotions, aggression, and morality in children: Bridging development and psychopathology* (pp. 177–198). Washington, DC, American Psychological Association.

Malti, T., & Buchmann, M. (2010). Socialization and individual antecendents of adolescents' and young adults' moral motivation. *Journal of Youth and Adolescence, 39*(2),138–149.

Minnameier, G. (2010). The problem of moral motivation and the happy victimizer phenomenon: Killing two birds with one stone. *New Directions for Child and Adolescent Development, 129*, 55–75.

Montada, L. (1993). Understanding oughts by assessing moral reasoning or moral emotions. In G. Noam & T.E. Wren (Eds.), *The Moral Self* (pp. 292–309). Cambridge, MA: MIT Press.

Murgatroyd, D. and E. Robinson (1993). Children's judgement of emotion following moral transgression. *International Journal of Behavioral Development, 16*, 93–111.

Nucci, L.P. and E. Turiel (1993). God's word, religious rules, and their relation to Christian and Jewish children's concepts of morality. *Child Development, 64*, 1475–1491.

Nucci, L.P. and E.K. Weber (1995). Social interactions in the home and the development of young children's concepts of the personal. *Child Development, 66,* 1438–1452.

Nunner-Winkler, G. (1999). Development of moral understanding and moral motivation. InF.E. Weinert and W. Schneider (Eds), *Individual development from 3 to 12. Findings from the Munich Longitudinal Study* (pp. 253–290). New York, Cambridge University Press.

Nunner-Winkler, G. (2008). From super-ego and conformist habitus to ego-syntonic moral motivation: Sociohistoric changes in moral motivation. *European Journal of Developmental Science, 2*(3), 251–268.

Nunner-Winkler, G. (2009). Moral motivation from childhood to early adulthood. In W. Schneider and M. Bullock (Eds.), *Human development from early childhood to early adulthood* (pp 91–118). New York: Psychology Press.

Nunner-Winkler, G., M. Nikele (2001). Moralische Differenz oder geteilte Werte. In B. Heintz (Ed.) Geschlechtersoziologie. *KZfSS Sonderheft, 41,* 108–135

Nunner-Winkler, G., M. Meyer-Nikele, et al. (2006). *Integration durch Moral. Moralische Motivation und Ziviltugenden Jugendlicher.* Wiesbaden: VS Verlag für Sozialwissenschaften.

Nunner-Winkler, G., & B. Sodian (1988). Children's understanding of moral emotions. *Child Development, 59,* 1323–1338.

Oliner, S.P. and P.M. Oliner (1988). *The Altruistic Personality. Rescuers of Jews in Nazi Europe.* New York: The Free Press.

Oser, F., & R. Reichenbach (2000). Moralische resilienz: Das phänomen des „Unglücklichen Moralisten". In W. Edelstein and G. Nunner-Winkler (Eds.), *Moral im sozialen Kontext* (pp. 203–233).Frankfurt a.M.: Suhrkamp.

Perner, J. (1991). *Understanding the representational mind.* Cambridge MA: MIT Press.

Perner, J. and H. Wimmer (1985). ""John thinks that Mary thinks that." Attribution of second-order beliefs by 5- to 10-year-old children." *Journal of Experimental Child Psychology, 39,* 437–447.

Putnam, H. (1994). *Words and Life.* Cambridge, MA & London: Harvard UP.

Putnam, R.D., R. Leonardi, et al. (1993). *Making democracy work. Civic traditions in modern Italy.* Princeton, NJ: Princeton University Press.

Rawls, J. (1972). *A theory of justice.* London/Oxford/NY: Oxford University Press.

Rest, J.R. (1986). *Moral Development. Advances in research and theory.* New York: Praeger.

Rest, J.R. (1999). Die Rolle des moralischen Urteilens im moralischen Handeln. In D. Garz, F. Oser & W. Althof (Eds.), *Moralisches Urteil und Handeln (*pp 82–116*).* Frankfurt a. M.: Suhrkamp.

Reuband, K.H. (1988). Von äußerer Verhaltenskonformität zu selbständigem Handeln: Über die Bedeutung kultureller und struktureller Einflüsse für den Wandel in den Erziehungszielen und Sozialisationsinhalten. In H.O. Luthe & H. Meulemann (Eds.), *Wertwandel Faktum oder Fiktion? Bestandsaufnahmen u. Diagnosen aus kultursoziologischer Sicht* (pp. 73–97). Frankfurt a.M., New York, Campus.

Reuband, K.H. (1997). Aushandeln statt Gehorsam. InL. Böhnisch & K. Lenz (Eds.), *Erziehungsziele und Erziehungspraktiken in den alten und neuen Bundesländern im Wandel. Familien* (pp. 129–153). Weinheim and München: Juvent a.

Schneider, W., & M. Bullock (2008). *Human development from early childhood to early adulthood: Findings from a 20 year longitudinal study.* New York: Psychology Press.

Selman, R.L., & D.F. Byrne (1974). A structural-developmental analysis of levels of role taking in middle childhood. *Child Development, 45,* 803–806.

Smetana, J.G. (2006). Socio-Cognitive Domain Theory: Consistencies and variations in children's moral and social judgements.In M. Killen & J.G. Smetana (Eds.), *Handbook of moral development* (pp. 119–153). Mahwah, N.J.: Erlbaum.

Sokol, B.W. (2004). *Children's conception of agency and morality: Making sense of the happy victimizer phenomenon.*Unpublished PhD, University of British Columbia, Canada.

Sokol, B.W., & M.J. Chandler (2003). Taking agency seriously in the theories-of-mind enterprise: Exploring children's understanding of interpretation and intention. *British Journal of Educational Psychology Monograph Series II, 2, Development and Motivation,* 125–136.

Solomon, R.C. (1976). *The passions.* Garden City: Anchor Press.

Tugendhat, E. (2006). Das Problem einer autonomen Moral. In N. Scarano & M. Suárez (Eds.), *Ernst Tugendhats Ethik* (pp. 13–30). München:C.H.Beck.

Turiel, E. (1983). *The development of social knowledge: Morality and convention.* Cambridge: Cambridge University Press.

Walker, L.J. (1999). Die Rolle des Urteils im Wirken der Moral. Moralisches. In D. Garz, F. Oser and W. Althof (eds). *Urteil und Handeln* (pp. 137–167). Frankfurt a.M..: Suhrkamp.

Walker, L.J., B. de Vries, et al. (1987). Moral stages and moral orientations in real-life and hypothetical dilemmas. *Child Development, 58,* 842–858.

Weinert, F.E., & W. Schneider (1999). *Individual development from 3 to 12. Findings from the Munich Longitudinal Study.* New York: Cambridge University Press.

Weyers, S., M. Sujbert, Eckensberger, L.H. (2007). *Recht und Unrecht aus kindlicher Sicht. Die Entwicklung rechtsanaloger Strukturen im kindlichen Denken und Handeln.* Münster: Waxmann.

Wittgenstein, L. (1984). *Philosophische Untersuchungen.* Frankfurt a.M.: Suhrkamp.

Yuill, N., J. Perner, et al. (1996). Children's changing understanding of wicked desires: From objective to subjective and moral. *British Journal of Developmental Psychology, 14,* 457–475.

AFFILIATION

Gertrud Nunner-Winkler
formerly head of the research unit 'Moral Development
of the Max Planck Institute for Human Cognitive and Brain Sciences
Munich, Germany

BETTINA DOERING

II. THE DEVELOPMENT OF MORAL IDENTITY AND MORAL MOTIVATION IN CHILDHOOD AND ADOLESCENCE

INTRODUCTION

Investigating moral identity and moral motivation from a developmental and criminological perspective accomplishes two contradictory research goals. On the one hand, developmental research on morality argues that establishing moral identity begins with adolescence and moral motivation further increases with age, especially between childhood and adolescence. On the other hand, research on delinquency identifies an increase of criminal behaviour between childhood and adolescence. Furthermore, adolescents are the most criminalized group according to data about reported and unreported crime. Although criminal or aggressive behaviour is explainable in different ways, morality should be one possible explanatory factor of delinquent behaviour. Assuming the truth of this hypothesis, how can adolescents be more morally motivated while they show also more delinquent behaviour? Looking further into the studies investigating moral motivation, the increase of moral motivation still requires adequate confirmation. Therefore, this chapter addresses the development of moral identity and moral motivation in childhood and adolescence and discusses the idea of an age-related increase of moral motivation.

THEORETICAL BACKGROUND

The Moral Identity and Moral Motivation

After a long period of focusing on cognitive moral development based on the Kohlbergian tradition, Blasi introduced the concept of the moral self (1983). The main difference between Kohlberg's and Blasi's position is best described by the following assumption of Lapsley (1996, p. 86): "For Kohlberg, moral motivation to act comes from one's fidelity to the prescriptive nature of moral principles. Responsibility is entailed by the formal, categorical character of a moral structure and flows directly from it. Hence not to act is to betray a principle. For Blasi, in contrast, moral motivation to act is a consequence of one's moral identity, and not to act is to betray the self." Indeed, a moral principle has an internal validity, but it is less binding if it is abstract, outside of the self and therefore less personally important.

K. Heinrichs, F. Oser & T. Lovat (Eds.), Handbook of Moral Motivation: Theories,
Models, Applications, 289–306.
© 2013 Sense Publishers. All rights reserved.

The idea to bridge the gap between moral cognition and behaviour by adding moral identity as a possible source of moral motivation was an important step within moral psychology. The moral self is defined by two different dimensions, moral self-integration and the centrality of morality within the self (Blasi, 1995, 2004, 2005). If morality is more integrated within the self and has a higher centrality, an individual will demonstrate a stronger motivation to behave morally, because the individual has a tendency towards self-consistent behaviour. To define moral behaviour as truly moral, a previous reasoning process with different action opportunities is important. Therefore, moral behaviour is defined by intention and choice. If the individual chooses the moral action alternative, then he/she is motivated to behave morally. Besides moral judgment, moral identity can be the source of this moral motivation. Moral motivation is defined as "an 'agents' willingness to do even at personal costs what they, to the best of their knowledge, judge to be right" (Nunner-Winkler, Meyer-Nikele, & Wohlrab, 2007, p. 28). It is evident that the self is not exclusively constructed around moral characteristics. Accordingly, other motives matter when an individual decides to act in a specific manner. Inter-individual differences exist because some individuals construct their self around moral characteristics and others give personal needs a more important role. Some however can integrate the above and so transform moral concerns into personal needs. This process is discussed critically within the literature because morality is by definition the orientation towards others' welfare and not towards personal needs.

In summary, moral identity will be understood in line with trait theories of motivation (Scheffer & Heckhausen, 2006). The motive to behave morally is driven by moral traits, which are part of an individual's identity. The moral motivation is therefore understood as the concrete manifestation of the moral identity defined by each person.

The Development of Moral Identity and Moral Motivation

A developmental perspective towards moral identity formation is required because "literature on moral self-identity and the moral personality seems largely preoccupied with sketching out what it looks like in its mature form in adulthood" (Narvaez & Lapsley, 2009, p. 5). Identity generally can be understood as the answer to the question: "Who am I?" It is a specific structure and combination of personal characteristics, which the individual is aware of (Oerter & Dreher, 2008, p. 303). Furthermore, that identity is not a static and unchangeable construct and is better represented as a relational and social context dependent structure has been indicated by research (Simon & Mummendey, 1997, p. 13). In contrast, Erikson (1981b) remarks that one of the important functions of identity is a feeling of continuity and coherence.

Various theoretical approaches to describe the process of identity formation have been attempted. First, Erikson's theory (Erikson, 1981a, 1981b) of identity development should be mentioned. His psychoanalytically orientated model claims that the best adapted development is observable when individuals are able to handle their specific psychosexual or psychosocial conflicts and crises (Straub, 2000). "Identity achievement and identity diffusion are polar alternatives of status inherent in Erikson's theory." (Marcia, 1966, p. 551) The former are the equilibrated solutions of identity crises, whereas the latter refers to the dis-equilibrated form. Following up Erikson, Marcia offers his Ego Identity Status-Model (Marcia, 1966, 1993). The model differentiates between four statuses of identity. The ideal status is the "identity achievement" as a product of identity crises accompanied by a self-reflexive exploration and this finally leads to a biographically relevant "self-constructed committed identity" (Straub, 2000, p. 294). The second status, also named "moratorium", is the self-reflexive process itself. The opposite of "identity achievement" is "foreclosure" and is regarded as a third status in Marcia's model. An individual showing this identity status does not engage in a self-reflexive process to achieve an autonomous identity. The fourth possible identity status is "identity diffusion". According to the definition of this status, individuals have no stable, cross-situational orientation (Marcia, 1993).

Over the life-span, Erikson's and Marcia's theories emphasize the importance of adolescence for "identity achievement". For Erikson (1981b), adolescence describes a time period where identity conflicts and crises can have long-lasting consequences. Additionally, Marcia (1980) assumes that the majority of adolescents explore different future identities and ways of life in this period. The development from "Identity diffusion" and "foreclosure" to "moratorium" and "identity achievement" is therefore mainly positioned in the period of adolescence. These theoretical assumptions are emphasized by further empirical research. Rosenberg (1986) discovered an increasing amount of cognitively elaborated reasons between late childhood and adolescence. Self-descriptions in adolescence compared to childhood are described as being more justified, differentiated, organized, and abstract (Harter, 1990; Harter & Monsour, 1992; Rosenberg, 1986). Assigned to the moral domain, abstract principles gain higher importance and are used to justify decisions and behaviour in older age-groups. The organization of more differentiated self-descriptions categorizes concordant and contradictory characteristics within the self and, in late adolescence the ability to integrate these contradictions develops (Harter & Monsour, 1992). In early stages of identity formation, moral principles are not integrated within the self. They are perceived as external and legitimated by authorities and, therefore, the identity status is "foreclosure" (Blasi, 1993). The question of justification and legitimization develops with increasing cognitive abilities and hence "identity achievement" becomes possible. In line with the described development, moral principles will be seen as intrinsically important and more central to the self. With higher centrality and integration of moral principles into the self, moral motivation will be strengthened and moral judgments will become more obligatory for an individual. The reason for this development is that an individual seeks for self-consistency, continuity and a positive evaluated self (Blasi, 1983; Erikson, 1981b; Higgins, 1987; Tajfel & Turner, 1986). The first study considering moral centrality and self-integration from a developmental perspective was presented by Arnold (1993). Arnold investigated subjects in Grades 6, 8, 10 and 11 and found no age-related differences for centrality. In fact, the author discovered a shift for self-integration, where younger children have a more external perspective on moral identity and adolescents a more internal perspective.

In line with these results comes a recent study by Krettenauer (2011) who investigated the centrality of moral characteristics and internal moral motivation. Three different research questions occurred within the study: first, whether moral centrality predicts internal moral motivation; second, whether an age-related change for moral centrality and internal moral motivation is observable; and, third, to what extent moral centrality and internal moral motivation predict responsibility judgments. Krettenauer (2011) hypothesized that moral centrality and internal moral motivation should be seen as different constructs, where moral centrality is not age-related but varies between individuals and internal motivation is correlated with age. For some adolescents, moral principles and values are not important because they construct their self around personal needs (e.g. sports, music, achievement or an employment). Instead, internal moral motivation is a case of development because, first of all, children perceive values and principles as external and, with age, "individual conscience becomes more salient" (Krettenauer, 2011, p. 311). For this reason, Krettenauer hypothesized an increasing internal moral motivation by age. Participants of the study were students of 7th, 9th and 11th grade. Additionally, investigations with undergraduate students have been carried out. Moral centrality and internal moral motivation are highly correlated in this study (r=.62, p < .01). In another study of Nunner-Winkler et al. (2007), the correlation was significant but lower (r=.40, p<.01). Furthermore, moral centrality was not significantly correlated with age. Finally, a relationship between moral centrality and internal moral motivation with responsibility judgments, measured as moral emotion expectancies, was found. Additionally, Nunner-Winkler (2008) investigated the development of moral motivation at the age of 4, 6, 8, 18 and 23 and detected an increasing moral motivation by age. The stability of moral motivation was interestingly very low and only for the extreme poles of moral motivation was a high stability found. Whereas Kohlberg (1996) stated that children are orientated towards sanctions and authorities, Nunner-Winkler and Sodian (1988) found, in line with Turiel (1983), an early developed moral knowledge but a later developed moral motivation. A further study by Malti and Buchmann (2010) detected no differences between 15 and 21 year old participants. Beside the influence of development, gender differences of moral motivation are discussed within literature, whereas boys show a lower strength of moral motivation compared to girls (Nunner-Winkler et al., 2007). Interestingly, these differences not only occur but also increase within adolescence (Nunner-Winkler, 2007).

After the theoretical and empirical results on developmental changes of moral identity and moral motivation have been discussed, what shall be marked as the essence of the development of moral identity and moral motivation? Two studies investigated moral centrality and found no age-related differences. Furthermore, that moral centrality shows inter-individual but no developmental differences has been pointed out. Both studies investigated adolescents between grade 6 and undergraduate students representing early and late adolescence as well as young adulthood. Even literature assumes a transitional process in that age period, if an increase between childhood and adolescence occurs is still questionable. For self-integration in terms of a change from an external to an internal perspective, the stage model of Kohlberg (1996) can be seen as good empirical evidence. The stage model shows in the pre-conventional stage authority based moral judgments (external) and within the post-conventional stage autonomous principle orientated moral reasoning (internal).

For the development of moral motivation, no clear evidence has been found. Whereas Krettenauer (2011) did not find a pattern throughout development, Nunner-Winkler (2008) detected a developmental change. A further problem is the persistent absence of a study, to the best of the author's knowledge, which has investigated the age groups between childhood and early adolescence. Except for the study of Malti and Buchmann (2010), a small sample size marks further limitations of the described studies. For developmental research, these sample sizes can be insufficient, since comparison of mean differences balanced samples in every age group are required. In order to fill these research gaps, the present study investigates if adolescence is important for the development of moral identity and moral motivation and if an increase of both is observable. As described earlier, moral identity is considered as one of the possible sources of moral motivation (Bergman, 2004; Blasi, 1983; Krettenauer, 2011) and a positive relationship between both constructs is hypothesized.

THE STUDY

Sample

A representative, standardized and administered student survey was conducted in 2010 within a rural area of Germany to answer the described research questions. To investigate the transition between childhood and adolescence, 4th, 7th and 9th grade students are considered. Only students with a written consent of their parents participated in the study. Table 1 shows the sample statistics. Within the 4th grade, the lowest response rate is observable. The percentage of girls shows a relatively equal gender distribution. Ethnicity was calculated out of six different questions about the nationality and origin of the child or adolescent and their parents. If one answer was not German, the participant was from a foreign ethnicity. Between 81.8 and 84.2% of all participants are German. The predominant foreign ethnicity is the former Soviet Union. Within 7th and 9th grade, a weighting coefficient was used to adjust the sample distribution to the population in reference to the school types.

Table 1. Sample statistics

	4th grade	*7th grade*	*9th grade*
Sample size	1.221	815	2.891
Response rate	64.0	74.9	72.0
% – girls	51.1	49.9	51.3
Age – M (SD)	10.05 (0.45)	13.18 (0.54)	15.18 (0.58)
% – German ethnicity	83.2	81.8	84.2

Moral Centrality

Moral centrality was measured with an adapted version of the Good-Self Assessment by Barriga et al. (2001). Within this measure, participants were asked to rate 16 moral or immoral characteristics regarding the importance for their self-concept. Because the original study investigated adolescents (16–19 years), it was not clear if the 16 characteristics are appropriate for children of the 4th grade. In order to meet this question, a pretest was conducted to generate moral and personal characteristics, which are relevant for 4th grade as well as for 7th and 9th grade students. On the one hand, children and adolescents were asked to freely determine 15 important characteristics and, on the other hand, 20 different traits with a closed answer format were presented. The 20 characteristics were selected out of previous studies using the Good-Self Assessment (Arnold, 1993; Barriga et al., 2001; Harter & Monsour, 1992; Nunner-Winkler, Meyer-Nikele & Wohlrab, 2006; Pratt, Arnold, Pratt, & Diessner, 1999; Pratt, Hunsberger, Pancer & Alisat, 2003). Subsequent to the pretest, the traits were analyzed and selected by the following criteria. First, the characteristics should be important to every age-group and the means and standard deviations of personal and moral traits should be similar. Second, from a theoretical and empirical perspective, the characteristics should be clearly moral or personal and, third, the traits should be equally important for girls and boys. In the end, 4 moral characteristics (fair, honest, helpful, considerate) and 4 personal characteristics (popular, humorously, sporty, smart) are used for the main study. The answer format ranged from 1 "not important to me" to 4 "very important to me." Only 8 traits were used to have a suitable measure for children of the 4th grade. In table 2, the results of the item analysis of the main study are presented. "Humorously" was removed from further analysis because of low factor loadings and item-selectivity. The correlation between moral and personal characteristics scale is .047 (p < .01). Both scales are sufficiently reliable considering the small item number and children as participants. After the items have been aggregated, a difference score was constructed. The mean of the personal traits was subtracted from the moral traits (M=.80, SD=.79). The difference represents the comparison between the importance of moral characteristics and personal traits. A larger positive difference represents a higher importance of moral compared to personal traits. A negative score occurs if personal traits are more central for the individual. Differences close to zero indicate low mean differences.

The specific feature of the difference score is the possibility to show the relative importance of morality compared to personal characteristics.

Table 2. Item analysis (Factor-Analysis with Kaiser-normalization, oblimin, delta = 0)

		N	M (SD)	Factor 1	Factor 2	r_{it}	α
Moral	fair	4.878	3.53 (.59)	.687		.45	
	honest	4.866	3.70 (.53)	.657		.41	
	helpful	4.895	3.46 (.61)	.760		.53	
	considerate	4.883	3.37 (.64)	.793		.57	.71
Personal	popular	4.866	2.47 (.88)		.701	.41	
	humorously	4.873	3.21 (.75)		.375	.19	
	sporty	4.874	2.84 (.96)		.780	.46	
	smart	4.895	2.83 (.85)		.746	.43	.63[1]

[1]Reliability without "humorously"

Moral Motivation

Moral motivation was measured on the basis of hypothetical decisions, moral judgments and emotion attributions (Nunner-Winkler et al., 2006; 2007). Compared to moral dilemmas, within moral conflicts, a personal need and moral principles contradict each other, whereas in moral dilemmas, two moral principles are incompatible. According to Malti and Buchmann (2010), two conflicts of medium gravity were selected out of the moral conflicts applied by Nunner-Winkler et al. (2006, 2007). The construction of the moral conflicts was guided along three criteria: first, the situations should be structurally familiar to the children and adolescents; second, the moral dimension should be easily comprehensible; and; third, it should be not too difficult to make the immoral decision (Nunner-Winkler et al., 2006).

The first vignette described the following story: "imagine you offered your bike for sale. You want to sell it for 400 Euro. A young man is interested. He bargains with you and you agree on 320 Euro. Then he says: 'Sorry, I don't have the money on me; I'll quickly run home to get it. I'll be back in half an hour.' You say: 'Agreed, I'll wait for you.' Shortly after he is gone, another customer shows up who is willing to pay the full price". In the second story, the following text was presented to the participants: "imagine that you have found a purse with 100 Euro in it and an identity card of the owner" (Malti & Buchmann, 2010, p. 142). Subsequent to the presentation of the moral conflicts, the participants were asked what they would do in this situation and the reason for doing this. Additionally, the participants were asked about their feelings and why they would feel this way. Because it was the first time the moral conflicts were used in a questionnaire, a manipulation check was presented to test whether the participants had read and understood the text or not. Children and adolescents, without reading or understanding the two stories, were not included in the analysis. For the first conflict (bike conflict), 5.8 % of the 4th grade children, 3.2 % in 7th and 2.2 % in 9thgrade answered wrong to the following question: "what is the story about?" 1.9 % of 4th and 7th grade students and 0.8 % of the 9th graders did not read or understood the second conflict (money conflict) correctly. Two trained coders transferred and coded the collected data. An inductive coding system was established to analyse the data. The reliability of the coding system was proved with 9.5 % of all cases. For all categories, the inter-rater-reliability exceeded .70, which generally is interpreted as a good agreement (Bortz & Döring, 2005, p. 277). For the following analysis, a combined measure of decisions, emotions, and judgments is used, which is partly adapted from Malti and Buchmann (2010). Table 3 shows definitions and examples for both conflicts.

Table 3. Categories of moral motivation with definitions and examples
(D: Decision, E: Emotion, J: Justification)

	Definition	bike-conflict	money-conflict
happy victimizer	pragmatic decision, positive emotions, pragmatic reasons	D: selling the bike to the second customer E: good J: because I can get more money	D: I keep the money. E: happiness J: because I get money
unhappy victimizer	pragmatic decision, negative emotions, pragmatic reasons	D: selling the bike to the second customer E: bad J: indeed I get more money, but I promised to wait	D: I keep the money and hand the pocket to the police E: bad J: because of the money But I would be anti-social.
unhappy moralist	moral decision, negative emotion, moral reasons	D: I would tell the second customer, that the bike is unfortunately sold E: I feel uncomfortable. J: because I sold the bike, but I like to get more money	D: bring it to the police E: bad J: indeed I could have more money, but I would also wish to get my money back
happy moralist	moral decision, positive emotions, moral reasons	D: I would tell the second customer, that the bike is unfortunately sold E: good J: because I promised the bike to the first customer	D: bring it to the police E: good J: because I do the right thing

Strong moral motivation is observable if an individual is willing to behave morally for moral reasons. If the moral decision is further accompanied by positive or neutral emotions, the individual does not value the personal need (e.g. to get more money) and has therefore the strongest moral motivation compared to a person having negative emotions. The latter, the unhappy moralist, indicates therefore a lower moral motivation compared to a happy moralist. In previous publications, the unhappy and happy moralist was combined within one category (Malti & Buchmann, 2010). As the importance of emotional consequences of self-inconsistency increases (Blasi & Glodis, 1995), however, it is vital to include both of the inconsistent categories, namely, the unhappy victimizer and the moralist. Individuals with pragmatic decisions for hedonistic reasons are categorized as victimizers. An unhappy victimizer, compared to the happy victimizer, reveals a bad conscience and is taking moral reasons into account, even though these moral reasons are less important to the person. The happy victimizer demonstrates the lowest moral motivation because potential moral reasons are not important for the decision.

Analysis of Age Cohorts

In the following part of the chapter, the age-related results are presented. It should be noted that no longitudinal data are provided and thus no developmental analyses are possible. First, the results for moral centrality and moral motivation are presented accompanied by correlational analysis of both constructs. Afterwards, separate analyses for girls and boys are provided, because studies found significant gender differences on moral centrality, moral motivation and moral respectively immoral behaviour (Arnold, 1993; Barriga et al., 2001; Nunner-Winkler et al., 2007; Van Roy, Groholt, Heyerdahl, & Clench-Aas, 2006). The age differences for moral centrality are illustrated in Table 4.

Table 4. Means (Standard Deviations) of moral centrality (moral traits, personal traits, difference of moral and personal traits), weighted data

	moral traits	personal traits	moral-personal traits
4th grade	3.63 (.42)	2.89 (.70)	.75 (.80)
7th grade	3.41 (.51)	2.71 (.70)	.70 (.84)
9th grade	3.49 (.41)	2.64 (.65)	.85 (.77)
p – value	< .001	< .001	< .001
partial n²	.029	.021	.006

Noticeable moral traits are very important within every age group, whereas personal traits are rated as less important for self-definition. Significant differences between the three age groups were found for moral and personal characteristics as well as for the difference score. Moral and personal traits are more relevant in 4th grade compared to 7th and 9th grade. The difference score shows a divergent pattern, whereas 9th graders have the highest difference score. The practical significance of the results is rather low but, for the difference score, the partial Eta² is less than one percent.

The gender dependent analysis revealed significant gender differences in every age group. Moral characteristics are more important for girls; for boys, personal traits are more important. The amount of differences between girls and boys is quite similar in every age-group. Referring to the difference scores, the amount is twice as high for girls, which is approximately true for every age-group. Thus, girls indicate a higher moral centrality compared to boys.

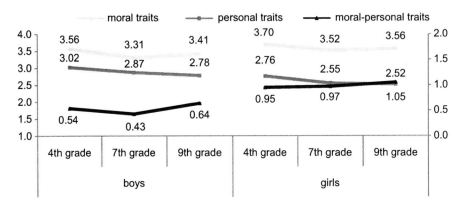

Figure 1. Means of moral centrality (moral traits, personal traits, difference of moral and personal traits) separated for boys and girls, weighted data.

In a next step, moral motivation was analyzed and overall results are presented in Figure 2. Relatively large differences between the two conflicts can be noticed and, compared to the bike conflict, more children and adolescents are happy moralists within the money conflict. Although the correlation between the two moral conflicts is low (r=.22, p<.001), the developmental pattern is similar. The comparisons between the age groups reveal for both conflicts a significant decrease of moral motivation by age (Cramer's $V_{bike\ conflict}$=.19, p<.001; Cramer's $V_{money\ conflict}$=.21, p<.001). The inconsistent categories (unhappy victimizer and moralists) were hypothesized to decrease, but empirical analysis presented a different result. The percentage of unhappy victimizers increases while the amount of unhappy moralists decreases with age.

The results for moral centrality revealed significant gender-differences, but no increase or decrease of these differences by age. The question arises if this result is also evident for moral motivation. Within the 4th grade, no significant relationship between gender and moral motivation in both conflicts appears but, for 7th and 9th grade, significant correlations between moral motivation and gender can be observed. To test if the correlational coefficients are significantly different among 4th and 7th respectively 9th grade, Fisher's z was used. Analysis revealed significant differences concerning the correlations between gender and moral motivation for comparisons between 4th and 9th grade. Comparisons between 4th and 7th grade are only significant for the money conflict. Conclusively, gender differences increase by age, whereas the amount of victimizers increases stronger for boys than for girls. Interestingly, within 4th grade, no differences of moral motivation between girls and boys emerge. The older age groups showed an equal result as observed for moral centrality: the strength of moral motivation is higher for girls than for boys.

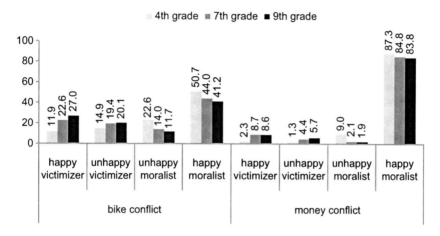

Figure 2. Moral motivation (%), weighted data.

Finally, the correlations between moral centrality and moral motivation will be presented. If moral centrality is the source of moral motivation, the correlation is expected to be of a medium size. The correlational analysis revealed significant (p < .001) coefficients between .14 and .20 depending on what conflict and what moral centrality measure (difference score or moral centrality) is used. The correlations do not systematically vary by age.

Table 5. Correlations between gender and moral motivation (Spearman's Rho, p<.001***)

		bike conflict	*money conflict*
4th grade	r	.044	.041
	n	964	739
7th grade	r	.139***	.259***
	n	628	710
9th grade	r	.199***	.221***
	n	2.399	2.587
Fisher's z	4th–7th grade	-1.9	-4.25***
	4th–9th grade	-4.1***	-4.4***

DISCUSSION

The chapter queries the assumption of an age-related increase of moral motivation. Results of the presented study reveal a decreasing importance of personal and moral traits. This leads to the highest rate of moral centrality (difference score) for 9th grade, when compared to the rate for 4th and 7th grade. The high ratio is caused by a decreasing importance of personal traits from 4th to 9th grade, rather than by a growing importance of moral traits. That moral motivation decreases from 4th to 9th grade questions the idea of an increase of moral motivation. Girls display a higher moral centrality and a stronger moral motivation compared to boys. For moral motivation, the gender differences increase with age, which is in line with former studies (Nunner-Winkler, 2007; Nunner-Winkler et al., 2007). One possible interpretation could be that girls compared to boys have to accommodate a more pro-social gender stereotype and therefore also show a higher moral motivation. As gender roles are less important within childhood, the differences according to gender increase.

For the first time, to the best of the authors' knowledge, the period between childhood and adolescence was investigated. "Identity achievement", respectively "moral identity achievement", is not completed in adolescence: this is one possible reason for the presented results. A study by Archer (1982) revealed that 81 % showed an ego identity status of "identity diffusion" or "foreclosure" within 12th grade. This might be an explanation for a weak relationship between moral centrality and moral motivation, because moral identity cannot be a source of moral motivation until identity achievement is completed. Previous studies demonstrate a developmental increase (Nunner-Winkler, 2007) or no age-related differences (Krettenauer, 2011; Malti & Buchmann, 2010), but the present study found a decrease of moral motivation from childhood to adolescence. Therefore, development of moral motivation cannot be regarded as a continuous and linear increase. In contrast to early (7th grade) and middle (9th grade) adolescence, a larger difference of the strength of moral motivation is observable between late childhood (4th grade) and early adolescence (7th grade). Therefore, the presented results are in line with Krettenauer (2011; Krettenauer & Eichler, 2006), who discovered no increase of internal moral motivation between grade 7th and 9th. The study of Krettenauer (2011) revealed a stability of moral motivation between middle adolescence and young adulthood, and the author (Krettenauer, 2011, p. 324) assumed that "an increase in internal moral motivation may have occurred earlier in development (i.e., in childhood rather than adolescence)." The empirical support for these assumptions is delivered by Nunner-Winkler (2007), demonstrating an increase of moral motivation between the ages of 4 and 8. But, the present study revealed a decrease of moral motivation between late childhood and early adolescence. Therefore, another turning point after the period of adolescence in terms of a very late increase of moral motivation should be taken into account. This would meet behavioural correlates of morality, e.g. delinquent behaviour (Barriga et al., 2001; Doering, 2012; Krettenauer & Eichler, 2006; Stams et al., 2006). According to the age-crime-curve (e.g. Farrington, 1986; Laub & Sampson, 2003), the peak of delinquent behaviour can be found in adolescence. Furthermore, Farrington (1986) determined a half peak for violent crime with 32 years and non-violent crime by age 21 for females and 23 for males. These age-related trajectories for delinquent behaviour emphasize the result of a decreasing moral motivation and, furthermore, a late starting point of a stable and developed moral motivation. Therefore, a u-shaped curvilinear developmental trajectory might be also possible for moral motivation.

Hence, theoretical and empirical research supports the present results. Reviewers might be critical, saying that younger children tend to answer in line with more socially acceptable attitudes and behaviours. If so, stronger moral motivation within 4th grade would be a result of social desirability rather than real developmental changes towards the strength of moral motivation. Therefore, three different assumptions were established. First, if social desirability is the reason for higher moral motivation within 4th grade, the correlation with the item "to some questions within the questionnaire, I do not answer truly" would be higher in 4th grade compared to 9th grade. Second, if 4th graders answer 'more social desirability', they would also indicate less delinquent behaviour compared to 9th grade. Third, the relationship between moral motivation and delinquent behaviour would be higher for 4th grade compared to 9th grade. The latter would be observable because children would answer to the moral conflicts and to the delinquent behaviour questions with more social desirability responses. Therefore, the correlation should increase. The three ideas were tested and analyses reveal falsifications of all of the three assumptions. Given that result, it follows that the effect is not based on age-related differences of social desirability responses.

Although the results are not due to social desirability, limitations of the present study should be mentioned. As stated earlier, the present study investigated different age cohorts in a cross-sectional design. For developmental analysis longitudinal data must be utilized, because a changing social context rather than age-related changes could be the reason for differences between age groups. In line with this argument, the different results of the pre-mentioned studies could be explained. Only the study of Nunner-Winkler (2007) employed longitudinal data and revealed an increase of moral motivation by age. With longitudinal data continuity and stability of a moral identity and moral motivation can also be investigated (Nunner-Winkler, 2007). Interestingly, low stabilities of moral motivation were found within the mentioned study with respect to methodological changes. Furthermore, 29 % of the participants between 17 and 22 display a decreasing moral motivation while the average effect shows an increase. Unfortunately, the study lacks on measurement points between 8 and 17. Therefore, the study is not able to assume developmental changes between childhood and adolescence. In line with Erikson (1981b), the fundamental function of identity is the perception of continuity. The point when moral identity begins to be more stable is still not known. But for different other personality traits a meta-analysis of longitudinal data shows that the stability of traits increases with age and peaks in adulthood (Roberts & DelVecchio, 2000). As assumed earlier, in adolescence moral identity as well as other parts of identity representation are still changing and therefore less stable. Similar assumptions can be applied for moral motivation as a result of moral identity.

Critical to the point above is the low correlation between the two moral conflicts. Although the two moral conflicts measuring moral motivation indicated just a low correlation, age-related differences can be assumed for both. If moral motivation is best understood as a trait or persistent motive, however, why do two different situations indicate such a large discrepancy? Hence, the original measurement combined four and, respectively, six moral conflicts (Nunner-Winkler, 2007; Nunner-Winkler et al., 2006), whereas the present study used only two conflicts. With more conflicts, the situational variability versus stability would be better investigated. Further research on moral centrality should be done. The personal domain, in particular, is hardly assessed by just three traits.

In order to close the circle, within adolescence, no increase of moral motivation is observable and therefore no contradiction to the age-crime curve appears. A moral identity that suits the characteristics of identity achievement, cannot be assumed as achieved within adolescence since no stable moral motivation is observable. But why moral motivation decreases between late childhood and early adolescence and shows lower values until the end of adolescence respectively early adulthood? In line with Erikson's and Marcia's theories of identity formation and empirical results, adolescence is a changing period, where dogmas of the childhood are questioned. This would completely meet Kohlberg's pre-conventional stage (Kohlberg, Levine & Hewer, 1983) and Arnold (1993), where moral principles and moral rules are perceived as external (e.g. based on authorities). Within adolescence, an individual seeks for autonomy and a self-defined identity. But just a few adolescents reach the status of "identity achievement", where again morality is a stable and integrated part of the identity. The other portion of adolescents searches for their own comprehension of morality, which could also result in deviant norms. For example, in adolescence deviant peers are one of the most important influencing factors of deviant attitudes and behaviour (Warr & Stafford, 1991). Therefore, it seems reasonable that also moral motivation resulting out of "moral identity achievement" decreases.

CONCLUSION

Looking at the results of the presented study, what implications could be mentioned for research on moral development? On the one hand, research on developmental trajectories of delinquent behaviour delivers hope, because the majority of delinquency in adolescence is "adolescent limited", whereas a smaller portion demonstrates "life-course persistent" delinquent behaviour (Moffitt, 1993). On the other hand, it might be not sufficient for research to believe, that the 'normal' developmental course will solve the problem of delinquency and low moral motivation in adolescence automatically. One reason for this assumption is that moral motivation is not only important to prevent delinquent behaviour, it is also necessary for positive behaviour, e.g. helping behaviour, altruism and civil courage.

A larger body on moral developmental research was focused on the moral judgment and how this part of the cognitive component of morality can be fostered. But Barriga et al. (2001) showed, that moral judgment is only marginal significant in reducing delinquent behaviour when moral self-relevance and self-serving cognitive distortion is taken into account. Therefore, Barriga et al. (2001) emphasize the importance of other cognitive constructs besides moral judgment, e.g. moral centrality and moral sensitivity. For example Frimer and Walker (2009) stated within their "reconciliation model" that self-interest and moral concerns must be integrated to establish moral motivation. Although, the idea would solve the conflict between self-interest and morality, it seems that the definition of morality in terms of an orientation towards others would be futile. For the same reasons, self-consistency and a positive evaluated self as motives for moral motivation and behaviour have been criticized earlier. If self-interest gives the motivational power to a consistent moral motivation, the same construct would motivate delinquent and moral behaviour. Therefore, it would be useful to learn more about the conditions for moral identity achievement. How can an elaborated moral judgment be integrated into a moral identity and therewith leads to moral motivation?

The presented study showed that moral motivation decreases between late childhood and adolescence and moral centrality cannot be assumed as the only source of moral motivation. Through a longitudinal study, the question how the development of a more elaborated moral judgment is related to a decrease of moral motivation in adolescence could be answered. Another research question could be, if the relation between moral centrality and moral motivation definitely increases in adulthood or only exists for a person who reached the status of identity achievement? Therefore, it seems important to understand the interrelatedness of the different moral components within development for a better understanding of moral motivation.

ACKNOWLEDGEMENT

The author would like to thank Dirk Baier, René Langheinrich, Melissa Nelson and the editors of the book for their helpful comments and proofreading of earlier versions of this chapter.

REFERENCES

Archer, S. (1982). The lower age boundaries of identity development. *Child Development, 53,* 1551–1556.

Arnold, M.L. (1993). *The place of morality in the adolescent self.* Harvard University, Cambridge, MA: unpublished thesis.

Barriga, A.Q., Morrison, E.M., Liau, A.K., & Gibbs, J.C. (2001). Moral cognition: Explaining the gender difference in antisocial behavior. *Merrill-Palmer Quarterly, 47,* 532–562.

Bergman, R. (2004). Identity as motivation: Towards a theory of the moral self. In D. Lapsley & D. Narvaez (Eds.), *Moral development, self, and identity* (pp. 21–46). Mahwah, NJ: Erlbaum.

Blasi, A. (1983). Moral cognition and moral action: A theoretical perspective. *Developmental Review, 3,* 178–210.

Blasi, A. (1993). The development of identity: Some implications for moral functioning. In G.G. Noam & T.E. Wren (Eds.), *The moral self* (pp. 99–122). Cambridge, Massachusetts, London: The MIT Press.

Blasi, A. (1995). Moral understanding and the moral personality: The process of moral integration. In W.M. Kurtines & J.L. Gewirtz (Eds.), *Moral development: An introduction* (pp. 229–253). Boston: Allyn and Bacon.

Blasi, A. (2004). Moral functioning: Moral understanding and personality. In D. Lapsley & D. Narvaez (Eds.), *Moral development, self, and identity* (pp. 335–348). Mahwah, NJ: Erlbaum.

Blasi, A. (2005). Moral character: A psychological approach. In D. Lapsley & F.C. Power (Eds.), *Character psychology and character education* (pp. 67–100). Notre Dame Ind.: University of Notre Dame Press.

Blasi, A., & Glodis. (1995). The development of identity. A critical analysis from the perspective of the self as subject. *Psychological Review, 15*, 304–433.

Bortz, J., & Döring, N. (2005). *Forschungsmethoden und Evaluation [Research methods and evaluation].* Heidelberg: Springer.

Doering, B. (2012). Die Bedeutung Moralischer Motivation bei der Erklärung delinquenten Verhaltens im Jugendalter [*The influence of moral motivation on delinqeunt behavior in adolescence*]. *Neue Kriminologische Schriftenreihe* (in press).

Erikson, E.H. (1981a). *Identität und Lebenszyklus [Identity and life cycle].* Frankfurt a.M.: Suhrkamp.

Erikson, E.H. (1981b). *Jugend und Krise [Identity: Youth and crisis].* Frankfurt a.M.: Klett-Cotta.

Farrington, D.P. (1986). Age and crime. *Crime and Justice, 7*, 189–250.

Frimer, J.A. & Walker, L.J. (2009). Reconciling the self and morality: An empirical model of moral centrality development. *Developmental Psychology, 45*, 1669–1681.

Harter, S. (1990). Processes underlying adolescent self-concept formation. In R. Montemayor, G. Adams & T. Gullotta (Eds.), *From childhood to adolescence: A transitional period* (pp. 205–239). Newbury Park: Sage.

Harter, S., & Monsour, A. (1992). Developmental analysis of conflict caused by opposing attributes in the adolescent self-portrait. *Developmental Psychology, 28*, 251–260.

Higgins, E.T. (1987). Self-discrepancy: A theory relating self and affect. *Psychological Review, 94*, 319–340.

Kohlberg, L. (1996). *Die Psychologie der Moralentwicklung [The psychology of moral development].* Frankfurt a.M.: Suhrkamp.

Kohlberg, L., Levine, C., & Hewer, A. (1983). *Moral stages: A current formulation and a response to critics.* Basel: Karger.

Krettenauer, T. (2011). The dual moral self: Moral centrality and internal moral motivation. *The Journal of Genetic Psychology, 172*, 309–328.

Krettenauer, T., & Eichler, D. (2006). Adolescents' self-attributed moral emotions following a moral transgression: Relations with delinquency, confidence in moral judgment and age. *British Journal of Developmental Psychology, 24*, 489–506.

Lapsley, D. (1996). *Moral psychology.* Boulder: Westview.

Laub, J.H., & Sampson, R.J. (2003). *Shared beginnings, divergent lives: Delinquent boys to age 70.* Cambridge, Massachusetts, and London: Harvard University Press.

Malti, T., & Buchmann, M. (2010). Socialization and individual antecedents of adolescents' and young adults' moral motivation. *Journal of Youth and Adolescence, 39*, 138–149.

Marcia, J.E. (1966). Development and validation of egoidentity status. *Journal of Personality and Social Psychology, 3*, 551–558.

Marcia, J.E. (1980). Identity in adolescence. In J. Adelson (Ed.), *Handbook of adolescent psychology* (pp. 159–187). New York: Wiley.

Marcia, J.E. (1993). The ego identity status approach to ego identity. In J.E. Marcia, A.S. Waterman, D.R. Matteson, S. Archer & J.L. Orlofsky (Eds.), *Ego identitity: A handbook for psychosocial research* (pp. 3–21). New York: Springer.

Moffitt, T. (1993). Adolescence-limited and life-course-persistent antisocial behaviour. *Psychological Review, 100*, 674–701.

Narvaez, D., & Lapsley, D.K. (2009). Moral identity, moral functioning, and the development of moral character. In D.L. Medin, L. Skitka, D. Bartels & C. Bauman (Eds.), *Moral cognition and decision making* (Vol. 50, pp. 237–274) Amsterdam: Elsevier.

Nunner-Winkler, G. (2007). Development of moral motivation from childhood to early adulthood. *Journal of Moral Education, 36,* 399–414.

Nunner-Winkler, G. (2008). Zur Entwicklung moralischer Motivation [Towards the development of moral motivation]. In J. Schneider (Ed.), *Entwicklung von der Kindheit bis zum Erwachsenenalter: Befunde der Münchner Längsschnittstudie LOGIK* (pp. 103–123). Weinheim: Beltz Verlag.

Nunner-Winkler, G., Meyer-Nikele, M., & Wohlrab, D. (2006). *Integration durch Moral: Moralische Motivation und Ziviltugenden Jugendlicher [Integration through morality: Moral motivation and civil virtues of adolescents].* Wiesbaden: VS Verlag für Sozialwissenschaften.

Nunner-Winkler, G., Meyer-Nikele, M., & Wohlrab, D. (2007). Gender differences in moral motivation. *Merrill-Palmer Quarterly, 53,* 26–52.

Nunner-Winkler, G., & Sodian, B. (1988). Children's understanding of moral emotions. *Child Development, 59,* 1323–1338.

Oerter, R., & Dreher, E. (2008). Jugendalter [*Adolescence*]. In R. Oerter & L. Montada (Eds.), *Entwicklungspsychologie* (pp. 271–283). Weinheim, Basel: Beltz.

Pratt, M.W., Arnold, M.L., Pratt, A.T., & Diessner, R. (1999). Predicting adolescent moral reasoning from family climate: A longitudinal study. *Journal of Early Adolescence, 19,* 148–175.

Pratt, M.W., Hunsberger, B., Pancer, S.M., & Alisat, S. (2003). A longitudinal analysis of personal values socialization: Correlates of a moral self-ideal in late adolescence. *Social Development, 12,* 563–585.

Roberts, B.W., & DelVecchio, W.F. (2000). The rank-order consistency of personality traits from childhood to old age: A quantitative review of longitudinal studies. *Psychological Bulletin, 126,* 3–25.

Rosenberg, M. (1986). Self-concept from middle childhood through adolescence. In J.M. Suls & A.G. Greenwald (Eds.), *Psychological perspectives on the self* (Vol. 3, pp. 107–136). Orlando: Academic Press.

Scheffer, D., & Heckhausen, H. (2006). Eigenschaftstheorien der Motivation. In J. Heckhausen & H. Heckhausen (Eds.), *Motivation und Handeln* (pp. 43–72). Berlin: Springer.

Simon, B., & Mummendey, A. (1997). Selbst, Identität und Gruppe [Self, identity and groups]. In A. Mummendey & B. Simon (Eds.), *Identität und Verschiedenheit. Zur Sozialpsychologie der Identität in komplexen Gesellschaften* (pp. 11–38). Bern: Huber.

Stams, J.G., Brugman, D., Dekovic, M., Rosmalen, L., Laan, P., & Gibbs, J.C. (2006). The moral judgment of juvenile delinquents: A meta-analysis. *Journal of Abnormal Child Psychology, 34,* 697–713.

Straub, J. (2000). Identität als psychologisches Deutungskonstrukt [Identity as a psychological construct of interpretation]. In W. Greve (Ed.), *Psychologie des Selbst* (pp. 279–301). Weinheim: Beltz.

Tajfel, H., & Turner, J.C. (1986). The social identity theory of intergroup behaviour. In S. Worchel & W.G. Austin (Eds.), *Psychology of intergroup relations* (pp. 7–24). Chicago: Nelson.

Turiel, E. (1983). *The development of social knowledge.* Cambridge: Cambridge University Press.

Van Roy, B., Groholt, B., Heyerdahl, S., & Clench-Aas, J. (2006). Self-reported strengths and difficulties in a large Norwegian population 10–19 years: Age and gender specific results of the extended SDQ-questionnaire. *European Child and Adolescent Psychiatry, 15,* 189–198.

Warr, M., & Stafford, W.H. (1991). The influence of delinquent peers: what they think or what they do? *Criminology, 29,* 851–866.

AFFILIATION

Bettina Doering
Criminological Research Institute of Lower Saxony
Hannover, Germany

LUCIANO GASSER, EVELINE GUTZWILLER-HELFENFINGER,
BRIGITTE LATZKO & TINA MALTI

III. MORAL EMOTION ATTRIBUTIONS AND MORAL MOTIVATION

INTRODUCTION

Ruby is complaining about Lucy who hit her in order to get on the swing. Lucy is swinging happily. Michael feels sorry for Ruby and tells Lucy to leave the swing to her, whereas Peter does not care, a common enough situation. One of the questions this example raises is why these children act in such different ways, although they are involved in the same situation. Why does Michael care for Ruby's welfare and try to help, and Peter does not? Or, generally, why do some people act morally in some situations and others do not? Does this in any way relate to the presence or absence of emotions (Michael feeling sorry and Peter not caring) and to the nature of these emotions?

In the present chapter, we offer some responses to these questions from a moral developmental perspective. Most of the moral psychological literature is concerned with the concept of moral motivation to explain why people act in different ways in morally relevant situations. In the moral developmental literature, moral motivation has often been related to children's moral emotions. Taking this relationship as a vantage point, we argue that moral emotions serve as a central source of moral motivation. In our view, this conceptualization lies at the core of explaining the link between moral motivation and (im)moral behaviour.

A prominent developmental approach, which elucidates the link between moral emotions and immoral action, is the so-called Happy Victimizer Paradigm – or Phenomenon. The happy victimizer phenomenon describes the finding that preschoolers attribute happiness to a moral transgressor in spite of judging the transgression as morally wrong (for reviews, see Arsenio, Gold, & Adams, 2006; Krettenauer, Malti, & Sokol, 2008). Only at primary school age do children begin to consistently attribute feelings of remorse or guilt to a moral transgressor. This finding is somewhat surprising, given that children already understand the intrinsic aspects of moral rules at three or four years of age (for a review, see Turiel, 2006). Accordingly, this asynchrony between the development of moral rule knowledge and negative (i.e., moral) emotion attributions has attracted much attention because it reflects our common sense that (a) moral emotions offer privileged access to a person's morality (Malti & Latzko, 2010); and (b) persons in real-life contexts

K. Heinrichs, F. Oser & T. Lovat (Eds.), *Handbook of Moral Motivation: Theories, Models, Applications, 307–322.*

often decide against their better judgment (Gutzwiller-Helfenfinger, Gasser, & Malti, 2010). In the following sections, we discuss the research on moral emotion attributions and moral behaviour according to the following questions: Are moral emotion attributions distinct indicators of moral motivation? Can they serve as indicators of the meaning morality has for a given person (i.e., what motivates individuals to act in accord with moral norms and obligations)?

To answer these questions, we first provide central defining characteristics of moral emotions. Second, we will introduce two central theoretical positions regarding the role of emotion attributions in predicting (im)moral behaviour. To evaluate the empirical soundness of the two approaches, we will then discuss selected studies on the relationship between emotion attributions and morally relevant behaviour. We use this evaluation to underpin our own theoretical position introduced above. Afterwards, we will again address the question whether moral emotion attributions can be considered as indicators of moral motivation and offer some conclusions. Finally, we will use these conclusions to substantiate our position, both theoretically and empirically, and present some implications for future research.

WHAT ARE MORAL EMOTIONS?

Developmental researchers conceptualize moral emotions as self-conscious or self-evaluative emotions, because they are evoked by self-reflection and self-evaluation (Eisenberg, 2000; Malti & Latzko, 2012; Tangney, Stuewig, & Mashek, 2007). Moral emotions represent central experiences in the context of moral conflicts. We speak of indignation because we heard of an instance of injustice; of guilt because we hurt someone; or of pride because we managed to resist temptation. Due to the subjective salience adherent to moral emotions in the context of moral conflicts, it is not surprising that they are ascribed an important role in situations calling for a decision. In such situations, moral emotions can serve as motives in the formation of moral action tendencies (cf. Malti & Keller, in press; Tangney et al., 2007).

The notion that moral emotions are relevant for moral motivation and moral behaviour has not remained unchallenged. Within cognitivistic approaches in moral philosophy and psychology, moral emotions were ascribed a minor role (Kant, 1781; 1785; Kohlberg, 1984). Because – as compared to moral arguments – moral emotions were viewed as not being intersubjectively accessible, they were considered unstable and unreliable for the prediction of moral behaviour. Along with an increasing insight into the interconnectedness between emotions and cognitions came the rehabilitation of moral emotions as motives for moral behaviour. For instance, moral emotions were no longer conceptualized as being independent of a person's cognitive representation of situations (Piaget, 1981; Montada, 1993; Nunner-Winkler, 1999; Turiel, 2006). Thus, emotions and judgments are inherently linked in moral conflict situations. For example, a child who is accidentally harmed by another child and ascribes harmful intent to that other child is more likely to show anger and revenge than a child (correctly) interpreting the incident as accidental (Arsenio & Lemerise, 2004). Moral values and the moral judgments associated with these values also play an important role in engendering moral emotions. Often, moral emotions are triggered by a conviction that a given action or behaviour is morally wrong (Turiel, 2006). Moral judgments can be highly automatized and internalized, resulting in their being perceived less as cognitive and more as emotional experiences in the first place (Turiel, 2006). Accordingly, emotions include cognitive aspects in various ways and can therefore be judged in their own right. And they can be adequate or inadequate, depending on the (correct or incorrect) assessment of a given situation or with respect to a given moral judgment. In line with recent integrative approaches to moral cognition and moral emotion (e.g., Arsenio et al., 2006; Malti & Latzko, 2010), we argue that cognitive moral processes and moral emotions are closely linked.

Nevertheless, moral emotions and moral judgments are not identical and do not necessarily correspond with one another. This can be explained by the differential physiological mechanisms associated with cognition and emotion. In contrast to moral cognitions, moral emotions are strongly related to the perception of physiological processes and states. According to William James, this marks emotions as distinct from "cold cognition": "Without the bodily states following on the perception, the latter would be purely cognitive in form, pale, colorless, destitute of emotional warmth." (1890, p. 450). Experiencing an emotion means to feel something which gives rise to specific sensations. Moral judgments lacking emotional evaluation are not accompanied by the experience of physiological reactions. In this sense, emotional reactions offer a different response to moral situations than non-emotional moral judgments (Nozick, 1989). They impart something about the way persons relate to situations as well as the aspects which are specifically relevant for a certain person (Blasi, 1999; Montada, 1993).

Accordingly, we argue that emotions, and in particular the accompanying physiological processes experienced in moral situations, trigger moral motivation. Before we can pursue this argument any further, we first need to consider two relevant theoretical approaches which address exactly this differentiation between moral cognition and moral emotion.

THEORETICAL EXPLANATIONS OF THE RELATIONSHIP BETWEEN MORAL EMOTION ATTRIBUTIONS AND IMMORAL BEHAVIOUR

Why should emotions attributed to a moral transgressor be considered indicators of moral motivation? Moral emotion attributions are usually assessed using everyday stories in which the protagonist is tempted to break a moral rule in order to satisfy his or her own needs (e.g., stealing a friend's candy). In a first step, children's moral rule knowledge is probed ("Is it right/okay or not to do x? Why?"). Next, children are asked to attribute emotions to the transgressors and to provide a justification for the emotion attribution ("How does [the protagonist] feel? Why?").

The hypothesis that moral emotion attributions can be viewed as indicators of moral motivation was first formulated by Nunner-Winkler (e.g., Nunner-Winkler, 1999; Nunner-Winkler & Sodian, 1988). The underlying assumption is that children's emotion attributions represent authentic expressions of what is important to them in a given moral conflict. Thus, moral emotion attributions are seen as indicating the degree to which a child feels personally committed to moral principles and hence also the degree to which moral principles are integrated into the self. In this sense, moral emotion attributions were interpreted as indicators of moral motivation and were expected to be closely related to morally relevant behaviour. To validate this hypothesis, Nunner-Winkler drew on a study of children aged 6 and 7 years, showing that moral emotion attributions predicted both children's cheating behaviour and their egocentric pursuing of their own goals in an experimental situation (Asendorpf & Nunner-Winkler, 1992).

Other approaches, however, see moral emotion attributions as a primary socio-cognitive competence. According to some researchers, for example, the transition from attributing positive to attributing negative emotions to a perpetrator parallels the development of an understanding that persons can have several emotions at the same time, that is, mixed emotions (Arsenio & Kramer, 1992; Arsenio & Lover, 1995, Harris, 1989; Sokol, 2004). Older children understand that a perpetrator can feel both good because of personal gain and bad because of the negative consequences of his/her action for the victim. This shows that children can take into account not only the perpetrator's perspective but also that of the victim. Therefore, moral emotion attributions are indicators of an individual's ability to coordinate social perspectives (Sokol, 2004). This shift from the perpetrator's to the victim's perspective constitutes an important, but not a sufficient precondition for moral behaviour, because perspective-taking may be used in the context of prosocial, as well as in the context of anti-social, goals. Accordingly, conceptualizing moral emotion attributions as a socio-cognitive competence cannot replace Nunner-Winkler's explanation, first and foremost because the ability to take someone's perspective does not guarantee that this capacity will be used for good (and not for evil) purposes. In the following chapter, we will examine the empirical literature on moral emotion attributions and immoral behaviour to evaluate the relative empirical basis of each of these two explanations.

RESEARCH ON MORAL EMOTION ATTRIBUTIONS AND IMMORAL BEHAVIOUR

To what extent does the empirical literature support the hypothesis that moral emotion attributions are indicators (a) of an individual's moral motivation or (b) of an individual's ability for perspective-taking? The following selective review of the literature critically discusses the predictive role of emotion attributions in immoral behaviour.

The present discussion focuses on aggressive behaviour, because most studies understand aggression as immoral action tendency (i.e., behaviour that is intended to harm others). To introduce a new perspective to the evaluation of this literature, we argue that different forms of aggressive behaviour need to be distinguished. A first possible distinction can be made between proactive and reactive aggressive behaviour. Each of these forms is supposed to have a unique relationship with moral emotional attributions. Another distinction refers to intentionality, arguing that there are different degrees of intentionality in aggressive behaviour: For example, owing to deficits in affect regulation, some children are less able to control their behaviour and may display increased levels of aggression, whereas others, suffering from no such deficits, may use aggression in a more premeditated fashion.

To account for these differences, the present discussion of the literature is organized along different forms of aggression. First, we discuss studies that related emotion attributions to behavioural disorders, physical aggression, or unspecific forms of aggression (such as externalizing behaviour problems or conduct disorders). Next, studies investigating emotion attributions in relation to specific forms of aggression with high intentionality are discussed. Such forms of aggression include proactive aggression, bullying, or highly sophisticated forms of aggression (e.g., relational aggression).

Moral Emotion Attributions and Conduct Disorder

Studies involving behaviourally disruptive children or physically aggressive children offer an equivocal picture. For example, in a study by Arsenio and Fleiss (1996), primary school children with behavioural disorders ($n = 24$) attributed happiness to a moral transgressor as often as control children ($n = 24$) did. Moreover, they attributed sadness more often than did control children, although children with conduct disorders were expected to be "prototypic happy victimizers". With respect to justifications of moral emotion attributions, however, results were as expected: Children with behavioural disorders gave more hedonistic justifications and used less reasoning based on fairness than control children. A study by Hughes and Dunn (2000), including 4 to 6-year-olds ($n = 80$), yielded similar results. Children with conduct disorders and control children only differed with respect to justifications of moral emotion attributions, not regarding emotion attributions themselves or regarding moral judgments. Children with conduct disorders more often used justifications involving fear of sanctions and less often moral justifications than control children. Finally, across both groups, negative correlations between justifications of moral emotion attributions and observed anger in social interactions were found. In another study including children aged 5, 7 and 9 ($n = 312$), attributions of happiness to a moral rule transgressor were positively related to aggressive behaviour, as rated by teachers (Malti, Gasser, & Gutzwiller-Helfenfinger, 2010). However, after controlling for verbal ability, social cognition (interpretative understanding) and moral judgments, only justifications of both moral judgments and moral emotion attributions remained significant predictors of aggressive behaviour.

That no difference was found between children with behavioural disorders and control children with respect to emotions attributed to a moral transgressor can be explained by the attribution task itself. Children had to attribute emotions not from their own perspective (self as perpetrator) but from an outside perspective (other as perpetrator) (see Krettenauer, Malti, & Sokol, 2008). Accordingly, it is highly probable that children did not identify with the protagonist (i.e., the perpetrator) and therefore reconstructed the situation merely from a factual and not from a moral point of view (see also Keller, Lourenco, Malti, & Saalbach, 2003).

This hypothesis has been confirmed in several studies which take into account the difference between the perspectives of self and other as perpetrator (Keller et al., 2003; Malti, 2007; Malti, Gasser, & Buchmann, 2009; Malti & Keller, 2009). For example, children aged between 7 and 11 years (n = 93) were asked to attribute emotions both to a hypothetical transgressor and to themselves in the role of transgressor in three situations involving moral conflicts (Malti & Keller, 2009). Parents' reports were used to assess externalising problem behaviour. Attributions to a hypothetical transgressor were not correlated with externalising behaviour. However, boys who consistently attributed negative emotions to themselves as transgressors across situations showed less externalising behaviour than boys who attributed less negative emotions to themselves as transgressors. For both boys and girls, a negative relationship was found between moral justifications of self attributed emotions and externalising behaviour. These findings were extended to include other age groups. Aggressive kindergarten children (n = 98) attributed negative emotions to themselves as perpetrators less often than prosocial kindergarten children (n = 137) (Malti et al., 2009). Finally, self-attributed moral emotions were also predictive of delinquent behaviour in an adolescent sample, after controlling for social desirability (Krettenauer & Eichler, 2006).

Still, the question remains why meaningful relationships were found between *justifications* of emotion attributions and problem behaviour in the studies by Arsenio and Fleiss (1996) and Hughes and Dunn (2000), whereas findings for *emotion attributions* are equivocal, depending on the perspective participants are attributing from. Another interpretation of the failure to detect a general relationship between moral emotion attributions and behaviour states that emotion attributions without accompanying justifications are bare of meaning and therefore do not predict social behaviour. Various, also non-moral, motives may underlie the attribution of a negative emotion to a perpetrator, like for example, fear of sanctions. Only by examining the justification given to a specific emotion attribution can its moral quality be assessed. Therefore, it is necessary to include justifications of emotions attributed to a perpetrator to gain insight into the motives underlying that emotion attribution in the first place.

Only some of the studies discussed have also included reference to moral knowledge. The study by Malti et al. (2009) showed that aggressive children more often referred to sanction-oriented reasons when justifying their moral judgments than prosocial children. And in the study by Malti et al. (2010), justifications of moral judgments were significant predictors of physical aggression. These findings raise doubts as to whether deficits in moral emotion attributions by themselves represent genuine motivational deficits or whether they are linked to delays in the acquisition of moral knowledge. This question becomes even more urgent as behavioural problems and physical aggression have been shown to relate to deficits in social cognition, like, for example, social information processing (Crick & Dodge, 1998; Orobio de Castro, Veerman, Koops, Bosch, & Monshouwer, 2002). Hence, if we want to more clearly distinguish between moral emotion attributions as indicators of social or moral cognition, on the one hand, and as specific indicators of moral motivation, on the other hand, we need to include additional forms of aggression which are not *a priori* related to social-cognitive deficits.

Moral Emotion Attributions, Proactive Aggression, and Bullying

Within aggression research, meaningful distinctions were established to differentiate between more impulsive, uncontrolled and more purposeful, targeted forms of aggression. A highly meaningful distinction, in this respect, is the distinction between *reactive* and *proactive* or, as some say "hot heated" and "cold-blooded", aggression (cf. Arsenio, Adams, & Gold, 2009; Dodge et al., 2006). Reactive aggression is defined as an impulsive and hostile reaction to a perceived threat or provocation. Reactively aggressive children often suffer from deficits in different areas of social competence and are usually rejected by peers. Proactive aggression, on the other hand, is not connected to any trigger and is both purposeful and calculating. It is positively correlated with various aspects of social adjustment and social competence, like, for example, popularity or communicative skills (e.g., Poulin & Boivin, 2000).

A study by Arsenio, Adams and Gold (2009) offers an interesting insight into the specific social-cognitive and moral-affective correlates of reactive and proactive aggression. Social cognition was operationalized on the basis of the *Social Information Processing* (SIP) *Model*. The SIP-Model encompasses six stages of social information processing: (1) encoding of the situation; (2) interpreting others' cues; (3) clarification of goals (instrumental versus relational); (4) response access or construction; (5) response decision; and, (6) behavioural enactment (cf. Crick & Dodge, 1994). In a sample of 100 adolescents, intent attribution, outcome expectancies of aggressive acts, and effectiveness of aggression were assessed using four stories describing ambiguous and deliberate provocations. Moral emotion attributions and justifications were measured using four stories of unprovoked aggression. Teachers rated adolescents' reactive and proactive aggression. For the prediction of aggressive behaviour by moral variables verbal ability, age, non-focal aggression (the opposite of the aggression form focused on, i.e., proactive or reactive aggression, respectively), and SIP variables were controlled for. Analyses showed that SIP variables were uniquely related to reactive and that moral variables were uniquely related to proactive aggression. These findings indicate that reactive aggression is more strongly related to social-cognitive deficits, whereas proactive aggression is specifically related to deficits in moral emotion attributions. We can therefore conclude that children who use aggression in a deliberate and controlled fashion do not suffer from deficits in social cognition but from specific affective-moral deficits, providing support to the hypothesis of moral emotion attributions as indicators of moral motivation.

More recently, a different form of aggression, bullying, has been increasingly investigated in relation to moral development. Bullying is defined as systematic aggressive behaviour enacted repeatedly over time against another, weaker or less powerful child (Olweus, 1978). Unlike impulsive and direct aggression, bullying is characterized by a complex social dynamic reflected in bullies' ability to win over other children and manipulate them for their own goals (Salmivalli, Lagerspetz, Bjoerkqvist, Oesterman, & Kaukiainen, 1996). Hence, bullies are another group of children presenting for testing of the hypothesis of a domain-specific deficit in moral emotion attributions.

An important distinction made in bullying research refers to *bullies* versus *aggressive victims* (e.g., Alsaker & Gutzwiller-Helfenfinger, 2009; Schwartz, 2000). Aggressive victims are involved in the bullying process, both as aggressors and as victims. They can be characterized as ineffective aggressors, showing impulsive and inadequate reactions to social challenges owing to problems in affect regulation (e.g., Hanish & Guerra, 2004; Veenstra et al., 2005). Bullies, on the other hand, act aggressively without being victimized. Unlike aggressive victims, they show advanced levels of social and social-cognitive competencies, giving them privileged access to material and social resources (Gasser & Keller, 2009; Hawley, 1999; Pellegrini et al., 1999). Bullies are popular and have a wider circle of friends (Estell et al., 2007). They also display comparatively high levels of Macchiavellian characteristics, like manipulative and exploitative strategies (Gasser & Keller, 2009).

In a study by Gasser and Keller (2009), social perspective-taking, moral rule knowledge, and moral emotion attributions were assessed in a sample of 7- to 8-year-old bullies and bully victims. Based on peer nominations and a short teacher questionnaire, 211 out of 624 children were selected for the study. They were classified as bullies, aggressive victims, passive victims, and prosocial children ($n =$ 50). Moral rule knowledge and moral motivation were assessed using four stories on moral rule transgressions. First, children had to judge if and why the transgression was right or wrong. Afterwards, they attributed an emotion to themselves in the role of the perpetrator and justified this attribution. If children justified moral transgressions as being wrong by giving moral reasons, moral rule knowledge was coded as 1 (versus 0). If children attributed themselves a negative emotion and gave a moral justification, moral motivation was coded as 1 (versus 0). A total score for both moral knowledge and moral motivation was computed by summing scores across the four stories. Strategic social-cognitive competence was assessed using tasks on cognitive and affective perspective-taking. Analyses indicated that bullies, along with prosocial children, possessed superior cognitive and affective perspective-taking ability as compared to aggressive victims. Furthermore, both bullies and aggressive victims had deficits in moral emotion attributions, as compared to prosocial children. Interestingly, only younger bullies displayed deficits in moral rule knowledge, whereas older bullies' moral rule knowledge remained intact. However, independent of age, moral emotion attributions were low. It seems that bullies' moral rule knowledge becomes more differentiated with age, along with gains in social perspective-taking ability, but without causing corresponding changes in moral emotion attributions. These findings suggest that bullies fail to integrate moral knowledge and moral motivation (cf. Gasser & Keller, 2009). However, this interpretation is based on the assumption that moral emotion attributions are indicators of moral motivation, which is in line with our position stated at the outset of the chapter. In the next section, we critically discuss this position by referring to two recent studies in the field.

Can Moral Emotion Attributions Serve as Indicators of Moral Motivation?

Two further studies suggest that the assessment of moral emotions by way of emotion attributions needs to be critically scrutinized if the latter are postulated to serve as indicators of moral motivation (Gasser & Malti, 2011; Hawley, 2003). In the study by Gasser and Malti (2010), the predictive power of moral rule knowledge and moral emotions on relational, as compared to physical, aggression was investigated. Similar to findings for proactive aggression and bullying, a positive relationship between relational aggression and both social and cognitive competencies, like deceptive ability (Ostrov, Ries, Staffacher, Godleski, & Mullins, 2008) or an advanced understanding of another's mind (Renouf et al., 2010), were found. The study included children aged 7 to 9 (n =237). Both physical and relational aggression were assessed using peer nominations and teacher reports. As expected, in older children, physical aggression was related to attributions of happiness, to less moral and more sanction-oriented justifications of emotion attributions, after controlling for gender, verbal abilities, and relational aggression. Surprisingly, exactly the opposite pattern emerged for relational aggression. Relational aggression was uncorrelated with attributions of happiness, but a positive relationship was found with moral justifications and a negative relationship with sanction-oriented justifications of emotion attributions (Gasser & Malti, 2011).

The study by Hawley (2003) yielded similar results. Based on resource control theory (e.g., Hawley, 1999), the relationship between kindergarten children's moral knowledge, self-attributed moral emotions, and resource control types was investigated (n = 163). Depending on the degree to which children used prosocial (PS) or coercive strategies (CS) for resource control (as assessed by teachers), she identified five distinct groups: (a) prosocial controllers (+PS, –CS); (b) coercive controllers (-PS, + CS); (c) bistrategic controllers (+PS, + CS); (d) non-controllers (-PS, –CS); and (e) typicals (medium levels of PS and CS). To some degree, bistrategic profiles correspond with the profile of cold-blooded bullies. They are aggressive but display the most effective resource control, and their social competencies and popularity are as high as those of prosocial controllers. Findings showed that the moral rule knowledge of bistrategic controllers was superior to that of prosocial controllers, typical controllers, and non-controllers. Moreover, bistrategic controllers gave more moral justifications of emotion attributions than prosocial controllers. The latter finding is surprising, as emotion attributions were assessed from the perspective of self as perpetrator. A possible explanation is that children with high levels of relational aggression, or bistrategic control, may have disengaged themselves from the moral conflicts as presented in the stories and therefore gave socially desirable answers. In such cases, moral emotion attributions can no longer be understood as indications of what children see as important in moral conflicts. Rather, children with relationally aggressive behaviour seem to refer to moral conflicts in a merely cognitive mode without being personally involved. Thus, alternative assessments of moral emotions need to be included in order to understand the full meaning of moral emotions as motives for (im)moral behaviour.

DISCUSSION

At the outset of this chapter, we introduced our theoretical position that moral emotions are of key significance to understand why some people act morally, whereas others do not. We raised the question whether moral emotion attributions can serve as indicators of an individual's moral motivation. Taking a developmental perspective, we revisited the relevant literature to address this question. Summing up the selected empirical literature, we conclude that, in most studies, moral emotion attributions were significantly related to aggressive behaviour, the prototypical operationalization of immoral behaviour in the developmental literature. More specifically, positive emotions attributed to the self as perpetrator were more strongly related to aggressive behaviour than emotions attributed to another as perpetrator. These findings show that some children – when attributing emotions to another as perpetrator – do not spontaneously identify with the perpetrator. This interpretation is supported by a recent meta-analytic study which showed that self-attributed moral emotions were more strongly related to aggressive behaviour than emotions attributed to hypothetical transgressors (Malti & Krettenauer, in press). Accordingly, moral emotions attributed to the self are especially relevant for one's own (im)moral behaviour, underlining the developmental importance of moral emotional growth.

Furthermore, in some studies, justifications of emotion attributions were more consistently related to aggressive behaviour than emotion attributions themselves. These results show that emotion attributions – as compared to justifications of emotion attributions – offer less information about the nature of underlying motives. This is particularly relevant for adolescence and young adulthood, when the motives underlying positive and negative emotion attributions become increasingly differentiated and diverse.

The present discussion also suggests that the differentiation between ineffective, impulsive aggression and effective, controlled aggression is highly relevant for research on the relationship between moral emotion attributions and immoral behaviour. Studies including physically aggressive or impulsively aggressive children found that these children suffer from deficits both in moral judgment and in moral emotion attributions (e.g., Malti et al., 2010), whereas studies including proactively aggressive children or bullies identified specific moral-affective deficits (e.g., Arsenio et al., 2009; Gasser & Keller, 2009). It seems that, for at least some aggressive children, an asynchrony exists between their perspective-taking ability and moral understanding, on the one hand, and their moral emotion attributions, on the other hand. These findings offer strong support to Nunner-Winkler's hypothesis of an analytical independence of moral cognition and moral motivation (Nunner-Winkler et al., 2007) and underpin our own, related position.

Notwithstanding, matters are more complex owing to equivocal findings with respect to so-called socially competent and effective aggressors. In some studies, relatively advanced justifications of emotion attributions were observed in relationally aggressive children or so-called bistrategic controllers. Against the background of these studies, it seems natural to interpret moral emotion attributions as reflecting a mere social-cognitive competence. This interpretation does not question the hypothesis of moral emotions as indicators of moral motivation, but rather doubts the appropriateness of operationalising moral emotions exclusively by means of moral emotion attributions in the context of hypothetical transgressions. At the outset of this chapter, we introduced two essential features of moral emotions: (a) Moral emotions are significantly interwoven with cognitive aspects; and, (b) moral emotions can be distinguished from cognitive judgments with respect to the perception of bodily processes. The first aspect is usually taken into account, both on the level of theoretical conceptions of moral emotions and on the level of their operationalisation, whereas the aspect of bodily experience is hardly ever considered. In many moral psychological deliberations, moral emotions are almost equated with moral judgments (e.g., Deigh, 1994; Montada, 1993; Nunner-Winkler, 1999; Turiel, 2006). Accordingly, the admonition that this conception of moral emotions represents a form of "judgmentalism" seems fairly reasonable (Greenspan, 1988).

Narratives also offer an encouraging approach to overcome some of the difficulties inherent in using a response measure to assess moral emotions in the context of hypothetical stories. Recent research indicates that emotions attributed in the context of hypothetical scenarios do not necessarily correspond with emotions children experience in real-life situations (Gutzwiller-Helfenfinger et al., 2010). As emotions experienced in real-life moral conflicts provide an important source for children's moral learning (Smetana & Killen, 2008), using an assessment method that taps into children's first-hand experiences may be an important first step to learn more about the way they refer to emotions in narrations of morally relevant situations. Real-life narratives provide reconstructions of real-life experiences and are well suited to assessing children's moral understanding (Wainryb, Brehl, & Matwin, 2005). They can be conceptualized as reconstructions of personal experiences, whereby those aspects that were salient at the time of the experience become part of the narrative (cf. Wainryb et al., 2005). A recent study by Gutzwiller-Helfenfinger et al. (2010), involving 5- and 9-year-old children (n = 190), found that the emotions and judgments constructed in the course of real-life narratives differed from those generated in the context of hypothetical transgressions. In the narratives, all emotions mentioned spontaneously were negative. In contrast, when affect ratings were offered, emotion attributions included also positive and neutral emotions. Moreover, children judged their own real-life transgressions (as recounted in narratives) as less severe and more justified than hypothetical transgressions. First, these initial findings show that using a response measure based on affect ratings results in the attribution of emotions differing in valence (positive, negative, and neutral) from emotions mentioned spontaneously when recounting a narrative (only negative). Accordingly, no indications of the happy victimizer phenomenon were found in narratives. Second, the differential findings regarding moral judgments and justifications generated in the context of real-life versus hypothetical transgressions clearly show that children's moral reasoning is complex and highly attuned to the circumstances in which it occurs, namely, reconstructing one's own experiences in the role of transgressor versus engaging in a more or less (emotionally) distanced act of deliberation about a hypothetical transgressor. As emotions experienced in real-life moral conflicts provide an important source for children's moral learning (Smetana & Killen, 2008), using an assessment method that taps into children's first-hand experiences may represent another important way to assess moral emotions. Moreover, narratives offer relevant insights into the affective/emotional side of moral experience. First, they (may) contain expressions relating to physiological reactions accompanying moral affect, e.g., "… and then my face turned very hot". Second, telling a narrative of a morally relevant situation may be accompanied by emotional reactions on the side of the narrator, which can be systematically observed, for example, by videotaping the process of narration.

CONCLUSION

In order to advance the development of methods to assess moral emotions, future research should additionally consider experiences of bodily processes as a core feature of moral emotions. Accordingly, assessment methods need to ensure that stories presented to participants trigger emotional involvement. For example, an extension of the happy victimizer paradigm might include assessing moral judgments and emotions in emotionally meaningful situations which occur naturally or are induced within an experimental setting (cf. Kochanska, Gross, Lin, & Nichols, 2002). In this sense, attempts at assessing judgments or emotions immediately after observed moral conflicts in real-life situations are especially promising (Smetana et al., 1999; Turiel, 2002).

Taken together, we draw two general conclusions. First, moral emotions – operationalized as moral emotion attributions – are of key significance in explaining (im)moral behaviour. Second, we showed that the field is in need of additional, innovative studies to elucidate the intricate relationship between cognitive, emotional, and behavioural aspects of moral development. Alternative, innovative assessment methods, including both real-life and experimental contexts, offer a promising avenue towards gaining further insights into the role moral emotions play in morally relevant behaviour.

REFERENCES

Alsaker, F., & Gutzwiller-Helfenfinger, E. (2009). Social behavior and peer relationships of victims, bully-victims, and bullies in kindergarten. In S.R. Jimerson, S.M. Swearer, & D.L. Espelage (Eds.), *The handbook of bullying in schools: An international perspective* (pp. 87–100). New York: Routledge.

Asendorpf, J.B., & Nunner-Winkler, G. (1992). Children's moral motive strength and temperamental inhibition reduce their immoral behavior in real moral conflicts. *Child Development, 23*, 1223–1235.

Arsenio, W.F., & Lemerise, E.A. (2004). Aggression and moral development: Integrating social information processing and moral domain models. *Child Development, 75*, 987–1002.

Arsenio, W., & Lover, A. (1999). Children's conceptions of sociomoral affect: Happy victimizers, mixed emotions, and other expectancies. In M. Killen & D. Hart (Eds.), *Morality in everyday life: Developmental perspectives* (pp. 87–128). New York, NY: Cambridge University Press.

Arsenio, W.F., & Fleiss, K. (1996). Typical and behaviorally disruptive children's understanding of the emotional consequences of socio-moral events. *British Journal of Developmental Psychology, 14*(2), 173–186.

Arsenio, W.F., Gold, J., & Adams, E. (2006). Children's conceptions and displays of moral emotions. In M. Killen & J.G. Smetana (Eds.), *Handbook of moral development* (pp. 581–610). New Jersey: Lawrence Erlbaum Associates, Publishers.

Arsenio, W.F., & Kramer, R. (1992). Victimizers and their victims: Children's conceptions of the mixed emotional consequences of moral transgressions. *Child Development, 63*(4), 915–927.

Askan, N., & Kochanska, G. (2005). Conscience in childhood: Old questions, new answers. *Developmental Psychology, 41*(3), 506–516.

Blasi, A. (1999). Emotions and moral motivation. *Journal for the Theory of Social Behavior, 29*, 1–19.

Blasi, A. (2005). What should count as moral behavior? The nature of 'early morality' in children's development. In W. Edestein & G. Nunner-Winkler (Eds.), *Morality in context* (p. 119–130). Amsterdam: Elsevier.

Crick, N., & Dodge, K. (1994). A review and reformulation of social-information-processing mechanisms in children's social adjustment. *Psychological Bulletin, 115*, 74–101.

Deigh, J. (1994). Cognitivism in the theory of emotions. *Ethics, 104*, 824–854.

Eisenberg, N. (2000). Emotion, regulation, and moral development. *Annual Review of Psychology, 51*, 665–697.

Eisenberg, N., Spinrad, T. & Sadovsky, A. (2006). Empathy-related responding in children. In M. Killen & J. Smetana (Eds.), *Handbook of Moral Development.* (pp. 517–549). Mahwah, NJ: Erlbaum.

Gasser, L., & Keller, M. (2009). Are the competent the morally good? Perspective taking and moral motivation of children involved in bullying. *Social Development, 18*, 798–816.

Gasser, L., & Malti, T. (2011). Relationale und physische Aggression in der mittleren Kindheit: Zusammenhänge mit moralischem Wissen und moralischen Gefühlen [Relational and physical aggression in middle childhood: Relations to moral judgment and moral emotions]. *Zeitschrift für Entwicklungspsychologie und Pädagogische Psychologie, 1*, 29–38.

Greenspan, P. (1988). *Emotions and reasons. An inquiry into emotional justification.* New York: Routledge, Chapman & Hall.

Gutzwiller-Helfenfinger, E., Gasser, L., & Malti, T. (2010). Moral emotions and moral judgments in children's narratives: Comparing real-life and hypothetical transgressions. *New Directions for Child and Adolescent Development, 129*, 11–31.

Hanish, L.D., & Guerra, N.G. (2004). Aggressive victims, passive victims, and bullies: Developmental continuity or developmental change. *Merrill Palmer Quarterly, 50,* 17–38.

Harris, P. (1989). *The development of psychological understanding.* Oxford: Blackwell.

Hawley, P.H. (1999). The ontogenesis of social dominance: A strategy-based evolutionary perspective. *Developmental Review, 19*(1), 97–132.

Hughes, C., & Dunn, J. (2000). Hedonism or empathy? Hard-to-manage children's moral awareness and links with cognitive and maternal characteristics. *British Journal of Developmental Psychology, 18,* 227–245.

James, W. (1890). *The principles of psychology.* New York, London: Holt and Macmillan.

Kant, I. (1781). *Kritik der reinen Vernunft, Prolegomena, Grundlegung zur Metaphysik der Sitten, Metaphysische Anfangsgründe der Naturwissenschaft.* (1. Aufl.).

Kant, I. (1785). *Grundlegung zur Metaphysik der Sitten,* Bd. IV.

Kohlberg, L. (1984). *The psychology of moral development: The nature and validity of moral stages.* San Francisco: Harper and Row.

Keller, M., Brandt, A., & Sigurdardottir, G. (2009). "Happy" and "unhappy victimizers: The development of moral emotions from childhood to adolescence. In W. Koops & A. Sanders (Eds.), *The development and structure of conscience* (pp. 253–267). Hove, UK: Psychology Press.

Keller, M., Lourenço, O., Malti, T., & Saalbach, H. (2003).The Multifacetted Phenomenon of 'Happy Victimizers': A Cross-Cultural Comparison of Moral Emotions. *British Journal of Developmental Psychology, 21*(1), 1–18.

Kochanska, G., Gross, J.N., Lin M-H., & Nichols, K.E. (2002). Guilt in young children: Development, and relations with a broader system of standards. *Child Development, 73*(2), 461–482.

Krettenauer, T., & Eichler, D. (2006). Adolescents' self-attributed emotions following a moral transgression: Relations with delinquency, confidence in moral judgment, and age. *British Journal of Developmental Psychology, 24,* 489–506.

Krettenauer, T., Malti, T., & Sokol, B. (2008). The development of moral emotions and the happy victimizer phenomenon: a critical review of theory and applications. *European Journal of Developmental Science, 2,* 221–235.

Malti, T. (2007). Moral emotions and aggressive behavior in childhood. In G. Steffgen & M. Gollwitzer (Eds.), *Emotions and aggressive behavior* (pp. 185–200). Göttingen, Germany: Hogrefe.

Malti, T., & Keller, M. (2009). The relation of elementary-school children's externalizing behavior to emotion attributions, evaluation of consequences, and moral reasoning. *European Journal of Developmental Psychology, 6,* 592–614.

Malti, T., Gasser, L., & Buchmann, M. (2009). Emotion attributions and moral reasoning of aggressive and prosocial children. *Aggressive Behavior, 35,* 90–102.

Malti, T., Gasser, L., & Gutzwiller-Helfenfinger, E. (2010). Children's interpretive understanding, moral judgments, and emotion attributions: Relations to social behavior. *British Journal of Developmental Psychology, 28,* 275–292.

Malti, T., & Keller, M. (in cooperation with F.X. Fang, A. Edele, & G. Sigurdardottir) (2010). Development of moral emotions in cultural context. In W. Arsenio & E. Lemerise (Eds.), *Emotions, aggression, and morality in children: Bridging development and psychopathology* (pp. 177–198).Washington: American Psychological Association.

Malti, T., & Krettenauer, T. (2012). The relation of moral emotion attributions to prosocial and antisocial behavior: A meta-analysis. Child Development. Early online publication, 24 September 2012. doi: 10.1111/j.1467-8624.2012.01851.x

Malti, T., & Latzko, B. (2010). Children's moral emotions and moral cognition: Towards an integrative perspective. *New Directions for Child and Adolescent Development, 129,* 1–10.

Malti, T., & Latzko, B. (2012). Moral emotions. In V. Ramachandran (Ed.), *Encyclopedia of human behaviour* (2nd ed., pp. 644–649). Maryland Heights, MO: Elsevier.

Montada, L. (1993). Understanding oughts by assessing moral reasoning or moral emotions. In G. Noam & T. Wren (Eds.), *The moral self* (pp. 292–309). Boston: MIT-Press.

Nozick, R. (1989). *Examined life. Philosophical meditations.* New York: Simon & Schuster.

Nunner-Winkler, G. (1999). Development of moral understanding and moral motivation. In F.E. Weinert & W. Schneider (Eds.), *Individual development from 3 to 12* (pp. 253–292). Cambridge: Cambridge University Press.

Nunner-Winkler, G., & Sodian, B. (1988). Children's understanding of moral emotions. *Child Development, 59*, 1323–1338.

Olweus, D. (1978). *Aggression in the schools*. New York: Wiley.

Orobio de Castro, B., Veerman, J.W., Koops, W., Bosch, J.D., & Monshouwer, H.J. (2002). Hostile attribution of intent and aggressive behavior: a meta-analysis. *Child Development, 73*, 916–934.

Ostrov, J.M., Ries, E.E., Stauffacher, K., Godleski, S.A., & Mullins, A.D. (2008). Relational aggression, physical aggression and deception during early childhood: A multi-method, multi-informant, short-term longitudinal study. *Journal of Clinical Child and Adolescent Psychology, 37*, 664–675.

Pellegrini, A.S., Bartini, M., & Brooks, F. (1999). School bullies, victims, and aggressive victims. Factors relating to group affiliation and victimization in early adolescence. *Journal of Educational Psychology, 91*(2), 216–224.

Piaget, J. (1981). *Intelligence and affectivity: Their relationship during child development*. Palo Alto, CA: Annual Reviews.

Salmivalli, C., Lagerspetz, K., Bjorkqvist, K., & Kaukiainen, A. (1996). Bullying as a group process: Participant roles and their relations to social status within the group. *Aggressive Behavior, 22*, 1–15.

Sokol., B. (2004). *Children's conceptions of agency and morality: Making sense of the happy victimizer phenomenon*. Dissertation, University of British Columbia, Department of Psychology, Canada.

Smetana, J.G., & Killen, M. (2008). Moral cognition, emotions, and neuroscience: An integrative developmental view. *European Journal of Developmental Science, 2*, 324–339.

Smetana, J.G., Toth, S.L., Cicchetti, D., Bruce, J., Kane, P., & Daddis, C. (1999). Maltreated and nonmaltreated preschoolers' conceptions of hypothetical and actual moral transgressions. *Developmental Psychology, 35*, 269–281.

Tangney, J., Stuewig, J., & Mashek, D. (2007). Moral emotions, moral cognitions, and moral behavior. *Annual Review, 58*, 345–372.

Turiel, E. (2002). *The culture of morality: Social development, context, and conflict*. Cambridge, England: Cambridge University Press.

Turiel, E. (2006). Thought, emotions, and social interactional processes in moral development. In M. Killen & J. Smetana (Eds.), *Handbook of Moral Development* (pp. 7–36). Mahwah, NJ: Lawrence Erlbaum Associates.

Veenstra, R., Lindenberg, S., Oldehinkel, A., De Winter, A.F., Verhulst, F.C., & Ormel, J. (2005). Bullying and victimization in elementary schools: A comparison of bullies, victims, bully/victims and uninvolved preadolescents. *Developmental Psychology, 41*, 672–682.

Wainryb, C., Brehl, B.A., & Matwin, S. (2005). Being hurt and hurting others: Children's narrative accounts and moral judgments of their own interpersonal conflicts. *Monographs of the Society for Research in Child Development, 70*, 1–114.

AFFILIATIONS

Luciano Gasser
Institute of Education and Diversity
University of Teacher Education of Central Switzerland
Lucerne, Switzerland

Eveline Gutzwiller-Helfenfinger
Institute of Pedagogical Professionalism and School Culture
University of Teacher Education of Central Switzerland
Lucerne, Switzerland

L. GASSER, E. G.-HELFENFINGER, B. LATZKO & T. MALTI

Brigitte Latzko
Faculty of Education
Universität Leipzig
Leipzig, Germany

Tina Malti
Department of Psychology
University of Toronto
Mississauga, Canada

DARCIA NARVAEZ

IV. NEUROBIOLOGY AND MORAL MINDSET

INTRODUCTION

Theories of moral motivation often focus on how central moral concerns are to the individual and the consistency of behaviour matching these concerns. Yet few people are consistently virtuous. Why might this be? Triune ethics theory suggests that humans evolved different moral mindsets that when triggered, vary in perceptions and affordances for moral action, thereby partly explaining human moral inconsistency. The three basic ethical mindsets are safety (self-protection), engagement (relational attunement), and imagination (abstraction). A mindset or its subtype can become a disposition and/or be evoked by situations — in person-by-context interactions. Normative moral mindsets for compassion and reflection may require optimal brain development during sensitive periods; otherwise a self-protective orientation can become dominant.

Moral self, moral identity and moral personality are terms used to indicate the centrality of moral constructs in a person's self-concept (Lapsley & Narvaez, 2004; Narvaez & Lapsley, 2009). According to Blasi (1980), an individual with a moral personality situates moral concerns centrally in the self-concept and feels obligated to live consistently with respect to moral concerns. A person with a moral identity has moral traits that are chronically accessible and automatically applied to social information processing (Lapsley & Narvaez, 2004; Narvaez, Lapsley, Hagele & Lasky, 2006).

Most of the time, moral identity and moral motivation are discussed as if they are unitary concepts, as if the normative understanding of moral personality (e.g., responsible, caring, fair) is universal across individuals and situations. In this chapter, I suggest that moral identity and moral motivation are not unitary constructs but that instead humans have multiple moral motivations rooted in the evolved strata of the brain. According to this view, moral motivation shifts when a different mindset is active. Mindsets energize moral behaviour, like motivation generally energizes behaviour (Kelinginna & Kelinginna, 1981). In the view of triune ethics theory, behaviour can be energized to self-protect, to attune with others or to abstract, detaching emotionally from the present.

MORAL MOTIVATIONAL MINDSETS

According to Triune Ethics Theory (TET; Narvaez, 2008b; 2009), three types of affectively-rooted moral mindsets emerged from human evolution based on evolved

K. Heinrichs, F. Oser & T. Lovat (Eds.), Handbook of Moral Motivation: Theories, Models, Applications, 323–340.

brain strata (MacLean, 1990), although anatomical details are much more complex. Nevertheless, the strata tend to govern distinctive brain states, upon which morality is presumed to emerge (Cory & Gardner, 2002). These mindsets arise out of biological propensities but are shaped by experience during sensitive periods. Rooted in basic emotional systems, these biological propensities propel human moral action on an individual and group level. When an individual uses a particular mindset to guide decisions and actions, it becomes an ethic, a normative imperative that trumps other values.

A mindset represents a "central motive" that colours perception and goal setting and comprises part of what Moll and colleagues call the event-feature-emotion complexes that drive moral cognitive phenomena (Moll, Zahn, de Oliveira-Souza, Krueger & Grafman, 2005). In other words, motivational cognition and emotion are inextricably linked (Allman, Hakeem, Erwin, Ninchinsky & Hof, 2001). As a type of motivated cognition, each ethic influences which affordances are salient for action, saturating ongoing experience with that ethic's values (Moll, de Oliveira-Souza, Eslinger, Bramati, Mourao-Miranda, Andreiulo et al., 2002).

Each ethic is *subjectively* moral, that is, to the individual in a particular moral mindset the actions undertaken feel like moral actions, like the right and good thing to do at that moment. The Ethic of Safety emerges under a sense of threat and is focused on self-preservation and self-protection. To most philosophers and religious traditions, the egoistic orientation or the Safety ethic is *objectively* immoral and because it is often reflexive instead of intentional, not moral. However, to the individual, the reflexive action feels good and right in that moment. The other two mindsets fit with normative theories of moral concerns. The Ethic of Engagement focuses on relational presence and social resonance. The Ethic of Imagination embraces reason, stepping back from present emotions to coordinate instincts and intuitions, adapt to ongoing social relationships, and address concerns beyond the immediate. An ethic can be primed by the context, in interaction with personality disposition. See Figure 1 for a schematic of the ethics.

The Safety Ethic: Innate Shaped Instincts

The Safety Ethic is rooted in the R-complex (MacLean, 1990), or the extra-pyramidal action nervous system (Panksepp, 1998). Dominant in reptiles, the R-complex in mammals relates to territoriality, imitation, deception, struggles for power, maintenance of routine and following precedent. The Ethic of Safety is based primarily in these and similar instincts, which revolve around survival and thriving in context, instincts shared with all animals and present from birth. Primitive emotion systems related to fear, anger and basic sexuality reside here. Because survival mechanisms are hardwired into the brain, they are not easily damaged and can become the default mindset when social support is lacking and brain development is suboptimal.

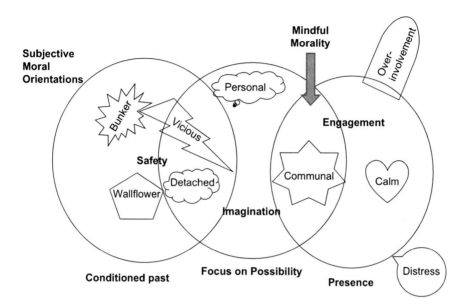

Figure 1. Triune ethics theory: Types and subtypes of ethics.

The safety mindset is about self-protection in view of perceived threat (real or imagined). The immediate goal for safety takes over the mind so energies focus there. When this occurs, the individual can take an aggressive stance (bunker safety), to ward off the threat, or a withdrawing, freezing stance (wallflower safety), to try to escape from the threat. A humorous example is when George Costanza on the television show *Seinfeld* thinks there is a fire at a children's party and pushes everyone else out of the way to escape to safety, thinking only of himself. The primary goal is to return to a sense of security, predictability and control, whether through harshness towards others, escape or some combination as with Costanza.

The ethic of safety is part of lower evolution, driven by goodness of fit and self-interest (Loye, 2002). It has its place in individual and group survival and as a more primitive moral expression. However, it is not the driving force of human evolution as identified by Darwin (1871/1981); that force is initiated in the systems underlying the Ethic of Engagement, an ethic that focuses on relational presence.

Engagement Ethic: Epigenetic Intuition

The second wave of brain evolution brought about the organization central to mammalian functioning, the limbic system and related structures ("paleo-mammalian;" MacLean, 1990). The foundational set of structures is identified as the visceral-emotional nervous system on the hypothalamic-limbic axis (Panksepp,

1998). This system lends a feeling tone to the functions of the R-complex, allowing for emotional signalling both internally (learning) and externally (sociality) (Konner, 2002). MacLean (1990) proposed that these paleo-mammalian structures are the seat of human emotion, personal identity, memory for ongoing experience, and an individual's sense of reality and truth. Notable are three signatory sets of behaviour that did not exist systematically in evolutionarily prior species (although these emerged separately in birds): nursing and maternal care, audiovocal communication between mother and offspring, and play. Human brains are reward-seeking structures, evolved to obtain gratification primarily from social relationships (Nelson & Panksepp, 1998). However, how well these structures function can depend on maternal and other caregiver care in early life.

A human infant's brain and body systems are dependent on experience, particularly through an attachment relationship that requires the caregiver to act as an "external psychobiological regulator" (Schore, 2001, p. 202) as the brain is socially wired and constructed in the early years (Eisenberg, 1995). "Development may be conceptualized as the transformation of external into internal regulation" where the "progression represents an increase of complexity of the maturing brain systems that adaptively regulate the interaction between the developing organism and the social environment" (i.e., caregivers; Schore, 2001, p. 202). For example, the caregiver plays multiple roles in regulating the physiological and psychological development of the infant. Hofer (1994; Polan & Hofer, 1999) describes how the caregiver's "hidden" regulation of infant development cuts across sensory systems (e.g., tactile, olfactory) and influences multiple levels of functioning. For example, maternal touch can lower an infant's heart rate during a distressing experience, supporting an adaptive behavioural response in the circumstance (Calkins & Hill, 2007, p. 240). When separated, the mother's absence causes multiple levels of disruption in the infant and the infant stops growing (Schanberg, 1995). In contrast, skin-to-skin contact promotes healthy sleep cycles, arousal and exploration levels (Feldman, Weller, Sirota& Eidelman, 2002).

Brain-building experiences are embedded in attachment relationships and are multivariate, little understood, but implicated in moral functioning (Schore, 2003a; 2003b). Here is one example. The basic regulatory processes of the parasympathetic nervous system appear to be deeply affected by caregiver behaviour. This occurs in part via the regulation of the vagus nerve (vagal tone), upon which emotional, behavioural, physiological and motor regulation are dependent (Calkins & Hill, 2007). The parasympathetic nervous system regulates cardio output through vagal tone under environmental stress (Porges, 1996). Responsive parenting with co-regulated communication patterns are related to good vagal tone, opening up sociality, whereas nonresponsive parenting leads to poor vagal tone and social distress (Porter, 2003; Haley & Stansbury, 2003; Calkins, Smith, Gill & Johnson, 1998; Kennedy, Rubin, Hastings & Maisel, 2004). In adults, good vagal tone function is related to greater compassion (Eisenberg & Eggum, 2008).

Evidence is increasing that engagement and its emotional components (e,g., secure attachment, empathy) are a primary force behind moral behaviour. For example, even among primates, empathy is a common occurrence (De Waal, 1996). Moreover, for most Gentile rescuers of Jews in World War II "caring compelled action"— most were driven by "pity, compassion, concern and affection" (Oliner, 2002; p. 125). The Engagement ethic is a capacity that dominates social interactions in ancestral social contexts (i.e., among hunter-gatherers; Ingold, 1999) where generosity and affability are fostered (see Narvaez, 2013).

To develop optimally, the Engagement Ethic may require compassionate reciprocal experiences during sensitive developmental periods, as evident in ancestral environments. My colleagues and I are studying whether this is true or not. We are examining ancestral parenting practices, practices that are variations on social mammalian caregiving evolved more than 30 million years ago. In early life these include natural childbirth, extensive breastfeeding, constant touch, responsiveness to the needs of the child, multiple adult caregivers, and free play (Hewlett & Lamb, 2005). Even after controlling for maternal income and education, we are finding that each is related to some aspect of three-year-olds' moral development (e.g., empathy, conscience, social engagement, inhibitory control; Narvaez, Gleason, Brooks, Wang, Brooks, Lefever, Cheng & Centers for the Prevention of Child Neglect, 2012; Narvaez, Wang, Deng, Cheng & Gleason, 2012). Although evolution has prepared the human brain for sociality and moral agency, ancestral parenting practices during development may be required for normal formation of brain circuitries necessary for optimal social engagement and moral functioning (Greenspan & Shanker 1999; Narvaez & Gleason, 2013; Panksepp 1998; Schore, 2003a).

The reciprocity learned in a mutually responsive relationship with the caregiver may form the basis of a sense of engagement and communion. Ideally, this is experienced in early childhood so that interpersonal respect and reciprocity form deeply in sensorimotor memory. Insensitive care may fail to foster the deep empathy of which humans are capable. Lacking mutually responsive care may result in a general insensitivity to others and perhaps to injustice itself (Lerner, 2002).

Despite the importance of empathy and communion in moral behaviour, most research in morality has focused on reasoning. Reasoning and related capabilities are central to the Ethic of Imagination.

Imagination Ethic: Cultivated Deliberation and Narrative

The third major brain formation to evolve was the neomammalian, which refers to the neocortex and related thamalic structures (MacLean, 1990). This somatic-cognitive nervous system on the thalamic-neocortical axis (Panksepp, 1998) is focused primarily on the external world, providing the capacity for problem solving and deliberative learning. The frontal lobes are considered the pinnacle of human evolution. They are the source of our deliberative reasoning, which includes much more than rational thought in the traditional sense. The mind thinks with feeling (Konner, 2002) and a mind without feeling makes poor judgments (Damasio, 1999). The frontal lobes provide the relay station between emotions and goals, planning and doing, coordinating systems from all parts of the brain. They maintain the sense of identity in cultural context through narrative self-explanation.

The development of brain areas related to the Ethic of Imagination, like those related to the Engagement Ethic, require a nurturing environment. The prefrontal cortex and its specialized units take decades to fully mature and are subject to damage from environmental factors both early (Anderson, Bechara, Damasio, Tranel & Damasio, 1999; Kodituwakku, Kalberg & May, 2001) and late in development (Newman, Holden, & Delville, 2005). Warm, responsive care fosters the emotion centers in the right brain (Schore, 2003a; 2003b) including the orbitofrontal cortex (OFC), vital to lifelong emotion regulation, whose inadequate or damaged development leaves one susceptible to psychiatric diseases such as depression and anxiety. The prefrontal cortex is susceptible to damage throughout development, not reaching completion until the third decade of life (Giedd, Blumenthal & Jeffries 1999; Luna, Thulborn, Munoz, Merriam, Garver, Minshew, et al., 2001). Binge drinking (Bechara, 2005) and violent video game play can turn normal brains into ones that look like those of aggressive delinquents (Mathews, Kronenberger, Wang, Lurito, Lowe & Dunn, 2005) as higher order development is halted. Of course, immature brain development influences moral expression, whether in the executive functions vital for the imagination ethic or the emotional regulation systems vital for the engagement ethic. The safety ethic is the default system when the Engagement Ethic and the Imagination Ethic have been poorly nurtured by the child's caregivers and community.

The Imagination ethic has several subtypes. *Communal imagination* combines the prosocial orientation of the engagement ethic with higher functioning, allowing for moral innovation and the extension of community beyond immediate relations into the future with those who are not present. *Vicious imagination* combines the self-protective mindset of the bunker safety ethic with the abstraction skills of the frontal lobe, creating plots and devices to impose one's will on others. When one has a powerful self-identity, it can propel one to take action (for better or worse). In terms of attacking USA interests, Osama bin Laden behaved from his vicious imagination mindset and, from what we are told in the gospels, Jesus usually behaved from an engagement or communal imagination mindset.

However, the human capacity for abstraction means that one can be detached from immediate social experience and reside in a personal realm. This happens when people have a personal goal such as the shopper who on an errand can be so single minded that she ignores social connections and misses opportunities to help others. In the modern world, this is a common occurrence. A dispositional *detached imagination* dissociates from emotion as a matter of course owing to right brain shut down, damage or inadequate socioemotional development (Siegel, 1999). Moral psychology experiments often focus on detached imagination by using decontextualized scenarios that do not require the intuitive insight provided by well-shaped emotions (Narvaez, 2010).

Adaptive Moral Motivation

Moral motivation fluctuates along with the changing needs and goals of the individual. As a shifting dynamic system, the individual moves through social space with general, built-in mammalian desires — to fit in, to connect with others, to be safe, to feel competent (e.g., Deci & Ryan, 1985) — but also with goal and dispositional habits shaped by experience. In each situation, an individual aims for what is perceived to be good and the most satisfying option. This is what all organisms do. Pattern recognition propels action. Learned patterns of response, especially sensorimotor memory built in early life, shape action choices and corresponding perception and action. Moral motivation is a momentary combination of immediate goals, longterm goals (e.g., identity, habits) and responses to the perceived context and the people (other dynamic systems) in the situation. If one has not had much social experience during sensitive periods, one may not notice social cues. If one experienced early trauma, one may have heightened thresholds for threat cues, seeing threat where there actually is none (Dodge, 1985).

Personality involves chronic schemas of perception, interpretation and action that interact with situations (Lapsley & Narvaez, 2004). Personality dispositions form a unique personal signature within situations. For example, a man may always become dismissive and insensitive around women but not around men and only when feeling threatened. Some personalities are more strongly consistent across situations (e.g., always helpful to others) whereas other personalities may only be helpful to family members. Cultural narratives and expectations matter but so do individual practices that build capacities over time.

TET mindsets are distinctive and lend themselves to different motivations. Each mindset is an orientation rooted in a different set of emotion systems with a distinctive set of concerns. Safety and Engagement are orthogonal. It is not possible to be in both mindsets at once (although there may be an oscillation between them). Safety is based in the sympathetic nervous system and the Engagement in the parasympathetic. In a safety mindset, the individual will operate reflexively with learned/conditioned patterns of self-protection and move within the emotion systems of FEAR, SEEKING, and RAGE (capitalized to reflect empirically identified systems, Panksepp, 1998). Memory and reasoning are diminished owing to self-protective sympathetic system arousal. Whether the person acts on preferred impulses for aggression or withdrawal depends on the skills of inhibitory control and how well the action fits with the goals of the moment. A person who has a habitual safety orientation may react internally with anger or insult but learn to inhibit external reaction. An individual may not run away physically but emotionally, as happens with avoidant attachment (Mikulincer & Shaver, 2007a). With emotional distancing and emotional detachment, harm to others is more likely (Bandura, 1999). However, one can learn to inhibit an ingrained safety ethic with meditation and other exercises, as well as immersion in safe social climates. Change can occur when one feels relationally calm and safe. Ideally, one learns to rewire the brain through intentional reshaping of habitual responses (Schwartz & Begley, 2003) and through maintaining moods that foster an engagement ethic, as when one focuses on gratitude or relational support (Mikulincer, Shaver, Gillath, & Nitzberg, 2005).

Whereas the Engagement Ethic is more of a right-brain orientation of openness and relational awareness, tapping into prosocial emotions of CARE, PLAY, LUST, the systems underlying the Imagination Ethic operate more from a left-brain orientation of analysis with linear thinking, categorization and so forth (for a review, see McGilchrist, 2009). These executive functions allow one to reflect on one's actions and imagine possibilities. Taking multiple viewpoints is a way to see alternatives to one's conditioned orientation. Human reflective capabilities allow for the selection of environments that foster preferred intuitions. However, reflective abstraction does not necessarily lead to changes in action. Changing habitual patterns of perceiving and acting takes more than reflection. It also requires guided practice (see Narvaez, 2006, 2007, 2008a, 2012).

Personality Effects

As noted previously, dispositional tendencies towards one ethical mindset or another may develop from experiences during formative years. The dispositional tendency may be manifested as a meta-agenda for interpersonal relationships. See Figure 2 for a simplified illustration of the three mindsets when online as "meta-agendas" and the subtypes that emerge.

Capabilities for the Engagement Ethic allow one to reach out to others in empathy when they are in distress (Mikulincer & Shaver, 2005). Good early care tends to foster an agreeable empathic, and conscientious personality (Kochanska, 2002) as well as openness to experience and good executive functions (Greenspan & Shanker, 2004), the characteristics typically found among moral exemplars.

In contrast, a person can have a foundational sense of insecurity based on early childhood experiences of extensive distress that together promote a distrustful view of the world. This is notable in attachment disorders, which can make a person less empathic toward and receptive to others (Eisler & Levine, 2002; Mikulincer & Shaver, 2005). The person whose personality is dominated by the ethic of safety may have a "stressed brain" formation from trauma or neglect (Newman, Holden & Delville, 2005) or one in which the right brain may be partially shut down from inadequate emotional nurturance (Schore, 2003b). A stressed brain is related to poor attachment and bonding and to compromised social abilities: "Stress during infancy that is severe enough to create insecure attachment has a dissociative effect, disrupting right hemispheric emotional functioning and species preservative

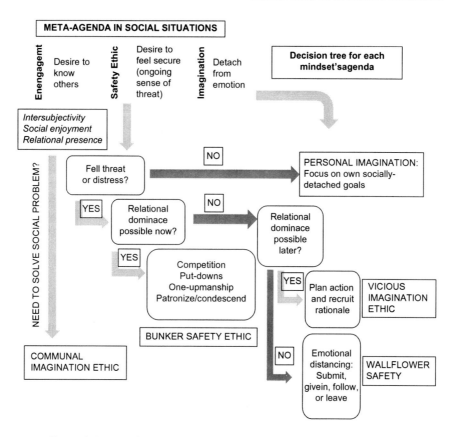

Figure 2. Triune ethics mindsets as meta-agendas with sample decision tree.

behaviour, and a permanent bias towards self preservation can become an adult trait" (Henry & Wang, 1998, p. 863).

In contrast, a personality that can integrate engagement and imagination into communal imagination is able to move beyond immediate self interest, to conceptualize alternative social systems, think impartially about moral problems, counteract harmful instincts and intuitions or behave altruistically in circumstances that evoke the safety ethic (e.g., Frankl, 1963). As pointed out earlier, however, when threat is high (and engagement ethic is low), a personality may be dominated by vicious imagination, focusing on maximizing safety and dominance, or disengage from emotion in detached imagination, making decisions like a distant bureaucrat (Bandura, 1999).

Situations may trigger a moral mindset, triggering self-situation memories (Freud's fantasies) except in the case of complete open-minded and openheartedness, which reflects a meta-agenda to avoid filters of judgment and analysis. TET mindset triggers can reflect a need for homeostatic balance restoration, setting up conditions for action (Franken, 2006). Action towards homeostasis can restore meaning and sense, diminishing threats to the self (Heine, Proulx, & Vohs, 2006).

What keeps moral behaviour going may be different from the moral mindset that instigates it. Disposition (practiced responses) and executive controls must keep it going. Persistence requires a meta-goal with ongoing monitoring of planned action. Expectancy theory (Vroom, 1964) may provide a framework for moral persistence, where motivation is influenced by expectancy (probability of success), instrumentality (connection of success and reward) and value of obtaining the goal. Using James' view of self-esteem (success/pretensions), those with low moral motivation may have had their prior attempts not succeed, affecting their sense of self-efficacy and self-esteem, and so they lowered their expectations for their own moral behaviour or shifted their attention and goals elsewhere — to more successful, better fitting endeavours (Higgins, 2011).

Situational Effects

Each of the three ethical mindsets is available to some degree in each person (unless there has been too much damage). Situations can stimulate different ethics. For example, terror management studies show that priming for safety (death) or for engagement (attachment) influences subsequent helping behaviour as well as attitudes towards and treatment of outgroup members (Hart, Shaver & Goldenberg, 2005; Mikulincer & Shaver, 2001). An environment characterized by safety and caring not only increases learning but prosocial behaviour as well (Solomon, Watson & Battistich, 2002). When a particular ethic is primed, it is presumed to influence perceptual sensitivities (Neisser, 1976), affective expectancies (Wilson, Lisle, Kraft & Wetzel, 1989), rhetorical susceptibilities (attractive fallacies), behavioural outcome expectancies and preferred goals (Mischel's "subjectively valuable outcomes," 1973, p. 270), as well as perceived affordances (social, physical and action possibilities). For example, when the safety ethic narrows one's perceptual and response systems, the affordances for behaviour centralize around self-advantageous and ingroup-advantageous actions.

Whether or not an ethic is evoked by a situation, culture or climate, varies from moment to moment according to personal history. Although situations can promote a mindset or put one in a mood for a mindset to be activated, habitually compassionate people keep themselves in a good mood (e.g., with gratitude) like the Dalai Lama. Priming varies in a person-by-context interaction. That is, some personalities are more primed by particular situations (Cervone, 1999). For example, although aggression cues promote hostile thoughts and actions generally, individuals high in agreeableness are not primed for aggression in these circumstances but activate pro-social responses (Meier, Robinson & Wilkowski, 2006). Moral exemplars likely have less variability in their responses and, instead, like the Dalai Lama, are able to maintain an engagement or communal imagination mindset.

Two Research Studies

To test triune ethics moral identities, my students and I have developed identity measures following Aquino & Reed (2002) where the respondent indicates the importance of moral goals represented by a set of terms (for *safety* identity: controlled, tough, unyielding, competitive; for *engagement* identity: caring, compassionate, merciful, cooperative; for *imagination* identity: reflective, thoughtful, inventive, reasonable). I report on two studies with college students using these measures.

Study 1 included 194 undergraduates who took questionnaires on computer which included Experience in Close Relationships-Revised (Fraley, et al., 2000), a measure of attachment; Basic Needs Effectance (sense of efficaciousness concerning areas of life identified as basic needs); Tomkins (1964) Humanism-revised; Big-5 Personality Scales (Goldberg et al., 2006); Triune Ethics Identity Scales (Narvaez, Brooks & Hardy, 2013); Action for the Less Fortunate (how often individuals have taken actions to help the less fortunate).

In the first study we expected that engagement and imagination ethical identities would be directly predicted by early experience. We used as proxies for early experience: secure attachment, humanistic orientation, basic needs effectance. We also expected early experience proxies to predict agreeableness and openness and that these would mediate effects of early experience on moral identity. The outcome variable was a 9-item self-report measure of action for the less fortunate. Regressions showed that two personality variables (Agreeableness & Openness) and two moral orientations (Engagement & Imagination) related to action for the less fortunate. Structural Equation Modeling (SEM) further investigated relations. Factor analysis showed attachment-related avoidance, effectance, and humanism formed a latent construct (we called early life effects). Early life effects predicted agreeableness and openness and moral mindsets. Openness and engagement identity predicted action for less fortunate. Figure 3 presents the results.

In a second study, we used ethical identity measures to examine engagement, imagination and two types of safety ethic, bunker and wallflower. We developed measures of how much a person lives their values and prefers their values be imposed on others. We expected that the ethical identities would have different attachment, personality and moral action signatures (engagement ethic predicts moral action and core values enactment; safety ethic predicts value imposition and negatively predicts moral action).

Study 2 participants were 191 undergraduates. They completed surveys online. We measured subtypes of the Safety Ethic: Bunker (combative and domineering) and Wallflower (withdrawn and timid). We used the Relationship Questionnaire (Bartholomew & Horowitz, 1991) was used to measure attachment style: secure,

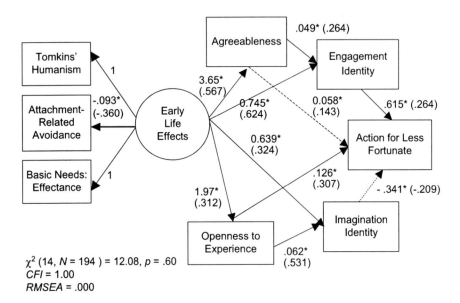

Figure 3. Study 1 path model for helping the less fortunate with unstandardized (Standardized) factor loadings. Solid lines represent significant factor/path loadings.
*p < .05

dismissing, fearful, preoccupied. We developed and factored two measures of value implementation: (a) Core Value Lifestyle (CVL; how much one consciously makes decisions based on core values in certain areas, e.g., "friends I cultivate," "purchases I make"); (b) Value Intrusion (how much one thinks that others should embrace one's own values, e.g., "I want authorities to ensure that others live the way I live").

Bunker safety identity was related to insecure attachment, value intrusion, and lack of core value lifestyle (CVL) while wallflower safety identity was related to insecure and fearful attachment and value intrusion. Engagement identity: related to secure attachment and CVL. Imagination identity: related to non-value intrusion and CVL.

Over both studies, the hypotheses were supported. Morality in college students was influenced by early life experience, affecting identity and moral behaviour. The three ethical mindsets (safety, engagement, imagination) appear to build on attachment orientation, relate to personality factors, and predict moral action, and value implementation. The results provide preliminary evidence that early life experience shapes brain and body systems for preferred moral functioning as triune ethics theory postulates. Additional evidence is available in Narvaez, Brooks and Hardy (2012).

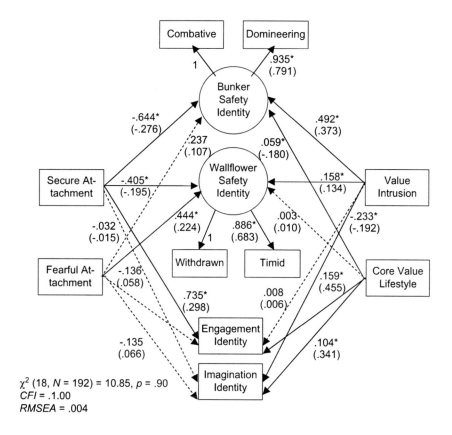

*Figure 4. Study 2 path model for how attachment and values influence identity with unstandardized (Standardized) factor loadings. Note: Solid lines represent significant factor/ path loadings. *p < .05*

CONCLUSION

Moral motivation may not be the unitary phenomenon it is often presumed to be. Triune Ethics Theory provides a way to consider the dynamic fluctuations in moral motivation and moral functioning as individuals perceive changes in situations, encounters and relationships. TET also offers a way to understand the importance of initial conditions (early life development) for moral motivational capacities and dispositions. In order to act with situation-appropriate compassion and reflection — the normative heart and mind of morality — individuals must have capabilities for self-regulation (e.g., self-soothing) and connecting to others (e.g., social resonance). These capacities initially rely on good early care (as represented in ancestral parenting practices), which is increasingly absent in modernized societies. Even if neglect is less than profound, its effects on the formation of systems that underlie optimal moral functioning can be long lasting. A child who spends a great deal of time alone in his or her room develops a different social orientation (embodied understanding of the social world) than a child who co-sleeps with parents and siblings and is never isolated. Starting life without the rich soil of mutually responsive caregivers may leave a child with shallow roots in socio-moral functioning, tenuous self-regulation, and a self-oriented neurobiology. Children with these characteristics are less compliant with adults and rules (Kochanska, 2002), more dangerous to themselves and their communities, and must spend a greater amount of more limited energy to self-regulate for life success (Sroufe, Egeland, Carlson & Collins, 2005). Returning to evolved principles for early care may be a place to start to enhance human moral capacities.

Anthropologists and other scientists often remark on the intelligence, sensitivity and moral engagement of nomadic hunter gatherer communities (e.g., Diamond, 1997; Everett, 2009). Although ancestral parenting practices may form a large part of these outcomes, so does culture. Cultures of peace support families and children and build narratives of peaceful character (Fry, 2006). In environments matching assumed ancestral conditions, extrapolating from anthropological reports, a great deal of attention was paid to keeping people from feeling threatened or being aggressive through cultural practices of equality and affection (Fry, 2006; Dentan, 1968), practices that are related to increased wellbeing (Caccioppo & Patrick, 2008; Pickett & Wilkinson, 2010). (For a description of these environments and the application to moral functioning, see Narvaez, 2013) Perhaps it is time to pay attention to the types of biologically-supportive environments that promote optimal moral formation and alleviate the maternal and familial stressors that impair moral growth.

REFERENCES

Allman, J.M., Hakeem, A., Erwin, J.M., Ninchinsky, E., & Hof, P. (2001). The anterior cingulate cortex: The evolution of an interface between emotion and cognition. *Annals of the New York Academy of Sciences, 935*, 107–117.

Anderson, S.W., Bechara, A., Damasio, H., Tranel, D. & Damasio, A.R. (1999). Impairment of social and moral behavior related to early damage in human prefrontal cortex.*Nature Neuroscience, 2*, 1032–1037.

Aquino, K., & Reed, A., (2002). The self-importance of moral identity. *Journal of Personality and Social Psychology, 83*, 1423–1440.

Bandura, A. (1999).Moral disengagement in the perpetration of inhumanities. *Personality andSocial Psychology Review, 3*(3), 269–275

Bartholomew, K. & Horowitz, L.M. (1991). Attachment styles among young adults: A test of a four-category model. *Journal of Personality and Social Psychology, 61*, 226–244.

Bechara, A. (2005). Decision making, impulse control and loss of willpower to resist drugs: A neurocognitive perspective. *Nature Neuroscience, 8*, 1458–1463.

Cacioppo, J., & Patrick, W. (2008). *Loneliness: Human nature and the need for social connection.* New York: W.W. Norton.

Calkins, S.D., Smith, C.L., Gill, K.L., & Johnson, M.C. (1998). Maternal interactive style across contexts: Relations to emotional, behavioral and physiological regulation during toddlerhood. *Social Development, 7(*3), 350–369.

Calkins, S.D., & Hill, A. (2007). Caregiver influences on emerging emotion regulation: Biological and environmental transactions in early development. In J.J. Gross (Ed.), *Handbook of emotion regulation*(pp. 229–248). New York: Guilford Press.

Cervone, D. (1999). Bottom-up explanation in personality psychology: The case of cross-situational coherence. In D. Cervone & Y. Shoda (Eds.), *The coherence of personality: Social-cognitive bases of personality consistency, variability, and organization* (pp. 303–341). New York: Guilford Press.

Cory, Jr., G.A., & Gardner, Jr., R. (Eds.) (YEAR???). The evolutionary neuroethology of Paul MacLean: Convergences and frontiers. Westport, CT: Praeger.

Damasio, A. (1999). *The feeling of what happens*. London: Heineman.

Darwin, C. (1871/1981). *The descent of man*. Princeton University Press, Princeton.

Deci, E.L., & Ryan, R.M. (1985). Intrinsic motivation and self-determination in human behavior. New York: Plenum Publishing Co.

de Waal, F. (1996). *Good-natured: The origins of right and wrong in humans and other animals*. Cambridge, MA: Harvard University Press.

Dentan, R.K. (1968). *The Semai: A nonviolent people of Malaya*. New York: Harcourt Brace College Publishers.

Diamond, J. (1997). *Guns, germs and steel: The fates of human societies*. New York: W.W. Norton.

Dodge, K.A. (1985). Attributional bias in aggressive children. In P. Kendall (Ed.), *Advances in cognitive-behavioral research and therapy* (pp. 75–111). New York: Academic Press.

Eisenberg L. (1995). The social construction of the human brain. *American Journal of Psychiatry, 152*, 1563–1575.

Eisenberg, N., & Eggum, N.D. (2008). Empathic responding: Sympathy and personal distress. In B. Sullivan, M. Snyder, & J. Sullivan (Eds.), *Cooperation: The political psychology of effective human interaction* (pp. 53–74).Malden, MA: Blackwell Publishing.

Eisler, R. & Levine, D.S. (2002). Nurture, nature, and caring: We are not prisoners of our genes. *Brain and Mind, 3,* 9–52.

Everett, D. (2009). *Don't sleep, there are snakes: Life and language in the Amazonian jungle*. New York: Pantheon.

Feldman, R., Weller, A., Sirota, L., & Eidelman, A.I. (2002). Skin-to-skin contact (kangaroo care) promotes self-regulation in premature infants: Sleep-wake cyclicity, arousal modulation, and sustained exploration. *Developmental Psychology, 38*, 194–207.

Fraley, R.C., Waller, N.G. & Brennan, K.A. (2000). An item-response theory analysis of self-report measures of adult attachment. *Journal of Personality and Social Psychology, 78*, 350–365.

Franken, R. (2006). *Human motivation* (6th ed.). Florence, KY: Wadsworth.

Frankl, Viktor E., (1963). *Man's search for meaning*. New York: Simon and Schuster.

Frederickson, B.L. (2002). Positive emotions. In C. Snyder & S.J. Lopez (Eds.), *Handbook of positive psychology* (pp. 120–134). New York: Oxford University Press.

Fry, D.P. (2006). *The human potential for peace: An anthropological challenge to assumptions about war and violence*. New York: Oxford University Press.

Giedd, J.N., Blumenthal, J, Jeffries, N.O., et al. (1999). Brain development during childhood and adolescence: A longitudinal MRI study. *Nature Neuroscience, 2*(10), 861–3.

Goldberg, L.R., Johnson, J.A., Eber, H.W., Hogan, R., Ashton, M.C., Cloninger, C.R., & Gough, H.C. (2006). The International Personality Item Pool and the future of public-domain personality measures. *Journal of Research in Personality, 40,* 84–96.

Greenspan, S.I., & Shanker, S.I. (2004). *The first idea*. Cambridge, MA: Da Capo Press.

Grosjean B., & Tsai, G.E. (2007). NMDA neurotransmission as a critical mediator of borderline personality disorder. *Journal of Psychiatry and Neuroscience, 32*(2), 103–115.

Haley, D.W. & Stansbury, J. (2003). Infant stress and parent responsiveness: Regulation of physiology and behavior during still-face and reunion. *Child Development, 74*, 1534–1546.

Hart, J., Shaver, P.R., & Goldenberg, J.L. (2005). Attachment, self-esteem, worldviews, and terror management: Evidence for a tripartite security system. *Journal of Personality and Social Psychology, 88*(6), 999–1013.

Heine, S.J., Proulx, T., & Vohs, K.D. (2006). The meaning maintenance model: On the coherence of human motivations. *Personality and Social Psychology Review, 10*(2), 88–110.

Henry, J.P., & Wang, S. (1998). Effects of early stress on adult affiliative behavior, *Psychoneuroendocrinology, 23*(8), 863–875.

Higgins, E.T. (2011). Beyond pleasure and pain: How motivation works. New York: Oxford University Press.

Hofer, M.A. (1994). Hidden regulators in attachment, separation, and loss. In N.A. Fox (Ed.), Emotion regulation: Behavioral and biological considerations. *Monographs of the Society for Research in Child Development, 59*, 192–207.

Ingold, T. (1999). On the social relations of the hunter-gatherer band. In R.B. Lee & R. Daly (Eds.), *The Cambridge Encyclopedia of hunters and gatherers*. Cambridge: Cambridge University Press.

Kennedy, A.E., Rubin, K.H., Hastings, P.D., & Maisel, B. (2004). Longitudinal relations between child vagal-tone and parenting behavior: 2 to 4 years. *Developmental Psychobiology, 45*, 10–21.

Kleinginna, P., Jr., & Kleinginna A. (1981). A categorized list of motivation definitions, with suggestions for a consensual definition. *Motivation and Emotion, 5*, 263–291.

Kochanska, G. (2002). Mutually responsive orientation between mothers and their young children: A context for the early development of conscience. *Current Directions in Psychological Science, 11*, 191–195.

Kodituwakku, P.W., Kalberg, W., & May, P.A. (2001). *Effects of prenatal alcohol exposure on executive functioning: Alcohol research and health: Alcohol-related birth defects: An update, 25* (3) (online document from NIAAA)

Konner, M. (2000). *The tangled wing*. New York: Owl Books.

Lapsley, D.K., & Narvaez, D. (2004). A social-cognitive view of moral character. In D.K. Lapsley & D. Narvaez (Eds.), *Moral development: Self and identity* (pp. 189–212). Mahwah, NJ: Erlbaum.

Lerner, M. (2002). Pursuing the justice motive. In M. Ross & D.T. Miller (Eds.), *The Justice motive in everyday life*. Cambridge, MA: Cambridge University Press.

Loye, D. (2002). *The moral brain. Brain and Mind, 3*, 133–150.

Luna, B., Thulborn, K.R., Munoz, D.P., Merriam, E.P., Garver, K.E., Minshew, N.J. et al., (2001). Maturation of widely distributed brain function subserves cognitive development. *NeuroImage, 13*(5), 786–793.

MacLean, P.D., 1990: *The triune brain in evolution: Role in Paleocerebral functions*. New York: Plenum.

Mathews, V.P., Kronenberger, W.G., Wang, Y., Lurito, J.T., Lowe, M.J., & Dunn, D.W. (2005). Media violence exposure and frontal lobe activation measured by functional magnetic resonance imaging in aggressive and nonaggressive adolescents. *Journal of Computer Assisted Tomography, 29*(3), 287–292.

McGilchrist, I. (2009). *The Master and his emissary*. New Haven, CT: Yale University Press.

Meaney, M.J. (2001). Maternal care, gene expression, and the transmission of individual differences in stress reactivity across generations. *Annual Review of Neuroscience, 24*, 1161–1192.

Meier, B.P., Robinson, M.D., Wilkowski, B.M. (2006). Turning the other cheek: Agreeableness and the regulation of aggression-related primes. *Psychological Science, 17*(5), 136–142.

Mikulincer, M., & Shaver, P.R. (2001). Attachment theory and intergroup bias: Evidence that priming the secure base schema attenuates negative reactions to out-groups. *Journal of Personality and Social Psychology, 81*, 97–115.

Mikulincer, M., & Shaver, P.R. (2007). *Handbook of adult attachment*. New York: Guilford.

Mikulincer, M., & Shaver, P.R. (2005). Attachment security, compassion, and altruism. *Current Directions in Psychological Science, 14*, 34–38.

Mikulincer, M., Shaver, P.R., Gillath, O. & Nitzberg, R.A. (2005). Attachment, caregiving, and altruism: boosting attachment security increases compassion and helping. *Journal of Personality and Social Psychology, 89* (5), 817–839.

Mischel, W. (1973). Towards a cognitive social learning theory reconceptualization of personality. *Psychological Review, 80*, 252–283.

Moll, J., de Oliveira-Souza, R., Eslinger, P.J., Bramati, I.E., Mourao-Miranda, J., Andreiulo, P.A., et al. (2002). The neural correlates of moral sensitivity: A functional magnetic resonance imaging investigation of basic and moral emotions. *Journal of Neuroscience, 22,* 2730–2736.

Moll, J., Zahn, R., de Olivera-Souza, R., Krueger, F., & Grafman, J. (2005). The neural basis of human moral cognition. *Nature Reviews: Neuroscience, 6,* 799–809.

Narvaez, D. (2006). Integrative ethical education. In M. Killen & J. Smetana (Eds.), *Handbook of moral development* (pp. 703–733). Mahwah, NJ: Erlbaum.

Narvaez, D. (2007). How cognitive and neurobiological sciences inform values education for creatures like us. In D. Aspin & J. Chapman (Eds.), *Values education and lifelong learning: Philosophy, policy, practices* (pp. 127–159). Dordrecht: Springer Press International.

Narvaez, D. (2008a). Human flourishing and moral development: Cognitive science and neurobiological perspectives on virtue development. In L. Nucci & D. Narvaez (Eds.), *Handbook of moral and character education* (pp. 310–327). Mahwah, NJ: Erlbaum.

Narvaez, D. (2008b). Triune ethics: The neurobiological roots of our multiple moralities. *New Ideas in Psychology, 26,* 95–119.

Narvaez, D. (2009). Triune ethics theory and moral personality. In D. Narvaez & D.K. Lapsley (Eds.), *Personality, identity and character: Explorations in moral psychology* (pp. 136–158). New York: Cambridge University Press.

Narvaez, D. (2010). Moral complexity: The fatal attraction of truthiness and the importance of mature moral functioning. *Perspectives on Psychological Science, 5*(2), 163–181.

Narvaez, D. (2013). Development and socialization within an evolutionary context: Growing Up to Become "A good and useful human being." In D. Fry (Ed.), *War, Peace and Human Nature: The convergence of Evolutionary and Cultural Views* (pp. 341–357). New York: Oxford University Press.

Narvaez, D. (2012). Moral neuroeducation from early life through the lifespan. *Neuroethics, 5*(2), 145–157. doi:10.1007/s12152-011-9117-5

Narvaez, D., Brooks, J., & Mattan, B. (January, 2011). *Triune ethics Moral Identities are Shaped by Attachment, Personality Factors and Influence Moral Behavior.* Annual meeting of the Society for Personality and Social Psychology, San Antonio.

Narvaez, D., & Gleason, T. (2013). Developmental optimization. In D. Narvaez, J., Panksepp, A. Schore, & T. Gleason (Eds.), *Human nature, early experience and the environment of evolutionary adaptedness* (pp. 307–325). New York: Oxford University Press.

Narvaez, D., Gleason, T., Brooks, J. Wang, L., Lefever, J., Cheng, A., & Centers for the Prevention of Child Neglect (2012). *Longitudinal effects of ancestral parenting practices on early childhood outcomes.* Manuscript under review.

Narvaez, D. Wang, L., Deng, L., Cheng, A., & Gleason, T. (2012). *Ancestral Parenting Practices and Child Outcomes in Chinese Three-Year-Olds.* Manuscript under review.

Narvaez, D., & Lapsley, D.K. (Eds.) (2009). Personality, Identity, and Character: Explorations in Moral Psychology. New York: Cambridge University Press.

Narvaez, D., Lapsley, D.K., Hagele, S., & Lasky, B. (2006). Moral chronicity and social information processing: Tests of a social cognitive approach to the moral personality. *Journal of Research in Personality, 40,* 966–985.

Neisser, U. (1976). *Cognition and reality.* New York: W.H. Freeman and Company.

Nelson, E.E., & Panksepp, J. (1998). Brain substrates of infant-mother attachment: Contributions of opioids, oxytocin, and norepinephrine. *Neuroscience and Biobehavioral Reviews, 22,* 437–452.

Newman, M.L., Holden, G.W., & Delville, Y. (2005). Isolation and the stress of being bullied. *Journal of Adolescence, 28,* 343–357.

Oliner, S.P. (2002). Extraordinary acts of ordinary people: Faces of heroism and altruism. In S.G. Post, L.G. Underwood, J.P. Schloss, & W.B. Hurlbut (Eds.), *Altruistic love: Science, philosophy, and religion in dialogue.* (pp. 123–139) New York: Oxford University Press.

Panksepp, J. (1998). *Affective neuroscience: The foundations of human and animal emotions.* New York: Oxford University Press.

Pickett, K., & Wilkinson, R. (2010). *The spirit level: Why greater equality makes societies stronger.* New York: Bloomsbury Press.

Polan, H.J. & Hofer, M.A. (1999). Psychobiological origins of infants' attachment and separation responses. In J. Cassidy & P. Shaver (Eds.), *Handbook of attachment: Theory, research, and clinical applications* (pp. 162–180). New York: Guilford.

Porges, S.W. (1996). Physiological regulation in high-risk infants: A model for assessment and potential intervention. *Development and Psychopathology, 8*, 43–58.

Porter, C.L. (2003). Coregulation in mother-infant dyads: Links to infants' cardia vagal tone. *Psychological Reports, 92*, 307–319.

Schanberg, S. (1995). The genetic basis for touch effects. In T. Field (Ed.), *Touch in early development* (pp. 89–104). Mahwah, NJ: Erlbaum.

Schore, A. (2003a). *Affect regulation and the repair of the self.* New York: Norton.

Schore, A. (2003b). *Affect dysregulation and disorders of the self.* New York: Norton.

Schore, A.N. (2001). The effects of early relational trauma on right brain development, affect regulation, and infant mental health. *Infant Mental Health Journal, 22*, 201–269.

Schwartz, J.M., & Begley, S. (2003). *The mind and the brain: Neuroplasticity and the power of mental force.* New York: HarperCollins.

Siegel, D.J. (1999). *The developing mind: How relationships and the brain interact to shape who we are.* New York: Guilford.

Solomon, D., Watson, M.S., & Battistich, V.A., (2002). Teaching and school effects on moral/prosocial development. In V. Richardson (Ed.), *Handbook for research on teaching* (pp. 566–633). Washington, D.C.: American Educational Research Association.

Sroufe, L.A., Egeland, B., Carlson, E.A., & Collins, W.A. (2005). *The development of the person: The Minnesota study of risk and adaptation from birth to adulthood.* New York: Guilford.

Tomkins, S.S. (1965). Affect and the psychology of knowledge. In S.S. Tomkins & C.E. Izard (Eds.), *Affect, cognition, and personality* (pp. 72–97). New York: Springer.

Vroom, V. (1964). *Work and motivation.* New York: Wiley.

Wilson, T.D., Lisle, D.J., Kraft, D., & Wetzel. C.G. (1989). Preferences as expectation-driven inferences: Effects of affective expectations on affective experience. *Journal of Personality and Social Psychology, 56*(4), 519–530.

AFFILIATION

Darcia Narvaez
Department of Psychology
University of Notre Dame
Notre Dame, Indiana, USA

DON COLLINS REED

V. A SIMILE OF MORAL MOTIVATION[1]

INTRODUCTION

Living morally is like going on a trip. You want to find the best road to get you where you are headed, avoiding wrong turns and other mishaps. You can use a map, a GPS, or oral directions from someone at a gas station along the route. Or perhaps you have often been this way before and can get where you are going without thinking. On some stretches you may have to negotiate heavy traffic, detours, or fallen limbs. Because you can get distracted, you need to keep your destination in mind and in some cases to remember the broader purpose for your trip. Still, if there is no ignition within or propulsion from the engine, all else is for naught. We guide ourselves toward our destination because firing spark plugs and controlled explosions get us and keep us moving.

The processes by which we get moving and those by which we guide our moving are both crucial to moral motivation, but psychologists have tended to focus on one or the other. The problem of "moral motivation," as it is often formulated, arises from the so-called "judgment-action gap," the gap between judging correctly the right thing to do and doing it. If failure to do what is right is not a question of ignorance, it may be a matter of inadequate motivation. So what motivates people to be moral? And how do humans develop moral motivation?

Nunner-Winkler (2007, 2009, see 1993; Nunner-Winkler et al., 2007) has pointed out that people can have various motives to do the right thing, such as self-interest (punishment avoidance, desire for rewards), an unreflective need to conform to other's expectations, or a severe superego. People may do the right thing from concern for others, personal integrity, or respect for moral rules as such. Also, people may develop motives to do the right thing because of a genetic predisposition to benefit close relatives (kin altruism), a social-class-based consistency of concrete norms across family, school, clubs, workplace, and community, or a strong gender-feminine identification that prompts care for others at the cost of opportunities to gain competitive advantage over them. Moral motivation may develop from secure attachments in early childhood, child-rearing practices such as inductive reasoning and authoritative parenting, and/or peer group involvements that prompt consensus-oriented strategies and provide role-taking opportunities that require taking responsibility for one's actions.

On this way of thinking, one may be motivated to do what is right but from ulterior motives. In that case, doing what is right would not be acting morally. Whether your

K. Heinrichs, F. Oser & T. Lovat (Eds.), Handbook of Moral Motivation: Theories, Models, Applications, 341–362.

actions are moral and morally motivated depends on whether you intend to do what is right because it is right rather than for some further end, that is, on what Kant (1994/1785) called having a "good will."

The aim of this chapter is to present a bi-level account of moral motivation as a foot-in-the-door first step toward an elaborated multi-level model. So the thesis is that at least two clearly distinct and easily distinguished levels of person functioning are required for ideal moral motivation: deliberate conscious guidance and non- or pre-conscious physiological activation. In order not to make too light a work of it, I show how two psychological accounts of moral motivation that seem opposed to each other are best understood as complementary: Blasi's account of moral self-motivation through conscious willing and Haidt's account of moral motivation through pre-conscious activation of physiological processes. The former is oriented by Kantian and the latter by Humean philosophical assumptions. Each of these two accounts is important and neither should be considered adequate on its own. Section II of the chapter outlines a model of ethical functioning and clarifies the often exaggerated contrast between Kant's and Hume's accounts of moral motivation, opening the possibility that psychological accounts based on them could be complementary. Section III describes Haidt's Moral Foundations Theory, noting its debts to Hume, and Section IV describes Blasi's model of moral self-motivation, highlighting his Kantian emphasis on conscious willing. Sections V and VI offer broadened definitions of morality and moral reasoning which highlight the Aristotelian emphasis on the purpose of morality and a social-pragmatist account of moral reasoning. This shows how we can situate Blasi's and Haidt's accounts as complementary components of a bi-level model.

BRIEF SKETCH OF A MODEL, LOCATING KANTIAN & HUMEAN EMPHASES

It is easy to exaggerate the disagreements between Kant and Hume and by the same token between Blasi and Haidt. The emphases of their nuanced accounts are different, but they need not contradict each other unless we suppose that their descriptions of processes at different levels of organization offer competing comprehensive explanations of a multi-level phenomenon.

A model of the person level of ethical functioning, leaving aside interactional and cultural levels, would have at least three components: motivation, guidance, and ends or goals (see Table 1). By "motivation" I mean the underlying processes of the onset and continuation of moving (the non- or pre-conscious physiological level of person functioning). As suggested in the simile in the first paragraph, we can imagine motive processes by reference to the ignition within an automobile's engine and the force produced externally by its operations. But since motivation is not moral motivation unless well guided toward proper ends (the conscious level of person functioning), an adequate explanation of moral motivation must account for all three components.

Table 1. Outline of a model of ethical functioning based on a simile of moral motivation

3 Components:	7 Processes:	Elements:	Emphases of 3 Moral Philosophers:
Motivation	Ignition	Impulses, drives, urges, needs, etc.	Hume's emphasis
	Propulsion	Emotions, compulsions, habits, etc.	
	Braking	"Self-control," including impulse inhibition, habit breaking, etc.	
Guidance	Steering (short)	Intuitions and short-range deliberations (means to immediate ends)	Kant's emphasis
	Navigation (long)	"Self-regulation" from deliberation (means to remote ends)	
Ends	Intended destination (narrow)	Narrow-scope, occasion-specific goal(s) (ends)	Aristotle's emphasis
	Sense of larger purpose (broad)	Broad-scope, life-course goal(s) (ends)	

The dispute between Kant and Hume is principally over which is primary morally, reason or passion, thinking or feeling. They agree, however, that reason and passion are both necessary.

Kantian (1994/1785 & 1797) construals of morality (e.g., Kohlberg, 1981; also see Nunner-Winkler, 2009; Blasi, 1999b, 2005a) treat impulses and emotions (Motivation rows in Table 1) as secondary, serving and motivating performance of duty as determined by reason. Such accounts emphasize conscious willing (Guidance rows) and downplay the goals of moral action (Ends rows), since acting for the sake of some further end or purpose makes the worth of one's action depend on something other than the form of one's intention. When one acts for an end, one exhibits obedience to imperatives that are merely "hypothetical" (*If* I want to achieve [a certain end], *then* I must....) rather than "categorical" (Whatever my ends, I must....).

However, Kant did consider feelings and impulses useful. In the *Grounding of the metaphysics of morals* (1785) he stated,

> In order to will what reason alone prescribes as an *ought* for sensuously affected rational beings, there certainly must be a power of reason to infuse a feeling of pleasure or satisfaction in the fulfillment of duty, and hence there has to be a causality of reason to determine sensibility in accordance with rational principles. (*Grounding*, p. 460)

In the *Metaphysics of morals* (1797), Kant went further:

> ...it accordingly is an indirect duty to cultivate our natural (sensitive) feelings for others, and to make use of them as so many means for sympathy based on moral principles and the feeling appropriate to them. Thus it is a duty not to

avoid places where the poor, who lack most necessary things, are to be found; instead, it is a duty to seek them out. It is a duty not to shun sickrooms or prisons and so on in order to avoid the pain of compassion, which one may not be able to resist. For this feeling, though painful, nevertheless is one of the impulses placed in us by nature for effecting what the representation of duty might not accomplish by itself." (*Metaphysics of morals*, p. 457)

For Kant (1994/1785 & 1797), reason was primary because only by pure practical rationality can one discern universal moral requirements. The passions are fickle in the moment and vary from here to there – but nonetheless the passions may when rightly cultivated move us to act morally in cases in which the recognition of having a duty may not by itself be adequately motivating.

On the other hand, Humean (1978/1739–40, 1983/1751) construals of morality (such as Moral Foundations Theory, or MFT: see esp. Haidt, 2012; Haidt & Joseph, 2004, 2007; and the Social Intuitionist Model or SIM: see esp. Haidt, 2012, 2001; Haidt & Bjorklund, 2008) make passion primary (Motivation rows) and reason secondary (Guidance rows). Reason, according to Hume (1978/1739–40, Book III, Part I, Section I, p. 463, see also Book II, Part III, Section III, p. 413), discerns (a) matters of fact, such as what means promote specific ends, and (b) relations of ideas, such as how some statements logically entail others. But information by itself does not move us unless we care about what it is about, yet then it is our caring that motivates us, not the information.

Still, it would go too far to suggest that reason performs no moral function on Hume's account. In the *Treatise of human nature* (1978/1739–40), he notes,

Human nature being compos'd (sic) of two principal parts, which are requisite in all its actions, the affections and understanding; 'tis certain that the blind motions of the former, without the direction of the latter, incapacitate men for society…. (*Treatise*, Book III, Part II, Section II, p. 493).

In the *Enquiry concerning the principles of morals*, Hume (1983/1751) notes that our sympathy varies proportionally to the familial or social nearness of the person who might be the object of our concern. We neglect these differences "in our calm judgments and discourse concerning the characters of men…." And in a passage echoed later (in Section IX, Part I), Hume then observes that the "intercourse of sentiments, therefore, in society and conversation, makes us form some general and unalterable standard" which suffices for our public interactions or for "society." In a note to the passage, he clarifies:

It is wisely ordained by nature, that private connexions (sic) should commonly prevail over universal views and considerations; otherwise our affections and actions would be dissipated and lost, for want of a proper limited object… But still we know here, as in all the senses, to correct these inequalities by reflection, and retain a general standard of vice and virtue, founded chiefly on general usefulness. (*Enquiry*, Section V, Part II, note 25).

Just as nearer objects appear larger, though we know they are not, the passions incline us too much to narrow sympathies. In this as in the case of vision, reason is necessary to correct this distortion in order to promote pleasure, which tends to be greater for each as it is shared more widely.

Though Kant emphasizes conscious deployments of practical rationality and Hume emphasizes the passions, each recognizes the important role of what the other emphasizes – and we can move toward reconciling their accounts, and by the same token those of Blasi and Haidt, if we recognize the extent to which their different emphases focus on different levels of organization in the multi-level phenomenon of moral motivation (for an account of the "dynamic systems approach" to multi-level systems, see Kim & Sankey, 2009; Witherington, 2007; Fischer & Bidell, 2006; Thelen & Smith, 1994).

MFT DESCRIBES PRECONSCIOUS-TO-CONSCIOUS PROCESSES

Haidt's Moral Foundations Theory (MFT; see esp. Haidt, 2012; Haidt & Joseph, 2004, 2007) assumes an evolutionary frame of reference and describes motivational processes without distinction between ideal and contra-ideal functioning. Presumably morality and moral motivation did not appear all of a sudden through an exception to natural processes but emerged during the evolution of our species, perhaps especially over the past 200,000 years, when the brain of *Homo sapiens* was fully in place. If we grant that the evolutionary origins of proto-moral and moral motivation should be sought in predecessor hominin species over the past six million years (when our line split off from that of modern chimpanzees and bonobos), increasing in social complexity especially 50,000–75,000 years ago (at what Jared Diamond, 1999, has called "the great leap forward" of civilization), we might suspect that the *first onset* of specific instances of moral motivation in *Homo sapiens* occurs a step or two prior to conscious reasoning. Before the emergence in evolution of explicit, conscious reasoning, the onset of proto-moral motivation likely occurred in the implicit recognition of objects and situations in the social world as matters of socio- or proto-moral interest.

It is like jerking your hand away from the stovetop before you begin to feel you fingers burn, but of course it is more complex socially. Imagine you are in a crowded room with about 150 people. You feel uneasy. Then you notice that, across the room, someone is watching you, frowning. Your initial, preconscious response included recognition/perception plus appraisal/evaluation plus emotion/impulse. Your response occurred in a flash, with conscious awareness dawning only after you already felt uneasy. We might reasonably suspect that the processing pathway to the emotion/ impulse was on hyper-drive through a neural short-cut to your brain's limbic system – through what Ramachandran (2011) calls visual Pathway 3 or the "so what stream" – but the conscious awareness of recognition/perception plus appraisal/evaluation took slightly longer to assemble and coalesce. Your conscious awareness in such a case, therefore, is a product of neural-cognitive processing, not the cause of it. The three components of this response-set are distinguishable conceptually but, in normally functioning people without brain damage, are not separable. They would typically occur so quickly (and pre-consciously) that it would be misleading to think of them as a chronological sequence in which separate, isolable moments could be discerned. Logically of course, recognition must precede the appraisal of what is recognized, but this happens in a flash and outside of, or in the penumbra of, consciousness.

In a typical or "prototypical" (unambiguous, non-conflicted) case, you don't take time to consider. Your appraisal and impulse have already been felt when you have a chance to consider what you recognize to be taking place. The point is not that the response-set is not a cognitive phenomenon but that it is not at first a conscious phenomenon. It is conscious only after it has begun. Thus, it cannot have begun in this instance *in virtue of* immediately prior conscious operations or processes.

For the purposes of the argument in this chapter, we should notice that MFT can help us understand the *first onset* of moral motivation. With the bi-level account outlined in this chapter, we need not be concerned whether impulses or "intuitions" (see Haidt, 2012; Haidt & Joseph, 2004, 2007) account for everything in moral motivation, let alone everything in ethical functioning. We do not need them to, at least not according to the argument of this chapter.

Haidt (2012; Haidt & Joseph, 2004, 2007) argues that morality evolved, not as a domain-general capacity but, instead, as a set of sub-domain response patterns ("moral foundations") that met adaptive challenges. In Table 2, the six moral foundations Haidt (2012) identifies are outlined by reference to adaptive challenge, original domain, current domain, and characteristic emotion(s). The crucial differences between the moral foundations (sub-domains) are the differences between their adaptive challenges and the original domains related in evolution directly to them. It will be sufficient for the purposes of this chapter to discuss one of the moral foundations by way of illustration: the Care/harm foundation.

The hominin brain and cranial area expanded along the lineage producing *Homo sapiens*, so that not only were tool making and using common but also funerary, graphic, and ornamental symbolism, and eventually spoken and written language and larger, hierarchically more complex social groups. In order to be born live with such large heads, human fetuses had to be born premature, relative to other mammal species. And though infant care is required in most mammal species, it became required for longer periods through hominin evolution, especially with modern humans. As a prolonged period of infant dependency emerged in mammalian evolution, parents had to respond (a) to infant and child hunger or other needs or suffering, (b) to intentional infliction of harm to infants and children, and (c) to their straying too far from watchful attention or (d) into direct or indirect danger, etc. Those parents who responded quickly, automatically, and/or consistently were more likely to have offspring who survived to rear their own offspring. Associated response patterns for (a) suffering-detection, (b) harmful intention-detection, (c) absence- and (d) danger-detection, etc., became over many generations standard issues in the motivational economy of typical members of mammalian species.

Table 2. Moral Foundations (adapted from: Haidt & Joseph, 2007, and Haidt, 2012)

	Adaptive challenge	*Original triggers*	*Current triggers*	*Characteristic emotion(s)*
Care/ harm	Protect & care for young, vulnerable, or injured kin	Suffering, distress, or threat to one's kin; benevolent intentions toward one's kin	E.g., non-kin infants, baby seals, dolls, cartoon characters, suffering non-kin youth and adults; altruistic people	Compassion, empathy
Fairness/ cheating	Reap benefits of cooperation with non-kin (in hunting, mutual defense, etc.) and protect access to vital resources (including reproductive rights)	Cheating, deception; one-with-one &/or group cooperation Poachers, thieves, seducers, rapists	E.g., marital infidelity, broken vending machine, cutting in line, political corruption; law enforcement personnel E.g., copyright violations in music file sharing, excessive taxation, close surveillance, violations of personal space, abortion doctors/ clinics, anti-abortionists; military personnel	Resentment; trust, gratitude Anger
Liberty/ oppression	Repel bullies & tyrants	Alpha males/ females who abuse subordinates, extortion	E.g., signs of male chauvinism, censorship, trade regulation, medical paternalism; freedom fighters	Indignation, rebelliousness
Loyalty/ betrayal	Reap benefits of group cooperation	Threat or challenge to group safety or cohesion	E.g., sports teamfanship, ethnic identity, economic protectionism; people who sacrifice for the group's benefit	Rage at traitors; group pride
Authority/ subversion	Cooperate in role-differentiated hierarchy; deferring to and obeying legitimate authority	Signs of dominance & submission; rebellion, insubordination	E.g., blasphemy, sacrilege; bosses, respected professionals & clerics	Respect, fear
Sanctity/ degradation	Avoid disease-causing microbes & parasites	Feces, vomit, snot, pus, diseased people, rotting corpses	E.g., maggots, rats, menstruation, masturbation, incest, taboo ideas (communism, homophobia)	Disgust, feeling degraded; elevation, awe

The response patterns that address this adaptive challenge (prolonged infant and childhood dependency) include narrow and broad domains. The narrow or "original domain" of the set of response patterns accounts for the adaptive effect of the sub-domain in the original environment of evolution. The broad or "current domain" includes that narrow group and also other objects and/or situations that are similar enough – relative to the detection-features of the narrow, directly adaptive set of response patterns (whatever the genetic and neural mechanisms turn out to be) – so that they trigger the response patterns of the sub-domain.

The original domain of the Care/harm set of response patterns is the narrow set of objects and/or situations that prompts care for and protection of offspring and vulnerable or suffering kin, since this is what makes these response patterns most directly adaptive. The current domain, more broadly, is the total set of objects and/ or situations that triggers these response patterns, when the adaptive benefit may be less direct, including other infant-kin-like individuals, such as non-kin infants, pets and companion animals, and even non-pet baby mammals of other species (baby chimps, puppies, kittens, bunnies, seal pups, etc.) or simulacra of them (cartoon characters, dolls, child-like story characters, etc.) (Haidt, 2012). The suffering and/ or vulnerability of non-kin youth and adults may trigger responses in the Care/harm foundation as well (think of the way the KONY2012 campaign was well designed for this effect). The characteristic emotions of the Care/harm foundation are compassion and empathy. That is, the objects and/or situations in the social world, in the original and current domains, which prompt response patterns in this foundation or sub-domain, more often than not trigger feelings of compassion and empathy.

For the purposes of this chapter, illustrating one of the "moral foundations" is sufficient to see how sub-domain response patterns may be preconscious, that is, how they may begin from a lightning quick recognition and appraisal, through a neural short-cut to the limbic system, before conscious awareness assembles and coalesces through different processing pathways. The response pattern is certainly cognitive; it is simply not from its beginning conscious.

Still, insofar as MFT, in combination with Haidt's (2001, 2012) Social Intuitionist Model (SIM), is taken to describe the bases of all ethical functioning, without distinguishing between ideal and contra-ideal functioning, it is liable to critique. MacIntyre (1981, Ch. 5) argued that the Enlightenment project for justifying morality was bound to fail because moral norms cannot be justified by reference only to untutored, untransformed human nature. In the Aristotelian scheme, the purpose of moral norms is their role in guiding the transformation of human nature, given at birth or as it happens to be, to optimal functioning and flourishing. But in the wake of the collapse of the Aristotelian teleological system in natural philosophy in the 16th and 17th Centuries, moral theorists began to reject teleological thinking in ethical philosophy as well (see esp. Hobbes, 1994/1651). Moral Foundations Theory plus the Social Intuitionist Model seem to refer only to a human nature produced by evolution, "given at birth," not to human personality or character transformed to virtue and capability for human flourishing. To put it differently, with MFT and SIM

Haidt is trying to describe *typical moral functioning*, not give a normative account of *optimal functioning*. To the extent that Haidt and Joseph (2007) do describe a virtue-centered ethics, they describe an ethics like that of arch-Enlightenment thinker, Hume (1978/1739–40), whose account of human nature and ethics is not teleological and, according to MacIntyre, suffers the fate of all Enlightenment attempts to justify morality (see MacIntyre, 1989).

Designating genuinely *moral* foundations, which are tuned up so as to foster flourishing, requires allusion at least to an account of optimal functioning. Ignitions and controlled explosions are not the onsets of and continued propulsion for a trip unless we understand them in the context of guidance toward some destination. The proper level of organization on which to locate optimal functioning is not the physiological level of initial onsets but instead the conscious level of moral self-motivation.

THE MORAL SELF-MOTIVATION MODEL DESCRIBES IDEAL CONSCIOUS FUNCTIONING

Blasi (see esp. Blasi 1980, 1983, 1988, 1993, 1999a, 1999b, 2004a, 2004b, 2005a, 2005b, 2009) and Nunner-Winkler (1993, 1999, 2007, 2008, 2009, this volume; Nunner-Winkler et al., 2007) have conducted a series of studies toward constructing a Kantian or neo-Kantian psychological model of moral motivation (see also Bergman, 2002). We might call it the moral self-motivation model. According to this model, moral knowledge and moral motivation not only are distinct conceptually; they also are separate in the lives especially of young children but also of a substantial minority of adults. At a relatively young age (4–6 years), children seem to know some simple, concrete moral rules (don't take what is not yours; don't kick or bite; etc.), which they hold to be valid everywhere, regardless of what the local rules are or what authorities say (see Turiel, 1979, 1983, 2002, 2006; Turiel et al., 1987). They are able, upon questioning, to distinguish these moral rules from concrete social conventions (boys don't wear dresses; children don't call their teachers by their first names; etc.), which they realize may not be valid everywhere and depend on what the local rules are and/or what authorities say.

However, if the LOGIC longitudinal sample (see Nunner-Winkler, 2009, this volume) is representative, about 70% of 5 year old children exhibit relatively low motivation or commitment to following concrete moral norms. They think they and others would feel good when violating a concrete moral norm if it gets them something they want, suggesting that their enjoyment and self-appraisal are more strongly influenced by fulfillment of personal desires than by fulfillment of moral duties. But this high proportion of children with low moral motivation decreases steadily at measurement points with children aged 7 years, 9 years, 18 years, and 23 years (Nunner-Winkler, 2009). About 18% of 23 year olds in their longitudinal sample exhibit low moral motivation. Also, only about 14% of 5 year olds exhibit high moral motivation, but this increases steadily to about 47% of 23 year olds.[2]

Sex differences in moral motivation appeared at age 9 and increased at age 18 (Nunner-Winkler, 2009). The difference was accounted for by differences in gender identification when matched with morally relevant gender stereotypes. According to responses of subjects in the study, the traits commonly associated with being a "true [or real] man" tend toward pursuit of personal interests over the good of others, where the opposite is the case in traits associated with being a "true [or real] woman." So the boys who more highly identified with their gender stereotype tended to be lower in moral motivation, whereas the girls who were more highly gender identified tended to be higher in moral motivation. Nonetheless, there were no significant sex differences in the lists of traits identified by the children as those of the ideal self or of the ideal life partner and thus apparently no significant sex differences in understandings of morality.

So, moral motivation tends to increase with age especially when role expectations are consistent with a high regard for the interests of others. Such changes in moral motivation can be explained by reference to the emerging organization of one's identity (self-identification) – including but not only gender identification – along moral lines. Doing what one morally ought, and being the sort of person for whom being moral is second nature, may become a central part of one's integrity as a person, who one really is.

How does moral identity develop? According to Blasi (2004b), the main themes include the development of agency and the agentic construction of identity upon moral values and ideals. Early processes concern agency. In an infant's earliest experience in the first year of life (Blasi, 2004b), she begins to recognize that she controls certain physical movements and that these movements are distinct from things that happen to her or that she only observes happening. She also wants or desires some things and wants to avoid or prevent others. These experiences of the earliest forms of agency correspond to two sets of processes fundamental to the formation of the self. One is self-mastery, or the self-control of organismic processes and impulses and the self-regulation of actions and emotions. The other is self-appropriation, or the hierarchical structuring of one's desires, volitions, and commitments through affirming and claiming some and denying and rejecting others. Self-mastery (self-control and self-regulation) concerns what we feel and do on any occasion. But self-appropriation (affirming/claiming and denying/rejecting) shapes who we are. One might say, "yes, I admit that I did that intentionally (lied to my partner, stole from my employer, yelled at my child, etc.), but that's not who I am." Through affirming some and rejecting other impulses, actions, and commitments, we form our identities.

Blasi and colleagues (Blasi, 1993; Blasi & Glodis, 1995; Glodis & Blasi, 1993; Blasi & Milton, 1991; Blasi & Oresick, 1986) conducted studies of the development of identity, based on the accounts of Erikson (1968) and Loevinger (1976). They found the following about the growing sense of self: in their samples, typical 11–12 year olds (pre- or early-adolescents) are not conscious of a self as an inner core of themselves. For them, being phony or betraying themselves means interfering with or interrupting the activities they like in order to conform to social expectations or peer pressure. Some 17–18 year olds (middle-adolescents), by contrast, are conscious of an inner self constituted by the spontaneous feelings and perceptions they experience as simply given. They are being phony or betraying themselves when they fail to express these feelings and perceptions outwardly in their behaviour. On the other hand, some adults (25–39 years old in their sample) are conscious of a self and identity consisting of the deeper values and ideals which they affirm and claim. These self-appropriated ideals and values constitute their integrity as moral persons, because these adults maintain and manage their ideal- and value-related characteristics and commitments as aspects of themselves for which they are especially responsible. For them, self-betrayal involves failure to maintain this responsibility to uphold their own core values.

Though the self-conscious maintenance of identity does not seem to occur until late adolescence or adulthood, the precursors begin much earlier. Blasi's (see esp. 1993, p. 117, 2004b, p. 13; 2005b, p. 89) account may be summarized as follows: before a child is conscious of an inner self that is the core of her identity, let alone before she feels responsible for its content, she engages in interactions that may provide her with "concrete sensual experiences…of the good of moral actions" (2005b, p. 89; a full account would need to say more here than Blasi offers). The opposite may of course be the case, and all manner of variations. Early on she processes these experiences largely unreflectively, in some ways consciously yet un-self-consciously. In these experiences, she encounters requests and rules, then role-based duties, and eventually moral obligations. Some she feels to be external expectations, imposed though perhaps voluntarily complied with. But some she appropriates as expectations she comes to have of herself. In childhood and early- and middle-adolescence she is not conscious of control over these self-expectations. They are just given. But by late adolescence or early adulthood she may begin self-consciously to take responsibility for the rules, duties, and obligations to which she holds herself accountable (This is likely related to the shift from conventional to post-conventional morality on a Kohlbergian scheme).

In the advanced, self-conscious phases of these processes of "structuring a morality based will" (Blasi, 2005b, p. 89), she will need to accomplish three sorts of task: to claim selectively, as her own, moral values and ethical ideals, while rejecting values and ideals at cross-purposes with those; to control and cultivate her impulses and emotions so that they at least do not prevent her realizing her values and ideals; and to acquire first-order and second-order desires (Frankfurt, 1971, 1987, 1988) and virtues, in the process turning her impulses and emotions to the service of her values and ideals. The first of these is what Blasi (2004b) describes as self-appropriation. The second and third are beyond self-appropriation, proceeding by two further steps.

Blasi (1999b) has sketched an account of emotion control along the following lines: spontaneous emotions spring from non- or pre-conscious needs and impulses.[3] The emotions prompt activity aimed at satisfaction of needs and impulses and first-order desires. We develop toward these spontaneous emotions (through processes mentioned in the summary two paragraphs earlier) certain reflexive, second-order desires, that is, desires that our emotions should be of certain sorts and be expressed in certain ways rather than others. Our reflexive desires motivate control of spontaneous emotions. These second-order desires depend on core concerns we have, such as the concerns to avoid harm and punishment, to pursue achievement and status, to do what is right, and/or to be consistent with our core values and ideals. As a contingent practical matter, if and to the extent that these concerns are priority ordered, as represented in our second-order desires, there will be a regular pattern of resolution when concerns and/or desires conflict, say, when a concern for achievement and status conflicts with a concern for helping others. The "morality based will" (Blasi, 2005b, p. 89) originates in self-appropriated core concerns which are arranged and activated as hierarchically ordered reflexive desires, which in turn motivate control of spontaneous emotions, so that at least these emotions do not prevent moral conduct, and ideally they foster it.

Not only is Blasi's (1999b) account of emotion regulation focused on the will, but also he (2005b) has outlined a will-centered account of virtue (see Blasi 2005b, p. 82, Table 2, Steps in the Development of the Moral Will). On this account (see p. 71, Table 1, List of Moral Virtues), the moral will is represented in a set of lower-order virtues, such as empathy and compassion, fairness and justice, loyalty and friendship, obedience and respectfulness, law-abidingness and civic-mindedness, and conscientiousness (compare the moral foundations in Table 2 above, from Haidt, 2012). In Kantian (1994/1785 & 1797) fashion, virtue is conceived as resoluteness of the will to conform to moral duty in various sub-domains. Blasi (2005b) adds a set of higher-order virtues, not strictly moral, but skills, like memory or intelligence. They include a "will cluster" and an "integrity cluster." In the will cluster, perseverance and determination are virtues of will for moving forward, whereas self-discipline and self-control are virtues of will for holding back. Resoluteness in moving forward might of course include moving forward with mass murder, and resoluteness in holding back might include inhibiting sympathetic response to one's victims. The integrity cluster includes responsibility and accountability (for honouring one's commitments), self-consistency (for seeking coherent organization of one's commitments), and integrity (for the unity of one's subjective sense of self).

A proper structuring of the will is at the same time a shaping and reforming of the passions. As some first-order desires, spontaneous emotions, and concerns are claimed and integrated, while others are disowned and rejected, a hierarchy of desires and concerns is constructed. Through self-appropriation of impulses, emotions, and first-order desires that support morality, one can develop a well-ordered and integrated set of core moral concerns and second-order desires so that inclinations serve rather than detract from moral actions and projects.

THE PURPOSE OF MORAL MOTIVATION

So Kant and Blasi emphasize what guides us: deliberate conscious willing – represented by braking, steering, and navigating in our opening simile. Hume and

Haidt emphasize what gets us and keeps us moving: pre-conscious cognitive and physiological processes – ignition and propulsion in our simile. Each is inadequate without the other, and on this Hume and Kant agree. Neither Hume nor Kant, however, offers much of an account of what we move for – both our destination and the broader purpose of our travels (see Hume, 1978/1739–40, pp. 620–621; and see Kant, 1994/1797, p. 480). This is Aristotle's emphasis (and it is explored by Haidt, 2006). We are motivated to be moral, on an Aristotelian account, to the extent that we recognize that the disciplines morality requires foster (without guaranteeing) flourishing. From this perspective, Hume and Kant, Haidt and Blasi, focus on different levels of person functioning both of which are essential for moral motivation for human flourishing. We get moving and navigate our route because there is somewhere we want to be.

The idea that being moral is required for and fosters flourishing is different from three other notions of morality that do not mention flourishing per se, that (a) morality consists of imperatives that are intrinsically binding irrespective of consequences (rather than instrumental), that (b) being moral is being pro-social or altruistic (rather than selfish), and that (c) being moral is required for maximizing pleasure and minimizing pain. There is something to each of these three notions, but they may best be understood as aspects of the broader Aristotelian construal (though a full defense of this suggestion is beyond the scope of the current chapter). According to such a construal, morality is caring reciprocal interaction guided by the minimal and/or optimal conditions of personal wellbeing and cooperation for mutual flourishing. The very definition of morality requires reference to ideal or optimal person functioning and its aim, human flourishing. A brief explanation of the components of this definition can help show its role in reconciling the accounts of Blasi and Haidt.

On this definition, mutual flourishing ("the good") is the purpose or end of morality ("the right"). The simple answer to the question, "Why be moral?" is that only if one is moral can one flourish. Flourishing cannot, of course, be a matter merely of gratification of one's untrained (spontaneous and un-self-appropriated) desires and appetites, for such gratification can be and is accomplished through immorality. We might think of Plato's characters, Thrasymachus (in *Republic*) and Callicles (in *Gorgias*), and a contemporary equivalent, Gordon Gekko (in the 1987 film, "Wall Street," and its 2010 sequel). So if the goal of life is not gratification, what constitutes flourishing?

Enlightenment and post-Enlightenment intellectuals in the West rejected traditional notions of flourishing and came to define morality by reference to minimum conditions for the possibility of flourishing on [almost] any understanding of it, and this understanding became embedded in formal legal systems in Western nation-states (see MacIntyre, 1981, 1989).[4] So, for instance, if family and friendships of various sorts are essential on [almost] any understanding of flourishing, then the minimum requirements of fostering family and friend relationships are universal moral requirements. Universally and irrespective of culture, one must not lie to family and friends, not steal from or short-change them, and not use unprovoked violence against them. Individuals came to be understood as endowed with rights against being treated these ways. These rights (as minimum conditions) may be extended to larger and larger domains beyond family and friends, to one's ethnic group or community, to one's motherland, to the point of a concept of universal human rights (see Reed, 2008, on the extrapolation of concrete reciprocity to an abstract ideal and a universal principle).

On the other hand, those committed to revealed and/or traditional norms and worldviews – to whom the norms and worldviews of out-groups seem other and defective relative to their own – went another way (the account here is similar but not identical to Haidt's, 2012, account of the contrast between liberals and conservatives). Their moralities have typically been a matter of optimal conditions for mutual flourishing. For instance, one must not only respect the minimum conditions for the possibility of good relations with family and friends (not lying, cheating, or assaulting). One must also do the things that foster such relations, such as spending time together, sharing common interests, enjoying shared activities, making sacrifices for each other, and experiencing personal and social intimacies not shared with others (see Aristotle, 1999/350 bce, Bk. IX, Ch. 4). One is required to do the things that foster good relationships, not merely refrain from doing the things that tend to destroy them. One is also required to become and be the sort of person who habitually does such things. So moralities requiring optimal and not only minimal conditions are filled with virtues, and not only rules, and primarily with duties to others.

Also, moral requirements include self-regulating self-disciplines and not only the imperative to respect the rights of others to non-interference and informed consent. You are obliged to become and be patient, temperate, and honest with yourself, for instance, whether these help others or yourself directly on specific occasions or not, because on the whole and for the most part they do. And though not all conservatives or traditionalists have been able to put it this way, some have noticed the irony in the liberal transcendence to an objective, neutral, multi-cultural worldview which has condemned revealed and traditional norms and worldviews as other and defective relative to the liberal paradigm.

Morality properly understood, therefore, fosters (without guaranteeing) flourishing through self-regulating self-disciplines and cooperative, mutually beneficial practices. It is the ground-rules (recall MacIntyre, 1981, Ch. 5) for the kind of shared life in which children are raised so that they will be able to engage in the types of relationships and practices that foster flourishing. Our understandings of what morality makes mandatory vary from the more minimal to the more comprehensive, depending on how liberty-centered and thin, or community-centred and thick, is a community's notion of what is normal/typical and normative/enforceable in promoting human flourishing. Nonetheless, it is possible to articulate some general features of human flourishing on [almost] any account.

Haidt (2006) summarizes results of research by social and positive psychologists as they relate to the components of happiness or human flourishing. His top six list follows Aristotle's (1999/ca. 350 bce) top five to a remarkable degree, despite Haidt's (2012) professed debts to Hume in his MFT. We need (a) "companionate love" and genuine friendships; (b) "vital engagements," or activities we find challenging and engaging that draw on our strengths; (c) an adequate minimum of material resources, but not too much, since both too little and too much lead to types of striving that are inconsistent with satisfaction with enough; (d) virtues, i.e., good habits and moderate desires so that by second-nature we tend to act automatically (without on-the-spot conscious deliberation) in ways that lead to flourishing; (e) good balances in our lives and communities between constraints and freedom and between commonality and diversity, and (f) the kind of self-awareness that enables us to notice our own biases and faults even though we are typically quick to point out hypocritically the biases and faults of others. Aristotle (1999/ca. 350 bce) himself affirms (a) – (d) and adds another: (g) good luck, so that we are not ruined by undeserved misfortune and we can live in conditions in which flourishing is possible with the right effort. Though Haidt (2006) discusses Aristotle on virtue, it is not completely clear he realizes how closely the findings he reports follow Aristotle's account of what is required for flourishing.

Haidt (2006) singles out two of these as most important: relationships and vital engagements. Notice briefly part of what the first these requires. To enjoy the types of relationships that make life meaningful and worthwhile, one must among other things cultivate "companionate love" and not be fooled into the "myth of 'true' love":

> True love is passionate love that never fades; if you are in true love, you should marry that person; if love ends, you should leave that person because it was not true love; and if you can find the right person, you will have true love forever. (Haidt, 2006, p. 124)

But, as Haidt (2006, pp. 124–128) argues, passionate love for a particular person (some combination of lust for and infatuation with that person) inevitably fades, and so "'true' love" is bound to fail. What has to happen for some of one's relationships not to be ruined by passionate love and the false hope of "'true' love"? One needs appealing, good models of companionate love as a child, traits of character that enable one to modulate one's spontaneous desires, impulses, and emotions, and some before-the-fact awareness and/or in-the-moment circumspection about the enthralling character of lust and infatuation and their inevitable fading. So some of what is important comes early in the processes of the formation of the self that Blasi describes. Some is from the conscious self-regulation, reflection, and discernment the affected individual can muster in the moment.

We can see another instance of the complementarity between Haidt's and Blasi's accounts in the case of the Care/harm foundation, as an instance of the other foundations. According to MFT, you and I exhibit evolved, pre-conscious response patterns in our encounters with objects and situations in our social worlds. They stem from various original domains in which quick and consistent responses were adaptive, but they now extend to wider domains of objects and situations. For instance, we may care about cruelty to dependent domesticated animals (the work of PETA comes to mind) or the depraved conditions of children quite remote from us who are conscripted into sexual slavery or brutal warfare (think again of KONY2012). But MFT has not so far explained why the current or wider domain of each moral foundation should or would ideally be shaped in one way rather than another. Why care about cruelty to animals or remote child sex slaves and child soldiers? Nothing in the evolution of the original domain of the Care/harm foundation requires that we care, and the account of the current or wider domain only explains how the original domain may be extended, or not, to others than vulnerable kin. MFT helps us understand *how* we are moved to care, through pre-conscious response patterns, but processes like "concrete sensual experiences …of the good of moral acts" (Blasi, 2005b, p. 89) and self-appropriation are involved in why we may have come to care, and some understanding of how this caring is related to caring reciprocal interaction for mutual flourishing is needed.

NATURAL MORAL REASON

There is still the question left from earlier concerning the primacy in morality of reason or passion. For Hume (1739–40 & 1751, and perhaps Haidt), we are sensitive beings who are capable of reasoning, but passion is primary. For Kant (1785 & 1797, and perhaps Blasi), we are rational beings who also have a sensual nature, but reason is primary. My argument in this chapter needs an account of reason that shows how neither reason nor passion is primary per se but that they are [ideally] two levels of an integrated functioning, an account which makes reason neither a non-natural faculty nor a natural but merely calculating faculty. Within the limits of this chapter, I can give only a sketch, but here is a start: We are natural social beings with complex capacities not only for first-order representations of objects and situations in our social worlds as stimuli for our responses, but also for second-order representations or meta-representations which enable us to consider our first-order representations and would-be responses as themselves objects for response. Such a social-pragmatist, symbolic interactionist account was offered by G.H. Mead (1934) and taken up by Kohlberg (1984/1969) in his revisions of Piaget (1932) (see Reed, 2008).

In recent moral psychology, moral reasoning has often been construed as the formulation and/or justification of judgments about what it is morally right to do in individual cases. This typically involves appeal to concrete moral rules and abstract moral principles. Some (including Haidt, 2001, 2012) suggest that this role of moral reasoning is merely or mostly post hoc, involving the invention of rationalizing accounts of actions for which we feel held accountable to others or ourselves. Such rationalization likely only performs its function, however, on the presumption that the primary function of moral reasoning is justification, the way a false smile (which is not recognizably mocking or ironic) only works on the presumption that it means what a genuine smile would mean in the circumstances.

Moral reasoning is a normal activity of natural social beings with our human capacities. Mead (1934) described the difference between the impulsive, biologic individual and the rational, socially self-conscious individual as follows:

It would be a mistake to assume that a man is a biologic individual plus a reason, if we mean by this definition that he leads two separable lives, one of impulse or instinct, and another of reason – especially if we assume that the control exercised by reason proceeds by means of ideas considered as mental contents which do not arise within the impulsive life and form a real part thereof. On the contrary, the whole drift of modern psychology has been toward an undertaking to bring will and reason within the impulsive life. The undertaking may not have been fully successful, but it has been impossible to avoid the attempt to bring reason within the scope of evolution; and if this attempt is successful, *rational conduct must grow out of impulsive conduct.* My own attempt will be to show that it is in the social behaviour of the human animal that this evolution takes place. (1934, pp. 347–348, emphasis added)

Only a brief summary of the relevant portions of Mead's (1934) account in the "Supplementary essays" to *Mind, self, and society* can be given here, but it can suggest how we should rethink the relationship between reason and passion in moral psychology.

The biologic individual lives in the immediate now, being present in the moment. It lives by its impulses (more flexible than instincts, by which "lower" animals live), and when it is brought up short, it shifts back and forth among impulses, until a solution is happened upon. But the socially self-conscious individual lives in a flow of time between a fixed past, in which it has adjusted to its world, adjusting impulses to objects that come to be their stimuli, in something like self-appropriation, and an uncertain future. The socially self-conscious individual also lives by its impulses, but it is able to reflect upon them (and we might add its intuitions, judgments, actions, habits, etc.) as objects, to hold them at a distance in the manner suggested by Blasi (1999b). The socially self-conscious individual does not say "yes" or "no" to impulses from some standpoint outside the impulsive life. "Control over impulse lies only in the shift of attention which brings other objects into the field of stimulation, setting free other impulses, or in such a resetting of the objects that the impulses express themselves on a different time schedule or with additions and subtractions" (Mead, 1934, p. 367, see p. 351). Recall the way some children in Mischel's (1974; Mischel et al., 1972; Shoda et al., 1990) marshmallow test of delayed gratification looked away or employed other self-diversion techniques, trying to redirect their attention from the marshmallow in front of them in order to resist the impulse to eat it too soon, before the wait to have the second marshmallow added had elapsed. The socially self-conscious individual controls impulses by refocusing its attention to other stimuli which prompt other impulses – and in that it is similar to the biologic individual shifting back and forth among impulses. But there is a difference.

On Mead's (1934) account, the self consists in large part of the organization of the responses of others to oneself as responses one comes to have to oneself. One responds to herself as she has learned others respond to her in similar circumstances, including not only immediate emotional responses and utterances but also expectations, rules, and moral obligations (Mead's, 1934, "generalized other"). The self takes the attitude of others toward herself, responding to herself, by implicitly representing her impulses and hypothetical action-scenarios to herself, responding to them as objects. Though Mead did not put it this way, the self makes meta-representations to which it can respond. Reflection, as reasoning, consists of one's representing to oneself one's organized reaction to a stimulus (an object calling out a response, from an impulse seeking expression, from an attitude) in such a way that he responds to his represented organized reaction as he has learned others respond to himself. This is made concretely possible early in life through what Mead calls the vocal gesture. The young child vocalizes his thoughts to himself, which calls out in the child the responses he has experienced to be called out in others. For instance, the child's fearful words are followed by a parent's soothing words uttered by the child himself, or the child's consideration of a forbidden action is followed by the child's vocalization of the parent's words of prohibition. In this way, the young child shifts his attention and the objects of his attention, calling out alternative impulses, by taking the attitude of another on himself through vocalization (which will eventually be internalized as silent thought).

The socially self-conscious child begins such reflective processes implicitly but is eventually able to conduct them explicitly, when her meta-representations are realized consciously and articulated formally. It is not that she is not an impulsive individual, or that she is an impulsive individual plus a reason – let alone that she is rational and also, incidentally, impulsive. She is rational just to the extent that she is capable of reflecting on both her impulses and her would-be actions as themselves material for evaluation, as she has learned in her household, community, and culture that such impulses and actions are valued.

CONCLUSION

We get moving (ignitions and controlled explosions) and guide ourselves along our route (braking, steering, and navigating) because there is somewhere we want to be (destination and broader purpose of our travels). An account of moral motivation needs to account for how we get moving, for how we guide our moving, and for what we move for. Haidt's MFT with its account of pre-conscious response patterns in sub-domains of morality can help us understand the first. Blasi's model of moral self-motivation and the role of deliberate conscious agency in modulating emotions and in willing can help us understand the second. And an account of human flourishing, as discussed by Haidt (2006) and Aristotle, supplemented by Mead's account of natural reason, helps us understand the third. Moral motivation is at least a bi-level phenomenon (conscious agency and pre-conscious physiological activation), involving the coordination of processes on different levels of person functioning. And what look like rival and incompatible accounts – Blasi's and Haidt's – are accounts of different levels of person functioning the insights of which should be saved in a comprehensive multi-level account.

NOTES

[1] Correspondence may be addressed to Don Collins Reed; Department of Philosophy; Wittenberg University; Springfield, Ohio U.S.A.; dreed@wittenberg.edu. I am grateful for the support of Wittenberg University for a 2010–2011 sabbatical during which research for this chapter was conducted and for comments on an earlier draft of this chapter by Larry Walker and Darcia Narvaez.

[2] These trends in the study population, however, were in spite of individual variability in change of moral motivation. At each age interval after 7 years old, about 40–45% of the children showed no change from their earlier high, middle, or low moral motivation level; about 30–35% showed an increase in moral motivation; and about 20–25% showed a decrease. So the clear age-trend of increasing moral motivation in the population as a whole was not mirrored in most individual trajectories.

[3] Blasi (1999b, p. 11) uses "motives" here, but I substitute "impulses" to eliminate the redundancy of having motives motivate by giving rise to emotions as motivational responses.

[4] Hume, Kant, and J.S. Mill are three of the most famous representatives of Enlightenment in Western moral philosophy.

REFERENCES

Aristotle (1999/ca. 350 bce). *Nicomachean ethics* (abbreviated EN, for *Ethica Nicomachea*). Indianapolis: Hackett Publishing Co.

Bergman, R. (2002). Why be moral? A conceptual model from developmental psychology. *Human Development, 45*, 104-124.

Blasi, A. (1980). Bridging moral cognition and moral action: A critical review of the literature. *Psychological Bulletin, 88*, 1–45.

Blasi, A. (1983). Moral cognition and moral action: A theoretical perspective. *Developmental Review, 3*, 178–210.

Blasi, A. (1988). Identity and the development of the self. In D.K. Lapsley & F.C. Power (Eds.), *Self, ego, and identity: Integrative approaches* (pp. 211–225). New York: Springer Verlag.

Blasi, A.(1993). The development of identity: Some implications for moral functioning. In G.G. Noam & T.E. Wren (Eds.), *The moral self* (pp. 99–122). New Baskerville: MIT Press.

Blasi, A. (1999a). Comment: Caring about morality: The development of moral motivation in Nunner-Winkler's work. In F.E. Weinert & W. Schneider (Eds.) *Individual development from 3 to 12: Findings from the Munich longitudinal study* (pp. 291–300).New York: Cambridge University Press.

Blasi, A. (1999b).Emotions and moral motivation. *Journal of the Theory of Social Behaviour, 29*, 1–19.

Blasi, A. (2004a). Moral functioning: Moral understanding and personality. In D.K. Lapsley & D. Narvaez (Eds.), *Moral development, self, and identity* (pp. 335–347). Mahway, New Jersey: Lawrence Earlbaum.

Blasi, A.(2004b). Neither personality nor cognition: An alternative approach to the nature of the self. In C. Lightfoot, C. Lalonde, & M. Chandler (Eds.), *Changing conceptions of psychological life* (pp. 3–25). Mahway, New Jersey: Lawrence Earlbaum.

Blasi, A. (2005a). What should count as moral behavior? The nature of "early morality" in children's development. In W. Edelstein & G. Nunner-Winkler (Eds.), *Morality in context* (pp. 119–120). New York: Elsevier.

Blasi, A. (2005b) Moral character: A psychological approach. In D.K. Lapsley & F.C. Power (Eds.), *Character psychology and character education* (pp. 18–35). Notre Dame, Indiana: University of Notre Dame Press

Blasi, A. (2009) The moral functioning of mature adults and the possibility of fair moral reasoning. In D. Narvaez and D.K. Lapsley (Eds.), *Personality, identity, and character: Explorations in moral psychology* (pp. 396–440). New York: Cambridge University Press.

Blasi, A., & Glodis, K. (1995). The development of identity: A critical analysis from the perspective of the self as subject. *Developmental Review, 15,* 404–433.

Blasi, A., & Milton, K. (1991).The development of the sense of self in adolescence. *Journal of Personality, 59,* 217–241.

Blasi, A., & Oresick, R.J. (1986). Emotions and cognition in self-inconsistency. In D. Bearison & H. Zimiles (Eds.), *Thought and emotion* (pp. 214–263). Hillsdale, New Jersey: Lawrence Earlbaum.

Diamond, J.M. (1999). *Guns, germs, and steel: The fates of human societies.* New York: W.W. Norton.

Erikson, E.H. (1968). *Identity, youth, and crisis.* New York: Norton.

Fischer, K.W., & Bidell, T.R. (2006). Dynamic development of action and thought. In W. Damon & R.M. Lerner (Eds.), *Handbook of child psychology, Vol .One. Theoretical models of human development* (pp. 313–399). Hoboken, New Jersey: John Wiley & Sons.

Frankfurt, H. (1971). Freedom of the will and the concept of a person. *The Journal of Philosophy, 68,* 5–20

Frankfurt, H. (1987). Identification and wholeheartedness. In F. Schoeman (Ed.), *Responsibility, character, and emotions: New essays in moral psychology* (pp. 27–45). New York: Cambridge University Press.

Frankfurt, H. (1988). *The importance of what we care about.* New York: Cambridge University Press.

Glodis, K.A., & Blasi, A. (1993). The sense of self and identity among adolescents and adults.*Journal of adolescent research, 8*(4), 356–380.

Haidt, J. (2012). *The righteous mind.* New York: Pantheon.

Haidt, J. (2006). *The happiness hypothesis.* New York: Basic Books.

Haidt, J. (2001). The emotional dog and its rational tail: A social intuitionist approach to moral judgment. *Psychological Review, 108,* 814–834.

Haidt, J., & Joseph, C. (2007). The moral mind: How five sets of innate intuitions guide the development of many culture-specific virtues and perhaps even modules. In P. Carruthers, S. Laurence & S. Stich (Eds.), *The innate mind* (Vol. 3, pp. 367–391). New York: Oxford University Press.

Haidt, J. & Joseph, C. (2004). Intuitive ethics: How innately prepared intuitions generate culturally variable virtues. *Daedalus, 133*(44), 55–66.

Haidt, J., & Bjorklund, F. (2008). Social intuitionists answer six questions about morality. In W. Sinnott-Armstrong (Ed.), *Moral psychology, Vol. 2: The cognitive science of morality* (pp. 181–217). Cambridge, Massachusetts: MIT Press.

Hobbes, T. (1994/1651). *Leviathan.* Indianapolis: Hackett Publishing Co.

Hume, D. (1978/1739–40). *A treatise of human nature.* New York: Oxford University Press.

Hume, D. (1983/1751). *An enquiry concerning the principle of morals.* Indianapolis: Hackett Publishing Co.

Kant, I. (1994/1785 & 1797). *Grounding for the metaphysics of morals* and excerpts from *The metaphysics of morals,* in *Ethical philosophy* (2nd ed.). Indianapolis: Hackett Publishing Co.

Kim, M., & Sankey, D. (2009) Towards a dynamic systems approach to moral development and moral education: A response to the *JME* Special Issue, September 2008. *Journal of Moral Education, 38*(3), 283–298.

Kohlberg, L. (1981). *The philosophy of moral development.* New York: Harper & Row.

Kohlberg, L. (1984).*The psychology of moral development.* New York: Harper & Row.

Loevinger, J. (1976). *Ego development: Conceptions and theories.* San Francisco: Jossey-Bass.

MacIntyre, A.C. (1981). *After virtue.* South Bend, Indiana: University of Notre Dame Press.

MacIntyre, A.C. (1989). *Whose justice? Which rationality?* South Bend, Indiana: University of Notre Dame Press.

Mead, G.H. (1934). *Mind, self, and society.* Chicago: University of Chicago Press. (see especially Supplementary Essays, pp. 337–378)

Mischel, W. (1974). Processes in delay of gratification. In L. Berkowitz (Ed.), *Advances in experimental social psychology* (Vol. 7, pp. 249–292). San Diego, CA: Academic Press.

Mischel, W, Ebbesen, E.B., & Zeiss, A.R. (1972). Cognitive and attentional mechanisms in delay of gratification. *Journal of Personality and Social Psychology, 21,* 204–21

Nunner-Winkler, G. (2009). Moral motivation from childhood to early adulthood. In W. Schneider & M. Bullock (Eds.), *Human development from early childhood to early adulthood: Findings from a 20 year longitudinal study* (pp. 91–118). New York. Psychology Press.

Nunner-Winkler, G. (2008). "From super-ego and conformist habitus to ego-syntonic moral motivation. Sociohistoric changes in moral motivation." *European Journal of Developmental Science, 2*(3), 251–268.

Nunner-Winkler, G. (2007). Development of moral motivation from childhood to early adulthood. *Journal of Moral Education, 36*(4), 399–414.

Nunner-Winkler, G. (1999).The development of moral understanding and moral motivation. In F.E. Weinert& W. Schneider (Eds.), *Individual development from 3 to 12: Findings from the Munich Longitudinal Study* (pp. 253–290). New York. Cambridge Univ. Press.

Nunner-Winkler, G. (1993). The growth of moral motivation. In G. Noam & T. Wren (Eds.), *The moral self* (pp. 269–291). Cambridge, Massachusetts. MIT Press.

Nunner-Winkler, G., Meyer-Nikele, M., & Wohlrab, D. (2007). Gender differences in moral motivation. *Merrill-Palmer Quarterly, 53*(1), 26–52

Piaget, J. (1997/1932). *The moral judgment of the child*. New York: Free Press.

Ramachandran, V.S. (2011). *The tell-tale brain*. New York: W.W. Norton & Company.

Reed, D.C. (2008) A model of moral stages. *Journal of Moral Education, 37*(3), 357–376.

Reed, D.C. (1997). *Following Kohlberg: Liberalism and the practice of democratic community*. Notre Dame, Indiana: University of Notre Dame Press.

Shoda, Y., Mischel, W., & Peake, P.K. (1990). Predicting adolescent cognitive and self-regulatory competencies from preschool delay of gratification: Identifying diagnostic conditions. *Developmental Psychology, 26*(6), 978–986.

Thelen, E., & Smith, L.B. (1994). *A dynamic systems approach to the development of cognition and action*. Cambridge, Massachusetts: MIT Press.

Turiel, E. (2006). The development of morality. In W. Damon and R.M. Lerner (Eds.), *Handbook of child psychology* (pp. 789–856). Hoboken, New Jersey: John Wiley & Sons.

Turiel, E. (2002). *The culture of morality*. New York: Cambridge University Press.

Turiel, E. (1983). *The development of social knowledge: Morality and convention*. New York: Cambridge University Press.

Turiel, E. (1979). Distinct conceptual and developmental domains: Social convention and morality. In C.B. Keasy (Ed.), *Nebraska symposium on motivation* (Vol. 25, pp. 77–116). Lincoln, Nebraska: University of Nebraska Press.

Turiel, E., Killen, M., & Helwig, C.C. (1987). Morality: Its structure, functions, and vagaries. In J. Kagan and S. Lamb (Eds.), *The emergence of morality in young children* (pp. 155–243). Chicago: University of Chicago Press.

Witherington, D.C. (2007). The dynamic systems approach as metatheory for developmental psychology, *Human Development, 50*(2/3), 127–153.

Trivers, R.L. (1971). The evolution of reciprocal altruism. *Quarterly Review of Biology, 46*, 35–57.

AFFILIATION

Don Collins Reed
Department of Philosophy
Wittenberg University
Springfield, Ohio, USA

PART 5

GOOD AND BAD MORAL MOTIVATION

It is interesting that moral motivation is related to doing the good but also to omitting moral necessities. In this part, different approaches provide fundamental ideas on how to consider, deliberate and study the motivation to act in both directions. Some of these chapters focus on how moral motivation might emerge, while others focus on how a lack of moral motivation might emerge, or if morality is intentionally omitted.

Beerthuizen and Brugman proclaim that the newly developed concept of moral value evaluation influences one's moral cognition which, in turn, shapes behaviour. Via structure equation modelling, they confirm moral value evaluation as an (indirect) predictor of externalizing behaviour. Additionally, self-serving cognitive distortions were identified as the strongest associates of immoral behaviour.

Weyers provides an outstanding qualitative interview study of adolescent criminals reconstructing their offences and their biographies. He tries to illustrate that there are different ways in which the young integrate moral and motivational aspects in the way they explicate themselves as offenders: some of them really lack moral motivation, while others hopefully could change their identities and increase moral motivation in future.

Power points out that the context of sports is highly relevant to moral issues and moral motivation, granted that it is a domain where fairness and moral aspects are struggling with motives of competition. We could assume that athletes do not primarily engage in sports in order to care about others, but to enjoy their sports or to win. Obviously, one can engage in sports morally or immorally and situational as well as cultural determinants influence how athletes behave.

Grün explicates his idea of ethical hostility. This concept mainly stresses that even if people seem to be highly motivated owing to moral issues, sometimes there are other "non-moral" drivers behind triggering "moral behaviour" because of "non-moral" reasons. Moreover, he proposes that sometimes fear could motivate individuals to hide their hostile interests or emotions behind moral language and moral action.

Klöckner provides an overview of how morality and motivation are grasped. He discusses moral and non-moral predictors of environmental behaviour. As the main result, he developed a model framework of environmental behaviour integrating moral and non-moral determinants of environmental action.

MARINUS G.C.J. BEERTHUIZEN & DANIEL BRUGMAN

I. MORAL VALUE EVALUATION

A Neglected Motivational Concept in Externalizing Behaviour Research

INTRODUCTION

For almost half a century, research into the development of one's morality has focused almost exclusively on the development of moral cognitive processes, stating that moral judgment (i.e., the evaluation of whether something is right or wrong, cf., Haidt, 2001) is founded in moral reasoning (i.e., the moral reasoning about *why* something is right or wrong, cf., Gibbs, 1979; 2010; Kohlberg, 1981, 1984). Not surprisingly, the research into the relationship between morality and both moral and immoral behaviour (e.g., respectively, pro-social and externalizing behaviour) focussed also on moral reasoning. However, while moral cognitive developmentalists were confident of an associative link between moral reasoning and (im)moral behaviour (e.g., Blasi, 1980), a causal explanatory relationship had (and has) yet to be confirmed. For instance, lower moral stage reasoning was more prevalent among delinquent individuals than among non-offending individuals (a phenomenon that has been thoroughly acknowledged, Stams et al., 2006). This suggests a negative association between moral reasoning and delinquent behaviour, though it offers no definitive proof in regards to causality. Subsequent research, inspired by the suggestion that there is more to the explanation of behaviour than moral reasoning (cf., Blasi, 1980; Kohlberg & Candee, 1984), therefore strived to investigate other moral characteristics besides moral reasoning.

For example, following the theoretical suggestion that the moral aspect of one's identity is related to behaviour as well (e.g., the moral self, Blasi, 1993), several studies examined and, indeed, confirmed this relationship between moral identity and moral behaviour. One of the first studies to investigate the link between moral identity and behaviour, found a positive relationship between the moral characteristics in one's identity and the occurrence of ethical behaviour (Arnold, 1993). Since then this relationship between moral identity and moral (or pro-social) behaviour has been widely established and acknowledged (cf., Hardy & Carlo, 2005). However, not only moral identity's relationship to moral behaviour was examined, as recent studies also investigated its relationship with immoral behaviour. In a similar sense, an increased moral identity was (either directly or indirectly) related to a relative absence of immoral (i.e., externalizing) behaviour (Barriga, Morrison, Gibbs & Liau, 2001; Johnston & Krettenauer, 2011).

K. Heinrichs, F. Oser & T. Lovat (Eds.), Handbook of Moral Motivation: Theories, Models, Applications, 365–384.

Other moral cognitive processes were investigated as well. One of these processes that recently received a lot of attention is the concept of self-serving cognitive distortions (as envisioned by Gibbs and Potter, 1992; often operationalized through the "How I Think"-Questionnaire [HIT-Q], Barriga, Gibbs, Potter & Liau, 2001). Self-serving cognitive distortions are biased or inaccurate cognitive processes that, if highly prevalent within an individual, facilitate externalizing behaviour (Barriga, Gibbs et al., 2001). Though clearly more an *immoral* motivator, rather than a *moral* motivator (cf., Rest, 1999), the notion that cognitive distortions are regarded as relevant in delinquents is nothing new (Sykes & Matza, 1957). For many decades, there have been reports of delinquents who blame others for their own externalizing behaviour (i.e., denying of responsibility), or say that their actions have little to no consequences (i.e., denying of injury). Such reports and attitudes have been interpreted as (the result of) distorted social information processes, now coined self-serving cognitive distortions. The claim that the high prevalence of such distortions would facilitate immoral behaviour has found empirical support (Barriga, Morrison et al., 2001; Helmond, Brugman, Overbeek & Gibbs, 2011; Nas, Brugman & Koops, 2008).

About one decade ago, a multi-process cognitive developmental model was suggested (Barriga, Morrison et al., 2001), with the intention to thoroughly bridge the gap between moral reasoning and externalizing behaviour (Blasi, 1980; Kohlberg & Candee, 1984). Between moral reasoning and externalizing behaviour, the above discussed concepts of moral identity and self-serving cognitive distortions were introduced as mediating processes. In Barriga, Morrison and colleagues' model, moral reasoning was hypothesized to contribute to shaping one's moral identity, as the use of higher stage reasoning (i.e., reasoning aimed at facilitating interpersonal accord on a micro- or macro-level) would be associated with an increased moral identity. Furthermore, both these processes would "buffer" against the use of self-serving cognitive distortions. More specifically, higher levels of moral reasoning and a moral identity would discourage (or motivate against) the use of immoral thoughts and attitudes to justify immoral behaviour. Lastly, these three so called moral cognitive processes (i.e., moral reasoning, moral identity and self-serving cognitive distortions) would each retain their respective direct influences on the occurrence of externalizing behaviour. While the theoretical implications of the moral motivational cluster held up fairly well, two major issues arose during the empirical examination – by Barriga, Morrison and colleagues – of the moral cognitive model for externalizing behaviour. First, no relationship was found between moral reasoning and moral identity. Second, the expected direct negative relationship between moral reasoning and externalizing behaviour was of marginal magnitude.

The arrival of the moral cognitive model (Barriga, Morrison et al., 2001) hardly brought any consensus to the field of externalizing behaviour research, as in the past decade the role of moral reasoning in behaviour was still disputed (cf., Brusten, Stams & Gibbs, 2007; Emler & Tarry; Tarry & Emler, 2007). As a result of this dispute, somewhat unexpectedly, a relatively under-researched moral motivational concept emerged as a possible co-contender for the explanation of moral behaviour. It is this concept, namely moral value evaluation, which is the main focus of this chapter and its relationship with (im)moral motivation and externalizing behaviour.

MORAL VALUE EVALUATION

Owing to the novelty of the term in empirical research regarding externalizing behaviour, we will first introduce the moral motivational term on a conceptual level (the term made its initial appearance in Beerthuizen, Brugman, Basinger & Gibbs, 2011). We do this by dividing the concept into two parts (i.e., moral value[s], and evaluation) and then discussing how these two parts intertwine.

Moral Values

Moral values are frequently believed to be values based around harm, or rather, the absence of inflicting harm (Turiel, 1983). Nonetheless, recent perspectives on what constitutes a moral value exhibit more complex and non-harm characteristics, such as purity (Graham et al., 2011). In the current chapter, we focus on those harm-based moral values. In his classical moral reasoning research, Kohlberg identified a total of twelve types of moral values, which he coined moral value domains that are central to everyday life (Colby & Kohlberg, 1987a, p. 42). It is upon these values that the measurement of Kohlbergian moral reasoning is based. Five of these value domains (i.e., contract and truth, affiliation, life, property and law, and legal justice) have frequently found their way into moral reasoning research regarding externalizing behaviour (e.g., Tarry & Emler, 2007). When discussing the concept of moral value evaluation in the current chapter, it is also these five value domains about which we speak.

Evaluation

Moral value evaluation clearly concerns an evaluation of moral values. Moreover, it is an evaluation of the *importance* of those moral values. Even more specifically, moral value evaluation implies the attribution of importance to the adherence of behaviours that *directly* uphold moral values. In its essence, it is a bipolar evaluative process (of importance versus unimportance), similar to the fundamental evaluation dimensions by Osgood, Suci and Tannenbaum (1957; e.g., strong versus weak). The concept reflects an individual's general sense of how important moral values are in everyday life, and how important it is to uphold these moral values. Furthermore, when compared with the moral cognitive processes mentioned above (e.g., moral reasoning), moral value evaluation is much more affective, intuitive and impromptu. Individuals are able to quickly report on whether they believe something to be important or not as this attribution is founded on their emotions; by definition, these are immediate, rather than mediated (Nunner-Winkler, 2007). Any reasoning about the substance behind one's intuitive judgment on the importance of moral values therefore has to come second (although one's reasoning might subsequently inform the importance).

As the concept of attribution of importance to moral values has barely existed before in externalizing behaviour research (Gregg, Gibbs & Basinger, 1994; Palmer & Hollin, 1998), little is known about moral value evaluation (Tarry & Emler, 2007). This sciolism includes its psychosocial origins and its developmental patterns, if any. When looking beyond the semantic label of moral value evaluation, however, its conceptual embodiment (i.e., immediate evaluations of importance) and operationalization[1] in previous literature does show overlap with another well-discussed moral concept, namely, moral judgment (according to Haidt, 2001). From a conceptual perspective, both are quick (i.e., they require little to no cognitive effort) and bipolar evaluations (i.e., good versus bad, important versus important) of actions, characteristics or values. Furthermore, both are expected to precede moral reasoning in everyday moral issues. In special issues, however, as elaborated by Haidt (2001), their role may differ. It could perfectly be the case that everyone agrees on the importance of moral values but does not agree on or is less sure about the decision to be taken, depending on the moral reasoning one is convinced to be the most adequate.

Previous Literature

Though moral value evaluation has been largely ignored in more "classical" externalizing behaviour research (e.g., only two out of a potential fifteen studies on juvenile delinquents' moral functioning examined by Stams and colleagues [2006], report peripherally on moral value evaluation), some recent studies do report on it more thoroughly. Two studies indicate that moral value evaluation is inversely related to self-reported, externalizing behaviour (Beerthuizen et al., 2011; Tarry & Emler, 2007). In other words, an increased attribution of importance to moral values is related to fewer self-reports of externalizing behaviour. Furthermore, the study by Beerthuizen and colleagues indicates that incarcerated delinquent adolescents exhibit lower levels of importance attribution when compared with non-incarcerated adolescents. These recent findings contrast with an assumption originating from two earlier studies (Gregg et al., 1994; Palmer & Hollin, 1998), the assumption being that both delinquents and non-delinquents attribute equal levels of importance to moral values, this as both groups rate most of the moral values as important (in contrast to unimportant). A critical difference between the earlier and recent studies, however, is that the recent two also incorporated the 'very important' indication within their scales of analysis, thus using the full range of the moral value evaluation operationalization, while the earlier two did not.

Even though it is now apparent that some empirical literature is available, fundamental literature on the specifics of moral value evaluation remains scarce. In other words, much room is left for speculation on *why* recent studies report a negative relationship between moral value evaluation and externalizing behaviour. We intend to provide a (preliminary) answer to this question by combining the elaboration of the concept moral value evaluation above, its operationalization in the empirical literature so far (i.e., the SRM-SF in Gregg et al., 1994; Palmer & Hollin, 1998; Tarry & Emler, 2007; and the SRM-SFO in Beerthuizen et al., 2011), and the literature of the relationship between moral cognition and externalizing behaviour (Barriga, Morrison et al., 2001).

ELICITOR OF MORAL COGNITION

Moral value evaluation is in itself a potential associate of moral motivation, especially owing to its close proximity to the concept of emotions, as discussed above, and its moderate to strong relationship with empathy, as demonstrated by a secondary analysis of a data-set evaluating an intervention for juvenile delinquents (Brugman & Van den Bos, 2007). It is plausible that when an individual holds certain moral values dear, s/he is more likely to adhere to those same values because acting in any other way could be self-threatening. More specifically, acting in a way not in coherence with one's own perception on moral values, has the potential for causing emotionally distressing internal dissonance, such as moral guilt or shame (especially when such moral values are omnipresent, Gibbs, Basinger, Grime & Snarey, 2007). Given the notion that the experience of moral emotions is closely related to an absence of externalizing behaviour (Haidt, 2001), this would explain the negative relationship between moral value evaluation and externalizing behaviour in the previously discussed studies. Empathy based moral motivators are weak, however, as their positive effects on moral behaviour fade quickly when other processes come into play (Prinz, 2011). This notion is also reflected in previous studies wherein an initial substantial relationship between moral value evaluation and behaviour existed, but lost its magnitude when paired with other attitudinal or socio-moral processes (Beerthuizen et al., 2011; Tarry & Emler, 2007). Given moral value evaluation's distinct relationship with "stronger" moral cognitive processes (in relation to externalizing behaviour, i.e., moral reasoning, moral identity and self-serving cognitive distortions), we expect that moral value evaluation's relationship in such multi-process contexts is mediated, rather than deflated. Building upon the moral cognitive model of Barriga, Morrison and colleagues (2001), we will now introduce moral value evaluation into this model.

Moral Reasoning

Moral value evaluation should, according to analogies with Haidt's social intuitionist model (2001) and moral value evaluation's operationalization in several moral reasoning instruments, precede moral reasoning. One process preceding another does not however automatically imply an association. Nonetheless, the essence of the moral values of those that have been used to conceptualize and operationalize moral value evaluation so far (i.e., Beerthuizen et al., 2011; Tarry & Emler, 2007), contain strong anti-harm elements, such as fairness and justice. In other words, these values represent facilitating factors for interpersonal accordance. As the higher stages of moral reasoning used in the present study embody reasoning embedded in a desire for interpersonal accordance (on a micro- and macro-level, contrasting the lower self-preservation stages), there is a strong similarity in moral content. We therefore expect the nature of the relationship between moral value evaluation and moral reasoning to be positive. That is, by analogy with the social intuitionist model, moral reasoning is (at least partially) influenced by one's evaluative stance on moral values. This positive relationship has been supported by previous empirical results (Beerthuizen et al., 2011; Tarry & Emler, 2007).

Moral Identity

Furthermore, its relationship with moral identity is expected to be of a similar nature as to moral reasoning (i.e., moral value evaluation preceding moral identity, and of a positive nature). We predict this as the process of self-reflection on one's identity resulting in the self-realisation of one's moral being is inherently founded in a review of personal moral values, goals and behaviour (Blasi, 1980). This identity process therefore plausibly incorporates evaluations of which (and if) moral values are important to the individual. We therefore believe that individuals who attribute increased importance to moral values will also perceive themselves to be more moral. Moral identity, just as moral reasoning, is a deliberate process and moral value evaluation is therefore expected to precede moral identity. Moreover, the preceding nature of moral value evaluation to moral identity is only "logical", as moral value evaluation is theorized to precede moral reasoning, which in turn precedes moral identity. The positive relationship claimed to exist between moral value evaluation and moral identity has been confirmed in a previous study (Beerthuizen et al., 2011), and was observed when performing secondary analyses on the data-set of an unpublished masters thesis (Tiebout, 2008).

Self-Serving Cognitive Distortions

Lastly, the relationship between moral value evaluation and self-serving cognitive distortions is expected to be of a negative nature[2]. We believe that cognitive distortions are more likely to occur if one attributes less or no importance to moral values, as the process of moral disengagement is less self-threatening when such moral values have less value to the self. In other words, if you do not care about upholding moral values, it is easier to assume a stance in which the violation of these values is facilitated. This is in line with the reasoning and empirical results of the relationship between moral value evaluation and moral identity discussed above, and previously established relationships between moral identity and self-serving cognitive distortions (Barriga, Morrison et al., 2001).

The Current Study

In sum, moral value evaluation is expected to precede the moral cognitive processes of moral reasoning, moral identity and self-serving cognitive distortions. Thereby it can be considered an influential elicitor of these moral cognitive processes. Its direct relationship to externalizing behaviour is expected to deflate to insignificance in the multi-process model, having its effect being mediated through the moral cognitive processes. To investigate these expectations, we have gathered empirical data concerning several moral and behavioural processes, similar to the processes as in the study by Barriga, Morrison and colleagues (2001). Besides the primary hypotheses discussed above, we also have some predictions (and exploration) of secondary importance. The relationships of the moral cognitive processes among each other, and self-reported externalizing behaviour are expected to change little, with two notable exceptions. First, we expect a positive relationship to emerge between moral reasoning and identity (something Barriga, Morrison and colleagues did hypothesize, but did not find). For the current study, an alternative operationalization of moral identity was applied, which showed improved validity in previous research in relationship to its theorized relationship with moral reasoning (Brugman, 2008). Second, the strength of the relationship between moral identity and self-reported externalizing behaviour is expected to be of a weaker nature than previously reported. Younger adolescents (as in the current study) are less likely to have construed a "full" moral identity, when compared to older peers as those participating in the study by Barriga, Morrison and colleagues. Therefore, moral identity's relationship with behaviour is not fully matured, which is expected to exhibit itself through a weaker relationship between the two (Hart, 2005). Lastly, the model will be explored for both males and females separately, to examine whether the null-findings reported by Barriga, Morrison and colleagues also hold up for a younger group of participants.

METHOD

Sample

For the current study, data from 191 Dutch adolescent participants were collected to investigate the relationship of moral value evaluation to moral cognitive and externalizing behavioural processes. To allow even relatively weak relationships to emerge within the model, these participants were combined with a similar adolescent sample of 351 Dutch participants from a previous methodological study (i.e., the non-offending sample from Beerthuizen and colleagues, 2011). The only major difference between the samples from the current and previous study was that the current sample consisted entirely of higher educated participants, while the sample from Beerthuizen and colleagues also contained lower educated participants.

This resulted in a total number of participants of 542 individuals, between 11 and 18 years of age (with an average age of 14.3 years, $SD = 1.4$) and evenly divided according to gender (i.e., 49.3% of the sample consisted of males). Most of the participants (67.2%) were following a higher level of education in respect to the Dutch educational system (i.e., higher secondary education and secondary pre-university education; known in the Netherlands as, respectively, HAVO and VWO). The remaining participants were following education at a lower level (i.e., secondary pre-vocational and vocational education; known in the Netherlands as, respectively, VMBO and MBO). Participants were recruited from, and assessed at, their respective educational institutions, with data being collected at a single point in time, allowing for cross-referential analyses. During assessment, participants were presented with a booklet containing the four instruments and measurements described below, and a form for background information.

Measures

First, to assess *moral value evaluation* and *moral reasoning*, the Dutch translation of the Socio-moral Reflection Measure – Short Form Objective (SRM-SFO, Basinger, Brugman & Gibbs, 2007) was used. The SRM-SFO is a relatively novel recognition measure for moral reasoning, which also assesses moral value evaluation. Contrasting classical production measures of moral reasoning, such as the previously mentioned SRM-SF (Gibbs et al., 1992) and the MJI (Colby & Kohlberg, 1987b), where participants have to write down or provide an interviewer with their reasons, the SRM-SFO provides its participants with a list of reasons to choose from. In addition, before each item assessing moral reasoning, participants indicate how important they believe the moral issue or value to be. For instance, one item assesses how important participants believe it is, in general, to tell the truth. An example of a moral reason one can select is "because a lie will sooner or later always be detected" (i.e., stage 2 reasoning, Kohlberg, 1984). Previous research has shown that the SRM-SFO exhibits acceptable validity and reliability for use in adolescent samples (Beerthuizen et al., 2011). Averaging the item scores for the moral value evaluation items created the overall moral value evaluation score. For more information on the coding and scoring process of the moral reasoning scores, see Beerthuizen and colleagues (2011). The internal consistency of the moral value evaluation scale was acceptable (Cronbach's $\alpha = .70$); and for the moral reasoning scale it was borderline acceptable (Cronbach's $\alpha = .59$).

Second, to assess *moral identity*, the Good Self Assessment questionnaire (GSA, as in Barriga, Morrison et al., 2001) was used. The GSA consists of a list of characteristics that one can possess, both of a moral and non-moral, albeit not immoral, nature. Participants indicate for each of these characteristics how much they believe themselves to possess those characteristics. For example, moral characteristics in the GSA include honest and helpful, while it also contains traits such as funny and energetic as non-moral characteristics. As the newly collected sample used a slightly different version of the GSA than the sample from Beerthuizen and colleagues, the moral identity scores were transformed into Z-scores separately for both samples to account for these differences. Averaging the item scores for the moral characteristics created the moral identity score, resulting in acceptable internal consistencies for both samples (Cronbach's α ranged from .70 to .73).

Third, to assess *self-serving cognitive distortions*, the Dutch translation of the "How I Think"-Questionnaire (HIT-Q, Barriga, Gibbs et al., 2001) was used. The HIT-Q measure consists of a list of statements one can relate to. Of these statements, the majority reflects a self-serving cognitive distortion, while other items assess one's anomalous responding (i.e., socially desirable and perfunctory responding) or positive statements to mask the purpose of the questionnaire. Self-serving cognitive distortion statements include "it is okay to tell a lie, if someone is dumb enough to fall for it" and "if you know you can get away with it, only a fool would not steal". The Dutch version of the HIT-Q has shown acceptable validity and reliability in samples similar to the ones in the current study (Nas et al., 2008). Averaging the item scores for the cognitive distortion items created the self-serving cognitive distortion score, resulting in an excellent internal consistency (Cronbach's α = .93). The anomalous responding scale was not used in the current study, as its discriminatory function has not been convincingly demonstrated among Dutch adolescents (Van der Velden, Brugman, Boom & Koops, 2009).

Lastly, to assess *externalizing behaviour,* the Self Report Delinquent Behaviour list (SRDB, as in Leenders & Brugman, 2005) was used. The SRDB consists of a list of (minor) acts of delinquency or externalizing behaviours, which are normative for the target population of the current study (i.e., Dutch young adolescents). Such behaviours and acts include, but are not limited to, aggression (e.g., hitting someone) and property offences (e.g., vandalism). Participants indicate for each of these acts how often they had engaged in such behaviour. As with the GSA, the SRDB was slightly different for the used samples, and Z-scores were created for externalizing behaviour scores to account for these differences. Averaging the item scores of the whole list created the self-reported externalizing behaviour score, resulting in acceptable internal consistencies for both samples (Cronbach's α ranged from .76 to .86).

RESULTS

Descriptives

Before we investigate the full-blown model on externalizing behaviour, as hypothesized above, we will first examine the respective variables (i.e., moral value evaluation, moral reasoning, moral identity, self-serving cognitive distortions and externalizing behaviour) on a smaller scale. The descriptives of the variables are shown, differentiated for males and females, in Table 1. When comparing the descriptives of the variables with those in similar studies with similar participants, no anomalies or extremities were detected. For instance, the moral value evaluation scores show (in respect to their scale) overall high scores (as was previously reported in Tarry & Emler, 2007), whereas the overall prevalence of self-serving cognitive distortions was well below the clinical level (as discussed in Nas et al., 2008).

Table 1: Means and standard deviations for moral value evaluation, moral reasoning, moral identity, self-serving cognitive distortions, and self-reported externalizing behaviour, differentiated for males and female

	Males		Females		
Variable	M	SD	M	SD	RNG
1. MVE	2.44	.30	2.53	.24	1-3
2. MR	2.90	.35	3.02	.31	1-4
3. MI$_A$	2.85	.57	3.08	.46	1-5
3. MI$_B$	2.79	.40	2.98	.32	1-4
4. SSCD	2.58	.72	2.20	.60	1-6
5. EB$_A$	2.03	.80	1.50	.41	1-5
5. EB$_B$	1.72	.40	1.55	.32	1-4

Note. As the current sample and the one imported from Beerthuizen and colleagues (2011) had slightly different operationalizations for moral identity and self-reported externalizing behaviour, the raw data for those variables are presented separately for each sample (A = current sample, B = Beerthuizen et al., 2011). MVE = Moral value evaluation; MR = Moral reasoning; MI = Moral identity; SSCD = Self-serving cognitive distortions; EB = Self-reported externalizing behaviour.

Correlations

Next, we investigated the zero-order Pearson correlations (i.e., without controlling for any factors) among the variables. The results, again differentiated for males and females, are shown in Table 2. As the operationalizations of both moral identity and self-reported externalizing behaviour differ slightly for different participants, Z-scores were used in the Pearson correlations to account for these differences.

Table 2: Zero-order correlations for moral value evaluation, moral reasoning, moral identity, self-serving cognitive distortions, and self-reported externalizing behaviour, differentiated for males and females

Variable	1	2	3	4	5
1. MVE	-	.13*	.23***	-.33***	-.14*
2. MR	.13*	-	.13*	-.23***	-.07
3. MI	.36***	.07	-	-.22***	-.20**
4. SSCD	-.41***	-.22***	-.28***	-	.50***
5. EB	-.21*	-.20**	-.21***	.52***	-

Note. As the current sample and the one imported from Beerthuizen and colleagues (2011) had slightly different operationalizations for moral identity and self-reported externalizing behaviour, Z-scores were used to account for these differences. Males are shown below the diagonal, females are shown above the diagonal; MVE = Moral value evaluation; MR = Moral reasoning; MI = Moral identity; SSCD = Self-serving cognitive distortions; EB = Self-reported externalizing behaviour; * $p < .05$; ** $p < .01$; *** $p < .001$.

Moral Value Evaluation

Table 2 indicates that the results for moral value evaluation in regard to its relationship with the other moral cognitive and behavioural processes are as expected. An increased attribution of importance to moral values is related to both higher levels of moral reasoning and an increased self-perception of moral characteristics. Furthermore, this increased attribution is also related to a lower prevalence of self-serving cognitive distortions and self-reported externalizing behaviour. Lastly, relations are roughly the same for both males and females.

Moral Reasoning

Furthermore, the results also exhibit most of the hypothesized relationships among the other moral cognitive and behavioural processes. Higher levels of moral reasoning were related to an increased self-perception of moral characteristics for females, as expected, but this was not the case for the male portion of the sample. On the other hand, as hypothesized, higher levels of moral reasoning were negatively associated with the prevalence of self-serving cognitive distortions, both for males and females. Such a similar negative association was also found between moral reasoning and self-reported externalizing behaviour for males, but not for females.

Moral Identity and Self-Serving Cognitive Distortions

Lastly, the expected relationships among moral identity, self-serving cognitive distortions and externalizing behaviour were all prevalent. An increased self-perception of moral characteristics was related to a lower prevalence of self-serving cognitive distortions, and less self-reported externalizing behaviour, in both males and females. Lastly, for both sexes, a higher prevalence of self-serving cognitive distortions was related to more self-reported, externalizing behaviour.

Model Path Analysis

To investigate the expectation of moral value evaluation's mediation through the other moral cognitive processes, a path model was constructed and analyzed with SPSS AMOS 16 (Arbuckle, 2007). To examine whether the relationships among the moral and behavioural variables differ for males and females, a multi-group approach was used, exhibiting the paths separately for both genders. The model is shown in Figure 1. The model itself is an untrimmed model, which means that all possible relationships between the variables are allowed to exist. More specifically, no paths are statistically removed, even if they are marginal or not significant. This approach was chosen to mirror as closely as possible the path model of Barriga, Morrison and colleagues (2001), which used a similar approach to allow for comparisons between the current model and theirs. As no parameters were excluded from the model, this results in a population discrepancy value of near zero. As model fit analyses require a non-null population discrepancy value, model fit indexes are not appropriate to evaluate (or even provided by AMOS). Two participants did not report on externalizing behaviour, with no indication of any severe issues associated with missing values (cf., Scheffer, 2002), and were excluded from the analysis.

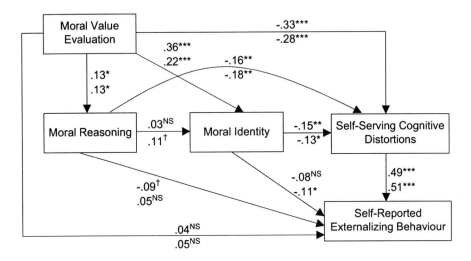

Figure 1. Path analysis of unrestrained multi-process model on externalizing behaviour for males and females.

Broadly speaking, the relationships among the model's variables show similar directional relationships compared to the zero-order correlations. There are some notable exceptions. Moral value evaluation is no longer directly related to self-reported, externalizing behaviour for both sexes. Furthermore, the relationship between moral reasoning and moral identity for females is now only marginally present, whereas it was originally of a stronger order. A similar phenomenon can be observed for the relationship between moral reasoning and self-reported externalizing behaviour for males. Moreover, the association between moral identity and self-reported externalizing behaviour is no longer statistically supported for males.

The primary association between moral value evaluation and externalizing behaviour was expected to be of an indirect nature. This association is confirmed by the results. The indirect effect of moral value evaluation on externalizing behaviour was the strongest indirect effect of all variables included in the model (the β value was, respectively for males and females, -.24 and -.19). This indicates that an increased attribution of importance is related to a lower prevalence of externalizing behaviour, but only through full mediation by moral reasoning, moral identity and self-serving cognitive distortions (as no direct effect remains for moral value evaluation). The remaining indirect effects of moral reasoning and moral identity were of a weaker nature (β values ranged from -.07 to -.11). The multi-process model as presented, explained 28% of the variance in self-reported externalizing behaviour in males, and 27% in females.

DISCUSSION

The current chapter primarily intended to introduce the motivational concept of moral value evaluation, which is the attribution of importance to moral values. Although this concept is theoretically important in the field of externalizing behaviour, research on moral value evaluation is extremely scarce. Moral value evaluation was expected to negatively relate to externalizing behaviour. Subsequent expectations state however that if other processes were introduced in the relationship between moral value evaluation and externalizing behaviour, the relationship between moral value evaluation and externalizing behaviour would persist merely as an indirect one. More specifically, moral value evaluation was expected to influence moral cognitive processes (i.e., moral reasoning, moral identity and self-serving cognitive distortions) which, in turn shape behaviour. When empirically testing these predictions, they were largely confirmed.

Moral Value Evaluation and Externalizing Behaviour

Most important, the lessening of relational strength between moral value evaluation and externalizing behaviour occurred when moving from the zero-order context to that of the multi-process path model. This certainly strengthens the argument that moral value evaluation is an elicitor of "stronger" cognitive processes (e.g., self-serving cognitive distortions) which, in turn, demote (or promote) externalizing action, although there is an alternative explanation. The assessment of externalizing behaviour consisted purely of retrospective report, also without addressing the context within which such behaviours took place. It is plausible that, besides its indirect relationship with the general occurrence of externalizing behaviour, it has a stronger relationship with impromptu externalizing behaviour (i.e., when there is little to no time for cognitive processes between intention and initiation of externalizing behaviour, such as unplanned shoplifting). This is likely, as moral value evaluation has a strong emotional, intuitive and thus immediate component, making it possible for it to "intervene", while other moral cognitive processes struggle for similar effects (Haidt, 2001). Future research into the relationship between moral value evaluation and externalizing behaviour should incorporate different contexts of externalizing behaviour, or measure "light" impromptu transgressions of moral conduct (e.g., cheating) in an experimental setting, to investigate these expectations.

Moral Value Evaluation and Treatment

These results also have implications for the forensic clinical treatment of incarcerated adolescents. While major treatment programs (e.g., EQUIP, Gibbs, Potter & Goldstein,

1995; and ART, Goldstein, Glick, & Gibbs, 1998) focus on improving the delinquent's moral reasoning and cognitive distortions, the observed effects of these interventions on such cognitions range from negligible to modest (cf., Brugman & Bink, 2011; Nas, Brugman & Koops, 2005). As the current effect sizes of the treatments leave something to be desired, research into improving the effects of these programmes is needed. A worthwhile process to focus upon in these investigations would be moral value evaluation, as several moral cognitive processes are founded within it (according to the discussed model). Actually, the process is already stimulated in these programmes, but is not yet recognized as important. By studying moral value evaluation, and particularly how it can be enhanced, one can potentially augment other effects. For instance, by first enhancing one's attribution of importance to moral values, one could indirectly improve upon one's moral cognitions as well (probably more so in combination with treatment focussing on those moral cognitions). Furthermore, there is evidence that the attribution of importance to moral values regresses in an incarcerated setting for individuals who do *not* receive treatment containing a moral competence component (Helmond, Brugman & Overbeek, 2011), further highlighting the need to pay attention to moral values in institutionalized contexts.

Cognitive Distortions and Externalizing Behaviour

In regard to the observed relationships among the other moral and behavioural processes, one relationship stands out, namely that of the immoral motivational process (i.e., self-serving cognitive distortions) and externalizing behaviour. While the directional relationship is as expected (i.e., higher prevalence of cognitive distortions are related to higher prevalence of externalizing behaviour), its magnitude is beyond expectations. More specifically, few studies report such extremely strong associations (especially if multiple processes are involved, Cohen's $d = 1.15$, very large according to Cohen, 1988) between cognitive processes and behaviour, as is reported in the current study for cognitive distortions. Moreover, within the current model (and for the current sample), it seems as though self-serving cognitive distortions "swallow" the respective (moderately small) effects of the other moral predictors towards externalizing behaviour. By itself, it explains 25% of the variance in self-reported externalizing behaviour, with the additional predictors adding a mere 2-3%. While previous studies have indeed reported large positive relationships between self-serving cognitive distortions and externalizing behaviour (Helmond, Brugman, Overbeek & Gibbs, 2011), the current study's relational magnitude outmatches these previous findings. This increased contribution of cognitive distortions to the explanation of externalizing behaviour is plausibly caused by the current study's inclusion of younger adolescents (perhaps in combination with a relatively high level of education). This claim is further strengthened by a similar study with children (aged 7 to 12 years), which exhibited an even larger magnitude of the relationship between cognitive distortions and externalizing behaviour than those currently reported (Van de Bunt, Brugman & Aleva, 2010).

Morality Versus Immorality

As the current book's focus is on moral motivation, a moral motivational interpretation of these results is in order. As discussed in the introduction, the concept of self-serving cognitive distortions is clearly an agent of immoral motivation. The cognitive effects from distorted social information processes facilitate the engagement in externalizing behaviour. Contrasting this immoral motivation are the "forces of the good", a moral cluster consisting of moral reasoning, moral identity and moral value evaluation. These processes, if "properly" developed (i.e., overall stage 3 reasoning or higher; adequate possession [and self-perception] of moral characteristics; and sufficient attributed importance to moral values) should ideally buffer against the temptations of "easy" immoral motivational processes. It appears however that these "good" forces are not doing too well among regular young adolescents (and children). The three moral processes are less associated with immoral behaviour *combined*, than immoral behaviour's relationship with a single process of immoral motivation. The concept of immoral motivation is by far the strongest predictor of immoral behaviour. This is not entirely unexpected, given the knowledge of the "weak" nature of moral motivators among young individuals (Prinz, 2011). The influence of the moral cluster (including the moral motivator of moral self-perseverance, as discussed earlier) increases when individuals grow older, as is suggested when comparing the results of this chapter to the study by Barriga, Morrison and colleagues (2001). Once again, this is also not entirely unexpected, as even classic developmental psychologists already detected a maturation of the childrens' and adolescents' morality, as they grow older (Kohlberg, 1958; Piaget, 1932). Nevertheless, the dominant influence of immoral motivation (such as self-serving cognitive distortions) remains, even among highly educated older adolescent (as studied by Barriga, Morrison and colleagues, 2001).

Remaining Issues

While we acknowledge the substantial impact of immoral motivational factors on antisocial behaviour among young individuals, we want to address some issues concerning this observed relationship. The current (and predominant) operationalization of self-serving cognitive distortions (i.e., the HIT-Q, Barriga, Gibbs et al., 2001) into externalizing behaviour research is potentially "contaminated". That is, the items assessing self-serving cognitive distortions incorporate explicit externalizing behaviour (i.e., lying, stealing, physical aggression and oppositional defiance) similar to those used in externalizing behaviour measures. Therefore, the HIT-Q does not assess cognitive distortions "pur sang" (i.e., "inaccurate or biased ways of attending to, or conferring, meaning upon experiences"; Barriga, Gibbs et al., 2001, p. 1), but cognitive distortions based heavily within behavioural contexts. It is therefore no surprise that the current and previous studies (Barriga, Morrison et al., 2001; Nas et al., 2008; Van de Bunt et al., 2010) find strong relationships with externalizing behaviour. The "inflated" nature of this relationship is further illustrated through a decrease in relational magnitude, when the behavioural component of self-serving cognitive distortions is neutralized (Berg, Meijer & Wouters, 2011). Again, we acknowledge the role of cognitive distortions regarding externalizing behaviour, but we do want to emphasize that behavioural context matters in the interpretation of such relations, also found with other moral cognitive processes (i.e., moral reasoning; cf., Beerthuizen & Brugman, 2012; Brugman & Aleva, 2004; Gregg et al., 1994; Palmer & Hollin, 1998).

On a final note, we want to address two issues associated with the current chapter's study. First, the collected data was of a cross-sectional nature, limiting us to associative relationships and *not* causal relationships (though we do hypothesize such relationships). It is entirely plausible and likely that the occurrence of immoral behaviour has a feedback loop back to the (im)moral cluster (as was demonstrated for moral reasoning, Raaijmakers, Engels & Van Hoof, 2005). With the current data, however, this cannot be confirmed or denied. Second, moral value evaluation is currently "handicapped". The width of the item indication span has always been limited to either two (i.e., unimportant and [very] important) or three (i.e., unimportant, important and very important) indication points. While it appears as a minor difference, its effect is notable, as the latter operationalization *did* produce significant results in the current study and previous research (Beerthuizen et al., 2011; Tarry & Emler, 2007), contrasting the studies using the former operationalization (Gregg et al., 1994; Palmer & Hollin, 1998). This indicates that the dyad in attribution between important and very important is crucial in determining moral value evaluation's relationship to externalizing behaviour, and *not* the dyad between unimportant and (very) important as previously studied (i.e., Gregg et al., 1994; Palmer & Hollin, 1998). Widening the item indication span (e.g., to a 7-point width, allowing for various degrees of importance attribution) in future research would allow moral value evaluation to be studied more extensively and, for example, be used in diagnostic assessments.

CONCLUSION

In conclusion, this chapter introduced the scarcely studied psychosocial concept of moral value evaluation, and its relationship with processes of moral reasoning and identity, and immoral motivation. The (preliminary) conclusion is that moral value evaluation is indirectly associated with externalizing behaviour, theorized to influence one's moral cognition which, in turn, shapes behaviour. Of these moral cognitive processes, the immoral motivators of self-serving cognitive distortions were by far the strongest associates with their behavioural counterpart of externalizing behaviour.

NOTES

[1] Moral value evaluation has been operationalized as an "elicitor of moral reasoning" in several successful measures of moral reasoning (e.g., SRM-SF, Gibbs, Basinger & Fuller, 1992; SROM-SF, Basinger &

Gibbs, 1987; and SRM-SFO, Beerthuizen et al., 2011). That is, the items of assessmentconcerning one's evaluation of moral values are presented first to the participant, with the moral reasoning items related to the moral value following. Moral value evaluation was originally meant as "just" an elicitor for moral reasoning and *not* as an autonomous measure (i.e., no registration protocols existed prior to the SRM-SFO, Beerthuizen et al., 2011; Gibbs et al., 1992).

[2] We want to note that from the more classical perspective on *why* self-serving cognitive distortions occur (i.e., to serve as a neutralizer of guilt/shame in individuals trespassing norms; Sykes & Matza, 1957), different relation valances can be expected. If one holds no value to morality, and trespasses them, then there is no need to distort one's own cognition to avoid guilt and shame. From this perspective, a positive relationship can be expected, as the presence of moral values creates the *need* for cognitive distortions when engaging in externalizing behaviour. However, such a positive relationship, also between similar moral concepts (i.e., moral identity), and self-serving cognitive distortions has yet to be found. This potentially might be because self-serving cognitive distortions do not necessarily have to neutralize moral shame (e.g., one regrets violating others), but also immoral shame (e.g., one regrets others discovering his/her immoral nature/actions and subsequent repercussions) and disequilibrium caused by implicit socialization processes on behavioural conduct.

REFERENCES

Arbuckle, J.L. (2007). *Amos^TM 16 user's guide*. Chicago: SPSS Inc.

Arnold, M.L. (1993). *The place of morality in the adolescent self* (Unpublished doctoral dissertation). Harvard University, Cambridge, United States.

Barriga, A.Q., Gibbs, J.C., Potter, G.B., & Liau, A.K. (2001). *How I Think (HIT) Questionnaire manual*. Champaign: Research Press.

Barriga, A.Q., Morrison, E.M., Liau, A.K., & Gibbs, J.C. (2001). Moral cognition: Explaining the gender difference in antisocial behavior. *Merrill-Palmer Quarterly, 47*(4), 532–562. doi:10.1353/mpq.2001.0020

Basinger, K.S., & Gibbs, J.C. (1987). Validation of the Sociomoral Reflection Objective Measure - Short Form. *Psychological Reports, 61(1)*, 139–146.

Basinger, K.S., Brugman, D., & Gibbs, J.C. (2007). *Sociomoral Reflection Measure - Short Form Objective (SRM-SFO)*. Unpublished instrument, Urbana University, United States.

Beerthuizen, M.G.C.J., & Brugman, D. (2012). Sexually abusive youths' moral reasoning on sex. *Journal of Sexual Aggression, 18*(2), 125–135. doi: 10.1080/13552600.2010.519126

Beerthuizen, M.G.C.J., Brugman, D., Basinger, K.S., & Gibbs, J.C. (2011). *Moral reasoning, moral value evaluation and juvenile delinquency: An introduction to the Sociomoral Reflection Measure - Short Form Objective*. Manuscript submitted for publication.

Berg, I., Meijer, F., & Wouters, T. (2011). *Delinquentie, depressie en denkfouten - De dynamiek van externaliserend en internaliserend gedrag [Delinquency, depression and thinking errors - The dynamics of externalizing and internalizing behaviour]* (Unpublished bachelors' thesis). Utrecht University, Utrecht, the Netherlands.

Blasi, A. (1980). Bridging moral cognition and moral action: A critical review of the literature. *Psychological Bulletin, 88*(1), 1–45. doi:10.1037/0033-2909.88.1.1

Blasi, A. (1993). The development of identity: Some implications for moral functioning. In G.G. Noam & T.E. Wren (Eds.), *The moral self* (pp. 99–122). Cambridge: MIT Press.

Brugman, D. (2008, July). *Perspectives on the moral self: moral self relevance*. Paper presented at the 20th Biennial Meeting of the International Society for the Study of Behavioural Development, Wurzburg, Germany.

Brugman, D., & Aleva, A.E. (2004). Developmental delay or regression in moral reasoning by juvenile delinquents? *Journal of Moral Education, 33(3)*, 321–338. doi:10.1080/0305724042000733082

Brugman, D., & Bink, M. (2011). Effects of the EQUIP peer intervention program on self-serving cognitive distortions and recidivism among delinquent male adolescents. *Psychology, Crime & Law, 17*(4), 345–358. doi:10.1080/10683160903257934

Brugman, D., & Van den Bos, J.K. (2007). *De effecten van herstelopvoeding op morele ontwikkeling bij delinquente jongens in een justitiële jeugdinrichting [The effects of restorative education on the moral development of delinquent boys in a youth detention center].* Utrecht University, Utrecht, the Netherlands.

Brusten, C., Stams, G.J., & Gibbs, J.C. (2007). Missing the mark. *British Journal of Developmental Psychology, 25*(2), 185–189. doi:10.1348/026151006X146044

Cohen, J. (1988). *Statistical power analyses for the behavioural sciences* (2nd ed.). Hillsdale: Lawrence Erlbaum Associates.

Colby, A., & Kohlberg, L. (1987a). *The measurement of moral judgment* (Vol. 1) *-Theoretical foundations and research validation.* Cambridge: Cambridge University Press.

Colby, A., & Kohlberg, L. (1987b). *The measurement of moral judgment* (Vol. 2) *-Standard issue scoring manual.* Cambridge: Cambridge University Press.

Emler, N., & Tarry, H. (2007). Clutching at straws: Is it time to abandon the moral judgment deficit explanation for delinquency? *British Journal of Developmental Psychology, 25*(2), 191–195. doi:10.1348/026151007X178084

Gibbs, J.C. (1979). Kohlberg's moral stage theory: A Piagetian revision. *Human Development, 22(2),* 89–112. doi:10.1159/000272431

Gibbs, J.C. (2010). *Moral development and reality: Beyond the theories of Kohlberg and Hoffman* (2nd. Ed.). Boston: Pearson Allyn & Bacon.

Gibbs, J.C, Basinger, K.S., & Fuller, R. (1992). *Moral maturity: Measuring the development of sociomoral reflection.* Hillsdale: Erlbaum.

Gibbs, J.C., Basinger, K.S., Grime, R.L., Snarey, J.R. (2007). Moral judgment across cultures: Revisiting Kohlberg's universality claims. *Developmental Review, 27*(4), 443–500. doi:10.1016/j.dr.2007.04.001

Gibbs, J.C., & Potter, G.B. (1992). *A typology of criminogenic cognitive distortions.* Unpublished manuscript, The Ohio State University, Columbus, United States.

Gibbs, J.C., Potter, G.B., & Goldstein, A.P. (1995). *The EQUIP-Program: Teaching youth to think and act responsibly through a peer-helping approach.* Champaign: Research Press.

Goldstein, A.P., Glick, B., & Gibbs, J.C. (1998). *Aggression replacement training: A comprehensive intervention for aggressive youths.* Champaign: Research Press.

Graham, J., Nosek, B.A., Haidt, J., Iyer, R., Koleva, S., & Ditto, P.H. (2011). Mapping the moral domain. *Journal of Personality and Social Psychology, 101*(2), 366–385. doi:10.1037/A0021847

Gregg, V., Gibbs, J.C., & Basinger K.S. (1994). Patterns of developmental delay in moral judgment by male and female delinquents. *Merrill-Palmer Quarterly, 40,* 538–553.

Haidt, J. (2001). The emotional dog and its rational tail: A social intuitionist approach to moral judgment. *Psychological Review, 108*(4), 814–834.

Hardy, S.A., & Carlo, G. (2005). Identity as a source of moral motivation. *Human Development, 48,* 232–256. doi:10.1159/000086859

Hart, D. (2005). The development of moral identity. In G. Carlo & C.P. Edwards (Eds.). *Moral motivation through the life span* (pp. 165–196). Lincoln: University of Nebraska Press.

Helmond, P.E., Brugman, D., Overbeek, G., & Gibbs, J.C. (2011). *A meta-analysis on the relationship between cognitive distortions and externalizing behavior: Can interventions reduce cognitive distortions?* Manuscript submitted for publication.

Helmond, P.E., Brugman, D., Overbeek, G. (2011). *Program integrity and effectiveness of the EQUIP intervention for incarcerated antisocial youth on cognitive distortions, social skills, and moral development.* Manuscript submitted for publication.

Johnston, M., & Krettenauer, T. (2011). Moral self and moral emotion expectancies as predictors of anti- and prosocial behaviour in adolescence: A case for mediation? *European Journal of Developmental Psychology, 8*(2), 228–243. doi:10.1080/17405621003619945

Kohlberg, L. (1958). *The development of modes of moral thinking and choice in the years 10 to 16* (Unpublished doctoral dissertation). University of Chicago, Chicago, United States.

Kohlberg, L. (1981). *Essays on moral development, Vol. 1: The philosophy of moral development.* San Francisco: Harper & Row.

Kohlberg, L. (1984). *Essays on moral development, Vol. 2: The psychology of moral development.* San Francisco: Harper & Row.

Kohlberg, L., & Candee, D. (1984). The relationship of moral judgment to moral action In L. Kohlberg (Ed.), *Essays on moral development, Vol. 2: The psychology of moral development* (pp. 498–581). San Francisco: Harper & Row.

Leenders, I., & Brugman, D. (2005). The moral/non-moral domain shift in young adolescents in relation to delinquent behavior. *British Journal of Developmental Psychology, 23*(1), 65–79. doi:10.1348/026151004X20676

Nas, C.N., Brugman, D., & Koops, W. (2005). Effects of the EQUIP programme on the moral judgment, cognitive distortions, and social skills of juvenile delinquents. *Psychology, Crime & Law, 11*(4),421–434. doi:10.1080/10683160500255703

Nas, C.N., Brugman, D., & Koops, W. (2008). Measuring self-serving cognitive distortions with the "How I Think" questionnaire. *European Journal of Psychological Assessment, 24*(3), 181–189. doi:10.1027/1015-5759.24.3.181

Nunner-Winkler, G. (2007). Development of moral motivation from childhood to early adulthood. *Journal of Moral Education, 36*(4), 399–414. doi:10.1080/03057240701687970

Osgood, C.E., Suci, G., & Tannenbaum, P. (1957). *The measurement of meaning.* Champaign: University of Illinois Press.

Palmer, E.J., & Hollin, C.R. (1998). Comparison of patterns of moral development in young offenders and non-offenders. *Legal and Criminal Psychology, 3,* 225–235.

Piaget, J. (1932). *The moral judgment of the child.* Glencoe: Free Press.

Prinz, J.J. (2011). Is empathy necessary for morality? In P. Goldie & A. Coplan (Eds.). *Empathy: Philosophical and Psychological Perspectives.* Oxford: Oxford University Press. Retrieved from: http://subcortex.com/IsEmpathyNecessaryForMoralityPrinz.pdf

Raaijmakers, Q.A.W., Engels, R.C.M.E., & Van Hoof, A. (2005). Delinquency and moral reasoning in adolescence and young adulthood. *International Journal of Behavioral Development, 29*(3), 247–258. doi:10.1177/016550250544000035

Rest, J.R. (1999).*Die Rolle des moralischen Urteilens im moralischen Handeln.* In D. Garz, F. Oser & W. Althof (Eds.), *Moralisches Urteil und Handeln* (pp. 82–116). Frankfurt a.M.: Suhrkamp.

Scheffer, J. (2002). Dealing with missing data. *Research letters in the information and mathematical sciences, 3,* 153–160.

Stams, G.J., Brugman, D., Deković, M., Van Rosmalen, L., Van der Laan, P., & Gibbs, J.C. (2006). The moral judgment of juvenile delinquents: A meta-analysis. *Journal of Abnormal Child Psychology, 34*(5), 697–713. doi:10.1007/s10802-006-9056-5

Sykes, G.M., & Matza, D. (1957). Techniques of neutralization: A theory of delinquency. *American Sociological Review, 22*(6), 664–670.

Tarry, H., & Emler, H. (2007). Attitudes, values and moral reasoning as predictors of delinquency. *British Journal of Developmental Psychology, 25*(2), 169–183. doi:10.1348/026151006X113671

Tiebout, C.L. (2008). *Morele ontwikkelingskenmerken als voorspellers van integriteit bij sollicitanten van de politie [Moral developmental characteristics as predictors of police recruits' integrity]* (Unpublished masters' thesis). Utrecht University, Utrecht, the Netherlands.

Turiel, E., (1983). *The development of social knowledge: Morality and convention.* Cambridge: Cambridge University Press.

Van de Bunt, J.A., Brugman, D., Aleva, A.E. (2010). *Moral evaluation and externalizing behavior in children with behavior disorders: The mediation role of self-serving cognitive distortions.* Manuscript submitted for publication.

Van der Velden, F., Brugman, D., Boom, J., & Koops, W. (2009). *The How I Think Questionnaire as a tool for evaluation of prevention programs and diagnostic purposes in young adolescents.* Manuscript submitted for publication.

AFFILIATIONS

Marinus G.C.J. Beerthuizen
Department of Psychology

M. G. C. J. BEERTHUIZEN & D. BRUGMAN

Utrecht University
Utrecht, the Netherlands

Daniel Brugman
Department of Psychology
Utrecht University
Utrecht, the Netherlands

STEFAN WEYERS

II. JUVENILE DELINQUENCY

Lack of Moral Motivation or Moral Ambivalence?

INTRODUCTION

The assumption that criminality is related to moral immaturity is strongly rooted in our everyday understanding. Even psychological approaches often connect delinquency with personality features, such as psychopathy or lacking empathy, implying a low degree of moral sense (Eisenhardt, 2005; Stams et al., 2006). In Kohlberg's influential theory of moral development, a low stage of moral judgment is seen as an important condition for committing criminal offenses (Kohlberg, 1978). However, there is generally only a weak correlation between moral stage and action (Blasi, 1983; Oser, 1999). Therefore, what concerns *moral* behaviour, especially moral *motivation* is considered a desideratum in stage theory (Blasi, 1993, 2004; Hardy, & Gustavo, 2005; Keller, 2004; Nisan, 1993; Nunner-Winkler, 1993). In my opinion, the same applies to the explanation of *im*moral behaviour, as it is probably connected with both cognitive as well as motivational moral immaturity.

The present article is directed towards the relationship between moral motivation and delinquency as one kind of immoral behaviour. In section one I will discuss the theoretical foundations the article is based on: First of all I will outline my understanding of moral motivation with respect to the conceptions of Blasi and Nunner-Winkler. Then I will discuss the relationship between morality and delinquency with regard to Kohlberg's theory and other approaches, which relate criminality to moral development. At the center of this article is a study on imprisoned juveniles and young adults. In the second section, I will present the results of this study which was aimed at moral judgments and biographical reconstructions. The focus is on the agents' criminal offenses and the ways in which they present and interpret their biographies. These self-presentations are expected to give an insight into the moral or immoral motives of the offenders. As a conclusion, I will discuss the relationship between morality and delinquency with respect to the empirical findings of the study, the moral self-concept and especially moral motivation. My thesis is that most delinquents have a weak moral motivation. However, they do not show a complete lack thereof but are highly ambivalent towards moral norms. This ambivalence seems to imply a low degree of the integration of moral norms and values into the self.

K. Heinrichs, F. Oser & T. Lovat (Eds.), Handbook of Moral Motivation: Theories, Models, Applications, 385–404.

THEORETICAL FOUNDATIONS

Moral Motivation as a Self-Commitment to Morality

My understanding of moral motivation is deeply influenced by the conceptions of Augusto Blasi (1983; 1993; 2004) and Gertrud Nunner-Winkler (1993), both of whom have modified the approach of Lawrence Kohlberg (1984). In Kohlberg's theory, moral motivation is strongly connected with the cognitive structure of moral judgment. From this perspective, the more elaborate the understanding of moral norms and principles, the higher the motivation to act morally – and vice versa: the lower the stage of moral judgment, the lower the moral motivation. In Kohlberg's conception, the knowledge of the good is seen as both necessary and sufficient in terms of the motivation to act morally (Bergman, 2004). In contrast, Blasi and Nunner-Winkler see the knowledge of the good as necessary but not as sufficient for moral motivation and moral action.

My thesis is that the significance of moral development for acting morally or immorally depends less on the stage of moral judgment than on developing a *moral self*. It is about the relevance of moral values and objectives for the individual as well as about the capability and readiness[1] to interpret situations morally. At first introduced by Blasi (1983) to explain the discrepancy between judgment and action, this concept aims at the interplay of the various dimensions of morality: sensitivity, judgment, motivation and action. Blasi (2004) emphasizes the cognitive content of morality, describing understanding as the "core of morality" (p. 338). At the same time, he emphasizes the necessity to "translate moral understanding into moral motives" (p. 341).

However, if the knowledge of the good does not provide sufficient motivation to act morally, how can moral *understanding* be translated into moral *motivation*? Blasi's model of moral self contains three main statements: First, moral understanding is closely connected to moral action only "if it is translated into a judgment of personal responsibility" (Blasi, 1993, p. 99). Second, "...moral responsibility is the result of integrating morality in one's identity or sense of self" (ibid.). Third, "from moral identity derives a psychological need to make one's actions consistent with one's ideals" (ibid.). According to this conception, three conditions are crucial and necessary for building up moral motivation: these are moral understanding, moral identity and self-consistency.

Moral cognition or understanding: The readiness to act *morally* presupposes a (reflective or intuitive) judgment about what is *morally right*. Even the reverse is possible: If someone is not willing to comply with moral norms, it may be useful or even necessary for him - if he has constituted the action as a moral one - to neutralize the moral dimension of his acting, that is, to justify or excuse one's own behaviour by rejecting the wrongness of the action or one's own responsibility for it. Therefore, moral motivation cannot be analyzed without considering moral understanding. Moral judgments are judgments of obligation. However, moral judgments often have only a limited motivational strength. According to Blasi (1993), *judgments of personal responsibility*, in particular, gain motivational strength because they are related to moral identity and to a feeling of *personal* obligation.

Moral identity: The growth of moral motivation is related to the development of identity. Blasi describes this development as "active processes of selection and hierarchical ordering. Only some of our own biographic data are appropriated to our sense of self [...] other aspects of ourselves are not rejected, but subordinated to core commitments" (Blasi, 2004, p. 344). From this perspective, developing a moral identity and a moral motivation means integrating morality into the self. It is required that somebody not only has a feeling of obligation toward moral norms but also builds up a self-commitment to morality. To describe this complex structure of motivation, Blasi and Nunner-Winkler refer to Harry Frankfurt's (1993) concept of "second-order desire". Here, the self is conceptualized "as an active agent, building up second-order desires that commit one to value orientations that guide life choices and determine personal projects [...] Moral motivation is understood as a second-order desire – in this case, a commitment to morality" (Nunner-Winkler, 1993, p. 269). From this perspective, moral motivation includes not only the dimension of being driven by moral motives but also volitional processes, especially seen in a state of commitment to morality. The content of this commitment is "...wanting to do what is right or wanting to be a virtuous person." (p. 286). This structure of motivation is strictly different from a first-order desire such as an altruistic desire. It is necessary that the moral motive is upheld in a conflict with an egoistic motive: "Moral motivation implies that one is willing to do what is right not only when one feels like doing it but also when doing it necessitates sacrificing personal desires" (ibid.).

Self-consistency: Why act morally? The model of Blasi and Nunner-Winkler implies two different reasons. The first reason – the moral reason – is related to the formal structure of morality: One should act morally and one is willing to act morally because *it is the right thing to do* – not because it leads to the feeling to be a good person, etc. The second reason – the motivational reason – is related to the structure of personality or identity. In this model, self-consistency is understood as a psychological need to maintain one's own identity. This need is seen as the "basic motivational spring of moral action" (Blasi, 2004, p. 344). The model of moral motivation as a self-commitment to morality connects both reasons: People are willing to act morally because it is the right thing to do *and* because they want to maintain their own identity. Upholding the moral identity is not a *selfish* motive, because the moral identity is strongly related to the *moral* reason. Therefore, it is not reasonable to separate the motivational reason from the moral reason – as Nucci (2004) does. Giving one's attention only to the moral reason ignores the psychological necessity to translate moral understanding into moral motivation.

This model is supported by empirical findings by Blasi (1993) and Nunner-Winkler (1993). It is also supported by a study by Colby and Damon (1992), indicating that the development of moral commitment did not depend on the achievement of higher stages of moral judgment: People arguing at stage 3 are as likely as those at stage 5 to have built up a strong commitment to morality. The moral self-model also achieves support by results of studies by Nisan (1993). Accordingly, humans do not orient their actions strictly according to rules but rather to the "principle of maintaining personal identity" (p. 253). Even in Nisan's concept, self-consistency is seen as the central motivational source of moral action.

This concept of moral motivation will be applied to the analysis of the biographical self-presentations of juvenile delinquents.

THE RELATIONSHIP BETWEEN MORALITY AND DELINQUENCY

It would be premature to assume a *close* relationship between morality and delinquency. For, delinquency is a *juridical* category, but *in the moral sense* delinquent acts are very different. A general relationship is not to be expected, because not all criminal offenses are immoral. In some cases, it is also doubtful whether a lack of moral motivation or another kind of moral immaturity is significant for committing crimes:

- This applies to mental illness, drug addiction or to other cases of diminished responsibility.
- If offenses are interpreted as violations of conventions, they do not appear to be morally relevant. For drug consumption, this has been proven (Priest, & McGrath, 1970), but this might as well be true for other offenses in the context of which nobody is directly harmed.
- If offenses are considered to be morally right, we may rather expect a high degree of moral motivation: Examples are actions such as civil disobedience, but also politically motivated violent offenses in the context of "false moral identities" (Moshman, 2004).
- People behaving in a criminal way in one context (e. g. business) may show a high degree of morality in other contexts, such as their family. Such segmentations suggest morality to be context-dependent, but they do not prove a general lack of moral motivation.
- Even serious crimes do not always indicate a lacking of moral motivation, in that, subsequently, the actors can react by remorse or feelings of guilt (Blasi, 1993).

Thus, we should not expect a correlation to moral motivation for all kinds of delinquency. What must be taken into account are the type of offense and the factual circumstances, the actors' motivations as well as the social context within which values orientations developed. Accordingly, the *theory of subcultures* postulates norms-related conflicts in respect of differences of social status (Cohen, 1955). Delinquency is connected to a sub-cultural norm system, according to which the actors behave. In contrast, Sykes and Matza (1957) emphasize the *moral ambivalence* of delinquents. They state that the latter do not reject the dominating norms but mostly accept them; however, they learn "techniques of neutralization" by which they fight off moral demands. Also Emler (1984) emphasizes the social nature of delinquency: The agents choose a "delinquent identity" (p. 227) to gain social reputation within their peer group. From the point of view of these approaches, delinquency is less the result of a lack of moral motivation as it is a connection to adopting deviant patterns of action and orientation.

According to Kohlberg (1978) and Jennings, Kilkenny and Kohlberg (1983), delinquents show strong developmental delays regarding their moral judgment. This assumption is based on 13 studies in the course of which juvenile delinquents reasoned primarily at the pre-conventional stages 1 and 2, whereas non-delinquents achieved conventional stages 3 and 4. The authors postulate that criminal offenses are rather compatible with *pre-conventional morality*. Although the latter is not the cause of delinquency, nonetheless, the lower the stage the easier it is to ignore or rationalize one's own judgment. According to Jennings et al. (1983), the pre-conventional thinker "...feels less obligated to conform" (p. 311) to social norms. This explanation does not focus on a cognitive, but on a motivational aspect; that is, it is a weak feeling of obligation. This argumentation is based on the assumption that moral motivation develops in close connection with moral judgment. Moral rules are known at the pre-conventional level, but the reasons for their validity are only insufficiently understood, and from this, a low degree of motivation results. In contrast, moral judgment from stage 3 onwards is considered as an important condition for the control of criminal stimuli: "Moral reasoning of increased maturity has an insulating effect against delinquency" (ibid.).

Kohlberg's theses are problematic, both from the empirical and the theoretical points of view:

- His results refer only to youth up to about 16 years of age, and generalizing these results for young adults lacks any empirical evidence.
- His theses are in contradiction to his own analyses, which indicate a close connection between moral judgment and moral action only for stage 5 or moral type B, but not for conventional stages 3 and 4 (Kohlberg, 1984, pp. 498-581).
- The thesis of motivation increasing at any higher stage is untenable (Oser, 1999).

The analysis of delinquency requires the integration of further dimensions of moral development, especially of moral motivation. In his later works, Kohlberg integrates motivational aspects more strongly into his theory. Following Piaget, he postulates a development from a heteronomous A-Type to an autonomous B-Type of moral judgment (Colby, & Kohlberg, 1987a, pp. 315-387). Essential for the "moral types" is less the cognitive *complexity* of judgments than their strength of obligation, as well as *generally applying them* to different contexts: The autonomous type "accepts the obligations inherent in moral rules and principles" (p. 351). In contrast, the heteronomous type "is constrained by rules and laws that he does not experience as intrinsically obligating" (ibid.). A number of studies provide evidence for the relevance of moral types; they are more closely related to moral action and to violent behaviour than stages 1 to 4 (Kohlberg, 1984, pp. 498ff.;

Krettenauer, & Edelstein, 1999). However, this concept contradicts the assumption that each higher stage is associated with increased consistency between judgment and action, since subjects of stage 3B act more consistently than those of stage 4A. With individuals of the B-Type, moral norms appear more motivationally rooted. Thus, the types may also be more relevant than the stages in attempting to analyze delinquency.

In general, criminality is a complex social problem which is not primarily the result of deficits of moral socialization. Nevertheless, moral judgments and motives or a lack thereof can play an important role. The way in which humans judge on moral norms, their own behaviour and themselves, the significance moral values and motives have for their selves, is important for preliminary considerations on criminal offenses and for their interpretation in retrospect: Moral motives may be completely missing or be superimposed by other motives; it may be that one's own actions are not at all recognized as being morally relevant; moral demands may be perceived but neutralized.

With respect to the relationship between moral motivation and delinquency, Nisan's (1993) observation is important that humans orient their actions more to the "principle of maintaining personal identity" (p. 253) than strictly to rules. Accordingly, it is not the case that any transgression endangers the identity; the crucial question is "*to what extent* an action harms one's personal identity" (p. 253). Generally, individuals are considerably different in respect of the value of morality for themselves and how much deviation from that what they consider right they can accept for themselves (Blasi, 1993; Hardy, & Gustavo, 2005; Nunner-Winkler, 1993). If people do not build up moral motivation, that is, if morality does not become a "core commitment" (Blasi, 2004, p. 344), this may result in an ambivalent attitude: namely, while norms are generally accepted, their violation does not really endanger one's own self-image.

Generally, most people do not need a moral commitment to obey the law or to comply with moral norms; a conformed morality appears sufficient. However, when criminal influences are strong, a commitment to morality is seen as a personal resource by which one can resist criminal impulses. We do not expect most juvenile delinquents to have a high moral motivation. However, we expect them to have internalized moral norms, at least to a certain degree. Thus, we assume that they have to neutralize moral demands when committing crimes.Using strategies of neutralization would indicate that they do not show a complete lack of moral motivation but are ambivalent towards moral norms (Sykes, & Matza, 1957). Telling about reactions as guilt or regret could indicate a more consistent and stronger integration of morality into the self.

Thus, important for the analysis of the moral development of delinquents is their *subsequent reaction* to their own behaviour, as this reaction is an indicator of their morality. As Blasi (1993) says: "A person can be deeply moral even if he or she engages in actions that are morally ambiguous or outright immoral; in this case, the integration of morality in personality could be seen in one's response to one's own action, e.g., regret, guilt, and concrete attempts to repair the damage and reconstitute one's values" (p. 120).

MORALITY AND DELINQUENCY: EMPIRICAL FINDINGS

In the following section, I will present the results of our study on imprisoned juveniles and young adults.The study was carried out in the context of a just community-intervention in a juvenile prison (Brumlik, 1998; Sutter, 2007; Sutter, Baader & Weyers, 1998). A wide empirical analysis is applied. Cognitive as well as motivational moral aspects were examined: moral judgment, general acceptance of moral norms and moral type. Additionally, the way in which the subjects reconstructed their own biographies and offenses were taken into account (Weyers, 2004). The moral stage and moral type were assessed, using Kohlberg's "Moral Judgment Interview" and his methods of analysis (Colby, & Kohlberg, 1987a, b). The biographical self-presentation and reconstruction of the offenses were obtained using biographical interviews and evaluated qualitatively (Schütze, 1983). The biographical descriptions were also compared with the factual reconstructions, as detailed in the official court documents. As moral motives develop in the context of biography, we may expect information about the patterns of moral motivation precisely from biographical narrations. For, the main focus of this chapter is on the analysis of the biographical self-presentations.

The sample consisted of 30 randomly selected male inmates of a German juvenile detention centre, between 16 and 23 years of age. The subjects had mainly committed more serious offenses - including murder, robbery and assault, and were given sentences ranging from 1.5 to 8 years. The reconstruction of their offenses, according to the verdicts, shows that all actors engaged in morally relevant actions which were meant to harm others (Weyers, 2004, pp. 139-149).

Acceptance of Moral Norms, Moral Judgment and Moral Type

Our findings contradict the thesis that juvenile delinquents reject essential moral norms because they have internalized deviant norms (Cohen, 1955; Emler, 1984). All 30 subjects were not only in support of keeping laws, but also of punishment for offenses such as theft or criminal assaults. In the context of the Heinz-Dilemma (Colby, & Kohlberg, 1987b), 29 subjects *support* breaking into the pharmacy to save a life. This suggests that herein the actor's reasoning is not primarily based on what is socially desired. However, the *general* acceptance of moral laws tells nothing about the *stage* and *type* of moral judgment as well as about how *one*'s own offense is judged.

Do delinquents judge primarily at the preconventional stages 1 and 2, as Kohlberg assumed? Our results show a different image: 19 people reached stage 3, five the transitional stage 3/4, and two even stage 4 (Weyers, 2004, p. 161). Thus, the great majority judges at the conventional level while only four juveniles reason at the transitional stage 2/3. The average is 309 (WAS[2]). These results argue – as do the results by Stams et al. (2006) – in favor of a developmental delay. However, the findings argue against Kohlberg's thesis, because the focus of his explanation is not concerning a delay, but rather the conception of "pre-conventional morality".

Kohlberg's concept of moral types includes more motivational aspects and is thus more relevant for action than the stages (Kohlberg, 1984; Krettenauer, & Edelstein, 1999). This typology was extended by an *ambivalent* type (A/B), as in the course of assessment many subjects achieved numerous A- *and* B-scores (Colby, & Kohlberg, 1987b, pp. 909-977). Whereas A and B depict ideal-typical developmental poles, type A/B represents an empirically mixed type. It represents a cognitively differentiated kind of type A and is similar to group morality: Moral obligations are hardly generalized but stay restricted to friends and family (Weyers, 2004). As type B implies a stronger obligation and generalization of moral judgments, there was the expectation that delinquency rather corresponds to types A and A/B. Indeed, the majority can be classified as belonging to type A (five subjects) or type A/B (16) but almost one third judges according to type B. For these nine subjects, morality appears to comprise an important component of their selves.

It seems reasonable to reverse the perspective: The actors must interpret their own behaviour and imprisonment and integrate both into their biographies. If type B comes along with an appreciable moral commitment, this must be reflected by the retrospective reaction to offenses.

Biographical Self-Presentation and Reconstruction

How do these juveniles and young adults present their offenses and how do they present themselves as agents in this context? Biographic-narrative interviews were conducted with 17 out of the 30 subjects (Schütze, 1983). To avoid any strategic orientation at social expectations, no *moral* question was asked, but the subjects were asked to tell their entire biography. After the narration, we added a few questions concerning the committed crimes and the subjects' expectations towards the future among others.

Biographical presentations reflect previous experiences but they are also structured according to the current situation and present the narrator's favorite self-image (Rosenthal, 1995). Even statements on *previous* motives and experiences are reconstructions from *today's* point of view. Thus, when analyzing them, we must distinguish the point of view of the past from that of today. The analysis is oriented at the chronological and topical structure of the narration. The main interest is in morally relevant categories: Previous and current patterns of orientation; moral (and immoral) judgments, motives and emotions; neutralization strategies; processes of biographical change. The narrations are then contrasted with how the offenses were presented by the verdicts. These juridical reconstructions are not objective judgments but they give an idea whether the biographical narratives were plausible and how important omissions and distortions were.

In the course of the analysis, six types of biographical self-presentation could be worked out. They included quite different perspectives of the juveniles and young adults towards themselves and their offenses. In the following, by way of short excerpts from interviews, I will explain three types in more detail and, due to lack of space, give short summaries of the three other types (Weyers, 2004, pp. 231-295).

The "Criminal Deviant".   Sven[3], 21 years old, was classified as stage 3/4 and moral type A/B. He was sentenced to six years of imprisonment. Sven describes himself as a *"loner"*[4], having had only one *"true friend"*. At the age of 14, he had become the friend of a 20 year old soldier who had *"fought with him"* and had shown him how to *"stand pain"* and to *"really hit back"*. In retrospect, he sees this as a key experience: *"I see this as the foundation stone of what became of me later"*. He tells that *"it"* started at the age of 14. His friend had told him about his own criminal offenses: *"Well, and then I thought: 'Now that's the real thing', somehow I liked it"*. Finally, he beat those guys who had beaten him before, and *"from that time on I knew that once I would belong to that side instead of the other side"*.

It is not clear if this statement is congruent with his experiences at that time: In *retrospect* he interprets himself as somebody who *already then* had understood himself to be deviant, as somebody belonging to the other side. He considers this deviant side to be more attractive and to fit his own inclinations (*"that's the real thing"*; *"I liked it"*) – and he constructs a biographical continuity from today back to his childhood. Accordingly, he interprets taking some money from his grandfather at the age of eight as evidence of his *"criminal"* personality: *"Already at an early age I found out that I have criminal dispositions"*. This is a construction from today's point of view and not the point of view of the child. But this interpretation makes clear that Sven sees delinquency as an inherent part of his personality, which he evaluates positively. This self-concept makes his behaviour look biographically coherent.

Sven gives *"fun"*, *"thrill"* and *"money"* as motives for his many burglaries. Taking out windows and lock-picking had been something he *"really liked"*, *"fascinating"*. He only implies the facticity of other offenses which had not been proven. They had been *"pure action"* and *"even more risky"*. He said that he is *"proud"* that these *"well planned"* offenses had *"never been detected"*. These formulations show that these are both previous and current motive structures: He *interpreted and still interprets* these actions in a very positive way.

Sven also mentions earlier *moral* interpretations: Once, when he imagined how he himself would feel if concerned, he had thought that stealing was *"ratty"*. But this insight was at once neutralized with the action normalized (*"also many others do it"*), the victim devalued (*"maybe he steals himself"*) and personal distance emphasized (*"I don't know him"*). Sven described this process as an active attempt: *"So I tried to suppress it"*; *"that what is to be expected, money and things, has more weight then, and so you prefer doing this"*.

Sven committed his main offense with an accomplice. The victim was a woman they knew, who shortly before had been interrogated by the police about these burglaries. Sven reports the severe physical and sexual act of violence (going as far as making plans for murder) like a sober chronicler; there are hardly any differences from the account by the court. He describes what he was feeling during the deed as a *"fight of emotions within"*. However, while admitting his aggressive stimuli, he *"fights down"* the moral emotion. He had seen the *"the plea in the eyes"* of the victim, but this had only made him *"even more furious"*. Neutralization strategies play an important role for his behaviour, most of all the interpretation of *"betrayal"*, through which the responsibility is shifted towards the victim. Sven describes what he did by a metaphor: He follows the insinuations of the *"bad angel"*, while, on the other hand, he fights off the *"good angel"* by *"covering his ears"*. Again, he describes his behaviour not as a loss of control but as intentional.

Indeed, in retrospect, Sven judges his violent deed very negatively: *"I do see, it was a cold deed, an emotionless deed, that was dirty, after all"*. But he judges from an observer's point of view; his judgment is not motivationally rooted. This is also suggested by his judgment concerning his punishment: *"Not such a severe punishment for a start, maybe it wasn't a great thing to do, but still"*. Here, a strongly minimizing interpretation of the deed becomes obvious. Sven has neither feelings of guilt nor any biographic conflict. Although he knows that what he did was not right and he sees the suffering of his victims, there is no compassion. For him, accomplishing self-related goals is much more important. Therefore, it does not come as a surprise that he pursues new criminal intentions. He is aware of the possible consequences of his behaviour (*"clink"*), so everything would have to be done *"101 per cent perfectly"*.

The "Hero".   *Martin*, 22 years old, was classified as stage 3 and moral type A/B. He presents himself and his actions as a heroic story. After at first telling about some minor offenses, he tells about three bank robberies which he had committed together with a friend. These robberies had been *"no problem at all"*, indeed *"child's play"*. They had robbed *"240,000 Deutschmarks"* and spent so much money that after three weeks it had *"gone"*: He tells about *"cars"*, *"motorbikes"* and *"fake IDs"*, about *"cocaine"*, *"parties"*, *"most expensive hotels"* and a *"brothel"*, where they had *"paid 2,000 Deutschmarks for one who only wanted 100"*. Moral aspects do not play any role here and the story completely lacks credibility. Only when asked later, did he report the first two robberies as failure. Moreover, according to the court, 240,000 had not been stolen. The figure was in fact merely 8,500 Deutschmarks.

At first, Martin tells about the later holdup of a passerby, only in passing and without any moral reservations. When asked later, he gives more details of the circumstances. When his accomplice told him to use his baseball bat, he had scruples: *"Somehow I couldn't do it, there was a brake, telling me you can't hit him"*. But, nevertheless, finally he hit *"two times"*; they took the money and left the heavily injured victim on the ground. From today's point of view, he does not condemn the deed, but shows a certain degree of distancing: "*What I also think these days is, if it was me to run in the street now and it was me to be beaten up there*". However, "*to be beaten up*" is strongly belittling. Only when Martin agrees to tell the deed in detail, are the scruples at that time, as well as the current distance, revealed. However, these emotions disturb his preferred self-image, just as the failed robberies do not fit to a success story.

The two other "heroes" of the study also present themselves as successful gangsters leading wild lives. To present themselves as strong, cool guys, events are exaggerated or simply invented. They hardly see, or they neutralize the moral relevance of their behaviour; negative self-evaluations or feelings of guilt do not play any role at all. Also, a biographical change and turning away from delinquency cannot be observed.

The "Remorseful Sinner".   A widely different way of presenting oneself is given by *Mahmut*, 18 years old. He was classified as stage 3 and moral type B. He tells at first about a number of calamities during his childhood: about war, being a refugee, the death of his parents and serious illness. At the age of 16, he had stabbed another youth to death. He had been hanging around with friends outside a youth club and a fight broke out with other boys. He describes his deed as a kind of accident: He only intended to "*show*" the knife and the victim – so to speak – ran into the knife. This is an exonerating interpretation; it reduces responsibility. It is undisputed that the deed was not planned; according to the court, he stabbed the boy but without intention to kill.

Mahmut describes his experiences after the deed as a mental breakdown, accompanied by acts of self-destruction: Drug use, depression and a suicide attempt are also documented in the prison files. His narration of the trial is dominated by moral shame: He wishes the ground would open and swallow him up; he says that he had not been able to look "*into anybody's eyes*", to "*keep his head high*". Also, other aspects suggest a moral way of interpreting his action: He tells that he had cried, had told the relatives that he was sorry, and that he had not been able to sleep anymore. The severity of his imprisonment (6.5 years) is not in the focus of his narrative; the focus is around his feelings of guilt. He clearly presents himself as the perpetrator: "*For me, all that was inside me was: `You have killed somebody`*".

The moral interpretation of what Mahmut did is the main aspect of his narration. However, he sees himself only partly as the acting subject: "*How could that happen?*", that was the "*only question*" he was "*constantly*" asking himself. He places this powerless suffering into a biographical frame: "*With me, it is always this way: that thing which I believe will never happen to me, that happens*". He mentions his mother's death, his operation, the threat of being extradited, and he also places his deed into this context. Mahmut interprets his life in the sense of a "trajectory" (Strauss, & Glaser, 1970). He does not see himself as the subject of his biography - too uncontrollable are the events which descend on him. Also, the killing he sees rather as something which has happened to him than as an action on others. This interpretation is the expression of a deep rift between the deed and his self-image, of being alienated from his own personality. This deed cannot be integrated into his biography. Nonetheless, he is able to maintain his self-image of being a good man, without denying what he has done - because he did not mean it, because it "*happened*".

The "Victim".   The two individuals of this type had committed homicides and experience serious identity crises. In contrast with the "sinner", however, they do not react with remorse or feelings of guilt but by rejecting responsibility, going as far as to completely deny their offenses or their own complicity: A planned homicide is reinterpreted as an act of self-defense, and complicity in the murder is denied. Accordingly, the actors emphasize that they are innocent: From this perspective, the offenders become victims of the judicial system. These massive strategies of rejection suggest that there are latent moral interpretations and feelings. However, both agents do not show any compassion towards their victims but only towards their mothers, whom they have failed. These latent feelings of shame and guilt seem less due to personal moral sentiments and judgments than to the reactions of the social environment, of their mothers in particular. By denying guilt, an attempt is made to maintain one's self-image and accompanying social relations, but their identity appears strongly fragmented. In both cases, neither a biographical change nor turning away from delinquency can be observed.

The "New Adult".   The most striking feature of the "new adults" is biographical change, which becomes obvious by strictly separating their points of view of the past and of today. The three actors of this type had committed narcotics offenses, bodily injuries and property offenses. They do not present themselves as "remorseful sinners"; they do not experience serious identity crises and have no (serious) feelings of guilt. The moral perspective is not predominant, but it is clearly recognizable: It becomes obvious by judging their offenses and their previous personalities negatively, by regret, shame and avoiding the rejection of responsibility. These actors maintain their moral integrity by having changed, by having become somebody else: Criminal deeds are no longer consistent with their own identity. It is only partly clear what has caused or motivated their change. Personal experiences in particular play a central role, but they also appear to come along with moral considerations: Two actors consider their times of imprisonment to be a positive experience, a time of penitence and thinking about their lives and offenses. For one actor, the birth of his child ("*the most important thing in my life*") and his responsibility for it plays a crucial role. What all actors have in common is a strong desire to leave their former lives behind and to start "*a normal, new life*".

The "Stupid Boy".   These actors also characterize their own offenses - most of all bodily injuries, narcotics offenses and robberies - as "stupidity". However, this characterization is a strategy of trivialization. Moral considerations or motives, as well as processes of biographical change cannot be observed. There is no negative judgment on one's own person or behaviour, also no indications of regret or guilt; instead, there is a frequent use of neutralization and justification strategies. The narrations of these actors reveal a naive perspective on their lives and crimes: They present themselves as somebody being quite okay, somebody without bad intentions, having not done anything bad, after all. Conspicuous is the relevance of the peer-group for their identities: "*Not to make a fool of myself in front of the others*" is what one actor gives as his main motive for a "*duel*" in the course of which he seriously injures his counterpart. Another actor takes part in a bank robbery, for "*I didn't want to be seen as the guy who is afraid*". The main motivation of these actors is gaining or maintaining reputation within the deviant peer-group and not losing face in front of it (Emler, 1984). This type seems to be connected to age: All five actors are between 16 and 18 years of age and belong to the youngest third of the sample.

Conclusion: These types of self-presentations show different patterns of integrating delinquency into their biographies. The actors' reactions to their behaviour reveal motivational structures in respect of delinquency and the significance of moral values and motives for their selves. The "sinner", as well as the "new adult" adopts a moral point of view. The "victim" totally rejects any responsibility; for the other types, moral aspects do not play any significant role. There are indications of a connection to Kohlberg's concept of moral types: The two "sinners" and the three "new adults" judge as expected of moral type B, that is, only for these *five* agents moral aspects are a relevant part of their self-presentation. In contrast, no relation to moral stage can be found (see Table 1).

Table 1: Types of biographical self-presentation (n=16[a])

Type	Frequency	Crucial criteria of self-presentation	Moral type	Moral stage	Main motives
Criminal deviant	1	deviant identity: on the other side; fascinated by committing crimes; criminal plans for the future	A/B	3/4	money, fun, thrill; revenge; self-image: belong to the other side
Hero	3	success story: presentation as strong, cool guy (as little Al Capone); biographical continuity	A/B	3	money; maintaining (self-) image as a strong/cool guy
Remorseful sinner	2	strong feelings of guilt and shame; identity crisis (intensity depends on the severity of the offense)	B	3	maintaining or reconstituting (self-) image as a good man

(Continued)

Table 1: (Continued)

Type	Frequency	Crucial criteria of self-presentation	Moral type	Moral stage	Main motives
Victim	2	denial of guilt and responsibility; presentation as victim of the justice; identity crisis (homicide)	A/B	3, 3/4	money; maintain social relations: rejecting attributions (murderer)
New adult	3	biographical change: having become somebody else; regret and negative self-evaluation (with respect to former offenses)	B	3, 3/4	maintaining (self-) image as a reformed man; leaving one's former life behind
Stupid boy	5	naivety; trivialization of the crimes ("stupidity"); biographical continuity	A, A/B	2/3, 3	gaining or maintaining peer-group reputation

a) one individual could not be classified according to any type.

DISCUSSION: MORAL AMBIVALENCE AND WEAK MORAL MOTIVATION

Moral immaturity is not the *cause* of delinquency, but moral judgments and moral motives may have an influence on *whether* people commit offenses, as they offer the possibility of self-regulation and self-control. Here, I follow Frankfurt's (1993) assumption that one is capable of influencing one's own desires and motives. The subject is not simply driven by stimuli but is capable - also in the light of moral norms - of reflecting on them, controlling them, and choosing from alternatives. Whether moral judgments and motives have a regulative function seems to depend more on motivational commitment to morality than on the notion of them being at a certain moral stage. The concept of moral motivation as a second-order desire (Blasi, 1993; Nunner-Winkler, 1993) is supported by our empirical results: The subjects in our study only show slight *cognitive* developmental delays; they know moral norms and understand them. However, in the context of their concrete actions, they often ignore or neutralize moral demands. Thus, cognitive and motivational aspects of morality have to be correlated.

The delinquents under analysis herein are not sociopaths. They accept moral norms in general but stay highly ambivalent towards them. Sykes and Matza (1957) described this ambivalence as well as several neutralization techniques. These techniques can be understood as a crucial condition for criminal behaviour: It is *negative moral judgments*, judgments about *a lack of* responsibility, the function of which is fighting off moral demands. As seen in the narrations of Sven and others, these strategies make it possible to minimize feelings of guilt and disapproval and thus to maintain one's own self-image as well as social relations (Scott, & Lyman, 1968). The more serious the offense, the stronger is the necessity to justify it towards oneself and others. Neutralization strategies are significant, not only *in retrospect* but also in *planning* the action (Agnew, 1994; Bandura, 2002; Shields, & Whitehall, 1994). The rejection of anticipated feelings of guilt supports the subject in performing the action and structures their later reactions to it. If there are strong feelings of guilt, the offense is not repeated or it is not committed at all. The delinquents' frequent application of neutralizations suggests that they are ambivalent towards moral norms but do not show a *complete* lack of morality. In this case, neutralizations would not be necessary.

According to Nisan (1993), humans orient their actions to the "principle of maintaining personal identity" (p. 253). He sees, as Blasi (1993) does, maintaining one's own identity as an important motivational source. A certain deviation from norms is seen as normal, because humans demand moral perfection neither from themselves nor from others. Thus, with respect to delinquency, the crucial question is *whether* and *to what extent* an action endangers one's identity.

Nunner-Winkler (1993) emphasizes the difference between the acquisition of moral knowledge and the growth of moral motivation. Whereas, at an early age, almost all children know about the intrinsic validity of moral rules, the development of a self-commitment to morality is a differentiated learning process which happens at different speeds and with different degrees of success. However, a strict separation of affective and cognitive learning is not reasonable because it is through moral socialization that one acquires knowledge of rules while, at the same time, learning about its affective significance. Apart from the *general* validity of norms, in social interaction one also learns about their *context-specific* relevance and the degree to which one might regard them as binding: How seriously must these rules be taken? Under which circumstances can a violation of norms be accepted? Children and juveniles who grow up in environments, which are morally inconsistent, seem to experience a strong discrepancy between the validity claim of moral norms and their realization in different contexts. As a consequence, many learn that moral norms must not always be taken seriously.

Under such conditions, moral norms and values hardly become an important part of the self and this results in a weak moral motivation and an ambivalent attitude: Norms are generally accepted, but in certain contexts they are not action-guiding, because their violation does not harm one's identity. This moral ambivalence is not restricted to criminal offenders. However, our findings show that with many of them the discrepancy between what they believe to be *actually right* and what they believe to be *still acceptable* is particularly large. They do not believe that their offenses were *right*, but they also do not consider them as *bad*. Even serious offenses are justified or not even recognized as being morally relevant. Moral judgments play an important role, but only *negatively*, in the sense of neutralization. Especially in the case of seriously injuring other people, it becomes obvious that moral impulses and interpretations do exist but are partly suppressed because they endanger the goal of the action – it may be a material or social one. As a result, the subsequent reaction is mostly characterized by rejecting responsibility and by moral indifference.

The self-presentations of the juvenile offenders reveal central biographical patterns and motivations. The agents do not present the beginning of their "careers" in the sense of intentional actions. Delinquency is not consciously strived for but learned in passing. They join criminal deeds of their clique or friends without seriously considering what they are doing. Herein, an acting subject can hardly be observed. This "letting go" reveals a low degree of orientation towards the future and a low degree of understanding oneself as an agency (Damon, & Hart, 1988). In the biographies of all subjects of our study, with the exception of Mahmut, the strong influence of delinquent peer-groups on the development of their identity and their learning of deviant patterns of orientation and behaviour is obvious. Almost all agents show a growing habituation to delinquency, moral interpretations hardly play any role – unless other people are seriously injured.

However, the biographical depictions also include "core narrations" (Keupp, 1999, p. 217) or "life themes" (Noam, 1993, p. 210) which point out very different motivational structures.

For the "*criminal deviant*", delinquency is a part of his life plan. This becomes obvious by his way of interpreting "*criminal dispositions*", by his "*fascination*" with committing burglaries as well as his plans for the future. These aspects are fundamental to Sven's deviant identity and provide biographical coherence and continuity. Obtaining money is one motive for his crimes, but his feelings of "fascination", "fun" and "thrill" indicate that committing crimes is also an end in itself. Sven presents himself as a born and professional criminal, who does not have any self-image as a good man – quite the contrary: "I belong to the other side".

The "*hero*" is likewise motivated by obtaining money and judges his offenses positively. The main aspect of this type is presenting himself as a cool and tough guy; this contradicts reality: He suppresses certain events and invents others, in order to present his preferred self-image, for which moral values and motives do not play any role at all. Nevertheless, his heroic stories indicate wishful fantasies of greatness rather than a criminal life plan or a deviant identity: "I would like to be a cool, tough guy".

Crucial for the "*remorseful sinner*" is a moral interpretation of his deed, accompanied by strong feelings of guilt and an existential crisis. Mahmut experiences a break between what he did and his identity, feeling alienated from his own personality. As his killing was not intentional, and by accepting his guilt, he is able to maintain his self-image as a good man and to distance himself from the killing: "It was not me, I did not mean it".

Those actors presenting themselves as "*victims*" also experience a severe existential crisis. They try to maintain a positive (self-)image by totally rejecting responsibility and the attribution of being a murderer. Denying their guilt is their essential biographical topic. But they do not succeed in "solving" the crisis; their identity appears fragmented. There are strong contradictions between the way in which they see themselves and the way they are perceived by others: "I am different from what they say, I am innocent".

Biographical change is essential to the identity construction of the *"new adult"*. This type is able to present a positive self-image by reformation and distancing himself from earlier behaviour. These actors construct a break between past and present. Their core narrations are leaving their former life behind and maintaining the (self-)image as being a reformed man: "Today I am not like I used to be"; "I would not do it today".

The identity construction of the *"stupid boy"* is still fragile. He positively evaluates his life up to now and maintains his positive self-image by trivializing his offenses: He did not intend or do anything really bad. An essential motive of these actors is gaining or maintaining reputation and recognition by the peer group: "I do not want to lose face in front of the others".

The biographical analyses suggest that only the "sinner" and the "new adult" have established an appreciable commitment to morality. This assumption is also suggested by classifying these actors under moral type B. Even if morality is not in the focus of their identity, this commitment is a resource to avoid further criminal offenses. The analyses also indicate that the other actors have not built up a moral motivation. With respect to Blasi's (1993) concept of moral self, the following can be concluded regarding these actors: Moral understanding is not translated into judgments of personal responsibility; morality is not or only weakly integrated in their identity; morality is subordinated to non-moral desires or commitments. Thus, morality is not a motivational force for acting.

However, with the exception of the "criminal deviant", the agents' plans for the future include ideas of normality which are deeply in contrast with delinquency and prison. The desire to *"lead a normal life"* or to start a *"new life"* is an often quoted motive which might initiate processes of biographical change. Whether this motive may contribute to turning away from delinquency depends not only on the actors but also on many conditions in their social environment.

CONCLUSION

Educational implications: The findings clearly indicate that the subjects differ strongly from one another. These differing conditions of moral development must be taken into consideration in social work with juvenile delinquents. The results also suggest that moral development can play an important role in biographical change and in turning away from delinquency. However, the results imply that purely cognitive approaches of moral education have only a limited impact. Measures for facilitating moral development in penal institutions have to take into account the motivational and biographical dimension of morality and the actor's neutralization strategies with regard to their criminal offences. When working with juveniles who present themselves in ways such as the "remorseful sinner" or a "new adult", there is entailed a great opportunity to encourage processes of biographical change. Due to their young age, this may apply to a lesser extent to the "stupid boys". The delinquent patterns of the "hero", the "victim" and especially the "criminal deviant" however, seem to be more firmly established. Thus, many different and substantial psycho-social measures are required.

In this context, there is some empirical evidence that just-community interventions have a positive influence on the moral development of juvenile offenders (Jennings, et al., 1983; Sutter, et al., 1998; Sutter, 2007; Weyers, 2010). The just-community intervention addresses both cognitive and motivational aspects of development; the focus is not on moral reasoning but on participation and cooperation in real-life issues and conflicts. However, further research is needed to clarify what works in this intervention. Should it be in establishing moral discussions and a moral atmosphere in the institution, as Jennings et al. (1983) argue, or facilitating processes of social negotiations, even if moral aspects play only a marginal role therein, as Sutter (2007) argues? Furthermore, we need further research focused on which other aspects of interventions are working. Generally, we need more investigation with respect to the impact of educational treatments in penal institutions and in social work with juvenile offenders.

There are several issues and questions for further research. The process of building-up a self-commitment to morality and the development of moral motivation in the course of life merits systematic attention, especially within a longitudinal framework. In this context, we need more investigation of the interplay of cognitive and affective aspects of moral development and of the relationship between moral motivation and biographical experiences in particular. This way, biographical processes and topics should come more into focus (Noam, 1993). Finally, with respect to delinquency, more information is needed about the ways in which strategies of neutralization and mechanisms of moral disengagement (Bandura, 2002) are learned and about their connection to the conditions of the social environment. As a consequence, we need a theoretical framework to bring together the development of morality with the development of identity and, furthermore, both of them with the individuals' biographical experiences within social contexts.

NOTES

[1] According to Thorkildsen (in this volume), readiness includes motivational and volitional processes.
[2] The "Weighed Average Score" is the mean value of the stage values of an interview: A value of 300 equates stage 3 (Colby, & Kohlberg, 1987b).
[3] All names have been changed, some biographic data were anonymized.
[4] All interview statements are given in Italics and with quotation marks.

REFERENCES

Agnew, R. (1994). The techniques of neutralization and violence. *Criminology, 32*, 555–580.
Bandura, A. (2002). Selective moral disengagement in the exercise of moral agency. *Journal of Moral Education, 31*, 101–119.
Bergman, R.M. (2004). Identity as motivation: Toward a theory of the moral self. In D.K. Lapsley & D. Narvaez (Eds.), *Moral development, self, and identity* (pp. 21–46). Mahwah, NJ: Erlbaum.
Blasi, A. (1983). Moral cognition and moral action: A theoretical perspective. *Developmental Review, 3*, 178–210.

Blasi, A. (1993). The development of identity. Some implications for moral functioning. In G. Noam & T. Wren (Eds.), *The moral self* (pp. 99–122). Cambridge: MIT Press.

Blasi, A. (2004). Moral functioning: Moral understanding and personality. In D.K. Lapsley & D. Narvaez (Eds.), *Moral development, self, and identity* (pp. 335–347). Mahwah, NJ: Erlbaum.

Brumlik, M. (1998). Just Community: A social cognitive research project in the penal system. *European Journal of Social Work, 1*, 339–346.

Cohen, A. K. (1955). *Delinquent boys. The culture of the gang.* Glencoe, IL: Free Press.

Colby, A., & Damon, W. (1992). *Some do care: Contemporary lives of moral commitment.* New York: Free Press.

Colby, A., & Kohlberg, L. (1987a). *The measurement of moral judgment. Vol. 1: Theoretical foundations and research validation.* Cambridge: University Press.

Colby, A., & Kohlberg, L. (1987b). *The measurement of moral judgment. Vol. 2: Standard issue scoring manual.* Cambridge: University Press.

Damon, W., & Hart, D. (1988). *Self-understanding in childhood and adolescence.* Cambridge: University Press.

Eisenhardt, T. (2005). *Dissoziales Verhalten. Ursachen und Prävention.* Frankfurt a.M.: Lang.

Emler, N.(1984). Differential involvement in delinquency: Toward an interpretation in terms of reputation management. In B. Maher, & W. Maher (Eds.), *Progress in experimental personality research* (Vol. 13, pp. 173–239). New York: Academic Press.

Frankfurt, H. (1993). On the necessity of ideals. In G. Noam, & T. Wren (Eds.), *The moral self* (pp. 16–26). Cambridge: MIT Press.

Hardy, S. A., & Gustavo, C. (2005). Identity as a source of moral motivation. *Human Development, 48*, 232–256.

Jennings, W., Kilkenny, R., & Kohlberg, L. (1983). Moral-development theory and practice of youthful and adult offenders. In W. Laufer, & J. Day (Eds.), *Personality theory, moral development and criminal behaviour* (pp. 281–355). Lexington: Heath.

Keller, M. (2004). Self in relationship. In D.K. Lapsley, & D. Narvaez (Eds.), *Moral development, self, and identity* (pp. 267–298). Mahwah, NJ: Erlbaum.

Keupp, H. (1999). *Identitätskonstruktionen.* Reinbek: Rowohlt.

Kohlberg, L. (1978). The cognitive developmental approach to behavior disorders: A study of the development of moral reasoning in delinquents. In G. Serban (Ed.), *Cognitive defects in the development of mental illness* (pp. 207–219). New York: Brunner-Mazel.

Kohlberg, L. (1984). *Essays on moral development. Vol. 2: The psychology of moral development.* San Francisco: Harper & Row.

Krettenauer, T., & Edelstein, W. (1999). From substages to moral types and beyond: An analysis of core criteria for morally autonomous judgments. *International Journal of Behavioral Development, 23*, 899–920.

Moshman, D. (2004). False moral identity: Self-serving denial in the maintenance of moral self-conceptions. In D.K. Lapsley, & D. Narvaez (Eds.), *Moral development, self, and identity* (pp. 83–109). Mahwah, NJ: Erlbaum.

Nisan, M. (1993). Balanced identity: Morality and other identity values.In G. Noam, & T. Wren (Eds.), *The moral self* (pp. 239–266). Cambridge: MIT Press.

Noam, G. (1993). "Normative vulnerabilities" of self and their transformations in moral action.In G. Noam, & T. Wren (Eds.), *The moral self* (pp. 209–238). Cambridge: MIT Press.

Nucci, L. (2004). Reflections on the moral self construct. In D.K. Lapsley, & D. Narvaez (Eds.), *Moral development, self, and identity* (pp. 111–132). Mahwah, NJ: Erlbaum.

Nunner-Winkler, G. (1993). The growth of moral motivation.In G. Noam, & T. Wren (Eds.), *The moral self* (pp. 269–291). Cambridge: MIT Press.

Oser, F. (1999). Die missachtete Freiheit moralischer Alternativen: Urteile über Handeln, Handeln ohne Urteile. In D. Garz, F. Oser, & W. Althof. (Eds.), *Moralisches Urteil und Handeln* (pp. 168–219). Frankfurt a.M.: Suhrkamp.

Priest, T., & McGrath, J. (1970). Techniques of neutralization: Young adult marijuana smokers. *Criminology, 8*, 185–194.

Rosenthal, G. (1995). *Erlebte und erzählte Lebensgeschichte.* Frankfurt a.M.: Campus.

Schütze, F. (1983). Biographieforschung und narratives Interview. *Neue Praxis, 13*, 283–294.

Scott, M., & Lyman, S. (1968). Accounts. *American Sociological Review, 33*, 46–62

Shields, I., & Whitehall, G. (1994). Neutralization and delinquency among teenagers. *Criminal Justice and Behavior, 21*, 223–235.

Stams, G.J., Brugman, D., Dekovic, M., van Rosmalen, L., van der Laan, P., & Gibbs, J.C. (2006). The moral judgment of juvenile delinquents: A meta-analysis. *Journal of Abnormal Child Psychology, 34*, 697–713.

Strauss, A., & Glaser, B. (1970). *Anguish. The case history of a dying trajectory.* Mill Valley, CA: Sociology Press.

Sutter, H. (2007). Demokratische Partizipation im Jugendstrafvollzug. *Sozialer Sinn, 8*, 131–158.

Sutter, H., Baader, M., & Weyers, S. (1998). Die "Demokratische Gemeinschaft" als Ort sozialen und moralischen Lernens. *Neue Praxis, 28*, 383–400.

Sykes, G., & Matza, D. (1957). Techniques of neutralization: A theory of delinquency. *American Sociological Review, 22*, 664–670.

Weyers, S. (2004). *Moral und Delinquenz. Moralische Entwicklung und Sozialisation straffälliger Jugendlicher.* Weinheim: Juventa.

Weyers, S. (2010). Demokratische Partizipation durch "Just Communities". In B. Dollinger, & H. Schmidt-Semisch (Eds.), *Handbuch Jugendkriminalität* (pp. 415–426). Wiesbaden: VS Verlag.

AFFILIATION

Stefan Weyers,
Institute for Educational Science
Johannes Gutenberg-University of Mainz
Mainz Germany

CLARK POWER & KRISTIN K. SHEEHAN

III. MORAL MOTIVATION AND SPORTS

INTRODUCTION

Largely neglected by moral psychologists, sports offer a special window into human motivation. Ryan and Deci (2007) note that "sport and exercise epitomize motivation" because of the "exertion, energy, focus, and ... discipline" they typically demand. Indeed, the leading investigators of motivation in education (Ames, 1992; Dwek, 1999; and Nicholls, 1989), as well as in psychology more generally, Ryan and Deci (2007), have found that their frameworks fit particularly well when applied to sport. Although athletes may need to be highly motivated to achieve success in sports, is there any reason to believe that their motivation is itself moral? Athletes do not play sports out of a sense of duty or obligation to others, nor do they play sports to better their communities or to overcome suffering and injustice.

The motivation to play sports is not even altruistic or prosocial in the sense that athletes choose to play primarily for to benefit others in need. The choice to play a sport is, however, a choice to engage in activity that should ideally bring enjoyment to oneself as well as to others. It is neither a selfish nor a selfless choice. It is also not a response to duty in the sense one does not have a moral obligation to play a sport in the same way that one has a moral obligation to respect the rights of others or to care for one's family. Although the choice to play a sport is not in itself a moral one, once one decides to play in sport, one tacitly agrees to abide by a set of conventional rules that the make the sport both challenging and fair. One can, of course, play a sport morally or immorally. Here is where moral motivation becomes especially relevant, given the competitive nature of sports. The importance given to winning in sports can distort an athlete's motivational orientation creating a strong temptation to cheat, to harm one's opponent, or even to ask oneself or a teammate to risk serious injury. Moreover, the culture in which one engages in a particular sport can blur the line between right and wrong, undermine moral responsibility, and lead to self-aggrandizement at the exploitation of others.

To put it simply, sports are rule-bound activities, which engage the human quest for excellence and which express human freedom and joy. Sports can teach us a great deal about moral psychology precisely because the complexity of the motives that surface at all levels of athletic competition. Sports are fundamentally "playful;" but we take them very seriously as we are willing enormous amounts of time, energy, and money to pursue them. In many sports environments today, the desire for personal and team success can and often does overwhelm the requirements of justice

K. Heinrichs, F. Oser & T. Lovat (Eds.), *Handbook of Moral Motivation: Theories, Models, Applications, 405–426.*

and civility robbing sports of their joy and threatening the foundations of sport itself. If sports are to survive as play, we must be able to sustain the critical role that moral motivation has in informing the way we compete.

MORAL MOTIVATION AND GOOD SPORT BEHAVIOUR

The philosopher, Randolf Feezel (2004) begins his inquiry into the ethics of sportsmanship with a familiar scenario of a coach taking advantage of the referees in order to win a basketball game. We have adapted it for use in our research:
At the end of a tie basketball game, a shot is taken from under the basket. The referee calls a foul but cannot see who was fouled. Coach Curran saw that the player fouled was the weakest free throw shooter. So he sends his best free throw shooter to the line.

> Did Coach Curran cheat? Was this an immoral act or was he simply doing what any competitor would do if offered the chance? Feezel (2004) judges Coach Curran to be acting unfairly and to be or at least to have acted as a "bad sport" (p. 84). In our view, he makes the high moral stage argument (Stage 5 in Kohlberg's scheme) that Coach Curran violated a constitutive rule of basketball, which he has a contractual obligation to uphold. Feezel goes on to note that in virtue theory, Coach Curran has shown himself to be lacking in "trust" and "integrity" (p. 84).

In discussing this scenario with high school and college coaches and athletes, we have encountered a sharp divide. A slight majority reported that they would do as Coach Curran did. Unlike Feezel, they did not see Coach Curran's decision as immoral or as lacking in virtue. They all noted that the culture of high school and college basketball is extremely competitive and that coaches are paid to win. Although some admitted that taking advantage of the referees' indecision was less than ideal, they also asserted that opposing coaches would do the same if they had the opportunity. Yet all of those who approved of Coach Curran's decision at the college or high school level disapproved of such a decision at the grade school level where they thought that the coach should be sensitive to the moral development of the young athletes. The fact that they regarded Coach Curran's behaviour as morally inappropriate in the context of younger players supports Feezel's judgment that no matter how excusable Coach Curran's decision may be in winning obsessed culture of professional, college, and even high school basketball, it is at the very least morally questionable.

Those who disagreed with Coach Curran's decision made two different arguments. The first focused on the importance of playing by the rules. For example, one college athlete stated, "The right things to do is to honor the rules of the game." He elaborated that following the rules is a matter of basic "fairness." The second argument appealed to the virtues of honesty and personal integrity. One athlete put it this way: "[it is] a decision of telling the truth when you know it." Several coaches and athletes pointed out that the coach should be a "role model" and that by putting winning before "character," Coach Curran had lost his moral authority as a coach.

Our ongoing research using this and other moral dilemmas involving cheating and aggression in sports suggests that there may be at least two sources of moral motivation for playing according the rules. The first focuses on the act itself and the importance of upholding the rules and the principle of fairness. The responses of this kind indicate that the motivation for following the rules comes from a love of or respect for the game itself. As one coach put it, "Coaches and players should be motivated by their love of the game to defend the fairness of competition." The second motivational source focuses on individual virtue and character. The responses of this latter kind refer to personal honesty and integrity. Some coaches regard this as a matter of personal integrity: "It [whether you cheat or not] reflects on your character." Other coaches view honesty and integrity as critical components of role of the coach as a "moral authority." The fact that same individuals often refer to both kids of justifications, leads us to believe that these two motivational frameworks are overlapping and mutually reinforcing. Loving the game and taking responsibility for upholding the highest standards of the game go hand and hand.

Yet we cannot fail to recognize that in spite of the strong motivational pull to do what is right, there is another motivation pull to do what it takes to win. Those who agree with Coach Curran believe that sending the best foul shooter to the line is all part of being competitive at the higher levels of organized sports. While some admit that they would rather not take advantage of the situation, they also believe that it is permissible and called for within the particular competitive context. Most who agree with Coach Curran are not saying that it is morally permissible to win at all costs. They agree that certain kinds of cheating are morally wrong, but that this not a situation in which a coach is taking an *unfair* advantage. They believe that they are operating within a social contract in which all coaches and players understand that they are free to exploit referees' indecision. In fact, coaches who agree with Coach Curran typically assume their opponents would do exactly the same thing if they were fouled.

Coaches who condone acting as Coach Curran did hesitate to excuse more overt attempts to influence referees' calls. For example, many believe that "flopping" in soccer and basketball goes too far and takes away from the game. Yet some still insist that flopping is an art form and a part of the game insofar as all teams engage in it. Our examples make clear that how individuals interpret their responsibility for upholding the rules of the game depends on their perception of the norms of the sport in which they are competing. In our view, as the competitive level increase, shared norms of fairness tend to devolve to the least common denominator as competitors think of each other as egoistically trying to get away with as much as the referees will allow. What gets lost in this devolution is respect for referees and respect for oneself as well as one's opponent. One does not respect referees when one tries to manipulate them; and one does not respect one's opponents, if there is a shared assumption that the only motivation to uphold the rules is purely extrinsic. We find it revealing that coaches and athletes defend manipulating officials as not on the basis of moral principle but of necessity. On some level, we all know that sports can and should be better than the way we sometimes play them, particularly at the highest levels of competition.

MORAL MOTIVATION AND TEAM UNITY

The moral motivation of sports is nowhere more evident than in the sacrifices that individuals make for their team. Anyone who has played a team sport will testify to the power of the team to elicit one's best effort. One of the great moments in the Olympics was when the gymnast Kerri Strug overcame the pain of a sprained ankle from her previous vault to clinch the gold medal for her team. Landing squarely on both feet at the completion of her vault, she tore the tendons in her ankle, which prohibited her from competing in later Olympic events. Yet Kerri's s willingness to sustain an injury for the good of her team made her a moral exemplar. Participating on a team encourages not only heroic acts of courage but also a commitment to cooperate for the sake of the team as a whole. This often means that the "stars" on the team have to adjust their play for sake of team cohesiveness. There is much truth to the well worn cliché, "there is no 'I' in team." All great coaches understand that team chemistry wins games. Knute Rockne, the legendary Notre Dame football coach and one the "fathers of the field of Sports Psychology" emphasized teamwork over talent: "The secret is to work less as individuals and more as a team. As a coach, I play not my eleven best, but my best eleven." We might object that the motivation that comes from belonging to a team is not purely moral but mixed with the recognition that that team cohesiveness contributes to winning. Yet our research with athletes from ages twelve to fifty suggests that concern for the team as a whole is a sufficient motivation for self-sacrifice. Most athletes believe that every member of a team has an obligation to put the welfare of the team ahead of her or his personal achievements for the sake of the team as a whole and for others on the team. Many athletes do not even mention that sacrificing for the team improves one's chances of winning, although this is certainly true. This sense of devotion to the team can extend beyond the sports field.

For example, we presented members of an urban high school team with the following dilemma:

> While the Cougars are waiting for their coach to take them into the locker room, a few players start kicking soccer balls at each other. One of the balls breaks a trophy in the trophy case. It is an expensive trophy that costs over $100. A few players sweep the floor up so no one will notice. Those who were throwing the ball ask everyone to keep quiet about what happened. A week later Coach White asks his players if they knew anything about a trophy that was found missing. Should anyone tell the truth? Why or why not?

After some joking about how members of the team should to stick together and deny knowing anything about the incident, one player spoke up, "We would let the coach know that we did and we would take care of it. If that had happened to our team trophy, we would have wanted the other team to pay for it." Another player explained, "Look we would want to do what is right and come up with the money for a new trophy." Asked who should be held responsible for paying for it, a third player responded, "All of us, we are brothers; we are in this together." Challenged whether it would be fair to ask teammates to pay for the trophy if they were one's who were kicking the ball, a fourth player smiled and said, look we are a team, we are all one. Those who weren't fooling around didn't stop those who were. We are in this together and we would all pay for this equally."

Many of the students on this team were immigrants from Africa, Latin America, and the Middle East. Their families and were poor and their parents rarely, if ever watched them play. The players told us that the year before we interviewed them, they were not a team at all but just a bunch of individuals, who quarreled and criticized each other. Things changed when their new coach, a custodian in their school, took a character-oriented coaching workshop that we designed (Play Like a Champion, 2010). That workshop emphasized encouraging the players to take ownership of the team and building a strong sense of community. The players told us that this season they had became a completely different team. The results showed in school where they helped each other to succeed in the classroom and on the soccer field where they won a league championship.

We can see from this example that sports teams can elicit a motivational power for self-sacrifice and devotion to the common good that extends beyond the playing field. Although that motivational power is exceedingly strong, it is moral only to the extent that the team's goals are moral. In the case of Kerri Strug's vault on an injured ankle, we may ask whether it was fair for her coach to have asked her to risk her future by taking that second jump. Does the end of winning a gold medal for her team justify the means of asking an 18 year-old athlete to compound an injury knowing that she would never let her team down? We may also ask what her teammates should and would have decided if asked. Would increasing their probably of winning the gold medal have outweighed any moral scruple they might have had?

IS WINNING EVERYTHING?

Anyone who follows or who has played sports knows that athletes will go to great lengths to achieve success for themselves and their teams. Whether their striving is morally motivated depends upon what they are willing to do to succeed. Anyone who competes must play to win. This is the whole point of engaging in any competitive game. There is little enjoyment participating in a race or in a basketball game if one does not believe that one's opponents are trying to win. In fact, there is little enjoyment in playing if winning comes too easily. Shields and Bredemeier (2009) argue, however, that not all competition is "true competition." They describe "decompetition" as playing to win by using whatever tactics one can get away with.

Decompetition undermines moral motivation by substituting the enjoyment of true competition for the extrinsic rewards that come from winning.

One of the most shocking illustrations of decompetition comes from a well known study conducted by Bob Goldman in the mid-1990s. He asked 198 Olympic or near Olympic level athletes to respond to two scenarios:

1. You are offered a banned performance-enhancing substance, with two guarantees: a) You will not be caught; b) You will win.
   Would you take the substance?
2. You are offered a banned performance-enhancing substance that comes with two guarantees: a) You will not be caught; b) You will win every competition you enter for the next five years and then you will die from the side-effects of the substance.
   Would you take it?

Goldman found that 193 of the athletes reported that they would cheat in the first scenario and over half would cheat in the second (Bamberger & Yaeger, 1997). Goldman noted that these responses have been consistent since he began his investigation in 1982 (Bamberger & Yaeger, 1997). Many commentators focused on the fact that more than half of these elite athletes were willing to die for their success. Yet when we think of all Olympic caliber athletes endure in order to attain world class status, we can better understand why so many would be willing to make the ultimate sacrifice. From this perspective, we can also appreciate why Kerri Strug would not let an injury keep her from taking her last vault.

What should disturb us more than the sacrifice athletes are willing to make for the ultimate recognition in their sport is the finding that practically every athlete would take the banned substance if they knew that they would not get caught. At the time of the study, a program to discourage the use of performance enhancing drugs through rigorous testing had been going on for over twenty years. It obviously had no positive effect on athletes' moral motivation. Nor apparently had it had much of an effect on athletes' behaviour as the use of banned substances had proliferated as new methods of cheating and avoiding dictation became available.

We may be tempted to conclude from the Goldman study that the quest to identify moral motivation in sports is a quixotic one. Sports pages are filled with stories of cheating scandals in almost every sport and at almost all competitive levels. Yet a study of the general population that Goldman's findings apply only to his elite sample (Connor & Mazanov, 2009). This leads to ask whether elite athletes are in a special category or whether the willingness to cheat and to put one's life on the line may be related in a linear way to the level at which one is competing. Research in this area is still at its infancy. The Connor and Mazanov (2009) study tells us what we may already suspect that the average person is not as willing to go to the lengths as the best athletes in the world. But we still may ask whether athletes at a high but not the highest level be willing to cheat and to sacrifice their lives to make it to the highest professional ranks. We have begun to explore this question with a very small sample of athletes at the Division I college level. Our findings at this point indicate that these athletes are far less willing to cheat (less than 50%) and far less willing to die (less than 10%) than those in Goldman's sample. One simple explanation for difference between our findings and Goldman's may simply be that that a gold medal is a far greater reward for achievement than a professional contract. Another explanation may be that Olympic level athletes have already gone to far greater lengths to achieve the successes they have won than college athletes who are not at the very top of their sport. While both of these explanations may have some truth, we believe that our college athletes were not all that dissimilar from Goldman's. Many of the college athletes admitted that they would be sorely tempted to cheat, and a relatively high percent (about 40%) said they would.

Can we conclude from these studies that sports have a corrupting influence on moral character, particularly as athletes become more accomplished and the rewards of competition increase? Although it may be true that the higher athletes rise in a sport, the greater the likelihood they will be motivated to do whatever they can to achieve the highest honors, is this simply owing to a lack of moral motivation? We believe that the problem is far more complicated. When we asked the varsity athletes in our sample whether they would be willing to take a performance enhancement drug that would guarantee success in a pickup game, they all found the question to be insulting. They all noted that competing in pickup games was entirely different from competing in college. The whole point of the pickup game, they explained, was for the joy of the competition itself. Taking unfair advantage robbed the game of meaning and of its enjoyment. Why then would athletes cheat in varsity competition? They told us that sports are more like a business at the college level, and that the "honor system" of the pickup game simply is not operative.

Much of the empirical evidence suggests that sports may be largely an amoral activity, which may even have a detrimental influence on moral development. Years ago, Bredemeier and Shields (1984) found that athletes' moral reasoning was lower than non-athletes on both hypothetical and practical sports dilemmas. Using a different measure of moral reasoning, Stoll and Beeler (2000) reported similar results. In an unpublished report, Stoll and Beeler (2005) noted that those findings have persisted and, in the case of women athletes, have grown worse. Finally, Kavussaunu and Ntoumanis (2003) found a negative correlation between the numbers of seasons that athletes participated in a sport and their moral functioning. Although one might be tempted to claim that participation in sports has a negative influence on moral development, we believe that it is more plausible that sports are for the most part largely morally neutral activities. By that we mean that sports do not ordinarily involve many moral decisions. Athletes who spend a great deal of time practicing and playing sports are, therefore, not spending time on other activities, such as community service or reading the newspapers that are more likely to engage their moral reasoning. Moreover, we find that few coaches or athletic administrators deliberately engage athletes' ethical judgment or sense of moral responsibility.

In fact, in some cases, coaches and athletes deliberately avoid bringing up potential contentious moral issues that might undermine team cohesiveness.

Bredemeier and Shields (1986) have gone so far as to suggest that sports competition can create a "morality-free" zone in which individuals do not feel bound by the same moral constraints and responsibilities that operate in other areas of life. This is an intriguing hypothesis, which draws some support in from athletes in high contact sports, like boxing and football, who describe themselves as undergoing a Dr. Jekyll to Mr. Hyde transformation from everyday life to the ring or playing field. Yet most athletes, even in high contact sports, recognize and accept moral as well as conventional restraints on their behaviour. In fact, sports by their very nature impose more restrictions on behaviour than there are in everyday life. For example, sports limit play to a bounded area and restrict the use of certain limbs, such the feet as in basketball or the hands in soccer.

The enjoyment that leads all people of all ages to play sports comes from developing the skills to meet the challenges that rule system imposes. It makes no sense to try to circumvent the very rules that give sports their individual character. Nor does it make sense to behave in ways that undermine the joy that comes from competition. Yet, as we shown, moral motivation in sport is often difficult to maintain, especially in certain environments that distort the nature of sport as play.

Our ongoing investigations into moral development and sports lead us to believe that we cannot understand moral motivation in sports by looking at only intra-psychic variables. The environment in which athletes play matters. Athletes' motivation to play fairly or to cheat appears to be a function of how they define the situation in which they are competing as well as what we may loosely describe as their moral character.

THE CONSTRUCT OF MORAL MOTIVATION

The concept of moral motivation has been a puzzle for moral psychologists since the discipline took shape at the beginning of the 20th century. Psychologists past and present have posited non-moral motives and mechanisms for acting in accord with moral norms. These range from behavioural reinforcements to praise and blame. Piaget (1932/1965) and Kohlberg's (1984) cognitive developmental approaches to moral development sidestepped such motivational explanations altogether by positing that the motivation for acting morally was built into the very logic of equilibrated social interaction. White (1959) described the inner need that leads to the exploration of and adaptation to the physical and social environment as effectance motivation. He noted that human beings have a natural desire for competence and mastery. Acting morally, as Piaget argued, is simply to accord in accord with logic of social relationships. Individuals do not need external inducements to act logically. Kohlberg's well-known stages of moral development (Colby, Kohlberg, Speicher, Hewer, Gibbs & Power, 1987) describe a progression from external to internal motivation, culminating in a commitment to universal justice. The higher individuals advance in their moral reasoning, the less they find external sanctions relevant as motives for moral behaviour. For example, an athlete reasoning at Stage 2 may decide not to cheat because she may get penalized. At Stage 3, she may find that even if she could get away without a penalty, she should play by the rules because she wants others to regard her as a good sport. At Stage 4, she may reason that whether or not others notice she is a good sport, the rules should apply to everyone. At Stages 5 and 6, she understands that the rules should be established through a social contract to guarantee fairness and enjoyment for all.

As is clear from these examples, individuals functioning at Stages 4, 5, and 6 see no "payoff" to being moral other than the peace that comes with following their consciences. Yet when the desire to win can become almost overwhelming, it is sometimes difficult to keep in mind the importance of fairness or winning the right way. It is even more difficult in highly competitive situation to play by the golden rule, which demands putting one's opponent's desire to win on the same moral plane as one's own. The challenge of maintaining one's moral motivation in sports demands a check on one's egoism as well as one's emotions. Kohlberg (1981) pointed out in his well known essay on the philosophy of moral development, "From Is to Ought: How to Commit the Naturalistic Fallacy and Get Away With It in The Study of Moral Development," that morality is unique among cognitive structures insofar as it alone involves "basic sacrifice" (p. 188). Athletes and coaches must always be prepared to sacrifice winning and the external rewards that come with it for the sake of fairness itself.

MORAL RESPONSIBILITY AND MORAL MOTIVATION

Experimental and educational research indicate that although moral reasoning plays an increasingly more powerful role in motivating moral action, even the highest moral stages of moral reasoning may be insufficient to determine how individuals will act in certain situations. For example, participants in the Milgram experiment believed that administering painful shocks as a teaching method was wrong but continued to obey out of a belief that they were following orders and were not responsible (Milgram, 1974). Similarly, in studying the moral cultures of high schools, we (Power, Higgins, & Kohlberg, 1989) found that although all students believed that stealing and cheating are generally wrong, many found their peers' stealing and cheating peers in school was morally acceptable. We learned that that loyalty to peers often excused students from acting in ways they otherwise knew to be right. When we asked why students did not feel responsible for even expressing their disapproval, they responded that it was up to adults and not the students to "police" the school.

In the Milgram experiment and in our school culture research, the participants failed to take to take responsibility for upholding moral precepts that they ordinarily support with because they believed that that the ultimate responsibility for enforcing the moral order belongs to those in positions of authority. We noted earlier in our discussion of the Coach Curran scenario that many athletes and coaches at the high school, college, and professional levels that taking advantage of the referees was a part of the game. In their view, it was up to the referees and only the referees to see to it that the correct player was sent to the foul line. In these very different contexts, the motivation to uphold rules depends not only on an understanding of the rightness of the rules but on a sense of feeling responsible for the rules themselves. The Milgram experiment challenged the participants to disobey an authority in order to follow the dictates of their conscience. The high school and sports settings demanded far less insofar as they challenged their participants to cooperate with the authorities instead of ignoring or deceiving them. Many of the participants in the Milgram experiment manifested and reported a moral tension between their personal judgments that they were wrongfully harming others and their trust in the authority who tried to absolve them of any moral responsibility for their actions. In the high school and sports situations, the participants appear to have experienced no such tension. The context seems to have canceled out their motivation even to make a personal moral judgment about what they should do in this situation.

As we noted in our study of the moral culture of schools (Power, Higgins & Kohlberg, 1989), the students' lack of motivation to act morally may be understood as a problem of moral responsibility, related to the system of making and enforcing school rules. When administrators and teachers make disciplinary rules that attempt to motivate conformity through external sanctions, it is not surprising that students would leave it up to the administrators and teachers to enforce the rules. Similarly, when sports organizations make rules that attempt to motivate conformity through external sanctions, it is not surprising that teams try to get away with as much as the referees will allow.

Competition and Responsibility

In our current work on moral development in sports, we distinguish between taking responsibility for acting morally within a given social framework (by not cheating or by playing unselfishly) and taking responsibility for the morality of the social framework itself (by cooperating with the officials). While both of these kinds of actions are moral, we believe that they make very different demands on the individual and arise from somewhat different motivational wellsprings. It is one thing to be responsible for playing by the rules out of a basic sense of fairness, and it is something else altogether to be responsible for upholding the rules at a cost to one's self or one's team. The motivation for upholding the rules by, for example, helping the referees to make the correct call, comes out of a love of and concern for the integrity of the game itself. Although a moral team culture can motivate fair play, only a wider moral sport culture can motivate actions that put moral principles before winning.

Sports can provide a lens for understanding how these two different kinds of responsibility and motivation function in business and politics. For example, individuals may feel highly responsible for the good of the firm even at the cost of great personal sacrifice. They may also feel highly responsible to uphold the laws governing the operations of the firm. Yet in the case of 2008 financial crash, many of those working on Wall Street took advantage of the lack of regulatory oversight. They engaged in highly lucrative financial practices without taking moral responsibility for their global and even national impact. We see a similar pattern in politics as party loyalty often trumps a concern for the public good. Like sports, business and politics are highly competitive arenas in which individuals may find little or no institutional and cultural support for acting on behalf of the common good. Yet sports teach us that individuals can rise above the limitations of their environments to open up new possibilities for collective action.

Motivation and The Moral Self

We believe that even in highly competitive contests, individuals are motivated by a sense personal responsibility rooted in their moral identity. Blasi (1980) posited that moral responsibility was motivated by a concern for self-consistency. As individuals develop their sense of agency and identity, they take ever increasing ownership of their action and inaction. Yet as Blasi (1993) and others e.g., (Arnold, 1993, Colby & Damon 1992; Power, 1997) have found, the motivational drive for consistency between one's judgments of right and wrong and one's actions depend to a large extent that moral values are perceived to be at the core of one's identity. We are currently investigating the extent to which coaches and athletes with a relatively strong moral identity will be more likely to feel responsible for cooperating with officials as well as playing fairly. We are also investigating the extent to which coaches and athletes have an identity specific to the sports context that is more or less moral than their overall sense of their identity. Our preliminary results indicate that individuals' base their sports' identities primarily on values related to high achievement, such as hard work, effort, and perseverance. To a lesser extent, some athletes will speak of themselves in social terms as cooperative or in moral terms as reliable. We are not surprised that sports' identities are built around the virtues related to competitive success rather than on virtues related to morality, such as justice. Yet we also believe that many individuals fail to develop strong moral identities as sportspersons because the sports culture itself overemphasizes winning over fair play and substitutes achievement for moral fidelity.

In our preliminary exploration of the moral identity of college level athletes, we find, however, that some regard certain kinds of cheating as a reflection of lack of character and as inconsistent with the way they want to see themselves as athletes. In describing their distaste for cheating, they often identify with like-minded athletes who hold themselves to a higher standard of play. This suggests that the development of a moral self in sports as in other contexts may be influenced by the interactions athletes have with significant others in the sport as well as the sports culture in which they participate.

Indeed, a growing body of research indicates that the moral quality of athletes' experience varies significantly by the social context, which is heavily influenced by the coach (Kavussanu, 2007). This research draws heavily on the moral atmosphere construct put forth to study schools by Power, Higgins, and Kohlberg (1989) and adapted by Shields and Bredemeier (1995) to explore influence of sports teams on moral functioning. Not surprisingly, researchers find that the perceptions that athletes have of team norms regulating aggression and cheating influence not only their own moral assessments of these actions but also their willingness to engage in them (Kavussanu, 2007). We are only beginning to understand how these norms come to be established, but we do know that coaches play a significant role (Kavussanu, 2007; Shields, Bredemeier, LaVoi, & Power, 2005). For example, coaches differ widely in the respect they show officials and their expectations for how their players treat officials (Sheehan & Power, 2010); and the perceived behaviour of the coach has a strong influence on the behaviour and attitudes of young athletes (Shields, Bredemeier, LaVoi, &Power, 2005).

ACHIEVEMENT GOAL THEORY AND MORAL MOTIVATION

Most of the research on teams' moral atmosphere suggests that it may be mediated by the achievement context that coaches, and to some extent parents and players, establish (Duda &Balaguer, 2007; Kavussanu, 2007; Kavussanu & Roberts, 2001; Ommundsen, Roberts, Lemyr &Treasure, 2003). Nicholls (1989) pointed out that individuals adopt two basic goal orientations in achievement settings. Some adopt a task orientation and focus on developing their competence and attaining mastery in their performances. Others adopt an ego orientation and focus on demonstrating their ability relative to others. Individuals with a task orientation are process-oriented and value the activity for its own sake. They use self-referenced criteria in evaluating their competencies. Those with an ego orientation focus on outcomes (wins and losses) and use social comparative criteria to evaluate their self-worth.

It should not be surprising that consistently strong correlations have been found between the strength of athletes' ego orientation and low moral functioning (Kavasunu, 2007). When winning or losing becomes the major if not sole criterion for judging one's worth, there is a powerful motivation to do whatever it takes to win. The desire to demonstrate one's superiority motivates many athletes, who are not anxious about their self-worth. Many of these athletes live in small self-contained worlds in which success in sports is all that matters. In such a world, sports cannot be what it is meant to be - social play. Athletes obsessed with winning or the fear of losing are no longer motivated to pursue the proper pleasure of sports, which is the shared joy of competing.

Kavasunu (2007) notes that achievement goal theory predicts that individuals with a strong task orientation should be motivated to play by the rules because they base their judgments of competence on how well they competed rather than simply whether they won or lost. To date, studies have yet to establish a consistent correlation between the strength of one's task orientation and moral functioning. This may be due to measurement issues or more likely to limitations in the achievement motivation construct itself. Because individuals with a high task orientation focus on their own performances rather than comparing themselves with others, they may be relatively indifferent to whether others are cheating or behaving without regard for the welfare of others. In our view, taking an active interest in promoting fairness and respect for others in sport requires much more than a benign achievement orientation. Sports demand a delicate moral balance in which the competitors try to best each other while deliberately maintaining conditions of fairness and mutual respect.

THE JOY OF SPORTS

Following Hunziga's (1955) classic treatment of play and culture, we maintain that sports are essentially a particular form of play and as such have as their goal pure enjoyment. As play, therefore, sports have what Hunziga (1955) calls a "not-serious" quality compared to other human activities (p. 13). Even when sports are played professionally, they are played for the sake of entertainment. Sports belong to life of leisure, as opposed to work. Sports offer a break from the cares and obligations of everyday life. When we play or even watch sports, we enter into the world of make-believe with arbitrary rules and bounded space and time. Through those rules and the traditions of our games, we channel a wide range of human passions from love to aggression into that make-up world that expresses our freedom and our commitment to justice. In the make-believe world of sports, we can all be champions if we strive with all our energy, put our team before ourselves, and take responsibility for playing by the rules and the spirit of the games.

Hunziga (1955) emphasizes that freedom is a defining characteristic of any kind of play. Play is not a necessity in the way that earning one's living or protecting oneself or one's family from danger is. There is, moreover, no moral duty to play. In fact, sports events are pre-empted in times of crisis and mourning. This is what we mean by play being non-serious. Sports have, of course, their own seriousness as any competitor or fan knows. Feezell (2004) calls this an "internal" seriousness because we make the choice to engage in the activity in the first place (p. 13) and undertake the rigors of conditioning and skill development voluntarily. The seriousness of sport is a playful seriousness and intensifies and purifies the joy of competition.

Renaissance scholar and former Commissioner of Major League Baseball, A. Bartlett Giamatti (1989), reminds us that regarding sports are play does not mean that they are less important than work. In fact, from the standpoint of human happiness, he claims that the opposite is true: "The issue is not a dualistic opposition between work and play. It is a progression from one to the other, from what is necessary to what is desirable, from the utilitarian to the liberal, or free" (p. 29). Bartlett also points out that the freedom experienced in sport as play is not that of a private individual but of a flourishing community.

The only rational motive for playing sports in the first place is for enjoyment. Although coaches and athletes may have all kinds of motives for engaging in sports from proving their superiority over others to maintaining their health, we maintain that sports are by their very nature games played for mutual enjoyment. We have learned through working with adults and children involved in youth sports that children understand better than many of their elders what sports are meant to be. Asked why they play sports, the vast majority of children rank having fun first over all other motives and far ahead of winning (Seefeldt, Ewing, & Walk, 1992). They give other reasons as well, but fun is their top choice. Many youth sport coaches are surprised to learn that children put fun first and are even more surprised that children rank winning as one of the lowest reasons for playing. The coaches see winning as the obvious goal of competing. They are right, of course; but they do not distinguish winning as the dominant conscious motivation within competition from winning as a motivation for competing in the first place.

Perhaps because they have not yet been corrupted by the more toxic influence in sports, children compete because, win or lose, they enjoy the activity. Although winning adds to pleasure of the activity, the activity is worthwhile and joyful itself. We cannot have an adequate approach to moral motivation without understanding how joy functions in relationship to morality in sports. In his Nicomachean Ethics (Irwin, 1999), Aristotle takes pains to discuss the proper role of pleasure in virtuous activity. Although athletes play sports for the enjoyment of the activity itself, they cannot experience the joy of sports in isolation from the play of the game itself. In fact, when individuals compete egoistically for the pursuit of their own pleasure exclusively, they cannot experience the proper pleasure that comes from competition, which is social one. Without denying the psychological fact that virtuous persons experience pleasure in virtuous activity, Aristotle, nonetheless, asserts against hedonists, that virtuous activity can only be virtuous if it is done for its own sake. The pleasure that accompanies any virtuous activity, he points out, is not the end toward which we should aim but a consequent end, that comes as a bonus. Aristotle makes very clear that the pleasures related to the virtues are tied intimately to the virtuous activities themselves and are unavailable apart from those activities. In the context of sport this means that the joy of sports is available only when individuals play sports with respect for their opponents and the conventions that give sports their identity. The joy of sports is not one that can be experienced privately or egoistically. It is a joy that cannot only be experienced along with others. In this sense, moral motivation in sport is bound with up with the anticipation of the joy that sports participation brings to the self and to others. That joy is accessible only to those who play morally and only as a consequent end.

PIAGET REVISITED: MOTIVATIONAL MECHANISMS OF CONSTRAINT AND COOPERATION

Piaget (1932/1965) began his classic, *The Moral Judgment of the Child*, with a surprising encomium that those studying moral development in sports have largely ignored: "Children's games constitute the most admirable social institution" (p. 13). Piaget investigated children's games because they were built on a system of rules. Piaget, like Kant, believed that respect for the rules was at the heart of morality. By carefully examining how children of different ages played marbles, Piaget demonstrated that children's understanding of and commitment to the rules made their enjoyment of these games possible. He noted that "mere competition is not what constitutes the affective motive-power of the game" (p. 42). Rather, motive-power of the game is bound up in the social experience of competing within a framework of "common rules." The game itself cannot be reduced to the mere demonstration of superior force or skill. Rules make the game a cooperative and engaging social experience. Probing further into children's consciousness of the rules, Piaget found that children were most likely to follow the rules when they understood the reasons for the rules and were capable of altering old rules and making new ones. Piaget studied children's games precisely because he wanted to observe how children interacted in a rule-governed context without adult interference or coercion. He found that children not only developed an appreciation for the function of rules but also became "a sovereign and a legislator in the democracy [of children playing the game]" (p. 71).

Piaget saw children's games as more than portals into children's thinking about rules and morality. Children's games in his view are one of the principal ways in which children develop as socio-moral persons. Piaget believed children could develop socially and morally only under the condition of cooperation: "The sense of justice .... requires nothing more for its development than the mutual respect and solidarity of the children themselves" (198). Piaget elaborates that "adult authority ... is not in itself sufficient to create a sense of justice" (319). This is because adult authority elicits submission to rules but not autonomous consent to them. In order to develop a sense of justice, children need the experience of cooperation among equals. Games thus provide a special opportunity for children to experience the benefits of rules and to alter the rules in order to better realize the ideal spirit of the game.

Piaget surely would have expected participation in sports to have promoted rather than inhibited socio-moral development. Yet his positive assessment of the developmental value of playing games was based on the fact that in the games Piaget studied, children controlled their own play. Today in the United States most children play on sports teams organized by adults. This organization robs children's play of its socio-moral worth. Adults choose which children play on which teams, who get to play on those teams, and which position the children will play. Adults establish and change the rules. Adult referees enforce them. Children play sports under what Piaget called the conditions of constraint rather than cooperation. Conditions of constraint foster moral heteronomy. When adults control children from the outside children lack not only the motivation but even the opportunity to regulate their own play.

The distinction that Piaget makes between conditions of constraint and those of cooperation also shed light on the problems that we raised earlier with organized sports at higher competitive levels. As sports organizations increasingly emphasize and reward winning, they recreate conditions of constraint that undermine intrinsic motivation generally and moral motivation more particularly. If sports are to be played at the highest moral level, the participants must be invested in supporting the integrity of the rules that give the game its character and maximize the competitive character of the game itself. Unfortunately the transformation of sports into high stakes tournaments of sports has taken control of the game away from the players. This is true in youth leagues starting at age seven all the way to the professional leagues. The higher the age and competitive level, the greater the importance attached to winning and the more sports become less intrinsically motivated play and more extrinsically controlled work.

If want to understand sports from a Piagetian perspective, we must turn to backyard and playground pickup games in which the participants, choose the teams, contractually establish the rules, act as their own referees, design fair procedures for resolving conflicts, and make sure that everyone had enough fun to come back for the next game. It is no wonder that organized sports do not resemble the marble games Piaget observed in Neuchatel.

A MODEL FOR UNDERSTANDING MORAL MOTIVATION IN CONTEXT

In our view, sports are morally motivating by their very nature as rule constituted activities. Moral motivation becomes a concern when the structure of the game itself becomes corrupted by internal and external factors that turn sports competition into decompetition. Research on moral motivation in sports must take into account a complex array of personal and environmental factors that can influence how athletes compete. We present a simple model for motivation in sport that pictures motivation arising from an interaction of internal personal conditions and external environmental conditions (See Figure 1).

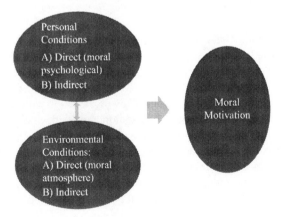

Figure 1. Moral motivation: Personal and environmental conditions.

The within person conditions are to two types: 1) Direct, which has to do with such moral psychological factors influencing sports participants' a) perceptions of their activity as morally relevant, b) judgments of right and wrong, c) and commitment to act responsibly as a good sport; and 2) Indirect, which has to do with such non-moral factors as: a) level of competence in a sport, b) attachment to the team, and 3) achievement orientation(task versus ego). These internal personal conditions do not operate in isolation from the environment, however, as Figure 1 shows.

The environmental conditions are also of two types: A) Direct, which has to do with the moral atmosphere of the sport environment; and B) Indirect, which has to do with such non-moral factors as 1) the competitive level (recreational to professional), 2) the external reward structure attached to winning, 3) the motivational climate, 4) the contact level of the sport, and 5) the extent to which the sport is revenue generating. Modifying the classification scheme used in investigating the moral atmosphere of schools, we propose that the moral atmosphere consists of three components: 1) the social aggregate (moral characteristics of the coaches, players, and administrators), 2) the organization of the sport at level of the a) team, b) the game itself, and the league), and 3) the culture of the sport at the level of the team, the league, and wider sport society.

The moral atmosphere of one's sport experience varies widely by social aggregate that is by the people with whom one plays, particularly one's coach. Coaches can and do put pressure on players to cheat and set high or low expectations for civility and respect for opponents and officials. Yet the atmosphere cannot be reduced to the qualities of individuals. Individuals act within organizational frameworks and these frameworks open or close opportunities for individuals to act in responsible ways. Sports are fundamentally competitive games. They should flourish insofar as their organizational structures uphold conditions necessary for sports to operate as games by providing for an equitable distribution of talent, equipment, and training facilities and by being responsive to the health, safety, and enjoyment of the participants. We have found that organizational settings characterized by constraint are heteronymous; they place the authority for rule making and rule enforcing outside of the control of the participants. This loss of control "outsources" moral responsibility thus undermining moral motivation. Within a sports team, such settings are established by autocratic coaches, who unilaterally set down rules and expectations and enforce them with extrinsic rewards and punishments. In the competitions themselves, organizational settings that rely on referees and external sanctions to maintain the rules, take the responsibility for enforcing the rules and fair play away from the players and their coaches.

On the other hand, organizational settings characterized by cooperation place the authority for rule making and enforcing under the control of the participants themselves. The purest example of such settings is pickup game in which the players take responsibility for assuring that their games are played fairly and with attention to the mutual enjoyment of all of the participants. The pickup game depends upon the players' commitment to uphold the rules and pursue the common good.

The absence of a "third party" regulating the game is itself a condition eliciting moral motivation. Within teams, democratic forms of organization appear to be the most conducive to the players' taking responsibility with coaches for building strong norms of caring and collective responsibility. We are finding that increasing numbers of coaches at the college and high school levels are using team meetings as a way of giving players a greater sense of ownership of their team. On the other hand, there is ample evidence that sports are becoming entertainment businesses, which encourage spectacle and celebrity.

Sports participants interact within organizational structures to develop cultures at the team, league, societal, and even international level. Moral cultures consist of shared norms, beliefs, and values based on principles of equity and respect for persons. As we have noted, sports by nature generate cultures of respect for persons, for the game, and for the rules that constitute the games. Yet, as we have seen, the cultures under which various sports are played can easily erode as toxic structural elements that have more to do with money and status take control of the game away from the players. With few exceptions, we have come to expect players and teams to do whatever it takes to win. We have created sports cultures that encourage coaches and teams to take full advantage of what they can get away with. It is a culture that encourages individual and collective egoism and robs sports of their morally motivating character.

CONCLUSION

Our preliminary analysis of moral motivation in sports indicates that the optimal environment for sports at any competitive level is one characterized by an organization of cooperation and a culture of mutual respect and love for the game. We are living in an era in which winning has become an end unto itself, detached from the fair play of the game itself. The winning at all costs mentality leads to one of two responses. The first and most common response is to try to curb the abuses in sport through more rigorous external controls, such as random drug testing and serious penalties for those who are caught violating the rules. This is the mentality of constraint and it attempts to bypass autonomous moral motivation altogether.

The second and less appreciated response is to build organizations and cultures of cooperation that encourage moral autonomy. One example of a sport that has developed rules and a culture that encourage moral motivation is golf. Golf is one of the few sports in which there is a strong expectation for players to regulate themselves and to self-report violations of the rules. In the playoff for the Horizon Heritage Tournament title with over $400,000 on the line, Brian Davis of England called a two-stroke penalty on himself for inadvertently nicking a reed on the backswing of his recovery shot from a hazard to the left of the 18th green. Only Davis was aware that he had barely touched the overhang, yet he did not hesitate to make his infraction known to an official. The reaction of the golf community was not surprise but affirmation. "What Davis did was what probably 90 percent of the players on the tour would have done" wrote Larry Dorman (2010). Dorman went on to recount golf's proud history of self-reporting going back to the legendary Bobby Jones, who in 1925 after calling the same penalty on himself said, "You may as well praise a man for not robbing a bank."

Ultimate Frisbee is another sport with a strong emphasis on fair play and self-enforcement. Key to Ultimate Frisbee is the principle known as the Spirit of the Game, which squarely puts responsibility for fair play and joyful competition on the individual players:

> Ultimate has traditionally relied upon a spirit of sportsmanship which places the responsibility for fair play on the player. Highly competitive play is encouraged, but never at the expense of the bond of mutual respect between players, adherence to the agreed upon rules of the game, or the basic joy of play. Protection of these vital elements serves to eliminate adverse conduct from the Ultimate field. Such actions as taunting of opposing players, dangerous aggression, intentional fouling, or other 'win-at-all-costs' behaviour are contrary to the spirit of the game and must be avoided by all players (Zaslow and Ultimate Players' Association Conduct Committee, 2005).

Ultimate Frisbee, which began as an informal countercultural movement is now played internationally.

We can learn from golf and Ultimate Frisbee that sports can be morally motivating at the highest levels of competition. The question is whether sports organizations from youth to the professional levels will develop the organizational structures and cultures that respect the moral agency of their participants and encourage them to engage in the moral reflection and deliberation needed to maintain the integrity of our games. Only when athletes take full responsibility for the play of games they love will sports bring forth the moral motivation imbued with joy that belongs to free and noble people.

REFERENCES

Ames, C. (1992). Classrooms: Goals, structures, and student motivation. *Journal of Educational Psychology, 84*(3), 261–271.

Arnold, M.L. (1993). *The place of morality in the adolescent self.* Unpublished Ph.D. dissertation, Harvard University

Bamberger, M., & Yaeger. D. (1997, April 14). Over the edge. *Sports Illustrated, 86*(15), 60–70.

Blasi, A. (1980). Bridging moral cognition and moral action: A critical review of the literature. *Psychological Bulletin, 88*, 1–45.

Blasi, A. (1993). The development of identity: Some implications for moral functioning. In G.G. Noam & T.E. Wren (Eds.), *The moral self* (pp. 99–122). Cambridge: M.I.T. Press.

Bredemeier, B.J., & Shields, D.L. (1984). Divergence in moral reasoning about sport and everyday life. *Sociology of Sport Journal, 1*, 384–357.

Bredemeier, B.J., & Shields, D.L. (1986). Game reasoning and interactional morality. *Journal of Genetic Psychology, 147*, 257–275.

Colby, A., & Damon, W. (1992). *Some do care: Contemporary lives of moral commitment.* New York: The Free Press.

Colby, A., Kohlberg, L., Speicher, B., Hewer, A, Gibbs, J.,& Power, C. (1987). *The measurement of moral judgment, Vol 1: Theoretical foundations and research validation.* New York: Cambridge University.

Connor, J. & Mazanov, J. (2009). Would you dope? A general population test of the Goldman Dilemma. *British Journal of Sports Medicine, 43*(11), 871–872.

Dorman, L. (2010, April 11). Davis's honesty was refreshing, but not unexpected [Web log comment]. Retrieved from http://onpar.blogs.nytimes.com/2010/04/19/daviss-honesty-is-refreshing-but-in-golf-its-par-for-the-course/

Duda, J.L., & Balaguer, I. (2007). Coach-created motivational climate. In S. Jowett & D. Lavallee (Eds.), *Social psychology in sport* (pp. 117–130). Champaign, IL: HumanKinetics.

Dweck, C.S. (1999). *Self-theories: Their role in motivation, personality and development.* Philadelphia: The Psychology Press.

Irwin, T. (Ed.). (1999). *Nicomachean ethic.* Indianapolis, IN: Hackett Publishing Company.

Feezell, R. (2004). *Sport, play and ethical reflection.* Urbana: University of Illinois Press.

Giamatti, A.B. (1989). *Take time for paradise.* New York: Bloomsbury USA.

Huizinga, J. (1955). *Homo ludens: A study of the play-element in culture.* Boston: Beacon Press.

Kavussanu, M. (2007). Morality in sport. In S. Jowett & D. E. Lavalee (Eds.). *Social psychology in sport* (pp. 265–278). Champaign II: Human Kinetics.

Kavussanu, M., & Roberts, G.C. (2001). Moral functioning in sport: An achievement goal perspective. *Journal of Sport & Exercise Psychology, 23,* 37–54.

Kavussanu, M. & Ntoumanis, N. (2003). Participation in sport and moral functioning: Does ego orientation mediate their relationship? *Journal of Sport & Exercise Psychology, 25,* 501–518.

Kohlberg, L. (1981). *Essays on moral development.Vol. 1:The philosophy of moral development.* New York: Harper and Row.

Kohlberg, L (1984). *Essays on moral development. Vol. 2: The psychology of moral development.* San Francisco: Harper & Row.

Milgram, S. (1974). *Obedience to authority: An experimental view.* New York: Harper and Row.

Nicholls, J.G. (1989). *The competitive ethos and democratic education.* Cambridge, MA: Harvard University Press.

Ommendsen, Y., Roberts, G.C., Lemyre, P.N., & Treasure, D. (2003). Perceived motivational climate in male youth soccer: Relations to social-moral functions, sportpersonship and team norm perceptions. *Psychology of Sport and Exercise, 4,* 397–413.

Piaget, J. (1932/1965). *The moral judgment of the child.* London: Free Press.

Power, F.C., Higgins, A., & Kohlberg, L. (1989). *Lawrence Kohlberg's approach to moral education.* New York: Columbia University Press.

Power, F.C., & Khmelkov, V.T. (1997). The development of the moral self: Implications for moral education, *International Journal of Educational Psychology, 27*(7), 539–551.

Power, C. & Sheehan, K.K. (2010). *Coaching for character.* Notre Dame: Play Like a Champion Educational Series.

Ryan, R.M., & Deci, E.L. (2007). Intrinsic and extrinsic motivation in exercise and sport. In M.S. Hagger, & N.L.D. Chatzisarantis (Eds.), *Intrinsic motivation and self-determination in exercise and sport* (pp. 1–19). Champaign, IL: Human Kinetics.

Seefeldt, V., Ewing, M., & Walk, S. (1992). *Overview of youth sports programs in the United States.* Washington, DC: Carnegie Council on Adolescent Development.

Sheehan, K.K., & Power, F.C. (2012). *Assessing coach ethics.* Unpublished paper. Notre Dame: Play Like a Champion

Shields, D., Bredemeier, B., LaVoi, N.M., & Power, C.F. (2005). The sport behavior of youth, parents, and coaches: The good, the bad & the ugly. *Journal of Research on Character Education, 3,* 43–59.

Shields, D., & Bredemeier, B. (1995). *Character development and physical activity.* Champaign, IL: Human Kinetics.

Shields, D., & Bredemeier, B. (2009). *True competition: A guide to pursuing excellence in sport and society.* Champaign, IL: Human Kinetics.

Stoll, S.K., & Beller, J.M. (2000). Do sports build character? In J.R. Gerdy (Ed.), *Sports in school: The future of an institution* (pp. 18–30). New York: Teachers College Press.

Stoll, S.K., & Beller, J.M. (2005). Male/female student athletes' moral reasoning 1987–2004. *University of Idaho center for ethics.* Retrieved from http://www.educ.uidaho.educenter_for_ethics /Measurements/HBVCI/findings.htm.

White, R. (1959). Motivation reconsidered: The concept of competence. *Psychological Review, 66,* 297–333.

Zaslow, G. & Ultimate Players' Association Conduct Committee (2005). *About Spirit of the Game: Excerpts from the* Official Rules of Ultimate: 11th Edition. Usa Ultimate Retrieved from http://www. usaultimate.org/about/ultimate/spirit_of_the_game.aspx.

AFFILIATIONS

Clark Power
Institute for Educational Initiatives
University of Notre Dame
Notre Dame, USA

Kristin K. Sheehan
Institute for Educational Initiatives
University of Notre Dame
Notre Dame, USA

KLAUS-JÜRGEN GRÜN

IV. FROM ETHICAL HOSTILITY TOWARD
COOPERATIVE ETHICS

INTRODUCTION

"The time has come for ethics to be removed temporarily from the hands of philosophers and biologicized" (Wilson, 1975, p. 562), E. O. Wilsons, the father of Sociobiology demanded almost 40 years ago. Meanwhile biologists and economists have gained much more knowledge about moral motivations than philosophers. Yet, still philosophers have the jurisdiction in defining ethics and morality. Nevertheless, if we want to understand moral motivation, standard ethics only assures us that it is the good which motivates us to follow the good.

STANDARD ETHICS

Standard ethics is based on the idea that there is something like a mental condition that makes us do something that is really good. This mental condition is imagined to be the motivation of ethical action. It shall not be caused by activity in our biology or in the emotion itself, but by pure reasoning about what is bad and what is good. An act is said to be moral, according to this deontological opinion, when it is not based on usefulness or utilitarian values. Moral actions are supposed to be based on categorical values, which are said to be totally different from utilitarian aims or the emotions of an individual, as Michael Sandel assumes (Sandel, 2009).

Is it really true that our moral sentiments are based on something that can be called good in an absolute sense? Deontologists take it for granted without proof that moral judgments are not to be compared with all the expressions of useful interests (Tanner, Medin & Iliev, 2008). Kant postulated – without proof – the "factum of reason" which established the categorical difference between usefulness and reasonableness. Wittgenstein, for example, suspects that every moral judgment referring to categorical or absolute good is based on misuse of language. He only accepts ethical rules expressed in a relative sense of the good – good for something else, not good for its own sake.

Without mentioning the utilitarian position, Ludwig Wittgenstein rejected any deontological point of view in ethics and morality. The idea of the "absolute good" he defined as a "state of affairs" that "would be one which everybody, independent of his tastes and inclinations, would necessarily bring about or feel guilty for not bringing about". Wittgenstein logically concluded "that such a state of affairs is a

K. Heinrichs, F. Oser & T. Lovat (Eds.), Handbook of Moral Motivation: Theories, Models, Applications, 427–446.

chimera. No state of affairs has, in itself, what I would like to call the coercive power of an absolute judge. Then what have all of us who, like me, are still tempted to use such expressions as 'absolute good', 'absolute value', etc., in mind and what do we try to express?" (Wittgenstein, 1929, para. 2). If there is only "good" in a relative sense, categorical values are excluded.

Misuse of language, in a more common way, means that we present a prescriptive intention as if it were a simple description of a situation. "To help Mary moving her piano is good" looks similar to the description: "To drive the car safely is good". However, only the second expression is a description of what objectively we must do in order not to cause harm. This misuse is a well-established maneuver to persuade others to accept my own preferences for Mary or helping women in general, because I treat the word "good" in a way as if it were a common duty, given by the laws of nature. In the prescriptive sense the motivation of helping Mary is imagined to be based on the moral meaning of "good" and not on the usefulness of the action.

More precisely than Wittgenstein's logical analysis of language, neurobiology has now brought up clear evidence that no action can be done without an expected reward. This scientific fact we have to consider in a strong sense. As long as we did not have empirical knowledge of the causal function of the mesolimbic award system, there was some evidence that moral activity like altruism could be not based on reward or benefit. Explaining ethics nowadays must notice that no human action can be fulfilled without the expectation of reward in the same way as a patient with Parkinson's disease cannot move his legs without the production of Dopamine in his substantia nigra (Schultz, 2009). We refer to this biological fact while using the word "reward" even in ethical contexts.

The reward can be the happiness of being good according to the sacred values an individual has established. It can be achieved by dropping names or avoiding names. In speaking politically correctly, for example, we produce euphemisms which are created to soften the blow of something taboo. Euphemisms quickly absorb any negative connotations; however, the reward can also be utilitarian reasoning. The expectation of reward in one of these senses is a necessary cause for moral action. There are no effects without causes and there will be no human action without activation of the reward system in the brain (Narvaez, 2008). That means that the mental condition of an idea like the absolute good of the categorical good itself will never be able to replace the motivation of any action.

It follows that every supposed "absolute value" is actually bound by conditions. Even sacred values such as deontological or religious goods can only be recognized as being good if the areas of the brain known to be associated with reward were activated. If there were anything like categorical values, as Kant and deontologists assert, they would not be bound by conditions like all the other values that are associated with activity in the reward-related regions of the brain. Categorical values are imagined to generate a duty to do what we ought to do only according to the rational system of thinking about the good – without any inclination of our emotions or individual interest. In fact there is reason to distinguish between deontological and utilitarian judgments (Berns, 2012), but these activities, located in different areas of the brain, must both create the expectation of reward. Therefore, every categorical value is actually a hypothetical value. Deontology with its sacred values does not differ much from utilitarianism as long as both describe aims of human actions that are done only if they activate the reward-related regions of the brain. If there is no reward expected but only punishment, or our sacred values are contradicted by their opposites, researchers find there is arousal in the amygdala, which is associated with negative emotions (Ibid).

In general, our moral and ethical standards are useful social rules that are simply read off and acted on when a relevant case arises. We have to evaluate the consequences and the harms and benefits that our actions impose on others. As long as we do not expect any other causes for moral action than the expectation of benefit within our social order, every ethical system and its moral judgments admits empirical investigation. The rejection of empirical ethics and the investigation of empirical causes in morality, however, have led deontology to the negligence of important biological and emotional motivations for morality. Deontology is the tradition of Kant's moral philosophy. It is justified by J. Habermas, J. Nida-Rümelin, M. Sandel e.a. They have in common the non-theologically idea if an absolute good or justice which is in no way reduced to economy, biology and strategic thinking. "Reasonably one does what has the best consequences", Nida-Rümelin writes. "This apparently trivial thesis is wrong. Why it is wrong will be illustrated in this chapter."[1] More explicitly, Habermas attempts "to defend the priority of the deontologically understood justice…"[2]

One of the most neglected motivations for moral judgment and action is fear and rejected hostility. Even if philosophical ethics has had little interest in this subject, ordinary life, fiction and poetry nonetheless tell us about it. I shall present some examples from ordinary life and literature to support the thesis that a large proportion of moral judgments produce the sensation of being good even if the individual pursues hostile aims. I shall try to explain the observation that moral judgments can produce a reward while diminishing the awareness of hostility and fear in an individual.

First of all, I shall consider the question of how it can be that the miraculous word "justice" is able to hide such a wicked trait as desire for revenge. Poets, writers and other artists are perfectly well acquainted with the magic of moral talk using this word. Nonetheless, scientists in the wide field of human sciences do not refer to the hostile implications of moral judgments that can be concealed by using the word "justice". Only few philosophers in the tradition of materialistic thinking emphasize this non-ethical origin of justice: "It is not accidental that justice occupied a key position for those philosophers who, although they are counted among the greatest of antiquity, have written not about natural law but of patriarchal, lordly law." The eye of law – this is Ernst Blochs conviction – "sits in the face of the ruling class" (Bloch, 1987, pp. 39 and 181).

ETHICAL HOSTILITY

On a beautiful afternoon in a small town in the middle of Europe, people are preparing for the arrival of a famous native of the town who left it 30 years ago. Since then, she has become a billionaire and now promises to provide the town with much-needed funds, to raise it from its state of disrepair. Residents are suffering considerable hardship and poverty. The twentieth-century Swiss writer Friedrich Dürrenmatt, dreamed up this town, gave it the name Guellen (which literally means "manure" and "to manure") and placed it in Switzerland. It could be anywhere in the civilized world.

The billionaire is the 63-year-old Claire Zachanassian, with red hair, an artificial leg and an artificial hand. She announces to the impoverished townspeople that she will donate one billion dollars, depending on one condition: she will only give it in return for the death of her former lover, Alfred Ill, the owner of Guellen's general store and the most popular man in town. As she became pregnant, Alfred Ill denied their love and together with former citizens organized her expulsion. Now, her donation is conditional on Ill's death.

Claire tells the residents that she wants *justice*. She only came with the intention of buying herself *justice* but everybody knows that she wants revenge. Yet the word "revenge" is not even mentioned in the whole play. Claire only talks about justice.

One could say this is fiction and has nothing to do with ordinary life. One would be wrong, as the following example shows. We quote this example because it shows clearly the concealed hostility in a moral action and in the feeling of being good. In the year 2007 the Pope reinstituted the Latin-language "Prayer for conversion of the Jews". Catholics are urged to pray for the Jews, to pray that the "Lord our God" may "illuminate their hearts so that they may recognize Jesus Christ as savior of all men." It is not important for us to discuss the pontiff's action in relation to the Good Friday Mass after the Second Ecumenical Council of the Vatican, which ended in 1965; and it does not diminish the meaning of ethical hostility that the prayer is only performed in the Easter Week and only in the Latin-language liturgy. It is important however to recognize that the prayer can have an outrageous, malicious meaning even when the conscious perception of a praying individual's intention does not show any hostility.

What are hostile implications of moral judgments? In our examples, one fictional and the other non-fictional, ethical hostility can be discovered as one side of the ambivalence of feelings. An individual's consciousness can have the dominant awareness that his praying for the Jews is a philanthropic gesture, even as he actually transmits hostility to the Jews. This is the moral implication of the ambivalence and it has priority in consciousness. In fact prior to that philanthropic feeling is the hostile intention. Human beings however usually do not like seeing themselves as hostile. Every row begins as fighting back. Aggressors never recognize themselves as the initiators of a row or a fight. There is only the perception of defending and doing something necessary or even doing their duty. Especially hostility in an anti-Semitic sense must be kept in repression.[3] The most efficient way of avoiding any recollection of one's own hostility is to overemphasize philanthropy and humanity.

Catholics, in the mentioned prayer, propose that the Jews are damned. To a pious and devout Catholic believer, this means that a Jew cannot belong to the chosen few who will be redeemed on the Day of Judgment. It makes the believer feel pity for the Jew. He wants to embrace the damned fellow and soothe his suffering. While feeling pity and sorrow, the believer enjoys the idea of being altruistic in a deep sense for humanity, which makes him forget the slightest sensation of hostility. The whole action depends however on the believer's conviction that being a Jew means something evil. The emphasis on the philanthropic implication of the action of praying arises from the fear of his own hostility in the character of the praying individual. Actually this action is one of harsh discrimination but the individual will never be aware of his prior motivation. So that is why the Vatican claims that no disrespect was intended. This might be right, because the conscious self and its intention have no idea of the discriminating hostility in the prayer.

Only the target of the altruistic gesture recognizes the hostility. One rabbi said the Good Friday prayer strikes Jews as "exclusivist and triumphalist."[4] So far the prayer has not been repealed.

A REMARKABLE OBSERVATION

In moral judgments we can discover a considerable amount of fear - especially the fear of one's own hostility and one's own pleasure. Fear of the concealed memory of one's own cruelty can be the concealed part of the ambivalence of feelings. One of the earliest sources of the awareness that moral emotions depend on the memory of cruelty in oneself or the group to which one belongs can be found in Georg Forster's *A Voyage round the World*. Georg Forster (1754-1794) spent almost four years of his youth on the ship *Resolution* during James Cook's second voyage around the world. In New Zealand, a group of lieutenants and sailors explored an island and just happened to witness an act of cannibalism. A dead young man in the sand close to the ocean attracted their attention. Obviously the man was a victim of cannibalism after hostility between two tribes. Except for the missing chin the head was almost undamaged, and one of the lieutenants took it as a souvenir onto the *Resolution*. Inhabitants approached in their canoes and even some sailors on the *Resolution* seemed to be very interested in the head when one of the Englishmen offered them a roasted piece of the cheek. "The rest lamented this action as a brutal depravation of human nature", writes Forster,

> "agreeable to the principles which they had imbibed. However, the sensibility
> of Mahine, the young native of the Society Islands, shone out with superior
> lustre among us. Born and bred in a country where the inhabitants have already
> emerged from the darkness of barbarism, and are united by the bonds of society,
> this scene filled his mind with horror. He turned his eyes from the unnatural

object, and retired into the cabin, to give vent to the emotions of his heart. There we found him bathed in tears; his looks were a mixture of compassion and grief, and as soon as he saw us, he expressed his concern for the unhappy parents of the victim. This turn which his reflections had taken, gave us infinite pleasure; it spoke a human heart, filled with the warmest sentiments of social affection, an habituated to sympathize with its fellow-creatures. He was so deeply affected, that it was several hours before he could compose himself, and ever after, when he spoke on this subject, it was not without emotion" (Forster, 2000, p. 279).

Mahine, the young passenger from the Society Islands, who was "born and bred in a country where the inhabitants have already emerged from the darkness of barbarism", showed the strongest emotional reaction, as Forster emphasizes. We could read: "... where the inhabitants have *just* emerged from the darkness of barbarism...", because of his proximity to the former cannibalism in his own society. The memory of cannibalism that his society has overcome must be kept under repression. He is not able to express the cruelty of cannibalism itself; he only expresses "his concern for the unhappy parents of the victim". To be concerned about the unhappy parents however is obviously something other than being concerned about "the unnatural object".

Forster's statement can be read as an example of Sigmund Freud's theory of emotional ambivalence, explicated in *Totem and Taboo*, where he compares taboo ceremonials to modern neurosis, to which religion still has to be attributed, in Freud's opinion. Excessive apprehensiveness and solicitude

"is very common in neuroses, and especially in obsessional neuroses, with which our comparison is chiefly drawn. We have come to understand its origin quite clearly. It appears wherever, in addition to a predominant feeling of affection, there is also a contrary, but unconscious current of hostility — a state of affairs which represents a typical instance of an ambivalent emotional attitude.

The hostility is then shouted down, as it were, by an excessive intensification of the affection, which is expressed as solicitude and becomes compulsive, because it might otherwise be inadequate to perform its task of keeping the unconscious contrary current of feeling under repression. Every psychoanalyst knows from experience with what certainty this explanation of solicitous over-affection is found to apply even in the most unlikely circumstances — in cases, for instance, of attachments between a mother and child or between a devoted married couple. If we now apply this to the case of privileged persons, we shall realize that alongside of the veneration, and indeed idolization, felt towards them, there is in the unconscious an opposing current of intense hostility that, in fact, as we expected, we are faced by a situation of emotional ambivalence." (Freud, 1961, p. 46)

We can compare moral actions like the one described to neuroses. The latter make people feel strong emotions – namely fear and angst – if they are restrained from doing things that are futile. "Will all great Neptune's ocean wash this blood / Clean from my hand? No, this my hand will rather / The multitudinous seas incarnadine, / Making the green one red" (Act 2, scene 2), Lady Macbeth cried out as she did her bloody work. As we all know, the habit of repeatedly washing one's own hands expresses a feeling of guilt. If someone is restrained from obsessively washing his hands, he will be attacked by panic. With the appearance of being interested only in the proper and the pure (state of his hands), the neurotic person has shouted down his remembrance of the contrary: the unconscious current of impurity and hostility.

Freud referred to James George Frazer's *The Golden Bough* and his studies of some particularities in king taboos: "Indeed", Freud writes,

"owing to the variety of outcomes of a conflict of this kind which are reached among different peoples, we are not at a loss for examples in which the existence of this hostility is still more obviously shown. 'The savage Timmes of Sierra Leone', we learn from Frazer, 'who elect their king, reserve to themselves the right of beating him on the eve of his coronation; and they avail themselves of this constitutional privilege with such hearty goodwill that sometimes the unhappy monarch does not long survive his elevation to the throne. Hence when the leading chiefs have spite towards a man and wish to rid themselves of him, they elect him king.'

Even in glaring instances like this, however, the hostility is not admitted as such, but masquerades as a ceremonial" (Freud, 1961, p. 46).

Even if no fear in an explicit sense can be observed, we count it as a kind of moral fear if people conceal their hostile intentions behind the mask of great humanity. Famous dramas and thrillers use this element of ethical hostility to highlight the sinister character of a criminal. Alfred Hitchcock's movies – for instance *Saboteur* from the year 1942 – give shape to the evil by drawing his figures with an excessive solicitude and over-emphasis on their humanity. One member of the gang, who is planning to blow up a huge dam and a power plant, mentions in a conversation while passing the plant in a car: "I'm glad we came this way, even if it adds some miles to our trip. But somehow I become a little bit sentimental. I want to take a last look at it. Beautiful isn't it? A great monument to men's unceasing industry." About the chief of the gang, whose crimes include responsibility for the death of hundreds of workers in an aircraft factory they have just burnt down, he declares in the same conversation: "You know Tobin very well?" – "No, not very well. I just met him once on his ranch." – "Did he have a child with him?" – "His grandchild? Yes. He seemed to be very vulnerable." – "Yes, that's one of the things that I like about Tobin, his love for that little girl. Evidence of a good heart."

The audience understands this very well and appreciates this tension between the conscious state of mind – "evidence of a good heart" - and the uncontrollable power of hostility, which is shouted down with that caressing affection. The conscious self obviously does not allow the awareness of both pleasure and hostility in our character. It provokes opportunities to "prove" the humanity of an individual.

FEAR AND MORALITY

Fear can be a special kind of motivation. It motivates people to do something that is only concentrated on diminishing the fear and not on the diminishing of danger. So far, we have neglected the distinction between angst and fear or fright but this distinction can help us to become aware of real dangers. What we have to be aware of, for our own safety, are real dangers. We must learn to fear dangers that really exist, but we should diminish our fear of things that are not dangerous at all. The German noun "angst" describes the emotion of someone who believes that harmless situations, things, words or thoughts could be dangerous. We have to remember how dominant fear in the sense of angst in taboos occurs, mostly in cases of politically correct speaking. We feel the strong emotion not to speak out the tabooed words but if we did name the taboo-word it would not cause any real danger.

The problem with this emotion is that it makes individuals do things that do not necessarily diminish real dangers but only hide this unreasonable fear or angst. For example, people often fear the number "13". This involves them in wasting lots of time and other resources to escape the number "13"; yet none of these activities avoids any real dangers because the number "13" isn't dangerous at all. The same is true of fear of the dead, fear of foreigners, fear of love or the fear of not being loved by God, fear of gays, fears about liberals and so on. Things like these are better described by the word angst. Angst is only concerned with making itself vanish. All these fears – or Ängste – can only create new dangers, instead of diminishing the original one. To handle a real danger, we must not hide a bad feeling but face it and find its causes in order to diminish them.

Gays are not dangerous in themselves but it is obvious that the moral condemnation of gays is caused by the fear of one's own interest in homosexuality, which has to be repressed.

If we start to ask why an increasing number of things occur that trigger angst, we find one reason in the alliance between fear – in the meaning of angst – and ethics or morality. Barry Glassner, who has investigated American society, states: "Our fear grows, I suggest, proportionate to our unacknowledged guilt" (Glassner, 1999, p. 72). Glassner's suggestion repeats Sigmund Freud's thesis that permanently repressed pleasure will become angst. Nonetheless, civilization always requires repression of pleasure. In some cases, that means repression of aggression. This can be easily achieved through an everyday phenomenon. We all know that above all communities with adjoining territories and other mutual interests and relations are engaged in constant feuds and in ridiculing each other. Freud recalls by name the Spaniards and the Portuguese, but we can add every local patriotic aggression which can arise between two towns or cities that are separated by a river or a valley.

It also happens whenever a nation strengthens the cohesion of its own people by provoking difficulties in foreign affairs. What Freud earlier named "the narcissism of minor differences" explains the hostile implications in the experience of being good or belonging to the good. "We can now see that it is a convenient and relatively harmless satisfaction of the inclination to aggression by means of which cohesion between the members of the community is made easier. ... When once the Apostle Paul had posited universal love between men and the foundation of his Christian community, extreme intolerance on the part of Christendom towards those who remained outside it became that inevitable consequence" (Freud, 1962, p. 61).

The angst behind our moral values appears in another commonly known phenomenon. Imagine you have a large amount of money that a friend gave to you, to save it for him. No one knows about this deal. Imagine now that you find yourself in financial difficulties. You think of the money and how urgently you need it. Your decision to take from your friend's money only depends on the strength of your moral values. This means it depends on the power of the demand: "Thou shalt not steal". If this demand fails to rule your action, then you know that you can no longer promise to stay clear of becoming corrupt but you fear your own hostile tendencies if you hold on to the high ethical demands. You know that you can no longer guarantee not to become a corrupt person if your moral standards fail. This strong uncertainty, where you no longer know how you will cope with a conflict over whether your "free will" to be fair and responsible can overcome your hostility and egoism, produces angst about your own weakness.

This is the meaning of the quotation people refer to when they say: "If God does not exist, everything is allowed" (Dostoyevsky, F., *The Brothers Karamazov*). Obviously this thesis is wrong. I am not allowed to steal, to kill, not even to smoke in restaurants if god does not exist. Even if it is not against the law, people will not allow each other to lie, to be unfair or even to be mean but I myself could fear ceasing to be moral if the strong claim has disappeared. I fear that I would allow myself too much, because I don't trust myself. It is a fear - in the sense of angst - of my own hostility, which I know could be stronger than my own free will not to be hostile. I fear the loss of a helpful motivation. "Do you wish my life to have no meaning?" (Camus, 1942, p. 46), Albert Camus lets the investigator ask the stranger who is accused of murder. The stranger has just explained to the investigator that he does not think his belief in god has anything to do with the trial. The investigator fears the idea that his utmost moral principle — god — could be less important than he believes. For in that case the investigator could no longer guarantee to be good. His life could be without meaning, because he fears that he is unable to give meaning to his own life. He fears the loss of his own humanity if God no longer tells him how to be human.

Erich Fromm has investigated this subject and named it the fear of freedom in one of his early works:

"...authority can appear as internal authority, under the name of duty, conscience, or super-ego. As a matter of fact, the development of modern thinking from

Protestantism to Kant's philosophy, can be characterized as the substitution of internalized authority for an external one" (Fromm, 2001, p. 143).

INSTRUMENT OF POWER

As long as ethics and morality give those who are at a disadvantage additional chances they must conceal their gain of power. Moral behaviour in the sense of marked simplicity can generate the feeling of being more powerful than those who are privileged. Many anecdotes about the cynic Diogenes generate humor time and again by making use of the same mechanism. Here are some examples:

One day while he was wasting time in his barrel, Diogenes was visited by Alexander the Great. As Alexander asked him where he came from, Diogenes answered: "cosmopolites" – that means: "I am a citizen of the whole world."

How small must Alexander the Great have felt. He, who had conquered India and Persia, subjugated Greece and owned almost everything in the eastern part of the Mediterranean, thought only that he was a citizen of Greece. And how grandiose must Diogenes have felt, who did not own anything, who held no position and lived in a barrel? It is said that once, while Diogenes was sunning himself, Alexander the Great came up to him and offered to grant him any request. Diogenes told him: "Stand away from the sun on me."

How small again must Alexander have felt, after hearing that Diogenes requested nothing more from him but what anybody else could grant, namely to get out of the way.

The mechanism of this humour is obvious. First there is a hostile implication, which is then masked by the predominant tone of affection in his words. Most of all, there is a remarkable gain of power for Diogenes when he answers in the way he does. It seems that people who appreciate Diogenes' answers especially like – and fear at the same time – this very cheaply gained amount of power. As game theorists have recently discovered, limiting one's own options brings a special kind of social power. Fasting and hunger strikes are methods of protesting injustice and pressuring opponents. This kind of pressure is carried out in a way that forces opponents to back down by limiting one's own freedom of behaviour into one single option. The fasting or hunger-striking person shows that he will maintain his strategy until the very end. The nonviolent strategy actually is based on self-interest and shows a manipulative element of suffering, for the others' compassion is used against their interest (Biggs, 2003).

Even Charity can be regarded as an instrument of power. Ethics and morality in the Western tradition are mainly based on the principle of charity. One concept of charity is the love of one's enemies, as Luke reports that Jesus told his audience: "Love your enemies, do good to those who hate you, bless those who curse you, pray for those who ill-treat you. If someone strikes you on one cheek, turn to him the other also. If someone takes your cloak, do not stop him from taking your tunic. Give to everyone who asks you, and if anyone takes what belongs to you, do not demand it back. Do to others as you would have them do to you. If you love those who love you, what credit is that to you? Even 'sinners' love those who love them. And if you do good to those who are good to you, what credit is that to you? Even 'sinners' do that. And if you lend to those from whom you expect repayment, what credit is that to you? Even 'sinners' lend to 'sinners', expecting to be repaid in full. But love your enemies, do good to them, and lend to them without expecting to get anything back. Then your reward will be great, and you will be sons of the Most High, because he is kind to the ungrateful and wicked. Be merciful, just as your Father is merciful" (Luke. 6, 27-35).

No one thinks about hostility on hearing those words of charity; and this is, as we stated, the main implication of morality. But - for instance - if we put Oscar Wilde's comment next to it: "Always forgive your enemies, nothing annoys them so much", we touch that unconscious current of hostility in the love for enemies. (This is one reason why we don't allow people to tell jokes or draw caricatures concerning our religious beliefs: we fear the reminder of the truth that can be transported by jokes and caricatures.) At least those who find Wilde's word funny reveal that they have an idea of the hostile implication. Otherwise they would not have felt like laughing. The Christian prescription of charity offers an undiscovered implication, if people read this with its humorous sense. In Oscar Wilde's sense, charity is bearing a quantity of hostility. It gives destitute people, who have no other means and opportunities, domination and sovereignty at no cost.

Sigmund Freud denied even the possibility of realizing the principle of charity in the gospel of Luke's "love for enemies". Much too tremendous are the costs for the resignation in love for enemies. It imposes duties on me for whose fulfillment I must be ready to make sacrifices. The economical system of our soul, in the psychoanalytical sense, does nothing for free, or to put it more scientifically: it does nothing without cause. Every emotion and every feeling has a corresponding relationship to pleasure. Resignation is not an original cause. It is the reaction to recognizing that there are no other possibilities. To make an individual disclaim an expectation of pleasure, it must have a prospect of happiness or pleasure - which also means diminution of unhappiness.

Freud quotes one of the ideal demands of civilized society, "Thou shalt love thy neighbor as thyself", and adds the questions: "Why should we do it? What good will it do us? Above all, how shall we achieve it? How can it be possible?" (Freud 1962, p. 56). One has to deserve my love otherwise love is worthless and occurs by accident. The loved one is selected by choice. If everybody is selected, no one is selected.

On closer inspection of the love for enemies, Freud found further difficulties, especially the problem that an "enemy" will appreciate my kindness to forgive him without cause, which leads Freud to the cognition: "... obedience to high ethical demands entail damage to the aims of civilization, for it puts a positive premium for being bad" (Ibid., p. 58). One can feel beloved by god while one dwells in comfort, as Freud describes with a quotation from the author Heinrich Heine: "Mine is the most peaceful disposition. My wishes are: a humble cottage with a thatched roof, but a good bed, good food, the freshest milk and butter, flowers before my window, and a few fine trees before my door; and if god wants to make my happiness complete, he will grant me the joy of seeing some six or seven of my enemies hanging from those trees. Before their death I shall, moved in my heart, forgive them all the wrong they did me in their lifetime. One must, it is true, forgive one's enemies – but not before they have been hanged" (Heine, H., *Gedanken und Einfälle*, quoted from ibid. p. 57).

To Freud it is obvious that the permanent threat of civilized societies is an underlying "primary mutual hostility of human beings". Because instincts are stronger than reasonable interests, civilization "has to use its utmost efforts in order to set limits to men's aggressive instincts and to hold the manifestations of them in check".

In fact, we have good reason to assume that almost every moral judgment is built on this gain of power. Ethics and morals are the easiest to use of all instruments of power, especially by those who lack any other such instruments.

THE TALKING OF "THE THEY"

In a very different way, Martin Heidegger had the intuition that the identification with the anonymous community arises from a specific fear (angst) about expressing individual emotions, feelings, interests and values. Instead of being oneself and being responsible, members of a community prefer the distance from themselves they achieve among others: "being-with-one-another has the character of distantiality", Heidegger states. He continues: "This being-with-one-another dissolves one's own Dasein completely into the kind of being of 'the others' in such a way that the others, as distinguishable and explicit, disappear more and more. In this inconspicuousness and non-ascertainment unfolds its true dictatorship" (Heidegger, 1996, p. 118).

This distantiality creates not only averageness but also a loss of individual responsibility. If one does what the average does; if one feels like "they" feel; and if one claims to have no other interests than "they" have, one has feelings and convictions that are not one's own. As we will see, this is the concept of a categorical imperative, which is the utmost secular principle of ethics and morality in the world of academic philosophy: to express the motive of an action not as the result of an individual desire, but as the common duty. In the course of thinking that he is analyzing the essence of pure practical reason, Kant does none other than describe what individuals do when they do not allow themselves to express their own interests: They hide their own distinguishable and explicit ideas behind the duty of doing what "the They" expects him to do.

Unfortunately, this seems to be the principle of every moral judgment. If we judge morally, we declare something that is in our own interest to be a common duty. Because Kant thinks that morality must consist mainly of a categorical imperative such as: "Act only on that maxim by which you can at the same time will that it become a universal law", Kant describes what an individual always wishes, without knowing or understanding Kant or being conscious of the wish. But Kant confused cause and consequence. The categorical imperative is not the beginning of an action, it is only a rational reflection on what I have done. What I have done is to have interpreted an individual interest – or angst – as a common duty. And this is what happens in every moral judgment, when I say that it must be a common interest, which I am about to do or to avoid.

Sometimes it really is a common interest. The universal prohibition "Thou shalt not lie" is empirically based on the wisdom that everybody has a tendency to lie if he can gain from lying. However, I never want to be the victim of a lie. This interest of mine as an individual would not impress the one I want to prevent from lying unless I present the appearance that this is a common interest, not my own, and I am only doing my duty to represent the common duty. In case of the prohibition "Thou shalt not lie" there is undoubtedly a common interest. But the assumption that I would do anything else but hide my own interest behind the common duty appears as pure metaphysical speculation. There is no need for this assertion, because we have no idea how to prove it, and the action is totally understandable without metaphysics. The categorical imperative appears to be nothing but a hypothetical imperative. It depends on empirical conditions and interests that are supposed to become invisible behind the strong command.

Kant's ethical theory is a rationalist version of "Strict Father morality, which Kant combines with the Family of Man metaphor and the Society of Mind metaphor" (Lakoff et al.,1999, p. 416).

What Kant and modern Kantians deem the utmost moral principle is on the other hand an example of Heidegger's theory of the fear of being oneself. "It is an existential character of the 'they'. In its being, the 'they' is essentially concerned with averageness. Thus, the 'they' maintains itself factually in the averageness of what is proper, what is allowed, and what is not. Of what is granted success and what is not" (Heidegger, 1999, p. 118).

STRATEGIC ETHICS

One can suspect that Freud, Kant, Heidegger and all the quoted poets above who give examples of the hidden fear (angst) of our repressed pleasure and repressed aggression are of poor scientific power, and that the morally good is nothing else but the morally good. But meanwhile, studies in empirical ethics and "Triune Ethics Theory (TET)" (Narvaez, 2008) have documented astonishing results. They give us a new impression of the hostile implication in moral motivation. Game theory offers a wide variety of experiments to answer the question of how people can be motivated to be fair and just (de Quervain et al., 2004). The simplest game that exhibits altruistic punishment is the Ultimatum Game. The game goes like this:

"Under conditions of anonymity, two player are shown a sum of money, say $10. One of the players, called the Proposer, is instructed to offer any number of dollars, from $1 to $10, to the second player, who is called the Responder. The Proposer can make only one offer and the Responder can either accept or reject this offer. If the Responder accepts the offer, the money is shared accordingly. If the Responder rejects the offer, both players receive nothing. The two players do not face each other again.

There is only one Responder strategy that is a best response for a self-regarding individual: accept anything you are offered. Knowing this, a self-regarding Proposer who believes he faces a self-regarding Responder, offers the minimum possible amount, $1, and this is accepted.

However, when actually played, the self-regarding outcome is almost never attained or even approximated in fact, as many replications of this experiment have documented, under varying conditions and with varying amounts of money" (Gintis, 2009, p. 57).

The game proves that a common rational choice theory does not describe how real people decide an action. It also proves however that real people are not driven by the Pareto optimum, which would be fulfilled with any amount the Proposer offers. Perhaps the most interesting result of the study of this game is that the Responder is not primarily motivated by moral feelings or moral rationality. The motive to reject unfair offers lies in the emotions of anger, revenge, and the power to punish the Proposer.

Gintis, de Quervain, Fehr, and others have discovered within this game that altruism normally is not pure altruism but is caused by the intention to punish individuals who make unfair offers. Those punishments are not primarily driven by a rational awareness of normative ethics, but are driven by emotions and feelings of aggression like anger, envy, rage or revenge. In these cases the motivation of morality is obviously a primary hostile emotion, not a rational decision in the sense of rational choice theories or theories of the free will. It is even less the result of a categorical imperative. Gintis summarizes these results of empirical ethics: "Recent neuroscientific evidence supports the notion that subjects punish those who are unfair to them simply because this gives them pleasure" (Gintis, 2009, p. 51).

While scanning a subject's brains with positron emission tomography and examining the neural basis for the altruistic punishment of defectors in an economic exchange, the first reaction toward moral judgment occurs in areas that are unconscious. We have no reason to expect that a rational will, acting only according to the maxim that one would wish to become universal law, initiates the action. An unconscious activity in the reward system in the limbic area forces the individual to act in a way that could be interpreted afterwards as if a categorical imperative had existed. But the empirical result shows that even the categorical imperative is based on the existence of a primary impulse in the limbic system. Consequently the categorical imperative is actually a hypothetical one, which means that the ideal demand of pure reason appears as nonsense. Every ethical judgment is dependent on a non-ethical supposition, which is best described in terms of the biology of the brain and the strategies of game theory. We can postulate a fear (angst) however in ethical theory to accommodate the empirical supposition in ideal demands.

The empirical conditions, at least in the case of the Ultimatum game, are summarized by Gintis too:

> "Punishment activated the dorsal striatum, which has been implicated in the promising of rewards that occurs as a result of goal-directed actions. Moreover, subjects with stronger activations in the dorsal striatum were willing to incur greater costs in order to punish. This finding supports the hypothesis that people derive satisfaction from punishing norm violations and that the activation in the dorsal striatum rejects the anticipated satisfaction from punishing defectors.

> Third, it may be that subjects really do not believe that conditions of anonymity will be respected, and they behave altruistically because they fear their selfish behaviour will be revealed to others.

> Fourth, and perhaps most telling, in tightly controlled experiments designer to test the hypothesis that subject-experimenter anonymity is important in fostering altruistic behaviour, it is found that subjects behave similarly regardless of the experimenter's knowledge of their behavior" (Gintis, 2009, p. 51).

THE FEAR OF LOSING ALL MORALITY

Our consciousness does not necessarily reflect what really happens in those areas of our brain that are unable to lie. Instead of reflecting the true beliefs and convictions of a character, our mind seems to fear those sensations and rejects them. In philosophical literature on ethics at least, there is even a powerful tendency to fear all of the work in the neurosciences demonstrating that the reflections of our consciousness do not have the meaning that self-confidence attributes to them. "Not my brain thinks, I am thinking", authors are shouting out, as if powerful dictums could save our sense that the conscious self primarily rules our moral actions. In analogy to the quotation: "If God does not exist, everything is allowed", they think: "If our conscious self does not exist in the way it is reflected in self-confidence, everything is allowed."

By explaining every categorical imperative in terms of hypothetical imperatives, the strategic considerations of game theory gain importance in founding even ethic rationality. If we follow the hypothesis that every ethical problem is to be described as the problem of transforming a zero-sum game in a non-zero-sum game (cooperative game), we no longer need to deny the interest in power and the elements if ethical hostility within most every moral judgment. Further studies should therefore investigate whether this hypothesis can be proved. The hypothesis goes back to considerations in Thomas Schelling's *Strategy of Conflict*: "If the zero-sum game is the limiting case of pure conflict, what is the other extreme? It must be the 'pure-collaboration' game in which the players win or lose together, having identical preferences regarding the outcome" (Schelling, 1980, p. 84f). The Freudian idea of ambivalence of emotions and feelings returns in a new sense in strategic game theory, as Schelling says: "If we accept the idea of two selves of which usually one is in charge at a time, or two value systems that are alternate rather than subject to simultaneous and integrated scrutiny, 'rational decision' has to be replaced with something like collective choice. Two or more selves that alternatively occupy the same individual that have different goals and tastes, ... have to be construed as engaged not in joint optimization but in a strategy game"(Schelling, 1982, p. 93f).

There is no need to fear the loss of ethics and morality if we step away from ethics construed by the imagined pure reason or the pure and absolute good. Strategic thinking and the need to cooperate, the natural tendency to establish fairness, and many economical and social reasons will always give us empirical reasons to establish normative principles and ethical systems. But strategic ethics will avoid the dishonesty of hiding hostile implications behind the masks of unrighteous philanthropy.

CONCLUSION

In this chapter, I showed that ethics is not only a matter of the good. One of its major tasks is the transformation of concealed hostility into moral feelings. Motivation of this transformation seems to be mainly the fear (angst) of an individual's own hostility. As long as standard ethics only concentrate on traditional concepts of the goodness, they cannot give answers to questions of how hostile emotions are going into moral sentiments and ethical systems and how we could avoid this.

Writers, biologists, psychologists and economists supply a wide range of examples which made clear that some kind of ethical hostility is well known. First of all, I have drawn attention to the naming of the word "justice" that is able to conceal the emotion of revenge. In order to understand the mechanism how the feeling of being good can make hostile motivations vanish I quoted the prayer for the Jews. This non-fictional and well known example describes clearly the action of charity (praying) as an act of hostility. The decisive factor in this example is the fact that a person who prays is not at all aware of his hostile emotions against the Jews. On the contrary, he may have the feeling of doing something for the Jews - namely to plead for redeeming them. It seems obvious that the more ardent the action of praying is carried out, the better it conceals the remembrance of hostile emotions of a praying individual. While Catholics estimate praying to be something good, it seems to be necessary to conceal and transform hostility.

Biologists have discovered that any human action can only be effective if the reward-system in the brain is activated. Therefore the investigation of moral actions must not generate the opinion that they could be done without a reward. Even altruism rewards an individual with good emotions, and the altruistic action would not be done without the expectation of this reward. Meanwhile economists and psychologists investigate the nature of fairness and altruism. They appear as forms of hostility (punishment) transformed into the feeling of good. Another element of hostility in ethical and moral behaviour is the interest in gaining power. Above all the aim of ethics is to provide those with additional chances who have fewer chances by birth or because of their social participation. Humor can be a clue to concealed angst of hostility in moral talking. Ethical theory as well as moral feelings conceal the instrument of power and declare ethics only to be interested in the good and not at all an instrument of power.

We called it moral fear, a special amount of fear or, better, angst, which motivates individuals to hide their hostile interests or emotions behind moral language and moral action. In the same way as fear – in the sense of angst – motivates individuals to do things that are able to diminish the angst but not to diminish dangers, moral fear arises from the individual's memory of what he has learned to be good or bad. We referred to Sigmund Freud's theory of motivating power of taboos. Therefore, moral fears have a close connection to neuroses. Like neuroses, they are not related to real existing danger but to the consciousness of an individual. Dropping names or avoiding names, as sometimes observed, in demands of political correctness, are not to be aimed at reducing discriminating factors but of avoid naming them precisely.

Looking at ethics in a strategic way, we understand much better the motivation of ethical values in modern society. Ethics is not the opposite of strategic thinking; it is one aspect of it. Strategic ethics does not deny the interests of individuals and opens the way to describe strategies to increase cooperation. If ethics is understood as the strategy to transform zero-sum games in non-zero-sum games, we have a major task for ethics: to describe the motivation for cooperation in cases one could consider might derive greater benefit by not cooperating. In strategic ethics, there is no need to produce fear of one's own desires or interests.

NOTES

[1] Nida-Rümelin, J. (1995). Vorwort: „Vernünftigerweise tut man das, was die besten Folgen hat. Diese scheinbar trivial richtige These ist falsch. Warum sie falsch ist, wird in diesem Buch zu zeigen versucht." (Translation by the author.)

[2] Habermas, J. (1991) p. 0 writes in the Vorwort "…den Vorrang des deontologisch verstandenen Gerechten vor dem Guten zu verteidigen." (Translation by the author.)

[3] Theologists who have detailed information about the Pope's state of mind, tell us, that the Prayer for the Jews is not only anti-Judaic, but even anti-Semitic. (Berger, D., 2010, p. 97.)

[4] http://www.newser.com/story/18484/jews-outraged-at-vatican-prayer.html.

REFERENCES

Berger, D. (2010). *Der heilige Schein. Als schwuler Theologe in der katholischen Kirche.* Berlin: Ullstein.

Berns, G. (2012). *The price of your soul: Neural evidence for the non-utilitarian representation of sacred values.* Social Science research network. Retrieved from http://papers.ssrn.com/sol3/papers.cfm?abstract_id=1817982.

Biggs, M. (2003). *When costs are beneficial: Protest as communicative suffering.* Sociology Papers Paper Number 2003–04, Department of Sociology, University of Oxford. Retrieved from www.sociology.ox.ac.uk/swp.html.

Bloch, E. (1987). *Natural law and human dignity* (D.J. Schmidt, Trans.). Massachusetts: MIT Press.

Buchanan, J.M., & Tullock, G. (2004). *Thecalculus of consent. Logical foundations of constitutional democracy.* Indianapolis: Liberty Fund, Inc.

Camus, A. (1942). *The stranger,* (S. Gilbert, Trans.). New York: Alfred A. Knopf, Inc.

de Quervain, D.J.-F., Fischbacher, U., Treyer, V., Schellhammer, M., Schnyder, U., Buck, A., et al. (2004). The neural basis of altruistic punishment. *Science, 305,* 1254–1258.

Fehr, E. (2006). *Neuroökonomik. Die Erforschung der Grundlagen des menschlichen Sozialverhaltens,* Walter-Adolf-Jöhr-Vorlesung. Forschungsgemeinschaft für Nationalökonomik. St. Gallen.

Forster, G. (2000). *A voyage round the world.* In O. Berghof & N. Thomas (Eds.), (pp. 254, 714) Honolulu: University of Hawai'i Press.

Freud, S. (1961). *Totem and taboo.* London: Routledge.

Freud, S. (1962). *Civilization and its discontents.* New York: Norton.

Fromm, E. (1942/2001). *The fear of freedom.* London: Routledge.

Gintis, H. (2009). *The bounds of reason. Game theory and the unification of the behavioral Sciences.* Princeton: Princeton University Press.

Glassner, B. (1999). *The culture of fear. Why americans are afraid of the wrong things.* New York: Basic Books.

Grün, K.-J. (2011). *Angst, die sich verschweigt. Über die falsche Konditionierung unseres moralischen Bewusstseins.* In P. Aerni& K.-J. Grün (Eds.), *Moral und Angst. Erkenntnisse aus Moralpsychologie und politischer Theologie* (p. 57–78). Göttingen: Vandenhoeck & Ruprecht.

Habermas, J. (1991). *Erläuterungen zur Diskursethik.* Frankfurt a.M.: Suhrkamp.

Heidegger, M. (1996). *Being and time.* New York: State University Press.

Knoch, D., Pascual-Leone, A., Meyer, K., Treyer, V.,& Fehr, E. (2006). Diminishing reciprocal fairness by disrupting the right prefrontal cortex. *Science, 314,* 829–832.

Lakoff, G.,& Johnson, M. (1999). *The embodied mind and its challenge to western thought.* New York: Basic Books.

Narvaez, D. (2008). Triune ethics: The neurobiological roots of our multiple moralities. *New Ideas in Psychology, 26,* 95–119.

Narvaez, D., & Vaydich J.L. (2011). Angst und Liebe als Motoren des moralischen Handelns. In P. Aerni & K.-J. Grün (Eds.), *Moral und Angst. Erkenntnisse aus Moralpsychologie und politischer Theologie* (p. 131–144). Göttingen: Vandenhoeck & Ruprecht.

Nida-Rümelin, J. (1995). *Kritik des Konsequentialismus.* München: Oldenbourg.

Sandel, M. (2009). *Justice: What's the right thing to do?* London: Allen Lane.

Schelling, T.C. (1980). *The strategy of conflict.* Massachusetts: Harvard University Press.

Schelling, T.C. (1982). Ethics, law, and the exercise of self-command. Tanner Lecture at the University of Michigan. In *Choice and Consequence. Perspectives on an errant economist* (p. 83–112). *Cambridge,* Massachusetts: Harvard University Press 1984.

Schultz, W. (2000). Multiple reward signals in the brain. *Nature Reviews Neuroscience 1,* 199–207.

Schultz, W. (2009). Midbrain dopamine neurons: A retina of the reward system? In P. Glimcher, W. Colin, F. Camberer, E. Fehr, & R. A. Poldrack (Eds.), *Neuroeconomics. Decision Making and the Brain* (p. 323–329). Amsterdam, Boston: Elsevier.

Tanner, C., Medin, D. L., Iliev, R. (2008). Influence of deontological vs. consequentialist orientations on act choices and framing effcts. When principles are more important than consequences, *European Jounal of social Psychology, 36,* 757–769.

Wilson, E.O. (1975). *Sociobiology. The new synthesis*. Cambridge, MA: Harvard U.P.
Wittgenstein, L. (1929). *A lecture on ethics*. Retrieved from http://www.geocities.jp/mickindex/wittgenstein/witt_lec_et_en.html

AFFILIATION

Klaus-Jürgen Grün
Institute of Philosophy
Goethe University Frankfurt
Frankfurt/Main, Germany

CHRISTIAN A. KLÖCKNER

V. HOW POWERFUL ARE MORAL MOTIVATIONS IN ENVIRONMENTAL PROTECTION?

An Integrated Model Framework

INTRODUCTION

Environmental protection has become a major issue in many contemporary societies (Inglehart, 1995) and it has multiple facets, reaching from the protection of a local wetland or an endangered species, on the one hand, to fighting pollution and opposing genetically modified crops or mitigating global climate change, on the other hand. Social and environmental psychology has a tradition of following this societal development, with research on how and why individuals and groups of individuals act in an environmentally friendly way, while others do not (see Steg & Vlek, 2009, for a review of environmental psychology's contribution to the field). A rather large number of models have been proposed to explain people's environmentally relevant actions, theory based intervention strategies have been developed to change people's behaviour and just recently the focus is shifting toward understanding and predicting processes of behavioural change in the environmental domain (see Steg, van den Berg & de Groot, 2012, for a recent synopsis of the developments from a European perspective). Many of these approaches include moral aspects of one kind or another, but the concept of morality in environmental psychology is heterogeneous and situated at many different levels. This chapter will therefore first discuss why environmental protection can be perceived as part of the moral domain then introduce different concepts of morality in the environmental domain and how they motivate behaviour. Afterwards, it will be discussed how moral and non-moral predictors of environmental behaviour relate to and interact with each other, before a model framework of environmental behaviour will be proposed that integrates moral and non-moral determinants of environmental action. Since most of the studies about moral determinants of environmental behaviour have been conducted with adults, the question of moral development in this particular domain is not discussed in depth, but selected studies will be presented that shed some light on how moral concepts in the environmental domain are achieved. Finally, some examples will be presented concerning how to strengthen the influence of moral motivations on environmentally relevant decisions.

K. Heinrichs, F. Oser & T. Lovat (Eds.), Handbook of Moral Motivation: Theories, Models, Applications, 447–472.

ENVIRONMENTAL PROTECTION SEEN AS A MORAL ACT

The first question that has to be addressed in a chapter about motivators of environmental conservation in a book about moral motivations is whether protecting the environment is an act that belongs in the moral domain or not. In fact, early research in environmental action was either dominated by an economic perspective or a utility maximizing approach: The first approach would expect that people show pro-environmental behaviour if the cost-benefit structure is in favour of it, meaning, if it is profitable in terms of money or in more extended versions of the economic perspective also in terms of effort, time, etc. The second, and very much related, perspective would assume that people engage in conservation if that action has the highest utility for them personally compared to alternative actions.

If one of the most influential definitions of the moral domain by Turiel (1983) as "prescriptive judgements of justice, rights and welfare pertaining how people ought to relate to each other" (p. 3) is applied, then environmental protection clearly falls out of the moral domain. Also, Gibbs (2003) characterizes the moral domain by two principles referring to human beings: "first, justice and respect for a person (autonomy) and, second, non-maleficence or beneficence (along with its corresponding virtue, benevolence)" (p. 6). However, as far as other living beings (animals and plants) are suffering or benefitting from a certain action and concepts of justice, rights and welfare might be applied to them as well, pro-environmental action is not structurally different from social actions between people. As long as other beings are ascribed rights and the welfare of such beings is strived for it becomes a moral question whether to harm or protect them. Furthermore, other people might be indirectly harmed by harming the environment, either at the same point in time or in the future. Already in the early seventies, Heberlein (1972) proposed that environmental actions have a lot in common with pro-social behaviour and that therefore moral motivs might, under certain conditions serve as powerful motivatorsfor pro-environmental action. It seems to make sense to analyse environmental behaviour via the same premises as pro-social behaviour and see how much understanding can be gained by such an approach and where it probably has its limitations. To do so, the next sections will analyse first which kind of variables have been discussed in environmental psychology in relation to moral motivs.

VALUES, NORMS, CONCERN AND MORAL OBLIGATIONS

The concepts of moral motivation that are used in environmental psychology vary a lot with respect to their specificity. At one extreme, stable basic value orientations have been related to environmental behaviour. At the other extreme, very specific feelings of moral obligation felt in (and only in) a certain situation have been analysed as determinants of environmental action. In between are concepts like environmental value orientations, environmental concern and social as well as different types of personal norms. Figure 1 displays the continuum of potential moral motivators of environmental behaviour with respect to specificity on the horizontal axis. Whereas the value concepts displayed in the left hand side of the figure are the most basic guiding principles in life (either across domains as basic value orientations or domain specific) and thus are extremely stable, norms are more situation-specific and imply certain variability. Environmental concerns occupy a special position on the continuum that will be discussed later.

Furthermore, the different constructs discussed in the following sections differ in how they assume the moral motivation is driven: Is it appliance to social rules and expectations to avoid social sanctions and gain acceptance that drives people's behaviour or is it an anticipated negative emotional reaction to a mismatch between deeply internalized values and one's own behaviour irrespective of what other people think? Are the drivers extrinsic or intrinsic, or under which conditions is moral motivation more likely intrinsic and when is it more likely extrinsic? Figure 1 displays the continuum of potential moral motivators of environmental behaviour with respect to intrinsic vs. extrinsic motivation on the vertical axis. Whereas the motivators in the left half can be located both on the extrinsic and the intrinsic side, depending on how much they are internalized, the norms to the right are clearly allocated to either the intrinsic or the extrinsic side. The relationship to a specific environmental behaviour should in general be the stronger, the more specific and the more intrinsic the moral motivator is, which means that it should increase from the bottom left to the top right corner of figure 1, although descriptive or injunctive norms can be very powerful predictors under certain conditions.

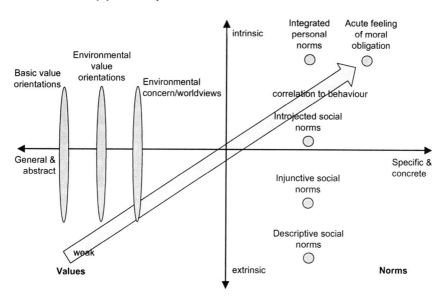

Figure 1: Types of moral motivators for environmental protection in a space defined by specificity and intrinsic vs. extrinsic motivation.

Basic Values

Basic value orientations are people's most fundamental and stable, but at the same time most abstract representations of morality. They tell us what we should strive for, what we should achieve and where we (have to) set priorities. They define where to look for the "right" and the "good" (Gibbs, 2003). Schwartz (1992) defines a value as "a desirable trans-situational goal varying in importance, which serves as a guiding principle in the life of a person or other social entity" (p. 21). There is a tradition to analyse basic values cross-culturally and determine people's and nations' prevalent value orientation in a system of a limited number of value dimensions. Several of such structuring basic value systems have been identified empirically, the two most prominent were proposed by a group of researchers around Ronald Inglehart and a group around Shalom Schwartz.

Inglehart and Welzel (2005) propose a value structure that assumes two basic dimensions of value orientations: One dimension depicts the degree of *survival versus self-expression* whereas the other dimension depicts orientation towards *traditional versus secular-rational values*. The survival-self-expression dimension subsumes how much weight a society and its citizens have to put on surviving as opposed to how much capacity can be freed to allow the citizens to express themselves by, for example, engaging in pro-social action. Developing countries usually score low towards the survival pole on this dimension whereas western, especially Scandinavian countries score high towards self-expression. The second dimension captures how much influence tradition and religion have in a society as opposed to a secular orientation of society. Islamic and Latin American countries score high on traditionalism whereas Confucian societies and the protestant Europe score high on secularity. Both dimensions can be further integrated into one dimension referred to as *materialism versus post-materialism*, where post-materialism means both high on self-expression and secular-rational values and materialism means both high scores on survival and traditional values. Although the Inglehart-Welzel-value system is not a value theory developed to describe individuals, it offers interesting insights into moral motives behind environmental action as it also allows for a description of individuals within the coordinate system. Individual members of a society might diverge from their country's predominant value orientation and create variability in value orientation that, in turn, might explain variation in environmental action. This raises the interesting question whether values understood in the presented way are intrinsic or extrinsic motivators of behaviour. The answer is most likely that they can be both. As long as a dominant value orientation in a society is either not internalized yet or in opposition to an individual's values, it may still have an impact on people's behaviour but the motivator comes from the outside. Anticipated social sanctions, the wish to be integrated into the group are then driving compliance with the values rules. However, as soon as a value is internalized and becomes part of an individual value system, it might become an intrinsic motivator, given that it becomes central enough for a person's identity (Blasi, 1980, 1983). The anticipated negative emotions if a mismatch between action and identity-relevant values occurs are an important motivator.

In fact, basic value orientations measured in the Inglehart-Welzel system show a relationship to support for environmental movements and action. Inglehart (1995) shows for example that support for environmental protection is the higher the more clearly post-materialistic goals are prioritized by a person. Interestingly, this effect can be most clearly found in advanced industrialized western countries whereas, in eastern or African countries, the relationship is weak. Inglehart interprets this finding as support for the thesis that post-materialistic values are generally strengthening support for environmental action but that under certain conditions this support can be also rooted in materialistic values. It might be for example that protecting the environment might become a question of survival for certain societies that are relying heavily on natural resources to sustain their population. In an early study of determinants of taking environmental action against climate change, Jaeger, Dürrenberger, Kastenholz, and Truffer (1993) found that post-materialism had a significant positive influence on the probability of taking climate action in a Swiss sample. This influence disappeared, however, when socio-cultural variables, like being exposed to cultural rules favouring climate-relevant environmental action, being involved in social networks emphasizing problems like climate change and political interest, were added to the equation. Also, Davis (2000) and Dunlap and York (2008) found only weak and partly contradictory relations between post-materialism and environmental action.

Schwartz and Bilsky (1987, 1990) empirically developed a value system based on multinational surveys that included people's ratings on how important each of 56 stated values (e.g., pleasure, politeness, self-respect, unity with nature, protecting the environment) is as a guiding principle in their lives. Schwartz and Bilsky identified underlying patterns in the ratings of people and grouped the values by similarity into ten value types: power, achievement, hedonism, stimulation, self-direction, universalism, benevolence, tradition, conformity and security (see figure 2). The ten sub-dimensions again are grouped into four clusters (self-enhancement, self-transcendence, openness to change, conservation). Self-enhancement and self-transcendence form the two endpoints of one basic value dimension in the Schwartz system, openness to change and conservationism[1] mark the other basic dimension. The basic value structure appeared to be stable across a variety of cultures, although the prevalence of specific value types varies (Bardi& Schwartz, 2003; Schwartz, 1992; Schwartz & Bardi, 2001; Schwartz, Sagiv & Boehnke, 2000).

Bardi and Schwartz (2003) report high correlations of embracement of a certain value type (e.g., universalism) and behaviour within that domain. As "protecting the environment" is explicitly mentioned in the list of 56 values, it is not surprising that there is a correlation between the value type "universalism", where this specific value is grouped into an environmental action. Several studies found a positive correlation between environmental behaviour and the two value clusters "self-transcendence" and "openness to change", whereas the clusters "conservation" and "self-enhancement" were negatively correlated to environmentalism (Karp, 1996; Thøgersen & Grunert-Beckmann, 1997; Nordlund & Garvill, 2002). Most of that influence however was not direct but mediated by other constructs, like attitudes and personal norms. Interestingly, conservation had an unexpected positive influence on recycling activities (Thøgersen & Grunert-Beckmann, 1997), probably indicating that recycling might be motivated by non-environmental motives (such as wanting to save resources, not wasting good material) which are in line with traditional values. In general, the impact of basic values on environmental protection seems to be small and mostly indirect, no matter if Inglehart's or Schwartz's value system is applied. As a reference system for shaping environmental attitudes, basic values seem however relevant.

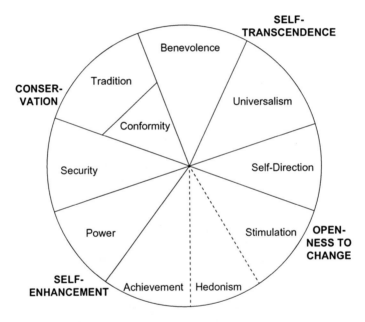

Figure 2: The Schwartz-value-system (Struch, Schwartz & van der Kloot, 2002, page 19, reproduced with permission).

Environmental values

Whereas basic values are unspecific with respect to the domain they are applied to and thus probably less potent to explain behaviour within specific areas are environmental values sets of value orientations that are specifically related to the environmental domain and should provide a better basis for environmental attitudes and behaviour. Within environmental values, it is common to differentiate different levels: the own person, other people and finally non-human life. Stern (2000) proposes to distinguish three kinds of environment specific value orientations that might be relevant for environmental action: (a) biospheric values, (b) altruistic values, and (c) egoistic values. The first value orientation emphasizes the environment and the biosphere directly and independently of its usability for humankind, the second prioritizes the usability of nature for the welfare of other people and the last set of values refers to maximizing the individual outcome. The latter value orientation should be negatively related to environmental protection whereas the first two should show a positive correlation, the one with biospheric values being the strongest. Some studies show this three-dimensional structure of environmental values (e.g., Karp, 1996; de Groot & Steg, 2007), while others fail to differentiate biospheric and altruistic values (e.g., Bardi& Schwartz, 2003). Another, very similar categorization was suggested by Merchant (1992) who differentiated ecocentric, homocentric and anthropocentric values (the first one assigning nature a value in itself, whereas the homocentric orientation derives nature's value from its utility to the individual person and the third one from its utility for humankind in general). In a cross-cultural study in six countries Schultz et al. (2005) found significant but only small to medium size correlations between basic value orientations and environmental values: Self-transcendence was positively related to biospheric values and negatively related to egoistic values, while the pattern for self-enhancement was inverse. Conservatism was only weakly positive related to egoistic values and weakly negative to biospheric values. Openness to change was not found to be related to environmental values at all.

Nordlund and Garvill (2002, 2003) show that ecocentrism is positively related to a general index of pro-environmental behaviour and car use, but that this relationship is indirect, a finding also reported by Barr and Gilg (2007). In an analysis of the willingness to pay for a wildlife protection programme, Ojea and Laureiro (2007) found that egoistic and altruistic environmental value orientations positively influence the willingness to pay. As for general values, also environmental values can be both extrinsic and intrinsic motivators of environmental behaviour, depending on the degree of internalization.

Environmental Concern - A Worldview Perspective

If environmental concern should be discussed in a chapter about moral motivators of pro-environmental behaviour might be open for debate. The theoretical concepts subsumed under the umbrella "environmental concern" are so diverse that some clearly are non-moral in nature and close to attitudes in their measurement while others have a clear reference to moral principles and reflect rather worldviews than attitudes (see Fransson & Gärling, 1999, for a discussion). In this section only the most prominent measure of environmental concern, the New Environmental Paradigm (NEP) shall be discussed. Theoretically seen, worldviews reside somewhere between basic values and very specific moral obligations. What makes worldviews interesting as a construct is that they contain beliefs about how the world functions, what is causing what, and how the different pieces of the world should go together. The beliefs constituting worldviews are not necessarily moral in nature but often have a moral undertone of what should be done, what is acceptable and what is right. This makes it relevant to analyse them in the context of this chapter. Furthermore, they have been discussed as a link between values and norms (see the section about the value belief norm theory below).

The original version of the NEP was introduced by Dunlap and van Liere in the late 1970s. In their paper (Dunlap & van Liere, 1978), they propose a twelve-item measurement instrument to capture how much a person embraces an ecological worldview, which by the time the instrument was developed was new and opposed to the predominant anti-ecological worldview. The scale was constructed to include three sub-dimensions: (a) *limits to growth*, which means recognizing that the potential to economic and population growth is limited, (b) *balance of nature*, which refers to recognition of the delicate equilibriums in nature that should not be tempered with, and (c) *human domination*, which is a negatively loading sub-dimension capturing how much a person agrees with that humankind has the right to dominate nature. The last dimension especially has a clear moral side as rights of non-human life are offset against rights of humans. Later, Dunlap, van Liere, Mertig and Jones (2000) published a revised version of the NEP scale. The dimensional structure of the scale has been subject to several analyses with ambiguous results: Some studies replicate the original structure (e.g., Geller & Lasley, 1985), some find that all NEP items load on just one factor (e.g., Noe & Snow, 1990), while others find two dimensions (e.g., Gooch, 1995) and limits to growth and balance of nature items usually load on the same dimension.

Less controversial than its dimensional structure is the positive relationship of environmental concern measured by the NEP scale to pro-environmental behaviour. In the original study, the NEP scores showed a substantial correlation with support for environmental regulations and funding of environmental programs and weaker correlations with personal environmental behaviour (Dunlap & van Liere, 1978). Since its publication, the NEP scale has been extensively used and its relationship to several types of environmental behaviours has been repeatedly shown (Davis, Green & Reed, 2009; Tarrant & Cordell, 1997). Other authors, however, showed that although NEP correlated with pro-environmental behaviour, the relationship was comparatively small compared to other constructs like personal norms, which indicates that the NEP scale is also not a direct predictor of behaviour but most likely an indirect one (Wiidegren, 1998; Scott & Willits, 1994). De Groot and Steg (2008) were able to show a substantial correlation of the NEP scale with environmental value orientations, especially with the biospheric values, which links them back to the more general value orientations.

Social Norms

Social norms are a mental representation of the perceived or anticipated expectations of relevant other people with respect to the behaviour in question - in other words, they are the internal representation of social pressure. By referring to social norms, an individual evaluates what other people might expect him or her to do in a given situation, if these people are important enough to consider their expectations, if they would support some behavioural alternatives, and if the individual is willing to give in to such expectations. If social norms are to be considered as moral motivators, they are clearly on the extrinsic side of the continuum. Complying to perceived social expectations occurs because people try to avoid social sanctions and punishment and try to gain social acceptance or group membership. Also participating in other people's prestige by complying to their expectations might be a motive active here. The function of social norms would therefore be to ensure that moral principles are followed even if the acting individual does not necessarily embrace them. Constructs like social norms can be found in many contemporary action models like the theory of planned behaviour (Ajzen, 1991)[3] or the norm-activation theory (Schwartz & Howard, 1981) and their relevant role in predicting behaviour or immediate determinants of behaviour is unquestioned. The strength of their influence varies, however, depending on the behavioural domain and context, as well as on the predominant culture.[4]

Also in the domain of pro-environmental behaviour, social norms have been demonstrated to be effective predictors. Goldstein, Cialdini and Griskevicius (2008) were able to positively influence people's behaviour in hotel rooms with respect to reusing towels by creating a social norm of reusing towels. Their message "*Join your fellow guests in helping to save the environment*" displayed in the bathroom was approximately 30% more efficient than the standard "*Help save the environment*" message. In a famous field experiment, Hopper and Nielsen (1991) found that the most effective way to influence people's participation in a recycling program was to make social norms salient by using well-known neighbours in a housing area as promotion agents for the program.

Social norms are, however, not a uni-dimensional construct. Thøgersen (2006) suggests a taxonomy of norms with a varying degree of internalization. The more external norms can be understood as social norms whereas the more internalized norms fall into the domain of the personal norms which will be described in the following section. The most external type of norm would be a descriptive social norm, meaning choosing a behaviour based on what other people *do* in a given situation, copying their behaviour. Motivations for repeating other people's behaviour could be observing other people to be rewarded for the behaviour (Bandura, 1965) or – more subtle – increasing interpersonal attraction and group cohesiveness. Injunctive social norms in contrast to that would capture how far a person perceives others to approve or disapprove with the considered behavioural alternatives irrespective of what they actually do themselves. In this case, anticipated feelings of shame would be the main motivation to avoid acting against other people's expectations. Schultz, Nolan, Cialdini, Goldstein and Griskevicius (2007) manipulated both types of social norms independently in an experiment to decrease personal energy use. Only providing people with a descriptive norm message (the average energy consumption of people in the same neighbourhood) had positive effects on people that had above average energy use before the experiment but negative effects of people that were below average. This boomerang-effect could be effectively counteracted when the descriptive norm message was combined with an injunctive norm message (indicating with an emoticon – a smiley – that below average energy use was approved while above average energy consumption was not approved).

The norm taxonomy by Thøgersen (2006) indicates that there is a continuum of internalization of norms and that the closer norms are to behaviour the more internalized they are. This means that both descriptive and injunctive social norms should not be a direct predictor of behaviour but mediated by more integrated types of norms or other constructs closer to behaviour. This is also reflected in the theory of planned behaviour (Ajzen, 1991) where social norms are a predictor of intentions but not behaviour and in the norm-activation theory where social norms impact personal norms but usually not behaviour over and above the influence that is mediated by personal norms (Schwartz & Howard, 1981).

Personal Norms and Feelings of Moral Obligations

Personal norms have been defined as a feeling of moral obligation and are tied to the self-concept of a person (Schwartz, 1977). According to that understanding, personal norms have some overlap with the concept of the "moral self" proposed by Blasi (1980, 1983). A personal norm would, in Blasi's terms, be referred to as morality that is central for definition of the identity of a person, a moral identity. Hence, personal norm theory would, in parallel to Blasi, assume that anticipated negative affect (feeling of guilt) for a mismatch between values or moral judgements and actions would lead to change of action. Personal norms reflect what a person feels morally obliged to do in a certain situation based on his or her value system. The difference between values and personal norms is that personal norms are very specific to a certain type of behaviour and in the strictest understanding to a certain situation and need to be activated before they become relevant (see below). Moral obligations are either felt or not felt in a specific decision making context. Values provide the background against which the feeling of moral obligation is generated in interaction with the individual interpretation of the situation and one's contribution to and responsibility for it and freedom of action in it. Again, a parallel to Blasi's theories (1980, 1983, 1993) is obvious: Also Blasi assumes that individuals only act according to their moral judgements if they accept responsibility for acting. Social norms also contribute to the formation of personal norms in a given situation. Although personal norms should be analysed as an acute feeling of moral obligation in a given situation, most measures of personal norm record personal norms (hence, feelings of moral obligation) aggregated to a certain extend across similar situations (e.g., "I feel morally obliged to use environmentally friendly modes of transportation when I need to go to the university."). This is why the author of this chapter likes to distinguish between what is referred to as "personal norms" in the literature and what could more accurately be described as an aggregated feeling of moral obligation across time and the acute feeling of moral obligation which is felt in a given situation, which is hard to measure and therefore only seldom analysed.

According to Thøgersen's (2006) norm taxonomy, personal norms are internalized social norms. The degree of integration differentiates between introjected personal norms which are only partly internalized and motivated basically by trying to avoid anticipated feelings of guilt towards external expectations and integrated personal norms. If the norm is, however, fully integrated, then the motivation to comply with the norm is internal, trying to avoid incongruence with one's own value system, which could be interpreted as part of Blasi's (1980, 1983, 1993) moral identity. The latter kind of personal norm is what most authors would refer to as a personal norm.

Personal norms have been shown to be an important predictor of pro-environmental behaviour. Furthermore, they seem to mediate the influence of basic and environmental values, worldviews measured by the NEP scale and social norms on behaviour to a large extent. Minton and Rose (1997) compared the influence of environmental concern, social norms and personal norms on three types of environmental behaviour (green consumerism, search for information about environmentally friendly products and recycling) and found personal norms to have the strongest impact. Thøgersen (2006) found that integrated personal norms were the best predictor of buying organic milk, buying energy saving light bulbs and source separation when analysed together with descriptive, injunctive and introjected norms. For using public transportation, however, introjected and integrated personal norms were equally strong. Nordlund and Garvill (2002, 2003) have shown both the close connection between personal norms and behaviour and the mediating function they have for more general values in the background. In the study by Thøgersen and Grunert-Beckmann (1997), personal norms came out as a much stronger predictor of waste prevention behaviour than attitudes and equally strong as attitudes in waste recycling. Furthermore, they mediated the influence of basic values.

THE VALUE-BELIEF-NORM THEORY

Whereas the preceding sections described variables that have been discussed in environmental psychology to reflect drivers for moral action in one way or another it was repeatedly concluded that the relationship between basic values and/or environmental values, on the one hand, and pro-environmental behaviour, on the other, is indirect. The next section will therefore introduce a theory that integrates several levels of moral decision making. With the value-belief-norm theory (VBN), Stern (2000) presented a framework that systematically structured the hierarchy of values and norms potentially impacting pro-environmental behaviour. As figure 3 shows, Stern grouped many of the previously discussed concepts into four main groups: Values, beliefs, personal norms, and behaviours. The variables are lined up in a linear progression from rather unspecific environmental values on the left side to concrete behaviours on the right side of the figure and also implemented some activating steps that to some extent reflect Blasi's "moral self" (1980, 1983, 1993).

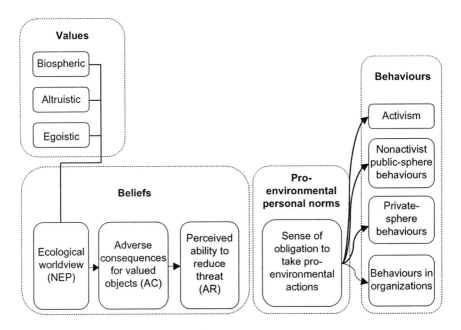

Figure 3. The value-belief-norm theory (adapted from Stern, 2000, page 412).

Interesting about the VBN theory are two things: (1) it differentiates between different types of pro-environmental behaviours and assumes that a person's felt moral obligation to take pro-environmental action does not necessarily express itself in all areas simultaneously. If only selected behaviours are analysed it might be missed that a person does something pro-environmental in another behavioural domain and the norm-behaviour relation becomes underestimated. It might for example be that a person is very active in the private sphere and recycles, saves energy at home or buys organic food but does not volunteer in any visible behaviour outside the home. (2) The VBN links environmental value orientations through a chain of specific constructs to the activation of acute feelings of moral obligation (personal norms) which then motivate behaviour. The first mediating step is that people form an ecological worldview if they have strong biospheric or altruistic and weak egoistic values. Given that this worldview is established, adverse consequences for a valued specific object (a nature reserve, a species, natural resources, etc.) may be perceived or anticipated. In the next step, the personal ability to reduce this threat is evaluated and if that leads to a positive outcome, feelings of moral obligation are activated. In other words, acting morally becomes part of identity. These feelings of moral obligation then are the motivators of specific behaviours, but trade-offs between behaviours are possible.

In a study, Stern et al. (1999) applied the VBN theory to predict support for environmental movements, environmental policy and private-sphere behaviour.

They found that the VBN theory predicted support for environmental movements and policy well compared to other theories. Steg, Dreijerink and Abrahamse (2005) tested the VBN theory in detail on the stated acceptance of energy policies and confirmed all proposed model relations. The only deviation from the original VBN model was that biospheric value orientations had *additional* direct effects on the perceived ability to reduce the threat and on perceived consequences. The models tested by Nordlund and Garvill (2002, 2003) are structurally similar to the VBN theory and provide good support for many of the assumed relations. Kaiser, Hübner and Bogner (2005), however, directly compared the VBN theory with the theory of planned behaviour (TPB, Ajzen, 1991) and found that the VBN theory was outperformed by the TPB although it was able to explain a large proportion of variation in general pro-environmental behaviour.

THE NORM-ACTIVATION THEORY

A theory that describes moral motivation's impact on behaviour is norm-activation (NAT, Schwartz, 1977; Schwartz & Howard, 1981). The theory focuses on the processes of how feelings of moral obligations are generated and activated in a given situation. It focusses on under which conditions moral judgements are actually translated into behaviour with the intermediate step of activated personal norms. Initially the theory was developed to explain altruistic behaviour but it has been applied repeatedly to environmental behaviour and has become one of the most prominent theories in this domain together with the theory of planned behaviour. Since the original version of the theory was never formalized or visualized in a proper way, several different versions of the theory can be found in the literature. All interpretations of the model build on a very similar set of variables: Central in all versions is the *personal norm* (PN), a feeling of moral obligation to act environmentally friendly, which is a direct predictor of environmental behaviour. In addition, variables like *awareness of need* (AN), *awareness of consequences* (AC), *ascription of responsibility* (AR), *perceived behavioural control* (PBC) and *social norms* (SN) are considered. Awareness of need describes the awareness a person has that an environmental problem exists and a solution is needed. Awareness of consequences is the representation that a person's own actions contribute to the problem.[5] Ascription of responsibility describes the feeling of being responsible for negative consequences when not acting environmentally friendly. Perceived behavioural control represents how far a person perceives him or herself in being in control over his or her action in a given situation. How much freedom of choice is there or are others or situational constraints already completely determining one's actions? PBC and AR are closely related constructs so that several versions of the norm-activation theory often either include one or the other. Social norms finally are the representation of the expectations of relevant other people as described in detail before.

The first version of the theory assumes that personal norms are a direct predictor of behaviour and that awareness of need, awareness of consequences, social norms and perceived behavioural control are independent predictors of personal norms. Perceived behavioural control is also assumed to have a direct impact on behaviour. This version of the NAT was proposed by Hunecke, Blöbaum, Matthies and Höger (2001) and is displayed in figure 4. They also assumed that external costs moderate the relationship between personal norms and ecological behaviour. Tested on travel mode choice, the theory received empirical support in their study. A similar model has also been successfully applied to the purchase of organic milk (Klöckner & Ohms, 2009). In a comparison of the NAT and the theory of planned behaviour, Wall, Devine-Wright and Mill (2007) found the NAT to be the more potent theory in explaining travel mode choice than the TPB, a finding that was not replicated by Bamberg, Hunecke and Blöbaum (2007).

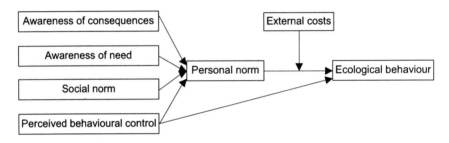

Figure 4. The norm-activation theory, version 1 (adapted from Hunecke et al., 2001, names of the variables have been adapted to the nomenclature used in this chapter).

Although the above presented model has received some support in the literature, the additive, independent influence of the constructs on the left side on personal norms might be questioned. Reading the initial papers by Schwartz (1977) and Schwartz and Howard (1981), two more complex understandings of the theory become evident: (a) Personal norms are the outcome of a norm-activation chain or cascade, starting with becoming aware of a need and/or the consequences of one's own behaviour, accepting responsibility for the action and perceiving control about the action and then generating a feeling of moral obligation to act which finally determines action. This mediator-hypothesis was proposed among others by Black, Stern and Elworth (1985), Steg, Dreijerink and Abrahamse (2005), and Stern and Dietz (1994). Also Klöckner and Matthies (2009) described a norm-activation chain in their extended norm-activation model. The mediation hypothesis is displayed in the upper half of figure 5. (b) The relationship between personal norms and environmental behaviour is moderated by the strength of the awareness of consequences and the ascription of responsibility. Personal norms are assumed to be potentially active in the background but only relevant for pro-environmental behaviour when both awareness of consequences and ascription of responsibility are strong. This moderator hypothesis was put forward by Schultz and Zelezny (1998), and Vining and Ebreo (1992), and is displayed in the lower half of figure 5. De Groot and Steg (2009) systematically tested the two hypotheses and found strong support for the mediator hypotheses and only weak support for the moderator hypothesis.

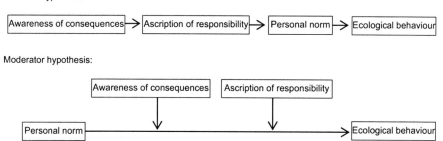

Figure 5. The norm-activation theory, version 2 & 3 (adapted from de Groot & Steg, 2009).

AN INTEGRATED MODEL FRAMEWORK

Discussion of both the value-belief-norm theory and the norm-activation theory has shown that integrating moral motivations of different kinds into more complex models provides a better understanding of the moral background of pro-environmental behaviour. The aforementioned theories have especially contributed to bridging the gap between moral judgements on the one hand that are guided by the more basic stable values and moral action that is assumed to be driven by concrete feelings of moral obligation (personal norms) in a certain situation. These feelings are not present in every situation to the same extend. Sometimes the need for action might be negated, sometimes responsibility is denied or the consequences of one's own behaviour are not linked to the outcome, sometimes the level of perceived control is low, sometimes acting moral is not part of the persons definition of identity in a given context. Thus, postulating the concept of "personal norms" as a trigger of moral action in a given situation has developed understanding considerably for when people act morally and when they do not.

Several studies, however, have questioned that even the relation between personal norms and behaviour is direct and have shown, that models that integrate personal norms into the theory of planned behaviour describe pro-environmental behaviour better (Gardner & Abraham, 2010; Klöckner & Blöbaum, 2010; Kaiser, 2006; Bamberg & Moser, 2007). The assumption is that feelings of moral obligation have to compete in a given choice situation against alternative motivations. Anticipated negative affects about value-action-mismatch can be traded off against other anticipated emotions and a costs-benefit-balance connected the behaviour in question. Sometimes, such trade-offs are even overridden by behavioural routines that short cut the decision-making process, especially if the behaviour is performed frequently. Klöckner and Blöbaum (2010) recently introduced an integrated model of pro-environmental behaviour that includes variables of the norm-activation theory, the theory of planned behaviour and situational constraints as well as habits as additional predictors of environmental action. Habits have been shown before to moderate the relation between personal norms and behaviour (Klöckner, Matthies & Hunecke, 2003; Klöckner & Matthies, 2004) and to be important determinants of pro-environmental behaviour (e.g., Verplanken, Aarts, van Knippenberg& van Knippenberg, 1994). The integrated model has been successfully applied to travel mode choice (Klöckner & Blöbaum, 2010; Klöckner & Friedrichsmeier, 2011), recycling (Klöckner & Oppedal, 2011) and investment in a wood pellet stove (Sopha & Klöckner, 2011). A new adapted and extended version of this comprehensive action determination model is displayed in figure 6 with a special emphasis on the moral activation cascade described earlier in this chapter and a linkage to basic and environmental values. In the study by Sopha and Klöckner (2011) part of this value-norm-chain has been modelled successfully already.

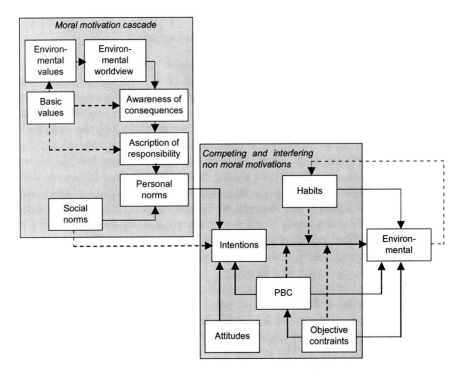

Figure 6. An adapted comprehensive action determination model.

The adapted comprehensive action determination model assumes that moral motivations enter the decision-making process about environmentally relevant behaviour in a highly indirect way. In line with the value-belief-norm theory, it assumes that basic values are first translated into environment specific values, which then constitute an environmental worldview. All three types of values might lead to moral judgements about how nature should be treated. The model assumes that such judgements are not necessarily translated into a feeling of moral obligation. They strengthen, however, the probability of becoming aware of possible negative consequences of one's own behaviour and the willingness to accept responsibility. The latter two variables might also be affected by other basic value sub-dimensions that are not directly related to environmental behaviour (e.g., to help other people). Given that the norm activation process was successful and (descriptive and injunctive) social norms do not stand against, personal norms become one determinant of intentions to act. Attitudes and perceived behavioural control are, however, other important factors that contribute to forming an intention that are not always in line with the personal norm. Sometimes, social norms can bypass the personal norms and have an independent impact on formation of intentions, especially if the values referred to are not central for self-definition. Usually their impact is, however, completely mediated by personal norms. Even if an intention to act was formed, counter-intentional habits, perceived behavioural control and objective constraints can still interfere with performance of the intended behaviour. All three factors are supposed to both have a direct impact on behaviour and moderate the relation between intentions and behaviour. Objective constraints shape perceived behavioural control but are not identical to it. Over time, repeated successful performance of behaviour in stable contexts strengthens the habit which then impacts repeated performance of behaviour (Klöckner & Matthies, 2012).

The model depicted in figure 6 makes it obvious how long the distance between moral processes and environmental behaviour is and how many variables can interfere with a successful performance of morally motivated behaviour. For the first time it combines assumptions about the transfer of moral judgements in the environmental domain to moral actions as described in the value-belief-norm theory and the norm-activation theory with assumptions about competing non-moral motivations as described in the theory of planned behaviour. Even if personal norms become activated and the felt moral obligation to act is strong, negative attitudes towards the behaviour or low perceived control can interfere with performance. And even if an intention is formed, habits and situational constraints can still interfere. To give an example of predictions this complex model of environmental behaviour would make the case of transport choice shall be used. What leads some people to take the bus instead of the car when travelling to university and others to prefer to sit in their car?

Let us sketch three prototypical persons: Anna, Hans and Magnus. Anna (student, 24 years old) embraces strongly self-transcendent and post-materialistic values. As a result, she also strongly believes in biospheric values and has a worldview that tells her that the natural equilibrium is fragile, that humankind is part of nature and that there are limits to the growth of modern mankind. Her values therefore tell her that nature should be protected. This leads to that whenever she has to make a decision how to travel, she perceives the need to choose the mode that has the least impact on the environment, she sees a relation between her actions and the environmental impact and she accepts that she is responsible for her actions. Being a moral person with respect to travel mode choice and the environment is central to her identity. Around her she has people who mostly support her in her way of thinking. She has a rather positive attitude about public transportation and cycling and dislikes the car. Most of the time she feels of having control about her travel mode choice and she lives in a big city where the public transportation is good. Actually, for environmental reasons she decided not to own a car and therefore she has limited access to a car although she can use the car of her co-habitant if she needs to. Thus, she has strong habits to use the bus when she travels. Not surprisingly, she will chose the bus or the bike whenever she travels with very few exceptions. Last time she used the car was when she needed to transport furniture that the bought in a second hand store, but that was long ago.

Hans (53, self-employed) believes in achievement and having the power to influence others. His values are more materialistic than post-materialistic. He thinks the environmental problems are overrepresented in the public debate. For him travel mode choice has nothing to do with morality, he sees neither a need to act, nor a connection between what he does and environmental impacts, nor any kind of responsibility on his side. Consequently he does not feel any moral obligation to use environmentally friendly travel modes. Sometimes his wife and his 18 year old daughter try to influence him to take the bus but he does not want to comply to that request. He feels that he actually has no choice but to use the car because he needs to be flexible in his job and he feels that public transportation is all too unreliable and too expensive, even if he lives in the same city as Anna. Thus, his attitude to public transportation is very negative. He uses the car every day, so when he decides he needs to get from A to B he actually chooses the car automatically, always!

Magnus (32, in paternity leave with his eight month old daughter) has as Anna a strong belief in post-materialism and self-transcendent values. He also thinks that nature is worth protecting and embraces a pro-environmental world view. Whenever he needs to decide how to travel he feels a strong obligation to travel environmentally friendly. However, since he now has to care for his baby and to transport the stroller as well as food and diapers, he feels sometimes not able to travel by bus. His positive attitude towards public transportation has somewhat deteriorated lately after some negative experiences where he was not able to enter the bus with the stroller. So Magnus torn between his pro-environmental norms and a perceived reduced control. Sometimes he takes the bus, sometimes he gives in and takes the car instead. His partner often pressuring him to use the car, so he does not get the social support he would need to take the bus despite the obstacles he now perceives. From being a habituated bus user he developed into a person that deliberately decides when to take the bus and when to take the car. So situational conditions like the weather, time pressure, if and what he has to transport now have a strong impact on his decisions and his value orientations have been pushed back a bit. All the three stories together tell us something about how difficult it can be to translate a moral judgement into an action. Whereas Anna and Hans act according to their values, Magnus sometimes feels able to act according to his values, sometimes not.

MORAL DEVELOPMENT IN THE ENVIRONMENTAL DOMAIN

How can the different moral judgements and the different behaviours of Anna, Hans and Magnus be explained from a developmental perspective? How did their different values and norms develop? The development of moral judgement and moral action is one of the main research foci in moral psychology. Interestingly, not much research effort in the domain of environmental psychology has been spent on how children develop moral motivations to act environmentally friendly. In a study by Matthies, Selge and Klöckner (in press) the relation between the parents' problem communication, injunctive norm communication and descriptive norms (the parents' behaviour) on the one hand and 8-10 year old children's personal norms, social norms and behaviour in the domain of reusing and recycling paper has been analysed. The strongest impact on children's recycling behaviour was by descriptive norms. If parents recycle themselves, then children perceive stronger social norms to recycle, have stronger personal norms and also more recycling behaviour. Injunctive norms (what parents tell their children to do) had significant but much weaker influence. Problem communication had an impact on the child's behaviour that was mediated by awareness of need and consequences. For reuse of paper the only the parents' problem communication had an influence, again mediated by awareness of need and consequences and then personal norms. Descriptive and injunctive norms had no significant influence, probably because reusing paper is something that is not very common in German households and is much more a practice in kindergarten and primary school. What can be learned here is that both parents' communication about environmental problems and their attempts to teach their children the moral background of acting environmentally friendly have an impact on their children's behaviour. What is, however, the most powerful teacher of moral behaviour is that one acts morally oneself, including as a parent. Acting as a moral model seems to be the best way to transmit morality to the next generation.

In another study Haustein, Klöckner & Matthies (2009) retrospectively analysed how the travel mode choice of young adults was impacted by communication with their parents' about the negative impacts of car use, how flexible their friends used different travel modes when they were about 15 years old and where acquiring a driving licence was perceived as an initiation to adulthood. All three variables had a significant impact on the participants' behaviour. Whereas experiencing acquisition of a driving licence mainly had an impact mediated by habits, was the impact of the peers' flexibility in mode choice mediated both by personal norms and habits. Discussions with parents about the impact of car use on the environment were finally seen to be affecting behaviour, mediated by social and personal norms. Whereas the mediating effect of habits is not relevant for this chapter and is discussed elsewhere

(Klöckner & Matthies, 2012), is the mediating role of social and personal norms interesting: It seems like what the parents tell their growing up children about car use and the environment leads to more or less internalized norms in their children. What the peer group did at the age of 14 also has an impact on travel mode choice of young adults. If the peer group used travel modes deliberately and made many different choices, young adults also are less locked into one travel mode and have stronger personal norms to use environmentally friendly modes. Again, behaviour of others seems to have a strong influence in norms.

INTERVENTIONS FOCUSSING ON MORAL MOTIVATIONS

Now that we know a little bit about how Anna, Hans and Magnus might have developed their set of values and norms and what might have contributed to why they behave the way they do, an interesting question is, what can be done to change the behaviour of Hans and Magnus. Environmental psychology has a strong tradition in developing and analysing intervention instruments. This research field is so extensive that within the remainder of this chapter only the surface can be scratched. For a more comprehensive review of intervention techniques other publications are recommended (e.g., Steg et al., 2012). What should be focussed on in this section are intervention techniques that have a strong connection to moral motivations of pro-environmental behaviour.

Among intervention techniques that can be assumed to have their main impact on behaviour mediated by the moral elements in the model presented in Figure 6, are social models, commitment, goal setting, and the foot-in-the-door technique. Social models are people who are either close to or admired by the target person. This means that they should have either a high similarity in terms of preferences, attitudes or even look or should be from a group of higher social status that the target person likes to belong to. Advertisement often makes use of the latter type of social models by employing celebrities in their campaigns. The former type of model is well illustrated by the already cited block leader study (Hopper & Nielsen, 1991), where already recycling citizens approached their neighbours and tried to convince them to take up recycling as well. Such a person has an impact on the target person both because of things he or she says (which would create injunctive norms) and even more importantly because of what he or she does (descriptive norms). If these social norms become internalized and, over time, become personal norms, then the change might become permanent. Social norms are also communicated in the studies by Schultz et al. (2007) and Goldstein et al. (2008), as described in the section about social norms. However, changing personal norms or even values like this is a long process. Another common technique is commitment. Here, the target person is asked to commit him or herself to perform certain behaviours in a defined time period. This can be either done in private in public, orally or written. Commitment enhances the likelihood that already existing personal norms are activated and thereby strengthens the link between personal norms and behaviour. Commitment has been shown to have smaller effects than other (non-moral) intervention techniques in the short run but the effects last much longer (Hopper & Nielsen, 1991). Commitment has stronger effects when it is given in written, as opposed to oral form, and when it is given public as opposed to private. However, commitment has the disadvantage that people with opposed attitudes or values tend to resist to commit. Sometimes they even show reactance and change their behaviour in the opposite direction. Goal setting means presenting people with a goal concerning how much certain behaviour should be performed in a time period. By doing this, a social expectation is expressed that could work in the same way as a model, depending on that the target person accepts the goal setter as a relevant social influence. The final intervention technique presented here is the foot-in-the-door technique (Freedman & Fraser, 1966). In the context of moral behaviour this technique would work as follows: First the target person is asked a small favour that is in line with his or her moral standards but easy to fulfil. Most people will agree on doing this. Then in a second step a larger action is asked for that the target person would usually not easily agree on performing. Because it is in line with the target person's moral standards and because the moral standards already have been expressed with the first action, the likelihood is strongly increased that also the second behaviour is performed. However, this intervention technique might be ethically questionable under certain conditions.

So what can be done with our three examples, Anna, Hans and Magnus? Hans is the most difficult case because he has no values and internalized norms that motivate him to use environmentally friendly travel modes. He would neither commit himself nor be open to goal settings. So for him non-moral intervention techniques seem more promising (e.g., a change of the incentive structure for the different travel modes). Most importantly, because he is strongly habitualized in his behaviour, an intervention to break his habits needs to precede any other kind of intervention (Verplanken & Wood, 2006). However, if a model can be found that has relevance for Hans the behaviour of this model might have a certain impact over time. Such a model might for example be one of his children (Klöckner, Sopha, Matthies & Bjørnstad, 2012). Magnus is probably the most promising candidate: He embraces pro-environmental values and norms but sometimes acts against them. This means that he would be the perfect candidate for a commitment campaign, goal setting or the foot-in-the-door technique. Asking him to commit himself to use public transportation instead of the car for one month might be easily possible; extending the plea to selling the car afterwards might have an effect, given that Magnus' experiences during the month were positive. Anna is, at first glance, not a relevant target for interventions, since she is already performing the behaviour that should be achieved. However, also Anna might benefit from interventions that make her maintain her behaviour. Social support might be relevant or supporting Anna in making decisions that sustain situational conditions in which she is able to easily us public transportation. Interestingly, very little research has been performed on how to make people who already behave in an environmentally friendly way maintain that kind of behaviour and not change to less beneficial behaviours once their living conditions change.

CONCLUSION

The chapter has shown that a variety of moral motivators on different levels of specificity are discussed to impact environmentally relevant behaviour. It has been further shown, that these motivators can be sorted in a hierarchical way and that even the variables that are closest to behaviour still only have a mediated influence on behaviour. This would seem to call into question if strengthening moral lines of reasoning with respect to environmental protection is promising success given the multiple possibilities for failure in the long process from values into action. On the other hand, relations between values and behaviour have been demonstrated and interventions with a moral focus have worked. Comparative studies of intervention strategies show, that interventions focussing on norms and values do not necessarily have the largest immediate effect, but they sustain and create long-lasting effects because values and norms are very stable variables compared with other variables (Hopper & Nielsen, 1991) and can repeat their influence over time, once they are changed.

Future studies should focus on the conditions under which people succeed in acting in accordance with their values and when they fail. The question should be answered how psychological intervention could contribute to removing or deactivating interfering variables once a change in values, worldviews or norms has been achieved.

NOTES

[1] The term "conservation" might be confusing in the context of environmental protection. Some authors therefor prefer the term "traditionalism" (Dietz, Fitzgerald, &Shwom, 2005).
[2] Also referred to as the "New Ecological Paradigm".
[3] In the theory of planned behaviour "social norms" are referred to as "subjective norms" but the content of the construct is identical.
[4] Studies show that social norms have a stronger impact in collectivistic cultures than in individualistic cultures (e.g., Abrams, Ando, & Hinkle, 1998).
[5] Sometimes AN and AC are collapsed into one construct and it has been difficult to differentiate the two empirically.

REFERENCES

Abrams, D., Ando, K., & Hinkle, S. (1998). Psychological attachment to the group: Cross-cultural differences in organizational identification and subjective norms as predictors of workers' turnover intentions. *Personality and Social Psychological Bulletin, 24*, 1027–1039.

Ajzen, I. (1991). The theory of planned behavior. *Organizational Behavior and Human Decision Processes, 50*, 179–211.

Bamberg, S., Hunecke, M., & Blöbaum, A. (2007). Social context, personal norms and the use of public transportation: Two field studies. *Journal of Environmental Psychology, 27*(3), 190–203.

Bamberg, S., & Moser, G. (2007). Twenty years after Hines, Hungerford, and Tomera: A new meta-analysis of psycho-social determinants of pro-environmental behaviour. *Journal of Environmental Psychology, 27,* 14–25.

Bandura, A. (1965). Influence of models' reinforcement contingencies on the acquisition of imitative responses. *Journal of Personality and Social Psychology, 1,* 589–595.

Bardi, A., & Schwartz, S.H. (2003). Values and behaviour: strength and structure of relations. *Personality and Social Psychology Bulletin, 29,* 1207–1220.

Barr, S., & Gilg, A.W. (2007). A conceptual framework for understanding and analyzing attitudes towards environmental behaviour. *GeografiskaAnnaler: Series B, Human Geography, 89*(4), 361–379.

Black, J. S., Stern, P. C., & Elworth, J. T. (1985). Personal and contextual influences on household energy adaptations. *Journal of Applied Psychology, 70,* 3–21.

Blasi, A. (1980). Bridging moral cognition and moral action: A critical review of the literature. *Psychological Bulletin, 88,* 1–45.

Blasi, A. (1983). Moral cognition and moral action: A theoretical perspective. *Developmental Review, 3,* 178–210.

Blasi, A. (1993). The development of identidy: It's role in moral functioning. In W. M. Kurtines & J. L. Gewirtz (Eds.), *Morality, moral behaviour, and moral development* (pp. 129–139). New York, NY: Wiley.

Davis, D. W. (2000). Individual level examination of postmaterialism in the U.S.: Political tolerance, racial attitudes, environmentalism, and participatory norms. *Political Research Quarterly, 53*(3), 455–475.

Davis, J.L., Green, J.D., & Reed, A. (2009). Interdependence with the environment: Commitment. interconnectedness, and environmental behavior. *Journal of Environmental Psychology, 29,* 173–180.

De Groot, J.I.M., & Steg, L. (2007). Value orientations and environmental beliefs in five countries. Validity of an instrument to measure egoistic, altruistic and biospheric value orientations. *Journal of Cross-Cultural Psychology, 38*(3), 318–332.

De Groot, J.I.M., & Steg, L. (2008). Value orientations to explain beliefs related to environmental significant behavior. *Environment and Behavior, 40,* 330–354.

De Groot, J.I.M., & Steg, L. (2009). Morality and prosocialbehavior: The role of awareness, responsibility, and norms in the norm-activation model. *Journal of Social Psychology, 149,* 425–449.

Dietz, T., Fitzgerald, A., & Shwom, R. (2005). Environmental values. *Annual Review of Environment and Resources, 30,* 335–372.

Dunlap, R.E., & van Liere, K.D. (1978). The "new environmental paradigm": A proposed measuring instrument and preliminary results. *Journal of Environmental Education, 9,* 10–19.

Dunlap, R.E., van Liere, K.D., Mertig, A.G., & Jones, R.E. (2000). Measuring endorsement of the New Ecological Paradigm: A revised NEP scale. *Journal of Social Issues, 56,* 425–442.

Dunlap, R.E., & York, R. (2008). The globalization of environmental concern and the limits of the postmaterialist values explanation: Evidence from four multinational surveys. *The Sociological Quarterly, 49,* 529–563.

Fransson, N., & Gärling, T. (1999). Environmental concern: Conceptual definitions, measurement methods, and research findings. *Journal of Environmental Psychology, 19,* 369–382.

Freedman, J.L., & Fraser, S.C. (1966). Compliance without pressure: The foot-in-the-door technique. *Journal of Personality and Social Psychology, 4,* 195–202.

Gardner, B., & Abraham, C. (2010). Going green? Modeling the impact of environmental concerns and perceptions of transportation alternatives on decisions to drive. *Journal of Applied Social Psychology, 40,* 831–849.

Geller, J.M., & Lasley, P. (1985). The new environmental paradigm scale: A re-examination. *Journal of Environmental Education, 17,* 9–12.

Gibbs, J.C. (2003). *Moral development and reality: Beyond the theories of Kohlberg and Hoffman.* Thousand Oaks, CA: Sage Publications.

Goldstein, N.J., Cialdini, R. B., & Griskevicius, V. (2008). A room with a viewpoint: Using social norms to motivate environmental conservation in hotels. *Journal of Consumer Research, 35,* 472–482.

Gooch, G.D. (1995). Environmental beliefs and attitudes in Sweden and the Baltic states. *Environment and Behavior, 27*, 513–539.

Haustein, S., Klöckner, C.A., & Blöbaum, A. (2009). Car use of young adults: The role of travel socialization. *Transportation Research Part F, 12*, 168–178.

Heberlein, T.A. (1972). The land ethic realized: Some social psychological explanations for changing environmental attitudes. *Journal of Social Issues, 28* (4), 79–87.

Hopper, J.R., & Nielsen, J.M.C. (1991). Recycling as altruistic behavior, Normative and behavioral strategies to expand participation in a community recycling program. *Environment and Behavior, 23*, 195–220.

Hunecke, M., Blöbaum, A., Matthies, E., & Höger, R. (2001). Responsibility and Environment: Ecological norm orientation and external factors in the domain of travel mode choice. *Environment and Behavior, 33*, 830–852.

Inglehart, R. (1995). Public support for environmental protection: Objective problems and subjective values in 43 societies. *PS: Political Science and Politics, 28*(1), 57–72.

Inglehart, R., & Welzel, C. (2005). *Modernization, cultural change and democracy. The human development sequence.* New York: CambridgeUniversity Press.

Jaeger, C., Dürrenberger, G., Kastenholz, H., & Truffer, B. (1993). Determinants of environmental action with regards to climatic change. *Climatic Change, 23*, 193–211.

Kaiser, F. (2006). A moral extension of the theory of planned behaviour: Norms and anticipated feelings of regret in conservationism. *Personality and Individual Differences, 41*, 71–81.

Kaiser, F., Hübner, G., & Bogner, F. (2005). Contrasting the theory of planned behaviour with the value-belief-norm model in explaining conservation behavior. *Environment and Behavior, 35*, 2150–2170.

Karp, D.G. (1996). Values and their effect on pro-environmental behavior. *Environment & Behavior, 28*(1), 111–133.

Klöckner, C.A., & Blöbaum, A. (2010). A comprehensive action determination model - towards a broader understanding of ecological behaviour using the example of travel mode choice. *Journal of Environmental Psychology, 24*, 319–327.

Klöckner, C.A., & Friedrichsmeier, T. (2011). A multi-level approach to travel mode choice - how person characteristics and situation specific aspects determine car use in a student sample. *Transportation Research Part F, 14*,261–277.

Klöckner, C. A., & Matthies, E. (2004). How habits interfere with norm directed behaviour - a normative decision-making model for travel mode choice. *Journal of Environmental Psychology, 24*, 319–327.

Klöckner, C.A., & Matthies, E. (2009). Structural modeling of car use on the way to the university in different settings: Interplay of norms, habits, situational restraints, and perceived behavioural control. *Journal of Applied Social Psychology, 39*, 1807–1834.

Klöckner, C.A., & Matthies, E. (2012). Two pieces of the same puzzle? Script based car choice habits between the influence of socialization and past behavior. *Journal of Applied Social Psychology, 42*, 793–821.

Klöckner, C. A., Matthies, E., & Hunecke, M. (2003). Problems of operationalizing habits and integrating habits in normative decision-making models. *Journal of Applied Social Psychology, 33*, 396–417.

Klöckner, C.A., & Ohms, S. (2009). The importance of personal norms for purchasing organic milk. *British Food Journal, 111*, 1173–1187.

Klöckner, C.A., & Oppedal, I. O. (2011). General vs. domain specific recycling behaviour - applying a multilevel comprehensive action determination model to recycling in Norwegian student homes. *Resources, Conservation and Recycling, 55*, 463–471.

Klöckner, C.A., Sopha, B. M., Matthies, E., & Bjørnstad, E. (2012). *Energy efficiency in Norwegian households - identifying motivators and barriers with a focus group approach.* Manuscript submitted for publication.

Matthies, E., Selge, S., & Klöckner, C.A. (in press). The role of parental behaviour for the development of behaviour specific environmental norms - The example of recycling and re-use behaviour. *Journal of Environmental Psychology.*

Merchand, C. (1992). *Radical ecology: The search for a liveable world.* New York: Routledge.

Minton, A. P., & Rose, R. L. (1997). The effects of environmental concern on environmentally friendly consumer behavior: An exploratory study. *Journal of Business Research, 40*, 37–48.

Nordlund, A., & Garvill, J. (2002). Value structures behind proenvironmentalbehavior. *Environment & Behavior, 34*, 740–756.

Nordlund, A., & Garvill, J. (2003). Effects of values, problem awareness, and personal norm on willingness to reduce personal car use. *Journal of Environmental Psychology, 23*(4), 339–347.

Noe, F. P., & Snow, R. (1990). The new environmental paradigm and further scale analysis. *Journal of Environmental Education, 21*, 20–26.

Ojea, E., & Laureiro, M.L. (2007). Altruistic, egoistic and biospheric values in willingness to pay (WTP) for wildlife. *Ecological Economics, 63*, 807–814.

Schultz, P.W., Gouveia, V.V., Cameron, L.D., Tankha, G., Schmuck, P., & Franek, M. (2005). Values and their relationship to environmental concern and conservation behavior. *Journal of Cross-Cultural Psychology, 36*(4), 457–475.

Schultz, P.W., Nolan, J.M., Cialdini, R.B., Goldstein, N.J., & Griskevicius, V. (2007). The constructive, destructive and reconstructive power of social norms. *Psychological Science, 18*, 429–434.

Schwartz, S.H. (1977). Normative influences on altruism. *Advances in Experimental Social Psychology, 10*, 221–279.

Schwartz, S.H. (1992). Universals in the content and structure of values: Theoretical advances and empirical. tests in 20 countries. In M. P. Zanna (ed.) *Advances in experimental social psychology* (Vol 25, pp. 1–65). Orlando, FL: Academic Press.

Schwartz, S.H., & Bardi, A. (2001). Value hierarchies across cultures: Taking a similarity approach. *Journal of Cross-Cultural Psychology, 32*, 268–290.

Schwartz, S.H., & Bilsky, W. (1987). Toward a universal psychological structure of human values. *Journal of Personality and Social Psychology, 53*, 550–562.

Schwartz, S.H., & Bilsky, W. (1990). Toward a theory of the universal content and structure of values: extensions and cross-cultural replications. *Journal of Personality and Social Psychology, 58*, 878–891.

Schwartz, S.H., & Howard, J.A. (1981). A normative decision-making model of altruism. In J. P. Rushton & R.M. Sorrentino (Eds.), *Altruism and helping behavior* (pp.89–211). Hillsdale: Erlbaum.

Schwartz, S.H., Sagiv, L., & Boehnke, K. (2000). Worries and values. *Journal of Personality, 68*, 309–346.

Schultz, P.W., & Zelezny, L.C. (1998). Values and pro-environmental behavior. A five-country survey. *Journal of Cross-Cultural Psychology, 29*, 540–558.

Scott, D., & Willits, F.K. (1994). Environmental attitudes and behavior. A Pennsylvania survey. *Environment and Behavior, 26*, 239–260.

Sopha, B., & Klöckner, C.A. (2011). Psychological factors in the diffusion of sustainable technology: A study of Norwegian households' adoption of wood pellet heating. *Renewable and Sustainable Energy Reviews, 15*, 2756–2765.

Steg, L., Dreijerink, L, & Abrahamse, W. (2005). Factors influencing the acceptability of energy policies: A test of the VBN theory. *Journal of Environmental Psychology, 25*, 415–425.

Steg, L., van den Berg, A. E., & de Groot, J. I. M. (2012). *Environmental psychology: An introduction.* Malden, MA, USA: Wiley-Blackwell.

Steg, L., & Vlek, C. (2009). Encouraging pro-environmental behaviour: An integrative review and research agenda. *Journal of Environmental Psychology, 29*, 309–317.

Stern, P.C. (2000). New environmental theories: Toward a coherent theory of environmentally significant behavior. *Journal of Social Issues, 56*, 407–424.

Stern, P.C., & Dietz, T. (1994). The value basis of environmental concern. *Journal of Social Issues, 50*, 65–84.

Stern, P.C., Dietz, T., Abel, T., Guagnano, G. A., & Kalof, L. (1999). A value-belief-norm theory of support for social movements: The case of environmentalism. *Human Ecology Review, 6*(2), 81–97.

Struch, N., Schwartz, S. H., & van der Kloot, W. A. (2002). Meanings of basic values for women and men: A cross-cultural analysis. *Personality and Social Psychology Bulletin, 28*(1), 16–28.

Tarrant, M.A., & Cordell, H.K. (1997). The effect of respondent characteristics on general environmental attitude-behavior correspondence. *Environment and Behavior, 29*, 618–637.

Thøgersen, J. (2006). Norms for environmental responsible behaviour: An extended taxonomy. *Journal of Environmental Psychology, 26*, 247–261.

Thøgersen, J., & Grunert-Beckmann, S.C. (1997). Values and attitude formation towards emerging attitude objects: From recycling to general, waste minimizing behavior. *Advances in Consumer Research, 24,* 182–189.

Turiel, E. (1983). *The Development of Social Knowledge - Morality & Convention.* New York, NY: Cambridge University Press.

Verplanken, B., Aarts, H., van Knippenberg, A., & van Knippenberg, C. (1994). Attitudes vs. general habit: Antecedents of travel mode choice. *Journal of Applied Social Psychology, 24,* 285–300.

Verplanken, B., & Wood, W. (2006). Interventions to break and create consumer habits. *Journal of Public Policy & Marketing, 25*(1), 90–103.

Vining, J., & Ebreo, A. (1992). Predicting recycling behaviour from global and specific environmental attitudes and changes in recycling opportunities. *Journal of Applied Social Psychology, 22,* 1580–1607.

Wall, R., Devine-Wright, P., & Mill, G.A. (2007). Comparing and combining theories to explain proenvironmental intentions: The case of commuting-mode choice. *Environment and Behavior, 39,* 731–753.

Wiidegren, Ö. (1998). The new environmental paradigm and personal norms. *Environment and Behavior, 30,* 75–100.

AFFILIATION

Christian A. Klöckner
Psychological Institute
University of Technology and Science (NTNU)
Trondheim, Norway

PART 6

MORAL MOTIVATION IN PROFESSIONS

Rest himself suggested engaging in research on moral behaviour as well as moral motivation in the context of professionalism. In this part, the discussion will be around a particular expectation that professionals have owing to moral concerns and how a professional identity and other motivational drivers could be developed to foster moral behaviour in different domains.

So, Bebeau and Thoma explain how moral identity as an important source of moral motivation could be grasped and developed in professions (dentistry, medicine, military, law). They found that the identity of exemplary professionals is contrasted with the identities of entering students, entering professionals, and professionals who have been disciplined by a licensing board.

Micewski takes a military philosophical approach to identify and discusses the expectations and challenges that the armed forces have to meet in that domain today. The decisive alterations in security affairs since the end of the Cold War have led to a paradigmatic change in missions and tasks assigned to armed forces. To deal with these challenges successfully, soldiers' and military leaders' identity should be grounded in a universe of ethical knowledge and lead to moral responsibility.

Campbell emphasizes how important moral motivation is in the teaching profession. She claims that the ethical intention of teachers is a strong component of moral motivation. To be morally sensitive and to know what was morally right, however, is not sufficient. Moreover, the teacher has to deal with contradictory desires (e.g. to maintain harmony and avoid personal conflict with administrators and parents) or structural conditions diminishing moral motivation.

Chi-Ming marks school leadership as a moral domain. Based on qualitative interviews of female school principals from Taiwan, she explored how the leaders become motivated to follow ethical standards while fulfilling their tasks at school, how they foster moral atmosphere and the influence of moral leadership on their moral motivation.

MURIEL J. BEBEAU & STEPHEN J. THOMA

I. MORAL MOTIVATION IN DIFFERENT PROFESSIONS

INTRODUCTION

Evidence from several professions (dentistry, medicine, law, and the military) supports constructivists' theoretical understanding of a developmental continuum of moral motivation and commitment (Rest's Component III). The continuum proceeds from self-interest and concreteness of thought characteristic of entering professionals to more other-oriented and abstract ways of making sense of the self in relation to others. At more advanced levels of moral motivation, the exemplary professional's personal and professional moral values are fully integrated and consistent across context and situation. Exemplary professionals are able to articulate the public duties of the profession, integrate them with personal value frameworks, and regularly and consistently engage in socially responsible actions. The identity of such exemplary professionals stands is contrasted with the identities of entering students, entering professionals, and professionals who have been disciplined by a licensing board.

MORAL MOTIVATION IN DIFFERENT PROFESSIONS

Rest's (1983) work on the components of morality coincided with an opportunity to study moral development in the professions. Rest thought the professions were a good place to begin the study of the four components for two reasons. First, much of the research on the moral functioning had been conducted with children, adolescents, and college students, which limited understanding of the upper levels of the developmental trajectory. Second, within the professions (especially the more developed professions) there were some clear "oughts" the profession agreed upon even if individual's within the profession didn't (1) "see the ought," a deficiency in moral sensitivity, (2) "understand the ought," a deficiency in moral reasoning and judgment, (3) see the self as responsible "to do the ought," a deficiency in moral motivation and commitment, or (4) have the will and competence to "do the ought," a deficiency in moral character and competence.

Our first collaboration (Bebeau, Rest & Yamoor, 1985) explored dentists' ability to interpret the ethical dimensions of unstructured problems. We discovered that professionals not only varied in their ability to interpret characteristics of the patient that had ethical implications for the professional, but in their recognition of their ethical duties in the situation. Similarly, as we engaged students in dilemma

K. Heinrichs, F. Oser & T. Lovat (Eds.), Handbook of Moral Motivation: Theories, Models, Applications, 475–498.

discussion in order to promote moral reasoning development, we found students disagreeing about professional responsibilities that were clearly articulated in the profession's code of ethics. These forays into professional ethics education highlighted the necessity to study Rest's third component. Thoma & Bebeau (in this volume) summarized the empirical literature generated by our efforts to study Rest's third component of morality—moral motivation and commitment. This chapter provides a more extensive discussion of evidence that bears upon moral motivation in the professions.

Before discussing moral motivation in different professions, we distinguish professions for which central and publicly stated purposes are to promote the public good and that are trusted by the public to do so, from "professions" or occupations that sell products and/or services that are desired, but are not deemed by society as essential to health and welfare. No one objects when the athlete or musician uses the term "professional" to convey both expertise and the expectation of monetary reward for their work, yet the term can also be used to convey particular moral expectations and responsibilities, which we will further elucidate. It is in this latter sense that the term profession is used.

The paper addresses a series of questions. The first, *What is a profession and who is a professional?*, builds on our general definition of a profession. Drawing on sociologists' studies of the emergence of professions in contemporary society, we specify features that distinguish among professions and the subsequent expectations society has for persons who have been granted a monopoly on a particular line of work. These expectations serve as criteria for assessing first, an individual's conceptual understanding of the expectations, and secondly, an individual's level of commitment to consistently act on the expectations, what is commonly referred to as professionalism, but is not necessarily understood as referring to the moral component of identity—what we refer to as professional identity formation. Our second question, *How are moral motivation and commitment (Rest's third component) and professionalism related?*, shows how Rest's conception of moral motivation is linked to professionalism when professionalism is understood as a fully evolved integration of the self with the profession's moral responsibilities to society.

To lay the foundation for a discussion of the evolving professional identity, Questions 3, 4, and 5 ask how entering professional students, exemplary professionals, and disciplined colleagues understand professional and societal expectations, and the extent to which their conception (a) is aligned with the profession's and society's expectation, and (b) reflects a level of integration between the self and the profession's expectations that leads to a life of committed moral action. In response to Question 6, we show how different levels of integration between professional expectations and the moral self are expressed. Question 7 asks for evidence of a developmental continuum of moral motivation and commitment within the profession.

Question 8 asks how professional identity (moral motivation and commitment) and professional effectiveness (moral action) are connected. Rest argued that the gap between moral reasoning and action was not just a function of moral motivation and commitment (Component 3) but also of moral character and competence (Component 4). As with moral motivation, Component 4 processes have not been extensively studied. Our response to the last question summarizes what is known and suggests areas for further attention by theorists and educators.

Finally, because professional identity formation has not been systematically addressed in professional education (Shulman, 2010), the paper concludes with implications for education, including barriers to implementation. Strategies for facilitating professional identity formation are cited, based upon what is currently known about the evolving professional identity. Directions for future research precede a general summary and conclusion.

(1) What is a Profession and Who is a Professional?

What is a profession? Both ethicists (e.g., Welie, 2004a-c) and sociologists (e.g., Hall, 1975) describe features that distinguish among occupational groups and differentiate some—often referred to as the "learned professions"—as occupations that have been given particular powers and privileges by society based upon a commitment to enhance the health or welfare of the individual and the larger society. Hall notes that as an occupation professionalizes over time, it tends to take on more of the distinctive features (italicized below) that characterize the more prestigious professions. Briefly, an occupation is given *authority* (i.e., to make judgments on behalf of clients or patients, to determine the standard of practice, to set standards for admission to professional school and standards for accreditation of professional schools, to self-govern) in proportion to the amount and stability of the *knowledge* it takes to gain access to the profession and in direct proportion to the amount of harm potentially caused by incompetent practice. *Power and privilege* are awarded in exchange for the profession's *promise* to place the rights of the client over self-interest and the rights of the society over the rights of the profession. To guide members of the profession in application of the promise, *codes of ethics* are developed. The canons of a code provide guidance to appropriate behaviour in various circumstances and enable the profession to monitor itself. Codes are expanded as new issues emerge or as views of professional morality change. Professions value the powers and privileges granted by society and, through *social organization*, strive first to achieve, and then to maintain them.

The goal of an occupation seeking professional status is to convince the public that the group ought to be granted powers and privileges to control access to the profession and essentially establish a monopoly for workers. As Welie (2004a) points out: "An occupation cannot simply claim professional status. That status must be granted by society." (p. 530) Whether the occupation is granted power and privileges is dependent upon whether the "collective of expert service providers have jointly and publicly committed to always give priority to the existential needs and interest of the public they serve above their own and who in turn are trusted by the public to do so." (p. 531) Society is understandably reluctant to grant an occupation powers to control who can practice, as doing so tends to create a monopoly that is likely to increase costs and decrease access to care.

Who is a professional? Hall argues that the possession of essential attributes implies that persons who wish to become members of one of the learned professions have particular responsibilities. Six expectations and responsibilities of the professional are presented in Table 1. These will be referred to in subsequent discussions within this chapter, especially as we explore how professionals understand these responsibilities. Further, these six expectations and obligations of the professional served as the basis for both the Role Concept Assessment used in the lead author's dental ethics curriculum, described under Question 5.

If, as Hall argues, power and privileges are granted to the profession on the basis of the assumption that each professional will take these responsibilities or obligations seriously, it would seem that a profession would have a right to expect that each individual who is chosen and then decides to become a professional will commit to these responsibilities. Of course, fulfilling these responsibilities is easier said than done. It may be relatively easy to say one is committed to a set of abstract concepts, especially if they haven't been explicitly taught, but more difficult to carry them out in real life professional settings. Professionals, and especially entry level professionals, often find themselves in situations where personal and professional values conflict or where professional obligations conflict. Many of the common conflicts are addressed in a profession's code of ethics. Yet the very nature of a profession, with its ever changing body of knowledge, requires that professionals develop skills in self assessment and ethical reflection that enable them to make good decisions about new problems that are likely to emerge during the course of professional life.

By specifying professional expectations, we are able to contrast the "moral" professional from the "good" person, or even the "good" professional. The "good" person is not required to put the interests of others—particularly strangers—before the self, to regulate peers, to keep abreast of the knowledge of his or her field, and so on. The "moral" professional is so required. In a series of articles designed to acquaint readers with distinctive features of a "moral" dental profession, Welie (2004c) captures our distinction between the "good" vs. "moral" professional. He says: "By definition, dentistry does not qualify as a profession when and to the extent that the interventions performed are purely elective instead of medically indicated. It therefore behooves dentists who focus their practices on aesthetic interventions to clearly state that they are not professionals. Doing so does not mean they are incompetent, dishonest or otherwise immoral. It simply means that the ethical structure of their practices differs from that of professional dentists. The ethical structure of such a dental practice "is akin to that of an interior designer rather than an oncologist." (p. 676).

Like the good musician or athlete, the cosmetic dentist exhibits the outward manifestations of the "good" professional (performs competently and is monetarily rewarded), but his practice is not consequentially linked to the profession's public purposes, a distinction we make as we explore the relationship between moral motivation and professionalism following Question 2.

(2) How are Moral Motivation and Professionalism Related?

Rest conceptualized moral motivation as the self's struggle to decide whether to pursue the moral value, arrived at through reasoning, or other values. For Rest, moral values were not the only values with which the individual had to contend. People value advancement in their careers, recognition and achievement, many things beside fairness or morality. As Bergman (2004) notes, Rest differed from Kohlberg's conception of the relationship between deontic judgments and responsibility judgment. For Kohlberg, as one advanced in moral judgment development, especially at post-conventional stages, deontic and responsibility judgments converged. For Rest, this appeared to be an empirical question. Rest (1986) cited Damon's studies showing how children's espoused moral ideals for fairness were compromised by other motives, when it came to dividing candy bars. Rest was particularly interested in moral motivation in adulthood. He often cited John Dean's disclosure in his book *Blind Ambition,* where Dean, a very competent lawyer, reported how his activities as special counsel to President Nixon were motivated by his ambition to succeed, and how questions of morality and justice were pre-empted by baser human values—a frequent refrain in accounts of wrong doing by politicians. In sum, professionals may agree that a profession has certain responsibilities or obligations, i.e., that an act is right and perhaps obligatory—what Kohlberg referred to as a first order deontic judgment—without making a second-order responsibility judgment, i.e., that the self is responsible to act in accordance with the deontic judgment.

As suggested under Question 1, whether moral motivation and professionalism are related depends on how professionalism is understood. If professionalism is understood as referring to the external manifestations of a role, i.e., whether the physician wears the white coat, or carries a stethoscope, uses the language of a professional, and displays a professional demeanor—what Hafferty (2006) refers to as "surface professionalism," then moral motivation and professionalism would not be seen as linked. The recent focus on measuring medical professionalism (Stern, 2006) appears to focus simply on the outward manifestations of behaviour.

If, on the other hand, professionalism is understood as the individual's underlying commitment to the values of the profession, what Hafferty refers to as "authentic professionalism," then moral motivation and professionalism would be linked—even if the individual failed to consistently pursue the moral value. The key for Hafferty is whether the behaviour "is consequentially linked to the individual's underlying identity (as a professional) rather than to how the job was carried out (in a professional manner)." (p. 283) As Rest would argue, in real life, professionals are under pressure to act in a variety of ways, and the alternatives may sometimes conflict with the moral ideal. The goal, of course, would be for consistency between deontic and responsibility judgments, but leading the professional moral life is incredibly challenging for many reasons, not the least of which is the complexity of professional practice.

Echoing Hafferty, Rule (2010) notes little consistency in the way the term professionalism is used in the literature, but opts, as do we, for a definition of professionalism (attributed to Welie) as "a cluster of *commitments* and *behaviours* (emphasis added), shared by the members of a profession, through which they exhibit the values, principles, and norms they hold in common as members of their profession." In our judgment, motive matters. Thus, a behaviour is moral only if it is consequentially linked to the social actor's underlying identity.

(3) How Do Entering Professional School Students Understand Professional and Societal Exceptions? Is Their Conception Aligned with the Professions' Values and Expectations?

Professional school applicants invariably express an altruistic desire to "help others" as their primary motive for becoming a professional. To capitalize on this native idealism, which is often seriously undermined during the rigors of education, dental and medical schools have instituted "white coat" ceremonies to symbolize the taking on of the profession's values and commitments. Typically, ceremonies, held at the very beginning of professional school, include an oath to uphold the professions values and expectations. In some cases, a brief introduction to the professions' values and expectations precedes the ceremony. The concern raised (Lantz, Bebeau & Zarkowski, 2011) is whether students are being asked to take an oath before professional values and expectations are fully understood.

To highlight this point, Bebeau (1994) found that after tracking entering dental students' initial understanding of the profession's expectations over a 10 year period, it became apparent that entering dental students could not articulate key professional expectations. Interestingly, even after carefully crafted instruction (including practice and individualized feedback) expectations were often misunderstood or miss-communicated. Some seemed to lack a conceptual framework for key professional concepts—like the responsibility for self-regulation and professional monitoring. More recently, Bebeau & Monson (2011) report that as many as 20 percent of entering cohorts of students question professional authority, feeling they should be free to develop their own values. In a similar vein, Rennie and Crosby (2002) reported that less than 40 percent of medical students agreed that physician misconduct should be reported (the deontic judgment), and only 13 percent said they would do so (the responsibility judgment). Interviewed about their reluctance to assume personal responsibility, they said it wasn't that misconduct shouldn't be addressed, it is just, they thought, that *someone else should do so [emphasis added]*. In an earlier study, Feudtner, Christakis and Christakis (1994) reported that at least part of the reluctance to report was attributable to discomfort at challenging members of the medical team over perceived wrong doing.

Concerned with how professional values are transmitted, Anderson (2001) was able to show that mentoring, presumed to be a key factor in professional socialization, did not enable doctoral students aspiring to become researchers to articulate basic expectations for integrity in research. Anderson's longitudinal study concluded that students do not seem to learn the values of their discipline from either mentors or the curriculum. Anderson's findings, coupled with the increased prevalence of research misconduct, prompted U.S. agencies to require training in the responsible conduct of research (IOM, 2002) as a condition for funding. A key question for all professional programs is whether simply informing learners of professional expectations will enable them to act upon them.

Individuals entering professional education and doctoral programs are clearly motivated to achieve. Acceptance at a highly rated professional school signals the beginning of yet another competitive pursuit for academic excellence in order to qualify for residency and/or specialty programs. Even when applicants express an altruistic desire "to help others" as a motivation for pursuit of a professional license, this idealist motive is not well grounded in an understanding of professional values and expectations. To further complicate the matter, evidence from cross-temporal meta-analyses of personal attributes (Twenge, 2009) reveals today's students as even more self-centered than previous generations. The increase in self-centeredness is also supported by recently reported declines in moral judgment development among college and professional students (Thoma & Bebeau, 2008). For these reasons the educator's challenge is enhanced. Even if students can be convinced that a profession should assume responsibility for self-regulation, their reluctance may go beyond an unwillingness to accept personal responsibility. They may feel uncertainty about the validity of their judgment, perceive danger in challenging a superior, and lack know-how—the person-level characteristics referred to in motivational theories as competence and control beliefs (Schunk & Zimmerman, 2005).

In summary, the definition of a profession provides a language to concretize professional responsibilities. Students may come to the professions with a general sense of altruism, but without a concrete understanding of professional expectations. Even when there is a general understanding of professional expectations, as exhibited by the 40 percent of medical students who acknowledged the profession's responsibility for self-regulation, they may see this responsibility as a duty of some generalized other, for example,—the professional school or the profession, but not as a responsibility that belongs to them, especially in their roles as entry level professionals. The challenge is to develop what Fisher and Zigmond (2001) describe as "survival skills"—the competence and confidence to act on these responsibilities.

The desired behavioural outcome, then, is likely a function of multiple factors: (1) acceptance of the profession's authority, (2) understanding what the profession expects of its members, (3) commitment to act on these expectations, and (4) the competence to follow through (Component 4). One unexplored issue (addressed under Question 8) has to do with Component 4 processes: How is the commitment to act connected to the competence to act? What is the role of education?

Next, with Questions 4 and 5, we contrast the understanding of professional expectations shown by those highly regarded by their peers because of their *exemplary behaviour* and those disciplined by a licensing board because of their illegal, and therefore *unprofessional, behaviour*. We show distinctions in levels of understanding, differences in level of moral motivation and commitment, and examples of some of the personal attributes that distinguish exemplary conduct from unprofessional behaviour.

(4) How Do Exemplary Professionals Understand Professional and Societal Expectations?

Rule and Bebeau's (2005) in-depth study of dental moral exemplars illustrates how moral motivation and commitment (the integration of the professional responsibilities with the self) and professionalism are connected. Not only can exemplars articulate professional expectations, they demonstrate nuanced understandings of these expectations in their daily lives. For example, Hugo Owens, in response to dental student complaints that they will graduate with a huge debt and, therefore, can't be "giving their work away," advises: "First excel; then help others" (p. 24). Jack Echternacht explains, "Dentists and physicians are servants of the people. We really are. There is a great deal of satisfaction derived from that" (p. 16). Expanding on his sense of obligation, he says: "I believe that if one lives in the community and makes his livelihood from it, he should return that benefit by participating in the activities of the community to better it in any way that he can" (p. 18). Illuminating an "other-centered" conception of community service, Jeremy Lowney argues that if you serve on the cancer board or on the school board in your community, you benefit from that. "Real service," he adds, "is the kind of giving where the only benefit is the satisfaction derived from helping someone who is really in need" (p. 84).

Exemplars demonstrate the person-level characteristics (self-efficacy, perseverance, personal agency, capacity beliefs, strategy beliefs and control beliefs—often referred to as learned optimism) associated with motivational theories (Schunk & Zimmerman, 2005). For example, capacity, strategy, and control beliefs are expressed by Dr. Owens, a highly effective dentist, community activist, and civil rights leader: "I could do things others thought should be done, but couldn't do for themselves" (p. 28). Emphasizing the importance of strategic planning, he says: "If you decide 'to take a stand' on an issue, you want to avoid a 'bad stand'" (p. 29).

Optimism about the basic goodness of people characterizes Dr. Benkelman's decision to never ask about a patient's ability to pay before initiating treatment. Ignoring the advice of practice management consultants, he says: "People will eventually pay. If I do this, it will work." And if they don't? He says he really wouldn't suffer. "I guess my basic philosophy of practice has always been to do things as easily for people as I possibly can, so that they don't feel like they've ever had to endure anything" (p. 39).

Nominated for their exceptional professional ethical identity, each dental exemplar was also regarded as highly successful and exceptionally competent, suggesting the presence of a strong achievement motivation capable of derailing entry-level professionals' commitment to moral values. Judged only by current activity, it might appear as though exemplars had pursued their personal and moral goals simultaneously. However, when asked to reflect on their own professional identity formation, they said they saw their sense of obligation to society and their profession as growing and changing over time. They gradually came to see professional and community service as what they must do, rather than what would simply be good to do if one were so inclined. Like Walker and Frimer's (2007) exemplars who exhibited the integration of personality characteristics of agency (achievement) with communion (service to others), the dental exemplars exhibited this integration, yet they saw this integration as something that had developed.

The interview data (Rule & Bebeau, 2005) illustrate tenants of developmental theory. (1) Exemplars are aware of transformations in their identity as it has unfolded across the life span. Concepts of professionalism (e.g., service to society, professional regulation, etc.) have undergone transformations since initial professional education. They now think of these responsibilities differently than they did as young professionals. (2) Aware of the value conflicts they have experienced, they know how to resolve them, and derive the satisfaction from living up to the profession's values. They have constructed "self-systems" (i.e., what will later be referred to as a stage 4 identity) that provide an internal compass for negotiating and resolving tensions among these multiple, shared expectations. (3) Highly competent and effective, they are self-aware and reflective. Competence is seen as an essential virtue employed in service to others, including their profession. They are aware of their multiple competencies, their values, and the forces that shaped their identity. They are able to critically assess aspects of their profession while remaining strongly committed to it. Viewed as authentic persons, they are leaders and change agents within their profession.

Rule and Bebeau's findings echo Colby and Damon's (1992) observations of the extraordinary integration of the self and morality. "Time and again we found our moral exemplars acting spontaneously, out of great certainty, with little fear, doubt, or agonized reflection. They performed their moral actions spontaneously, as if they had no choice in the matter. In fact, the sense that they lacked a choice is precisely what many of the exemplars reported" (p. 303). We see the same integration of the self and morality in Janet Johnson, a dental resident who, after unproductive discussions with her supervisor and then hospital administration, reported her supervisor for flagrant disregard for basic requirements for safe administration of sedation for anxious and uncooperative patients. Unlike the residents who preceded her in the position and took no action, she illustrates her conviction: "There was no way I could leave the situation the way it was" (Rule & Bebeau, 2005, p. 66). Whereas Dr. Johnson suffered from the kind of retaliation whistle blowers often fear, she did not waver in her conviction to act. Before acting, however, she carefully amassed evidence to support her judgment. "If someone is really guilty," she said, "the evidence should bear that out" (p. 74). Some years later, when nominated as a moral exemplar, she agreed to tell the story, but only if names and circumstances were modified. Her rationale was two-fold. Her colleague, having accepted the licensing board's sanction and modified the harmful practices, should not be forever identified with a lapse in professional behaviour. More importantly, she should not be honored for doing what is expected of a professional.

Next, a group of practicing professionals who were sanctioned by their profession for unprofessional conduct is examined to see how they conceptualize professional expectations and commitments to fulfill them.

(5) How Do Disciplined Colleagues Understand Professional and Societal Expectations?

For over 20 years, a state licensing board has been referring professionals sanctioned for violations of the rules[1] governing dental practice, for an ethics assessment (Bebeau, 2009a) and subsequent instruction, if so indicated. Bebeau (2009b) describes instructional outcomes for a sample of 44 professionals who completed the program. At pretest, these dentists typically displayed a shortcoming on at least one other measure of Rest's four component model of morality, but the one consistent shortcoming (for 41 of the 44 dentists in this sample) was their difficulty articulating the professional expectations listed in Table 1 and italicized below.

Table 1. Expectations and Obligations of the professional[a]

---

1. To acquire the knowledge of the profession to the standards set by the profession.
2. To keep abreast of changing knowledge through continuing education.
3. To make a commitment to the basic ethic of the profession-that is, to place the interests of the patient above the interests of the professional, and to place the oral health interests of society above the interests of the profession.
4. To abide by the profession's code of ethics, or to work to change it if it is inconsistent with the underlying ethic of the profession.
5. To serve society (i.e., the public as a whole)-not just those who can pay for services.
6. To participate in the monitoring and self-regulation of the profession. There are at least three dimensions to this expectation: to monitor one's own practice to assure that processes and procedures meet ever evolving professional standards; to report incompetent or impaired professionals, and to join one's professional associations in order to participate in the setting of standards for the continuation of the profession. The latter is not a legal, but rather an ethical responsibility

---

[a] Bebeau, M.J., & Kahn, J. (2002). Ethical issues in community dental health. In G.M. Gluck & W.M. Morganstein (Eds.), Jong's community dental health (5th ed., pp. 425–445). St. Louis: Mosby.

Most respondents cited a responsibility *to serve society,* yet a third of the respondents seemed to limit the responsibility to serve to those who could pay for their services.

Of particular interest were 15 individuals cited for Medicaid or insurance fraud who clearly articulated a responsibility to serve society. Interestingly, these individuals also had exceptionally high scores on the responsibility dimension of the PROI (See Thoma & Bebeau, this volume, for a discussion of the PROI), undermining the typical assumption that such individuals are manipulating the system for personal gain. In fact, assertions—that their actions were motivated by a desire to help a patient who seriously needed care for which they were unable to pay—appeared authentic. The combined data suggest an unbounded sense of responsibility to serve that borders on martyrdom.

With respect to the responsibility to *place the interest of patients before the self,* more than half (55%) expressed this duty. Yet, even when prompted, only one person expressed the profession's collective responsibility *to place the oral health interests of society before the interests of the profession.* Recall that exemplars saw this larger responsibility to society as obligatory. They worked tirelessly to promote the oral health of their community in addition to competently serving the needs of individuals.

Most frequently omitted by referrals was the responsibility *to abide by the profession's code of ethics* (76%), followed by the *responsibility for life-long learning (68%).* Although a majority (60%) made a general reference to the responsibility for *self-regulation and monitoring of one's profession,* the three dimensions of this responsibility (Table 1) were seldom mentioned. In contrast, exemplars spontaneously describe each of these dimensions, and see membership in professional associations as essential, as they work to fulfill the public's rightful expectations.

Whereas referrals exhibit various difficulties articulating professional expectations, unlike some entry level students, none questioned the profession's authority to hold them accountable. In fact, they willingly engaged in the assessment and subsequently completed a rigorous educational requirement. The following excerpts from interviews illustrate differences in understanding, commitment, and some downgrading of moral considerations.

Dentists A, B, and C were sanctioned for various rule violations. Dentists A and B were cited (among other things) for failure to maintain OSHA[2] standards for cleanliness and infection control. Asked to comment, Dentist A said: "Well, perhaps we weren't up to date on all the latest standards, but it's not like we weren't sterilizing our instruments! I think you can go overboard on cleanliness. Heavens, when I trained we didn't even wear gloves and masks."

Dentist B, similarly cited, shifted the blame to a staff member: "I've given that task to a dental auxiliary. She evidently hasn't been keeping up with the standards."

Dentist C was not cited for failure to maintain OSHA standards, but for "fraudulent billing" (i.e., using a billing code which upgraded the level of the procedure performed) and for questionable competence. When the interviewer remarked that Dentist C had not been cited for failure to maintain OSHA standards, he was aghast, exclaiming: "I must see that all infection control standards are met! I wouldn't want someone's health endangered by coming here." Asked about the "fraudulent billing," he acknowledged having given the responsibility to the office manager, "which I should have been more carefully monitoring. The idea that someone would think I was deliberately dishonest, is very upsetting." When probing about the challenge to his technical competence, his misunderstanding of responsibilities to self-monitor became apparent.

Commenting on the importance of patient satisfaction to his professional reputation, Dentist C had, he thought, bent over backward to satisfy a denture patient who had filed a complaint. He redid the patient's dentures multiple times, attempting to "make her happy." Aware that her oral health behaviours contributed to her dissatisfaction, he had informed her of this fact, but admitted he lacked skill in helping patients modify behaviour. He also hadn't thought to refer her to someone who could, or even to discontinue denture modifications until the contributing problems were resolved. More importantly, when his dental work was reviewed by specialists, it became clear that technical aspects of the work had not been adequately addressed. Dentist C's reaction to the Board's requirement to take additional continuing education courses in prosthodontics was met with a willingness to do so, but doubts about the remedy's usefulness: "I've taken all kinds of CE courses in this area, including hands-on courses and I have over 20 years of experience." The challenge was to help Dentist C to better articulate and then to implement the responsibility for self-assessment and self-regulation. During instruction, it became evident that Dr. C he had developed relationships with relevant specialists, but had not consulted regularly about patient problems or referred to a specialist at the first sign of a patient's dissatisfaction. He has since set in motion a plan to elicit frequent peer review of his technical competence from trusted colleagues.

What distinguishes Dentist C (with respect to infection control and billing practices) is his sense of personal responsibility, even when he failed to live up to professional expectations. Whereas Dentist A or B implicitly acknowledge that they can be held accountable for their failure to meet the standards, they don't seem to see the self as responsible.

The reactions of referrals who completed the instructional program has relevance for the design of programs to promote identity formation. They said that the instruction on professional values and expectations was the most inspiring dimension of instruction, and contributed to a sense of professional renewal (Bebeau, 2009b). Recall, that up to 20 percent of entry level students complain (anonymously) that the instructor is "imposing values" and they "should be able to develop their own values" (Bebeau & Monson, 2011). The idea that the instructor or the profession is imposing values reflects an individualistic and egocentric view that characterizes aspects of Kegan's stage 2 identity (described following Question 6, in the text accompanying Table 2). This perspective provides particular educational challenges.

To address Question 6, we present findings from systematic efforts to uncover the level of integration between the self and professional expectation within groups of professionals or aspiring professionals. Our interest is to understand how a professional moral identity forms, as well as how varied the perspectives are at particular points in professional development. Our long-term interest is to understand strategies to promote development.

(6) How are Different Levels of Integration Between Professional Expectations and the Moral Self Expressed?

To explore the integration of the self with professional identity, we adopted Robert Kegan's (1982) life-span model of self development. Kegan suggests, in contrast to trait or personality approaches to differences, that all humans are continuously involved in a process of constructing meaning. As individuals gain an increasing amount of experience in an extremely complex world, they construct progressively more complex systems for making sense of it. Similarly, each person constructs an understanding of what it means to be a professional, and a professional's understanding may be qualitatively different from that of the general public. For the exemplary professional, putting the interests of others before the self isn't just "good to do"—as in the Golden Rule, it is obligatory.

Before describing how the integration of the self with professional identity appears, we briefly describe how the adaptation of Kegan's life-span model came about. Motivated by a need to enhance professional identity formation of military leaders, Forsythe and colleagues (2002) used the Kegan interview (Lahey, Souvaine, Kegan, Goodman, & Felix, 1988)—a reliable, but costly and time-consuming assessment strategy—to study identity formation for a cross-sectional sample of military leaders, with a longitudinal follow-up for a sample of entry level cadets. Upon learning of the diversity of cadet's professional identity formation (discussed next, under Question 7), and believing the profession had a responsibility to promote identity formation, Forsythe devised four short writing exercises to prompt personal reflection on the way the cadet carried out the various professional roles (leader of character, servant of the nation, warfighter, member a profession) in practice. At the time, Phil Lewis, an expert on the Kegan interview, and Bebeau were visiting scholars at the United States Military Academy. Bebeau and Lewis (2003) found they were able to reliably code cadet essays for key elements that distinguished three levels of "The Evolving Professional Identity" (described below).

Subsequently, Bebeau and Forsythe designed essay questions that could be used with students in post baccalaureate professional programs to tap the cognitive, structural, and emotional content that the interviewer attempts to elicit. These questions have been used with five cohorts of dental students (Monson, Roehrich, & Bebeau, 2008; Monson & Bebeau, 2009) and have recently been adapted to elicit professional ethical identity formation of law students (Monson & Hamilton, 2010). Findings from these studies are reported in the next section.

The evolving professional identity. Following are brief descriptions of three levels of *The Evolving Professional Identity* commonly observed in professions.

The Independent Operator. These individuals understand professionalism as meeting fixed, concrete, black and white role expectations, rather than a broader understanding of what it means to be a professional. Motivation for meeting standards is wholly individual and based on a desire to be correct and effective. Said one aspiring professional, *"There are professional guidelines and codes that shape your life."* Table 2, presents excerpts from entering students' responses to four of the eight essay questions used to elicit professional identity. Excerpts coded a stage 2 are presented in column 1.

Table 2. The evolving professional identity[a]

Excerpts from Entry-level Professional Student's Responses to Essay Questions

Independent Operator	Team-Oriented Idealist	Self-Defining Professional
What does being a member of the profession mean to you?		
I will be working along with lots of other people who will be doing different tasks than I, myself, am doing. I will need to communicate well with these other individuals to get my job done. I will also be able to have good working hours and wonderful pay for the work I am doing. (entering dental student)	*Becoming a member of the dental profession to me means growing/ developing into a professional guided by a set of standards established by my peers, a lifetime of peers, already in the profession...*	*It means being morally responsibility [sic] to this profession. It means have empathy towards all of my patients, co-workers, and people that I have contact with in the dental profession. I came to this understanding by truly learning what drives me as a person. I love helping others and want to use this quality in a professional dental setting (coded as in transition to stage 4).*
[Being a professional] entails a lot of little things, such as showing up to work on time, dressing appropriately, completing assignments by or before deadlines, etc Professionalism means the way you conduct yourself while at your job. To be professional means to conduct yourself in a manner that expresses that you mean business. (entering law student)(Monson & Hamilton, p. 14)	*... you act in a respectful manner towards those with whom you are working with (sic). As a professional, you have been entrusted to provide a service to the best of your ability. Clients or customers are often placed in a vulnerable position, professionalism is not taking advantage of that vulnerability. (Monson & Hamilton, p. 14)*	*Professionalism is an obligation that I have to my profession and to the broader society. I need to know the law, how the legal system operates, what my client's needs are, and how to meet those needs without creating unnecessary conflict between opposing counsel, opposing parties and the public trust. (law graduate, content coded as stage 4; Monson & Hamilton, p. 14)*

(Continued)

Table 2. Continued

Excerpts from Entry-level Professional Student's Responses to Essay Questions		
Independent Operator	*Team-Oriented Idealist*	*Self-Defining Professional*

What does the profession expect?

That I act in accordance to their ideals.	*[h]old myself accountable for my practice – be a respectful person – give back to the profession in some way.*	*From observing other dental professionals, being a dentist myself would seem to imply that I too would be included in the elite group of health care [professionals], that I would join the ranks as a respected member of the doctoral community. However, being fully aware of the reputation dentists have among the general population, I would see my position as a mediator, to bridge the gap between the dental profession and the population we serve (in transition to stage 4).*

What conflicts will you experience?

How many MA [medical assistance] patients should I see – as I will actually be losing some money in doing this.	*There will be many conflicts I could face along the path of my career including conflicts between my professional career & personal life. Also, my moral capacities will be tested during the span of my career.*	*...what I think to be the 'right' thing in my heart and mind may not be what society or others think to be the best thing. I will always try to use my best judgment and keep as neutral a perspective as possible, but each event may make me act differently.*

What would be the worst thing for you if you failed . . .?

. . . to belabeled as incompetent and I would probably lose some of my patient base and possibly be sued for malpractice & lose my license to practice.	*Knowing that I have let others down would be the worst feeling for me. Other people will depend on me and I will do my best to not let them down."*	*The hardest thing? Knowing I have failed my patients, peers, etc. As I said, I try to set expectations for myself so high that only I am disappointed in myself (transitioning to stage 4).*

[a] *Descriptions of Kegan's stages 2–4 of his five stage model of identity formation. Adapted for professional ethical identity assessment by Bebeau & Lewis (2003).*

The Team-Oriented Idealist. Unlike *Independent Operators*, these professionals are both idealistic and internally self-reflective. They understand and identify with (or worry that they are not yet fully identified with) their chosen profession. They no longer see professionalism as enacting specific behaviours or fixed roles. Rather, they *see* professionalism as meeting the expectations of those who are more knowledgeable and legitimate, and even more professional. As one professional remarked, *"We must always hold ourselves to the highest professional standards."* See Table 2 (column 2) for excerpts from responses coded a stage 3.

The Self-Defining Professional or Integrated Professional. These individuals, unlike *Team-Oriented Idealists,* are no longer identified solely with external expectations of their professional role. Instead, having freely committed themselves to being a member of the profession, they have constructed a self system comprised of personal values integrated with those of the profession. These provide principles for living. While their identity is not wholly embedded in their profession, they have created a vision of the "moral" profession that is grounded in reflective professional practice. Among entering dental students and entering law students, we did not find excerpts that clearly meet coding criteria for stage 4. This is not surprising, as this level of identity is typically not achieved until mid-life. It did mean that we needed to code for transitions between stages.

Transitions. In the lifelong process of identity development, individuals spend a considerable amount of time (typically many months) in the transition between stages. Transitions are characterized by the process of encompassing one's current way of making meaning within the broader and more complex framework of the next developmental stage. Both stages may be demonstrated, with the higher stage expressed in a tentative and less well-articulated manner. Table 2 (column 3) presents excerpts from responses coded as in the transition to stage 4, with only one excerpt coded as stage 4.

Transitions to Kegan's stage 5. As *Self-Defining* individuals continue to transition to the next level (Kegan's [1982] *Humanist* or Rule & Bebeau's [2005] *Moral Exemplar),* they are able to stand aside from their own profession and even look across professions. They are able to see limits of their own ideological stance, seeing it as one system. They critically assess aspects of the professions, yet remain strongly committed. They are authentic persons who may emerge as leaders within the profession as they are able to see limits of their own ideological stance, thus being open to entertaining contradictions and seeing the merits of alternative systems and perspectives. Thus, *Self-Defining* individuals often become change agents within their profession.

With Question 6, we contrasted moral motivation and commitment evident among individuals at different levels of professional identity formation. Next, with Question 7, studies that tap the cognitive, emotional, and social structures that comprise an ethical professional identity are examined in order to show the prevalence of various levels of professional identity formation based upon available evidence.

(7) Is There Evidence of a Developmental Continuum of Moral Motivation and Commitment Within the Profession? How Varied Are Conceptions of the Moral Self Within Professions?

The first set of studies conducted by Forsythe and colleagues (Forsythe, Snook, Lewis, & Bartone, 2002) used the Kegan interview to assess identity formation for a cross sectional sample of entry level military cadets, mid-level military leaders, and senior military leaders, with longitudinal follow-up for second year and fourth year cadets. Supporting Twenge's (2009) findings that entering students are more self than other centered, (1) entry-level cadets were less developed than Kegan had assumed, (2) cadets did develop, particularly between the second and fourth year, (3) senior cadets perceived as effective leaders by peers, superiors, and subordinates had made key transitions in identity formation that enabled them to attend to the interests of others, and (4) advanced levels of identity formation characterized military leaders selected for further professional development.

A second set of studies initiated by Bebeau and colleagues used essay questions to elicit cognitive, emotional, and social structures that comprise an ethical professional identity. A scoring guide that integrated the professional expectations assessed with the Role Concept Essay with the structural elements of Kegan's stages and transition phases (Bebeau & Lewis, 2003) was refined and augmented with examples from dental and legal education. Table 3 shows the proportion of entering dental and law students at each stage or transition phase based on coding of essays. What stands out is the variability in identity formation within entering classes of both dental students and law students. Corresponding with the proportion of students who complain that the educator is imposing values, we see similar proportions of entering students at a stage 2 or 2/3.

Table 3 enables the reader to see more generally how success within their profession (Forsythe's senior military officers) or within business and industry (Eigel's CEOs and middle managers) is associated with more advanced identity formation. Notice that none of Eigel's CEOs or Forsythe's senior leaders exhibited the stage 2 or Stage 2/3 identity so common among entering cadets and even entering students in law and dentistry. One word of caution about the interpretation of the studies reported in Table 3. Forsythe, Snook, and Eigel used the Kegan interview, whereas the other studies used an essay designed to assess Kegan identity levels. There is only preliminary evidence (Hamilton & Monson, 2012) to support the comparability of the two measures. Given that it is often easier to articulate ideas than it is to put them in writing, we can only speculate whether the essay underestimates identity formation. Typically, students in dentistry and law, while on average at least four years older than entering cadets, are more articulate than entering college students. Similarly, law students may be somewhat more able to express their ideas in writing than the more scientifically minded dental student.

The studies cited here suggest varied levels of identity among cohorts and the presence of a less developed identity among entry level students that is not

Table 3. Summary of kegan identity assessment studies in the professions*

Study	Stage 2	Stage 2/3	Stage 3	Stage 3/4	Stage 4	Stage 4/5
Forsythe et al. (2002) [a]professional military cadets (freshmen) *n*=38	8 (21%)	24 (63%)	6 (16%)	0	0	0
Forsythe et al. (2002) [a]professional military cadets (senior) *n*=32	2 (6%)	10 (31%)	14 (44%)	6 (19%)	0	0
Forsythe et al. (2002) [a]senior service military officers n=28			3 (11%)	6 (22%)	5 (18%) 4 (3) 14 (50%)	Not reliably coded beyond stage
Monson, Roehrich, & Bebeau (2008) [b]entering dental students, 2005 *n*=46	6 (13%)	32 (70%)	4 (7%)	4 (7%)	0	0
Monson, Roehrich, & Bebeau (2008) [b] entering dental students, 2006 *n*=94	12 (13%)	48 (51%)	18 (19%)	12 (13%)	4 (4%)	0
Monson & Hamilton (2010) [b]enteringlaw students, 2009 *n*=73	11 (15%)	18 (25%)	23 (32%)	20 (27%)	1 (1%)	0
Snook (2007) [a]MBA students, *n*=26	9 (35%)		7 (27%)		9 (35%)	
Eigel (1998) [a] CEOs, n=21	0	0	0	0	17 (81%)	4 (19%)
Eigel (1998) [a] middle managers, n=21	0	2 (10%)	7 (33%)	0	10 (48%)	1 (5%)

*Adapted from Hamilton & Monson (2012)
[a]*Assessed with Kegan interview*
[b]*Assessed with Bebeau & Forsythe's Professional Identity Essay*

aligned with the profession's espoused value frameworks. The studies also confirm that identity formation is a life-long process, subject to influence by both culture and context. Educators' professional responsibility is to attend to their students' professional identity formation.

(8) How are Professional Identity and Professional Effectiveness Connected?

A comparison of exemplary professionals with disciplined colleagues and emerging professionals highlights moral motivation's central role in professional decision making. Referrals came to our attention because of violations of the laws governing professional practice. In fact, the licensing board saw the violations as serious enough to warrant a required ethics educational intervention. Assessment revealed that nearly all the referrals had a significant shortcoming in their ability to articulate professional and societal expectation. Coupled with this shortcoming was a shortcoming in at least one of Rest's other components.

In contrast, exemplars came to our attention because of their consistent, committed, and effective moral action. It was only during the interview process that their remarkable understanding of professional and societal values became evident. However, one critical difference between exemplars, emerging professionals, and disciplined colleagues is exemplars remarkably consistent interpersonal and problem solving effectiveness. It isn't that emerging professionals and disciplined colleagues aren't nice people; they often display a kind of dispositional goodness that makes them a joy to be around. Certainly, we notice strength of conviction on the part of exemplars, but exemplars are identified in large part because they are seen as competent—professionally, technically, and interpersonally competent as they engage in the public duties of the professions, which they see as obligatory. Yet, it is not that they never make mistakes. They do, but it is what they do not do when they make a mistake that sets them apart. They do not deny, shift blame, or hire lawyers to help them avoid responsibility. Instead, they self-assess, reflect, apologize, learn, and modify behaviour if needed. Furthermore, they work to influence change from within their profession, if change is needed. The "self-defining" professional identity appears to be an essential element of professional competence-broadly defined.

For emerging professionals, even when professional expectations are well understood, they are not easily enacted. Confirming the difficulty health professions students experience when expected to act on professional expectations, a recent analysis of senior dental students' reflective essays on the easiest and hardest professional expectations to fulfill[3] found that 44 percent of the 91 students perceived professional self-regulation and professional monitoring to be the hardest responsibilities to fulfill, whereas achieving the knowledge of the profession and meeting responsibilities for lifelong learning were considered easiest. Putting patients' interests before the self and serving the underserved were considered difficult, but not as difficult as questioning a superior about a judgment that seemed questionable or admitting an error in one's own judgment. Curriculum studies (Bebeau & Monson, 2008) reveal that reluctance to report instances of misconduct stems less from unwillingness than from uncertainty about how to do so and the negative reaction of colleagues expected to follow such actions.

IMPLICATIONS FOR EDUCATION

Young people who choose to endure years of education to enter a profession are achievement oriented. They value learning as a way to achieve personal goals that lead to the "good life"—perhaps conceptualized as a life of accomplishments that bring material goods, prestige, recognition, power, and influence. Whereas many young people express altruistic goals and value fairness, morality, and service to others, recent evidence (Twenge, 2009) strongly suggests that societal influences are inhibiting, rather than enhancing, the development of the moral self. The societal focus on idealism may also be responsible for recent declines in moral judgment development among college and professional students (Thoma & Bebeau, 2008). For these reasons, we find it important to assess the moral component of a professional identity so we can engage the young person in reflection about who they are and who they wish to become.

A significant barrier to implementing this recommendation is the prevalent view of the lay person, including many professionals—that values are established in childhood, and if not then, are certainly fully formed by the end of adolescence. As we have shown, this view is not supported by the evidence from studies of professional identity. Studies of entering professional students show no consistency in understanding of professional roles, but varied meanings depended upon the student's stage of identity formation. Clearly, not all persons in the professions achieve the more advance levels of identity typical of exemplars. Nonetheless, exemplary professionals were particularly aware that their understanding of professionalism had changed and developed over their professional lifetime. In fact, they viewed the very act of reflecting upon their inner lives and the forces that had shaped them, as affirming and revealing just how much they had grown and changed. Even Monson & Hamilton's early career lawyers—when asked—75 percent reported their understanding of professionalism has increased, whereas the others said their fundamental understanding hadn't changed, but the importance had increased. We agree with Kegan (1994) that "professionalism is less about external forces that grant privilege and authority, or shape personality or character, but about the internal psychological capacities involved with knowing, thinking, and forming relationships."

Recognizing the potential power of self-reflection and self assessment on development of professional goals and values and noting that such opportunities are rarely included in professional ethics curricula, Bebeau and Monson (2011) describe educational strategies to engage professional students in the kind of self-reflection on professional values and commitments that are likely to facilitate professional identity formation. These strategies are being tested in law and medicine.

IMPLICATIONS FOR RESEARCH

This chapter and the earlier chapter (Thoma & Bebeau, this volume) describe strategies for assessing the developmental aspects of moral motivation and commitment as they present themselves in the professions. The original approach (The Role Concept Essay) asked participants to reflect on various aspects of the profession, including what being a professional means to the individual. Responses are assessed for the degree to which participants can articulate what society expects of a professional. This approach assesses awareness and understanding of professional responsibilities, but not the extent to which the individual sees the self as responsible to act on these responsibilities in situations requiring such action. A second approach, the Professional Role Orientation Inventory, requires individuals to rate a series of statements that reflect different moral considerations. Different patterns of rating are associated with differing conceptions of professional responsibilities observed in society. The measure is sensitive to individual and group differences and to the educational interventions. The PROI does not directly assess professional identity, but infers it from ratings.

A third approach, described herein, is based on constructivist notions that individuals are engaged in meaning making and as they encounter professional education, they may also encounter the profession's values that may or may not become integrated into the development of the self. To date, we have observed that content from essay questions can be reliably coded for stage of identity formation given our current coding guides. However, data from essay questions has not been compared with data from interviews. Interviews have the potential for eliciting depth of understanding which may be missed with essay questions. Whereas the Subject-Object Interview has greater potential for eliciting precision in assessing developmental positions, the costs of administering the measure prohibit its use in educational settings. Nonetheless, a small scale study may enable the refinement of essay questions to elicit better understanding of developmental differences. Similarly, it may be possible to use findings from interview studies to design a measure similar to the Defining Issues Test that enables educators to judge the effectiveness of educational interventions aimed at promoting the moral component of professional identity.

CONCLUSION

The foundation of a professional moral identity lies in the social contract a profession has with society. This contract specifies particular duties and responsibilities of would be members. A first step in the development of a professional moral identity is to accept that the duties agreed to by the collective profession apply to the self. As was evident from a review of the literature, not all persons who claim to be professionals or aspiring professionals have accepted the responsibilities the collective profession has agree to as applying to the self. Even when individuals generally accept the profession's responsibilities as applying to the self, other values may pre-empt the moral value, resulting in a failure of professional moral motivation and commitment. Thus, moral motivation, as Rest conceptualized it, is linked to professional identity through the understanding of the self's and the profession's responsibility to society. Such a professional moral identity is exemplified by professionals, who have lived a life of committed moral action. These individuals not only can articulate the profession's responsibilities, but have elevated moral considerations over other considerations.

As psychologists have argued, identity formation is a lifelong developmental process. Thus, educators should not expect young people to come fully prepared to take on professional roles and responsibilities, or to demonstrate the kind of integration of personal and professional values that are exhibited by exemplars in the profession. The main question then is not whether young people are self, rather than other-centered, but the degree to which societal influences may be inhibiting, rather than enhancing, the development of the moral self. Irrespective of the cause, the long-term survival of a profession is dependent on the education of its members.

This paper presented evidence of a developmental continuum of moral motivation and commitment that is consistent with the perspectives of developmental psychologists such as Blasi (1984) and Kegan (1982), who have long argued that people differ in how deeply moral notions penetrate self-understanding. Understanding the self as responsible is at least part of the bridge between knowing the right thing and doing it. Evidence from studies of professionals in training, suggests that, in the final analysis, competence in Rest's component 4 processes may be even more important than the development of an ethical professional identity.

Summarizing the findings of five major studies of professions undertaken by the Carnegie Foundation, Lee Shulman (2010) remarked that "the most overlooked aspect of professional preparation was the formation of a professional identity with a moral core of service and responsibility around which the habits of mind and practice should be organized" (p. ix). New approaches, Shulman argued, are needed. Rest's four component model of moral functioning provides the theoretical grounding for education and studies grounded in Rest's model of moral motivation provide support for their potential effectiveness.

NOTES

[1] The state's dental practice act covers a wide range of possible violations including professional competence, oversight of the dental practice, and personal lapses that night interfere with the practice of the professional.

[2] Occupational Safety and Health Administration – Policy Statement On Bloodborne Pathogens, Infection Control and The Practice Of Dentistry. http://www.ada.org/1851.aspx

[3] Students were asked to reflect (based on clinical experience to date, and portfolio entries) on what they now viewed as the easiest, the hardest, and second hardest expectations of the professional to fulfill. Portfolio entries written during the first semester of the first year that were relevant to this activity included (a) the Kegan essay written as a baseline assessment, and (b) an essay "What does it mean to you to become a professional?" written as part of a course exam following a series of learning activities designed to enhance understanding of professional and societal expectations.

REFERENCES

Anderson, M. (2001). What would get you in trouble: Doctoral students' conceptions of science and its norms. *Proceedings of the ORI Conference on Research on Research Integrity*. Washington, D.C.: Office of Research Integrity.

Bebeau, M.J. (1994). Influencing the moral dimensions of dental practice. In J. Rest & D. Narvaez (Eds.), *Moral development in the professions: Psychology and applied ethics* (pp. 121–146). New York: Erlbaum Associates.

Bebeau, M.J. (2009a). Enhancing professionalism using ethics education as part of a dental licensing board's disciplinary action: Part 1 An evidence-based process. *Journal of the American College of Dentists, 76*(2), 38–50.

Bebeau, M.J. (2009b). Enhancing professionalism using ethics education as part of a dental licensing board's disciplinary action: Part 2 Evidence the process works. *Journal of the American College of Dentists, 76*(3), 32–45.

Bebeau, M.J., & Kahn, J. (2002). Ethical issues in community dental health. In G.M. Gluck & W.M. Morganstein (Eds.), *Jong's Community Dental Health* (5th ed., pp. 425–446). St Louis, MO: Mosby.

Bebeau, M.J., & Lewis, P. (2003). *Manual for assessing and promoting identity formation.* Minneapolis, MN: Center for the Study of Ethical Development, University of Minnesota.

Bebeau, M.J., & Monson, V.E. (2008). Guided by theory, grounded in evidence: A way forward for professional ethics education. In L. Nucci & D. Narvaez (Eds.), *Handbook on moral and character education* (pp. 557–582). Hillsdale, NJ: Routledge.

Bebeau, M.J., & Monson, V.E. (2011) Professional identity formation and transformation across the life span. In A. McKee& M. Eraut (Eds.), *Learning trajectories, innovation and identity for professional development: Innovation and change in professional education* (pp. 135–163). Dordrecht: Springer.

Bebeau, M.J., Rest, J.R., & Yamoor, C.M. (1985). Measuring dental students' ethical sensitivity. *Journal of Dental Education, 49,* 225–235.

Bergman, R. (2004). Identity as motivation: Toward a theory of the moral self. In D.K. Lapsley & D. Narvaez (Eds.), *Moral development, self, and identity* (pp. 21–46).Mahwah, NJ: Erlbaum.

Blasi, A. (1984). Moral identity: Its role in moral functioning. In W.M. Kurtines & J.L. Gewirtz (Eds.), *Morality, moral behavior, and moral development* (pp. 129–139). New York: Wiley.

Colby, A., & Damon, W. (1992). *Some do care: Contemporary lives of moral commitment.* New York: Free Press.

Eigel, K. (1998). *Leader effectiveness* (Ph.D. dissertation). University of Georgia, as cited in Kegan & Lahey (2009).

Feudtner, C., Christakis, D.A., & Christakis, N.A. (1994). Do clinical students suffer ethical erosion? Students' perceptions of their ethical and personal development. *Academic Medicine, 69,* 670–679.

Fisher, B.A. & Zigmond, M.J., (2001). Promoting responsible conduct in research through "survival skills" workshops: Some mentoring is best done in a crowd. *Science and Engineering Ethics, 7,* 563–587.

Forsythe, G.B., Snook, S., Lewis, P., & Bartone, P.T. (2002). Making sense of officership: Developing a professional identity for 21ˢᵗ century army officers. In D.M. Snider & G.L. Watkins (Eds.), *The future of the army profession* (pp. 357–378). Boston: McGraw-Hill.

Hall, R.H. (1975). *Occupations and the social structure* (2nd ed. pp. 63–135). Englewood Cliffs, NJ: Prentice-Hall.

Hafferty, F. (2006). Measuring professionalism: A commentary. In D.T. Stern (Ed.), *Measuring medical professionalism,* (pp. 81–306). New York, NY: Oxford University Press, Inc.

Hamilton, N.W., & Monson, V.E. (2012). Ethical professional transformation: Themes from interviews about professionalism with exemplary lawyers. *Santa Clara Law Review* 52. Available at SSRN: http://ssrn.com/abstract=1804419

Institute of Medicine. (2002). *Integrity in scientific research.* Washington D.C.: Institute of Medicine, National Research Council.

Kegan, R. (1982). *The evolving self.* Cambridge, MA: Harvard University Press.

Kegan, R. (1994). *In over our heads: The mental demands of modern life.* Cambridge, MA: Harvard University Press.

Lahey, L., Souvaine, E., Kegan, R., Goodman R., & Felix, S. (1988). *A guide to the subject object interview: Its administration and interpretation.* Cambridge, MA: Harvard University Graduate School of Education, Subject-Object Research Group.

Lantz, M.S., Bebeau, M.J. & Zarkowski, P. (2011). The status of teaching and learning of ethics in US Dental Schools. *Journal of Dental Education, 75*(10), 1295–1309.

Monson, V.E., Roehrich, S.A., & Bebeau, M.J. (2008, March). *Developing civic capacity of professionals: A methodology for assessing identity.* A paper presented at the American Educational Research Association Annual Meeting, New York.

Monson, V.E., & Bebeau, M.J. (2009, March). *Dental student professional identity development: Themes illustrative of developmental stage differences.* Paper presented at the American Educational Research Association Annual Meeting, Denver, CO.

Monson, V.E., & Hamilton, N.W. (2010). *Entering law students' conceptions of an ethical professional identity and the role of the lawyer in society.* Available at SSRN: http://ssrn.com/abstract=1581528

Rennie, S.C., & Crosby, J.R. (2002). Students' perceptions of whistle blowing: Implications for self-regulation. A questionnaire and focus group study. *Medical Education, 36*(2), 173–179.

Rest, J.R. (1983). Morality. In Mussen (Ed.), *Manual of child psychology* (4th ed., Vol.3). New York: Wiley.

Rest, J.R. (1986). *Moral development: advances in research and theory.* New York: Praeger.

Rule, J.T., & Bebeau, M.J. (2005). *Dentists who care: Inspiring stories of professional commitment.* Chicago, IL: Quintessence Publishing Co, Inc.

Rule, J.T., (2010). How dentistry should approach its problems: A vote for professionalism. *Journal of the American College of Dentists, 77*(4), 59–67.

Schunk, D.H., & Zimmerman, B. (2005). Competence and control beliefs: Distinguishing the means and ends. In P.A. Alexander & P.H. Winne (Eds.), *Handbook of educational psychology* (2nd ed., pp. 349–367). Mahwah, NJ: Erlbaum.

Shulman, L. (2010). Foreword. In M. Cooke, D.M. Irby & B.C. O'Brien (Eds.) *Educating physicians.* San Francisco: Jossey-Bass.

Snook, S. (2007, August 4). *Teaching leadership in business schools.* Address at the Annual Academy of Management Meeting.

Stern, D.T. (2006). *Measuring medical professionalism.* New York, NY: Oxford University Press, Inc.

Thoma, S. J, & Bebeau, M.J. (2008, March 24). *Moral judgment competency is declining over time: Evidence from twenty years of Defining Issues Test data.* Paper presented at the annual meeting of the American Educational Research Association. New York, NY.

Twenge, J.M. (2009). Generational changes and their impact in the classroom: teaching Generation Me. *Medical Education, 43*, 398–405.

Walker, L. & Frimer, J. (2007). Moral personality of brave and caring exemplars. *Journal of Personality and Social Psychology, 93*, 845–860.

Welie, J.V.M. (2004a). Is dentistry a profession? Part 1. Professionalism defined. *Journal of the Canadian Dental Association, 70*(8), 529–532.

Welie, J.V.M. (2004b). Is dentistry a profession? Part 2. The hallmarks of professionalism. *Journal of the Canadian Dental Association, 70*(9), 599–602.

Welie, J.V.M. (2004c). Is dentistry a profession? Part 3. Future challenges. *Journal of the Canadian Dental Association, 70*(10), 675–678.

AFFILIATIONS

Muriel J. Bebeau
Department of Primary Dental Care
School of Dentistry
University of Minnesota
Minneapolis, USA

Stephen J. Thoma
Educational Psychology
College of Education
University of Alabama
Tuscaloosa, USA

EDWIN R. MICEWSKI

II. MORAL MOTIVATION OF MILITARY PROFESSIONALS

A Military-Philosophical Approach

INTRODUCTION

It is inherent in the nature of the military world that soldiers are always close to issues of ethics and morality as the core of soldiering is the application of physical force and the use of violent means in exceptional circumstances. This remains true under the contemporary conditions of international relations and security affairs that behold the rise of political radicalism of non-state actors of mainly religious and ethnic provenance, who manifest their claims in asymmetrical warfare on a global scale. Questions of war and peace therefore do not only seem to encompass and affect the whole of mankind but they present themselves as ever more complex and intricate to answer. The onset of the post-Cold War scenario ushered the world into a "new season of bellicosity" (Luttwak, 1996) and shifted the armed services of most nations from instruments of national defense to instruments of international crisis-prevention and conflict-resolution. This entailed a profound alteration in the self-awareness of soldiers and armed forces and has brought about a host of new challenges, especially for military leaders. The new cultural and truly human underpinning to military operations resulted in increased cooperation with civil organizations and a broadened horizon for efficient military leadership. Due to the new shapes of conflict, the tactical, operative and strategic levels have mingled and the presence of electronic media, in many cases providing real-time coverage, has become a constant factor at all levels and in all areas of mission conduct. Rapidly changing conditions and circumstances require military leaders of all ranks to rely on their own judgments and sense of responsibility, simply because swift action is frequently required in a context wherein no orders are available and concrete law provisions and rules of engagement do not provide sufficient and immediate instructions upon which to act.

In the overall context of military leadership responsibility, the altered face of war and conflict has induced new moral and ethical challenges at all levels of the military establishment. As an example, let us think about the challenges arising from asymmetrical warfare with non-state actors and irregular forces intentionally violating the laws of war, and thus, human rights and the idea of humanity. How are we to fight these forces? May we turn away from a military ethos and the laws of

K. Heinrichs, F. Oser & T. Lovat (Eds.), Handbook of Moral Motivation: Theories, Models, Applications, 499–516.

war in order to cope with such challenges? Can the end of defeating an enemy that neglects the laws and ethics of war justify the usage and implementation of any and all means? With what mission regulations shall we come forth? Can the potential scope of actions and situations be totally covered by laws and rules of engagement? Beyond that, quite a few are irritated by the very idea of military ethics and soldierly acting upon individual moral incentive. For many, the strict connection between command and obedience as the backbone of the profession in arms obviously clashes with the idea of resorting to a personal moral judgment.

For these reasons, professional military education of the past two decades has seen a resurgence of the discipline of military ethics in leadership instruction in order to assure appropriate moral and human capacities on all levels of the military hierarchy in potential mission scenarios. Military leaders should be enabled, more than ever before, to translate ethical norms and standards, by way of their own personal leadership responsibility, into proper orders and actions in situations where critical moral authority is required.

The notion of moral motivation, given as a task here, arises in the context of military duty as a most fundamental one: What motivates somebody to engage in the military ethos of potentially "killing (injuring, mutilating) and getting killed (injured, mutilated)"? How can somebody be motivated to do that? On the level of military leadership, this question turns into an even more staggering notion: What motivates a military leader to send not only himself but also others into harm's way? How can that be ethically and morally justified? Above all, how can we build ethical competency, assure moral behaviour and reconcile the tension between obedience and conscience for the most morally challenging situations of war and armed conflict? How can we help the individual soldier to find the proper moral motivations to act justly and righteously in situations of utmost distress and danger? How can we enable the military leader to find the proper motivations to give morally justifiable orders under such circumstances?

This chapter will present some philosophical thoughts on the notion of motivation in moral philosophy, specifically examining the possibilities and limits of motivation in the realm of ethical and moral decision-making. The results will be put in the perspective of military life and the challenges that military professionals are facing in their particular environment of the potential use of force and violence. Ideas on how moral motivation can be taught and fostered in educational efforts and how the ethics of military leaders – a military ethics – can be embraced by society at large will conclude the chapter.

MOTIVE AND MOTIVATION IN ETHICS – EPISTEMOLOGICAL FOUNDATION

In my understanding ethics and morality are concerned with human acting and aim at the formation of meaningful and sensible human coexistence. Thus, normative ethics attempts to detect the supreme principles for the morally good and right that can serve as the ultimate criteria and guidelines for human action. Applied ethics, accordingly, pursues the task of relating these principles to the various fields of human acting in respective occupational and professional environments; hence: medical ethics, business ethics, military ethics, media ethics, etc.

In consequence, moral motivation must deal with the subject matter of how the principles of the morally good and right translate and can be translated into individual moral incentives to act. The essential question is this: How can it be achieved that what motivates human beings to act morally corresponds with the principles of the good and right, thus contributing properly and suitably to any given circumstance of human coexistence?

Since morality is concerned with the actual conduct of men, we encounter a critical problem when it comes to presuming the motivations that lie behind human actions. We face the fact that only the deeds themselves are visible and empirically traceable as well as comprehensible, whereas the motives that triggered the action remain in the dark. We use the notion of motive in the context of moral philosophy merely as internal motivations in the sense of incentives that drive a person's actions, rather than as an external motive or cause. From experience, we know that each individual acts or may act differently in the face of external facts, circumstances and conditions. For instance, a car accident is an external fact. One drives by and does not care whereas the other stops and tries to help. What are the internal motivations that make different people act differently when encountering the same circumstances? The same external fact apparently does not have the same influence on all. It appears obvious that a person's character in conjunction with his/her wider sphere of knowledge and emotional dispositions that remain largely unknown to others, modify the effect of any externally influencing and activity-triggering fact.

The internal motives or incentives to act are never apparent, but they are crucial whenever an action of moral worth is being discussed. This is why the philosopher as well as the jurist and the psychologist inquire into the intentions that lie behind the act and, by this alone judge the deed as far as its moral relevancy and value is concerned. On the other hand, everybody attempts to clear their character and vindicate their doings by pointing to the incentives and good motivations when they see their deeds misinterpreted or having gone awry.

This circumstance alone confers a certain "transcendental"[1] quality on investigations into the realm of ethics and morality and establishes the proven necessity that ethical questions can never be dealt with exclusively by science alone. It moreover makes clear why the discipline of ethics, in more than two millennia, has not delivered the kinds of results that can be shared as one single acknowledged paradigm by all disciplines of knowledge and reasoning. Indeed, it supports Immanuel Kant's point of view that ethics as a scientific discipline will never attain to ultimate answers. The most intrinsic human question for freedom as the condition of the possibility of responsible human acting represents one of the three transcendental ideas, and therefore irrefutable questions of metaphysics. While it is forever impossible to find a scientifically exact answer to this question, it is a perennial task with which human reasoning should concern itself. This is why Kant posits:

> "Metaphysics must come first, and without it there can be no moral philosophy at all" (Kant, 1993: Preface)

When it comes to the ethical significance of human conduct, we encounter an occurrence that is visible in the objective world but, at the same time, grounded in human consciousness. In the language of transcendental philosophy, this means that the fact of human action, as far as observable, can be no more than a phenomenon for whose further explanation metaphysics is demanded. In other words, morally relevant acts of human conduct carry both a phenomenal and intelligible side to them. The human way of acting has a significance that goes beyond the possibility of experience and touches upon the intelligible, the *noumenal*[2] world.

This twofold image of human acting is a reflection of the dual nature of the human character. Kant introduced the concept of the "intelligible character" (Kant, 1998, B 567) which, in combination with the empirical character as the phenomenal expression of itself in the empirical world, brings about the individual act of any given human being. In his subjective idealism, Arthur Schopenhauer, whose philosophical edifice should later on exert great influence on the emerging scientific discipline of psychology, considers this distinction to be the only way to resolve the problem of freedom and determinism. He substantiates the self-determining quality of the innate character that exists independent of experience and establishes the unique personality of all humans. This very Platonic view explains why every individual action is the both spatial and temporal manifestation of our respective intelligible character and thus could not have been other than it is. The intelligible character is basically what a person fundamentally is and defines a person's "inner essence" (Schopenhauer, 1969: Section 28). However, the fact that our consciousness tells us that we have "an unshakable certainty that we are the doers of our deeds" (Schopenhauer, 196: Conclusion) corroborates the existence of this innate character and gives us freedom in a more generic, yet limited, sense. As we learn more about ourselves, we can manifest our intelligible Self more appropriately and efficiently in life. The scholastic principle of "Operari sequitur esse"[3] resonates with Schopenhauer and will eventually lead to Friedrich Nietzsche's famous instruction "to become what one is" (Nietzsche, 2007, Section 9).

When there is an intelligible side to our character as the core unalterable element of our personality, then we grasp the significance that motives and motivation play in ethics and morality while, at the same time, we realize their limits. Any morally relevant act is a result of our character and the dominant motive that was present at the time. An action can therefore not be predetermined from the external motive and manifest circumstances alone; the other factor, the individual character and the data and awareness accompanying it, needs to be added to the equation. Indeed, the context of character and motivation constitutes the only law to which the human will is subjected, namely, the law of motivation. This law is a variation of the law of causality and refers to causality brought about through the medium of knowledge. It implies that every action can only take place in consequence of a sufficient motive, which can appear in the form of an intuition, perception, or abstract conception (Schopenhauer, 1995: p. 53).[4] The law of motivation bears transcendental quality as it applies with necessity, is independent of all experience and can be assumed without proof. This is why any action could only have taken place the way it took place. While a person might wish to have acted differently, he/she could only have acted in a different way if possessing a different character wherefore

"Man can do what he wants, but he cannot want what he wants" (Schopenhauer, 1999, p. 18).

Through all this, we become aware that influencing human acting can only happen via the realm of motives. As a result, while character development involves increasing the knowledge of our innate Self, it must incorporate ethical instruction in order to expand the horizon for potential motivation and thus enable and facilitate moral behaviour. While external motives trigger human action, the way of acting depends primarily on the intrinsic condition of the acting entity, referring to the individual character disposition of a human being at any given moment. Moral motivation, thus, aims at the formation of the essential ethical components of any person's consciousness. Those components, in connection with external motives and incentives to act, bring about the specific manifestations of individual human actions.

MOTIVE AND MOTIVATION IN ETHICS – MORAL-PHILOSOPHICAL FOUNDATION

The social nature of human existence necessitates an awareness of ethics and morality being primarily and almost exclusively concerned with interpersonal relations. Ethics comes to the fore when one's behaviour begins to affect others and thus applies in all aspects of human affairs, be it at the level of individual coexistence or the collective stage of social and political organization. This 'givenness' resides in the ontological capability of humans to have freedom to act and assume responsibility for their actions. Whatever we do with reference to others carries potential moral quality in and by itself and must therefore be guided by an ethical sense of responsibility. To be responsible thus means to make ethically appropriate use of one's freedom. Responsibility has to be considered to be an inference of freedom, an inevitable manifestation and complementary of it.[5] Thus is the human condition from whose ethical character there is no escape.

Since ethics and moral responsibility are directly linked to the use one makes of freedom, ethical behaviour steps in at the point that one's inclination towards freedom is restrained by respect for the freedom of others. An ethical situation is a circumstance between human agents in which one person or group of persons have a bearing on another person or group of persons. If we break a situation of ethical decision-making into its basic dimensions, we arrive at three distinctive and *a priori* self-evident elements that need to be involved and placed in context to each other. Any decision of moral or ethical relevance includes the inevitable parameters of goals-means-results. *Goals* relate to the end, the aim, objective, incentive, or purpose of any action; *means* speak of the resources and ways that are being used to attain to the desired goal; and, the *results* refer to the consequences that any action finally brings about. To make decisions within this ethical triad of decision-making, as well as for a trade-off among these elements, the history of ethical reasoning presents us with two dominant strategies: the *ends-based* and the *rule-based* approaches. While the former places the emphasis on the outcome, meaning the consequences and results of an action, the latter underscores incentive and intention as the deciding factors for any deed of ethical relevance.

The ends-based approach is generally defined as consequentialism, or teleological[6] ethics, and assumes that the morality of an action must be ultimately judged by the good and desired results that are realized. Consequentialists are convinced that the most important moral criterion for judging a deed is the overall outcome and gives priority to the consequences of human actions. The moral legitimacy of an action ultimately depends on its consequences, which is why the goals and means of an action must be morally justified by the results of such actions. Radical consequentialism would justify the usage of all means necessary to bringing about the best possible result.

In contrast, rule-based thinking, known as "deontological"[7] ethics, denies what the consequentialist analysis asserts, namely that an action is good or bad depending on the goodness or badness of its consequences. Deontologists assert that actions should be judged by their inherent rightness and validity, not by their outcomes. As a result, the righteousness of ethical decision-making is determined mainly by the morality of goals and intentions. Deontological moral obligations should be fulfilled not because they create a more effective result, but because they represent what moral actions require. Under deontology, therefore, the ends of any supposed action can never justify the usage of any or all means, for one must also act out of respect for the (moral) law or any other concept of moral righteousness.

Deontological and teleological (consequentialist) ethics agree that any action is triggered by a desired result, making clear that the reason for acting stems from the outer, empirical world. Every action is undertaken to bring about a desired result and even somebody who is motivated by the idea of moral duty has an interest in seeing the end of his action materialize.[8] However, deontology and teleology are at variance regarding the attainment of the result. While teleological ethics argues that the right thing to do is what produces the best consequences, deontological ethics claims that any ethically relevant striving for a specific result must be tempered by the transcendental regulative of the idea of justice. By adding this regulative dimension to moral acting, the deontological approach breaks through the teleological dualism of means and ends and manifests itself practically in self-imposed constraints regardless of even potentially unwanted consequences for the acting entity.

In the context of moral motivation, thus the question arises: How can one make moral decision-making work in the three-dimensional context of goals, means, and results? How to combine consequentialist and deontological claims? What could an appropriate approach to necessary trade-offs between means and results look like? How can ethical intentions and purposes be translated into actions that will maximize desirable outcomes without violating moral principles?

Already with the ancient Greeks we can find the convention for the prudent and wise praxis of human conduct. Aristotle suggests:

> "The work of man is achieved only in accordance with practical wisdom as well as with moral virtue; for virtue makes us aim at the right mark, and practical wisdom, prudence, makes us chose the right means"(Aristotle, 1998, p. 155 [1143b-1144a]) .

The deontology-based perspective, in the tradition of Immanuel Kant, guards against the relativism of consequentialism as it rejects the maxim that the end justifies (all) means and levels any action against the backdrop of a categorical principle. This principle features two key dimensions: First, all persons should be treated as having value in themselves, and second, individuals should act in accordance with maxims that can be universalized.[9]

The prudence tradition, on the other hand, joins deontology by insisting on the definitive authority of morality over circumstances, of "ought" over "is", while it also regards human virtue and personal character to be crucial factors to morality. Furthermore, it gives a first idea that the moral quality of any human being hinges upon character and personal integrity, rather than religious or political authority.

It was Schopenhauer who attempted to tie morality not to an abstract norm but rather to a concrete experience that all people can share. If we do not shut ourselves off to others, we are able, by way of personal introspection, to experience immediate solidarity with our fellow humans and encounter the intuitive certainty of compassion as the only true foundation of morality. If we do not keep our prescriptive norms for ethical behaviour tied to empathy as the true source of moral motivation, they will remain powerless and ineffective. Normative orientations need to be combined with the strong empirical elements of compassion and empathy in order to be effective. Here we encounter a variation of deontological ethics that derives moral responsibility not from an abstract operation of reasoning, but rather from an inner experience of humaneness.[10] It is again the moral motivation and an incentive based upon empathic sympathy, rather than the actual result of an action, that decides the moral worth of human deeds.

Teleological or deontological approaches constitute only two major strands of ethical theories and ways of categorizing different ethical models. Over time, these two approaches ramified further into several different schools of thought. In the end, it is the comprehensive totality of the moral philosophical heritage that is foundational to the understanding of morality and the ability to ascertain appropriate moral judgment. To the vast array of philosophical and religious ethical theories, modern science has added the cognitive theories of developmental psychology, constructivism, ethical naturalism and descriptive ethics as subject matters of the social sciences.

Broad knowledge and lasting occupation with ethics as a philosophical and scientific discipline can provide essential assistance for the acquisition of a habitual inclination to act morally. Moral motivation cannot mean a constant reasoning and rational deliberation about ethical theories at any moment when a morally relevant decision is required. Ethical enlightenment and the development of an appropriate moral consciousness will depend on profound educational instruction and formation. While there is no recipe and never a guarantee for appropriate moral behaviour, the holistic insight into and availability of the enormous anthology of ethical theories helps to shape an ethical sense of responsibility that provides profound moral motivation and incentive whenever needed.[11] This is what character development is all about, at the same time emphasizing its possibilities and limitations.

MOTIVE AND MOTIVATION IN MILITARY ETHICS

In consequence of the analysis up to this stage, the challenge for moral motivation in the context of soldiering and military affairs relates to instilling the knowledge and values that help and enable righteousness in situations ranging from everyday peacetime routine to the potentially violent and dangerous situations of wartime and armed conflict.

Due to its direct correlation with the use of violent means and the potential for killing and being killed, the military world touches upon the most profound basis of human existence. This is in itself frightening and scares many away from even being willing to deal with the subject of military ethics. Some dismiss the problem by pointing to an alleged inherent contradiction between military duty and ethics and render thus the subject of military ethics forever incomprehensible; others avoid any ethical responsibility in the military context by submitting the issue to obedience and unconditional deference that leaves no room for personal moral accountability.

Both approaches are clearly deficient as no dimension of human conduct can be devoid of ethics and no human being of sound mind can escape moral accountability. Even if somebody commits illegitimate actions upon orders it cannot exonerate them from their liability. Human acting, and in particular responsible leadership, cannot be tied to legal provisions alone. Ethical thinking and moral conduct transcend sheer legality and any concept of obedience to enacted norms and values, and thus point to an inward realm of human individuality. As a philosophical discipline, military ethics operates with the capacity of human reason to ask and answer crucial questions regarding all possible relations between military and soldierly action and moral norms.

Military ethics addresses crucial moral issues related to both the military world and the individual soldier, specifically the one in a leadership role. The scope of topics ranges from everyday challenges of peacetime conduct and the question of legitimacy toward society to the core dimension of military ethics, the subject matter of which perennially remains whether the use of violent means can ever be justified, be it at an individual or collective level.

As a segment of applied ethics, military ethics deals at the individual level with the moral integrity of the soldier, specifically with his ethically responsible behaviour in combat and armed conflict. The aspect of the leadership responsibility of the military officer and the moral implications that derive from his command authority presents itself in the context of the mission conduct of military formations and collectives. Another significant strand of military ethics looks at the social-ethical significance of the military organization in the sense of how the value cosmos of the armed forces and professional military identity can be reconciled with the civilian logic of open and democratic societies (Micewski, 2003, pp. 41–52).

In comprising these individual, collective and political-social aspects, military ethics has to be dealt with on the basis of two pragmatic conditions: The purpose and distinct organizational culture of the military organization, on the one hand; and, the conditions of the social and political environment within which armed forces exist and operate, on the other. Military ethics is closely linked to military and soldierly identity and has to be aware of the fact that the occupational field of the military, as any other, is formed by the purpose of the organization, the resulting professional and functional requirements, and the social and political environment. An appropriate understanding of military ethics requires therefore close acquaintance with certain disciplines of the social sciences, particularly sociology and political science.

The proximity of the military world to war with all its strain, suffering, and exertion made moral considerations a major concern throughout history and posed a most serious challenge to any concept of humanism. Since the military is an instrument of politics and acts under the supremacy of policy, armed conflict and war are political enterprises and any ethics of military and soldiering finds itself within the boundaries of political ethics.

As the idea of the inseparability of politics and ethics stems from ancient times, so does the idea of ethical restraint upon the waging of war and its embodiment in moral codes and legal norms. The proposition that war, when waged legitimately, should be based on ethical principles has been pushed by theologians and philosophers, such as St. Augustine, St Thomas Aquinas and Hugo Grotius, and has developed into the theory of Just War as the basic moral underpinning for military ethics. As a result of the embedded nature of the military in politics, the ethical approach to war and armed conflict has evolved on two levels, aiming firstly at those who hold the decision-making power to go to war, and secondly, at those who have to wage war when it finally comes to it.[12]

Therefore, the basic ideas with regard to a morally justified use of force as they are expressed in the Just War theories fall into two categories: The first set of principles, the Jus ad Bellum (Right to War) criteria, concern the conditions that make the use of force permissible. Under the assumption of the primacy of policy, the *Jus ad Bellum* principles constitute a political responsibility in the first place and affect the military only in its advisory function to politics. Among the most prominent criteria are: a) there must be just cause; b) war must be prosecuted for rightful intentions; c) war must be declared by a lawful authority; d) war must be a last resort; e) there must be reasonable hope for success; f) the political objectives must be proportional to the costs of war; and, g) war must be publicly declared (in terms of causes and intents). While these principles were designed for conventional war and the classical interstate conflict between politically established communities, and certainly not for the contemporary conditions of privatized war and asymmetrical conflict, their ethical power and justified moral claims persist. Any entity that intends to use forceful means has to be held accountable as to the justice of their cause, if their intentions are righteous and morally justifiable, and if their use of violent means is indeed the last resort to serve their purpose.[13]

The second set of principles, the Jus in Bellum (Right in War) criteria, concern the conduct of war by military formations and soldiers and thus express largely a military responsibility. The Jus in Bellum principles basically posit that a) war must be fought justly; and, b) discrimination (between combatants and non-combatants) must be observed.

The basic moral motivation for the individual soldier to observe the ethical rule of fighting justly revolves around the normative ethical principles of inevitability (necessity), proportionality, and discrimination. Under the premise of war being waged and military forces being used for rightful Jus ad Bellum criteria, the moral legitimacy for the use of violence plays out mostly by way of how soldiers fight and what means they use. The principles of proportionality and discrimination refer to the means themselves as well as against whom they are being used. While in the latter respect the differentiation between combatants and non-combatants is in the foreground, the former question refers to the means used in the sense of their sustainability with regard to humanitarian and technological conditions. The principle of inevitability and (military) necessity refers to the conduct of military and soldierly activity only when indispensable for the accomplishment of the mission and task at hand.

The general motivation for individual soldiers and military leaders to act and fight justly is most profoundly based on the concept of the Justus Hostis, the just enemy, which places war fighting and military combat in an all-encompassing human context. The essential motive for a just warrior is the acknowledgement of the enemy and opposing adversary as a human being, thus making it imperative to consider him an integral part of our moral decision-making calculus in intentional acting. This basic motive prevents the true military man (and woman) from "hating" the enemy, from dehumanizing him and denigrating him to a mere means for somebody's objective. The empathy for the human image of the opponent in violent conflicts is the core motive that prevents cruelty and war crimes – such as killing of innocents or execution of wounded adversaries or prisoners – from taking place and has become the major stumbling block in the new conflict scenarios of asymmetrical warfare.

As the recent history of the War on Terrorism demonstrates, the asymmetrical fighter applies violence in an indiscriminate way. Not only does he negate the discrimination between combatants and non-combatants, but he even denies the adversary the recognition of being equal in the sense of his humanity. Not only the opposing soldier or policeman, but rather every exponent of different creed or ethnicity is considered to be an enemy whose existential aspirations as a human being can be neglected. This is why the instrumental understanding of war as it was represented by the classical armed conflict between sovereign states that shared common ethical principles and norms of international and humanitarian law is being transformed ever more into an existential conception of warfare.[14] The difference results mainly from how the war-waging adversary is being viewed and recognized and from the fact that unconditional claims and aspirations thwart any attempt that could foster moderation, restraint, and implicit understanding. The new, ideological war, which is waged with asymmetric means and methods negates the stakes of morality. Whoever is considered to be an adversary is being combated in every possible manner since what is being fought can be destroyed and annihilated because it is not granted the same, if any, human quality.

The loss of moral substance in the realms of contemporary armed conflict and de-nationalized as well as privatized war has far-reaching consequences. The targeting of women, children and non-involved individuals by irregular forces, rogue military formations, organized crime, and terrorists is being used to further break down the moral boundaries of armed conflict. The conjoining of technical with moral asymmetries confronts the regular soldier and policeman with calamitous challenges as they are bound by moral symmetries and must never rid themselves of the idea of the humane and ethical.

The post-Cold War era of de-nationalized and increasingly privatized war has shaped a new identity of regular armed forces and military organizations that have been defined as postmodern. The postmodern paradigm sees the central task of armed forces no longer in the context of classical national defense, but rather in international conflict prevention, conflict de-escalation and resolution, and humanitarian assistance. This shift in the identity of Western military establishments brings about the need for an increased ability to deal with the complex configuration of conflict scenarios, characterized by structural and cultural interpenetration of civil and military spheres, the presence of irregular forces and sub-national actors, the internationalization of military staffs and formations, as well as the merging of strategic, operational, and tactical levels in the procedural progress of mission accomplishment. As the history of recent conflicts as well as the ongoing War on Terrorism proves, lower-level military leaders and individual soldiers find themselves ever more in ethically relevant situations where moral decisions have to be made for which existing legal provisions and Rules of Engagement (ROE) do not necessarily provide sufficient guidance. When immediate action is required and circumstances allow no time to refer to higher echelons of the military-political hierarchy, military leaders and individual soldiers have to fall back on their own moral competencies and sense of ethical responsibility. At this juncture in particular, responsible behaviour becomes linked to conscience and the moral proficiency of the individual character. While, in human affairs, there is no guarantee that proper moral behaviour will occur, it is that only the informed and instructed and well-inclined individual character finds increased chance to generate appropriate decisions and bring forth proper action.

In order to ensure, with high likelihood, humanely appropriate acting of soldiers and military formations, even and particularly under the challenging conditions of asymmetrical conflict and warfare, the instruction of the individual moral consciousness of soldiers and military leaders rests at the forefront of military ethics.

As the account of Just War Theory made clear, the ethical and moral challenges arise on three relevant levels that present themselves as normative for the realms of security and defense: First, the level of politics and political decision-making; second, the level of military formations and collectivities; and, third, the level of individual human conscience.[15] Due to the aforementioned fact that in (post-) modern armed conflict the tactical levels can gain strategic relevance and import, more than ever before is the third level of paramount significance. This is why educational efforts in military ethics focus on the moral competency of individual soldiers, particularly of military leaders on all levels of the military hierarchy, acknowledging the fact that moral competency represents a major dimension of adequate soldier identity in a postmodern world.

MORAL MOTIVATION AND MILITARY ETHICS IN EDUCATION

If we interpret morals as the motivational inclinations of a person in how he observes and exercises his social responsibilities, we become aware of the ethical significance of individual moral dispositions for all social and political interrelations in human affairs. This understanding also shields us against the dissolution of individual morals in collective morality and the reduction of individual responsibility to compliance with rules and regulations.

Through the era of political modernism, we have witnessed reiterated efforts to replace personal morals by ethical prescriptions as a universal remedy for human behaviour. The "moral law within myself", of which Immanuel Kant had spoken, was thus replaced by an ethical code that reduced individual moral conduct to following socially approved rules. In the military world, this approach condensed itself to what has become known as an almost obligatory obedience, a literal dutifulness to military orders and Rules of Engagement, in final consequence an incitement to wait and to do nothing if there is no respective order or the order arrives belatedly. The cases of Srebrenica and Rwanda are but two examples that made the devastating consequences of such understanding visible to the whole world in stark magnitude. These instances proved that responsible individual conduct must not be linked to rules and laws alone, but can in difficult and specific circumstances only be achieved if individual moral consciousness can unfold in a full and unconstrained way.

"The I always has one responsibility more than all the others" (Lévinas, 1985, p. 101)

said the philosopher Emanuel Levinas when making clear that the final responsibility of a human being, which one can only find within oneself, together with one's conscience, is bigger and more powerful than any ethical or legal norm. This is also true for the soldier and military officer. People are not moral because of society or their occupational environment; these can only provide for ethical or lawful behaviour (Bauman, 1995, p. 97). Beyond this, to be moral means that a person is fundamentally relegated to one's own Self and thus, to one's own freedom.

The classical, symmetrical armed conflict, in which regular forces were opposing each other on the grounds of a mutually acknowledged international law and minimal humanitarian standards, including the clear distinction between combatants and non-combatants, is no longer the primary challenge to military formations. The new dimensions of armed conflict and war no longer foster coping with moral and ethical challenges by clear hierarchical attributions and military operational procedures. Instead, ambiguous and complex situations, with indistinct actors who neglect the procedural and ethical principles of regular combat, present intricate and difficult challenges to soldiers and military leaders.

Taking this trend into consideration, the past years have seen a surge in ethical instruction in the armed forces of the Western hemisphere, particularly within the framework of transatlantic collaboration.[16] While the cooperation allowed for the negotiation of the political, cultural, military-institutional but also methodological and semantic differences, it brought to light the major procedural difference in conveying ethics and conducting moral education. The difference relates to whether ethics should be taught in the sense of a comprehensive instruction in abstract ethical and moral theory, or rather in the understanding of an empirical and pragmatic ethos orientation. The latter approach is mainly pursued in the nations of the Anglo-American world according to the principle that ethics should be "caught" rather than "taught". This particular approach features virtue ethics and attempts to prescribe virtues and values as a recipe for moral motivation and rejects any intellectualization of moral instruction.

From my viewpoint, an appropriate comprehension of ethical questions and moral challenges regarding the military world can only be achieved by philosophical reflection and cannot be construed without instruction in metaphysics, philosophical anthropology and ontology, and must be communicated within a comprehensive tutoring in military philosophy. Virtue and duty must never become routine, as habitual custom can easily lead to the inhumane as far as ethical challenges are concerned.

Each and every ethically relevant situation has to be considered to be specific and unique and has to be decided upon genuinely, based on the respective circumstances. The attempt to provide normative orientation by a methodological reduction of the subject matter and blinding out the metaphysical totality can come at the cost of forfeiting quality in moral decision-making.

CONCLUSION

The polemological reality of human existence becomes visible to us through the reality of everyday life with its technological and societal developments, but also with the manifestations of the perennial dichotomy of peace and war. While we recognize a surge in moral orientation and ethical counselling in various walks of life such as medicine, gene technology, economics, media and education, the world of security politics has equally witnessed a boom in ethics and moral scrutiny. The decisive alterations in security affairs since the end of the Cold War, featuring denationalization and privatization of international relations and the efficacious appearance of sub-national and non-governmental forces claiming their causes with asymmetrical means and methods, have led to a paradigmatic change in missions and tasks assigned to armed forces. The move from classical national defense to international conflict resolution and humanitarian missions in multinational formations, closely operating with civilian organizations of global, regional and local provenance, confronts the representatives of armed forces with new challenges that demand the increased consideration of ethical and moral viewpoints.

If soldiers and military leaders are supposed to find appropriate moral motivation for their actions and military conduct, a profound cultivation of ethical-moral dispositions is needed that can only be grounded in holistically informed moral consciousness. Adequate moral motivation cannot be the result of imitating historical examples or the blind observance of predetermined guidelines, but neither can it be a constant reasoning over a categorical imperative or philosophical conceptions. This is why the objective of ethical instruction in the military, as elsewhere, should be the attainment of an inner disposition, a moral inclination of the will that needs constant nourishment and further development.

The history of warfare abounds with examples of situations in which the internal morality of soldiering proved more decisive in humanitarian and ethical respects than orders, legal provisions, international law, or personal endangerment. Moral sentiment and an unwritten military honor code, based on individual conscience and a distinct sense of humane moral duty, has always shown itself in situations of high ethical tension. One recent example was the decision of Joint Chief of Staff General Powell in Operation Desert Storm not to pursue and hunt down retreating Iraqi Republican Guard troops, although admissible under the laws of war. Powell considered the destruction of those troops "un-American and unchivalrous" (Osiel, 2002, p. 25) and demonstrated that a strong moral sentiment can serve as a restraining factor in combat and war.

If moral motivation is accomplished for representatives of the military organization, then they will be able to comprehend existential questions regarding soldierly duty and military purpose and thus engage aptly in efficient discourses with their political and social environments. Ethical consciousness, human dignity, and the demonstrated virtue of soldiers help to better integrate them into society. It also enables military personnel to better cope with the institutional difference that sets the armed forces apart from other organizational entities in the environment of civil societies.

In our day and age, the need for military organizations to generate legitimacy and acceptance for their goals and conduct has become paramount. The distinctive character of the military and the resulting gap of values between the armed forces and society mostly owes to the incompatibility between a civilian logic that is mainly utilitarian and self-centered, and a military ethos that is altruistic and directed toward a collective immaterial good. At the most serious end of military duty, the exclusive chance of physical sacrifice still awaits the individual soldier. While the military has integrated itself into a political structure that is characterized by the supremacy of policy and has adapted itself to the bureaucratic arrangements of modern political administration, it retains the exclusive task to prepare and, if need be, apply violence and force. This is why, in the end, the tensions and even, at times, irreconcilable differences between a soldier's and a civilian's mind derive from a dilemma that is essentially ethical in nature.

Even though the distance between civil and military elites has diminished in the wake of the paradigm change in post-Cold War security affairs, the lasting mission to fight and endure armed conflict remains the key to the understanding of the distinctive nature of the military and its members. Particular vocations require, as already Aristotle has stated, people of suitable temperament and character. Carl von Clausewitz, in this vein and with officers and military leadership in mind, made clear that "every special calling in life, if it is to be followed with success, requires peculiar qualifications of understanding and soul" (Clausewitz, 1976, Book One, p. 138).

Only a soldier's and military leader's identity, formed around such perceptions and including a universe of ethical knowledge and moral responsibility, can enable military personnel to accomplish their tasks and missions successfully. At the same time, it is this ethical knowledge and moral responsibility that also facilitates their efforts to be solidly and insightfully embraced by society and its politics.

NOTES

[1] Transcendental refers to the fact that aspects independent and irrespective of experience play a role or are at work. In Kant's understanding transcendental stands for being "the condition of the possibility of experience" (Kant 1998, B 25), thus inferring the constitutionality of transcendental qualities for all empirical occurrences.

[2] In its classical meaning the term noumenon refers to what is known without the use of the senses, meaning forms or ideas that exist in a realm beyond space and time.

[3] Acting derives from being (translated E.R.M.)

[4] The context of moral reasoning, the psychologically-motivating forces that serve as incentives to act with necessity, based upon one's individuality, are outlined in detail in Schopenhauer's "The Fourfold Root of the Principle of Sufficient Reason" (1974), specifically Chapter VII, Section 43, pp. 212–214.

⁵ For more on the relation between responsibility and morality compare: Jonas, Hans 1985.

⁶ From the ancient Greek word *telos*, meaning end.

⁷ From the Greek term *deon*, meaning duty or obligation.

⁸ This is important to note as one of the more profound misunderstandings in the interpretation of deontological ethics is the assumption that the deontological motivation would be totally dissociated from results. The fact is that even the deontological act is triggered by some empirical circumstance and aspires some result, however, reaching the result does not determine whether or not the act was ethical or, in the least, of ethical relevance.

⁹ The first dimension corresponds with Kant's third formula of his categorical imperative: "Act in such a way that you treat humanity, whether in your own person or in the person of another, always at the same time as en end and never simply as a means"; the second represents the well-known first formula of Kant's moral imperative which defines the norm of universality as follows: "Act only according to that maxim through whereby you can at the same time will that it should become a universal law" (Kant 1993: pp. 36 [429] and 30 [421].

¹⁰ This thought derives from Schopenhauer 1995: Section 21 and 22; pp. 199–214.

¹¹ This assertion is based on the author's scholarly experience of dealing with ethics and moral philosophy in both a military and academic environment.

¹² For a more comprehensive account of the Just War Theory consider Christopher, 1994.

¹³ I have dealt with moral and ethical challenges deriving from asymmetrical warfare and the application of just war principles to the altered security environment of our day in my essay "On the Moral-Philosophical Legitimacy of Asymmetrical Warfare" in: Schroefl/Cox/Pankratz (eds.) 2009, pp. 75–86.

¹⁴ For more on the instrumental and existential understanding of war compare the respective chapter in Muenkler, 2002: pp. 91–115.

¹⁵ The author provides a comprehensive analysis of these three levels of ethical legitimacy in Micewski, 1998, specifically pp. 163–178.

¹⁶ The author of this paper has initiated and conducted a host of international projects in the field of military ethics within the Partnership for Peace Initiative of the North Atlantic Treaty Organization and in cooperation with the US Center for Civil Military Relations. Virtually all of these endeavors resulted in book publications most of which are accessible online for free. For publication reference see bibliography.

REFERENCES

Aristotle (1998). *Nicomachean ethics* (translated by David Ross), Oxford/New York:Oxford University Press.

Bauman, Z. (1995). *Postmoderne Ethik*, Hamburg: Hamburger Edition.

Christopher, P. (1994). *The ethics of war and peace. An introduction to legal and moral issues.* Englewood Cliffs: Prentice Hall.

Clausewitz, C. Von (1976). *On war*, New Jersey: Princeton University Press.

Jonas, H. (1985). *The imperative of responsibility.* Chicago: University of Chicago Press.

Kant, I. (1998). *Critique of pure reason.* Cambridge, New York: Cambridge University Press.

Kant, I. (1993). *Grounding for the metaphysics of morals.* Indianapolis: Hackett Publishers.

Lévinas, E. (1985).*Ethics and infinity. Conversations with Philippe Nemo*, Pittsburgh: Duquesne University Press.

Luttwak, E.N.. (1996). A post-heroic military policy.(post-Cold War US military policy)." *Foreign Affairs.* accessmylibrary. (September 14, 2010). http://www.accessmylibrary.com/article-1G1-18419996/post-heroic-military-policy.html

Micewski, E.R. (ed.) (2003). *Civil-military aspects of military ethics.* Volume One, Vienna: Publication Series of the National Defense Academy.

Micewski, E.R. (1998). *Grenzen der Gewalt – Grenzen der Gewaltlosigkeit. Zur Begründung der Gewaltproblematik im Kontext philosophischer Ethik und politischer Philosophie*, Frankfurt a. M: Peter Lang Publisher.

Nietzsche, F. (2007). *Ecce Homo: How one becomes what one is*. New York: Oxford University Press.

Osiel, M.J. (2002). *Obeying orders. Atrocity, military discipline and the law of war*, New Jersey: Transaction Publishers.

Schopenhauer, A. (1995). *On the basis of morality* (translated by E.F.J. Payne). Oxford: Berghahn Books.

Schopenhauer, A. (1969). *The world as will and representation* Volume One (translated by E.F.J. Payne). New York: Dover Publications.

Schopenhauer, A. (1974). *The fourfold root of the principle of sufficient reason* (translated by E.F.J. Payne). Illinois: Carus Publishing Company.

Schopenhauer, A. (1999). *Prize essay on the freedom of the will* (translated by E.F.J. Payne). New York: Cambridge University Press.

AFFILIATION

Edwin R. Micewski
Freelance Philosopher and Author
Formerly Director of the Institute for Human and Social Sciences
National Defence Academy Vienna, Austria.
He lives in San Luis Obispo, California, U.S.A. and Vienna, Austria

ELIZABETH CAMPBELL

III. ETHICAL INTENTIONS AND THE MORAL MOTIVATION OF TEACHERS

INTRODUCTION

We (teachers) have a lot of moral obligations to our students and we are very serious about them. I don't come here to collect a pay cheque and go home… there is some sense of satisfaction in what you do when I can walk out of here feeling good about what I do. Sometimes, however, I feel terrible because I worry that I wasn't fair to somebody during the day or that I didn't get back to somebody who needed to talk to me…So, you find that your day is all over the place and you think, what did I do today? What did I get accomplished because it just seemed like such a hectic day? I'm not a superhuman being, but I too have to make sure I make good choices. (Gina, grade six teacher, in Campbell, 2003, p. 46)

So, what is it that motivates teachers like Gina to conceptualize their work in moral terms, to revisit their own practice in all its daily complexity in order to assess its ethical defensibility, and to strive to honour such principles as fairness and responsibility in all that they do as professional practitioners? And, what is it that compels such teachers to act in moral ways, to translate their understandings of and perspectives on moral and ethical teaching practice more broadly into noble and responsive actions infused with compassion, fairness, honesty, and integrity? In his commentary on Richardson and Fenstermacher's well-known "Manner in Teaching" study (2001), David Hansen identifies "moral passion" as a driving force for teachers such as those studied in the "Manner" project who share much with Gina and many others; he writes, "the moral passion these teachers seem to hold toward their work fuels both their individuality and reveals the terrific rewards teaching can bring to its serious-minded practitioners . . . Their outlook appears to enable them to persevere, not to be thrown off their stride by any particular challenge but rather to meet challenges to the best of their available means" (Hansen, 2001, p. 734). While the "sense of satisfaction" and "terrific rewards" may be both a compelling force for, and a consequence of, teachers' moral choices and behaviour, what spurs them on to act morally or ethically right in the first place may also include other factors rooted deeply in the teacher's professional role and very being as both a moral person and ethical practitioner.

K. Heinrichs, F. Oser & T. Lovat (Eds.), Handbook of Moral Motivation: Theories, Models, Applications, 517–532.

MOTIVATION IN PRACTICE

As is explored in this chapter, such factors that teachers discuss as rationales for behaving in ways they believe to be morally imperative may include a deep sense of service in the best interests of others, notably their pupils; a personal commitment to the relational connections fostered by a sense of caring as well as a professional sense of duty and responsibility; fervent beliefs about students' rights and their will to uphold a respect for such rights in all that they do; a self-concept that defines them as moral guides, exemplars, and role models for their students; and, a deliberate dedication to enacting their moral intentions and achieving their moral goals that influence both their own ethical treatment of students and their aspirations for the students' moral growth and enlightenment. In her argument about the similarities and differences between character educators and care theorists, Noddings (2002) states that both "believe that moral motivation arises within the agent or within interactions" (p. 1). The factors that the teachers introduced in this chapter recognize as intrinsic to their moral practice are indeed rooted within their inner character and fostered through their relational experiences with students and others.

The aim of this chapter is to consider the following two questions from an applied perspective on moral motivation: What moves teachers to conduct themselves in morally and ethically sound ways, attentive to how virtues such as justice and kindness, truthfulness and constancy provide a foundation for their actions? And, what compels them to assume the influential persona of moral educator in the hope that their modelling, lessons in virtue, and admonitions in the classroom will somehow encourage students to grow in morally sound ways themselves? This largely conceptual essay explores what motivates teachers to conduct themselves ethically and morally in their daily interactions with students; it also considers what motivates them to engage in curricular lessons of a moral nature, whether they see them as forms of moral education or not. It discusses the term "motivation" not as a psychological construct, based on a specific theory of human development, but rather as a theoretical concept defined by its etymological roots in the Latin words *motivus* (stirred, moved) and *movere* (move, stir, agitate); in other words, it interprets moral motivation as something — a force, influence, or incentive for action — that moves, stirs, drives, and compels people, in this case teachers, to conduct themselves and their practice morally and ethically. For the purpose of this discussion, the terms "moral" and "ethical" are used for the most part interchangeably; this use reflects the combined literature in the field that refers to both the moral and ethical dimensions of teaching in conceptually and empirically compatible ways, and is a practice explained and defended elsewhere (Campbell, 2003, 2008b; Colnerud, 2006).

In exploring teachers' motivation, this chapter revisits data from some of my own qualitative research studies[1] (Campbell, 2003, 2008c, 2011) as well as empirical evidence and analytical conclusions from well-known studies by others (e.g., Hansen, 2002; Jackson et al, 1993; Richardson & Fenstermacher, 2001; Simon, 2001; Tirri & Husu, 2002). The following section on "compelling forces" or motivating factors that seem to influence teachers' moral practices speculates on the ethical intentions and moral motivation of selected teachers, some of whom participated in Jackson, Boostrom, and Hansen's (1993) "Moral Life of Schools" project, which was based primarily on extensive observation in 18 U.S. classrooms over two and a half years, and clearly captured the moral potency of spontaneous interactions among teachers and pupils that characterize much of the schooling day. The study itself provides vivid portraits in rich detail of how "moral considerations permeate the everyday life of schools and classrooms" (p.xiv). Also included is Hansen's account of one inner city Catholic boys' high school in an "economically disadvantaged" U.S. urban centre (Hansen, 2002); this empirical report was based on data collected initially as part of the "Moral Life of Schools" project, of which Hansen was a co-investigator. Also reviewed are several articles from the notable "Manner in Teaching" project (Fenstermacher, 2001; Richardson & Fenstermacher, 2001), a study of 11 teachers in two U.S. schools that initially focused on the relationship between a teacher's "manner" and the moral and intellectual development of students, and evolved into an analysis of the methods teachers use for fostering moral conduct in the classroom. "Manner," seen as synonymous with the "moral character" of the teacher (Fenstermacher, 1990, p. 134), is defined as a concept rooted in Aristotelian moral philosophy and highlights the desirability of such virtues as truthfulness, caring, justice, honour, friendliness, magnanimity, mildness, and practical wisdom in teaching. Two of the articles that are relevant to the consideration of the teacher's moral motivation or ethical intentions are written or co-written by members of the project's research team. One provides case study descriptions of two teachers that "focus on who a teacher is, what a teacher believes and how these beliefs are manifest in the teacher's conduct" (Richardson & Fallona, 2001, p. 705). The other describes two different teachers and seeks "to understand what morality and their own moral agency meant to them, and to note how they responded to discussing the topic in general, and the language they used to convey their intended meaning" (Sanger, 2001, p. 688).

As well as considering these two projects – the "Moral Life of Schools" project and the "Manner in Teaching" project – the subsequent exploration of those factors that motivate or compel teachers to conduct their work in morally attentive ways includes brief references to Simon's 2001 study of three U.S. high schools. Her observations of multiple classrooms in one public and two religious schools examined how teachers weave moral and existential issues into their teaching and classroom discourse. The section also includes references to Tirri and Husu's analysis of ethical dilemmas experienced by early childhood and elementary teachers in Finland who were both motivated and challenged by a concern for their students' "best interests" (2002). I also briefly revisit some of my own empirical work on the moral agency and ethical knowledge of teachers in Canada (Campbell, 2003) and the cultivation of ethical knowledge in pre-service and novice teachers who graduated from a range of teacher education programs in Canada (Campbell, 2008c, 2011). The purpose of this discussion of existing studies is to use limited snippets of their data and/or analytical conclusions as catalysts for considering a variety of moral motives that seem to drive teachers' work as moral agents.

The subsequent section addresses the moral character of teachers as a kind of intuitive driving force for them. It focuses on the centrality of the teacher as a person, and considers the importance of personal conscience and its link to intentionality. By way of comparison and conclusion, the chapter also briefly considers the kinds of forces that thwart teachers' intentionality to act in moral and ethical ways. It proposes that negative forces that arise within schools can serve as deterrents to moral motivation; however, it leaves unanswered the question of how to overcome them and focuses instead on the positive examples of teachers committed to moral action.

COMPELLING FORCES

In his discussion of the moral base of teacher professionalism, Sockett (1993) writes that "the value of an ideal of service lies not in attainments but in its worth as a moral guide" (p. 130). Presumably, that which guides could also compel. Teachers, many of whom feel the need to serve the interests of others, notably children, express what they "want" for their students and their teaching; these goals and intentions emanate from within them and serve to motivate their practice. As extensions of their character in that they reflect their beliefs, sense of ethics, and "moral passion," to recall Hansen's previous descriptions, such goals and intentions can become compelling forces that both guide and move teachers to fulfill their work as moral agents.

Often, teachers explain what they "want" is what they believe to be in the "best interests of the child"; for those in Tirri and Husu's study (2002), this now ubiquitous goal of education was defined in moral terms relating to human relationships, although they perceived "best interests" in different and frequently competing ways: teachers "may interpret the needs of children in a light different from that of their colleagues or parents. These differences in perceptions often lead to competing moral judgments; pedagogically, teachers are often called to mediate between these rival interests" (Tirri & Husu, 2002, p. 68). Notwithstanding the potential for ethical conflicts over competing visions of "best interests," as described in this study, teachers are driven by their commitment to serve such interests. Those who are thoughtful moral agents would assume also the responsibility for considering closely the ethical justification for their own interpretation of "best interests." By way of example, Darlene, one of the teachers in the "Manner in Teaching" project "was very clear about her need to treat individual students differentially. It is, however, her responsibility to determine what is best for each child to allow them to reach their and her goals. She reflected constantly on this differential treatment, particularly on treatment that she thought was not natural for her" (Richardson & Fallona, 2001, p. 713). Her constant reflection on issues of fairness among other considerations in relation to differential treatment suggests that Darlene is morally attentive to her judgements about "best interests" in ways that consequently would influence her practice.

For some teachers, the best interests of children are linked closely to idealistic goals of making a difference in children's lives, and helping them to become good people morally. Mrs. Johnson, a grade nine teacher from the "Moral Life of Schools" project, was shown to do this through a kind of "motherly caring" (Jackson *et al*, 1993, p. 156) that is evidently intentional and driven by her belief that her students, many of whom live harsh and difficult lives, "are far more vulnerable today . . . (and) need her nurturing in order to be better prepared for the challenges they face" (Hansen, 2002, p. 190). Middle school teacher, Kai, stated that, "In the end, I guess I'd like them (the students) to be the best human beings that they can be. If they don't learn anything else, then I would like for them to just be good people, know how to treat one another, respect themselves" (Richardson & Fallona, 2001, p. 717). In fact, all of the other teachers in the "Manner in Teaching" project as well as Kai "seem to share the aim of trying to help students become good people, a conviction that again spotlights the person in the role" (Hansen, 2001, p. 734). The concepts of shared aims and conviction imply that these teachers are not only strongly motivated to exert a positive moral influence on their students, but also aware of this goal and how it drives their interactions with the students.

The same is true in Simon's (2001) research; she discusses teachers as being "moral guides" and reports that "all the teachers I interviewed see themselves in that role at least to some degree" (p. 192). So too did all of the teachers in one of my projects (Campbell, 2003); they spoke at great length about their role as moral agents and educators and how an ultimate goal is to prepare students for a morally sound life in the future. And, they spent endless hours in class, often in unplanned, spontaneous, and reactive situations, emphasizing moral "lessons" about respecting others, developing empathy, being honest, and so on. As one high school teacher said, "Who knows, but I'm optimistic, and if I can reinforce in them the right behaviour, at some point in their lives, they'll get it. They'll understand" (Marissa, in Campbell, 2003, p. 56). Some connect this to a larger societal obligation in that they feel it is their responsibility to help students develop into good citizens (Tirri & Husu, 2002) who will be able to "function in a society like ours" (Shannon, grade three teacher, in Campbell, 2003, p. 48).

Closely related to the conceptualization of the teacher as a moral guide, is the teacher as role model — a moral exemplar and moral model. Many teachers discuss not only what they believe is the inevitability of this role, but also the desirability of it. They *want* to be positive role models, suggesting intentionality on their part, at least in a generalized way if not in each instance of every action; they recognize the importance of fulfilling this responsibility, and they are motivated by it. Ultimately, the kind of role model a teacher becomes is a reflection of his or her own character.

Speaking of the troubled lives and low self-esteem of his students, one teacher believes he provides them with a stabilizing influence and exclaims, "I have to be a role model . . . I have to be. Because I am one of the persons who affect the lives of the people that I teach" (Father Maran, in Hansen, 2002, p. 194). Also at the same high school, that has a "self-conscious intent to shape its students morally" (Hansen, 2002, p. 202) is Mrs. Johnson. Described previously as driven by a need to engage in "motherly caring," she is seen to "offer herself as a role model, who is unambiguous about the importance of trying hard, respecting others, and having hope for the future" (Hansen, 2002, p. 191). Similarly, teachers in the "Manner in Teaching" project discussed what they see as "conscious modeling" (Richardson & Fallona, 2001, p. 713); one of them, Darlene, was explicit about "how she models virtuous behaviour she wants the students themselves to develop" (Richardson & Fallona, 2001, p. 712). And, Simon (2001) "found that the teachers in the religion courses took very seriously their role as models of moral behaviour for their students" (p. 172).

This "modeling morality," as Simon describes it, is in these cases deliberate and intentional; it suggests a level of self-conscious awareness that teachers in my study also discussed quite consistently. As one stated, "I have to model proper ethical behaviour in terms of fairness, in terms of respect, in terms of honesty and just generally instilling some sense of kindness really. I mean the obvious point is to treat the students as I would want to be treated" (Judith, in Campbell, 2003, p. 37). Others spoke of being attentive to how they dress and how they speak to students as part of their concern about good modelling. However, as Colnerud (2006) points out, teachers are necessarily role models whether or not they are aware of it. And, not all teachers have the same level of ethical knowledge (Campbell, 2003). She believes the quality of their awareness ultimately determines the quality of the modelling relationship with students. Those with heightened awareness seem also to have the enhanced motivation to fulfill this role in exemplary ways.

In her summary of Kant's moral philosophy, Boss (1998) notes that, "A person of good will, according to Kant, has good intentions. They are motivated to act for the sake of duty" (p. 391). Whether or not duty is truly capable of motivating action has been debated, mostly as a philosophical but also an empirical question, for centuries and certainly will not be resolved in this discussion. Nonetheless, teachers do "live under an obligation to be as considerate and understanding as possible in dealing with their students . . . It is a moral duty" (Jackson et al, 1993, p. 292). And, many teachers have been shown to take very seriously their moral obligations to students; this is a result of their sense of duty, to paraphrase Gina's opening quotation at the beginning of this chapter. For example, Simon (2001) describes the weekly ritual of one of her teacher participants, Larry. At the end of each Friday afternoon, he says goodbye to his students by wishing them a good weekend and instructing them to "Stay sober!" He doubts that it has any real influence on them, but nevertheless believes it important that they know he is serious about his disapproval of their drinking habits. Simon concludes that, "whether it 'does good' or not, Larry sees it as his duty to express his care for his students . . . in this way" (Simon, 2001, p. 194). And, this sense of duty manifests itself in a variety of intentional actions the teacher feels compelled to take.

It is worth considering the potential influence that a sense of moral and professional duty can exert on a teacher's development of goals, aims, and self-established standards for his or her own conduct and that of the students. Those teachers with a heightened level of ethical knowledge are aware of how their goals and standards reflect moral imperatives. Many of the teachers in my "Moral Agency" project (2003) spoke "of the ethical intentions and judgements about their successes and failures in meeting self-established standards for being fair, kind, honest, and respectful to students. They spend a good deal of time and energy adjudicating in their own minds what these and other ethical principles mean in the complex and varying circumstances of school life. And, they are able to articulate moral rationales for their choices" (Campbell, 2003, p. 41). Similarly, Jackson, Boostrom, and Hansen (1993) describe the "moral climates" the teachers they studied created in their classrooms as being expressions of their own moral beliefs to which they "passionately subscribe" (p. 170). And, all of the teachers in the "Manner in Teaching" project were seen to "have a vivid conception of the kind of place they want their classrooms to be. Mutual respect, sharing, tolerance, orderliness and productive work are the notions most often mentioned by the teachers when describing their aspirations for their classrooms" (Fenstermacher, 2001, p. 642).

The goals that teachers establish, and the moral standards of conduct they hold themselves and their students to, are both the articulation of their overall ethical intentions and a motivating force for the way they interact with students. All of the empirical studies discussed here describe multiple situations in which teachers reprimand students for conduct that is unacceptable in their classrooms, such as ridiculing other students, or praise them for their kind, helpful, and honest behaviour. The "Manner in Teaching" project refers to such frequent episodes as "call-outs" and "showcasing" (Fenstermacher, 2001). While these are intended to serve an educative purpose for the moral instruction of students, other incidents in all of the studies show teachers monitoring their own actions as well. For example, many spoke of their conscious efforts to avoid embarrassing individual students and to be fair to all.

For some teachers, the motivation for treating students in what they see as moral or ethical ways is not only driven by personal caring or a sense of professional duty, but also by a fervent belief in students' fundamental rights. For example, one of the "Manner in Teaching" teachers believes students have a right to be given a rationale from her about "why" she teaches in the way she does, and she spends a good deal of time explaining this to them. The researchers conclude that, "This goal goes beyond being a means to an end. Providing the whys seems to be a moral necessity for her, as a teacher" (Richardson & Fallona, 2001, p. 710). In my own study (Campbell, 2003), teachers spoke about the "right" of students to feel safe in class without being ridiculed, singled out, or embarrassed by the teacher or anyone else; the right to an appropriate education for all children regardless of differences in ability; the "right to be informed of their marks for everything they do and their right to question the teacher, without fear, about any errors in the grading or calculating of marks" (p. 35); the right to have their property, work, or "stuff respected" (p. 41) that compels one teacher to find a way to keep all unclaimed student work for as long as the student remains in the school, even for years, despite a lack of storage space. For such teachers, their belief in student rights is a kind of personal moral conviction that serves as a compelling force to motivate their daily and sometimes fairly routine decisions and actions.

Compelling forces like those reviewed here – the aspiration to serve the best interests of children, make a difference in their lives, and help them develop into morally good adults, the need to conduct oneself at all times as a moral guide and role model, the sense of professional duty, the need to honour self-established moral goals and standards, and the conviction that students have rights that should be upheld — are internally fueled by each teacher's character and conscience. They are often also rooted in prior experiences that they have had, both positive and negative, as children, students, and student teachers. As Buzzelli and Johnston (2002) claim:

> Would-be teachers come to our teacher education programs with their own views and notions about teaching and about the teachers they hope to become. They have shaped their views through their own experiences in schools. Some may want to emulate teachers who have encouraged and inspired them; others may want to be teachers as a form of resistance, to change teaching practices they experienced and felt were intolerable. (p. 132)

Certainly, the student teachers interviewed for my study discussed at great length and with a clear sense of moral outrage the negative examples of teaching they had witnessed such as gossiping about students and their families, assessing student work dishonestly, treating students unfairly, publicly frightening, ridiculing, or disparaging students, neglecting their wellbeing, and misrepresenting curricula. As one of them stated emphatically, "I don't want to become like them (teachers she witnessed)" (Campbell, 2008c, p. 12).

Moral outrage, seen to be a motivating factor for moral action (Boss, 1998) lingers well into teachers' future practice as well. Experienced teachers in my study of moral agency (Campbell, 2003) recalled negative experiences they themselves had as students long ago. One teacher spoke of a teacher who continually made fun of her academic ability and called her stupid in front of the class; another had her read aloud sections of the textbook that she could not pronounce well because of her accent and the embarrassment this situation caused her. She explained that, "It's extremely important that I don't do that to any student" (high school teacher Carol, in Campbell, 2003, pp. 39–40). Another high school teacher, Marissa, had a similar experience when she was in grade nine with a teacher who bullied her; she stated, "This crushed me, and I don't want anybody in my class to ever feel that way" (p. 40). Richardson and Fallona (2001) wrote of one teacher whose father was a teacher with a very "severe" style; she said that all her teachers were similarly harsh and demanding and that, as a consequence, "she has attempted to right this wrong as a teacher" (p. 710).

Happily, past experiences that serve to motivate teachers to conduct their own practice in moral ways are not uniformly negative. Richardson and Fallona (2001) describe Kai, whose decision to go into teaching was influenced by the thought of her own "loving and caring and nurturing" (p. 717) teachers she had as a child and her desire to emulate them. Similarly, Sanger (2001) introduces us to Baba X who references his own childhood experiences in his frequent classroom discussions of moral imperatives: "I translate everything my Momma's ever done into my lesson plans somewhere, and wisdom somewhere" (Baba X, in Sanger, 2001, p. 693). It is not surprising that teachers recall past experiences as children both in and out of school in their reflections on their present interactions with children in their classes. It is notable that the strength of their memories helps to inform the moral motivation that guides their work as moral agent teachers.

The purpose of this section has been to consider the moral motivation teachers feel as they carry on in their daily practice — to ponder what it is that drives them to teach fairly, honestly, and with care and practical wisdom, and what compels them to engage their students respectfully and responsibly in moral lessons that abound in classrooms in planned and unplanned ways. Such forces include idealistic goals relating to helping children and serving their best interests, a dedication to broader societal goals by enabling students to become "good people," a desire to be a role model, a sense of professional duty, a commitment to self-established standards, and a belief in students' fundamental rights. Teachers speak of these forces as being influenced by personal and professional memories — good and bad — of past experiences as students and student teachers themselves. Such forces inform teachers' ethical intentions that underpin their daily practice in the classroom. The motivation, it seems, is entirely intrinsic; it springs from the very being of the people they are — from their characters.

MOTIVATION FROM WITHIN: CHARACTER AND CONSCIENCE

Virtuous people have a well-developed moral character. Virtue is integral to their self-concept . . . Virtuous people place moral motives above other considerations. They do not have to consider their motives before rushing to save someone in distress. (Boss, 1998, p. 413)

It is often presumed that teachers such as those described in the previous section are naturally good people drawn to the vocation of teaching by an inner sense of care for children and desire to exert a positive influence on their lives. Like Boss' definition of virtuous people, their moral motives are an intuitive extension of their personal character. And, this character is essentially formed as a defining personal quality long before teachers are initiated into their chosen career. While I believe the presumption of the teacher's natural goodness is arguable, it makes sense to accept that those entering teacher education programs do indeed have some kind of moral and ethical foundation as human beings (Buzzelli & Johnston, 2002; Fenstermacher, 2001; Joseph & Efron, 1993; Sockett, 1993).

In my study of the curricular inclusion or lack of inclusion of professional ethics and the moral aspects of teaching in pre-service teacher preparation programs, the student teacher and novice teacher participants I interviewed uniformly asserted that ethics, professional or otherwise, is a matter of personal character and "common sense." As one commented, "unless I am ethical, I believe that integrity is something that I need to stick to, I don't think that any amount of faculty training is going to help me get there . . . I think that all morals are already in you and that you are not going to pick this up from a course. I don't think that a course is going to teach me how I should be treating people from a moral or ethical standpoint" (Campbell, 2008c, p. 14). The sense of morality and ethics that they believe influences their intentions and actions as teachers is perceived to be personally cultivated based on their own intrinsic nature or character, their family and upbringing, and their life experiences. Four other novice teachers from the same research study offered the following beliefs:

> Most of my ideas (about ethics) were kind of ingrained in me and were probably pre-set before going into teachers college . . . I was lucky enough to have parents who raised me with morals and ethics. I think a lot of it comes from the people I interact with, the teachers I've had too who have been good . . . When I was a kid, my parents brought us up on good morals. I mean I live my every day by them. I think if you didn't have any to start with it must be hard to get them . . . To be honest, it's sort of something that you have to live and breathe. Do you know what I mean? I think it's hard for me to actually break down what is ethical in my teaching practice and what is not because I go in there everyday and *I live what I teach*, and this has to do with my background before my teacher training and being raised with a very good set of morals instilled in me, and I think that comes out in my teaching practice: everything from what kind of materials I present to my students to where I sit them in the classroom to how I speak to them is very important. (Campbell, unpublished data from the "Cultivation of Ethical Knowledge" project, 2005–2008)

These sentiments reinforce the importance of Osguthorpe's (2008) claim that teachers should be of good disposition and moral character. He notes, "we want morally good teachers because we want morally good teaching. We want teachers to teach in moral ways, to allow their moral inclinations to inform their practice" (p. 293). Similarly, this line of thought echoes Sockett's (1993) important point that the individual character of a teacher is a critical component of professional virtue and that it is "impossible to give a comprehensive account of what a teacher does without describing the person within the teaching act" (p. 7). Others have also remarked on "the centrality of the person in the role of teacher" (Hansen, 2001, p. 729); Hansen goes on to explain, "the reason why the person in the role matters so decisively is that the moral and intellectual efficacy of the methods pivots around who the person is" (p. 734). And, in one of their empirical studies, Tirri and Husu (2002) concluded, "teachers cannot separate their own moral character from their professional self.

Teachers' moral character functions as a moral approach in teachers' reasoning, guiding their ways of interaction with others" (p. 78). Ultimately, "...qualities of personal character would appear to play a significant role in the professional conduct of teachers" (Carr, 2007, p. 369). Like the novice teacher in my study who believed that she lives what she teaches, Jackson, Boostrom, and Hansen's study (1993) concluded that the teachers they observed all seemed to reflect the popular saying, "We teach ourselves" (p. 285). So, if, as Boss (1998) claims, "the motivation to behave morally is intimately tied in with how we define ourselves" (p. 224), then the motivation for teachers to engage in moral practices in their classrooms seems likely to come from within themselves, as an extension of their character.

It would seem that the human conscience is a mirror to one's character. It is a powerful motivator of moral action (Boss, 1998) and moral reflection (Buzzelli & Johnston, 2002). As Coles notes, "the conscience is the voice within us that has really heard the voices of others (starting with our parents, of course) and so whispers and sometimes shouts oughts and naughts to us, guiding us in our thinking and our doing. The conscience presses its moral weight on our feeling lives, our imaginative life" (Coles, 1997, p. 105). While we should be cautious in assuming that the characters of all teachers are uniformly positive in a moral sense, we can recognize the force of character in framing and even compelling their behaviour. One would hope that teachers whose practice is driven by their sense of conscience and whose self-understanding is filtered through an appreciation of moral and ethical principles such as fairness, honesty, care, respect, and integrity are better situated to fulfill their responsibilities as moral agents.

Sockett (1993) defines moral agency as a state in which "a person considers the interests of others, does not make discriminations on irrelevant grounds, and has a clear set of principles or virtues in which he or she believes and on which he or she acts" (p. 108). Moral agency is principle-based, exemplified in a teacher's conduct and daily practice, and reflective of a range of "dispositions" (Sockett, 2006) or virtues such as honesty, fairness, integrity, compassion, diligence, empathy, courage, and respect for others (Campbell, 2003; Colnerud, 2006; Fallona, 2000; Richardson & Fenstermacher, 2001; Sockett, 1992). The teacher as a moral agent (Buzzelli & Johnston, 2002; Huebner, 1996, Reitz, 1998) makes choices, uses judgement, cultivates inclinations, expresses intentions, and engages in actions and practices that illuminate the moral aspects of the curricular, pedagogical, evaluative, and interpersonal work that characterizes the inherent nature of teaching (Campbell, 2003; Jackson et al, 1993; McCadden, 1998; Simon, 2001). Intricately connected to the ethical imperatives that underlie the professional role of the teacher (Campbell, 2008a; Carr, 2000; Hostetler, 1997; Nash, 1996; Strike & Ternasky, 1993), moral agency is quite simply "that quality possessed by a person to act morally" (Fenstermacher, 2001, p. 650).

This quality, as I have argued previously (Campbell, 2003), carries a dual expectation with it for the teacher: "the first relates to the exacting ethical standards the teacher as a moral person and a moral professional holds himself or herself to, and the second concerns the teacher as a moral educator, model, and exemplar whose aim is to guide students towards a moral life. These dual characteristics of moral agency are obviously and inevitably interrelated as teachers, through their actions, words, and attitudes, may be seen to be living by the same principles that they hope students will embrace" (p. 2). Colnerud (2006) makes the same observation and refers to the "double set of reasons" for teachers to take heed of their own moral conduct (p. 373). In his essay on the need for teachers of good moral disposition and character, Osguthorpe (2008) similarly notes a commonly presumed causal relationship between the teacher as moral exemplar and the moral education and development of students.The teachers introduced previously in this chapter reveal attributes of moral agency in teaching.

For the moral agent teacher, the cultivation of conscience in one's students may be the ultimate goal of efforts to engage them in the moral world, whether or not this is perceived formally as "moral education." However, the conscience is also, as it was for Gina, in her worrying about being fair enough and responsive enough to students, the voice inside the teacher that judges his or her own actions and intentions. And, the conscience that the teacher listens to in order to guide personal and professional practice is likely grounded in the same virtues that the teacher seeks to impart to the students as integral to their own development of conscience. So, the teacher's character and the conscience that reflects it have a potentially pervasive influence in the classroom.

Whether teachers are actually aware of this influence and intentional in their exercise of it has been the source of some discussion (Buzzelli & Johnston, 2002; Campbell, 2003; Jackson *et al*, 1993). However, it seems plausible to regard some teachers' assertions that they "live what they teach" and "teach themselves" as indicative of at least some level of self-understanding and intentionality. Sockett (1993) argues, "many teachers have a moral vision, a moral sense, and a moral motive (however mixed up it may be in any individual person)" (p. 14). He believes psychologists would see this as "intrinsic motivation." If moral sense or vision, as an expression of one's character and conscience, provides a basis for motivation, intentions based on it must inevitably hover over one's practice, even if they seem to be at times unspoken, unplanned, or unrecognized.

Even in the many classroom moments when a teacher's specific intentions may not be obviously apparent, more general moral intentions in the form of overall goals, aims, and aspirations may well be infused into all that the teacher does as an extension of who he or she is as a moral agent. Influenced by character and conscience, the teacher is compelled to initiate as well as respond to a staggering range of curricular, pedagogical, and interpersonal situations. Many of these cannot be methodically planned or formally anticipated. Yet, to suggest that, as a consequence of the often-spontaneous nature of teaching, teachers are neither conscious of nor deliberate about how they conduct themselves in such moments may be to considerably underestimate the motivating power of their moral sense or vision, to recall Sockett (1993).

Some teachers have shown a profound level of awareness or astuteness of how the nuances of their actions, whether part of a formal lesson or a result of an unplanned classroom exchange, reflect their attentiveness to moral and ethical principles or virtues. In my study of such teachers, I have identified this capacity to recognize and honour abstract virtues as they are embedded in the specifics of the practice of teaching as "ethical knowledge" (Campbell, 2003). As I have written elsewhere, "Ethical knowledge is a personal and professional capacity that compels teachers to examine their own conduct and question their own intentions and actions. It requires them to apply a virtue-based lens to their professional experiences in order to anticipate and understand how moral and ethical values such as justice and fairness, honesty and integrity, kindness and care, empathy and respect for others can be either upheld or violated by seemingly routine and normative practices" (Campbell, 2011, p. 82). Such practices include choosing curricular materials, deciding on preferred pedagogical techniques, assessing and evaluating students, engaging in disciplinary practices, and navigating the social and interpersonal landscape of teaching: in short, any "aspect of their daily practice that has the potential to influence student well-being emotionally, intellectually, and physically" (Campbell, 2008c, p. 4).

Those with a keen sense of ethical knowledge clearly articulate their understanding of moral conduct and often trace it back to prior experiences and formative lessons they believe have influenced their own character. And, they have found ways to relate their personal virtues to their professional work. Although not using the language of "ethical knowledge," Buzzelli and Johnston (2002) have made a similar observation in their argument that, "the first morally significant feature of classroom interaction is that it involves teachers' personal and professional beliefs and values and the way they are enacted in the public setting of the classroom. Teachers continually make judgments about what to teach and how to teach, and such judgments involve deeply held beliefs and values" (p. 12). The teacher's making of moral judgements, the application of virtue-based perspectives to elements of practice, and the articulation of one's awareness of doing these things, either in a general sense or in a more specific situational respect, all seem to indicate that many teachers carry with them ethical intentions that drive their professional work.

CONCLUSION

The focus in this chapter has been on teachers who have been recognized for their moral orientation to teaching, not on all teachers as a uniform group. There is clearly empirical evidence to show that there are still many examples of unethical conduct in schools (Campbell, 2003, 2008c; Colnerud, 1997; Tirri, 1999; Tirri & Husu, 2002). In some of these studies' empirical examples that reveal teachers' failure to act in morally and ethically defensible ways, there seems to be a lack of moral motivation on their part. Or, perhaps it is that teachers, caught in ethical dilemmas caused by the dynamics of the collective school culture, are negatively motivated or, in other words, motivated not to take moral action. Specific reasons for such negative (as opposed to moral) motivation may vary; however, most seem to relate to the pressure of group norms to behave in certain conforming ways, even when they are not moral ways, and to a very real fear about taking moral stands in isolation of one's colleagues or, even worse, against them (Campbell, 2003; Colnerud, 1997; Tirri & Husu, 2002). As Boss (1998) notes, "many otherwise good people know what is right and are sensitive to the moral issues involved; however they lack the motivation to put this knowledge into action or praxis . . . Group mores can also weaken our motivation to do what we know is right" (pp. 223–224). The tendency for teachers to avoid moral actions if they require going against other teachers and exposing their ethically problematic practices has been addressed in the research as "collegial loyalty" (Campbell, 2003; Colnerud, 1997); teachers try to avoid engaging in interpersonal conflict with those with whom they work for their own personal reasons; "some allude to an overwhelming feeling of powerlessness and cowardice, fear and self-preservation, as well as a lack of clarity about limits of professional responsibility" (Campbell, 2003, p. 85). The desire to maintain harmony and avoid personal conflict with administrators and parents, as well as colleagues, can seem to trump one's motivation to pursue the right course of action, to the extent that Colnerud (2006) concludes from her research that "teachers' actions often seem to conflict with their own conscience" (p. 377). In this regard, the internal motivation to conduct oneself morally and ethically based on the driving force of one's inherent character and the insistent voice of one's conscience dissipates.

By contrast, the teachers described in this chapter are represented as those whose actions are driven by "something inside me that just said, go with what is true and right" (Marissa, in Campbell, 2003, p. 76). Some of them may also experience from time to time moments of negative motivation as discussed above. However, the research does not clarify this, so the complex question about the consistency and integrity of moral motivation within individuals remains empirically open and unresolved. Nonetheless, anecdotally and philosophically, the researchers do report that teachers have "multiple reasons" (Fenstermacher, 2001, p. 648) for saying what they say and doing what they do. These reasons are inevitably based on the moral sensibilities that the teachers themselves embody. Having reasons implies a level of ethical intentionality on their part. It may be that their intentions are mostly generalized reflections of their overall moral vision and a pervasive sense of moral purpose that come out in often spontaneous and unplanned ways. Or, their intentions may be more deliberately executed in the details of their specific actions, and their capacity to articulate this is an expression of their ethical knowledge. As McCadden (1998) claims, many teachers do "sincerely want to do the right thing . . . as they understand it" (p. 15) even though it is not always easy. They may have what Buzzelli and Johnston (2002) refer to as "moral commitment" (p. 14). And, commitment, like ethical intentions, is surely a strong component of moral motivation in teaching.

NOTES

[1]   I gratefully acknowledge the Social Sciences and Humanities Research Council of Canada for its support of this research.

REFERENCES

Boss, J. A. (1998) *Ethics for life: An interdisciplinary and multicultural introduction.* Mountain View, CA: Mayfield.

Buzzelli, C.A., & Johnston, B. (2002). *The moral dimensions of teaching: Language, power, and culture in classroom interaction.* New York & London: Routledge Falmer.

Campbell, E. (2003). *The ethical teacher.* Maidenhead, UK: Open University Press McGraw-Hill.

Campbell, E. (2008a). Teaching ethically as a moral condition of professionalism. In L. Nucci & D. Narváez (Eds.),*The international handbook of moral and character education* (pp. 601–617). New York: Routledge.

Campbell, E. (2008b). The ethics of teaching as a moral profession. *Curriculum Inquiry,* 38(4), 357–385.

Campbell, E. (2008c). Preparing ethical professionals as a challenge for teacher education. In K. Tirri (Ed.), *Educating moral sensibilities in urban schools* (pp. 3–18). Rotterdam: Sense Publishers.

Campbell, E. (2011). Teacher education as a missed opportunity in the professional preparation of ethical practitioners. In L. Bondi, D. Carr, C. Clark, & C. Clegg (Eds.),*Towards professional wisdom: Practical deliberation in the 'people professions'* (pp. 81–93). Farnham, UK: Ashgate Publishing Ltd.

Carr, D. (2000). *Professionalism and ethics in teaching.* London: Routledge.

Carr, D. (2007). Character in teaching. *British Journal of Educational Studies, 55*(4), 369–389.

Coles, R. (1997). *The moral intelligence of children: How to raise a moral child.* New York: Plume.

Colnerud, G. (1997). Ethical conflicts in teaching. *Teaching and Teacher Education, 13*(6), 627–635.

Colnerud, G. (2006). Teacher ethics as a research problem: Syntheses achieved and new issues. *Teachers and Teaching: theory and practice, 12*(3), 365–385.

Fallona, C. (2000). Manner in teaching: A study in observing and interpreting teachers' moral virtues. *Teaching and Teacher Education, 16*(7), 681–695.

Fenstermacher, G.D. (1990). Some moral considerations on teaching as a profession. In J.I. Goodlad, R. Soder & K.A. Sirotnik (Eds.),*The moral dimensions of teaching* (pp. 130–151). San Francisco: Jossey-Bass.

Fenstermacher, G.D. (2001). On the concept of manner and its visibility in teaching practice. *The Journal of Curriculum Studies, 33*(6), 639–653.

Hansen, D.T. (2001). Reflections on the manner in teaching project. *Journal of Curriculum Studies, 33*(6), 729–735.

Hansen, D.T. (2002). The moral environment in an inner-city boys' high school. *Teaching and Teacher Education, 18*(2), 183–204.

Hostetler, K.D. (1997). *Ethical judgment in teaching.* Boston: Allyn and Bacon.

Huebner, D. (1996). Teaching as a moral activity. *Journal of Curriculum and Supervision, 11*(3), 267–275.

Jackson, P.W., Boostrom, R.E., & Hansen, D.T. (1993). *The moral life of schools.* San Francisco: Jossey-Bass.

Joseph, P.B., & Efron, S. (1993). Moral choices/moral conflicts: Teachers' self-perceptions. *Journal of Moral Education, 22*(3), 201–220.

McCadden, B.M. (1998). *It's hard to be good: Moral complexity, construction, and connection in a kindergarten classroom.* New York: Peter Lang.

Nash, R.J. (1996). *'Real world' ethics: Frameworks for educators and human service professionals.* New York: Teachers College Press.

Noddings, N. (2002). *Educating moral people: A caring alternative to character education.* New York: Teachers College Press.

Osguthorpe, R. (2008). On the reasons we want teachers of good disposition and moral character. *Journal of Teacher Education, 59*(4), 288–299.

Reitz, D.J. (1998). *Moral crisis in the schools: What parents and teachers need to know*. Baltimore, MD: Cathedral Foundation Press.

Richardson, V., & Fallona, C. (2001). Classroom management as method and manner. *Journal of Curriculum Studies, 33*(6), 705–728.

Richardson, V., & Fenstermacher, G.D. (2001). Manner in teaching: The study in four parts. *Journal of Curriculum Studies, 33*(6), 631–637.

Sanger, M.G. (2001). Talking to teachers and looking at practice in understanding the moral dimensions of teaching. *The Journal of Curriculum Studies, 33*(6), 683–704.

Simon, K.G. (2001). *Moral questions in the classroom*. New Haven & London: Yale University Press.

Sockett, H. (1992). The moral aspects of the curriculum. In P.W. Jackson (Ed.),*Handbook of research on curriculum* (pp. 543–569). New York: MacMillan.

Sockett, H. (1993). *The moral base for teacher professionalism*. New York: Teachers College Press.

Strike, K.A., & Ternasky, P.L. (Eds.). (1993). *Ethics for professionals in education: Perspectives for preparation and practice*. New York: Teachers College Press.

Tirri, K. 1999. Teachers' perceptions of moral dilemmas at school. *Journal of Moral Education, 28*(1), 31–47.

Tirri, K., & Husu, J. (2002). Care and responsibility in 'the best interest of the child': Relational voices of ethical dilemmas in teaching. *Teachers and Teaching: theory and practice, 8*(1), 65–80.

AFFILIATION

Elizabeth Campbell
Department of Curriculum, Teaching and Learning
Ontario Institute for Studies in Education
University of Toronto
Toronto, Canada

CHI-MING (ANGELA) LEE

IV. FEMALE PRINCIPALS' MORAL MOTIVATION AND THE MORAL ATMOSPHERE OF SCHOOLS

INTRODUCTION

Several scholars have emphasized moral domain as a critical component of school leadership. Fullan (2003) addressed principalship as a moral enterprise and school leadership as following moral imperatives. Sergiovanni (1992) stressed three dimensions of leadership called "head", "heart" and "hand", which are connected and interactive. The leadership of heart has to do with the person's interior world and moral facet, such as what a person believes, values, dreams about and is committed to. Furthermore, moral leadership of school principals is an issue that focuses not only on the individual or the circumstances of a particular campus but also on cultural and societal contexts. Schrader (2008) indicated that an important aspect of moral leadership is in recognizing self in leadership contexts, both personally and organizationally. The percentages of female principals in a number of countries constitute a tiny minority of principals overall. For example, the percentages of female principals in Taiwanese elementary, junior high and senior high schools were 27.20%, 28.38%, and 16.6% respectively in 2009. There is little gender-related research regarding school leaders and the moral domain conducted by scholars. It is valuable to visualize leadership research in a more expansive way and to reveal the increased diversity which exists in schools today, particularly through the moral experiences of female principals in a socio-cultural context.

Moral motivation is a central and complicated element of moral functioning. The topic of moral motivation addresses the question: *"why be moral?"* and *"What is it that motivates moral behaviour and prioritizes moral values over other concerns that people may have?"* (Walker, 2002, p. 358) From L. Kohlberg's liberal enlightenment stance, true moral understanding is self-motivating, sufficient to stimulate moral action but leaving gaps in moral life. (Kohlberg, 1981, p. 302; Walker, 2002, p. 358) Besides cognitive-developmental perspective, Schroeder, Roskies and Nichols (2010, pp. 72–78) indicated four comprehensive theories of distinctively moral motivation to answer the aforementioned questions. These were named the instrumental, cognitive, sentimental and personality theories. The instrumental theorists hold that people are motivated when they form moral beliefs about how to satisfy pre-existing desires; the cognitive theorists advocate motivation as a central part of moral judgment so that we have a reason to act in a particular way; the sentimental theorists stress sympathy and other feelings of affective domain usually

K. Heinrichs, F. Oser & T. Lovat (Eds.), Handbook of Moral Motivation: Theories, Models, Applications, 533–548.

as arousing people's moral behaviour; and the personality theorists display people's identity, disposition and virtues as closely related to their moral judgment and action. In theory, people with moral motivation, involving multiple dimensions of moral desire, rationality, sympathy and identity, will prioritize moral values over other goals and their moral behaviour will be self-motivated.

This chapter extensively examines moral motivation in real life situations. The researcher applied the concept of moral motivation to moral education in the school context and referred the work to female principals through conducting a qualitative study. The hypothesis was that being a principal is usually motivated by a moral vision and the vision spurs them forward. As a result, several issues need to be addressed. These are as follows: what is the school principals' moral motivation when they serve as a leader? Why are they "moral" or "immoral" when they face moral dilemmas and conflict in schools? What is it that motivates moral behaviour and prioritizes moral values over other concerns that they may have in schools? How does moral motivation affect their moral action and interact with other factors in practice? The researcher selected Taiwanese female principals as examples in order to examine their moral motivation and its relationship with moral judgment and strategies for fostering the moral atmosphere in Taiwanese elementary, junior high and senior high schools. The purposes were: 1. to explore female principals' moral motivation and moral judgment; 2. to understand what strategies female principals applied to foster moral atmosphere and its moral motivation of their schools; 3. to examine which factors, especially the interaction of gender and culture, influence female principals' moral leadership and moral motivation, as well as how to interpret the similarities and differences.

MORAL MOTIVATION, MORAL JUDGMENT AND MORAL ATMOSPHERE

L. Kohlberg's theory of moral judgment, employing a cognitive-developmental approach, reveals a close connection of moral motivation, moral judgment and moral action. Kohlberg's six stages of moral development are (Kohlberg, 1981, pp. 409–412): Level A (Pre-Conventional) including "stage 1 punishment and obedience" and "stage 2 individual instrumental purposes and exchange"; Level B (Conventional) including "stage 3 mutual interpersonal expectations, relationships and conformity" and "stage 4 social system and conscience maintenance"; Level C (Post-conventional and principled) including "stage 5 prior rights and social contract or utility" and "stage 6 universal ethical principles". Additionally, Kohlberg (1981, pp. 121–122) listed a table, entitled "Motives for engaging in moral action", fitting in with the above six stages, and stressed mainly the points as follows: stage 1 action is motivated by avoidance of punishment; stage 2 action is motivated by desire for reward or benefit; stage 3 action is motivated by anticipation of disapproval of others, actual or imagined; stage 4 action is motivated by anticipation of dishonor, that is, institutionalized blame for failures of duty, and by guilt over concrete harm done to others; stage 5 action is motivated by a concern about maintaining respect of equals and of the community based on reason rather than emotion; and stage 6 action is motivated by a concern for self-respect and self-condemnation for not violating one's own principles. Neo-Kohlbergian scholars also suggested that *"moral functioning is the result of four component processes: moral sensitivity, moral judgment, moral motivation and moral character operating together and in interaction."* (Thoma, 2006, p. 72)

Furthermore, Power, Higgins and Kohlberg (1989) revealed a positive relationship between institutional moral atmosphere and individual moral development. They constructed "stages of sense of community valuing*"* by assessing the moral culture of schools (Power, Higgins & Kohlberg, 1989, p. 119): stage 2 *"There is no clear sense of community apart from exchanges among group members…Community is valued as it meets the concrete need of its members"*; stage 3 *"The sense of community refers to a set of relationships and sharing among group members. The group is valued for the friendliness of its members."*; and stage 4 *"The community is perceived as an organic whole composed of interrelated systems that carry on the functioning of the group."* It shows that differing moral atmosphere indicates diversified moral motivation.

Consequently, moral motivation, moral judgment and moral atmosphere are all developmental by stages and interrelated. The researcher explored female principals' moral motivation, moral judgment and their visions of moral atmosphere of schools, and analyzed further their approaches and developmental stages based on the aforementioned theories.

MULTIPLE APPROACHES AND FEMINIST PERSPECTIVE OF ETHICS

Besides moral motivation theories, this article stressed both multiple approaches and feminist perspectives of ethics on moral education and school leadership. Shapiro and Stefkovich (2005) introduced a multiple approach of ethical paradigms, including the ethic of justice, the ethic of critique, the ethic of care and the ethic of profession, to assist educational leaders in grappling with complexities, uncertainty, and diversity. Similarly, the researcher conducted a two-year (Aug 2005-July 2007) study focused on the planning, implementation and evaluation of a character-based school culture (CBSC) project in Taiwan. The CBSC project integrated the principles of justice, caring and developmental discipline, which was multidimensional and suitable for the Taiwanese context (Lee, 2009).

The ethic of justice is part of a liberal democratic tradition (Shapiro & Stefkovich, 2005). Kohlberg's theory of moral developmental stages following the above tradition has had a profound impact on moral judgment. Kohlberg (1981) stressed that the philosophical assumption inherent in the moral stages is the concept of justice. Kohlberg, Power, Higgins-D'Alessandro and other colleagues constructed the Just Community approach beginning in the 1970s. The justice orientation is embodied in the democratic process and in the focus on moral discussions, consideration of fairness, rights and duties (Higgins-D'Alessandro, 1995).

The ethic of caring was borrowed from Gilligan's Morality of Care and Noddings's Caring approach to moral education. Gilligan advocated caring and relationship as an additional and essential moral dimension, and allegedly brought a stronger women's voice to the domain of psychological theory in order to reframe the conversation between women and men (Gilligan, 1982/1993, p. xxvi). Noddings (2003), in her book, "*Caring: a feminine approach to ethics and moral education*", uses caring to describe a certain kind of relationship or encounter. Caring is a mutually satisfying relationship between caregivers and cared-for persons, without regard to gender. She regarded modeling, dialogue, practice and confirmation as four components of moral education from the caring perspective (Noddings, 2002, pp. 1–21). Moreover, Tronto (1995, p. 112) stressed a feminine approach to caring needs to begin by broadening our understanding of both in terms of the moral questions it raises and the need to restructure broader social and political institutions.

The above approaches were in some respects in reaction to the "discipline" approach originated from the moral theory of Durkheim (2002), who identified morality as having three basic elements: the spirit of discipline, attachment to social groups and autonomy (Lukes, 1973, pp. 112–119). Durkheim advocated that discipline is essential to ensuring consistency and regularity of conduct and also a sense of authority, which serves to evoke the desired behavioural responses and also has a restraining effect (Durkheim, 2002, pp. 17–32; Saha, 2001, pp. 26–27). The Developmental Approach to Discipline is different from the Durkheimian"traditional" approach (Watson, 2008, p. 198). In general, while traditional discipline relies on authoritarian practice to control classroom and maintain school order, Developmental Discipline focuses on building respectful and cooperative relationships, establishing shared norms and goals and promoting moral discussion and reflection in order to establish a caring, just and democratic learning community (Watson, 2008, pp. 181, 197–198). In broad terms, it might be referred to as a 'moral approach' to instill discipline.

Various moral approaches to justice, caring and discipline share commonalties and are largely complementary (Lee, 2009). In Kohlberg's view, caring and justice were not two moral values that connected in the life cycle, but facets of the same morality (Power & Makogon, 1995). Gilligan asserted a two-voice model of moral maturity and addressed justice and caring as coherent moral perspectives or languages intertwined in dialogue with each other (Reed, 1997, p. 236). Feminist ethics transcend a purely feminine perspective and disrupt gendered dualism. It argues "justice is not possible without care; care without justice is oppressive." (Porter, 1999, p. x) Therefore, the researcher utilized the multiple approaches and feminist perspective of ethics for analyzing female principals' moral motivation and therelationship with moral judgment and strategies for instilling a moral atmosphere in schools. In addition, the researcher relied on five overarching themes that characterize feminist ethics to make a thorough exploration offemale principals' moral motivation and experiences as follows (Brabeck & Ting, 2000, p. 18):

1. the assumption that women and their experiences have moral significance;
2. the assertion that attentiveness, subjective knowledge, can illuminate moral issues;

3. the claim that a feminist critique of male distortions must be accompanied by a critique of all discriminatory distortions;
4. the admonition that feminist ethics engage in analysis of the context and attend to the power dynamics of that context; and,
5. the injunction that feminist ethics require action directed at achieving social justice.

TAIWAN EDUCATIONAL SETTINGS AND STRATEGIES FOR IMPROVING MORAL EDUCATION

Taiwan's educational system and moral education are facing great changes and challenges owing to an open, free and diverse society developing, beginning especially with the abolishment of Martial Law in 1987. There were three characteristics of changes and challenges (Lee, 2004): First, Taiwanese elementary and junior high schools had taught "*Morality*", "*Life and Ethics*" or "*Civics and Morality*" subjects for approximately five decades, beginning with the Nationalist Government's move from China to Taiwan in 1949. However, the government and certain non-governmental organizations (NGOs) have implemented revolutionary educational reforms since the 1990s. The main reason for educational reforms was to decrease the pressure being placed on Taiwanese students in National Entrance Examinations. Unexpectedly, one result of these momentous educational reforms for moral education was to move from a separate timetable subject to diversified and generalized morally related education. Therefore, certain educators believe this to be a turning point to redefine a new style of moral education, while others see it as a crisis owing to a lost heritage. Second, since conventional school ethics and authority structures have gradually eroded, the relationships between school administrators, teachers, students and parents are sometimes adversarial on Taiwanese campuses. The school atmosphere is varied owing to differing leadership and relationships. Third, traditional Confucian moral values and authoritarian-political ideologies have weakened, so schools are struggling to reconstruct a suitable and modern moral values system to replace them. There are a few Taiwanese scholars and educators who thought Confucianism to be similar to the modern theory of caring ethics. However, Noddings (2010, pp. 137–141) has clarified the differences between ethics of caring and Confucianism, at least in her view. She argued that Confucianism is a form of particularism which has emphasized the importance of virtues, prescribed roles and duties and the central duties of Confucianism are male-defined, while care ethics emphasizes female equality and relation between care-givers and care receivers instead of role-identified system. (Noddings, 2010, pp. 137–141)

In response to the aforementioned changes and challenges, the Taiwan Ministry of Education (TMOE) released the "*Moral and Character Education Improvement Project* (MCEIP)", which was drafted by the researcher, in late 2004, and amended twice, in 2006 and 2009. The program's main goals (TMOE, 2006) are: "*to facilitate the development of students' moral thinking and their ability to select, reflect on, cherish and identify with core ethical values and codes of conduct; to develop a character-based moral culture in Taiwanese schools, involving teachers, students, administrators, parents and community leaders; to strengthen the roles of parents and community leaders playing in schools' moral and character education; and to give non-political organizations, cultural and educational foundations, as well as the mass media, a larger role in schools' moral and character education."* Moreover, Lee (2008) conducted a TMOE project and provided ten respective and complementary dimensions of strategies and indicators for schools to implement and evaluate moral and character education. Those ten dimensions were characteristics of school, administrative leadership, teachers' professional development, resources integration, formal curriculum, informal curriculum, hidden curriculum, student progress, school atmosphere and sustainable development. The framework was available for the researcher to analyze female principals' strategies for fostering their schools' moral and character education.

School principals played a crucial role during the periods of Taiwan's educational reform, in particular regarding moral education. The route to become a principal takes at least ten years from being a teacher through examinations and training. The TMOE revised *"the Law of Compulsory Education for elementary and junior high schools"* in 1999 and this resulted in two significant changes for principals' selection systems. One was that central government empowered local governments in the systems; the other was that the principals' selection method previously controlled by governmental officials changed to a democratic form of voting by a committee, including representatives of teachers, students' parents, scholars and community leaders. The current system's advantages and disadvantages bear scrutiny, but there are certainly more challenges in moral issues and dilemmas for school principals because they need to coordinate various interests from teachers, students, parents, government and society.

RESEARCH DESIGN AND IMPLEMENTATION

This study focused on an inquiry into female principals' moral motivation and its relationship with moral judgment and their strategies for fostering school moral atmosphere in Taiwanese schools. In Asian culture, female principals usually confront more challenges than males because of existence of gender stereotype and inequality in society. Therefore, one of the main purposes was to examine which factors, especially the interaction of gender and culture, influence female principals' moral leadership and moral motivation. The researcher mainly applied a method of qualitative research interviews for this study. As a female Taiwanese scholar, the researcher has long paid attention to the theories of moral motivation, moral judgment, moral atmosphere and moral education. Particularly, she also focuses on the similarities and differences between feminism, culture and their interrelated issues concerning school leadership. Before the interviewing, the researcher consulted with eight scholars and principals in two symposia. Then, the researcher interviewed eight female principals and visited their schools from December 2008 to April 2009. The sample selection of participants in this study represented a purposeful rather than random sample. The criteria for the selection of participants were that all of them previously received awards as excellent principals or their schools received awards of excellence in moral and character education from TMOE in the previous three years. In addition, the researcher took diversity of certain variables into consideration, including educational level, school location, school size, principals' age, and principals' working experience.

A qualitative research interview relies heavily on the researcher as the primary instrument for obtaining data. The researcher visited eight campuses and conducted in-depth, open-ended and semi-structured face-to-face interviews with their principals. The principals introduced their campus and then provided a rich representation of their stories to the researcher. The researcher and the interviewees had a relaxed and kind dialogue during the visiting period (around two hours) due to the integrity of the researcher's prestige, knowledge, experience and trustworthiness. The researcher used a digital recorder to record interviews with the participants and reviewed carefully the transcriptions written by assistants. The participants in this study received a copy of the interview transcripts for review, clarification, and suggestions. The researcher utilized coding and then categorizing ideas and statements of experiences from the text based on theories of moral motivation, moral judgment and strategies of improving moral atmosphere to formulate analytic and interpret conclusions. The basic data of the interviewed eight female principals and the characteristics of their schools listed as Table 1. The researcher utilized code names for those principals interviewed with eight Confucian virtues, common used in Taiwanese society, in Chinese pronunciation. The similarities of those female principals were that they graduated from Teachers Universities/Colleges and have been educators for more than 30 years except a 23-year teaching experience of Principal *Ping*.

FEMALE PRINCIPALS' MORAL MOTIVATION AND ITS RELATIONSHIP WITH MORAL JUDGMENT AND STRATEGIES OF MORAL ATMOSPHERE

The main findings and discussions of this study to fit in with the research purposes were as follows.

Moral Motivation of Female Principals Were Derived from Passion, Voluntarism and Responsibility Respectively

Three of the female principals mentioned their moral motivation of being a moral leadership based on passion, voluntarism and responsibility. They all emphasized that becoming a principal is an arduous process so they need to inspire themselves with strong moral motivation to avoid giving-up. The researcher found that these

Table 1. Basic data of eight female principals and their schools

Code name (literal meaning)	Age	Being a principal in this school	School type	School location in Taiwan	Student enrollment
Principal *Zhong* 忠(loyalty to ruler or nation)	58	11 years	private girls' middle school	Taipei City (metropolis)	1200
Principal *Xiao* 孝(filial piety)	64	8 years	public junior high school	Taipei City (metropolis)	2200
Principal *Ren* 仁(benevolence)	55	11 years	public junior high school	Taoyuan County(urban)	1300
Principal *Ai* 愛(love)	52	8 years	public elementary school	YunlinCounty (rural)	1500
Principal *Xin* 信trustworthiness	54	7 years	public senior high girls' school	GaoxiongCity (urban)	2500
Principal *Yi* 義(justice)	64	11 years	public elementary school	Miaoli County (rural)	800
Principal *Ho* 和(harmony)	61	8 years	public junior high school	Taipei City (metropolis)	2200
Principal *Ping* 平(peace)	46	1 year	public junior high school	Xinzhu County(urban)	1200

principals share various sources of moral motivation: passion inclined to affective perspective, voluntarism inclined to personality perspective and responsibility inclined to cognitive perspective. Therefore, these principals' moral motivation was inclined to sentimental, personality and cognitive approaches without the instrumental one (Schroeder, Roskies& Nichols, 2010). In addition, the interviewed principals' moral motivation tended to Kohlberg's (1981) conventional and post-conventional levels of "Motives for engaging in moral action" without pre-conventional level.

> Principal *Zhong* mentioned, "…*I am an alumnus of this school, so I succeeded the leadership with passion. …And hope to promote efficiently moral and character education which is a traditional culture in my school.*"

> Principal *Ren* emphasized,"… *I insist 'equity in education for every student' as my core value.... To be a principal makes me like a superwomen who is able to rescue the minority of students.*"

> Principal *Ai* stressed, "…*You are compulsory to play the role well as soon as you are a principal. You are able to do something good for children. This is a responsibility of being a principal.*"

Female Principals Shared Comprehensive Moral Values as a Core of Moral Motivation

The principals stressed that they usually placed importance on a number of moral values as a core of moral motivation in their job as follows. Principal *Zhong* stressed justice, fairness and empathy. Principal *Xiao* stressed responsibility, honesty and respect. Principal *Ren* stressed equity and honesty. Principal *Ai* stressed responsibility, honesty, politeness and punctuality. Principal *Xin* stressed politeness, rule of law, respect, responsibility, and gratitude. Principal *Yi* stressed fairness, rule of law, respect, justice and harmony. Principal *Ho* stressed fairness, honesty and frugality. Principal *Ping* stressed honesty, courage and tolerance. Consequently, those moral values they stressed could be divided into and across three categories: justice (i.e. fairness, respect, rule of law, equity); caring (i.e. empathy, responsibility, harmony, tolerance); and discipline (i.e. honesty, confidence, punctuality, courage, politeness, gratitude, frugality). Those moral values shared comprehensive moral values as a core of moral motivation as well.

Female Principals Confronted Resembling Moral Conflicts and Made Decisions Based on Reason, Laws and Emotion, which would Influence their Moral Motivation

The majority of the principals indicated the moral dilemma as they faced mostly were conflicts of interests and rights between students and teachers, pressure from student parents' on school administrators, and proper ways to deal with incompetent teachers in schools. In addition, principals of high schools encountered a great pressure on how to keep balance between academic achievement and moral growth of students. For example:

Principal *Zhong* mentioned, "... *I faced a moral dilemma between an incompetent teacher's interest and students' rights of learning. Finally, I insisted students' rights with impartiality and led to the teacher's retirement.*"

Principal *Ping* mentioned, "...*The first year when I came to this school, I felt depressed last year because of distrust on my leadership from students' parents. They usually accustomed to principal's authoritarian methods misunderstood as efficiency. However, my professional major is psychological guidance and I stressed democratic leadership...*"

Principal *Ren* mentioned, "...*There are two main obstacles for principals to promote moral and character education. One is there is no time for implementing moral education in class due to timetable curricula to be highly concentrated for the National Entrance Examinations. The other is a conflict sometimes existed between traditional teaching/discipline and modern human-rights education, i.e. regulations of students' hair and uniform.*"

Besides, almost all the principals emphasized they usually based moral judgment and decision-making with consideration to three elements, namely, reason, laws and emotion when they faced moral dilemmas. Therefore, the female principals' moral judgment depended on a balance with multiple approaches considering justice, caring and discipline. Furthermore, their moral judgment and moral motivation were interwoven together.

Female Principals had Resembling Visions of Moral Motivation for their School Moral Atmosphere

The interviewed principals advocated with one voice that their schools were to be a moral atmosphere with rationality, confidence, respect, self-identity, autonomy and sharing. For example:

> Principal *Zhong* mentioned, "...*I'd like to construct a school atmosphere with mutual trust between administrator, teachers and students.*"

> Principal *Ren* mentioned, "...*I inspire students' rationality and autonomy through all the curriculum and school activities.*"

> Principal *Xin* mentioned, "...*I hope to build a school culture of sharing for all members and taking part in school activities. We voted for the ethical core values of our school.*"

> Principal *Yi* mentioned, "...*Although my school is situated in a rural district and the majority of my students' family backgrounds are disadvantaged, I am devoted to providing a platform for students to perform their talent. It improves their self-identity, confidence and respect for others by means of combination of moral education and traditional artistry, like Hakka songs and diabolo skills.*"

Therefore, the principals' visions for their school stressed sharing and participating and corresponded to the stage 3 and stage 4 of "stages of sense of community valuing" of moral atmosphere and moral motivation (Power, Higgins and Kohlberg, 1989).

Female Principals Fostered their School Moral Atmosphere and Moral Motivation by Fruitful and Creative Strategies

The principals indicated that their strategies for fostering moral atmosphere and consolidating moral motivation were being role models, caring for students and teachers, empowering teachers, cooperating with parents and community leaders, cultivating a comfortable and aesthetic physical environment, infusing moral and character education across all subjects and students' extra-curriculum, offering opportunities of critical thinking and experience-learning to students, and strengthening students' conventional practice. For example:

Principal *Ai* stressed, "...*I think it's the most important thing for a principal as a role model for teachers and students.*"

Principal *Xiao* stressed, "...*I believe emotion is very crucial in moral and character education. To be a good principle, you need to have affections and love to your school, including education itself, students and teachers. You also need to be emotional-responsive to all of them.*"

Principal *Ren* mentioned, "...*We provide a number of creative and various extra-curriculum, i.e. Camp of Astronomy and Boy/Girl Scouts, instead of ordinary memory and test classes in summer/winter vacations to foster intellectual and moral development of students. In addition, I would like to build a caring campus in my school. Several years ago, I took the initiative in encouraging teachers to donate NT$ 100 (around US$ 3) every month to help the disadvantaged students. It has done a great contribution in my school.*"

Principal *Ho* mentioned, "...*I consider there is a close linkage between moral education and all the academic subjects. Therefore, I endeavour to infuse moral lessons into all subjects and provide opportunities and environment for students' inquiry, thinking and experience.*"

Comparing Lee's (2008) ten respective and complementary dimensions of moral and character education, the principals' strategies for fostering moral atmosphere and consolidating moral motivation manifested a number of dimensions in characteristics of school, administrative leadership, teachers' professional development, resources integration, formal curriculum, informal curriculum, hidden curriculum, and school atmosphere. However, they failed to mention strategies of how to improve and evaluate student progress, and how to promote sustainable development of school moral/character education.

A Few Female Principals Uncovered the Dark Side of Moral Atmosphere and Collision of Moral Motivation in their Present/Previous Schools

Three principals disclosed their experiences of misunderstanding, capability being questioned and disappointment when they exercised their administrative responsibility. Such as:

Principal *Zhong* mentioned, "...*I was very rigid in teaching, administrative works and students' life of dormitory when I just received the principal leadership around ten years ago. Occasionally my anger scared some teachers and students. They misunderstood me as an authoritarian leader. However, I gradually become more and more moderate and democratic when I am getting older and more experienced.*"

Principal *Ren* mentioned, "...*I returned a subsidy of infrastructure to the local government at the first year when I came to this school due to some problems*" *of communicating with teachers. A number of teachers and student parents questioned my capability of leadership. I felt very frustrated at that time... Later I spent lots of time to learn how to do things properly and changed their impressions of me."*

Principal *Ho* mentioned, "*...I had a terrible experience at my previous school. I met a troublesome teacher who was the chairperson of teachers' association. He opposed most of my policies with no reasons and led to a hostile atmosphere between two groups of teachers and parents. I felt disappointed and then left the school finally because I did not want to compromise myself under the unreasonable pressure."*

Although the principals uncovered the dark side of moral atmosphere and collision of moral motivation in their present/previous schools, they all expressed that they insisted on their moral judgment and were supported by their moral motivation to conquer all the frustration and difficulties they faced.

FACTORS INFLUENCING FEMALE PRINCIPALS' MORAL LEADERSHIP AND MORAL MOTIVATION

A Number of Personal Factors Influencing Moral Experience and Moral Motivation of Female Principals

The personal factors, which influenced those principals' moral leadership and moral motivation, were approximately their educational background, experience of student clubs when they were at their colleges/universities, their administrative experience, encouragement and guidance of colleagues or senior principals, and moral development through in-service learning. For example:

Principal *Zhong* mentioned, "*...I was interested in Ethics when I had an in-service workshop regarding moral and life education. I learned what moral dilemma was and how to think over critical issues in school. It helped me in my moral leadership."*

Principal *Xin* mentioned, "*...I was a chairperson of student club when I was a University student. Those valuable experiences inspired me and induced creative ideas for me in applying to the practice of school leadership."*

Principal *Yi* mentioned, "*...We have regular meetings for principals' professional development supported by the local government. We meet each other for around every month. The functions of the meetings have two: one is to improve principals' knowledge in their profession through speeches and books-introduction; the other is to reinforce principals' enthusiasm for moral leadership through discussions and sharing with each other."*

The Structural Factors Influenced Moral Experience and Moral Motivation of Female Principals Disclosed Ideologies of Traditional Patriarchy and Gender Inequality

According to the interviews of female principals, there were two issues uncovering ideology of traditional patriarchy and gender inequality from feminist and cultural perspectives. One issue was almost all the female principals expressed they had never actively planned to be a school principal during their career due to family factors. They were usually encouraged by their colleagues or thanked for good luck to be a principal when they had fewer household duties over time.

Principal *Ren* mentioned, "*...I am a single-parent family with two daughters. I had to take care of them when they were young. Until they grew up I have sufficient time in school and take the job of principal...Now I don't need to cook for my family hurriedly like other female colleagues when getting off duty. I am able to stay in school until night or weekend without overtime pay.*"

Principal *Xin* mentioned, "*...The main reason why I become a principal was encouragement by colleagues. At the beginning, I did not have enough self-confidence and then I found myself with great potential. Sometimes I do not like administrative jobs because of exposure of human's negative nature during the process. However, I keep going on as there is no road back.*"

Principal *Ping* mentioned, " *...My father encouraged me to study National Taiwan Normal University because he expected me to be a principal in the future when I graduated from high school...However, I did not have the intention to carry it out until two years ago because my children were young and my husband were very busy in his job.*"

The other issue affecting most female principals' moral experience and moral motivation was how to insist their moral values and to refuse unnecessary social contact and activities outside the school when they were under certain pressure from parliamentarians of city/county or community leaders. For example:

Principal *Xiao* mentioned, "*...When I receive this leadership, I devote myself in this school with all my heart and avoid unnecessary matters outside of my duty...It is hard to insist on this principle.*"

Principal *Ho* mentioned, "*...I do not want to spend too much time to take part in several community activities which are not related to education as a result a number of students' parents and community leaders dissatisfy with mybehaviour. The existing regulation of principal selection is not beneficial for some principals, like me, who hope to concentrate on schools' affairs and educational profession.*"

Principal *Ping* mentioned, "*...As you know every Parliament member of local government possesses certain power to distribute budget and rights* *of interrogation during the sessions. Few principal dare to offend them intentionally in this culture. However, it is a great suffering and reluctance for me when some Parliament members invite me to have a drink. (note: heavy drinking and drunkenness)...I am still learning how to persist in my profession and conscience facing this situation."*

Female Principals Still Face Challenges of a Number of Cultural and Gender Issues on Moral Motivation

Taiwanese government proclaimed *"Educational Law for Gender Equality"* in 2004. However, the interviewed principals face changes and challenges of a number of cultural and gender issues, i.e., possessing gender stereotype and hard to implement preferential treatment for female teachers, in their schools. For examples:

Principal *Zhong* mentioned, "...*There are a number of excellent alumni of my school, who are doctors, lawyers and so on....However, there are some people ask me if our students are too independent to have happy marriages. I do not have the good answer to the question although we claim this is a modern society of gender equality in Taiwan."*

Principal *Xin* mentioned, "...*I think girls are more considerate than boys. I am fortunate to work at this Girls' school, so the environment of this campus is clean. ...My daughter suggested me not be a talkative principal because most Mom are talkative to their children."*

Principal *Yi* mentioned, "...*Sometimes I have to deal with a number of complaints from teachers regarding fairness. Such as there are teachers who take breast-feeding for their children, so they demand more time during lunch break to come back home or make preparation for their babies. However, it's hard for some teachers, who is single, male or doesn't have child, with empathy on this situation."*

CONCLUSION

This chapter focused on an inquiry into female principals' moral motivation to fulfill their moral leadership and its relationship with moral judgment and their strategies for fostering school moral atmosphere in Taiwan's elementary, junior high and senior high schools. The researcher mainly applied a method of qualitative research interviews and also paid attention to the similarities and differences between feminism, culture and their interrelated issues concerning moral leadership and moral motivation. The findings of this study were: 1. Moral motivation of female principals were derived from passion, voluntarism and responsibility respectively; 2. Female principals shared comprehensive moral values as a core of moral motivation; 3. Female principals' moral motivation confronted similar moral conflicts and made decisions based on reason, laws and emotion; 4. Female principals had resembling visions of moral motivation for their school moral atmosphere; 5. Female principals fostered their school moral atmosphere and consolidating moral motivation by fruitful and creative strategies; 6. A few female principals uncovered the dark side of moral atmosphere and collision of moral motivation in their present/previous schools; 7. A number of personal factors influencing moral experience and moral motivation of female principals; 8. The structural factors influencing moral experience of female principals disclosed ideologies of traditional patriarchy and gender inequality; 9. Female principals still faced challenges of a number of cultural and gender issues on moral motivation.

The results of this study are beneficial for educators and administrators to understand and communicate with female principals as well as to cultivate competent and morally motivated female principals. In addition, this study indicated that female principals' moral motivation is not only influenced by individual factors but structural ones. Finally, this article, based on a Taiwanese context, displayed the interrelationship between gender, culture and leadership on the topic of moral motivation. It showed up the importance of uniqueness, complexity and difference apart from educational theories and practices of mainstream, homogeneity and universality.

(This paper was partial results of a research project funded by the Taiwan National Science Council from August 2008 to July 2010. The previous version was presented at the 36th annual conference of the Association for Moral Education, St. Louis, USA in 2010. My gratitude goes to the editors' insightful comments and suggestions of this book.)

REFERENCES

Brabeck, M.M. and Ting, K. (2000). Feminist ethics: Lenses for examining ethical psychological practice. In M.M.Brabeck (Ed.), *Practicing feminist ethics in psychology* (pp. 17–36). Washington,D.C.: APA.

Durkheim, E. (E.K. Wilson & H. Schnurer, Trans.)(2002). *Moral education: A study in the theory and application of the sociology of education.* New York: Dover Publications.

Fullan, M. (2003). *The moral imperative of school leadership.* Thousand Oaks: Corwin Press.

Gilligan, C. (1982/1993). *In a different voice.* Boston: Harvard University Press.

Higgins-D'Alessandro, A. (1995). Educating for justice and community: Lawrence Kohlberg's vision of moral education. In W.M. Kurtines and J.L. Gewirtz (Eds.), *Moral development: An introduction* (pp. 49–81). Boston: Allen & Bacon.

Kohlberg, L. (1981).*The philosophy of moral development: Moral stages and the idea of justice.* New York: Harper & Row.

Lee, C.-M. (2004).Changes and challenges for moral education in Taiwan.*Journal of MoralEducation, 33*(4), 575–595.

Lee, C.-M.(2008).*Strategies and indicators for implementing and evaluating moral and character education in Taiwan's elementary and secondary schools.* Paper presented at the 34th annual conference of Association for Moral Education, November 13–16, South Bend: University of Notre Dame.

Lee, C.-M. (2009). The planning, implementation and evaluation of a character-based school culture project in Taiwan. *Journal of Moral Education, 38*(2), 165–184.

Lukes, S. (1973).*Emile Durkheim—his life and work: a historical and critical study.* New York: Penguin.

Noddings, N. (2002). *Educating moral people— a caring alternative to character education.* New York: Teachers College, Columbia University.

Noddings, N. (2003). *Caring: A feminine approach to ethics and moral education* (2nd ed.). Berkeley: University of California Press.

Noddings, N. (2010). *The maternal factor: Two paths to morality.* Berkeley: University of California Press.

Porter, E. (1999). *Feminist perspectives on ethics.* New York: Pearson Education Inc.

Power, F.C., Higgins, A. and Kohlberg, L.(1989). *Lawrence Kohlberg's approach to moral education.* New York: Columbia University Press.

Power, C., & Makogon, T.A. (1995). The just community approach to care. *Journal for a Just and Caring Education, 2,* 9–24.

Reed, D.C.(1997).*Following Kohlberg: Liberalism and the practice of democratic community.*Notre Dame: University of Notre Dame.

Saha, L.J. (2001). Durkheim's sociology of education: A critical reassessment. *Education and Society, 19*(2), 21–23.

Schroeder, T., Roskies, A.L. and Nichols, S. (2010).Moral motivation.In J.M. Doris and the moral psychology research group (Eds.), *The moral psychology handbook* (pp. 72–110). Oxford: Oxford University Press.

Sergiovanni, T.J.(1992). *Moral leadership: Getting to the heart of school improvement.* San Francisco: John Wiley & Sons.

Shapiro, J. & Stefkovich, J. (2005).*Ethical leadership and decision making in education* (2nd ed.). New Jersey: Lawrence Erlbaum Association.

Schrader, D.(2008). Teaching moral leadership In F. Oser and W.Veugelers (Eds.), *Getting involved: global citizenship development and sources of moral values* (pp. 227–248). Rotterdam: Sense.

Taiwan Ministry of Education (TMOE) (2006).*Jiaoyu bu pinde jiaoyu cujin fangan* [TMOE Moral and character education improvement program, MCEIP]. Retrieved on 4 February
2008 from: http://ce.naer.edu.tw/index3-1.html.

Thoma, S. (2006). Research on the defining issues test. In M. Killen and J. Smetana (Eds.), *Handbook of moral development* (pp. 67–91). New York: Erlbaum Associates.

Tronto, J.C. (1995). Women and caring: What can feminists learn about morality from caring. In V. Held (Ed.), *Justice and care: essential readings in feminist ethics* (pp. 101–116). Colorado: Westview.

Walker, L.J. (2002). The model and the measure: An appraisal of the Minnesota approach to moral development. *Journal of Moral Education, 31*(3), 353–367.

Watson, M. (2008) Developmental discipline and moral education. In L. Nucci & D.Narvaez (Eds.), *Handbook of moral and character education* (pp. 175–203). New York: Routledge.

AFFILIATION

Chi-Ming (Angela) Lee
Department of Civic Education and Leadership
National Taiwan Normal University
Taipei, Taiwan

PART 7

MORAL MOTIVATION AND MORAL EDUCATION

In this part, moral motivation is discussed in the context of education. Interestingly, education has a different theoretical basis than moral psychology and especially than moral development. Whereas these academic fields can describe moral motivation from a functional point of view, education is interested in intentional change. We could argue why then not put these chapters at the beginning of our handbook? We put them at the end because of their originality and theoretical rootedness in influencing, stimulating and guiding humans.

Kwok and Selman concentrate on students' informed social reflection to conceptualize and to teach moral motivation in schools. The ability to recognize the fullest range of social actions and their potential consequences, the social dimension of moral reasoning, is important because moral decisions typically involve others directly or indirectly. They claim that informed social reflection, historical understanding and ethical awareness should be integrated into civic orientation in order to have motivational impact that serves to trigger one towards (or against) acting in a particular way.

Althof and Berkowitz focus on character and citizenship education. They argue that educating for moral development (or more specifically moral motivation conceptualized in line with self-determination theory) cannot target individuals only but needs to address interpersonal relationships and social communities that shape the lives of humans as well.

Oja and Craig focus on professions that prepare students at the undergraduate level, such as, for instance, recreation management or teaching in order to internalize ethical standards. The authors advocate for the need to design internships carefully in order to develop moral motivation (e.g. cultivating professional ethical identity) leading interns to prioritize professional values over competing non-moral values. They prefer programs providing the student with opportunities to integrate classroom-acquired theory and skills in a working environment with a qualified practitioner.

Esteban and Burraixis proclaim that moral philosophy, moral education and moral motivation are in constitutive relationship with each other. Postmodernism can be understood as the result of a process, including as the consequence of a moral educational project. Moreover, they identify four motives for engaging in the moral education of new generations of citizens and they interpret these four motives in accordance with the philosophical debate previously noted between the individual (liberalism) and the community (communitarianism).

JANET KWOK & ROBERT L. SELMAN

I. MORAL REASONING, MORAL MOTIVATION AND INFORMED SOCIAL REFLECTION

INTRODUCTION

"The psychological rule says that when an inner situation is not made conscious, it happens outside as fate."- Carl Jung, Aion (1951)

If the development of moral motivation requires active engagement and inquiry, schools have been failing for decades to prepare young people to become moral citizens. Drawing an argument for human development as the aim of education over forty years ago, developmental psychologist and moral education theorist Lawrence Kohlberg described a troubling phenomenon made visible by his close friend and fellow University of Chicagoan Phil Jackson. An educational psychologist, Jackson creatively unveiled the "hidden classroom curriculum" (1968), or rather, the social and moral values underlying the rules, regulations, and goals traditional schools imposed upon students as a form of social control. These hidden or implicit values, Kohlberg claimed, are at odds with the maturation of ethical reasoning. High school students may be developmentally ready to explore the issue of protecting individual rights, an essential tenet of Western democracy that requires exploration and understanding to be upheld, but the school administration continues to insist upon structured directives to maintain order, motivated by the ascendant need for safety, control, and institutional rule (Kohlberg, 1970). Such anxieties prize dominance and order over the development of aware moral behaviour which is impossible without moral motivation. While some situations might merit command and control, students need to be given the opportunity to understand the forces of context, climate and culture. These can be built up through the encouragement of reflective engagement.

The "hidden curriculum," Jackson and Kohlberg argued, serves the rules of social reproduction —stay out of trouble, do your work— but not the dialogue that yields the capacity for informed social reflection (Selman & Kwok, 2010) necessary for the development of a reflective and engaged citizenry that will protect democracy and promote social justice. "The educational use of exposing the hidden curriculum is not to prevent the dialogue by calling classroom 'law and order' moral character, nor to cast it out on the ground that the child needs only freedom," Kohlberg wrote, "but to…bring the dialogue of justice into the classroom" (1970, pp. 123). Exposing the hidden curriculum asks schools and students alike to identify the various motivations

K. Heinrichs, F. Oser & T. Lovat (Eds.), Handbook of Moral Motivation: Theories, Models, Applications, 551–566.

behind daily school operations and expectations, even if they discover that these are anything but moral.

In this essay, we will explore how moral motivation can be better understood, supported, and perhaps even taught through developing students' informed social reflection (Selman & Kwok, 2010), the ability to recognize the fullest range of social actions possible for us, and their potential consequences. The social dimension (or orientation) of moral reasoning is an important component of understanding moral motivation because moral decisions typically involve others directly or indirectly and, as with the hidden curriculum, often occur in contexts where we did not create the rules. When looking back in time, informed social reflection allows us to understand the moral motivations and social orientations we access in order to decide looking forward in time to what options are available to us in interpersonal and civic situations, and which one we will ultimately choose as we navigate our social and cultural environment.

DO GOOD INTENTIONS REALLY PAVE THE ROAD TO HELL? MORAL MOTIVATION AND MORAL ACTION

Does moral behaviour come from moral reasoning? That is, if you have the capacity for moral reasoning, can one expect your actions to be moral? Micha Brumlik and colleagues' work (Brumlik, 1998; Brumlik, et al., 2000, cited in Oser, Althof, & Higgins-D'Alessandro, 2008) suggests that the answer is no: they claim that not only do delinquent and non-delinquent youth seem to display no significant differences in their moral reasoning stages, there also appears to be no association between moral stages and the seriousness of delinquent acts. In addition to these similarities in moral stages, Weyers (2002, cited in Oser et al., 2008) noted that non-delinquent and delinquent adolescents appear to have the same average intelligence level and similar social perspective-taking abilities. If moral reasoning capacity and intelligence do not appear to be the line between moral and immoral behaviour, what marks the territory?

Nunner-Winkler (1993) describes moral learning as comprised of the acquisition of moral knowledge – made possible by developmental changes in cognitive ability and the awareness of cultural expectations – followed by the process of establishing moral motivation. The latter's acquisition and expression varies across individuals, and it is this deeply idiosyncratic factor that explains how two people with similar backgrounds, with the same moral reasoning abilities and intelligence, might make vastly different moral choices in the same situation. Moral motivation is the "intrinsic desire to do what is right" (p. 411, Nunner-Winkler, 2007), and it is significant, she claims, because it is the crucial link between moral (and pro-social) action to moral reasoning: in other words, moral motivation is the leap from theory to practice, thought to action. Since one's moral motivation(s) are built in part upon individual reasoning, skills, and systems that are opaque to others, we will use informed social reflection as a microscope to see the moral motivation present or absent in an action.

Some clarification is required of the word "motivation": why not "justification"? ("Reasons" broadly captures all possible types of rationale for moral choices.) We have chosen "motivation" because we conceptualize moral motivation as occupying a causal role in moral decision-making: the individual applies his moral reasoning to the situation and *then* chooses to act based upon this information. "Justification" implies approaching moral decision-making as a retroactive process wherein the individual commits an action first and only afterwards chooses a reason to explain the action. This reason may be the one preferred by the individual or that seems most valid, but it may not be the *actual* reason that guided the action. "Motivation" emphasizes the catalytic dimension of moral reasoning that we have made the foundation of our exploration. As Inspector Clouseau of the Pink Pantherfilms declared in *A Shot in the Dark* (1964), "You are forgetting the most important fact: motive."

INFORMED SOCIAL REFLECTION: UNDERSTANDING MORAL REASONING IN THE REAL WORLD

In the instant (or instances) in which an individual must decide how to handle an interpersonal or civic (community) issue, she tacitly draws on the perceived range of available choices that are created, not strictly as a matter of her social cognitive maturity, but also from her informed understanding of her own past, the common past shared by those in her context, and the affordances and constraints of her experience of social context and culture. Clear is her awareness of, and reflection on how her choice will affect her and those in her close personal relationships and those beyond (Selman, 2003).

We have been able to articulate and understand informed social reflection through using a battery of hypothetical dilemmas involving cases of social exclusion and injustice. These scenarios are grounded in the reality of a past series of in depth interview studies of middle and high school climate, referring to actual incidents described by students (Feigenberg, Steel King, Barr & Selman, 2008; Selman & Feigenberg, 2010).

Through our interviews of students in middle and high schools and our observations of their school life, we identified situations that could serve to foreground ethical social relations (teasing, bullying, harassment, ostracism from cliques), civic issues and initiatives (mandatory school uniforms, racist graffiti on the walls) and historical consciousness (understanding the socio-historical basis for unfamiliar religions and customs as they were experienced in school). It has led us to portray a psychological picture of informed social reflection that draws upon the three primary colours of our definition [Figure 1: Informed Social Reflection and its components]: civic orientation, ethical awareness, and historical understanding (Selman & Kwok, 2010).

Informed social reflection is most effective in those instances in which moral motivation necessarily precedes moral actions: it allows the actor to understand his own ability and practice of understanding *before* action, not the retroactive

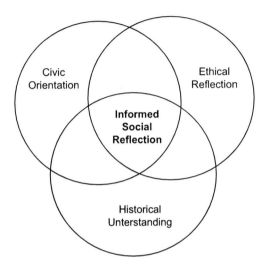

Figure 1. Informed social reflection.

justification of his actions, nor being at the mercy of one's evolutionary reactions and temperamental impulses. In its most complete form, informed social reflection parallels Jurgen Habermas' proposition concerning rational reconstruction through its integration of, on the one hand, what an individual believes to be the better and best (and less and least preferable) ways to act and react in a societal situation, and on the other hand, a fuzzier or clearer recognition of *how* she came to see those options as available to her (Outhwaite, 2009). Habermas conceptualized this kind of understanding by drawing upon Lawrence Kohlberg's six moral stages: when someone advances to a higher stage, she is required to refute the moral judgments she had once held to be valid at the previous stage through describing how and why she was equivocating (Habermas, 1995). Gaining this skill elevates one's orientation from one of personal action to social discourse: it is not that the individual has been transformed by environment or some cognitive quantum leap, but that she has had a cognitive shift of existing capabilities that has synthesized new solutions and directions (Habermas, 1995) in some specified period of time, be it chronological (as in ontogenesis over the life span) or situational (as in over the course of an incident, situation, or ongoing relationship).

It is not that the individual is justifying her actions after the fact so much as it is her perception of her environment and conceptualization of its related forces that affect how she and her peers interpret the options available to them. Habermas illustrates the directionality of this concept: "to act morally is to act on the basis of insight... Moral action is action guided by moral insight" (1995, p. 162). Yet, while rational reconstruction provides a worthy developmental approach to moral decisions, it does not address the crucial issue of how social context and development interact, or in other words, how moral motivation delivers moral action. It is here that informed social reflection allows us to see how some aspects of ethical conduct and moral reasoning interact with our social world and rules.

MORAL REASONING IN THE WILD: THE SOCIAL SIDE OF MORAL CHOICES

When we are confronted with a moral or ethical decision, our moral motivation is shaped not only by our access to our own highest level of reasoning attained through development (cognition) and through our discussion and debate (communication) as Habermas has suggested, but also by the societal and cultural forces that influence what actions we believe are available to us —these are the social orientations of our moral motivations. We might think of moral motivation as emerging from within ourselves interacting with the social factors acting from without. Although we are burdened by the formidable cultural, contextual and biological forces that inevitably shape our decisions, developing informed social reflection allows one to be more stable and more flexible through accessing a greater range of options in various social contexts, rather than rigid or labile in the moment of action. Informed social reflection allows us to become aware that we rely on *both* social and moral intelligence to make our choices, as well as how we act upon these types of information.

We posit from our own program of research, including this analysis, that we can reliably identify four distinct types of "sociological lessons" disseminated by the hidden curriculum of schools – and by extension, from society – that can motivate or guide students' perceptions of social and civic choices in school contexts, or in other words, their social orientations. The rational reconstruction of the options in the social world of school as a society or culture yields orientations predominantly toward: (A) Safety, both physical and psychological preservation; (B) Rules and Power; (C) Relationships and Need for Inclusion; and, (D) Societal and Civic Incentives (Feigenberg et al., 2008; LaRusso & Selman, 2011).

These Orientations can reflect the developmental aspect of an individual's social motivations: like a ripple on water, when thrown into the maelstrom of a moral dilemma, the individual usually begins the process of choice identification by running through the various possible immediate effects on oneself *before* broadening one's analysis to consider the potential consequences for others (Figure 2). With a supportive environment and opportunities to explore and experience the challenges and rewards of perspective coordination and interpersonal negotiation with others, the individual can begin to think of the consequences of his actions for those further removed from him, physically, psychologically, socially, and temporally. Not surprisingly, the "chronologically" later arrival (ontogenesis) of a more future focused or civically-minded orientation in adolescence dovetails with developmental neuroscience: not until well into the second decade of life is the prefrontal cortex fully developed in the regions which control planning (Geier & Luna, 2009) and the accurate assessment of perceived rewards and consequences (Romer & Hennessy, 2007). These Orientations represent reasoning that is rooted

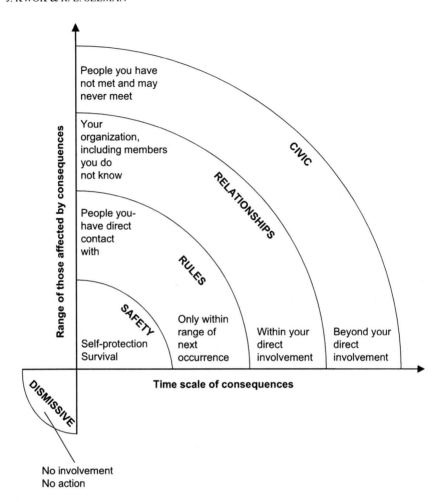

Figure 2: Four fundamental social orientations.

in but not necessarily direct reflections of the competencies of an individual. An individual could be developmentally advanced but may not express a fully Civic (i.e. fully contextualized) Orientation (D) for a variety of reasons, an issue which we will explore next in this discussion.

RECOGNIZING THE OFFSPRING: KNOWING WHAT TO LOOK FOR

As described above, we were originally able to understand and articulate the construct of informed social reflection through student interviews about the different kinds of problems students might experience at school. To understand how informed social reflection both makes us aware of and alert to the various social and moral tensions that influence our actions, we will use as an example an interpersonal difficulty surprisingly common in schools (Hoffman, 2010) for these internal and external tensions to act upon.

In the hypothetical scenario (representing the civic domain in Figure 1) presented below, participants in our studies are asked to *rate* each of the possible responses separately. Each strategy offered is meant to represent one of four types of civic *choices* that the individual imagines to be within the range of possibilities of ways to react in a societal situation: 'bystand', 'passive and active upstand', or 'escalate/retaliate'[1]. Then, they are asked to *rank* the best (and least preferable). Finally, they are asked to select the choice they think they would make if they were in that type of situation:

> Several students at your school have been targeted by anonymous threatening racist messages posted on a Facebook page for the school. The messages seem to suggest that they are sent from someone who knows the students from school. One of your friends is among the victims and has asked you for help. Among the following choices, which one would you do? [We have included our classifications of each response's type of civic choice, but these would not be included in the version distributed to students]
>
> a) Let the students deal with the problem. (Retaliate)
> b) Organize a school wide meeting to discuss racism. (Active Upstand)
> c) Offer to moderate the Facebook page to prevent re-occurrence. (Passive Upstand)
> d) Let the principal handle it. (Bystand)

Note that, on the surface, none of the options is necessarily inappropriate or uncivil[2]. It is important to remember that, in our program of research, a student is asked to both rate the effectiveness of each separately, and then rank (or compare) them. Finally, the students are asked which solution is the one to be chosen *in their own context* (that is, the school they attend), cleaving the meaning of "best" from the action to be taken. Often, students do not select what is to be done locally in alignment with how they rate each option in a highly de-contextualized (hypothetical) situation. For example, a student might rate the community meeting (Choice B, active upstand) as the best option in principle, but say that in their school, telling the principal (Choice D, bystand) is actually the best course of action. It is at this point that space is provided for the survey taker to tell us why. Using this method, we can obtain a glimpse of a student's own sense of what the relationship is between possibilities in thought and action or, more specifically, between moral motivation and moral action. Therefore, the method in actuality provides a way to take into account the respondent's recognition of how she came to see those options as available to her.

Our fundamental focus in this discussion will be on the students' selection of what choice (selected strategy plus the orientation of the written response) they would recommend for their *actual* school, and the reasons provided for this choice. We refer here to the students' stated reason for their choice as a (backward looking) *motivation*. We impose an Orientation (Safety, Rules/Power, Relationships, and

Civic) on the students' motivations in order to capture the moral and social factors driving students' choices.

In the attempt to assess informed social reflection, implicit is a reminder that by the stage of adolescence (by which time cognitive development has provided the "opportunity" that all orientations have "emerged"), a range of orientations is valid *only* for the current context. Each context presents a unique set of attractive actions by which to address the same dilemma, driven by a range of motivations. Students whose motivations are driven contextually or otherwise by a smaller range of available orientations may not make the optimal choice for their own well being or that of their community.

In the above scenario, describing the digital desecration of a Facebook wall, for instance, the student who imaginatively is able to attach motives to each "potential" choice and reject other choices based upon their related motives is moving toward demonstrating the ability to use well-informed social reflection. We should, however, avoid almost all temptation to only impose a hierarchy upon these responses, even though one fits.

Consider the following pairs of motivations provided for the same choice, in this case choice B (propose a school meeting to discuss racism), organized by two of the four (imposed) orientations. Now, Figure 3 [Figure 3: Orientations with examples of motivations] demonstrates that, although it is tempting to impose a hierarchical order of preference upon these orientations (i.e. options closer to the top rungs are "ethically better"), context still plays a crucial role. It may not, for example, make sense to use the broadest level of reflection in all cases, such as in one of imminent physical danger.

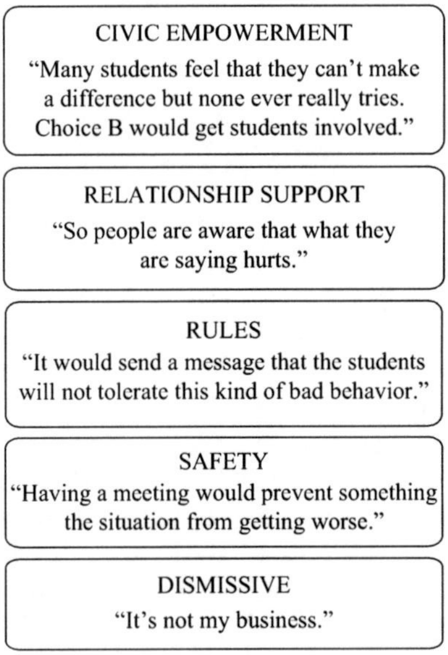

> **CIVIC EMPOWERMENT**
> "Many students feel that they can't make a difference but none ever really tries. Choice B would get students involved."

> **RELATIONSHIP SUPPORT**
> "So people are aware that what they are saying hurts."

> **RULES**
> "It would send a message that the students will not tolerate this kind of bad behavior."

> **SAFETY**
> "Having a meeting would prevent something the situation from getting worse."

> **DISMISSIVE**
> "It's not my business."

Figure 3: Orientations with examples of motivations.

Motivations tell us *why* you should or want to do something. The quality of one's informed social reflection is per Jung's quote, the awareness of how you arrived at that decision, and this is what needs to be understood and to be developed. But how can we do this?

THE LESSONS OF THE "HIDDEN CURRICULUM"

To more closely analyze the dualism of reflection and rational reconstruction, or, in our terminology, developmental and contextual affordances and constraints on social choices, let us turn to the comparative analysis of pairs of possible individual responses. Each response within the pair is drawn from a (real) student in an (imagined) different school, each with its own "culture."

Same "Objective" Choice, "Different" Motivations

Consider this pair of two motivations where two respondents selected Choice D ("Let the principal deal with it") but provided divergent justifications.

1. "If the students get involved they will fight. Leave it to an adult" (Safety)
2. "Because they don't know who did it even if they did, they're just kids. The culprit won't show respect or even be scared of a fellow student. You need some kind of authority." (Rules/Power)

These respondents have selected the same action, but their expressed motives appear to be quite different. The first respondent dismisses any obligation to the community without further explanation, and chooses to deflect responsibility to authority. The second respondent directs, but does not deflect, responsibility to authority in order to guarantee order and care for the community that he or she feels cannot be obtained otherwise.

Now, for the moment returning to our initial discussion of the "hidden curriculum," suppose Respondent 1 attended a school where command and control was the cultural and sociological orientation owing to many previous incidents of violence. In that circumstance, it would not be surprising if the average Orientation of the student responses from that school sample was Safety. If Respondent 2 attended a School wherein order and discipline were the rule of the day, such as in the archetypal military school, it would not be surprising if student B oriented toward Power/Rules. The first respondent's reasons for suggesting a motivation with a Safety orientation are unknown, but perhaps it points toward self-protection through keeping one's distance from conflict, and the second response draws upon the need for authority and order. Can we really say with certainty where each response sits in a developmental hierarchy? Schools, parents, internalized moral maturity, cultural norms, lived experience, or their emotions at the moment of answering the question can all play a part in how the respondent arrived at the answer. Individually, it is hard to know, but with larger samples comes greater understanding of the distribution (and meaning) of responses.

Different Choices, "Similar" Motivations

Examine, now, respondents who selected different choices but provided motivations with similar orientations.

3. Choice B ("Organize a meeting to discuss racism"): "Many students feel that they can't make a difference but really none ever really tries. Choice B would get students involved." (Civic Empowerment)
4. Choice C ("Offer to moderate the Facebook page"): "The people who wrote those things will probably not come out and say that they did it, and there will be nobody to stop it from happening again. Changing the Facebook page will send a message that students won't stand for that kind of stuff" (Civic Empowerment)

Although these two respondents have selected different actions to address the digital vandalism, both responses appear to share the same motivation, an orientation toward students achieving and demonstrating student responsibility and mutual care. These two students may have different *reasons* for their selections, such as locating the trauma of the event in the psychic versus the physical or social domain, but the responses appear to be in the service of seeking the same result. Both seem to believe that there are opportunities for civic participation in their school, but they interpret the mechanism of civic action differently. Suppose Respondent 3 attended a school which had a preponderance of Orientations coded as Relationships, whereas Respondent 4 attended a school where the overall Orientation was Power/Rules. Respondent 3 expresses a desire to change the attitudes of other students and ultimately build future collective action, as reflected in the Relationships Orientation, whereas Respondent 4 advises combating the problem of others' inaction through directly addressing the vandalism itself without attempting the (possibly futile) task of instigating large-scale change in the student body. In the absence of a supportive, caring school climate, why or how might students still manage to develop a sense of responsibility toward each other, as well as a belief in the efficacy of their efforts? Once again, to 'put the shoe on the other foot', would we be willing to conclude, should the empirical evidence support the claim, that social structures are driving student choices? If so, where are developmental differences across individuals?

Different Choices, Different Justifications (or are they?)

While there appear initially to be profound differences behind this following pair of responses, closer examination suggests that they may be quite similar in nature.

5. Choice A ("Let the students handle it"): "Because the adults don't care." (Dismissive Orientation)
6. Choice B ("Organize a meeting to discuss racism"): "Because awareness is usually a good way to solve problems." (Relationship orientation)

Although these choices – and even their associated motivated justifications – seem different, they may be more similar than they first appear. If one is prepared to dig a bit deeper into the interpretive realm, they at least have some elements in common. Respondent 6 provides what at first glance is the developmentally "preferred" motivation: "Acknowledge that racism is wrong and is bad for the community." But is it any more reflective than the other response? Taken by itself, without further clarification, Response 6 does not really reveal any understanding of *why* racism hurts the school community, nor does it consider that the people who wrote the graffiti did it *because* they wanted to be hurtful. Response 5 seems like a cynicalnon-motivation, but it is closer to providing an answer that describes the process of how Choice D would be most suitable for that student body: the adults do not care, and thus it is left up to the students to manage their circumstances. Neither student response, however, suggests any understanding of how the situation came to be, how it could be resolved, or why these responses are preferable to the others available because neither student response demonstrates that he or she is truly engaged in deep reflection.

While we claim none of the action responses as objectively civic or uncivic – one could easily suggest civically-minded motivations to any of the four choices – the results suggest that if students' responses within a given school were aggregated at the school level, students organized by school might very well prefer, on average, certain choices and certain orientations. A quest for empirical evidence to test this hypothesis, which we are now undertaking, will be very valuable.

It is also not surprising that there might be a clear grouping of choices with certain Orientations because the choices express distinct types of participation that may guide these responses: Choice B can be read as the most explicitly community-action driven, Choice C (police the web site) implies autonomous action, and Choice D (let the principal handle it) declines participation. Thus, perhaps students in schools where the hidden curriculum favors connections and community building, select Choice B as individuals who value Relationships. Meanwhile, students in schools which emphasize the importance of directives and maintaining order (perhaps due to the greater potential for a chaotic environment), choose Choice C which prescribes action to return order through removing the disorder, and students in disorganized or unstable environments believe Choice D is the solution to use because of their efforts to preserve Safety, both of or for themselves and others. Are some of these choices preferable to others?

In context, certain motivations might simply be untenable. For instance, would it be "illogical" or "irrational" and possibly in conflict with the survival instinct for a student in an unsafe school where most students have a Safety orientation to their decisions to attempt to adopt a civic future-minded orientation to the challenges faced there? Put another way, if choices involve both the strategy and the motivation (justification) for it, then the two can only be cleaved in theory (research) but not in practice (real life).

Is it enough to evaluate or portray these schools based upon the most common of their students' choices and orientations? Could we ascribe the scores of a developmental hierarchy to the hidden curriculum of these schools based upon whether students are more or less civically minded, and whether they made the more community-centric choice? Yet, in doing so, we are missing the crucial dimension of reflection: do students understand how the choice they have selected ultimately brings about some kind of result? What is it about having a meeting about racism that might go some way towards reducing it? Let us never forget that the school is nested in a community and a society.

A SENSE OF PURPOSE

What, then, is the *purpose* of reflection generally, and informed social reflection in particular, if it is not to promote some kind of specific goal? If reflection does not direct people toward a certain kind of decision, does its refinement provide any true utility to the individual and especially to others? After all, would Jung agree that the failure of psychoanalysis as a practice (i.e., as a treatment to help anyone change one's behaviour) does not negate its success as a method in gaining greater self-understanding. Can there be deep reflection, of self and society, simply for its own sake?

The nuances of meaning of the choices in the measure we describe yields one index that the broadest, most inclusive level of (informed social) reflection may not always be suitable: aware or not, the role of context is significant in helping/ influencing an individual to determine what choice is most appropriate (Selman & Feigenberg, 2010). When we understand our current context, whether it is a peer group or school rules and climate, we have the opportunity to envision and create a different context by becoming aware, but the context may also impose restrictions on what we perceive as possible, and shape our motivations for action. Optimally, students would learn and develop in climates that allow or encourage them to use their imagination to explore all choices and *then* decide whether or not to align their actions with the climate in which they actually exist. Toward this end, Kohlberg advocated and tried to design a Just Community School movement of self-governing democratic schools. Of course, he was thwarted by the constraints and affordances of others' rational reconstructions, that is, others in the educational world and society.

The construct of informed social reflection allows one to know what is at stake in moral and civic education, but it is not valuable simply for its own sake. It is not simply toward selecting the most socially appropriate or even the most civically engaged action. It is in fostering students' capacity to become aware of *the connections* that implicitly and explicitly exist between choices and justifications in their lives that renders them socially informed.

CONCLUSION

Can good performed without awareness be as dangerous as evil done blindly? Consider the German word *Kadavergehorsam*. Its meaning cuts across languages: "the obedience of corpses." Adolf Eichmann, the infamous Nazi leader responsible for the planning and administration of the systematic extermination of the Jewish people, used this word to describe himself at his war crimes trial in the 1960s. Social philosopher Hannah Arendt (1963), who documented the proceedings, observed that all present were perhaps more shocked that Eichmann did not attempt to justify his behaviour throughout the war as the product of psychological coercion or an inurement to mass murder, but rather as the "virtues and vices of blind obedience" (p. 135).

When Eichmann's superiors sensed that the "Final Solution," as Adolf Hitler referred to the Jewish genocide, could not and should not be sustained, they began to issue their own renegade orders to spare more Jewish lives and ultimately dismantle concentration camps. Yet was it Eichmann's "fanaticism" that drove him to reject these orders and clash openly with a growing shift in opinion? Was he morally stunted? A product of his times and place? Or both? Eichmann argued that he had only been drawing upon the guidelines set out by Immanuel Kant, whom he claimed to have read, that "the principle of my will must always be such that it can become the principle of general laws" (Arendt, 1963, p. 136). Arendt doubted whether Eichmann could have truly relied upon this mutation of the categorical imperative as a moral guideline: would Eichmann seriously accept living in a society where others could have freely executed him as well?

Eichmann's testimony stands as a troubling instance of self-reflection uninformed by social reflection, that is, one that had a profound cleaving from social awareness. It is especially memorable because of its cruelty and for its apparent failure to acknowledge anyone —including his own motivations— but the will of whoever handed him his orders. Yet we must also caution against the unexamined acceptance of less harmful, or even beneficial, motivations: Even if there are certain beliefs whose value has been proven beneficial to society, these will not necessarily lead to the right (or righteous) action if the participants do not understand why these testaments should guide them. It is at this juncture that civic education and the developmental moral sciences meet.

Michel Foucault invokes Marcus Aurelius, the Stoic Roman emperor, as a figure who encapsulates both profound and humble devotion to personal behaviour where the greatest care for oneself coincides with regard for self and others. Each day, the emperor had an "evening examination in which he reconstructed the deeds of the day in order to measure them against what he ought to have done, then the morning examination in which he prepared himself for the tasks he was to perform." Foucault suggests, "You review your use of future time and equip yourself; you reactivate the principles that must be enacted in order to exercise your duty" (Foucault, 2005, p. 300). While most of us likely fall short of this dedication to building self-awareness of our motivations, these two tasks come together as informed social reflection —the consideration of what we did, held in the same thought with what we think is best to do, with what we could possibly have done. Consider again the quote that appears at the beginning of this discussion: "The psychological rule says that when an inner situation is not made conscious, it happens outside as fate." What is moral motivation but the acknowledgement that we are the sum of our choices, and we must be fully awake for each one? In accessing our moral motivation, we ensure that we select the shape we wish for our lives to take. We have the opportunity to experience and learn each day if we accept its demands and embrace the commitment to include our past, present, future in our decisions.

NOTES

[1] Note the ambiguity of the Retaliate response (Choice A) as it could be interpreted as student agency, usually seen as an admirable feature.
[2] Please note that we are also aware that the identification of what type of strategy an item response represents is (etically) imposed by us on that item response

REFERENCES

Arendt, H. (1963). *Eichmann in Jerusalem.* New York: Penguin.
Feigenberg, L.F., Steel King, M., Barr, D.J., & Selman, R.L. (2008). Belonging to and exclusion from the peer group in schools: Influences on adolescents' moral choices. *Journal of Moral Education, 37*(2), 165–184.
Foucault, M. (2006). *The hermeneutics of the self: Lectures at the college de france, 1981–1982.* New York: Picador.
Geier, C., & Luna, B. (2009). The maturation of incentive processing and cognitive control. *Pharmacology, Biochemistry & Behavior, 93*(3), 212–221.
Habermas, J. (1995). *Moral consciousness and communicative action* (C. Lenhardt & S.W. Nicholsen, Trans.). Cambridge, MA: MIT Press.
Hoffman, J. (2010). Online bullies pull schools into the fray. *New York Times.* http://www.nytimes.com/2010/06/28/style/28bully.html?pagewanted=all [Accessed December 5, 2011].
Jackson, P. (1968). *Life in classrooms.* New York: Holt, Rinehart and Winston.
Kohlberg, L. (1970). The moral atmosphere of the school. In N. Overley (Ed.), *The unstudied curriculum: Its impact on children.* Monograph of the Association for Supervision and Curriculum Development, Washington, D.C.
LaRusso, M.D. & Selman, R.L. (2011). Early adolescent health risk behaviors, conflict resolution strategies, and school climate. *Journal of Applied Developmental Psychology, 32*(6), 354–362.
Nunner-Winkler, G.(1993). The growth of moral motivation. In G.G. Noam & T.E. Wren (Eds.), *The moral self* (pp. 269–290). Cambridge, MA: Massachusetts Institute of Technology.
Nunner-Winkler, G. (2007). Development of moral motivation from childhood to early adulthood. *Journal of Moral Education, 36*(4), 399–414.
Oser, F.K., Althof, W., & Higgins-D'Alessandro, A. (2008). The Just Community approach to moral education: System change or individual change? *Journal of Moral Education, 37*(3), 395–415.
Outhwaite, W. (2009). *Habermas: A critical introduction* (2nd ed.). Malden, MA: Polity.
Romer, D., & Hennessy, M. (2007). A biosocial-affect model of adolescent sensation seeking: The role of affect evaluation and peer-group influence in adolescent drug use. *Prevention Science, 8*(2), 89–101.
Selman, R.L. (2003). *The promotion of social awareness: Powerful lessons from the partnership of developmental theory and classroom practice.* New York: Russell Sage Foundation.
Selman, R.L., & Feigenberg, L.F. (2010). Between neurons and neighborhoods: Innovative methods to assess the development and depth of adolescent social awareness. In P.D. Zelazo, M. Chandler, & E. Crone (Eds.), *Developmental social cognitive neuroscience* (pp. 227–250). USA: Taylor & Francis Group, LLC.
Selman, R.L. & Kwok, J. (2010). Informed social reflection: Its development and importance for adolescents' civic engagement. In L. Sherrod, J. Torney-Purta, & C. Flanagan (Eds.), *Handbook of research on civic engagement in youth* (pp. 651–683). Hoboken, NJ: Wiley.

AFFILIATIONS

Janet Kwok
Harvard Graduate School of Education
Cambridge, Massachusetts, USA

Robert L. Selman
Human Development and Education
Harvard Graduate School of Education
Cambridge, Massachusetts, USA

WOLFGANG ALTHOF & MARVIN W. BERKOWITZ

II. CHARACTER AND CIVIC EDUCATION AS A SOURCE OF MORAL MOTIVATION

INTRODUCTION

Character education, civic education, or any education aimed at the development of moral or pro-social characteristics, must consider the nature of a moral agent; i.e., what psychologically comprises an individual who is both motivated and capable of acting in morally justifiable ways. In the case of character education, the focus is more all-encompassing and is applicable to all spheres of life. In the case of civic or citizenship education, particularly in democratic societies, the focus is more on public life and engagement. Regardless, if schools are to nurture the moral proclivities and capabilities of their future adult citizens, then they must take seriously what is known about the development of such proclivities and capabilities.

In this chapter, we look through the lenses of character and citizenship education, and in particular their intersection (cf. Althof & Berkowitz, 2006; Berkowitz, Althof & Jones, 2009), to better understand a particular aspect of that psychological nature, namely, moral motivation. In doing so, we will examine some core frameworks for both character and citizenship education, identifying the motivational pieces. We will also examine what theory and research tell us about educating for those specifically motivational components of the moral person.

WHERE MOTIVATION FITS IN FRAMEWORKS OF CHARACTER AND CITIZENSHIP

There is a strong parallel between two tri-partite frameworks of educational outcomes. The first comes from the Character Education Partnership and relies on a trichotomy that dates back at least to the work of Johan Pestalozzi. In the words of the Character Education Partnership, character consists of "understanding, caring about and acting upon core ethical values" (www.character.org). This model suggests that there are cognitive, affective/motivational, and behavioural aspects to the complete moral person (person of moral character). In a more concrete sense, merely knowing what is right or wrong is necessary but not sufficient for moral action to ensue. This can be seen in various pro-social and anti-social behaviours (e.g., Blasi, 1980; Kohlberg & Candee, 1984) and in the prevention of self-harmful behaviours (Schinke, Botvin & Orlandi, 1991). Rather, motivation to act upon what one cognitively understands as the good is also necessary to generate moral behaviour. In some cases, where the

K. Heinrichs, F. Oser & T. Lovat (Eds.), Handbook of Moral Motivation: Theories, Models, Applications, 567–584.

moral behaviour that is prescribed is not easy to enact, the skills ("acting upon") are also necessary. This parallels other models in psychology, such as behavioural intentions and attitudes (Fishbein & Ajzen, 2009).

In a similar model, the campaign for the Civic Mission of Schools (www. civicmissionofschools.org) identifies three key qualities of educated and active citizens to be targeted by civic education: civic knowledge, skills, and dispositions. Clearly the knowledge element maps directly onto the Character Education Partnership's "understanding" element, and likewise the CMS skills element parallels the CEP "acting upon" element. From the motivational standpoint, the "caring about" element in the CEP definition of character parallels the "dispositions" element postulated as necessary by the CMS. In other words, to be a democratic citizen, ready to participate in the civil and political life of a society, one needs to be disposed to act in ways that support the democratic process and serve the common good. If schools are to foster the development of such people, then they must strategically and intentionally adopt pedagogical strategies that can justifiably be expected to promote those dispositions or motivations.

From a more psychological perspective, Berkowitz (2012) has presented a model of the moral person using this tri-partite conception of character which differentiates the three areas of cognition (knowing), affect/motivation (caring about), and behavioural competencies or skills (acting upon), as well as the distinction between the moral domain and other areas of psychology that are not inherently moral but can serve to support or buttress moral agency (e.g., achievement motivation or perspective-taking). Finally, this model adds at its core the concept of the moral self (Colby & Damon, 1992; Lapsley & Narváez, 2004; Noam, Wren, Nunner-Winkler & Edelstein, 1993).

Whichever rendition of this psycho-anatomy one considers, it should be clear that doing the good requires a motivation to do the good, and that any intervention, educational or otherwise, that is designed to foster moral development, whether generically or as applied to public life, must include a focus on the promotion of moral motivation.

INTRINSIC VS. EXTRINSIC MOTIVATION

While it is beyond the scope and intention of this chapter to chronicle the complexity of human motivation, it is important to note that humans are multi-motivated organisms. For our sake, we also posit that the goal of character and citizenship education is for students to internalize and integrate relevant values, especially moral values. The concept of internalization, whether from psychoanalytic (Gilligan, 1976; Kochanska, 1991) or more cognitive perspectives (Bandura, 1996; Ryan & Deci, 2002), implies that some external valuing becomes part of the self-system. With regard to moral development, the goal then is for students to come to "own" a moral perspective as a product of the experiences they have in school (and of course in other spheres of their lives) and that they are integrated into their self-understanding and "brought into congruence with [their] other values and needs" (Ryan & Deci, 2000, p. 73).

An interesting dialogue exists in both psychology and education concerning this path of moving from external values/motives to internal values/motives. In a sense, it is an eternal quandary for all societies to know how to get each subsequent generation to embrace desirable motives and values. Of course, this can be understood from different perspectives. If one desires youth to simply adopt those beliefs, values, and motives that already exist in the adult culture, then veridical internalization may be presumed (a theoretical version of this concept can be found in Talcott Parsons' structural-functional sociology; in particular, Parsons &Shils, 1951). Or one may simply settle for compliance without internalization. If however one's goal is the development of pro-socially motivated independent moral agents, then a different socialization model is in order. Such a socialization model would combine pedagogical and other socialization processes that focus on (1) the transmission of cultural concepts and values but also on (2) the fostering of the aspects of the moral self that promote both independent and collaborative thinking towards desired values and motives. This has been a basic tenet of progressive education (Dewey; Kohlberg) and it is precisely the perspective that we take in this chapter.

One way to address this distinction is to differentiate between intrinsic and extrinsic motivation. On the most superficial level, intrinsic motivation is involved when a person engages in behaviour because it is pleasing or inherently satisfactory to do so. On the other hand, we speak of extrinsic motivation when a person engages in a behaviour not because of itself but because of some instrumental reason; that is, it is focused on outcomes that are separable from the action per se (Ryan & Deci, 2000). In fact, there are multiple levels to what may seem, at least on the surface, to be a clear dichotomy.

First, whereas intrinsically motivated behaviour is the clearest case of self-determined activity, not all behaviour that is extrinsically motivated is also non-autonomous, that is, under external control. Both Deci and Ryan's Self-Determination Theory (SDT) and Vallerand's Hierarchical Model of extrinsic and intrinsic motivation (Vallerand & Ratelle, 2002) posit a continuum of multiple types of extrinsic motivation, representing varying degrees of internalization and integration of values and behavioural regulations; these levels are: external regulation; introjection (focus on approval of others); identification (with the importance of a behaviour and the underlying value; self-endorsement of goals) and integration which is established when values and goals have been internalized, that is, fully and consciously assimilated to the self and the personal value hierarchy (Deci & Ryan, 1985; Deci, Vallerand, Pelletier & Ryan, 1991; Ryan & Deci, 2000). On the level of integrated regulation, actions are no less self-determined than when motivated intrinsically, although they are still carried out for an instrumental value, like being successful in school - or making moral choices. Ryan and Deci (2000) report evidence that more autonomous extrinsic motivation is associated with greater engagement, higher learning quality and greater psychological well-being - which are the very same effects as those of intrinsic motivation (p. 63). The fact that self-determined motivation that leads to considerate, reflective, responsible and engaged behaviour can have both intrinsic and extrinsic sources is good news for educators in general and character educators in particular who cannot always rely on intrinsic motivation: Not all topics and tasks at school are genuinely interesting and enjoyable. More dramatically, morality is not a matter of joy and good-weather relationships and moral action often demands transcending inner resistances of all sorts, including fear and selfish desires. Evidently, social and moral rules initially are external to the individual; it is only in a slow developmental process that they become more and more fully understood and internalized. Self-determined motivation, then, means "an inner endorsement of one's action – the sense that an action is freely initiated and emanates from within the self" (Reeve, 2002, p. 196).

Second, there is the distinction between means and ends. As discussed above, one can focus on the ends of character and citizenship education as either compliance with external forces or values despite not personally holding those values (i.e., behaviour without internalization). Or one can focus on promoting the authentic personal adoption of the targeted motives and values, that is, behaviour based on internalization. If, on the other hand, one focuses on means, rather than ends (and in reality, the focus is always on both), then a distinction can be made between using more extrinsic strategies (e.g., rewards, punishment, social recognition) or strategies designed for internalization (e.g., role models, advocacy by valued social groups, strategic relationships, critical reflection). The assumption then is that extrinsic motivators (means) lead to extrinsic motivation (end) and intrinsic motivators (means) lead to intrinsic motivation (end). While the empirical picture is not that dichotomous, on balance this is generally accurate. In a meta-analysis of 128 studies, Deci, Koestner and Ryan (1999, 2001) reviewed experiments, examining the effects of extrinsic rewards on intrinsic motivation. They found that tangible rewards (material gratification or awards) "significantly and substantially undermine intrinsic motivation, and this effect was quite robust. Furthermore, the undermining was especially strong for children" (Deci, Koestner & Ryan, 2001, p. 15). Students who initially were intrinsically motivated experienced the rewards as a means of control, thus calling into question the inherent value of the rewarded activity. The only exceptions from the general result were tangible rewards given unexpectedly after a task was completed and "verbal rewards" – positive feedback or social praise that appeared to have either a neutral or positive motivational impact (except, again, when in a controlling context). It is of particular importance for character and citizenship educators that the undermining effect of rewards can also reduce pro-social behaviour (e.g., altruism). This has been found in college students (Houlfort, et al., 2002), school aged children (Fabes et al., 1989), pre-school children (Lepper, Green & Nisbett, 1973) and even in toddlers (Warneken & Tomasello, 2008).

Yet a further complication comes from whether the target of a tangible reward is a particular behaviour or an outcome of that behaviour. As Ryan and Brown (2005) point out, behaviourism is intended to focus on rewarding behaviours, not outcomes of behaviours. So if a teacher uses rewards to increase attention in a distractible student, it is consistent with behavioural principles. On the other hand, if a teacher uses rewards to increase the scores on a test, it is not. The problem lies in the fact that there are many types of behaviour that can produce a higher test score, including immoral ones like cheating.

WORKING MODELS OF STUDENT MOTIVATION

Those who intentionally influence the development of children do it on the basis of either reflective or un-reflective models about what motivates children. They assume that children will be more highly motivated by whatever strategies they adopt. They may or may not be aware that they are doing this or even aware of what they believe, but nonetheless the choice to praise, ignore, hit, reward, discuss, etc. at least implies an assumption of how children function. This applies as much to educators as to others (e.g., parents, juvenile justice professionals, social workers). Given what we have just seen about the impact of extrinsic motivators, especially performance-contingent material consequences, it is indeed disheartening to see the nearly ubiquitous presence of such rewards in schools. Teachers and schools tend to not only favour rewards, but to institutionalize them and seem even to be proud of them. They give candy and stickers for behaviour. They offer additional play time or snacks for behaviour. They institutionalize reward programs and hold whole school assemblies or use public announcement systems or hallway postings to announce the "winners." Their working models seem typically to be that children will be motivated to be "good" (whether in an ethical sense or a social conformist sense or in the sense of task performance) if they get extrinsic rewards for such behaviour or see others receiving such material consequences for exhibiting "good" behaviour. They assume that the larger the incentive, the greater the motivational effects. Research, however, does not support these assumptions.

Reese and Overton (1970) once described two broad developmental families of theories of human development that they referred to as "models of man." The organismic (interactive, dynamic) model suggested that humans develop as a complex interaction of internal and external forces, and that humans co-construct both reality and themselves. The mechanistic (reactive) paradigm suggested that humans are essentially a product of external forces and are therefore more passive recipients of such forces. In the case of working models of children, educators seem disposed to fall on the mechanistic side rather than the organismic side, despite the empirical evidence to the contrary. This is not to say that external forces have no impact on children. Indeed, this may be one of the reasons for the seeming paradox in classrooms.

We propose two groups of reasons for the frustratingly intractable educator reliance on extrinsic rewards and other means of controlling student behaviour (also see Reeve, 2002, pp. 190-193). One is modeling, tradition, and training. Schools and educator preparation programs have long relied on behaviourist models and behaviour modification principles. This is most apparent in special education, but is rampant in education in general. Therefore, educators' own experiences in schools (both as students and as prospective teachers) frequently expose them to such strategies. Controlling teachers are considered more competent than autonomy-supportive teachers, by parents, supervisors and even students; the desire to be in control also mirrors the controlling and pressuring conditions in schooling.Accordingly, educators are not challenged to develop nor prepared to use forms of instruction that appeal to students' sense of autonomy and self-determined motivation. The second reason is that reward and control strategies often work, at least in the short run and, under conditions of educational "efficiency", the short run tends to be much more salient than the long run. For example, if a student is engaging in misbehaviour that is disruptive or even dangerous, a teacher may directly apply negative consequences (punishment). The behaviour is likely to stop immediately. The teacher sees the application of extrinsic consequences and the ensuing decrease in the undesirable behaviour and concludes that this strategy works (or more ironically is reinforced for this educational strategy). What the teacher does not see as clearly are the long term consequences of the punishment, such as alienation from school, damage to self-esteem if the punishment is public, and an increase in future misbehaviour. In other words, long-term damage to character development is the result of this strategy, but that is much less salient to the educator than the short-term decrease in the undesirable behaviour.

A TALE OF TWO MODELS

It may be helpful to contrast two current models being used to design educational systems, each at least in part aimed directly at promoting moral behaviour and motivation. The first is Positive Behaviour Interventions and Supports (PBIS) and the second is Self-Determination Theory (SDT). PBIS can be construed as mostly mechanistic and SDT as mostly organismic (Reese & Overton, 1970).

PBIS originated as a more humane alternative to punitive behavioural control mechanisms with severely developmentally-delayed students and adults (Carr et al., 2002). It then spread to other special needs populations and eventually was reconceptualized as a generic school-wide approach to behaviour management (Horner et al., 2005), sometimes called School-wide Positive Behaviour Supports (SWPBS; Vincent et al., 2011). The model applies behavioural principles to fostering a school climate that promotes academic and social success, while offering a multi-tiered approach to primary, secondary and tertiary prevention. What is of most relevance here is the primary prevention aspect.

> The primary prevention tier of SWPBS involves defining, teaching, monitoring, and rewarding a small set of behavioural expectations for all students across non-classroom and classroom settings. In addition, a clearly defined and consistently implemented continuum of consequences and supports for problem behaviours are established. (Horner et al., 2009, p. 134)

In essence, a set of behaviours is defined, a curriculum teaching those behaviours is implemented, and a clear set of consequences for misbehaviour and appropriate behaviour is applied. This is supported in numerous ways including through professional development and data collection and application. This approach is receiving strong government support at the federal, state and local levels and being implemented very widely across the US. There is a substantial empirical base for PBIS and SWPBIS.

Alternatively, Self-Determination Theory (Ryan & Deci, 2002) assumes that all individuals are in part self-constructing, that is, that they engage the environment (including the contingencies that behaviourist theories highlight) and construct meaning of it, of oneself, and of the relationship between self and other. SDT also assumes that this self-constructive tendency can and should be enhanced, including in schools by promoting autonomy-supportive schools and classrooms. This is where SWPBS and SDT tend to part ways. Whereas SDT recognized that both intrinsic and extrinsic motivation impact behaviour, SDT argues that intrinsic motivation is a stronger influence on behaviour, especially longitudinally. More specifically for this chapter, this applies to values and valuing (Kasser, 2002). It is also argued that valuing derives from both the self and from fundamental human needs. SDT focuses on three such needs: the need for autonomy and voice; the need for social connection and belonging; the need for a sense of personal competence. Hence, SDT's focus is on creating educational (and other) environments that support the development of a sense of self as a competent agent in positive relationships with others.

The child for SWPBS is seen more as a set of behaviours in a context that either supports or thwarts those behaviours. The child for SDT is seen as a self-defining organism with specific human needs that, when met, produce desirable motives central to the self-system (for an experience-loaded account of the two paradigms and their educational consequences, see Kohn, 1993).

CHARACTER AND CITIZENSHIP EDUCATION AND MORAL MOTIVATION

Ultimately, the concept of moral motivation has to do with the broad philosophical (and theological) question of "Why be moral?" (cf. Bergman, 2002). While well beyond the scope of this chapter, it is important to note that this question has taxed philosophers and others for millennia. Regardless of where one lands in the philosophical debate, the question continues to have great import for psychologists and educators who try to understand moral motivation and then to positively impact its development in schools and elsewhere. Both character education and citizenship education, at least in part, are focally concerned with fostering the development of moral motivation. In both fields, schools want to educate humans who have the understanding of moral and civic goals and values and are motivated to act upon what they understand to be good.

This wording implies that cognitive processes of active meaning-making (Blasi, 1999, 2005) enter the formation of moral motivation. In this regard, Malti,

Gummerum, Keller & Buchmann (2009) offer a useful definition when they conceptualize moral motivation as "the readiness to abide by a moral rule that a person understands to be valid, even if this motivation is in conflict with other, amoral desires and motives" (p. 443); these authors emphasize that by this definition, "moral motivation has a strong cognitive component, as a child must first understand the validity of moral rules" (ibid.) Similarly, Nunner-Winkler (2007) considers a person morally motivated "if an individual's judgment contains an understanding of the obligatory character of the moral ought and the concern motivating the imperative behaviour is intrinsically oriented to this understanding" (p. 401). This conception is in accordance with cognitive-developmental and social-cognitive theoretical traditions and with Deci and Ryan's conceptual discussion of sources for self-determined motivation that includes the integration of regulations by way of conscious evaluation and assimilation to the self.

It is clear from developmental research and theory that humans are multi-motivated. While pleasure is clearly a human motive, and hence extrinsic factors will therefore have an impact on human behaviour, it is the satisfaction of higher human needs such as those identified in SDT (autonomy, competence, belonging) that more deeply and permanently impact the development of competent moral agency, in large part by promoting deeply and personally held moral values and motives (Dalton & Watson, 1997). Evidence of the power of intrinsic motivation over extrinsic forces ranges from Harlow's demonstration that baby monkeys are more attracted to contact comfort than to the satiation of hunger or thirst to Warneken and Tomasello's (2008) demonstration that 20 month old toddlers reduce pro-social behaviour when rewarded for it to health psychology demonstrations that adults on an intrinsically-motivated health regiment become less compliant when rewards are given for their behaviour. What we want as the result of schooling (and other socialization of youth) are self-managed, self-aware individuals who can and do act as competent moral agents. Especially in a democratic-society, this is not only desirable but essential.

THE "HOW TO"

As SDT suggests, a good place to start is with fundamental human needs, such as autonomy, belonging and competence. Schools need to be places that are structured to intentionally meet those needs in children. Caring School Community (formerly the Child Development Project) has achieved powerful results by creating schools and classrooms designed to meet these three fundamental needs (Dalton & Watson, 1997). Autonomy is achieved by increasing student voice through class meetings and other forms of empowerment. Belonging is achieved by structurally promoting relationships (e.g., through cross-age buddying structures) and creating a welcoming school and classroom environment. And competence is promoted through child-focused academic pedagogies such as cooperative learning. Reeve and Halusic (2009), in answering common teacher questions about SDT, point out that rather than opposing undesirable behaviour teachers should instead acknowledge student resistance and use it to improve practice.

If schools are to promote democratic citizenship (Berkowitz, Althof & Jones, 2008; Berkowitz & Puka, 2009), it is essential that they promote autonomy and competence. Democratic citizens must have a sense of the power of their own voices (autonomy) and the self-efficacy (competence) to enter into the public sphere in a way that they can help promote the common good. Unless schools and classrooms are democratic microcosms of the democratic society envisioned by the Founding Fathers, optimal citizenship education becomes impossible (Dewey, 1899/1915, 1916). A behaviourist approach will focus the light on the consequences of behaviour (the rewards given for desired behaviour) and not on the pro-social motivations that should generate such behaviours. Lawrence Kohlberg argued years ago that a behaviourist approach would produce individuals whose moral motivations never transcend what he considered to be a highly immature stage of understanding the right as that which produces positive consequences for him or herself. In fact, we have long argued that schools that focus on reward and recognition send two messages to students: (1) do more of what we are rewarding you for and (2) we, as authorities and role models in your life, so deeply value a life chasing rewards and recognition that we have built your classrooms and schools around that. We are essentially socializing youth to follow the extrinsic motivators (the rewards and recognitions). Little wonder that employers are despondent over the recent generations of new workers who seem to demand and expect rewards and recognitions simply for doing what they are paid to do. We have socialized them to do so.

Educating for moral character (Berkowitz, 2012) likewise relies on schools and classrooms that foster the moral character, and moral motivation necessary for moral character, of youth. The Character Education Partnership (CEP; www.character.org) has outlined eleven principles of effective character education. The seventh is "The school fosters students' self-motivation." It is defined as follows:

> Character means doing the right thing and doing our best work "even when no one is looking." The best underlying ethical reason for following rules, for example, is respect for the rights and needs of others – not fear of punishment nor desire for reward. We want students to be kind to others because of an inner belief that kindness is good and an inner desire to be a kind person. We want them to do a good job – work that applies and further develops their best abilities – because they take pride in quality work, not just because they want a good grade. Becoming more self-motivated is a developmental process that schools of character are careful not to undermine by an emphasis on extrinsic incentives. Intensive focus on rewards and behaviour modification is consciously limited.

> Schools of character work with students to develop their understanding of rules, their awareness of how their behaviour affects others, and the character strengths – such as self-control, perspective taking, and conflict resolution

skills – needed to act responsibly in the future. Rather than settle for mere compliance, these schools seek to help students benefit from their mistakes by providing meaningful opportunities for reflection, problem solving, and restitution.

Consequences are relevant (logically related to the rule or offense), respectful (not embarrassing or demeaning), reasonable (not harsh or excessive), restorative (restoring or repairing the relationship by making restitution), and resource-building (helping students develop the character qualities – such as empathy, social skills, and the motivation to do the right thing – that were not put into practice when the behaviour problem occurred). Staff routinely deal with behaviour issues in positive ways that encourage reflection according to the core values, offer students opportunities for reparation and moral growth, and respect students as individuals. (Character Education Partnership, 2010).

The motivation to do the good comes from a variety of psychological roots. It comes from a developing system that includes a sense of self as a moral agent with a strong moral identity. It comes from healthy relationships with pro-social and nurturing others. It comes from belonging to social communities that collectively value morality (Power, Higgins, & Kohlberg, 1989). It comes from role models who advocate for and model moral behaviour and values. Finally, it comes from guided reflection on moral issues in both structured and unstructured settings. These five conditions then serve as the pedagogical blueprint for educating for moral motivation.

Educating for a Moral Self-System

Moral motivation is both a source and a function of the moral self. A number of scholars maintain that children's morality, in terms of their moral understanding and convictions, is more or less separate from their self-system. Only in adolescence self and morality become gradually connected and a moral identity develops (Bergman, 2002; Blasi, 1995, 2001; Colby & Damon, 1992; Nucci, 2001, 2004). "It is, thus, the integration of moral values into the adolescent self concept that gives rise to a moral self (i.e. a self that profoundly cares about matters of morality and ethical conduct)" (Krettenauer, 2011, 309). This process of moral self-integration, first described by Damon (1984), can be observed by the increased use of moral self-descriptors. In early and even middle childhood, moral terms rarely are used in a self-evaluative manner (see Hardy & Carlo, 2005, for an overview). Only when this capacity is developed, can the self serve as a stable source of moral motivation (Nucci, 2001, 2004).

While small children do develop an understanding of moral rules, they often do not act on them because they lack a sense of responsibility; this has been demonstrated for instance by research on the 'happy victimizer" phenomenon (Nunner-Winkler, 1998; for a review see Krettenauer, Malti & Sokol, 2008). However, moral understanding and the concern for moral issues develop over the years, and so does the understanding of emotions and interpersonal dynamics, resulting in increases of the self-evaluative competence to reflect upon their own motives in specific moral situations, so generating moral motivation (Hardy, 2006; Malti et al., 2009). All these developmental processes – moral reasoning, emotion understanding, interpersonal cognition, and empathy – can be promoted in educational settings. "As children start to reflect on how their characteristics and behaviours affect others, they begin to view themselves in moral terms (e.g., kind, honest, or fair). Further, through interactions with peers, parents, and others, children to varying degrees develop appreciation and concern for morality; hence, moral ideals become not only understood as objectively important, but important to them personally" (Hardy & Carlo, 2005, p. 248). This growing centrality of moral issues for children's self-understanding and the corresponding growth of moral motivation - the self-evaluative readiness to keep oneself responsible to act according to moral standards considered as valid - seems to be one of the mechanisms that leads to the integration of self and morality.

The moral self is constructed gradually and in a variety of ways. One way schools can contribute to an emerging moral self system in childhood is by making it an explicit part of the curriculum. Education can focus on studying moral motives in others, such as characters in literature and historical figures. Particularly in adolescence, it can support the development of a moral identity by focusing on self-reflection and making character a self-project as is done in the John Templeton Foundation's Laws of Life program (Elias et al., 2006) or the Youth Purpose Project (Damon, 2009).

Educating for Pro-social Relationships

Developmental science repeatedly demonstrates that human flourishing of a variety of sorts, including moral character, depends on healthy pro-social human bonding (Berkowitz, 2009; Berkowitz & Bier, 2005). Schools therefore need to be strategic, structural and intentional in promoting such relationships as widely as possible. When meeting this fundamental need for belonging or relatedness, as highlighted in Self Determination Theory, students are more prone to valuing pro-social outcomes and internalizing pro-social values and motives. Hal Urban, a high school teacher for 35 years, spent the first 3 weeks of school in part getting to know his students and getting them to know each other (Urban, 2008). Laura Ecken, an elementary school teacher, promoted the moral development and self-management of her troubled students by focusing on attachment theory and nurturing positive relationships with and between them (Watson & Ecken, 2003; Watson, 2006). Relationships can be built through mentoring. They can be built through cross-age pairing structures. They can be built by intentional self-disclosure or other means of learning about each other. They can be built through cooperative learning (Johnson & Johnson, 2008) and other collaborative practices. The key point is that schools and classrooms need to intentionally adopt or create such policies, procedures, and structures to maximize the likelihood that all members of a school community (students, teachers, administrators, support staff, etc.) build a set of healthy relationships with others.

Educating for Pro-social Communities

School climate has become a rallying concept for the fields of character education, social-emotional learning, and pro-social education (e.g., Cohen, 2006). In essence, this reflects the understanding that educating for moral development (or more specifically moral motivation) cannot target individuals only but needs to address interpersonal relationships and social communities that shape the life of humans. Relationship building as described above contributes to community building. Providing opportunities to serve others and practicing a pedagogy of empowerment that promotes collaboration beyond the classroom and participation in democratic decision-making (Battistich, 2008; Oser, Althof & Higgins-d'Alessandro, 2009) establishes further arenas of practicing social skills and of learning to understand, by experience, what active care and responsibility for individuals and a healthy polity look like and what makes them morally significant. Whether one is dealing with the individual classroom (Developmental Studies Center, 1996; Durlak et al., 2011), a school within a school (Power, Higgins & Kohlberg, 1989), a whole school (Gauld, 1993; Althof, 2003), or therapeutic communities (Gibbs et al., 1995), strategically building communities that authentically embrace, employ practices and structures consistent with, and model and advocate moral values will help promote the development of a generalized motivation to live up to such values and standards of justice, care, interpersonal respect and the common good - the development of moral motivation.

Educating by Role Models

One of the more challenging aspects of this approach is to convince educators that they are role models, and in fact are powerful role models. Mahatma Gandhi said that we need to be the change we want to see in the world. As adults responsible for engineering the moral development of students, we need to be the moral character we want to see in our students. We need to walk the talk (Lickona, 2008). Sizer and Sizer (1999) make this point powerfully, not only in their line of argumentation but even in the title of the book: *The students are watching: Schools and the moral contract*. All adults in schools must make the commitment to be and demonstrate the moral motives that they wish to nurture in students. But walking the talk is not enough. Adults also need to talk the walk. They need to advocate for that which they value and demonstrate. Often students do not get the message just from seeing the behaviour. That is why induction is important as well (Berkowitz & Grych, 2000). Induction entails explaining one's behaviour to children with a focus on the consequences of one's behaviour for others. This is why adult advocacy became so central in Just Community Schools (Althof, 2003, 2008; Oser, Althof & Higgins-d'Alessandro, 2008; Power, Higgins & Kohlberg, 1989).

Educating for Reflectivity and Autonomous Reasoning

Schools can be places where moral discussion abounds, but they can also be places where moral issues are avoided. Sizer and Sizer (1999) introduce the concept of "grappling" which transcends the more didactic proclivities of schools to "teach about."

> The habits of civil behaviour can do much to bring safety to a school's halls. But the meanings of civil behaviour are much tougher to present. They transcend one's immediate environment….One has to *grapple* with those meanings. (pp. 22-23)

A constructivist approach to moral education demands a curriculum and culture that not only allows for moral discussion, but actually demands it and creates the opportunities for developing moral reasoning competencies and bridging the gaps between moral judgment and action. This means staff trained in how to create a critically discursive curriculum and how to facilitate such discussions in the classroom. It means a classroom and school climate that stimulates the critical consideration of moral issues and even is permissive of civil disagreement when it comes to choices and participatory decisions (Berkowitz &Puka, 2009). Research related to Self Determination Theory shows that teacher behaviour and learning activities that support autonomy (e.g., give freedom of choices) and appeal to students' sense of competence lead to integrated forms of self-determined motivation and, thus, advance conceptual understanding as well as personal well-being, engagement, growth and adjustment (Deci, Vallerand, Pelletier & Ryan, 1991; Deci, Koestner& Ryan, 2001; Reeve, 2002, 2006, Reese &Halusic, 2009; Reeve, Jang, Carrell, Jeon &Barch, 2004). If students are to be morally motivated the school cannot be one that finds morality off-putting and frowns on open discussions of moral issues.

CONCLUSION

Moral motivation is ultimately a psychological phenomenon whose development can be nurtured in schools. To foster the development of future citizens of a democratic society who are motivated to do good in the world and have the knowledge and competencies to be effective moral agents acting in accord with their moral motives, schools must look at what psychology can tell us about how students develop, both in general and specifically in the domain of moral motivation.

Taking a developmental and more particularly a constructivist, organismic approach to child development will allow schools to implement strategies that impact moral motivation in a positive way. More specifically, promoting the development of a self-reflective and self-constructed moral self-system in the context of pro-social communities and healthy relationships with pro-social role models and relying on open civil and critical moral discourse will maximize the likelihood that the students leaving our schools will be agents of good in the world because they genuinely care about the good. On the other hand, if we conceive of our students as organisms to be trained and shaped by external forces through a behaviouristic lens, then we are likely to have students with weak moral motives who are easily derailed by the lure of extrinsic consequences for which we have socialized them.

REFERENCES

Althof, W. (2003). Implementing "Just and Caring Communities" in elementary schools: A Deweyan perspective. In W. Veugelers & F.K. Oser (Eds.), *Teaching in oral and democratic education* (pp. 153–172). Bern: Peter Lang.

Althof, W. (2008). The Just Community approach to democratic education: Some affinities. In K. Tirri (Ed.), *Educating moral sensibilities in urban schools* (pp.145–155). Amsterdam: Sense Publishers.

Althof, W., & Berkowitz, M.W. (2006). Moral education and character education: Their relationship and roles in citizenship education. *Journal of Moral Education, 35*, 495–518.

Bandura, A. (1996). *Self-efficacy: The exercise of control.* New York: Freeman.

Battistich, V.A. (2008). The Child Development Project: Creating caring school communities. In L.P. Nucci & D. Narváez (Eds.), *Handbook of moral and character education* (pp. 328–351). New York and London: Routledge.

Bergman, R. (2002). Why be moral? A conceptual model from developmental psychology.*Human Development, 45*, 104–124.

Berkowitz, M.W. (2012). Moral and character education. In K.R. Harris, S. Graham & T. Urdan (Eds.), *APA educational psychology handbook: Vol. 2. Individual differences, cultural variations, and contextual factors in educational psychology* (pp. 247–264). Washington, DC: American Psychological Association.

Berkowitz, M.W. (2009). Teaching in your PRIME. In D. Streight (Ed.), *Good things to do: Expert suggestions for fostering goodness in kids* (pp. 9–14). Portland: Council for Spiritual and Ethical Education Publications.

Berkowitz, M.W., Althof, W., & Jones, S. (2008). Educating for civic character.In J. Arthur, I. Davies & C. Hahn (Eds.), *SAGE Handbook of education for citizenship and democracy* (pp. 399–409). Thousand Oaks, CA: Sage.

Berkowitz, M.W., Battistich, V.A., & Bier, M.C. (2008). What works in character education: What is known and what needs to be known. In L.P. Nucci & D. Narváez (Eds.), *Handbook of moral and character education* (pp. 414–431). New York and London: Routledge.

Berkowitz, M.W. & Bier, M.C. (2005).The interpersonal roots of character education. In D.K. Lapsley& F.C. Power (Eds.), *Character psychology and character education* (pp.268–285). Notre Dame, IN: University of Notre Dame Press.

Berkowitz, M.W., & Grych, J.H. (2000). Early character development and education. *Early Education and Development, 11*, 55–72.

Berkowitz, M.W., & Puka, B. (2009). Dissent and character education. In M. Gordon (Ed.), *Reclaiming dissent: Civic education for the 21ˢᵗ century* (pp. 107–130). Amsterdam: Sense Publishers.

Blasi, A. (1980). Bridging moral cognition and moral action: A critical view of the literature. *Psychological Bulletin, 88*, 1–45.

Blasi, A. (1995). Moral understanding and the moral personality: The process of moral integration. In W.M. Kurtines & J.L. Gewirtz (Eds.), *Moral development: An introduction* (pp. 229–253). Needham Heights, MA: Allyn& Bacon.

Blasi, A. (1999). Emotions and moral motivation. *Journal for the Theory of Social Behavior, 29*, 1–19.

Blasi, A. (2001). Moral motivation and society: Internalization and the development of the self. In G. Dux & F. Welk (Eds.), Moral und Recht im Diskurs der Moderne. Zur Legitimation gesellschaftlicher Ordnung (pp. 313–329). Opladen: Leske + Budrich.

Blasi, A. (2005). Moral character: A psychological approach. In D.K. Lapsley & F.C. Power (Eds.), *Character psychology and character education* (pp. 67–100). Notre Dame, IN: University of Notre Dame Press.

Carr, E.G., Dunlap, G., Horner, R.H., Koegel, R.L., Turnbull, A.P., & Sailor, W., et al. (2002). Positive behavior support: Evolution of an applied science. *Journal of Positive Behavior Interventions, 4,* 4–16, 20.

Character Education Partnership (2010). *11 principles of effective character education: A framework for school success.* Washington, D.C.: Character Education Partnership.

Cohen, J. (2006). Social, emotional, ethical, and academic education: Creating a climate for learning, participation in democracy, and well-being. *Harvard Educational Review, 76(2),* 201–237.

Colby, A., & Damon, W. (1992). *Some do care: Contemporary lives of moral commitment.* New York: The Free Press.

Dalton, J., & Watson, M. (1997). *Among friends: Classrooms where caring and learning prevail.* Oakland CA: Developmental Studies Center.

Damon, W. (1984). Self-understanding and moral development from childhood to adolescence. In W.M. Kurtines & J.L. Gewirtz (Eds.), *Morality, moral behavior, and moral development* (pp. 109–127). New York, NY: Wiley.

Damon, W. (2009). *The path to purpose: How young people find their calling in life.* New York: Free Press.

Damon, W., & Hart, D. (1988). *Self-understanding in childhood and adolescence.* New York, NY: Cambridge University Press.

Deci, E.L., & Ryan, R.M. (1985). *Intrinsic motivation and self-determination in human behavior.* New York: Plenum.

Deci, E.L., Koestner, R., & Ryan, R.M. (1999). A meta-analytic review of experiments examining the effects of extrinsic rewards on intrinsic motivation. *Psychological Bulletin, 125,* 627–668.

Deci, E.L., Koestner, R., & Ryan, R.M. (2001). Extrinsic rewards and intrinsic motivation in education: Revisited once again. *Review of Educational Research, 71(1),* 1–27.

Deci, E.L., Vallerand, R.J., Pelletier, L.G., & Ryan, R.M. (1991). Motivation and education: The self-determination perspective. *Educational Psychology, 26*(3&4), 325–346.

Developmental Studies Center (1996). *Ways we want our class to be: Class meetings that build commitment to kindness and learning.* Oakland CA: Developmental Studies Center.

Dewey, J. (1899; revised 1915). *The school and society.* Chicago: University of Chicago Press; reprinted in: Middle works of John Dewey. Carbondale, IL: Southern Illinois University Press, 1976, Vol. 1, pp.1–109.

Dewey, J. (1916). *Democracy and education. An introduction to the philosophy of education.* New York: Macmillan.

Elias, M.J., Klein, D.A., DeLuca, A., Smith, D.F., Fattal, L.F., Bento, A., & Leverett, L. (2006). Reflections on the laws of life. *Principal Leadership, 6,* 39–43.

Fabes, R.A., Eisenberg, N., Fultz, J., & Miller, P. (1988). Reward, affect, and young children's motivational orientation. *Motivation and Emotion, 12,* 155–168.

Fishbein, M., & Ajzen, I. (2009). *Predicting and changing behavior: The reasoned action approach.* New York: Psychology Press.

Gauld, J.W. (1993). *Character first: The Hyde School difference.* San Franscisco: Institute for Contemporary Studies Press.

Gibbs, J.C. Potter, G.B.; Goldstein, A.P. (1995). *The EQUIP program: Teaching youth to think and act responsibly through a peer-helping approach.* Champaign, IL: Research Press.

Gilligan, J. (1976). Guilt and shame. In T. Lickona (Ed.), *Moral development and behavior: Theory, research and social issues* (pp. 144–158). New York, NY: Holt Rinehart and Winston.

Hardy, S.A. (2006). Identity, reasoning, and emotion. An empirical comparison of three sources of moral motivation. *Motivation and Emotion, 30,* 207–215.

Hardy, S.A., & Carlo, G. (2005). Identity as a source of moral motivation. *Human Development, 48,* 232–256.

Higgins-d'Alessandro, A., & Power, F.C. (2005). Character, responsibility, and the moral self. In D.K. Lapsley & F.C. Power (Eds.), *Character psychology and character education* (pp. 101–120). Notre Dame, IN: University of Notre Dame Press.

Horner, R.H., Sugai, G., Smolkowski, K., Eber, L., Nakasato, J., Todd, A.W., & Esperanza, J. (2009). A randomized, wait-list controlled effectiveness trial assessing School-wide Positive Behavior Support in elementary schools. *Journal of Positive Behavior Interventions, 11*, 133–144.

Horner, R.H., Sugai, G., Todd, A.W., & Lewis-Palmer, T. (2005). School-wide positive behavior support: An alternative approach to discipline in schools. In L. Bambara & L. Kern (Eds.), *Positive behavior support* (pp. 359–390). New York: Guilford.

Houlfort, N., Koestner, R., Joussemet, M., Nantel-Vivier, A., & Lekes, N. (2002). The impact of performance-contingent rewards on perceived autonomy and competence. *Motivation and Emotion, 26*, 279–295.

Johnson, D.W., & Johnson, R.T. (2008).Social interdependence, moral character and moral education. In L.P. Nucci& D. Narváez (Eds.), *Handbook of moral and character education* (pp. 204–229). New York and London: Routledge.

Kasser, T. (2002). Sketches for a Self-Determination Theory of values. In E.L. Deci & R.M. Ryan (Eds.), *Handbook of Self-Determination Theory* (pp. 123–140). Rochester NY: University of Rochester Press.

Kochanska, G. (1991). Socialization and temperament in the development of guilt and conscience. *Child Development, 62*, 1379–1392.

Kohlberg, L., & Candee, D. (1984). The relationship of moral judgment to moral action. In W.M. Kurtines & J.L. Gewirtz (Eds.), *Morality, moral behavior, and moral development* (pp. 52–73). New York: Wiley Interscience.

Kohn, A. (1993). *Punished by rewards.The trouble with gold stars, incentive plans, A's, praise, and other bribes.* Boston and New York: Houghton Mifflin.

Krettenauer, T. (2011). The dual moral self: Moral centrality and internal moral motivation. *Journal of Genetic Psychology, 172*, 309–328.

Krettenauer, T., Malti, T., & Sokol, B. (2008). The development of moral emotion expectancies and the happy victimizer phenomenon: A critical review of theory and application. *European Journal of Developmental Science, 2*, 221–235.

Lapsley, D.K., &Narváez, D. (Eds) (2004). *Moral development, self and identity.* Mahwah, NJ: Erlbaum.

Lepper, M. R., Greene, D., & Nisbett, R. E. (1973). Undermining children's intrinsic interest with extrinsic rewards: A test of the "overjustification" hypothesis. *Journal of Personality and Social Psychology, 28*, 129–137.

Lickona, T. (2008).The power of modeling in children's character development. In D. Streight (Ed.), *Good things to do: Expert suggestions for fostering goodness in kids* (pp. 33–50). Portland: Council for Spiritual and Ethical Education Publications.

Malti, T., Gummerum, M., Keller, M., & Buchmann, M. (2009).Children's moral motivation, sympathy, and prosocial behavior. *Child Development, 80*, 442–460.

Noam, G.G., Wren, T.E., Nunner-Winkler, G., & Edelstein, W. (Eds.) (1993). *The moral self. Studies in contemporary German thought.* Cambridge MA: The MIT Press.

Nucci, L. (2001). Education in the moral domain. Cambridge, UK: Cambridge University Press.

Nucci, L. (2004). Reflections on the moral self construct. In D. Lapsley& D. Narvaez (Eds.), *Moral development, self, and identity* (pp.111–132). Mahwah, NJ: Erlbaum.

Nunner-Winkler, G. (2007). Development of moral motivation from childhood to early adulthood.*Journal of Moral Education, 36*, 399–414.

Nunner-Winkler, G. (1998): Zum Verständnis von Moral – Entwicklungen in der Kindheit. In F. Weinert (Ed.),: Entwicklung im Kindesalter, (p.133–152). Weinheim/Basel: Psychologie Verlags Union

Oser, F., Althof, W., & Higgins-D'Alessandro, A. (2008). The Just Community approach to moral education: system change or individual change? *Journal of Moral Education, 37*, 395–415.

Parsons, T., & Shils, E.A. (1951).*Toward a general theory of action.Theoretical foundations for the social sciences.* Cambridge, MA: Harvard University Press.

Power, F.C., Higgins, A., & Kohlberg, L. (1989). Lawrence Kohlberg's approach to moral education. New York: Columbia University Press

Reese, H.W., & Overton, W.F. (1970). Models of development and theories of development. In L.R. Goulet& P.B. Baltes (Eds.), *Life-span developmental psychology: Research and theory* (pp. 115–148). New York: Academic Press.

Reeve, J. (2002). Self-determination theory applied to educational settings. In E.L. Deci& R.M. Ryan (Eds.), *Handbook of self-determination theory* (pp. 184–203). Rochester, N.Y.: University of Rochester Press.

Reeve, J. (2006). Teachers as facilitators: What autonomy-supportive teachers do and why their students benefit. *The Elementary School Journal, 106*(3), 225–236.

Reeve, J., & Halusic, M. (2009). How K-12 teachers can put Self-Determination Theory principles into practice. *Theory and Research in Education, 7,* 145–154.

Reeve, J., Jang, H., Carrell, D., Jeon, S., &Barch, J. (2004).Enhancing students' engagement by increasing teachers' autonomy support. *Motivation and Education, 28*(2), 147–169.

Ryan, R.M., & Brown, K.W. (2005). Legislating competence: High-stakes testing policies and their relations with psychological theories and research. In A.J. Elliot & C.S. Dweck (Eds.), *Handbook of competence and motivation* (pp. 354–373). New York: Guilford.

Ryan, R.M., & Deci, E.L. (2000). Intrinsic and extrinsic motivations: Classic definitions and new directions. *Contemporary Educational Psychology, 25,* 54–67.

Ryan, R.M., & Deci, E.L. (2002). An overview of Self-Determination Theory: An organismic-dialectical perspective. In E.L. Deci & R.M. Ryan (Eds.), *Handbook of Self-Determination Theory* (pp. 3–33). Rochester NY: University of Rochester Press.

Schinke, S.P., Botvin, G.J., & Orlandi, M.A. (1991). *Substance abuse in children and adolescents: Evaluation and treatment.* Newbury Park CA: Sage.

Sizer, T.R., & Sizer, N.F. (1999). *The students are watching: Schools and the moral contract.* Boston, MA: Beacon.

Urban, H. (2008). *Lessons from the classroom: 20 things good teachers do.* Redwood City CA: Great Lessons Press.

Vallerand, R.J., & Ratelle, C.F. (2002). Intrinsic and extrinsic motivation: A hierarchical model. In E.L. Deci & R.M. Ryan (Eds.), *Handbook of Self-Determination Theory* (pp. 37–63). Rochester, NY: University of Rochester Press.

Vincent, C.G., Randall, C., Cartledge, G., Tobin, T.J., & Swain-Bradway, J. (2011). Toward a conceptual integration of cultural responsiveness and Schoolwide Positive Behavior Support. *Journal of Positive Behavior Interventions, 13,* 219–229.

Warneken, F., & Tomasello, M. (2008). Extrinsic rewards undermine altruistic tendencies in 20-month-olds. *Developmental Psychology, 44,* 1785–1788.

Watson, M. (2006).Long-term effects of moral/character education in elementary school. In pursuit of mechanisms. *Journal of Research in Character Education, 4*(1&2), 1–18.

Watson, M., & Ecken, L. (2003).*Learning to trust: Transforming difficult elementary classrooms through developmental discipline.*San Francisco: Jossey-Bass.

AFFILIATIONS

Wolfgang Althof
Center for Character and Citizenship
College of Education
University of Missouri
St. Louis, USA

Marvin W. Berkowitz
Center for Character and Citizenship
College of Education
University of Missouri
St. Louis, USA

SHARON NODIE OJA & PATRICIA J. CRAIG

III. MORAL MOTIVATION AND THE ROLE OF THE INTERNSHIP IN PROFESSIONAL PREPARATION

INTRODUCTION

A number of theories of moral functioning have been proposed (Blasi, 1995; Colby & Damon, 1992; Hoffman, 1970; Kohlberg, 1969; Rest, Narvaez, Bebeau, & Thoma, 1999), each with its own assumptions about what motivates moral action (Hardy & Carlo, 2005), and although each model points to different sources of moral motivation, they all are "increasingly convinced that identity may play an important role in moral functioning, but links between identity and morality remain unclear, both conceptually and empirically" (p. 233).

Our conception of moral functioning is grounded in Neo-Kohlbergian theory of morality.[1] Moral motivation emphasizes two critical aspects: 1) the importance of ordering and prioritizing moral values over competing non-moral values, and 2) the formation of role concept or professional identity.[2] Although individuals may know what the moral action may be in an ethical situation, they may not choose moral values over other non-moral values. Individuals make decisions and act upon moral situations for a variety of reasons; they may be motivated by moral concerns such as the welfare of others or by non-moral concerns such as self interests, which may include avoiding punishment or reaping rewards (Nunner-Winkler, Meyer-Nikele, & Wohlrab, 2007). The prioritization of moral values in one's value system "…impacts the likelihood of moral values being acting upon in moral situations" (Hardy & Carlo, 2005, p. 234). A person who can put aside a self-serving action over an alternative ethical action has a strong desire to do what is most "morally defensible" (Duckett & Ryden, 1994, p. 61) and exhibits a strong caring for other humans. A deficiency in moral motivation occurs when a competing value is given higher priority or overshadows a moral value. When a person chooses an action that is self-serving rather than based on moral values, the person's values have replaced a concern for doing what is right.

MORAL MOTIVATION TOWARD PROFESSIONAL IDENTITY

In a professional context, each discipline's code of ethics emphasizes professional values and behaviours. A professional who exhibits moral motivation has an internalized understanding of and commitment to these ethical standards and thus places a high priority on professional values. According to Hardy and Carlo, "when

K. Heinrichs, F. Oser & T. Lovat (Eds.), Handbook of Moral Motivation: Theories, Models, Applications, 585–606.

morality is important and central to one's sense of self and identity, it heightens one's sense of obligation and responsibility to live consistently with one's moral concerns" (p. 235). A professional who exhibits moral motivation successfully prioritizes moral values above competing values because he/she is directed by an organized structure of moral identity (Narvaez, 2005).

Although many professional preparation curricula include goals related to professional identity development among students, there is still a "discrepancy between the intent of professional school education and the outcome" (Bebeau, 1994, p. 133).[3] We propose that students' professional identity can be influenced during the formal internship experience; however, the structure of the internship curriculum is critical in this process.

ROLE OF THE INTERNSHIP EXPERIENCE IN PROFESSIONAL PREPARATION

In this chapter we speak to professions that prepare students at the undergraduate level, such as recreation management, teaching, counseling, social work, nursing, etc. Internship programs in these types of professional preparation curricula are typically characterized by four criteria: 1) a specific number of hours worked in a practice setting, 2) exposure to essential competencies for practice, 3) academic credit is awarded, and 4) supervision is provided by a university faculty coordinator and an internship agency counterpart (Beggs, Ross, & Knapp, 2006). The internship is a time of intense skill acquisition, when students are challenged to make the critical transition to more autonomous professional functioning (Hambrick, Pimental, & Albano, 2009). A successful internship provides the student with opportunities to integrate classroom-acquired theory and skills in a working environment with a qualified practitioner. The student is placed in a demanding, yet protected position as he/she learns the varied aspects of service delivery in unique settings.

Although the internship has traditionally been valued for its role in fostering professional competencies for practice among students, it is less recognized for its role in the promotion of moral behaviour among students. If interns are to elevate to a level of professional autonomy, they not only need discipline-specific knowledge, skills, and an understanding of professional ethics, but they need to demonstrate moral behaviour in the face of adversity. Although many professional preparation programs provide a basic foundation in managing ethical dilemmas through didactic education in the classroom, this training is necessary, but not sufficient, for moral action among student interns. Socializing students to develop an internalized understanding of professional ethical codes through didactic means such as lectures and seminars may pose challenges for educators because these contexts may lack "motive force" (Hoffman, 2000, p. 239) for moral behaviour. We contend that when students engage in a complex new helping role during the internship experience, where they are exposed to ethical agency norms and values, supported and challenged by more experienced mentors and supervisors, and encouraged by academic supervisors to regularly reflect on their learning and development, they begin to understand and internalize professional ethical values, and thus take steps towards developing a professional identity.

Cultivating a Professional Identity during the Internship

During the internship experience, interns quickly face many personal and professional transitions that can lead to a number of ethical conflicts. In order to successfully manage these dilemmas, interns must resolve the tensions between their personal identity and the unique ethical and professional demands of their profession (Hambrick et al., 2009). Although professional education programs present students with the values of the profession through didactic training, authentic professional integration means that students have successfully assimilated those values, attitudes, behaviours, and culture in their work (Treizenberg & Davis, 2000). The ability to order and prioritize professional values over other competing values is a critical step in this integration process. Experts in the skills of moral motivation successfully prioritize ethical goals because they are directed by an organized structure of moral identity, whereas less mature professionals, such as interns, have less organized understandings of moral knowledge and may choose to conform to ethical standards in order to get rewards or avoid negative consequences (Narvaez, 2005). Even though such actions might reflect "right conduct," their motivation is deemed low because narrow self-interests have undermined the motivation to act on moral judgments. According to Rest et al. (1999), interns who are motivated by self-interests rather than by moral considerations have yet to develop the conceptual frameworks for a professional identity; they have yet to internalize the norms and values of the profession, rather remain motivated by competing personal values such as self-preservation, reward, or avoidance of punishment.

Although the internship is a time when interns are provided opportunities to practice ethical action, it is also a time when interns will likely be introduced to constraints or barriers to ethical action. While we hope that interns can learn to give priority to professional values over self interested values, in reality, they are often challenged by many conflicting value systems operating at the same time within the context of their internship experience (Triezenberg & Davis, 2000). These conflicting value systems may be associated with organizational, contextual or policy factors that compete for the intern's attention, acting as potential barriers to moral behaviour (Swisher, 2002). For example, interns across various professional settings may experience organizational policies that place values of productivity or profit over professional values such as fairness, fidelity, autonomy, or beneficence.

Because intervening variables may exist between ethics education in the classroom and the real life context of professional practice, educators must "seek creative ways to help [interns] anticipate, reflect on, and respond to such dissonance" (Mastrom, 2005, p. 265). We contend that we can influence the development of an intern's professional identity through fieldwork experiences; however, the structure of the internship curriculum is paramount in this training in order to bridge moments of interference and to guide the formation of professional identity among students engaged in an internship experience. Our study described in the next section provides insights into ways educators and intern supervisors might design fieldwork programs to cultivate a professional ethical identity among interns, leading them to prioritize professional values over competing non-moral values, thus becoming more morally motivated.

A STUDY OF HOW INTERNS LEARN TO BE MORALLY MOTIVATED

The Four Component Model of morality framed a study that explored aspects of the internship experience that appeared responsible for moral growth changes among undergraduates in a recreation management discipline (Craig & Oja, 2012).[4] For the purpose of this chapter, we focus on aspects of the internship experience that emerged as constraints to and resources in moral motivation for ten intern cases comprising the collective case study.

Recreation Management as a Helping Profession

Like many human service professions, recreation management is a line of work that requires a high degree of generalized and systematic knowledge as well as a primary orientation to others' interests rather than to individual self-interest (Barber, 1963). The leisure service delivery system comprises a vast network of government sponsored, non-profit, for-profit, and specialized organizations that provide recreation, therapeutic recreation, park, sports management, hospitality, and tourism experiences for individuals and communities (Stevens, 2010). Although these sectors differ in service focus, they are similarly driven by the needs of individuals, communities, and environments. Recreation professionals assume many different roles in practice; they are alternately seen as change agents, advocates, servant leaders, therapists, managers, planners, programmers, guides, and experts in sustainability. Through these varied roles, recreation practitioners are in a position to act on many value-laden decisions in everyday practice as they provide direct services, consultation, education, research, and advocacy to diverse sets of individuals and groups including consumers, clients, patients, families, employers, policy-makers, and third party payers. This diverse work may present practitioners with a variety of complex ethical dilemmas.

Examples of administrative ethical dilemmas that cut across various leisure service sectors include fraud, sexual harassment, conflicts of interest, safety, whistle blowing, child abuse, and dishonesty or stealing (Jamieson & Wolter, 1999). Setting-specific dilemmas are prevalent as well. For example, outdoor recreation managers encounter environmental and wildlife issues, and/or dilemmas associated with preservation, conservation, and ecosystem management; practitioners in the tourism industry may encounter issues related to the exploitation of Indigenous cultures, the negative consequences of sex tourism, and/or the impact of tourism on the physical environment; and commercial recreation business owners deal with issues related to business reciprocity, the marketing of controversial goods and services, and/or the generation of profits (McLean & Yoder, 2005). Therapeutic recreation specialists deal with problems related to the therapist-patient relationship, patient/client confidentiality and privacy, ethical implications associated with managed health care, fairness in the distribution of services, competence, and/or fidelity (Jacobson & James, 2001). Across the various service sectors, recreation practitioners are cast into conflicting roles requiring them to be open to "multiple styles of learning, diverse populations, and social concepts, values, and ethical behaviours that enable them to fulfill their responsibilities to society" (Kinney, Witman, Sable & Kinney, 2001, p. 90).

There is strong evidence suggesting that recreation practitioners deal with ethical issues on a regular basis, therefore it makes sense to prepare students majoring in recreation careers to handle the ethical dilemmas associated with practice. Although educators present students with the values of the profession through didactic training in the classroom, in order for students to successfully integrate into the profession, they must be socialized to develop an internalized understanding of these ethical codes. The professional internship experience offers an ideal opportunity to experience moral issues and practice ethical decision-making as students assume the role of a pre-professional across a variety of leisure service sectors.[5]

Internship Themes Related to Moral Motivation

A collective case study method (Stake, 2005) was utilized to gain an in-depth understanding of the aspects of the internship experience that appeared to foster or constrain moral motivation among ten intern cases.[6] Multiple forms of qualitative data were gathered from the ten intern cases including artifacts[7], observations/ fieldnotes[8], and interviews.[9] Case study is defined as a research strategy that is an all-encompassing method covering design, data collection techniques, and specific approaches to data analysis (Yin, 2003). This case study is framed within an interpretivist paradigm, which assumes that there are many points of entry into any given reality (Schram, 2003). This case study attempted to understand the complex and constructed reality from the point of view of ten interns who completed their internship experiences in 2007. A collective case study constitutes several cases because it is believed they will lead to better understanding and theorizing about a larger collection of cases (Yin, 2003). The end products are rich, narrative accounts that offer new insights into aspects of the internship experience that fostered or limited moral motivation among the ten interns who had experienced it.

If interns are to elevate to a level of professional autonomy during the internship experience, they must begin to demonstrate an internalized understanding of and commitment to professional ethics. This is not an easy task because internship experiences differ in the constraints and opportunities they present to interns. Some aspects of the experience have the potential to cultivate professional ethical identity among interns, while others pose significant challenges to identity formation. How interns learn to be morally motivated appears to be influenced by three critical aspects of the internship experience: 1) exposure to ethical agency norms and core values, 2) significant supervision and mentoring, and 3) opportunities for guided reflection. In this section we provide case examples to illustrate ways in which these aspects fostered and/or constrained moral motivation among the intern cases. We further suggest ways in which pedagogical strategies may be utilized during the internship experience to help interns prioritize moral values over competing values and thus begin the formation of a professional ethical identity.

THEME I: PRESSURES TO CONFORM TO AGENCY NORMS AND
CORE VALUES OF THE INTERNSHIP SETTING

A common phenomenon for individuals who are being inducted into a profession is the pressure to conform to the norms of the agency. Many novices tend to comply with institutional norms, even when the values and behaviours reflected by the norms are at odds with their own beliefs about best practices. For example, this emerged in our study as a potential constraint to moral motivation for seven of the ten interns. Interns tended to adopt the existing norms of their settings, rather than express independent judgment and action as they encountered ethical situations in practice. Intern conformity appeared to stem from a perception of being "powerless" because of their intern status. They failed to speak up when they observed questionable behaviour because they did not see themselves as having the right to do so; in their view, they were "only the intern." As a result of this perception, these interns became easily discouraged when challenged with ethical situations and were often unable to stand up to the pressure. This was evident in Lauren's case, an intern who worked with a private event planning firm in a large urban city in northeast U.S.A. Lauren observed co-workers using her company's equipment without their knowledge for their own catering event. In her mind, she questioned their actions, however she chose to remain silent and did not speak directly to the perpetrators and/or alert her superiors. During her interview after the internship, Lauren explained her motivation for this decision: "I didn't think that I should say anything. The guy that took the equipment was just laughing about it. He was like 'why not take it, they have such a huge warehouse full of stuff,' and so he felt it was okay to do that. I didn't say anything because I was an intern and it would have been stupid to say anything about him because he had been there for so long. I felt that I didn't have the right to do that." It appeared that Lauren's inability to articulate her concern directly to the perpetrators or her superiors was influenced by her perception that she was not in a position to do anything about it.

In addition to the perception of lacking authority to speak up during ethical situations, three interns were constrained by a self-interested need to succeed during the internship in order to receive a passing grade for the internship and graduate on time. They appeared "handcuffed" by the fact that their grade, and ultimately their graduation, hinged upon their successful performance during the internship. As a result, these interns emphasized a need to please others, which often meant that they would not speak up when they observed apparent injustices. Some of the interns passively conformed, while others were a bit more strategic, maintaining strong private reservations about doing so as evidenced by their reflective academic assignments. This was true for TJ, an intern who worked for a motorcycle rental business in northeast U.S.A. TJ was challenged by "unfair" customer service expectations and challenging work practices including long hours, forced overtime, and heavy amounts of responsibility for direct line staff. Rather than speak up and voice his displeasure with these working conditions, he chose to remain silent. He noted, "I was forced to quiet down and not speak my mind because I didn't want to lose my job. I wanted to complete the internship and graduate; that was my driving factor." TJ appeared motivated toward behavioural conformity despite the recognition that the norms in his agency's practices were not always consistent with professional values. He utilized his reflective journal and the online Blackboard® discussion assignment to vent his frustrations and "talk through" these situations. Although there was no evidence to suggest the other seven intern cases were so substantially motivated by the need to graduate on time, this issue needs to be addressed by university academic supervisors.

In contrast, Tara, an intern who worked for a small harbor boat tour business in the northeast U.S.A. appeared to perceive her internship role differently as she was able to withstand pressures to conform to an entrenched practice of poor supervision at her internship site. Tara recognized that staff morale was low because the owner of the business, her supervisor, failed to provide them with positive feedback and support. She indicated that "He lacks many of the qualities found in a successful manager; I feel like I only receive criticism and never any praise…further, he was difficult to read and his cold/harsh approach was intimidating." Even though Tara's morale was equally impacted by the owner's lack of attention and positive feedback, she was able to put that aside and focus on the wellbeing of her co-workers. Rather than sit idly by allowing this continued practice to occur, she focused on how his poor supervisory approach affected others and ultimately decided to take it upon herself to fill this void for her co-workers by initiating a morale-building project that included positive feedback notes for the staff. When asked to explain her rationale for this project, she noted, "I genuinely care about what is going on in their [staff] lives. I feel it is important as a supervisor to make sure everyone is performing at their best and the only way for this to happen is if everyone is content with their job." Her caring approach was reflected in one of these notes to a staff member: "Karen, thank you so much for all the time and energy you put into making this boat a fun and beautiful place. Your hard work does not go unnoticed – nor does your positive attitude. Your presence makes this boat a wonderful place for crew and customers. Keep the great ideas coming!" Tara valued her co-workers and was committed to promoting their dignity; this was something the owner was "not capable of doing." Tara's ability to stand up in the face of adversity, and respond to a challenging situation with a risky effort to change the status quo, suggests that not all interns are influenced by the perception of being "powerless" because of their intern status or intimidated to speak up or act because their internship grade might be hanging in the balance.

Core Values of the Internship Agency

The internship is one of the first real opportunities for students to get exposed to context-specific core values of the profession. Out of the ten interns, seven worked in commercial recreation agencies, two worked in municipal settings, and one worked in a community-based therapeutic recreation setting. In these various service settings, interns were engaged in new relationships with consumers, clients, patients, family members, site supervisors, co-workers, academic supervisors, and other interns. These interactions presented interns with ethical situations that challenged them to reflect on their own values in relation to the values of others and the institutional context.

Ethical dilemmas associated with the commercial recreation sector, for instance, emerged as potential constraints to moral motivation for three of the seven interns working in this type of setting. These interns were exposed to questionable situations such as conflict of interest, dishonesty, unfair work practices, and an emphasis on profits at all costs, which are common ethical pitfalls associated with the commercial recreation service sector (McLean & Yoder, 2005). This thematic finding appears to support the growing business literature that explores the paradoxical relationship between a company's profit-driven motive and core ideology. According to Collins and Porras (2002), highly successful visionary companies succeed because they can effectively balance their core values with their profit motive. Such core values may include a genuine care for their customers, employees, products/services, and a culture of support and innovation, and these companies actually take steps to make the core professional values pervasive throughout the company. Rather than observing a business culture that was effectively balanced between profit motive and professional core values, these three interns perceived profit maximization as the driving force at their agencies and expressed in their reflective writing their anxiety, frustration, confusion, anger, and self-doubt which appeared to motivate all three interns to actions that tended to emphasize their own personal interests, rather than the wellbeing of their clients.

For example, Riley, an intern who worked with a for-profit entertainment and booking agency in northeast U.S.A., encountered a recurring ethical dilemma that revolved around the owner's focus on making money. In one particular situation, she struggled with the owner's decision to charge a client $1,000 for terminating his contract upon learning of a cancer diagnosis that would preclude him from holding this event. Riley was struck by the owner's response as she noted:

> The fact that the client canceled his event for a health reason and not a business reason was tough to take; I had a hard time with the owner's decision. I thought

the client had enough to worry about and feel that extra financial strain was something he should not have to deal with. It was probably just business to the owner…I guess I am just a softy, but I had a hard time looking at this situation from a business standpoint.

Riley was acutely aware of and affected by the owner's questionable business decision, yet did not speak up about her concerns because "There wasn't much that I could do because I didn't have the authority there to do anything." Riley appeared to be sensitive and aware that ethical issues existed that risked potentially negative effects for the clients. Despite this awareness, however, she was not able to carry out a moral action, such as articulating her displeasure about these questionable business practices to the owner or her co-workers. Riley did not want to be viewed as a "troublemaker" and did not want to disturb the way things had been done at the agency. This factor motivated her thinking and actions. She was clearly challenged by what she saw as the reality of the business world as she continually allowed the owner's competing values to overshadow her own value of what she felt was right. Her lack of moral action appeared to be a result of deficiencies in moral motivation.

In contrast to the value incompatibility experienced by commercial recreation interns, two of the three interns working in public/non-profit recreation sectors encountered core values and behaviours in their settings that seemed to enhance their ability to prioritize professional values over non-moral competing values. The message they received on the job was one of genuine care and concern for others, and they appeared to be positively influenced by the consistent delivery of this message, which was often relayed to them through responsible site supervisors and coworkers who served as strong ethical role models. These interns seemed more at ease as they worked through ethical situations, and if they were challenged by a particular situation, they looked to their supervisor and/or co-workers to model professional behaviours or offer guidance in the resolution of the dilemma. For example, Amy, an intern who worked for a municipal recreation department in northeast U.S.A., encountered ethical situations that revolved around politics and fair use of the public facilities and services provided by her agency. While money seemed to be at the center of the majority of these conflicts for the town residents, her agency's bottom line was not about generating revenue, but rather was clearly focused on providing the best possible recreation service for as many residents as possible. During moments of resident conflict, Amy remained open to all viewpoints despite the fact that she did not always appreciate the manner in which they expressed their concerns to the staff. She articulated the need to remain open to their ideas and treat them with respect. She noted, "You should listen to the suggestions, and you can make changes and improve things, but that doesn't mean you have to change everything to align with their suggestion. You can't please everyone, but you always need to show respect so people can speak up about things, because that is their right." Amy's understanding of the values of the public service sector is reflected in a comment she made about her supervisor, who had worked for the agency for over 10 years:

My supervisor is not in this industry for the money or for having a pool just to say you have a pool. He's in it to have a pool so kids and families can use it, and so you can provide programs. I really respect him. That is what it is all about; you do your job and have passion for it, and he really does. All of the kids that play basketball are like his kids, all of the camp kids are like his kids, he takes care of everyone, and he has a great relationship with all of the people that he has worked with over the years.

The type of ethical situations that arose in Amy's public setting and the availability of strong ethical role models enabled her to recognize the impact of her work on the lives of others. Perhaps it was her internalization of the agency's public service philosophy that allowed her to take steps towards developing a professional identity.

Mediating Conformity Constraints

If educators are to appreciate the moral decisions our students make during the internship experience, we need to understand the ethical perspective those decisions are based on and recognize the factors that may influence those decisions. For example, in our recreation management program, we have a required pre-internship course that takes place one to two semesters before the internship semester. The course is designed to prepare students for the internship experience through the identification of career goals and the selection of an approved internship site. Course topics include an orientation to the philosophy, goals, and purpose of the internship experience; review of career settings; importance of networking through professional associations; understanding of ethical principles as applied in practice; and, issues related to the transition from college to professional life, including supervision, conflict management, and stress/self-care. At the conclusion of the course, students submit a summative portfolio emphasizing self-assessment, internship goals and objectives, skills in resume and cover letter construction, and interviewing techniques. The pre-internship course gives academic faculty the opportunity to get to know students, their professional goals, and their strengths and weaknesses.

While the professional preparation curriculum teaches students to uphold the ethical codes of practice, it is important to recognize that interns may be up against institutional control mechanisms that work to ensure that they are following accepted procedures and agency norms. We must continue to help students develop awareness and understanding of the potential ethical pitfalls associated with diverse service sectors of the field and the motivation to choose professional values over non-moral agency norms. We can achieve this outcome not only through didactic training in the classroom and requiring fieldwork experiences before the internship, but also by being attuned to the values and behaviours presented to our students during the internship experience. If we commit to *contextualized learning and instruction*, we should be able to effectively match students to internship agencies based on more than just their practical knowledge and experiences. As seen in this study, we may need to consider an intern's ability to withstand the considerable pressure of conforming to agency norms and values, especially when these values are non-moral in nature. We need to be sensitive to the fact that some interns may be a poor fit for a commercial recreation internship agency known for its profit-driven culture because they are more likely to stay focused on their own interests, do what they're told by authority, and passively conform to potentially questionable practices of their internship agency. On the other hand, some student interns may be better equipped to withstand the pressures of such an environment and may have a better chance of demonstrating moral behaviour in practice. Furthermore, when values other than professional values are at the center of the internship experience, educators should be prepared to proactively address these shortcomings through guided inquiry opportunities and reflective coaching. Through timely and skilled feedback, educators can provide interns with assurances that their attempts to uphold ethical principles in practice, even when these attempts are at odds with the agency's norms, will not result in failure of the internship experience. If educators can succeed in these intentional pedagogical efforts, we might be able to lessen the "reality shock" experienced by interns who encounter setting-specific ethical dilemmas in practice for the first time. Through ethics education in the classroom, such as a pre-internship course, and carefully designed fieldwork experiences, we can help prepare interns to choose professional values and begin developing their professional identity amidst the reality of practicing in the field.

THEME II: DEVELOPMENT OF PROFESSIONAL IDENTITY THROUGH SIGNIFICANT SUPERVISION AND MENTORING

Supervision, mentoring, and emotional support emerged as influential aspects of the internship experience for the moral motivation of interns. Six of the ten interns characterized their site supervisors and/or coworkers as strong ethical role models because they were available to them during daily interactions as well as at times when they needed guidance on the ethical front. For example, Lauren indicated that her site supervisor was a positive role model for motivating her throughout the internship experience. Lauren valued her supervisor's knowledge base, experience in the industry, and willingness to provide a diverse learning experience in all areas of the business. She appreciated her supervisor's graduated mentoring approach and remarked that it was this approach that led to her increased confidence in the field:

> My supervisor was trying to give me the opportunity to do a little bit of everything, and tell me all about the business, and then go out and do it. She trained me in a good way; at the beginning she talked about it, and then I watched her doing things, and then I would go out with her and do it, and then I actually did it on my own.

Lauren viewed her site supervisor as a vital link to her successful adjustment to the profession because she was available to her as she faced challenges associated with daily practice, and provided her with problem-solving assistance as she encountered and worked through ethical dilemmas. Her supervisor was invested in Lauren's learning experience, providing her with meaningful and challenging learning opportunities that motivated her to reach beyond her current skill set and comfort zone.

This type of mentoring relationship emphasizes *support and challenge* and *reflective coaching*. Effective site supervisors in this study appeared to be more attuned to interns' needs and were more committed to providing them with practical and emotional support as they struggled to accommodate new and ambiguous experiences in practice. They assumed a caring and empathic stance with interns, were genuinely invested in fostering intern development, and were committed to providing regular feedback that was at times both positive and constructive in nature. Effective supervisors not only supported interns in their adaptation to the new practice environment; they also challenged interns by providing them with tasks and responsibilities outside of their comfort zone. They achieved a good balance between support and challenge, and modeled responsible professional behaviours throughout the experience that appeared to positively motivate interns' understanding of and commitment to professional ethical values.

Conversely, ineffective site supervisors were less aware of interns' practical and emotional needs. Four of the ten interns experienced ineffective site supervisors whom they characterized as being poorly organized, intimidating and unapproachable, punitive in their approach, and/or too busy to provide interns with an adequate level of support and guidance. These types of supervisors were often unavailable during times of crisis, which required interns to look to their co-workers for advice. Unfortunately, these co-workers were not always willing to nurture interns or help them problem solve solutions to dilemmas, and some even participated in unprofessional work behaviours that proved to be the original source of ethical conflict for the intern. Overall, these types of supervisors and co-workers failed to create a supportive and nurturing environment, which subsequently led to anxiety for interns as they began to negotiate their new professional role. This was the case for TJ, an intern who became increasingly angry, frustrated, and disillusioned by his supervisor's poor motivational style. TJ recognized that this lack of mentoring resulted in low staff morale and contributed to their general lack of trust for those in authority at the site. He characterized his supervisor as the "type of manager that sits back and watches his troops, tells them what to do, and never gets dirty, or never does anything." In his academic assignments, he articulated his desire to have a "manager that is a motivator and gets involved with his employees, can interact with you in a positive manner, and is somebody that wouldn't ask you to do something that they wouldn't want to do." Although TJ articulated his thoughts about this situation in his academic assignments throughout the internship, he did not speak up directly to those in charge because he was conflicted by the need to complete the internship so that he could graduate on time. TJ's approach ultimately led to burnout and his performance suffered as a result, reflected in low scores on his final performance evaluation. His feelings were evident in his online discussion post towards the end of the internship, "I feel tired, worn out, a bit frustrated and ready to complete this internship ASAP. I want to complete my internship and put in my two week notice so that I can move on to something more enjoyable for myself." Rather than commit to the job after his internship ended, a verbal agreement he made with the site prior to starting the internship, TJ quit at the end of the internship experience amidst a great deal of tension and conflict. The lack of a significant mentor who was committed to supporting and challenging TJ during the internship clearly influenced this unfortunate outcome.

Mediating Lack of Mentoring

As reflected in the case narratives, when supervisors and/or co-workers failed to demonstrate moral behaviour themselves, or were unavailable to provide interns with an appropriate level of ethical guidance, interns turned to personal resources for emotional support as they negotiated difficult situations in practice. For some interns, these supports were parents or bosses in other jobs, while others leaned on friends at work or their intern peers. The online Blackboard® discussion assignment associated with this internship curriculum emerged as an important tool for interns who used their intern peers for this emotional support. This tool was beneficial because it fostered a sense of community for interns who felt isolated in their experience because their sites were in different parts of the country, far from the university. Through the Blackboard® mechanism, interns actively sought their peers' opinions and advice, or simply used them as a sounding board as they vented their frustrations. Interestingly, interns rarely sought assistance in these ethical situations from academic supervisors who they emailed regularly with written assignments; however, these assignments did not solicit discussion about moral dilemmas and ethical issues. Perhaps interns were unwilling to seek this guidance because they were fearful of appearing vulnerable, which might have had a negative impact on their ability to pass the internship. Or maybe the interns felt that they would be removed from their site had they shared some of their agency's business practices. This would result in having to start over by finding a new site, potentially further delaying their graduation date. This is an area for future research. It would be important to examine how educators can adequately respond to interns in isolated sites who are struggling with ethical dilemmas in practice, even when those interns don't seek out academic support.[10]

The recreation management internship case study showed that site supervisors and co-workers are critical role models and their ethical behaviours leave a lasting impression on interns. Educators have long valued the need for effective mentoring during the internship experience; however, as reflected in the case study findings, supervisors' influence reaches well beyond teaching interns requisite skills for successful practice—they must also motivate interns to practice with moral character and integrity. Although we expect site supervisors to be competent in practice, we tend to assume, because they hold a credential to practice or have a minimum number of years of experience in the field, that they are ethical practitioners able to model professional behaviours for our students. These findings suggest the need to adjust our assumptions and seek evidence of supervisor ethical competence during our site approval process. We need to make a conscious effort to ensure that appropriate professional core values are being presented to our students during the internship in order to facilitate the formation of a professional ethical identity.

THEME III: CULTIVATING A PROFESSIONAL IDENTITY THROUGH
GUIDED REFLECTION OPPORTUNITIES

Another aspect of this internship curriculum that appeared to positively motivate interns' moral growth was the opportunity for regular reflection through the academic assignments. Distributing written assignments throughout the internship helps to achieve a *balance* between interns' actions in the internship and their reflection. If there is too much time in between the action and reflection cycle, growth may be limited. For example, in this internship curriculum the various formative and summative written assignments (reflective journal, three analytical papers, online discussion forum with peers and academic supervisor, special project report, and summative portfolio document) were staggered throughout the internship in order to provide interns with regular guided inquiry opportunities to
reflect on their experience. Interns utilized different assignments to express their concerns and frustrations, acknowledge what they were learning, and help them make sense of the experience. For instance, Tara and TJ appeared to use the journal assignment to reconcile the conflicting values of their agencies, while Riley and Lauren found the final reflection paper and summative portfolio assignments most beneficial to their overall understanding of the experience.

One element that appeared to be missing from these guided inquiry activities was an intentional focus on eliciting ethical reflection from the interns. With the exception of one Blackboard® discussion thread, the reflective activities in this internship program did not request a more formal ethical analysis of the specific issues in which interns were involved. Despite this limitation, interns in this study appeared to be motivated by these reflective activities to advance their thinking around difficult issues; they used the assignments to "talk through" and, in some instances, simply vent about the intense problems or issues they encountered at their agency.

In order to foster professional ethical identity among interns, educators may need to consider the inclusion of more formal strategies designed to motivate ethical reflection about various ethical issues encountered during the internship experience. For instance, interns can be required to write a personal philosophy statement that challenges them to articulate their understanding of the nature of their discipline and view of themselves as change agents, and begin to express their understanding of and commitment to the professional ethical codes guiding their practice. These reflective activities can be useful tools for helping interns begin to develop a systematic understanding of ethical issues and the consequences of their behaviours in practice. Therefore, it is essential that internship programs in general, provide ample opportunities for engaging in these types of reflective activities and remain attentive to the need for strategies that foster ethical reflection.

Guiding intern reflection and inquiry is important in the internship as the mentor or supervisor provides timely and on-going feedback, probes for more detail, and offers advice or suggestions as interns grapple with certain elements of practice. In our internship program, guided inquiry by academic supervisors varied in the amount, quality, and timing of their feedback. As evidenced in the ten intern case narratives, site supervisors' efforts at guided inquiry were also limited, although the study was unable to assess these efforts. However, the analysis was done in relation to the academic supervisor's efforts in this study. Ideally, *guided inquiry* should take place during the course of intern action; however, academic supervisors in this study were restricted in providing timely feedback by their lack of proximity to interns who were scattered throughout the northeast U.S.A. and by the assignment submission method. At the time of this study, interns were processing their written work via a traditional postal service method, which produced a significant delay in receiving formative feedback from academic supervisors. As a result of this realization, and the recognition of the benefits of using technology in instruction, this internship program has since shifted its assignments to an electronic submission and feedback process. This simple shift in assignment submission method has enabled academic supervisors to provide interns with "real time" feedback. Although this adjustment has improved the internship program under study, it is evident that academic supervisors still need more training in guided inquiry strategies. Academic supervisors associated with this internship curriculum viewed themselves as "peripherally involved" in the internship experience and failed to recognize the significant role they actually can play in motivating interns toward professional identity formation.

DISCUSSION

We contend that there is value in exploring the internship experience as a primary pedagogical resource for intern moral motivation. The themes frame our ideas about how specific aspects of the internship experience may limit or foster moral motivation among recreation management interns.

Like Mead (1934), we contend that the stimulus for the moral growth of interns is more likely to occur in fieldwork experiences where students assume real-world helping roles and are supported and challenged by more experienced "others" to develop their professional ethical identity. Ethical issues experienced during the internship "exceed the hypothetical ethical problems discussed in seminars and classrooms, and prepare students for autonomous ethical functioning as an adult in the field" (Hambrick et al., p. 191). Professional practice does not exist in a vacuum, but rather is deeply embedded in an institutional context with a web of interactions with others (Carpenter & Richardson, 2008). Students who are immersed in professional practice through the internship are likely to be exposed to these context-specific values and behaviours for the first time. These diverse interactions and relationships bring interns face-to-face with ethical dilemmas that challenge them to reflect on their own values and understand how their values coincide with or differ from the values of others and/or the institutional context. These new patterns of interaction require interns to come to terms with the "moral dimensions of their new role" (Triezenberg & Davis, 2000, p. 48) and are likely to stimulate the development of a "moral self-identity" (Narvaez, 2005, p. 138).

Our conceptualization of how interns can learn to be morally motivated is comprised of three themes that emerged from case studies of ten interns (See Figure 1). These three themes include: 1) pressures to conform to agency norms and core values of the internship setting can impact the intern's ability to prioritize professional values over other competing values 2) the development of professional identity can be enhanced through significant supervision and mentoring, and 3) cultivating a professional identity can be positively impacted through guided reflection opportunities. Elements highlighted in the three themes are: *contextualized learning and instruction, support and challenge, reflective coaching, balance between action and reflection, and guided inquiry.* These elements are part of an integrated learning framework (Oja & Reiman, 2007) that has been used in teacher education[11]. We contend that an internship program that focuses on these elements can provide an optimum environment for interns to become morally motivated.

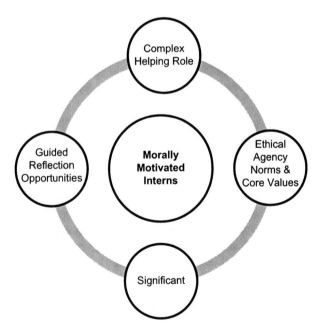

Figure 1. How interns can learn to be morally motivated.

As interns encounter ethical conflict, incongruity, ambiguity, and discrepancies in the obligations, commitments, and responsibilities in their new professional role, they experience disequilibrium as the new information challenges their usual mode of thinking. With significant support of the mentor (coach, supervisor) who guides and challenges them to further inquiry, they can begin to interpret and understand the new experience, and develop alternative ways of thinking about these dilemmas; their ways of thinking may shift from concrete to abstract, simple to complex, and self-centered to other-centered. As a result their ethical reasoning may become more integrated over time enabling them to better understand ethical problems in their professional work, to choose moral values over competing non-moral values, and to work cooperatively with others as they construct a professional identity that incorporates the ethical values of their profession.

CONCLUSION

This chapter is based in the Neo-Kohlbergian two-part concept of moral motivation that we stated in our introduction: 1) the importance of ordering and prioritizing moral values over competing non-moral values, and 2) the formation of role concept or professional identity. Narvaez' writings on expertise in moral motivation have been helpful to our understanding; she suggests that experts in the skills of moral motivation have developed an ethical self-identity that leads them to prioritize ethical goals over non-moral goals (Narvaez, 2005, p. 137). Interns are apprentices in the profession, and, as evidenced in the ten case studies, may be novices in the skills of moral motivation. They may be less able to prioritize ethical goals over non-moral goals; and they are just beginning to develop their professional identity. The intern cases illustrate the many conflicting value systems that confront interns. Their testimonies illustrate how interns can succumb to pressures in agency norms and exhibit deficiencies in moral motivation when competing values overshadow ethical values. Their testimonies also suggest elements that foster interns' moral motivation. The three themes in this chapter provide insights into ways educators and intern supervisors might design internship programs to develop moral motivation e.g. cultivating professional ethical identity leading interns to prioritize professional values over competing non-moral values. Through a carefully designed internship, interns may be assisted in demonstrating moral motivation in the face of adversity. Narvaez and Lapsley (2005, p. 155) emphasize curriculum techniques needed for developing ethical expertise that include simultaneous learning and using theory while building skills in a well-structured environment that provides corrective feedback and focused practice. The internship design elements highlighted in themes from the case studies in this chapter reinforce and further specify the curriculum techniques. We propose that the design elements of *reflective coaching* and *support and challenge* can form a well-structured environment that can provide the intern with corrective feedback. Using *guided inquiry*, the interns are encouraged to learn and use theory while they build a professional repertoire of skills. Deliberate focused practice emphasizes the internship as a series of *complex new helping experiences;* and practice over time with *support and challenge* provides *continuity* in new learning. A well-designed internship can assist interns as they begin to internalize professional ethical values and take steps toward developing a professional identity so that they are more able to prioritize moral values over competing values, thus exhibiting and developing moral motivation.

NOTES

[1] According to Rest et al. (1999), moral action is generated by the interaction of four components: moral sensitivity (i.e., interpreting situations in terms of the consequences one's own actions have on others); moral judgment (i.e., understanding and deciding upon "right" action in a given situation); moral motivation (i.e., ordering and prioritizing moral values over competing non-moral values); and moral character (i.e., command over the ego-strength and self regulatory abilities necessary to actually execute one's decisions). The four components "do not follow each other in a set temporal order" (Rest et al., p. 102), but rather are integrated in complex and unique ways to provide a dynamic feedback system that leads to moral behavior. Narvaez and Rest (1995) indicate that the Four Component Model depicts an "ensemble of processes" and that deficiency in any of the four components can result in a failure of moral action.

[2] Rest et al. use the terms "role concept" and "professional identity" interchangeably; we use the term "professional identity" in this chapter.

[3] Bebeau (1994) points to a lack evidence describing specific methods for influencing professional identity among students in professional preparation programs. As a result, she continues to develop and study the Professional Role Orientation Inventory and the Role Concept Essay as two means of measuring moral motivation among students and professionals across a variety of professional disciplines (Bebeau, 2002).

[4] This mixed methods study explored moral growth in undergraduates in a recreation management internship experience. The quantitative phase reported moral judgment gains in Personal Interest and Post-Conventional schema, and N-2 scores as measured by the Defining Issues Test 2 (Bebeau & Thoma, 2003) among 33 interns. The case study method used a pattern matching technique to show congruence between the theoretical patterns of Neo-Kohlbergian theory of moral development and observed patterns of judgment and action among 10 intern cases representing low and high levels of Post-Conventional reasoning.

[5] Student interns typically work in the following leisure service sectors: public and government (local, state, federal); non-profits (YMCA/YWCA, boys/girls clubs); event planning (firms, resorts, entertainment); private membership organizations (country clubs); employee services (corporate team building); sport management (recreational sports); armed forces (morale, well-being & recreation); tourism and hospitality (cruise industry, convention centers, visitor's bureau, theme parks, fairs, festivals, zoos, hotels); campus recreation (colleges and universities); and therapeutic recreation (recreation for disability populations).

[6] The setting for this study was a nationally accredited recreation management curriculum at a public university in northeast U.S.A. The sample was selected from two student cohorts who completed the pre-internship class during either the fall or spring semester, prior to their summer internship experience. Utilizing a criterion sampling strategy (Patton, 2002), ten case study participants were selected from a sample of 33 interns who volunteered to participate in the study during their internship. All ten of the intern cases were seniors, seven were female, and three were male.

[7] Artifacts were academic assignments associated with the internship program and included formative and summative papers submitted by the intern throughout the internship, weekly reflective journals maintained by the intern throughout the internship experience, bi-weekly online asynchronous discussions, and a summative internship portfolio document submitted by the intern at the conclusion of the internship.

[8] Researcher observations/field notes were generated for each of the ten interns cases throughout the internship experience. Field notes were generated during the mid-term on-site visit where the researcher questioned interns and their site supervisors about the intern's roles and responsibilities, performances, and situations in which the intern was required to demonstrate moral behavior. Additional field notes were recorded in intern case files as warranted based on the emergence of issues or concerns.

[9] At the conclusion of their internship, semi-structured interviews were conducted with each of the ten intern cases. In order to address issues of authenticity and reliability, the interview guide was developed through a series of observations, focus groups, telephone interviews with experienced site supervisors, and a pilot test study. Interview topics included background on the internship/logistics, work responsibilities, supervision, performance, role negotiation, impact of academic assignments on learning, and ethical situations encountered by interns that posed problems and contradictions for their current understanding.

[10] For example, in our recreation management program, interns may be placed with internship sites throughout the U.S.A. and a few have been placed internationally. Interns who are placed with sites that are a great distance from their home and the university may experience feelings of social isolation and homesickness, as their typical sources of emotional support are no longer close in proximity.

[11] Elements of a practice-based applied theory of learning and development were tested by Sprinthall and colleagues in a series of teacher preparation and training projects e.g. Reiman, 1999; Reiman & Thies-Sprinthall, 1998; Sprinthall & Thies-Sprinthall, 1983; Sprinthall, Reiman, & Thies-Sprinthall, 1996). Reiman and Oja (2006) consolidated the elements to seven conditions (principles) they referred to as an Integrated Learning Framework (ILF) to guide curriculum and pedagogy within a professional education program. The overall goals of the ILF are the development of more complex and more integrated understanding of oneself; the formation of greater conceptual complexity and flexibility as one interprets and acts in practice; the growth of moral decision making in response to professional dilemmas; and the acquisition of new behaviors that exemplify best practices in one's profession.

REFERENCES

Barber, B. (1963). Some problems in the sociology of the professions.*Daedalus, 92*, 669–688.

Bebeau, M.J. (1994). Influencing the moral dimensions of dental practice. In J. Rest & D. Narvaez (Eds.), *Moral development in the professions* (pp. 121–146). Hillsdale, NJ: Lawrence Erlbaum Associates.

Bebeau, M.J. (2002). The Defining Issues Test and the Four Component Model: Contributions to professional education. *Journal of Moral Education, 31*(3), 271–295

Bebeau, M.J., & Thoma, S.J. (2003). *Guide for DIT-2.* University of Minnesota: Center   for the Study of Ethical Development.

Beggs, B.A., Ross, C.M., & Knapp, J.S. (2006). Internships in leisure services: An analysis of student and practitioner perceptions and expectations. *Schole: A Journal of Leisure Studies and Recreation Education, 21,* 1–19.

Blasi, A. (1995). Moral understanding and the moral personality: The process of moral integration. In W.M. Kurtines & J.L. Gewirtz (Eds.), *Moral development: An introduction* (pp. 229–253). Needham Heights, MA: Allyn & Bacon.

Carpenter, C., & Richardson, B. (2008). Ethics knowledge in physical therapy: A narrative review of the literature since 2000. *Physical Therapy Reviews, 13*(5), 366–374.

Colby, A., & Damon, W. (1992). *Some do care: Contemporary lives of moral commitment.* New York, NY: Free Press.

Collins, J.C., & Porras, J.I. (2002). *Built to last: Successful habits of visionary companies.* New York, NY: HarperCollins.

Craig, P.J., & Oja, S.N. (2012). Moral judgement changes among undergraduates in a capstone internship experience. *Journal of Moral Education.* doi: 10.1080/03057240.2012.677603

Duckett, L.J. & Ryden, M.B. (1994). Education for ethical nursing practice. In J. Rest & D. Narvaez (Eds.), *Moral developmen in the professions* (pp. 51–69). Hillsdale, NJ: Lawrence Erlbaum Associates.

Hambrick, J.P., Pimentel, S., & Albano, A.M. (2009). From theory to practice: Facing ethical challenges as a clinical intern. *Cognitive and Behavioral Practice, 16*(2), 191–204.

Hardy, S.A., & Carlo, G. (2005). Identity as a source of moral motivation. *Human Development, 48*, 232–256.

Hoffman, M.L. (1970). Moral development. In P. Mussen (Ed.), *Handbook of child psychology* (pp. 261–361). New York, NY: John Wiley.

Hoffman, M.L. (2000). *Empathy and moral development: Implications for caring and justice*. New York, NY: Cambridge University Press.

Jacobson, J.M., & James, A. (2001). Ethics: Doing right. In N.J. Stumbo (Ed.), *Professional issues in therapeutic recreation: On competence and outcomes* (pp. 237–248). Champaign, IL: Sagamore Publishing.

Jamieson, L.M., & Wolter, S.A. (1999). Management—What is it? In B. van der Smissen, M. Moiseichik, V.J. Hartenburg, and L.F. Twardzik (Eds.), *Management of park and recreation agencies* (pp, 1–18). Ashburn, VA: National Recreation and Park Association.

Kinney, W.B., Witman, J.P., Sable, J.R., & Kinney, J.S. (2001). Curricular standardization in therapeutic recreation: Professional and university implications. In N.J. Stumbo (Ed.), *Professional issues in therapeutic recreation: On competence and outcomes* (pp. 87–103). Champaign, IL: Sagamore Publishing.

Kohlberg, L. (1969). Stage and sequence: The cognitive-developmental approach to socialization. In D. Goslin (Ed.), *Handbook of socialization theory and research.* (pp. 347–480). Chicago, IL: Rand McNally.

Mastrom, E. (2005). Teaching and learning about ethical and human dimensions in clinical education: Exploring student and clinical instructor experiences in physical therapy. In. R.B. Purtilo, G.M. Jensen, & C.B. Royeen (Eds.), *Educating for moral action: A sourcebook in health and rehabilitation ethics* (pp. 265–283). Philadelphia, PA: F.A. Davis Company.

McLean, D.J., & Yoder, D.G. (2005). *Issues in recreation and leisure: Ethical decision-making.* Champaign, IL: Human Kinetics.

Mead, G.H. (1934). *Mind, self and society.* Chicago, IL: University of Chicago Press.

Narvaez, D. (2005). The Neo-Kohlbergian tradition and beyond: Schemas, expertise, and character. In R.A. Dienstbier, G. Carlo, & C.P. Edwards (Eds.), *Moral motivation through the life span* (pp. 119–163). Lincoln, NE: University of Nebraska Press.

Narvaez, D. & Lapsley, D.K. (2005). The psychological foundations of everyday morality and moral expertise. In D.K. Lapsley & F.C. Powers (Eds.), *Character psychology and character education* (pp. 140–165). Notre Dame, IN: University of Notre Dame Press.

Narvaez, D., & Rest, J.R. (1995). The four components of acting morally. In W.M. Kurtines & J.L. Gewirtz (Eds.), *Moral development: An introduction* (pp. 385–399). Boston: Allyn & Bacon.

Nunner-Winkler, G., Neyer-Nikele, M., & Wohlrab, D. (2007). Gender differences in moral motivation. *Merrill-Palmer Quarterly, 53*(1), 26–52.

Oja, S.N., & Reiman, A.J. (2007). A constructivist-developmental perspective. In M.E. Diez & J. Raths (Eds.), *Dispositions in teacher education* (pp. 91–115). Greenwich, CT: Information Age Publishing, Inc.

Patton, M.Q. (2002). *Qualitative research and evaluation methods.* Thousand Oaks, CA: Sage.

Reiman, A.J. (1999). The evolution of social role-taking and guided reflection framework in teacher education: Recent theory and quantitative synthesis of research. *Teaching and Teacher Education, 15*, 597–612.

Reiman, A.J., & Oja, S.N. (2006). Toward a practice-based theory for professional education: Fostering teachers' ethical and conceptual judgment. In F.K. Oser, F. Achtenhagen, & U. Renold (Eds.), *Competence oriented teacher training: Old research and new pathways* (pp. 129–147). Rotterdam, Netherlands: Sense Publishers.

Reiman, A.J., & Thies-Sprinthall, L. (1998). *Mentoring and supervision for teacher development.* New York, NY: Addison Wesley Longman, Inc.

Rest, J., Narvaez, D., Bebeau, M.J., & Thoma, S.J. (1999). *Postconventional moral thinking: A Neo-Kohlbergian approach.* Mahwah, NJ: Lawrence Erlbaum Associates.

Schram, T. (2003). *Conceptualizing qualitative inquiry: Mindwork for fieldwork in education and the social sciences.* Upper Saddle River, NJ: Merrill Prentice Hall.

Sprinthall, N.A., Reiman, A.J., & Thies-Sprinthall, L. (1996). Teacher professional development. In J. Sikula (Ed.), *Second handbook of research on teacher education.* New York: Macmillan.

Sprinthall, N.A., & Thies-Sprinthall, L. (1983). The need for theoretical frameworks in educating teachers: A cognitive-developmental perspective. In K. Howey & W. Gardner (Eds.), *Education of teachers: A look ahead,* (pp. 74–97). New York: Longman.

Stake, R.E. (2005). Qualitative case studies. In N.K. Denzin & Y.S. Lincoln (Eds.), *The Sage handbook of qualitative research* (pp. 443–466). Thousand Oaks, CA: Sage.

Stevens, C.A. (2010). Recreation and leisure in North American life. In C.A. Stevens, J.F. Murphy, L.R. Allen, & E.A. Sheffield (Eds.), *A career with meaning: Recreation parks, sport management, hospitality, and tourism* (pp. 3–24). Champaign, IL: Sagamore Publishing.

Swisher, L.L. (2002). A retrospective analysis of ethics knowledge in physical therapy (1970–2000). *Physical Therapy, 82*(7), 692–706.

Triezenberg, H.L., & Davis, C.M. (2000). Beyond the code of ethics: Educating physical therapists for their role as moral agents. *Journal of Physical Therapy Education, 14*(3), 48–58.

Yin, R.K. (2003). *Applications of case study research.* Thousand Oaks, CA: Sage.

AFFILIATIONS

Sharon Nodie Oja
Department of Education
University of New Hampshire
Durham, New Hampshire, USA

Patricia J. Craig
Department of Recreation Management and Policy
University of New Hampshire
Durham, New Hampshire, USA

FRANCISCO ESTEBAN BARA & MARIA BUXARRAIS ESTRADA

IV. WHY MORAL EDUCATION IS MOTIVATING BY NATURE

INTRODUCTION

Moral education has been a constant in Western thought, a proprium of our history (Jaeger, 1957). Morality is a human condition, an ontological question. It is what makes it possible for us to be able to give value to what happens around us and to what happens to ourselves. Also, and more interestingly, morality allows us to go from what we are now to what we are not yet. In an Aristotelian sense, we are beings in act and in potency, our condition of incompleteness and indeterminacyplacing us on a path of perfection towards the good (bonum), the truth (verum) and the beauty (pulchrum).

Therefore, it is relatively easy to find a reason that allows us to affirm that moral education is motivating by nature. What can be more motivating than to show us how to live in a way oriented to goodness, truth and beauty, and so to foster the development of human nature in a moral sense? Yet, it is not as easy as it may seem. Motivation, etymologically speaking, is the mental preparation for an action to be carried out with consciousness and interest that is, the determination of purposes that are the result of a rational approach and worthy to be pursued. The words 'interest' and 'consciousness' are crucial. To put it another way, the motivation, if it is well understood, arises from reasons that have internal value by themselves, for the mere fact of being how they are. The motives for moral education can be of one kind or another. History shows that the reasoning behind certain ways of educating in morality have made it one of the causes of social problems and injustice (Arendt, 1968) which has even led, in some cases, to the destruction of educational institutions as buildings of thought.[1]

The current variety of views on moral philosophy may suggest that there exist different versions of motives for which moral education is worthy. This fact is certainly important because whichever moral philosophy is supported and whichever moral education is sustained, the argued reasons will differ. Some moral motivations will be defended while others will be rejected. Moral philosophy, moral education and moral motivation are in constitutive relationship with each other. All moral philosophies are set in the classical coordinate axis that places the individual at one end and the community at the other. We can say that the different versions are reasonable but not complete. Moreover, it would be a mistake to regard them as immeasurable, as if they alone could explain the whole reality since this would hinder the dialogue between them.

K. Heinrichs, F. Oser & T. Lovat (Eds.), Handbook of Moral Motivation: Theories, Models, Applications, 607–622.

The aim of this chapter is twofold. On the one hand, it aims to present the current reality in relation to moral education with motivations that, in one way or another, have caused us to arrive at our current reality. Postmodernism can be understood as the result of a process, as the consequence of a moral educational project. On the other hand, there are four motives or reasons that we consider vital in order to engage with interest and consciousness in the adventure of morally educating the new generations of citizens, that is, four reasons for moral motivation. These reasons need to be interpreted in the philosophical debate previously suggested between the individual (liberalism) and the community (communitarianism), and, as we shall see, they cannot be considered only from one end because this would distort reality.

WHERE MOTIVATION IN MORAL EDUCATION IS SITUATED AT PRESENT

We can say that we live in a new era, in a reality that began to take shape in modernity and that it is now showing its face, gestures and ways of being. This new reality or historic moment is known as postmodernism. Social, cultural, economic and technological developments have participated in shaping a reality that in many respects has little to do with its predecessor. Postmodernism should not be understood as a continuation of modernity, but as a truly new era. This new reality has been identified, described, and analysed (Bauman, 1993, 2007) not many years ago and, as it could not be otherwise, there are still many issues unidentified and unresolved, a fact that has facilitated the emergence of a truly thought-provoking debate.

The vast majority of insights made so far concern, explicitly or implicitly, moral education, its past, its present, and its future. In other words, the moral education of recent years, while preserving the singularity of each community and individual, is being identified as one of the main causes that have brought about the appearance of certain situations we are living out today (Bauman, 1993). Overall we can say that the conclusions being reached are not very encouraging and point to an uncertain future.

We shall be pointing out some conclusions with no intention of being exhaustive. The first one and perhaps most powerful is the one that would encompass everything regarding contemporary individualism (Lipovetsky, 1983). Individualism can be noticed and perceived as being especially strong in recent years; it seems to be one of the hallmarks of postmodern identity. The individual subject is in vogue and bypasses all other questions. For example: our young people seem to identify increasingly less with political institutions and what they represent, with their inherited customs, etc., and take on independent and individualistic lifestyles governed by personal desires that change depending on the occasion (Beck, 1992; Giddens, 1991).

The implications of this postmodern trend are, among others, community absenteeism, social exclusion of certain minority groups and youth violence (Sloam, 2008). So far, the solution to this problem that actually concerns quite a few countries seems to be the support of a civic education. Some examples of this international trend are seen in the introduction of "civic, legal and social education" (éducation civique, juridique et sociale -ECJS-) in France in 1999, the introduction of citizenship education classes in English schools in the year 2002, and the program "Learn and Live in a Democracy" (Demokratie Lernen & Leben) developed in Germany. Investigations such as those carried out by the IEA (Association for the Evaluation of Educational Achievement) show the positive effects of such education. Nonetheless, we should not be satisfied with the implementation of solutions to specific problems. The situation needs to be analysed at its root, that is, from moral philosophy. What kind of values education is behind the rise of contemporary individualism? What is considered right in the moral education of recent years? Which reasons have been emphasized and in which versions?

The second issue has to do with the fragmentation of life or, as some have called it, the corrosion of character (Sennett, 1998). Postmodern life looks like the participation in a set of fragmented circumstances made up of disjointed chapters, independent of one another. Until recently, the connection of work and personal life, regardless of their different interpretations, facilitated the construction of a unitary project of life that the postmodern era is shattering (Sennet, 1998). The ego is breaking into various selves; each of them comes and goes depending on the situation, thereby destroying any possibility of unity. We are one person at work, another at home, another in the community and another in front of the computer screen. How can you build a character in such conditions? How can you form a unitary and real personal project for life?

Current reality also appears to be a tsunami of assumed truths, many of which are only mere opinions or quackery, as illustrated in the excellent reflection, *On Bullshit*, by the moral philosopher Harry G. Frankfurt (2005), according to which we do not have any theory yet. It seems as if each person represented a unique and special truth, a fact indeed quite curious at a time when dialogue is presented as the instrument par excellence by which to build a fairer and more egalitarian world. We want to think together but are not willing to think the same (Steiner, 2004). So here we have the paradox.

Finally, and very closely related to this, postmodernity involves the appearance of consumers of statements with no semantic or intellectual depth. There is some tendency to buy and sell outlandish statements with no semantic foundation that advertise a good life but not necessarily fulfilling (Cortina, 1997; 1999). The power of such statements among the youngest can be noticed in TV shows of world influence like Big Brother, Star Search and the like. Once more, this situation invites us to think about the moral education that has been carried out in the last years. What has been deemed right and valuable when it comes to morally educating the new generations? What has been considered motivating as something worth pursuing at all costs?

The different versions of moral philosophy that are in operation today may shed some light on the matter. Each one from its particular position brings out the essential reasons for a moral education and so they help us to understand why we are in the situation we are in. This does not mean, of course, that we are placed in the worst of possible scenarios. In short, what is most interesting is that the debate between liberals and communitarians can give us some clues to answer our first question: why is moral education motivating by nature?

However, before getting into this discussion, we would like to point out the model of moral education in which we are currently functioning. The moral education that we sustain draws from the theoretical and practical model that we call "construction of a moral personality" which has been implemented for over 20 years in school-age students (Buxarrais, 1997; Martínez, 1998). This is a model that brings together inputs from other models such as those focused on development and moral reasoning (Kohlberg, 1981, 1984; Colby & Kohlberg, 1987; Gibbs, 2003), those based on emotional and sensitive aspects (Prinz, 2009), and those addressing the issue from the formation of a moral character (Lapsley & Clark, 2005; Nucci & Narváez, 2008; Doris, 2010). At the same time, it also considers the contributions of integrative models of moral development such as those of Turiel (1984) and Rest (1986). We sustain a moral education that allows students to achieve moral ground, either individually and privately or publicly and collectively (Veugelers, 2011). The premises of our model of construction of a moral personality can be summarized as follows. It is the learning within the cognitive-behavioural tradition that favours the resolution of disputes following a communicative rationality and the use of dialogue. From the perspective of a Kantian foundation (Kant, 2008), it treats people as ends in themselves, respecting their freedom and individuality. It regards, in the Aristotelian sense (Aristotle, 1998), the teleological dimension of the student as a virtuous person. Finally, it considers that people are called to be someone engaged in the community in a decisive and influential manner (Aristotle, 2003).

This model is based on the pedagogical work of eight dimensions of development (Puig & Martín, 1998). These are self-knowledge, autonomy and self-regulation, dialogue, the ability to transform the environment, empathy or social perspective, social skills, critical understanding of reality, and finally, moral reasoning. These dimensions of moral development are grouped into three macro categories, namely, the construction of self, fellowship, and socio-moral reflection.

KEY ASPECTS OF THE LIBERAL-COMMUNITARIAN DEBATE
FOR A MORAL EDUCATION

In the last years, liberals and communitarians have engaged in a philosophical discussion (Mulhall & Swift, 1992) that allow us to discern the premises on which we will be building the moral education of the century that has just begun. These premises clearly recover the primary motivations for moral education as a transformative process of the person in the same way that we understand it.

This is not a contemporary discussion but the continuity of the classical and well known debate between Kantian and Hegelian philosophy, or as we have suggested already, between the individual and the community. In this chapter, the discussion that we are referring to begins with the presentation of John Rawls' (1971) book, *A Theory of Justice.* Since that time, there have been a number of criticisms, among which are those of Michael Sandel (1982), Alasdair MacIntyre (1981, 1990), Charles Taylor (1990) and Michael Walzer (1983). These authors and others have been classified as representing the communitarian current despite their open disagreement with the label that has been placed on their way of thinking. Certainly, more than a school of thought itself, it consists of a set of criticisms to the liberal principles espoused by Rawls, and amendments to liberal thought overall. The diversity of positions is large and goes beyond the strict duality between liberals and communitarians. A proof of this is that, in the course of this debate, authors have appeared such as Joseph Raz (Raz, 1986) and Will Kymlicka (Kymlicka, 1989) whose contributions are halfway between the liberal and communitarian ideas.In any case, and as a matter of clarity in this dissertation, we will be using the liberal and communitarian labels to refer to each other despite the fact, we insist, that their actual characteristics do not allow for such simple categorization.

Having said this, we will try to recover those issues that have been addressed in the liberal-communitarian debate. They will allow us to discern more clearly some of the insights that have been gained directly or indirectly into moral educationand its potential motivations. As noted above, both philosophies emphasize different moral motivations. On the one hand, according to Rawlsian philosophy, the main motivation lies in the autonomy of the person as a means and end. On the other hand, communitarian philosophy maintains that moral motivation concerns community and the person being engaged in it. Hereafter, we will analyse the different options. In the following section, we will attempt to clarify why we deem these reflections appropriate in allowing us to state that moral education has a number of reasons that make it a subject inherently motivating.

Topics Of Discussion and their Impact on Moral Education

Rawls' liberalism (Rawls, 1971) assumes that all people are free and equal, and therefore, in order for this to be true, we should think of justice as fairness among people. Very briefly, the Rawlsian principles of justice are those that should arise from a sort of agreement that people would reach if they were unaware of their beliefs, particular circumstances, social condition, and physical characteristics, if they were, as Rawls himself suggests, in utter ignorance about their selves. It would be as if we were to divide a cake without knowing in advance what portion would be up to each of the diners. Obviously, each part should be equal so that no one is jeopardised. Principles of justice as fairness put people, using Rawls' words, in the *original position*, a position where one should not be aware of the socioeconomic status, personal strengths or weaknesses that he will have after applying such principles. Rawls calls this the *veil of ignorance.* We could say that people are not accountable for being born in such-and-such cultural context, in this or that family, nor for being how they are; therefore, it is not fair to ask for benefits or advantages for social and personal conditions. Justice as fairness also requires ignoring the conception of Right in the person, or at least, that it should not be taken into account within the public space. What is important is not the different conceptions of Right but what is behind them, which is nothing else than the freedom to choose between them or to make a different choice. In any case, private morality should not interfere in public life.

This brief explanation of Rawlsian liberalism results in a series of philosophical issues that have become part of what is known as the communitarian critique (Mulhall & Swift, 1992). These issues require analysis so that a proposal for moral education can be suggested according to the needs of the current time.

The first issue has to do with the conception of person. For Rawlsian liberalism, the individual should be conceived as something different from his individuality, his personal qualities, his particular social condition, and his own idea of Right. Above all, the person should be conceived as someone in possession of a highest-order interest to develop and pursue different conceptions of Right. This conception may be valid for the formation of fair and equitable communities, a valid moral motivation. In light of communitarianism, however, this is the wrong way to conceive of the person. Authors such as Michael Sandel (1982) and Alasdair MacIntyre (1981) argue that the Rawlsian *original position* ignores that people are actually shaped by moral purposes, values and conceptions of Right, that the relationship between person and moral purposes is constitutive, that is, part of the person and therefore much stronger than the account to be found in liberalism. Otherwise, they say, how can a rational person conceive of the reality and its circumstances regardless of what he ethically and morally thinks and argues? Can a person exchange values as easily as liberalism believes, or is a person fundamentally constituted by his/her values? The debate is set. For liberalism, the individual is seen as a free being, independent and choosing his/her own life project, whereas, for communitarianism, the individual is conceived of according to the personal values that are constitutive of self; it is these values and the life project constituted by them that allow us to speak of someone as a person. Both positions have a reasonable and logical moral motivation but none of them offers a complete explanation of reality.

The second question is referring to asocial individualism. For Rawlsian liberalism, society is a partnership between individuals who are privately associated and whose interests are defined outside the community to which they belong. To put it another way, the individual is individualised prior to the choice of his purposes; his identity is already fixed beforehand and, therefore, there will always be some distance between what one is and what one values. In Kantian terms, we could say that what makes us human beings is not our goals, interests, or ideas, but the ability to think and act with autonomy, and that this is actually shown in our personal and private choices. Fostering this ability is a first-order moral motivation. However, for communitarian authors, especially Alasdair MacIntyre (1981) and Charles Taylor (1990), liberalism ignores the extent to which the communities in which people live are giving them their identity and values. The person is, if we may say, a community parasite because the very concept of person has a social and community origin. This version responds to another not inconsiderable moral motivation since it is a motive to educate in that moral choice.Liberalism understands society as a cooperative of individuals, whereas the community is actually much more than this.

The third aspect is related to universalism. Rawls' theory is devised in a universal manner, coming as it does from the philosophical field. The mere fact that philosophy is dedicated to the pursuit of truth forces him to move away from his surrounding circumstances and context. For liberalism, any rational community can apply the principles of justice as fairness regardless of its characteristics. This is a far-reaching moral motivation because it means supporting moral education in an ethics of universal minimums. However, for the communitarian perspective (Walzer, 1983), this view ignores moral and cultural particularity, the fact that different cultural groups also represent different ways of understanding values and ethical principles. Communitarianism is accusing liberalism of having some universal aspirations that today cannot be accepted. We are therefore facing another topic that is clearly educational. Our educational institutions are a cluster of moral communities, and any aspiration of universalism could spoil the moral project of one or several moral communities, usually the most defenceless, minority and disadvantaged ones. Now, is any moral project valid for the simple reason of being so? The current situation suggests not. The motivation to reason about what is morally good and valuable is more than justified.

The fourth issue is referring to subjectivism versus objectivism. From what has been said so far, we can assume that, for Rawlsian liberalism, the choice of purposes, values, and conceptions of Right are arbitrary expressions of preference and therefore not subject to rationale. The rational and autonomous individual decides on his preferences without being forced to justify such a decision. In short, the person is the beginning and the end of morality. Moral preferences regard the individual as both the creator and the object of such creation. Autonomy is a moral motivation worth the effort. Communitarianism, however, does not quite agree with this assumption. Human beings are moral beings on the basis of the moral traditions of their own community (MacIntyre, 1981) or in relation to an inner voice or ideal of authenticity (Taylor, 1994) based on horizons of meanings outside themselves. Communitarianism does not believe that autonomy explains why we are moral subjects but rather that our moral formation is directly related to the community we live in, and hence some objectivism is true in its own nature. Again, we can see how the liberal-communitarian debate puts on the table an issue of major importance for postmodern values education and its moral motivations.

The fifth and last themes are what we might call anti-perfectionism and neutrality. Liberalism relies on States, including the institutions that form them – the educational ones also – that will remain neutral to the different conceptions of Right. In other words, the public sphere should not defend any life choices, as these belong to the private life of every individual and not in the field of justice and equality that the States must guarantee. The moral motivation is simply to defend the neutrality of the public space. Communitarianism, on the other hand, argues that the States have to ensure the function of human and community perfection and that this requires positioning themselves. According to the communitarians (MacIntyre, 1981), there exist some valuable forms of life that are above others; forms that, for instance, dignify the human condition more than others. If the States do not foster them they run the risk of getting dissolved or simply disappearing. Moreover, they argue that under presumed neutrality and behind the speech of justice as fairness, is hidden conviction about how individuals should live and which are the accepted forms of life.

These five topics pointed hint at the importance of the liberal-communitarian debate and its deep relationship with moral motivation and its different meanings, therefore, with different ways of dealing with moral education. We consider that this is a discussion on moral philosophy that, as already mentioned, brings to light the main motives for moral education and this in turn only raises questions for the world of education. Choosing some moral motives or others will make us take separate ways and go for different models of moral education.

Postmodern educational institutions, and especially the professionals who work in them day after day with the youngest members of our communities, are called to speculate about education in order to feel solid in a liquid environment (Bauman, 2007). Are the students independent of their values and the real figures in the election of their life projects or are they determined as long as they acquire certain values and not others? Should the students be trained in a partnership between people and in defence of justice, or should they feel that their life is a community life that requires commitment and defence of the Good (*bonum*), the Truth (*verbum*) and the Beauty (*pulchrum*)? Should moral education aim at universal ethical principles, or should it focus on the particularities of each cultural group, its moral history, and its rational arguments? Should we think that the student is sovereign over him/herself, over body and mind, or that s/he will be sovereign only as long as s/he acquires the values of the community to which s/he belongs? Finally, should education be a neutral non-aggressive act and therefore not interfere with the different conceptions of Right, or should it be a prospective action that complies with certain conceptions of Right and rejects others?

WHY MORAL EDUCATION IS MOTIVATING BY NATURE. THREE POSSIBLE REASONS

As already noted, the liberal-communitarian debate leaves a number of topics on moral education on the table. We believe that all of them can be grouped into three reasons that are not only appealing for its mere analysis but that also condition moral education, so that it turns into a truly motivating subject at all levels from the most theoretical to the very practical. These reasons are presented on the basis of two propositions. The first one tries to find the best of both positions, in other words, all that can encompass the reality of the whole and not just a part of it. The second one is the respect for humanistic ideals, such as those that swept Europe in the fourteenth and fifteenth centuries and that were so clearly expressed by the young

Italian scholar, Pico della Mirandola (1956), in his *Oratio de hominis dignitate,* as the exaltation of human dignity.

We want to emphasize once again that, in light of the liberal-communitarian debate, these reasons can be distorted and, in some cases, they may not even respect the humanitarian principles we have just noted. In other words, the motives for moral education can be many but they are not all equally valid.

The Person as a Reason for Moral Education

The object of action in moral education is the person, something as obvious to accept as it is easy to forget. It is safe to say that, although not intentionally, a large number of teachers in our schools and universities put their attention more on the construct of the student, the citizen, or the professional than on the person who is behind the construct. The person may be understood as a being contingent in nature or as someone to whom things happen that might not have happened and that in one way or another condition his existence. For example, there are some students with varying intellectual capacities to learn certain content, students with varying degrees of emotional development, whose circumstances are what they are but that might have been different. Regarding morality we can think similarly. The student is just a person defending certain values that ultimately respond to a matter of choice; that is, they are the product of an exercise of will and personal desire.

The respect for the autonomy of the person is something fundamental in moral education, and consequently each person must be considered different and unique within the variety of different and unique persons with whom one lives, even if his moral preferences do not correspond with those of the majority including his teachers. Liberalism has fostered autonomy as the basic principle of democracy.

Understanding moral education purely in this way however can distort the educational task *per se*. Moral education is not only a matter of autonomy and personal will. It is not about displaying a showcase of values from which one can choose according to his personal situation. Should that be the case, what would be the motive to morally educate the new generation of citizens? What would be the function of moral education other than presenting a list of moral choices from which one could select? The student is something more than a contingent and independent person because s/he also belongs to a community that shapes his personal identity. Considering the student merely as an independent being prevents him from understanding some of his moral experiences, ways of doing things and attitudes that are embedded in his community. The student seen from an absolutely liberal point of view will not be able to embrace all the variety of values that are rooted in his community and, in any case, will not be able to be accountable for the values that he doesnot regard as his own and that nevertheless are distinctive of his community. Responsibility understood as the expression of personal freedom and the taking care of one's own actions and thoughts (Jonas, 1995) is the purpose of moral education, now more than ever, as has been noted in the first section.

The awareness of living in community and embodying its values, although these have not been chosen in an autonomous way, is not a goal of moral education but an inherent ingredient of it. A moral education project supported by the most absolute liberalism creates a communal system of partnerships between people with the purpose of obtaining those gains that one cannot obtain by oneself, but does not favour engagement through relationships that might condition one's personal identity (Cortina, 1997). Values are qualities that shape personal identity rather than contingent attributes of the self. The notion of personal identity is entangled with the interrelationship between community, family and educational institution. The communitarian contributions to liberal thinking let us discern the reality from a wider and more comprehensive perspective.

From all this, we can draw two conclusions that turn moral education into something truly motivating, in other words, that bring strong motives to moral education. On the one hand, participating in educational action is a way of developing free, unique, and personal identities at the same time that civic community practices are developed. On the other hand, goods provided by historically built communities – a key aspect of humanism – are difficult to grasp in an independent and individual manner and, in any case, leaving them in the hands of one's own personal will is too great a risk if the aim is to build more equitable, freer and fairer communities.

Rationality as a Reason for Moral Education

The student must develop himself in an educational environment that allows him to reach a rational conclusion about values, where such conclusion is of course respected insofar as it is the final product of a rational and personal exercise. In a sense, liberalism upholds that we are free and equal persons. The person is autonomous and is presumed to possess ability to reason. As such, the person is solely responsible for seeking the truth. Heteronomy – searching for values outside the individual or through others – is an illegitimate source of morality because the Kantian categorical imperative, the source of liberalism, requires autonomy. In this sense, moral education has to favour the autonomy of the students and respect their absolute freedom. At the same time, educating for autonomy and defending its moral motivations can lead to controversial situations. In this regard, it is worth retrieving a case (Sandel, 2009). William Bulger, who came to preside over the Senate of the State of Massachusetts (1978-1996) and was later Chancellor of the University of Massachusetts for seven years, was the brother of James "Whitey" Burger, head of the savage criminal group of Winter Hill and still today, one of the "ten most wanted" by the FBI. Both brothers kept in contact by telephone. In 2001, a federal prosecutor urged William to provide information about his brother. "Do you feel more loyalty to your brother than to the people of Massachusetts?" asked the prosecutor. "I've never seen it that way, but frankly I am loyal to my brother and I care about him [...] I have no intention of helping anyone to capture him," said William, in a classical assertion of autonomy.[2]

In contrast, or the communitarian, criticismof autonomy does not explain why we are subjects with values. People are moral beings on the basis of the traditions of our communities or on the basis of horizons of moral meanings outside ourselves (Taylor, 1990). In this regard, let us present another case (Sandel, 2009). David Kaczynsky reported in 1996 to the FBI his suspicions that "Unabomber", a domestic terrorist who sent several mail bombs that killed three people and injured twenty-three more, was his brother. Federal agents arrested the brother and he was condemned to a life sentence without probation.[3] In the second case, loyalty to solidarity with the victims, a moral tradition rooted in most communities, was more important than the loyalty to the principle of autonomy and freedom of choice.

In this, we have a possible solution to one of the well-known desiderata in moral education, the one referring to the formation of real people. A moral education that hopes to achieve this should introduce students to the horizons of moral meanings aimed towards the Right of the community. An analysis of the current situation, as has been pointed out in the first section, warns us that it is not clear that the different moral positions of students are a rational product, nor that, contrary to the popular belief they have been acquired in the strictest autonomy. Students are living in a time that is encouraging them – in an apparent manner but not always real – to develop their own self-definition. The ideal of self-fulfilment or self-knowledge without external horizons of moral meanings creates, as can be seen in environments clearly relativistic, something like a "culture of narcissism", self-centred forms of identity (Lipovetsky, 1983) or the construction of the emotivist self (MacIntyre, 1981; Elzo, 2006; 2011). In the process of building their own self-definition as moral beings, students do not always know the point of arrival. They do not always have an external reference since in the current context there is no distinction between personal and impersonal reasons (Elzo, 2006; 2011). We consider that moral education is the ideal framework to point at the aim of the person, to show the essence of all that as individuals we are called to be. A moral education must provide a proposal, some rational criteria that allow one to distinguish between different moral perspectives; otherwise everything can be criticized even from one's own perspective. Being rid of the notion of the rational aim of the person, whatever that is, involves denying the fact that the person can reach a higher or more perfect state than he currently possesses. We understand that transmitting the knowledge of the aim of the person is a motive of first order in moral education because it helps to realize that morality is rational and objectively reasonable and helps us to move from facts to values in in the form of ethical duties. For example: from this perspective moral education should teach through actions that we are vulnerable beings and that we are called to help each other, to show our friendliness (Lévinas, 2003). Only in this way can we see that we are beings who need to help each other, and that this must constitute a moral duty.

In short, moral education has an additional motivation, another reason that makes it worth embarking on. It is not about reaching a particular point of arrival translated into moral values because we believe in the pluralism of moral and virtuous practices.

What is clear to us, however, is that this point of arrival must be the one that makes the student regard in a rational way what is best for him and the community.

Fellowship as a Reason for Moral Education

If there is one kind of education typically universal in the deepest sense of the term, this is moral education. It is needless to mention the universal nature of ethics and morality, its fundamental human nature, and its transcendence in time and space. Postmodernism is a particular reality in this regard and our educational systems are a reflection of that reality. The vast majority of teachers are facing the problem of continuing to defend the universality of values, advocating for a global citizenship (Cortina, 1997), at the same time that they are conditioned by the presence of a variety of cultures and patterns of moral thinking in the same classroom. Educating for the universality is not the same as educating in the universality, and nowadays universality is present in the same space, in the day-to-day educational task.

A liberal approach promotes civic fellowship and an absolute respect for different cultures, particularly minorities. The principles of intercultural education (Kymlicka, 1995) have been orchestrated on this basis, understanding intercultural education as a civic and harmonious exchange between coexisting cultures. There are intercultural education projects that have certainly achieved the expected success, but we cannot hide that the beginning of the new century is being marked significantly by problems of cultural fellowship.[4] On the other hand, what is the meaning of intercultural education from a moral education point of view? Does it have any other purpose besides knowing the other from an information perspective and maintaining detached tolerationthe other's way of conceiving and understanding reality?

Communitarianism reminds us again of the importance of the community in the development of personal identities and its influence on moral education. From this standpoint, the danger is that the obsession with intercultural education causes cultural education to fall into oblivion, and a proof is the rise of cultural nationalisms. It is true; we are essentially intercultural beings (Maalouf, 1998). We can tell by just looking at our ancestral past, but this should not prevent us from being also cultural beings. The moral frameworks, closer or further from our moral community, are the means we have to guide us in certain ethical and moral issues. These moral frameworks or values are there regardless of our ability to find our position in them. We could say that this is an aspect of moral education as important as it is to have a map when we need to locate ourselves in a new city. In this case, the problem lies not only in the ignorance of universal rights like equality, freedom and fraternity, but also the lack of knowledge of one's own location with respect to those values. Multicultural fellowship should not hamper the instruction in the cultural background of the individual, and as much as possible, it should be in harmony with the different coexisting cultural backgrounds. We do not intend to enter the debate of cultural Darwinism according to which there are cultures morally superior to others, nor whether the education policies of our States should be open to other cultures. We simply want to point out that intercultural education requires being educated in one's own culture, that it is unlikely that we can appreciate the other if we do not previously appreciate the self.

CONCLUSION

Moral education is an important subject of postmodernity as it has always been throughout the history of Western thought. The present times and the social and educational circumstances in which we are living place moral education at the centre of the educational debate. We need to find reasons so that the moral education we offer to the new generations of citizens is of good quality, motives that make us understand that values are the greatest of the legacies we can leave to the next generation.

As we have mentioned, the debate between liberals and communitarians that has been established in the field of moral philosophy helps us to recover the reasons that turn moral education into something inherently motivating, reasons that become worthwhile motives to be pursued with interest and consciousness. We have identified four reasons that have been presented in several versions but that impel us to retain the best of each perspective.

The first reason mentioned has to do with the person. The person's own account is sufficient as a motivation for moral education. The person may be deemed a being essentially autonomous and free in regard to the choice of values, but can also be regarded as a social being considering that it is actually one's community that leads one towards autonomy and freedom. A moral education that ignores the community fails to care for the person as the person deserves. A moral education that does not deem the person the main player of one's own choices does not respect personal dignity.

The second reason deals with rationality. Moral education is also the education of reason. The path to human perfection that takes us from what we are now up to what we are not yet should take place in the light of reason. Morality should be forged in an atmosphere of freedom and autonomy, but this does not mean that we do not need our community to achieve such an environment. We are beings embedded in horizons of moral meanings and that should be the basis for the development of the students as unique persons.

The third reason analysed concerns fellowship. Ours is a multicultural reality that has different ways of understanding the person and reality. Respect for autonomy and freedom can lead us to fellowship agreements, information about the other, and not much more. We are called however to understand, to comprehend each other and to criticize rationally those moral projects that do not dignify the person. Moral education in this sense is also an education in the commitment to human perfection, in the choice of a fulfilling life project.

In short, It has reasons that make it something worth pursuing. Be that as it may, these reasons need to undergo thorough thinking because their account can lead moral education towards one position or another and not all grounds seem to be reasonably valid and morally right.

NOTES

[1]   We are referring to Th . Adorno, M. Horkemeier and W. Benjamin, thinkers of the first generation of The Frankfurt School.
[2]   Scot Lehigh, "Burger Chose the code of the Street", *Boston Globe,* December 4th, 2002, p. A19
[3]   David Johston, "Judge Sentences Confessed Bomber to Four Life Terms", *New York Times,* May 5th, 1998.
[4]   We are referring to the armed conflict between different cultural groups and States, and the new aftermath following the attacks in New York in 2001, Madrid in 2004, and London in 2005.

REFERENCES

Aristotle. (1998). *The Nicomachean Ethics.* New York: Oxford University Press.
Aristotle. (2003). *Politics.* In L.P. Pojman (Ed.), *Classics of philosophy* (2nd ed.). New York: Oxford University Press.
Arendt, H. (1968). *The origins of totalitarism.* Florida: A Harvest Book.
Bauman, Z. (1993). *Postmodern ethics.* Oxford : Blackwell Publishers.
Bauman, Z. (2007). *Liquid times: Living in an age of uncertainty.* Cambridge: Polity Press.
Beck, U. (1992). *Risk society. Towards a new modernity: Theory culture and society.* London: Sage.
Buxarrais, M.R. (1997). *La Formación del Profesorado en Educación en Valores. Propuestas y Materiales* [Teacher Training in Values Education. Proposals and Materials]. Bilbao: Desclée de Brower.
Colby, A.,& Kohlberg, L. (1987). *The measurement of moral judgment* (Vol. I, II).Cambridge: Cambridge University Press.
Cortina, A. (1997). *Ciudadanos del mundo. Hacia una teoría de la ciudadanía*[Citizens of the World. Towards a Theory of Citizenship].Madrid: Alianza Editorial.
Cortina, A. (1999). *Los ciudadanos como protagonistas*[Citizens As Protagonists]. Barcelona: Galaxia Gutenberg.
Della Mirandola, P. (1956). *Oration on the dignity of man* (A.R. Caponigri, Trans.). Chicago: Regnery Publishing.
Doris, J.M. (2010). *Lack of character. Personality moral behaviour.* New York: Cambridge University Press.
Elzo, J. (2006). *Los jóvenes y la felicidad* [Youth and Hapiness]. Madrid: PPC
Elzo, J. (2011). *Valors tous en temps durs.* [Fragile values in hard times]. Barcelona:Barcino.
Frankfurt, G.H. (2005). *On bullshit.* New Yersey: Princeton University Press.
Gibbs, J.C. (2003). *Moral development and reality: Beyond the theories of Kohlberg and Hoffman.* Thousand Oaks, CA: Sage Publications.
Giddens, A. (1991). *Modernity and self identity Self and society in the late modern age.* London: Polity.
Jaeger, W. (1945). *Paideia: The ideals of greek culture.* Oxford: Oxford University Press.
Jonas, H. (1995). *El principio de la responsabilidad. Ensayo de una ética para la civilización tecnológica* [The Principle of Responsibility. Essay of an Ethics for The Technological Civilization]. Barcelona: Herder.
Kant, I. (2008). *Fundamentación de la metafísica de las costumbres* [The Groundwork of the Metaphysics of Morals]. Madrid: Espasa-Calpe.
Kohlberg, L. (1981). *The meaning and measurement of moral development.* Worcester, MA: Clark University Press.
Kohlberg, L. (1984). *Essays on moral development. The psychology of moral development.* San Francisco: Jossey Bass.
Kymlicka, W. (1989). *Liberalism, community and culture.* Oxford: Oxford University Press.

Kymlicka, W.(1995). *Multicultural citizenship. A liberal theory of minority rights.* Oxford:Clarendon Press.
Lapsley, D., & Clark, F. (2005). *Character psychology and character education.* Indiana: University of Notre Dame Press.
Lévinas, E. (2003). *Humanism of the other* (N. Poller, Trans.). IL: Illinois University Press.
Lipovetsky, G. (1983). *L'ère du vide. Essais sur l'individualisme contemporain.* Paris: Éditions Gallimard.
Maalouf, A. (1998). *Les identités meurtrières.* Paris : Grasset & Franquelle.
MacIntyre, A. (1981). *After virtue.* London: Ducworth.
MacIntyre, A. (1990). *Three rival versions of moral enquiry. Encyclopedia, genealogy and tradition.* New York: Scott Meredith Literacy Agency.
Martínez, M. (1998). *El Contrato Moral del Profesorado* [The Moral Contract of Teachers]. Bilbao: Desclée de Brower.
Mulhall, S., & Swift, A. (1992). *Liberals & communitarians.* Oxford: Blackwell Publishers.
Nucci, L., & Narváez, D. (2008). *Handbook of moral and character education.* New York: Routledge.
Prinz, J. (2009). *The emotional construction of morals.* New York: Oxford University Press.
Puig, J.M. & Martín, X. (1998). *La educación moral en la escuela. Teoría* y *Práctica.* [Moral Education at the School: Theory and Practice]. Barcelona: Edebé.
Raz, J. (1986). *The morality of freedom.* Oxford: Oxford University Press.
Rawls, J. (1971). *A theory of justice.* Cambridge: Harvard University Press.
Rest J.R. (1986). *Manual for the Defining Issues Test.* Minneapolis: Center for the Study of Ethical Development.
Sandel, M. (1982). *Liberalism and the limits of the justice.* Cambridge: Cambridge University Press.
Sandel, M. (2009). *Justice. What's the right thing to do?* New York: Farrar, Straus and Giroux.
Sennett, R. (1998). *The corrosion of character: The personal consequences of work in the new capitalism.* New York: W.W. Norton & Company.
Sloam, J. (2008). Teaching democracy: The role of political science education, *British Journal of Politics and International Relations, 10,* 509–524.
Steiner, G. (2004). *The idea of Europe.* Tilburg: Uitgeverij.
Taylor, Ch. (1990). *Sources of the self.* Cambridge: Cambridge University Press.
Taylor, Ch. (1994). *The ethics of authenticity.* Cambridge: Harvard University Press
Turiel, E. (1984). *El Desarrollo del Conocimiento Social. Moralidad y Convención* [The Development of Social Knowledge. Morality and Convention]. Madrid: Debate.
Veugelers, W. (Ed.). (2011). *Education and humanism. Linking autonomy and humanity.* Rottterdam: Sense Publishers.
Walzer, M. (1983). *Spheres of justice.* New York: Basic Books.

AFFILIATION

Francisco Esteban Bara
Department of Theory and History of Education
University of Barcelona
Barcelona, Spain

Maria Rosa Buxarrais Estrada
Department of Theory and History of Education
University of Barcelona
Barcelona, Spain

KARIN HEINRICHS

MORAL MOTIVATION IN THE LIGHT OF ACTION THEORY

Perspectives on Theoretical and Empirical Progress

INTRODUCTION

Rest's Four Component Model (Rest et al., 1999) proclaimed moral motivation as the third component on the way to action. He himself admitted moral motivation was associated with a lack of sophisticated research, moreover, to a lack of systematization of different approaches and studies in this field. To fill this gap, the current book provides an overview of currently discussed approaches to moral motivation.

All in all, it has become obvious that moral motivation has been studied based on a variety of theoretical and empirical approaches. The great challenge to gain scientific progress will be to cross borders of disciplines and research traditions: to build bridges between moral and motivational or social psychology (Baumert et al., this volume, Agerström & Björklund, this volume, Oser, this volume; Krapp, this volume; Thorkildsen, this volume; Vollmeyer, this volume; Weiner, this volume;), to philosophical (Wren, this volume; Esteban, this volume, Grün, this volume; Lovat, this volume; Micewski, this volume) or educational research (Althof & Berkowitz, this volume; Campbell, this volume; Oja & Craig, this volume; Lee, this volume).

Therefore, a Process Model of Acting (Heinrichs, 2005) provides a theoretical framework which reconstructs the way a situation is constituted towards evaluating the behaviour systematically. In this chapter, this general model of acting will be applied to the context of moral issues. Facets and perspectives on moral motivation presented in this book and their impact on moral behaviour will be discussed. The model especially focusses on motivational and volitional processes and allows explication of the role of motivation on the way to action with greater detail than Rest's model.

In this chapter, moral motivation will firstly be explicated along the lines of Rest's Four Component Model because this model is very prominent and often referred to in addressing the judgment-action-gap and to point to motivational processes as relevant to act responsibly in morally relevant situations (Thoma & Bebeau, this volume; Rest et al., 1999). Afterwards, Rest's assumptions on moral motivation will be contrasted with those proclaimed in the Process Model of Acting, because it is presumed that the main assumptions of the process model provide a chance for theoretical progression, for reframing and for integrating the approaches on moral

K. Heinrichs, F. Oser & T. Lovat (Eds.), Handbook of Moral Motivation: Theories, Models, Applications, 623–658.

motivation presented in the different chapters of the book. In other words, referring to Lakatos (1982, pp.47-49), the strategy of negative heuristics is applied in order to gain theoretical progress by using the process model as a framework where the different approaches to moral motivation could be discussed and reinterpreted.

MORAL MOTIVAITON IN REST'S FOUR COMPONENT MODEL

Rest reviewed a wide range of literature to collect and systematize the state of research owing to internal processes relevant for moral action in real situations. As a result, he proclaimed four categories, pointing to four components (and to four different kinds of internal processes), all determining the movement from situation constitution to behaviour in a morally relevant situation (Thoma & Bebeau, in this volume; Rest et al., 1999). Moral motivation is the third component, indicating a category in Rest's thinking (as a result of his literature review) which pools internal processes contributing to how an individual feels when being driven towards "moral behaviour". Rest concentrates on how responsibility to act in a morally justified way evolves. He defines moral motivation as "the degree of commitment to taking the moral course of action, valuing moral values over other values, and taking personal responsibility for moral outcomes" (Rest et al., 1999, p. 101). Thus, the third component refers to responsibility, including motivation, and – in some applications – commitment as well (see Bebeau & Thoma, this volume)[1].

So, in that sense, moral motivation is seen to be important on the way to moral behaviour. Nonetheless, neither the feedback loops to other (cognitive, emotional or volitional) processes nor the sources of motivation were explained by Rest sophistically. At the same time, he did not differ between moral motivation as a personal determinant which does not vary over time, on the one hand, and motivation as a state of being driven in the process of acting, on the other hand. In Rest's model, moral motivaiton could be discussed as a trait or a state. That is why Rest's idea is somehow a source of speculation and, of course, a source for new and more precise conceptions of moral motivation. Thus, obviously there is a need to sharpen the concept and functioning of moral motivation, both in order to explain the development of moral motivation and to describe the relevant processes leading to a state of being powered towards moral action.

GOING BEYOND REST'S MODEL: CONTRASTING ASSUMPTIONS
ON MORAL MOTIVATION

Compared to the Four Component Model, the Process Model of Acting provides a theoretical framework by which to discuss moral motivation from an action-based view. The Process Model does not claim to reconstruct the specifics of dealing with conflicts and challenges in the moral domain but allows for enriching the discussion within moral psychology by pointing "outside of the box" to moral as well as non-moral drivers of acting in morally relevant situations (Heinrichs, 2005). Additionally, the Process Model reconstructs the way to an intention as input-output-relations connected to each other systematically. It assumes that there usually are feedback loops and interacting processes between the different sub-processes, as well as that cognitive, emotional, motivational and volitional facets are to be considered for their impact towards acting in morally relevant situations.

Moral motivation, in the sense of the Process Model, addresses a state of being driven and powered towards action in situations regarded by the agent as morally relevant and, owing to this more general concept, the need for specifying what "moral motivation" in situational circumstances could mean is obvious.

In the next sections, first, the basic assumptions of the Process Model as an action-based framework are presented in more detail before secondly the concept of moral motivation is outlined.

Core Assumptions of the Process Model of Acting

1. Acting in real situations is defined as purposeful, intentional and controllable and it requires a minimum of consciousness. The minimum target is to solve an individually constituted problem (to copy with a particular situation) (Heinrichs, 2005, pp. 193-202).
2. The process of acting is determined by cognitive, emotional, motivational as well as volitional processes; this assumption is based on the idea that the agent has to be described in multi facets (Heinrichs, 2005, pp. 87-100).
3. The process of acting can be divided into four phases: intention formation, action planning, conducting the behaviour, evaluating (Heinrichs, 2005, pp. 128, 182-185, 207).
4. Forming an intention includes four components: (a) a constituted problem (situation), (b) an idea of aims and ways of acting (minimum a state of conviction to be able to solve the constituted problem, (c) motivational power in line with the anticipated aims and (d) volitional power as a feeling of commitment to solve the problem (Heinrichs, 2005, pp. 140-161, 207).
5. The process of acting is elicited by the individually constituted problem as constituted, if a difference between 'is' and 'ought' is perceived. The identified problem is the core of an individually constituted situation. (Heinrichs, 2005, pp. 115, 141).
6. The Process Model aims to explain judging and acting in a wide range of situations and problems, including morally relevant situations of – again – different types. It could be applied to hypothetical dilemmas as well as to "real", morally relevant situations in everyday life (Heinrichs, 2005, pp. 260-270).
7. Real morally relevant situations are considered as multi facets and related simultaneously to different domains (e.g. social, conventional, prudential or moral), and not limited to moral realms (Smetana, 2010, pp. 123-124).
8. Perceiving and defining a situation is determined by mental models of a situation, by experience-based knowledge (Heinrichs, 2005, pp. 137, 185-188).

9. The processes of acting (even the starting process of defining a situation) could pass off in different modes of data processing: in an automatic-intuitive mode (if the perceived situation is fitting to the associated mental model of the situation) or in a reflective mode (Heinrichs, 2005, pp. 188-192).

10. Acting in everyday life is normally going off in the automatic-intuitive mode. To change into the reflecting mode will only happen if the person has not associated a fitting mental model of the situation, if he or she is motivated to reflect and if there is an opportunity to reflect. This opportunity might be lacking (e.g. under time pressure) (Heinrichs, 2005, p. 208).

Concept of Moral Motivation in Line with the Process Model of Acting

The assumptions concerning motivation, and especially "moral motivation", could be explained in terms of the Process Model of Acting as follows:

1. Motivation is considered as a state during the process of acting, one that influences the pathway to action especially in the first phase (in the phase of forming an intention) (Heinrichs, 2005, pp. 150-154), but also in the following steps towards behaviour (action planning or initiating and conducting action).

2. There might be feedback loops and interactions between motivational and cognitive, emotional or volitional processes on the way to forming an intention as well as on the way to behaviour.

3. Motivational power as a state has not been specified as linked to one particular concept of motivation studied in motivational psychology (see Oser, this volume).

4. Moreover, the action-theoretical framework allows for integrating different perspectives on how an individual could get into a state of being motivated. The state of being motivated might be influenced and evolve because of different situational and personal determinants (situational: e.g. the constituted (moral) problem, constituted situation, associated objectives and ways of acting); personal: e.g. moral self, moral reasoning, basic needs, personal needs, experience-based knowledge).

5. A person could only get in a state of being *morally* motivated if he or she has constituted a moral problem, meaning that he or she has perceived a difference between "is" and "ought" owing to the current setting and to a morally relevant criterion (Heinrichs, 2005, pp. 115, 116, 141, 226, 227).

6. This moral problem is embedded in a constituted real situation. The situation could have associations not only to the moral but also to other (e.g. the convention, prudential) domains.

7. Moreover, the motivational power to cope with – in the individual's view - morally relevant real situations, is called "*moral motivation*" and could evolve because of (i) "moral" (e.g. the moral self as a kind of commitment to act consistently with one's own moral judgment or a kind of commitment to obey particular principles (justice, fairness, etc.) as well as of (ii) "non-moral" drivers (e.g. physical needs

like hunger or the need for sleep, basic social needs as to be socially integrated or to be perceived as competent) (Heinrichs, 2005, pp. 137, 152-154).

8. The process model claims to provide a framework which can be applied without being linked to a particular moral standpoint or moral content. Furthermore, the Process Model of Acting maintains itself as "morally neutral" insofar as it could be used by researchers to represent processes of acting independently of the agent's moral standpoint. Additionally, the process model could be applied to different kinds of morally relevant problems, defined by the individual's leading moral criterion, its preferred moral value relevant for defining the problem (Heinrichs, 2005, pp. 225-231).

9. Moral motivation does not cover all processes leading to the state of being energized towards a particular goal. Especially in a particular situation, if ambivalent ways of acting could be associated and empowered by different motivational (moral and non-moral) sources, there will be a need for decision-making about what way of acting should be preferred. That means that there will be a need for reflecting before an intention is formed and a need for "volitional power" insofar as cognitive control processes are necessary to being decided and committed to act in a "moral" way, on the one hand. On the other hand, especially those individuals who are not of a strong moral self, might define moral problems, but nonetheless use disengagement strategies to reject moral standards and responsibility and to follow self-interests or other "non-moral" motives and then be committed to a "non-moral" way of acting (Bandura, 1991; Bandura et al., 1996).

THE ROLE OF MOTIVATION AND VOLITION ON THE WAY TO FORMING AN INTENTION – AN ACTION-BASED VIEW

So, the Process Model of Acting provides a general action based view appropriate for application and reflecting the specific challenges on the way to dealing with moral issues (Heinrichs, 2005, pp. 84, 115). The Process Model additionally underpins the need for differentiating motivational and volitional processes more explicitly than is the case in Rest's Four Component Model. Additionally, it hopefully could contribute to a sophisticated discussion about the role of motivational processes on the way to action and the interaction of motivational and other kinds of internal (e.g. cognitive, emotional or volitional) processes.

Therefore, the role of motivation and volition on the way to action will be explained. The general action-based view represented by the Process Model will be applied to morally relevant situations. In order to sharpen the role of moral motivation, to summarize its impacts and to draw conclusions for further research on moral motivation, one could refer especially to the chapters included in this book.

Even as Rest points out in his third and fourth component, not only motivational but also volitional processes are relevant on the way to action. Rest stresses that motivation on its own is not enough to account for feeling responsible. Moreover, commitment is necessary as well (component III). Furthermore, ego-strength and other personal determinants may help to implement an intention to which the individual feels committed (component IV; see Rest et al., 1999; Bebeau & Thoma, this volume).

Referring to the Process Model of Acting, these volitional processes were differentiated systematically from those which will be relevant to forming an intention (and achieving a state of commitment) (Sokolowski, 1993, p. 120; 1996, p. 487; Heinrichs, 2005, pp. 154-165) and those volitional processes which will be necessary in the phase of action planning and implementing the formed intention and coping with difficulties in initiating the particular action, struggling with other intentions, and maintaining the power of the intention for a longer time in the case of dealing with complex problems (Sokolowski, 1993, p. 122; Heinrichs, 2005, p. 160-161).

The discussion in this chapter focuses on the first phase of acting, ending up with a formed intention. The first phase of acting includes four sub-processes which could be separated at least analytically: the constitution of a (moral) situation (1), anticipating objectives and ways of acting (2), getting motivationally energized (3), and, being volitionally powered (4). These four sub-processes have necessarily to be completed when an individual formed an intention, felt committed to it and decided to solve a constituted (moral) problem (Heinrichs, 2005, pp. 161-162). In line with the Rubikon Model (Gollwitzer, 1996; Heckhausen, 1987), commitment is perceived as a necessary condition to initiate and realize the anticipated action.

Furthermore, the process model is not restricted to "rational decision-making" as is the focus in the Rubikon Model and which Heckhausen himself admitted to taking place in everyday life only in some very specific situations (Gollwitzer, 1996, p. 540; Heckhausen, 1989, p. 213). If we want to enrich the discussion on moral motivation from hypothetical dilemmas to real, morally relevant situations (Heinrichs, 2005, pp. 254, 259-260; Krebs & Denton, 1999, p. 225), it seems to be fruitful to study how individuals become committed to a particular way of acting in either an intuitive-automatic mode of information processing or by passing an extensive phase of reflecting. The Process Model allows for reconstructing, both forming an intention via rational-reflective decision-making as well as via gaining a feeling of being committed to an intention in an intuitive mode of data processing.

In the following, each of the four sub-processes necessary for forming an intention (see figure 1) will be described: first, in line with a general view on acting and secondly specified owing to acting in morally relevant situations. However, this step by step reconstruction of the process of acting seems to be associated with the same sequence of sub-processes in the time elapsed; this is not assumed. Moreover, the different sub-processes are assumed to be connected analytically by input-output relations. During the processes, there might be feedback loops between all these processes as well.

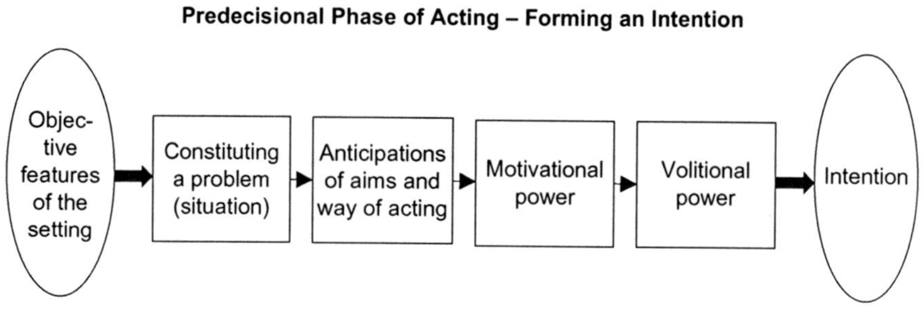

Predecisional Phase of Acting – Forming an Intention

Figure 1. Process of forming an intention (see Heinrichs, 2005, p. 161; translated from German to English).

Constituting a (Moral) Situation – Reconstructed Referring to the Process Model of Acting

In the Process Model, it is assumed that the definition of the situation determines the process of acting. On the way to forming an intention, constituting a situation is the first and very important step. This is the case especially if the constituted situation points to a problem, to a discrepancy between the "is" and the "ought". Only if a problem is defined, can the agent feel energized to solve the problem and be impelled towards acting. To answer the question whether this state of being energized to solve a problem has to be described in a specific way if a moral problem is constituted, remains an open question. Vice versa, we could not answer the question, as yet, whether sources of "moral motivation" would influence the process of defining the situation itself. To gain deeper insights, it would be necessary to discuss more sophistically what impact situational and personal determinants have on motivation as a state of being energized to act.

Based on Esser's model (Esser, 1996) and the idea of Fazio (1990), the process model proclaims that perceiving a situation means to associate a mental model of the situation (as an element of the individual's experienced-based knowledge) that fits the current setting. Defining a situation is determined by cognitive and affective processes, together called "the attitude towards a situation". A person constitutes a situation by associating a kind of "leading motive", "leading idea", usually in a spontaneous, intuitive mode of information processing. He or she associates a main theme to the situation (Esser, 2001, p. 221-223; Heinrichs, 2005, pp.134-135, 142-143). This "leading motive" is included in the relevant mental model of the situation and could – in the sense of Kohlbergian tradition of moral psychology or the theory of the moral domain – be a "moral" one. Moreover, if the subject discovered a moral problem, this could be linked to justice, as well as to other moral values or principles.

To sum up, we can assume that motivational drivers (e.g. the moral self) determine the process of defining a situation. Second, it is obvious that otherwise the defined problem itself has motivational impact towards acting. Third, Esser points to another kind of motivational power relevant during constituting a situation, namely, the motivation to reflect and to change the mode of information process.

In settings well known to the agent or of less complexity, there might not be any need to reflect. Referring to his or her experience-based knowledge, the individual knows intuitively how to interpret the situation. Then the process of constituting a situation might pass off in an automatic spontaneous mode of data processing, determined particularly by affective processes. If there was a lack of experience-based knowledge in situations meeting the current conditions, however, the agent might feel bemused and would not know how to interpret the situation or what to do. Then, it could happen that the mode of data processing is changed into reflection if there is an opportunity to do so (e.g. enough time) and if the agent is *motivated* to deliberate (Esser, 1996, pp. 12-17, 2001, pp. 205, 272; Heinrichs, 2005, pp. 133-138, 140-145).

Constituting a Morally Relevant Situation – Perspectives for Studying Moral Motivation

Depending on situational as well as on personal determinants, we could distinguish types of morally relevant situations which might differ in respect to situational aspects, for example, to the context or the complexity of the constituted (moral) problem. Dilemmas could emerge as well as demands of obeying or rejecting a moral norm or a need for helping or pro-social behaviour. At the same time, the constituted situation referring to a given stimulus might vary between individuals because of the idiosyncratic characteristics of the individual's experience in similar situations, because of their mental models of the situation as elements of their experience-based knowledge, their domain specific knowledge or their moral sensitivity. Though we have already gained relevant results on content specificity of moral judging and acting (Beck, Heinrichs, Minnameier & Parche-Kawik, 1999; Krebs & Denton, 2005; see Bebeau & Thoma, this volume; Baumert et al., this volume), it will be a challenge to further research to study systematically what "context-specific" means, especially for "moral motivation".

In this chapter, we try to explicate the relevance of constituting a morally relevant situation for getting morally motivated. Therefore, we try to make a first step towards explicating interactions of situational and personal determinants on motivation:

1. I will look back to the claim of the later Kohlberg (Kohlberg, Levine & Hewer, 1984, p. 222) as well as of Rest (1999, p. 85) that, in research, it is necessary to focus on real morally relevant situations and not limit concepts of moral motivation to hypothetical dilemmas.
2. We discuss different interactions of the type of a morally relevant problem, of situational circumstances or contexts framing the (moral) problem as well as personal sources of moral motivation.

3. It is reasoned for a more basic methodological claim that researchers should be conscious of and explicate the types of situations or moral problems which their approach to moral motivation should be valid for.
4. It will be discussed why cognitive and affective processes are relevant for studying motivational processes in situations constituted individually as morally relevant.
5. Afterwards, I will discuss the impact of subjectively constituted situations from a methodological view, if measures of moral motivation are developed or discussed.
6. Finally, I point out the impact of certain situational features (e.g. temporal distance) on moral motivation.

(1) Moral motivation in real morally relevant situations – activating and applying moral principles. Looking back to Kohlberg's work, we recognize that he had started to study moral development from the basis of a broad understanding of morality (Kohlberg, 1986, p. 500). Even so, the more he and his co-workers continued, the more they focused on the reconstruction of the development of moral-cognitive structures. Finally, Kohlberg admitted that they had concentrated on moral judgments owing to (hypothetical) morally relevant situations which were assumed to be dealt with adequately by referring to decisions preferred by the majority of individuals arguing on moral stage 5, thinking post-conventionally (Kohlberg & Candee, 1984a, p. 492; Kohlberg, Levine & Hewer, 1984, p. 222).

In his later research, Kohlberg acknowledged that it would be necessary to go beyond studying moral reasoning in hypothetical dilemmas towards explaining how behaviour evolved in morally relevant real situations (Kohlberg, Levine & Hewer, 1984, p. 222). To meet these challenges, Kohlberg and Candee developed first ideas to bridge the gap of judging and acting via the thesis of monotonic relationships between judgment and behaviour, the moral types and the idea of responsibility judgments (Kohlberg & Candee, 1984a, b; Candee & Kohlberg, 1987). In their sequence model, they proclaimed that, after perceiving a situation as morally relevant, a moral principle was activated and, afterwards (in a second step), had to be accepted to form a responsibility judgment. The responsibility judgment was – in the sense of internalism – assumed to have motivational power towards acting consistently with the deontic judgment. It is maintained that a person wanted to act as though he or she was convinced that it was morally right (Kohlberg & Candee, 1984a, p. 403-417; see Minnameier, this volume). Kohlberg's and Candee's conceptions on how moral acting evolved were, however, more like initial ideas rather than sophisticated models. Rest agreed with the "late Kohlberg" that it would be fruitful and necessary to study moral judgment and behaviour not only in hypothetical dilemmas, but in "real situations" (Rest, 1999, p. 85).

Minnameier (this volume) encouraged a deeper discussion about the concept of moral motivation. In a recent publication, he made the provocative claim that the third component in Rest's model was neither necessary nor fruitful (Minnameier, 2010, 2012). In his view, the question of whether moral values or other personal values are more important is a moral problem itself and therefore not to be separated from the process of moral judgement. In line with Kohlberg's and Candee's sequence model (Kohlberg & Candee, 1984a, p. 430), Minnameier argues that, in such a morally relevant situation within the moral domain, in a first step, the agent might activate a moral principle (as an abductive process), secondly, apply the principle to the situation and form a deontic judgment (deduction) and, thirdly, assess whether the resulting action is appropriate or acceptable under these particular situational circumstances (induction) (Minnameier, this volume). The so-formed moral judgment itself then has - according to Minnameier - inherent motivational power towards action, and he therefore endorses a weak notion of so-called moral internalism.

Contrasting Minnameier's assumptions on how a "moral judgment" emerged with the Process Model of Acting and the sequence models of Kohlberg and Candee leads to two critical points on how the moral judgment interacts with moral motivation. First, if we reflect on the role of a moral judgment in terms of Minnameier in the phase of forming an intention, we could reconstruct moral judgment as a motivational driver powering a particular way of acting. Possibly the moral judgment has such intensive motivational power that the subject becomes committed to this way of action. In line with Minnameier's term, moral judgment, he admits that a person does not always have to intend to act in consistency with the deontic judgment. Moreover, it is claimed that, via induction, the agent could accept moral reasons of lower quality (in moral stages) compared to his individual moral competence under particular circumstances. Owing to those cases, Minnameier would admit that the intention does not have to be in line with the (initial) deontic judgment (Minnameier, 2012). Not only the stages of moral reasoning, but also the preferred way of action could vary. To sum up, the intention includes a moral judgment as a result of abduction, deduction and induction. It points to a decision about what kind of acting the person feels responsible to implement. This moral judgment represents a decision about what kind of acting is acceptable to solve the constituted moral problem and under situational circumstances.

Additionally, Minnameier's notion of "moral judgment" persists with the idea that a person might form a deontic judgment first and afterwards has to decide whether to follow this deontic judgment or to deviate. This idea is not in line with Esser's assumptions about how a situation is constituted, however, and also not in line with the Process Model of Acting. According to Esser, the moral principle as well as the circumstances for application are considered to be elements of the associated mental model of the situation and insofar as they are relevant to constituting the eliciting situation. To this point in time, we do not know enough about the criteria relevant for changes in the structure of moral reasoning or the preferred way of acting because of the same "core and moral problem". Contrasting the idea of internalism, changes in the preferred way of acting might not only be explained by moral stages because stages as schemas could be applied for reasoning towards different, even conflicting ways of action. The problem of situational specificity of moral reasoning has already been discussed in terms of moral differentiation as well as structural heterogeneity and variation of moral judgments (Beck et al., 1999; Lapsley & Narvaez, 2005; Minnameier, 2010; Krebs & Denton, 2005; Heinrichs, 2005, pp. 235-251).

So Beck, for example, proclaims moral differentiation to be grounded in socialization and different moral principles forming the main principles in particular contexts or life domains. Minnameier argues that there were situational circumstances as well as types of morally relevant problems, maybe linked to preferred patterns (especially stages) of moral reasoning typical for particular moral cultures or special contexts (Beck, 1999; Heinrichs, Minnameier & Beck, submitted). Those typical situational cues may cause application of particular moral principles or changes in moral stages. Moral differentiation in that sense, however, is discussed mainly in reference to the concept of moral stages and to problems within the moral domain. At the same time, it has to be admitted that, up to now, there is a lack of empirical evidence concerning what kinds of situational cues persons with certain characteristics may consider as relevant for changing the structure of moral reasoning. It also has not been sophisticatedly studied how an identified moral problem is related to other, maybe prudential or conventional, problems in the same situation. It would be interesting to identify when individuals change their quality of moral reasoning. Maybe they differentiate between situational circumstances as elements of the core of the moral problem (e.g. conflicting moral values, a transgression or the protagonist being treated in an unfair way) or as cues of how the moral problem is situationally framed (e.g. expectations to form a deontic judgment, to act efficiently, to achieve additional aims and fulfil other needs, to communicate a moral judgment in an interview or to act conssstently with this moral judgment) (Heinrichs, 2005, pp. 264-267). So, I like to point to the fact that we should do more than merely try to model moral judging and acting in situations typical for the moral domain. Compared to Rest's definition of moral motivation, we should not only concentrate on the motivation to prefer moral judgments and values against other judgments and values, but to specify what kinds of non-moral problems and situational facets are strengthening or - in contrast - weakening the individual's power to act morally.

Additionally, it may not be enough to assess situational conditions as the only drivers for changing decisions in morally relevant situations. Hopefully, it could be fruitful to study in a contrasting approach whether moral judgments differ in stages or in the preferred way of acting depending on situational circumstances forming a situational framing of a moral "core" problem. Then, we would expect changes in the moral judgments when a certain moral core problem is put into different domains (i), contexts (ii) or action-relevant situational frames (iii): (i) domains: conventional or prudential problems as additional facets of the morally relevant situation (ii) action-relevant situational cues as a frame of the core problem: actions to conduct like evaluating a way of acting to be adequate to be included in a deontic judgment, arguing in an interview, solving this problem by his own, discussing about the best solution with other people, justifying a former behaviour; (iii) contexts: e.g. due to moral problems a particular professions, moral problems in family context, among peers, among children, young or older people.

(2) Impact of types of problems and of the context on moral motivation. We could anticipate that it will be very fruitful to add studies, taking a social psychological perspective in order to investigate how states of being motivationally powered and of commitment evolved, (a) in different types of moral problems as well as, (b) in different contexts, how, (c) personal sources drive motivational power and, moreover, (d) because of other situational or cultural conditions (Power, this volume). Additionally, (e) there are more and more approaches preferring to study how personal as well as situational determinants interact and influence moral motivation.

(a) So maybe in moral dilemmas or value conflicts, a need to reflective moral reasoning might emerge. Maybe the thesis of internalism could be empirically confirmed, and mainly cognitive processes could explain the variance in moral motivation. At the same time, what about moral decision-making in situations provoking a decision to obey one moral norm or to reject it (see Nunner-Winkler, this volume, or Gasser et al., this volume), in situations where self-interest empowers the same way of action or in situations wherein no motive activated countering the moral one? Maybe in those cases, the process of forming an intention will be passed over in the intuitive mode of information processing while affective processes have greater impact on urging the individual towards action. In cases where there is a need but no opportunity or time to reflect or change the mode, the individual might accept a solution considered suboptimal. He or she will accept this, but maybe he or she is not as motivated or committed in strength towards the chosen way of acting as he or she would be via sufficient deliberation and moral reasoning. Thus, a reduced motivation or opportunity to reflect on moral conflicts, when no fitting mental model of the situation could be associated, might lead to a reduced motivational or volitional power to act consistent with the moral judgment. Additionally, the motivational power of the situation may vary depending on whether the constituted moral problem is embedded in a real and multi-faceted situation and maybe in contrast to other situational cues pointing to prudential or conventional problems (Smetana, 2010). In those cases, it might be important to study how the problem is defined, what is the leading motive as well as the motivational impacts on all these constituting facets of the situation and their interactions.

(b) Moreover, it is not only a certain type of morally relevant situation or conflict that impacts on the state of motivation. We could assume that the context influences the motivational power to solve a moral problem as well. Looking at the different contributions in this book, we see approaches to moral motivation focussing on very different contexts and each approach has taken a particular perspective on motivation (e.g. Bebeau and Thoma studied moral identity as a source of feeling responsible in the context of professions (Bebeau & Thoma, this volume). Klöckner (this volume) focussed on personal determinants on the motivation to conduct environmental behaviour and environmental education. Micewski (this volume) argued that the military has special expectations and conditions of morality. Campbell (this volume) thought about the relevance of moral motivation in teaching. Oja and Craig (this volume) investigated how to foster moral motivation in internships and Althof and Berkowitz (this volume) thought about moral motivation as a goal in character and civic education. In all these contexts, there seem to be particular expectations to moral agents or exemplars: in professions, individuals are responsible for a public good but expected at the same time to meet a specific code of ethics. So, there are explicit moral norms to be applied or not in particular situations. Otherwise, because of environmental conservation, we are conscious that the individual's contribution to environmental protection is very small. To achieve the goal, the society or even the world's population has to act in concert. In the military, very often the key issue is about life or death, and also many people are concerned with one action. In teaching, the agent not only has to act in a morally adequate way him or herself, but also should try to foster others' moral development.

(c) Moreover, as we see in other approaches to moral motivation, we have to admit that it is often discussed with reference to personal determinants, more or less stable over time or to some extent (in childhood, youth or adulthood). We discuss the development of the moral self (Blasi, 1982; Nunner-Winkler, this volume; Döring, this volume; Krettenauer, this volume; Wren, this volume; Lovat, this volume), moral identity (Bebeau & Thoma, this volume), moral exemplars (Colby & Damon, 1992; Walker, this volume) or moral interests as a source of motivation in the sense of self-determination (Krapp, this volume). These personal determinants are assumed to support moral motivation as a state of being driven during the process of acting (e.g. because people develop a feeling of being responsible in particular situations to behave in accordance with moral values "central" to their sense of self. So, we assume that there are people at higher and others at lower levels of moral motivation in terms of personal determinants that are stable over time. This level of moral motivation again has impact on the strength of being motivationally driven to constitute moral problems and, moreover, to form moral judgments, to commit to moral behaviour or, finally, to act morally.

(d) Power (this volume) demonstrates very well what impact situational determinants, like role models or a "moral atmosphere", have on the current state of motivation as well as on the development of relevant sources of moral motivation like the "moral self". He emphasises how moral values of others who are in an "intensive" relationship with the individual (e.g. the coach) influence the "moral self" in the context of sports.

(e) Considering upcoming approaches in moral psychology, the interaction of personality and situation is more and more the subject of investigation in attempting to explain the judgment-action-gap in general and moral motivation in particular. Even Blasi emphasized two dimensions of the moral self being relevant to bridging the gap between judgement and behaviour. These are the centrality of moral values (as explained above) and the integration of moral values to other ideas and motivations relevant to the self (Blasi, 1995, p. 229; Walker, 2004, p. 3). He explicitly stressed that the state of being motivated to solve a moral problem does not only depend on personal, but also on situational determinants which work to activate moral issues in a particular situation. This assumption is in line with the action-based view in the Process Model of Acting where both situational as well as personal variables (of different stability over time) have impact on the state of being motivationally powered (Heinrichs, 2005, p. 139). Thus, Narvaez proclaims different mental mind sets of ethics (security, engagement and imagination) and these mind sets to be elicited by particular situational conditions as well as preferred to an inter-individually varying extent (Narvaez, 2009, this volume).

(3) Challenge of border crossing – what about moral motivation in morally relevant situations? Approaches to moral motivation strictly in line with Kohlberg's assumptions are accused of being tied to the moral domain, to a well-defined, but specified idea of moral development and moral judgment as well as moral behaviour. These approaches focus on cognitive processes, proclaim moral internalism and restrict their stimuli to moral dilemmas as representative of eliciting situations within the moral domain. Some authors keep on preferring these assumptions to conceptualize and investigate moral motivation (see Wren, this volume, and, to some extent, Minnameier, this volume). Others might blame these authors for ignoring important critical feedback from associated fields of research, and for overestimating the role of cognitive processes and structures in the process of acting (Hoffman, 2000; Keller, 2007, p. 23; Nunner-Winkler, this volume).

Following Turiel's results (Turiel, 1983; Smetana, 2010), researchers in moral psychology mostly claim to be concentrating on studying the "moral domain". They do not intend investigating how to deal, for example, with social conventions. Moreover, they concentrate on situations where the other's welfare is endangered or on situations where the agent has to foster the other's welfare even though he will have to adhere to his own needs.

In fact, we have to acknowledge that we include different kinds of eliciting situations in psychological studies on moral issues, and this fact seems to have escaped our notice. On the one hand, we might be jeopardized in generalizing our results inadequately if moral judgment, motivation, emotions or behaviour are studied in specific situations and applied to broader contexts (Modgil & Modgil, 1986, p. 1). On the other hand, we should take care not to conduct empirical studies when their results could not easily be compared or integrated to identify the scientific progress. Thus, it is time to explicate and reflect more deeply upon what situations we focus on in our projects. Do we concentrate on moral dilemmas, conflicts or demands for obeying a moral norm, hypothetical or real situations, stimuli, including transgressions, injustice, immorality or "good behaviour"? Even Popper (1994, p. 53) has pointed to the researcher's obligation to explain what the developed model is thought to be valid for: that means that it is really important to identify criteria to describe the area of validity of his studies or theoretical approaches.

More and more studies in moral psychology do, or at least would, benefit from research in other disciplines and contexts (Lapsley & Narvaez, 2005). We find studies not investigating situations at the core of the "moral domain" in order to study moral reasoning, but regarding situations linked to issues which could become morally relevant in particular situations, like, for example, research on pro-social behaviour (e.g. Gutzwiller-Helfenfinger, Gasser & Malti, 2010; Malti & Krettenauer, 2011; Malti et.al., 2009). These studies could help us to gain scientific progress resulting from motivation in order to solve problems within the moral domain.

Narvaez and Lapsley (2005) cross disciplinary borders in applying ideas of research on (cognitive) expertise to the moral domain and in particular to moral motivation. Although Narvaez & Lapsley's approaches to moral expertise and social-cognitive personality are based on similar assumptions to the Process Model of Acting (Heinrichs, 2010,), the Process Model, as a general action model, provides a theoretical framework to go beyond the moral domain by provoking two questions: (1) What is typical for problem solving in the moral domain, if an individual has to deal with a morally relevant situation? and, (2) What is the similarity in acting and becoming motivated in moral situations compared to other, non-moral contexts? – Also, what makes "moral motivation", in the sense of the feeling of being driven to a particular course of action, assessed as morally adequate? Hopefully, to take an action-based view could help to enrich research on moral motivation and support border crossing between moral psychology and other relevant disciplines (Lapsley & Narvaez, 2005). Even if we endorse the study of moral motivation and behaviour in sophisticated and defined contexts, as explained before (teaching, other professions, etc.), there obviously is a great demand for connecting the scientific discussion within moral psychology to the state of the art in research on motivational issues in general in order to prevent research in moral psychology from "isolation" and to gain scientific progress (Heinrichs, 2005; see introduction this volume; Krapp, this volume; Ugazio, Lamm & Singer, 2012; Vollmeyer, this volume, Weiner, this volume).

(4) Constituting a morally relevant situation - How do cognitions and emotions trigger motivation? Although it is a clearly defined and narrow universe of discourse, Kohlberg had nonetheless concentrated on deontic judgments in hypothetical dilemmas, in order to provoke and measure the stage of moral reasoning and reflection. These stimuli were chosen to ban the agent from being emotionally involved in (moral) emotions in this research project. Even Kohlberg and his scholars nonetheless admitted that these constraints, in the name of "good empirical work", were not appropriate to study moral acting and in particular moral motivation in real situations.

Countering Kohlberg's position, Hoffman emphasized the impact of empathy and moral emotions on moral motivation in particular situations. Since Haidt's provoking article "The emotional dog and its rational tail" was published in 2001, the discussion on moral emotions as well as the research in that field has been expended. Today, we find a wide range of research on social and moral emotions and on the impact of emotions on moral motivation, moral action (see also Gasser et al., this volume; Malti et al., 2009, Ugazio, Lamm & Singer, 2012; Maxwell & Racine, 2011) or moral development (see Döring, this volume; Krettenauer, this volume).

Considering the process of defining a situation (the first process on the way to an intention), we could ask in particular: Do affective and emotional processes play an important role during the process of constituting an eliciting morally relevant situation? Referring to the Process Model of Acting, constituting a situation describes the attitude towards an incident. A mental model of the situation - an element of the individual's experience-based knowledge - fitting to the current incident is associated. Affective and emotional processes are highly relevant for interpreting a current situation, for identifying a (moral) problem and for the motivational impact of the problem as confirmed in the social psychological approach on justice sensitivity (Baumert et al., this volume). This construct refers to the concern for justice as a moral principle in a particular situation (Baumert et al., this volume) and points to the fact that "perception of (potential) injustice triggers emotional reactions" (Baumert et al., this volume, p. 163), especially negative (moral) emotions like anger, moral outrage, compassion or guilt. Thus, if the individual has experienced negative emotions, he or she might associate them with a particular situation later on. These negative emotions (anticipated or experienced in the current situation) might, granted exceptions, drive the individual to restore justice in the current incident or avoid injustice in the future. The individual might feel motivationally empowered to redress injustice by the experienced or anticipated injustice[2]. Baumert et al. (this volume) showed that "people differ systematically in their *readiness* to perceive injustice and in the *strength* of their cognitive, emotional, and behavioural reactions to injustice". (p. 168) To achieve deeper insights into how people constitute morally relevant situations, it would be interesting to investigate the following questions: Could injustice sensitivity occur after negative moral experiences of injustice and negative emotions? Are the results of justice sensitivity pointing to a specified concept compared to moral sensitivity and would it be fruitful to test whether both concepts (justice sensitivity and moral sensitivity) correlate? Or, should we concentrate on investigating value-specific concepts of moral sensitivity (e.g. justice sensitivity, ownership-sensitivity, assault-sensitivity, need-for-help-sensitivity) rather than more general concepts?

(5) Constituting a morally relevant situation – How valid are our methods of measurement to grasp emotional and motivational issues? One prominent approach to moral motivation is research identifying the so-called happy-victimizer-phenomenon as a particular phase in childrens' moral development, pointing to a lack

of moral motivation in childhood (see Nunner-Winkler, this volume; Krettenauer, Malti & Sokol, 2008). Thus, this approach counters the idea of internalism with externalism and proclaims emotion attributions and especially justifications of attributed emotions as indicators of motivation to act morally. What I want to pinpoint subsequently are critical issues concerning how valid emotions and motivation are measured in transgressions.

To ask for emotion attributions has been fruitful in identifying the happy-victimizer-pattern for the first time and illuminating that special phase of children around 4-6 years of age. In further projects, this phenomenon has been studied in youth, adolescence and even in adulthood. Enriching the universe of discourse and varying methods of data collecting, it has become increasingly obvious that this phenomenon is not unique to the early years of childhood. The happy-victimizer-phenomenon, as well as the attributed emotions and justifications, seem to differentiate owing to methods of measuring (emotion attributions to the perpetrator as another person or to the self) or because of the presented stimuli or age (Nunner-Winkler, this volume; Döring, this volume; Gasser et al., this volume; Gutzwiller-Helfenfinger, Heinrichs, Latzko & Minnameier, 2012). So, interesting questions remain, such as: Is this phenomenon really age- and context specific or did we grasp artificially varied patterns caused by inappropriate measures (see Gasser et al., this volume), especially by provoking answers and by presenting inappropriate stimulating situations?

Empirical studies have confirmed that the situational conditions really made a difference in the thrust and structure of moral judgment, as well as in the kind and strength of the attributed emotions (see Gasser et al., this volume). I recommend that we should be careful to make sure we measure moral judgments, moral emotions, moral motivation as well as moral behaviour in particular situations. It will be important to cross the disciplinary border and to integrate moral and social psychological approaches in order to grasp how people constitute morally relevant situations, how they judge, get motivationally powered and committed to act in order to solve the defined problem.

(6) Constituting a morally relevant situation - Temporal distance and its motivational impact. In a more distinctive view "moral sensitivity", differs among individuals. Agerström and Björklund (this volume) investigate temporal distance as a facet of morally relevant situations and discuss its impact on motivational strength. Additionally, they consider emotional processes as important drivers towards action. They proclaim that temporal distance is not morally relevant itself, but influences constituting a moral situation and the motivational power of the constituted situation. The authors have reviewed substantial evidence, showing that temporal distance affects the extent to which people (1) construe an event as being morally relevant in the first place, (2) endorse morality by condemning moral transgressors and praising moral acts, and (3) are motivated to act morally and resist "moral temptations" (Agerström & Björklund, this volume). So, we could assume that not only moral, but also

non-moral issues determine the motivational impact of the defined situation towards forming an intention and action. Moreover, both researchers found that moral values and principles were the more salient for people the more they were highly motivated to act in accordance with their moral ideals. Moreover, the more the situation was in the proximate future, the more relevant situational influences beyond the protagonist's control became, and the less important became those internalized moral values that push the individual towards their own moral self. The impact of non-moral and situational conditions increased compared to situations characterized by temporal distance. Goals of the "moral self" might struggle with non-moral goals or aims. The need for volitional processes and for a moral judgment, in the sense of induction (to reflect upon whether the moral principle is to be applied in this particular situation or whether to deviate from the deontic judgment in this particular situational circumstances) (see Minnameier, this volume), might arise.

So, "temporal distance" is a constitutive determinant of morally relevant situations. The temporal distance could be considered less a criterion to constitute the problem, however, as it is the difference between the "is" and the "ought" in the current situation that is instrumental, rather than a criterion of the situational frame (conditions) in which the problem is embedded (Heinrichs, 2005, pp. 264-266). So, temporal distance could be regarded less as a concern of the moral "core" problem than as a constitutive part of the situational conditions in which to apply a moral principle (Minnameier, this volume).

If we assume, as it is proclaimed in the Process Model, that the constituted problem is determining the whole process of acting, if we continue to attend to this social psychological idea, the following questions remain to be answered: Do the different conditions in the various contexts influence the way how people become motivated to act morally correctly in a particular situation? Is there a need for referring to different concepts of "moral motivation" in different contexts or types of morally relevant situations in order to explain motivation to act morally correctly? Or, can we suppose that "moral motivation" could be defined as a more general concept? Rest and his co-workers, at least in the beginning, assumed that it was possible to develop a general concept, but Rest himself has suggested investigating moral motivation in the context of professions as a first step. He considered the professions as very appropriate to start with (Bebeau & Thoma, this volume).

Anticipating Objectives and Action Plans – Reconstructed Referring to the Process Modell of Acting

The second process (see figure 1) - "anticipating objectives and action plans" -addresses mainly processes of problem solving. In the following section, again, the assumptions of the Process Model based on "anticipating objectives and action plans" will firstly be explained in accordance with a general action-based view.

Second, the assumptions of the Process Model of Acting will be applied to discussion of the impact on one's motivation to solve moral problems.

After the problem has been defined in well-known situations, the agent might have associated a suitable script and so be sure about the way of acting on which he would decide. Esser (1996, p. 13) pointed to habits or routines as typical cases for choosing the automatic-intuitive mode of data processing[3]. In other incidents that are new to the individual, or include complex problems, the person cannot easily associate relevant mental models of the situation or scripts or activate her experience-based knowledge. He or she might not "just know" what to aim for or what to do in order to solve the constituted problem. In that case, the process "anticipating aims and action plans", there are three different ways to solve the constituted problem and to form an intention: (a) the agent could change the mode of data processing and reflect on how to find a solution; (b) the agent could be highly self-confident to find a good way to cope with the particular situation later on even if he could not solve the problem at the moment of forming an intention; or, (c) the agent could accept a sub-optimal solution (Heinrichs, 2005, p. 143).

In complex situations, or when there is a lack of mental models of the situation, he or she: (a) might have to start a process of cognitive problem solving in a broader sense in order to substantiate objectives and to develop action plans. The agent might feel urged to reflect, to make a decision and therefore to change the mode of data processing. To form an intention in this case demands reflection and volitional power in order to find a good solution. The intention includes a concrete idea of how to act. Second, (b), even if the agent was confronted with new or complex problems and not able to anticipate concrete aims or action plans at once, he could feel confident in his own competence in solving this problem adequately later on (Heinrichs, 2005, pp. 146-150) and so be urged to solve this problem. So, intentions can be formed and commitment can evolve whenever the agent is sure about his competence to solve this particular problem in the (near) future and when he is motivationally driven to solve it, even if he has not developed an adequate solution yet. Third (c), if he or she had not anticipated suitable aims and action plans, but if additionally he or she is not willing to change the mode of data processing (because of situational circumstances or because of a lack of motivation to reflect), he or she could form an intention by accepting a sub-optimal solution. Maybe, however, the intention is minor in volitional power and strength of commitment more so than it might have been after sophisticated reflection. Additionally, it might be that there is no intention to solve the problem because of a lack of ideas about what to aim for or how to act. So, a lack of motivation to solve a moral problem could emerge – as pointed out in this section - by a lack of experienced-based knowledge fitting the currently perceived situation, that is, a lack of self-efficacy to get the problem solved in future, even if one has no pre-prepared solution at the time. Choosing sub-optimal solutions, because of a deficit in time or the opportunity to reflect, might diminish the strength of motivational power to act.

Anticipating Objectives and Action Plans – Perspectives for
Studying Moral Motivation

What are the consequences of applying these action-based assumptions on "anticipating objectives and action plans" to decision-making and problem solving in morally relevant situations? This question refers to one well-known criticism of Kohlberg's assumptions in his developmental theory. Kohlberg proclaimed moral-cognitive stages to be schemes applied to moral dilemmas independently from the "content", from the preferred value and the thrust of the decision. If we consider moral structures as content-independent schemes, associated with a particular moral problem as a cognitive structure included in the mental model of the situation, there is no determinant mentioned by Kohlberg which explained why an individual prefers the one or the other value, one or another way of acting. If we want to explain what aims or action plans an individual chooses to solve a constituted problem, however, we need an idea about how this decision regarding aims and action plans develops.

Minnameier (this volume) persists with Kohlberg's tradition in so far as he continues to refer to moral stages as relevant criteria to differentiate (deontic as well as inductive) moral judgements in situations in the moral domain. Similar to Kohlberg, Minnameier cannot explain what kinds of objectives or ways of action for which the agent will decide. The question about why a person chose one alternative or another seems to be ignored. Even in terms of moral segmentation, it is mostly seen how heterogeneous moral stages are applied to varying situations. Why people differ in the thrust of their moral judgement remains an open question which obviously cannot be explained merely in terms of moral stages.

Especially if we include real morally relevant, multi-faceted situations in our research, we could ask whether research on problem-solving or the explained assumptions on acting in general could help us to explain what aims and action plans the individual anticipates as possible solutions in morally relevant situations. If the agent had appropriate experiences in solving similar moral problems successfully, he could probably associate a script or sophisticated ideas on how to act properly. Otherwise, if the individual has not adequate experience-based knowledge available, he might have to apply his problem-solving competencies to the moral domain. Presumably, he will not need only problem-solving competence as a context-independent personal determinant, but he will also need to activate and adopt moral principles to the particular situational conditions and make a moral decision. Decision-making in morally relevant situations therefore is more than moral reasoning and applying moral-cognitive stages. It is also a matter of moral knowledge or internalized moral values and so is linked not only to cognitive processes, but also to emotional (e.g. as emotions are triggered by injustice-sensitivity (see Baumert et al., this volume) and motivational components or the moral self (or the moral identity) (see Bebeau & Thoma, this volume; Krapp, this volume; Krettenauer and Walker, this volume).

Before I focus on motivational and volitional processes, in the sense of the third and fourth sub-process on the way to an intention (Heinrichs, 2005, pp. 150-162),

I will go back to the cognitive processes of anticipating the aims and action plans of Boesch (1976, p. 20; see also Heinrichs, 2005, pp. 146-150) and ask what would happen if the agent could not conceive of a good solution intuitively, but had to apply his problem-solving competencies to the moral problem. The individual might try to anticipate and weigh the consequences of the particular behaviour in order to find the best solution. The result of this deliberation could, on the one hand, be considered as a moral judgment which has – in the sense of internalism – its own motivational impact. On the other hand, this process could be interpreted as cognitive motivational theories, anticipating expectations and consequences of the action, developing expectations and evaluating them by applying "values" (in the sense of expectation-value-models of motivation). Moreover, I would suggest discussing more sophistically how these "values" evolve in a particular situation. Kwok and Selman (this volume) emphasize how important it is in morally relevant situations to anticipate the effects of the behaviour in social systems, on interaction, other people, social relationships, groups, organizations or society. Therefore, the agents need to be socially informed and have experiences in how social interactions and systems work. As well, we might be able to identify other relevant situational factors influencing how an associated way of action is assessed.

It is therefore obvious that it could be fruitful to study in ways that go beyond the moral-cognitive perspective to explain how an individual gets into a state of being driven towards a particular way of acting in morally relevant situations. We could assume that if the person has identified a course of action as an adequate solution of the (moral) problem, as well as an adequate response to the real situation the moral problem is embedded in, the person may feel driven towards this way of acting. Otherwise, if a person could not imagine how to solve this problem successfully, the individual may feel demotivated, even in cases wherein the situation was considered as very important to cope with. If there is a lack of ideas, knowledge or (moral) competencies concerning how to solve this problem, there might emerge a state of confusion and uncertainty about how to act which might decrease the motivational power towards action. In contrast, in the literature studying moral judging in dilemma situations, this kind of uncertainty is not mentioned, probably because, if moral conflicts are constituted as value conflicts, the options concerning how to act were mostly quite clear and easy to anticipate: they would follow the one or the other value. In contrast, in real situations anticipating a good solution, often it is not as easy because there are more than the moral cues constituting the multi-facets of the situation.

To sum up, the latter reflections point to a need for more sophisticated modelling on how motivational power towards action could evolve or decrease depending on the experience-based knowledge in similar situations, as well as on the competence of solving moral problems embedded in real situations. I suppose that an individual who is not sure about what to aim for or how to act will be less motivationally empowered than another person who intuitively feels committed to one way of acting. Similarly, we could assume that a person of low self-confidence or self-efficacy trying to find good solutions might feel at least less motivationally driven towards solving this moral problem than an agent of high self-confidence or high self-efficacy. Low self-efficacy and self-confidence in solving such (moral) problems, insufficient situation-specific experience-based knowledge or accompanied negative emotions and affects (like e.g. fear, guilt, desperation, anger) could reduce the motivation to solve the constituted moral problem up to a state of indecisiveness or even capitulation. We could imagine that the more intensive the motivational impact of the constituted problem is and, especially if there is a lack of knowledge about fruitful ways of acting, the more the individual will experience an inner tension. The agent might try to reduce this cognitive dissonance. So, in some cases, the drive towards action (as motivational and volitional power) could increase and the individual will engage more intensively in further problem-solving. In other cases, the probability and strength of an evolving commitment to act morally might decrease (e.g. by applying disengagement strategies in order to reduce cognitive dissonance). The latter examples underpin that the strength of motivational power varies across individuals and types of morally relevant situations, and it would be good to get more insights about the determinants causing those variations. Additionally, because in moral psychology, and especially in the Kohlbergian tradition, problem solving competence, self-efficacy or self-confidence as determinants of how easily the agent managed to develop (morally) adequate solutions is nearly ignored and points to an interesting field of research.

Motivational Power - Reconstructed Referring to the Process Model of Acting

Referring to the Process Model of Acting, "motivation" as a general and not a specific concept for the moral domain is mainly considered as a state of being energized towards engaging in solving the constituted problem. If the individual is motivated, he/she would feel urged and motivationally powered to act in order to cope with a constituted situation. Emphasizing "motivational power" points to basic internal states associated with corporal conditions which have not been focused on or even mentioned in motivational psychology since the 1940s. In other words, researchers in the field have let aspects of emotions and energizing slide in their research on motivation (Sokolowski, 1993, pp. 23-25; Heinrichs, 2005, p. 95).

Resorting to those basic corporal states as indicators of a state of being motivationally empowered allows discussion of many different approaches geared towards explaining personal and situational determinants of this state of motivation (Heinrichs, 2005, pp. 150-151). Probably the state of being urged towards action could be owing to a mixed-bag of drivers, and each of the drivers might contribute to the strength of motivational power (Heinrichs, 2005, pp. 95-96; Oser, this volume; Vollmeyer et al., this volume). Applied to motivation in morally relevant situations, drivers towards action might support the individually identified "moral course of action", while others reduce the motivational power towards the morally preferred way of acting. To explore and specify how the different moral, as well as non-moral, drivers interact and contribute to moral acting could be one important aim of future research.

Additionally, in line with the process model, it is assumed that these drivers in morally relevant situations could point to personal determinants conceptualized as personality traits and so stable over time, but also to states only stable for a few moments and expected to vary depending on the context or situation (see Klöckner, this volume).

Motivational Power - Perspectives for Studying Moral Motivation

Moral motivation, in the sense of Rest's model, comes up as a category integrating very different approaches in moral and motivational psychology for describing why people are driven or pushed towards the moral course of action in morally relevant situations. Up to now, this third component of "moral motivation" has mostly been discussed within moral psychology and almost without any links to motivational psychology. Moral motivation within moral psychology is mainly considered to be a domain-specific internal driver to act morally and to withstand temptations and to prefer moral to non-moral values. In contrast, the Process Model provides a theoretical framework for crossing the borders from moral to motivational psychology. The action-based view supports reference to different (moral as well as non-moral) personal and situational determinants triggering motivation in morally relevant situations.

So, even the constituted moral problem itself could empower the individual to act (Euler, 1989, p. 35). In turn, the motivational impact of the constituted problem is grounded in individual personal sources of motivation which are considered to be more or less stable over time, especially the construct of "motives" (morally relevant - e.g. the justice-motive). Thus, as mentioned before, Baumert et al. (this volume) considered justice-sensitivity as theoretically linked to the more basic justice motive which itself is assumed to provide the drive for goal-directed behaviour. Moreover, motives are closely linked to affective reactions that signal whether relevant goals have been attained or not.

Nonetheless, studying *motives* will not be sufficient to grasp the different facets and determinants of moral motivation. Owing to justice-sensitivity, Baumert et al. (this volume) have to admit that the theoretically assumed correlation between the justice-motive and justice-sensitivity could not be confirmed empirically. Moreover, in motivational psychology, research on motives in general has been accused of being old-fashioned and considered as empirically failed (Krapp, this volume). As well, there is a great consensus that motivation as a state in a particular situation is influenced by personal as well as by situational determinants (v. Cranach & Ammann, 1999, pp. 257-258; Gollwitzer & Liu, 1996, p. 210; Heckhausen, 1989, p. 136; Heinrichs, 2005, pp. 95-96). Thus, concepts contrasting motives as motivational attributes of personality were developed posting motivation and moral motivation in particular as facets of "intrinsic" motivation, like self-determination or moral interests. Additionally, the latter constructs open the door to studying development and ways to foster moral motivation (see e.g. Krapp, Krettenauer, or Althof & Berkowitz, this volume). Other important ideas to conceptualize personal determinants as drivers towards a state of moral motivation are the moral self or moral identity (see e.g. Bebeau & Thoma, Walker, Döring, or Nunner-Winkler, this volume). These constructs also allow the study of their impact on behaviour as well as taking a developmental perspective.

All the approaches to personal determinants with motivational impact on moral behaviour mentioned above (the moral motives, self-determination towards moral behaviour, interest in moral issues, the moral self or moral identity) are based on the assumption that an individual could only behave morally if he or she has internalized a particular idea of morality and is intending to act in coherence with his or her preferred values, attitudes or moral judgments. Countering this position, the state of motivation towards moral action could also be grounded in extrinsic motivation. For example, if stimuli in the social environment were set as incentives for moral behaviour, and if they meet the individual's moral or non-moral needs (e.g. if employees were offered incentives, the organization would be aiming to meet the individuals' needs and to foster moral behaviour). Parents might also use different ways of applying incentives up to sanctions to urge their children to behave in a morally adequate way and to foster moral development. Even if we look at Kohlberg's moral stages, we could assume that extrinsic motivation to moral behaviour could evolve, especially if the individual formed a moral judgment on stage 1 or 2 as appropriate in this particular situation. In other words, sometimes there might be other than moral issues more relevant to the individual. Then, intrinsic moral motivation is lacking and moral behaviour might be fostered by implementing situational determinants with positive impact on the expected way of acting.

In addition to social motives, intrinsic or extrinsic motivation, it is apparent that, owing to moral issues, basic physical needs like thirst, hunger or bodily harm could constrain moral motivation and even enhance immoral behaviour. Consequently, not only social wishes, motives (as traits) or basic social needs (focused for example in the Rubikon model (Gollwitzer, 1996; Heckhausen & Kuhl, 1985; Krapp, 1999)) but also substantial physical needs should be taken into account as potentially triggering motivational power in morally relevant situations – not in terms of intrinsic sources of moral motivation, but to explain the strength of motivational power (Esser, 2001, p. 240).

Otherwise, we could ask whether there are motivational concepts prominent in psychology which do not fit at all with moral issues and so could be excluded from research on moral motivation. Vollmeyer et al. (this volume) assume that experience of flow could emerge in morally relevant situations (e.g. if a person is engaged in helping others). In contrast, there are also critical voices expressing doubt that, for instance, helping behaviour itself is perceived as joyful and the cause for getting into a state of "flow" or whether this state of being intrinsically motivated can evolve because basic needs are being met by conducting this behaviour in social settings. Maybe the need to be perceived as competent or to feel socially integrated is accompanying the helping behaviour, but not the 'joy' of helping injured people after an accident, for instance. Whether flow can emerge through solving moral problems is an issue that could be addressed theoretically and empirically.

Finally, if we are interested in the consequences of research on moral motivation for moral education, it will be important to study which concept of "moral motivation" could be considered as fruitful in an educational perspective. On the one hand, it would be interesting to know how to develop sources of motivational power like the moral self (see Krettenauer, Döring, Gasser et al. or Nunner-Winkler, Weyers, this volume), moral interest (Krapp, this volume) or moral identity (see Bebeau & Thoma, this volume). On the other hand, we might ask how to design an appropriate atmosphere for the situational context of moral acting as well as for fostering moral development (Power, Althof & Berkowitz, Oja & Craig, this volume).

In summary, there are many different approaches on motivation, all contributing to explaining states of being motivationally powered towards moral as well as immoral behaviour. It will be a matter of empirical research to decide which driver might best explain both kinds of behaviour. Focussing on adequate environmental behaviour, Klöckner (this volume) has collected and systematized variables linked to different concepts between intrinsic and extrinsic motivation into one model. Maybe this idea could be applied to other contexts within the moral domain (for example, to typical moral challenges in the different professions).

In order to grasp "motivational power towards the moral course of action", it might not be sufficient to focus on situations in which the "moral aim" or the moral way of acting is clearly preferred (all motivational drivers push towards a particular (the moral) way of acting) and in which one aim is of distinctively higher motivational power than others. Especially in the moral domain, we often assume that different ways of acting, aims or values are associated and have to be weighed (e.g. in moral dilemmas). As Rest implicitly supposes, one might be driven to one way of acting by moral values and to the other by non-moral values, and the individual has to prefer one of them – and these are the cases where "moral motivation" in this sense of preferring moral to non-moral values and accepting personal disadvantages becomes important.

Referring however to the Process Model, this assumption seems to simplify the influences of motivational drivers in many morally relevant situations. Moreover, in other cases, or when looking at particular moral agents, the motivational power of moral values or motives might trigger the same way of action as would non-moral drivers. As a result, the motivational power might increase – just as Walker points to caring moral exemplars as driven by agency as well as communion (Walker, this volume).

In multi-faceted situations associated with moral, as well as with aspects of other domains, the motivational pattern can be even more complex. The individual could anticipate more than one, or even more than two possible ways of action in addressing the same problem, and all of these ways of acting may be powered by some, but not only, morally special motivational sources. Then, a need for decision-making about which alternative to prefer can arise. If two or more ways of acting were nearly equal in their strength of motivational power, then there is a need for decision-making and, in a morally relevant situation, moral judging might evolve and the need for moral motivation emerge: the need to prefer moral values over non-moral values (Rest, 1999, p. 101) or the need for accepting personal disadvantages in order to care for others (see Walker, this volume) or prevent harm from others. In these cases, according to the process model, the individual might be urged for applying volitional (or cognitive control) processes to come to a decision and to become committed to a particular way of acting. How motivational and volitional processes interact on the way to forming an intention will be explained in the following section: first, referring to action in general, and, second, owing to morally relevant situations.

Volitional Power - Reconstructed Referring to the Process Model of Acting Within the Rubikon model, forming an intention is an act of rational decision-making and only needed in a few types of situations. If there was a need for such a deliberative decision towards how to act, and if the agent made the decision to act, then he would cross the "Rubikon" and enter the second phase of acting, namely, action planning. According to the Rubikon model, this transition from the first to the second phase of acting (from forming an intention to action planning) does not necessarily have to be passed by a decision made in the reflecting mode of data processing (Heckhausen, 1989, p. 213; Heinrichs, 2005, pp. 154-162). Moreover, in everyday life, often there might arise a state of feeling committed to an associated aim via an intuitive mode of data processing. This state of being decided and committed could also be sufficient to merge into implementing the intention. Still, we need to ask: how does this way of commitment develop?

Even Lewin and his co-authors found that motivation does not always lead to a sufficient plan about how to cope with a defined situation or problem. Sometimes, the motivation is not strong enough to overcome barriers for implementation. In other cases, motivation can be too strong and can interfere with an adequate solution (Heckhausen, 1989, pp. 80-81, 215, 467; Heinrichs, 2005, pp. 154-155). To be in a state of being strongly energized towards solving the constituted problem sometimes means more than being motivationally energized. Moreover, the need for volitional power might arise, a need for processes of cognitive control and self-regulation in order to gain a state of feeling self-committed (Beckmann, 1996, pp. 415-416; Heinrichs, 2005, pp. 157-158). Volitional power might be necessary if there were cognitive, emotional and motivational states geared towards different aims or action plans or that led to a state wherein different action plans were empowered to a similar extent. The agent would only decide to act if he made a decision that he "really wanted to..." reach the aim (Rheinberg, 1995, p.161; Gollwitzer, 1996, p. 54; Sokolowski, 1993, p. 121). In other words, volitional processes, in terms of such an "imperative approach to volition" (pointing to cognitive control processes), support negotiating ambivalent aims and weigh in on an inner soliloquy in order to achieve a state of commitment and form an intention (Heinrichs, 2005, pp.159-160). We could assume that the more the anticipated aims are differing in their strength of motivational power, the more there is a need for volitional processes to balance the different drivers and the more cognitive control is relevant to becoming committed.

Therefore, imperative approaches to volition provide a different perspective on volitional processes than models like the Rubikon model (at least in the early publications; Heckhausen, 1987; proclaiming a sequence of motivational and volitional phases during the process of acting). Referring to an imperative approach to volition, Sokolowski (1996, p. 487; see also Heinrichs, 2005, pp. 96-97; Vollmeyer et al., this volume) emphasizes that if different ways of acting were triggered by cognitive, motivational or emotional power, there would arise a need for self-regulation and coordination. Cognitive control processes might enable a person to reduce an experienced ambivalence between different ways of acting, in order to focus on realizing a certain aim and coming to action. All in all, however, these imperative volitional processes are not assumed to add motivational power in strength. However, volitional processes could support the person to focus one way of action and to bundle the internal drivers towards one particular way of acting. They foster the "will power" to initiate a preferred action and to withstand difficulties on the way to implementation as well. They increase the current state of "readiness" to act (Gollwitzer & Liu, 1996, p. 221; Heinrichs, 2005, p. 97).

Volitional Power - Perspectives for Studying Moral Motivation

How to get committed towards coping with a morally relevant situation in a particular way?

In order to apply these assumptions on volitional power of acting to morally relevant situations, we assume that an action plan could be motivationally empowered by "moral" as well as by "non-moral" motives, for example, by the motive to help (Vollmeyer et al., this volume) or by the justice-motive, on the one hand (Baumert et al., this volume), or by the power-motive, on the other hand (Vollmeyer et al., this volume; Grün, this volume). Even if a person stresses his or her intention to "be good", there could be "non-moral motives" which increase or even decrease the commitment to act in a particular "moral" way (Vollmeyer, in this volume). So, in contrast to Rest's definition of moral motivation, to become committed to a moral way of acting is not precisely described in terms of preferring moral values to non-moral values or preferring the moral way of action to a "non-moral way" (in the sense of internalism attributing a relevant motivational power to the deontic judgment). In applying the terms of the Process Model, we have to distinguish two different cases, as discussed before: first, when – even owing to motivational processes – only one way of acting was triggered by the high motivational power. Second, in contrast, there might evolve cases wherein two ways of acting are motivationally empowered to a similar extent. In the latter cases, the person experiences ambivalence, might feel pushed to different ways of acting and perceive a kind of conflict. Then, besides motivational power volitional and cognitive control processes might play an important role in forming a responsibility judgment in order to form an intention.

Again, referring to Minnameier, he concentrates on the impact of cognitive structures on the way to forming an intention. Based on his approach, it is not possible to explain why a single person would decide for one and not the other way of acting (e.g. in moral conflicts), in cases wherein the individual has already constituted a morally relevant situation and when he or she tried to fulfil the task of moral reasoning. The agent had to decide whether the deontic judgment (the moral principle) should be implemented in this particular situation or whether it would be morally right to accept acting deviantly in this particular situation (see Minnameier, this volume).

In the context of those cases, the Process Model of Acting could help to enlighten deviations by pointing to interactions between cognitive, emotional, motivational or volitional determinants. Assuming that different sources could support motivational power in a morally relevant situation, we could reconstruct that sometimes there might be ambivalence between the preferred way of acting motivationally triggered by the deontic judgment and another way of acting triggered by other, for example, motivational or emotional processes. Then, there might be a need for volition in the sense of an imperative approach. The individual might apply cognitive control processes to deal with this situation and to come to a decision about how to act.

If the agent has constituted a morally relevant situation and intends to solve the moral problem adequately, he or she might deliberate about how to act responsibly and form a moral judgment. Moral reasoning and moral-cognitive structures might mainly contribute to decision-making. If, in contrast, other (non-moral) motives have great motivational impact as well, we could assume that, besides moral reasoning, other cognitive-control strategies influence the decision about how the agent dealt with the experienced ambivalence. Or, maybe cognitive control strategies could be reconstructed as elements of induction, along the lines of Minnameier's inferential theory (Minnameier, this volume). In some cases, the agent might apply disengagement strategies in order to give more space to egoistic motives or self-interest (see Beerthuizen & Brugman, this volume; Weyers, this volume). Furthermore, he or she would give up solving the constituted problem before having formed an intention because he or she does not feel able to solve this problem and to apply volitional strategies adequately. Or, the agent does not stand by the process of forming an intention because there is a lack of motivational power.

To discuss the role of volitional processes in the sense of cognitive control strategies (e.g. justification, disengagement or copying strategies) could also be interesting in a developmental perspective. Maybe those kinds of volitional strategies become more and more differentiated during the lifespan. They might depend on the individual's moral-cognitive structures, but also on the individual's experienced-based moral knowledge or on metacognitive competencies.

In summary, we could imagine that, on the one hand, volitional processes are especially needed to form an intention in cases of ambivalence or when the anticipated ways of action are motivationally powered to a similar extent. These volitional processes lead to the state and determine the strength of being committed to the particular way of acting included in the intention, also in morally relevant situations. In reference to sequence models of volitional psychology (e.g. the Rubikon model, Gollwitzer, 1996), it is additionally assumed that the intention has a great impact on further phases of acting, especially on action planning and conducting. If difficulties evolved to implement the intention during the further phases of action planning and other competing intentions might result (Kuhl, 1987), further volitional processes might help to initiate and conduct behaviour (Gollwitzer & Malzacher, 1996, pp. 438-439). Neither Kohlberg nor. Candee nor Rest have neglected this need for volitional power. Moreover, in the Four Component Model, these processes were considered as challenges for the fourth component, the "moral character" (Rest, 1999, p. 101). In the Process Model of Acting, these latter kinds of volitional processes, relevant during the second and third phase of acting, are reconstructed in detail and also could be applied to moral issues. In this paper, however, the discussion of motivational and volitional power was limited in order to enlighten the impact of moral motivation in the first phase of forming an intention.

CONCLUSION

On a Way to a New Concept of Moral Motivation

Referring to the action-theoretically based discussion about the impact of motivational processes on the way to an intention and to action, finally, it is intended to point to perspectives on how to reach scientific progress in this field owing to content-related, strategic as well as methodological aspects. Thinking about how to conceptualize and investigate moral motivation in future studies, I suggest achieving a more complex imagination about how motivational processes determine acting in morally relevant situations. Therefore, I prefer not to limit our studies to one theoretical or empirical approach to moral motivation. Moreover, it would be fruitful to create research projects grasping motivational processes: (a) from different perspectives, (b) integrating emotional, cognitive or volitional facets or, (c) testing empirically what theoretical approach to motivation could explain more variance of the conducted behaviour.

There is a great chance not to reduce the discussion on moral motivation to research in moral psychology, rather than thinking laterally and taking an interdisciplinary approach. Let us build a bridge between disciplines and schools of research and let us apply results on cognition, motivation, emotions, volition and action in general to moral issues.

Moral psychology in the Tradition of Kohlberg`s approach focuses on the personal determinants of moral judging and acting. There are, however, situational determinants as well which foster or prevent individuals from engaging in moral action, and even the interaction between situational and personal determinants seems to be important to investigate. So, let us explicate in what kinds of situations a particular approach to moral motivation (as well as to moral sensitivity, judgment or action) can be claimed to be valid and let us start investigating moral motivation and acting without neglecting, but rather stressing, context-specific effects.

Additionally, I am convinced that sometimes the approaches within moral psychology stumble over their definitions of even the basic term, "morality". Many concepts in the Kohlbergian tradition use "morality" in terms widely unsharpened, first, from the perspective of the philosopher, who would wonder how the difference between "morality" and "ethics" is represented in terms of moral psychology. Second, it seems to me that we, as moral psychologists, accept the limited scope of the 'moral domain theory, based on its associated results. This could be considered as necessary and fruitful, on the one hand. On the other hand, however, it could also be interesting and supportive of scientific progress to study to what extent the mechanisms of problem solving and decision-making in general differ from the ways that intentions are formed and implemented in morally relevant situations (or owing to special kinds of moral problems). Moreover, the question remains whether we really should try to bond our psychological studies to a particular moral standpoint. Popper's idea of the value freedom of science might help to differentiate: first, we as psychologists might try to explain the important determinants of the process of acting and want to gain knowledge about how acting in morally relevant situations is triggered. Second, we might want to discuss the aims of moral education. The need for committing to particular moral values or moral philosophical standpoints is certainly necessary for evaluating whether a single problem is morally relevant, whether a single behaviour is adequate or not, for developing curricula for moral education or for creating developmental and learning environments to foster moral competence and motivation. If however we are investigating how moral motivation or behaviour develops, we should be careful when tying our psychological explanations to moral philosophical positions (Heinrichs, 2005, pp. 221-231).

Perspectives for Further Research on Moral Motivation

As discussed above, one of the main aims of this book was to collect ideas about how to be precise and sharpen the concept of moral motivation. Conceptual and theoretical progress in this regard is at least a first step but many different questions could follow which should be empirically studied as well. In the following, you will find some interesting research questions:

— How does moral motivation in its character and strength vary between contexts, eliciting situations as well as individuals?
— How does moral motivation develop over the lifespan and in different contexts? (Narvaez, Krettenauer, Walker, Gasser et al., Döring, all this volume) Are there different sensitive phases during the individual's development depending on age, progress in development or contexts?
— What do we think of when we proclaim a lack of moral motivation? How could this motivational lacking be assessed and how could we describe the agents'

personality of those individuals who show this lack of moral motivation? (see Weyers, Gasser et al., Power, Beerthuizen & Brugman, Döring, all this volume)
- How do motivational and volitional processes interact on the way to behaviour?
- How do we foster moral and to prevent immoral behaviour?

Moreover, there will be strategic as well as methodological challenges on the way to studying the questions above or gaining theoretical and empirical scientific progress on moral motivation. To investigate moral motivation as a multi-facetted concept empirically would require bundling resources across institutes, countries, schools of thinking and disciplines and initiating not only small but larger strategically planned projects. I recommend that we should try to foster in the future coordinated research on moral motivation, in the sense of Lakatos's idea of implementing research programs to gain scientific progress systematically without the tendency towards atomization (Heinrichs, 2005, pp. 41-43). So, we could try to test contrasting hypotheses to explain the same phenomena associated with moral motivation (like the happy-victimizer-phenomenon, pro-social behaviour, deviant or aggressive behaviour, moral exemplars, moral identity in professions) (see a project on the happy-victimizer-pattern among adults, Gutzwiller-Helfenfinger et.al, 2012). We could try to explain moral (or immoral) behaviour by including motivational determinants grounded in different theoretical approaches or grasping moral motivation by different measures in order to test what concept or instrument could explain the variance of the independent variable best (see Klöckner, this volume). In a similar way, it could be very interesting to include situational as well as personal drivers of motivation in one study to enlighten their impacts and interactions.

Considering even the open questions in the field of moral motivation mentioned above, it becomes obvious that gaining progress demands complex and costly research designs, longitudinal as well as experimental studies and, especially, projects which grasp behaviour itself and focus not merely on language about or indicators of behaviour.

Moreover, to meet the need for interdisciplinary projects, we are challenged to realize border-crossing successfully. Therefore, we should be prepared for effortful and effective communication and cooperation. The researchers themselves need to be open minded and "ready" to learn the other discipline's "language", to get used to the terms and methods of other schools of research. So, future research on moral motivation, claiming to build a bridge between different approaches and disciplines, points to a great challenge which should not be underestimated for more than practical reasons.

All in all, we could sum up that moral motivation is truly an important emerging field of research. In this book, we present quite different approaches. So now it is time to collaborate and start new projects in order to gain scientific progress systematically. It is up to the reader of this book and to us as researchers to continue to strengthen research in this field. We can be prepared and contribute to knowing more about why people act morally and what we in education can do help people avoid immoral behaviour and, as a result, foster their own positive morality.

NOTES

[1] That means that Rest accepted that motivational and volitional aspects were merged in terms of responsibility and pointed explicitly not only to the third component of motivation, but also to volition as part of moral character.

[2] This idea is coherent with the construct of negative moral experience-based knowledge (Oser, 2005). Moreover, Oser does not only study the role of experiences in a current process of acting, but points out the relevance of negative experiences to moral development. Maybe to perceive injustice and experience the consequences of injustice by your own or a person who is strongly related to you, may lead to developing mental models of morally relevant situations powered by negative emotions which could evolve again if this mental model of the situation will be activated in future settings.

[3] Dörner (1979, pp. 10-11; 13-14) also refers to such situations and calls them "tasks" in contrast to "problems". But in this literature the term "problem" is used differently compared to the process model. "Problems" in the process model include "problems" as well as "tasks" in terms of Dörner's approach. In the process model "problems" additionally include the case the agent has constituted a difference between "is" and "ought", but has not anticipated an appropriate, concrete aim despite of "redressing the difference towards the "ought". Additionally in terms of the process model a problem could emerge if a person had no idea which kind of behaviour would help to reach the aim (Heinrichs, 2005, pp. 145-146).

REFERENCES

Bandura, A. (1991). Social cognitive theory of moral thought and action. In W.M. Kurtines, & J.L. Gewirtz (Eds.) *Handbook of moral behavior and development*, Vol. 1 (pp. 45–103). Hillsdale, NJ: Erlbaum

Bandura, A., Barbaranelli, C., Caprara, G., & Pastorelli, C. (1996). Mechanisms of moral disengagement in the exercise of moral agency. *Journal of Personality and Social Psychology, 71*(2), 364–374

Beck, K. (1998). *Ethische Differenzierung als Grundlage, Aufgabe und Movens Lebenslangen Lernens.* Arbeitspapiere WP, No 15, Mainz: University of Mainz. Retrieved from http://www.wipaed.uni-mainz.de/ls/ArbeitspapiereWP/gr_Nr.15.pdf

Beck, K. (1999). Wirtschaftserziehung und Moralerziehung – ein Widerspruch in sich? Zur Kritik der Kohlbergschen Moralentwicklungstheorie. *Pädagogische Rundschau, 53*, S. 9–28

Beck, K., Heinrichs, K., Minnameier, G., & Parche-Kawik, K. (1999). Homogeneity of moral judgment? - Apprentices Solving Business Conflicts. *Journal of Moral Education, 28*(4), 429–443

Beckmann, J. (1996). Entschlußbildung. In J. Kuhl, J. & H. Heckhausen (Hrsg.). *Motivation, Volition und Handlung* (pp. 411–425). Göttingen et al.: Hogrefe, (Enzyklopädie der Psychologie: Themenbereich C, Theorie und Forschung, Ser.4, Motivation und Emotion; Volume 4).

Blasi, A. (1995). Moral understanding and the moral personality: The process of moral integration. In W.M. Kurtines & J.L. Gewirtz (Eds.), *Moral development: An introduction* (pp. 229–253). Boston: Allyn & Bacon.

Blasi, A. (1982). Kognition, Erkenntnis und das Selbst [Knowledge in social cognition]. In W. Edelstein, & M. Keller (Eds.), *Perspektivität und Interpretation* (pp. 289–319). Frankfurt: Suhrkamp Verlag

Candee, D., & Kohlberg, L. (1987). Moral judgment and moral action: A reanalysis of Haan, Smith and Block's Free Speech Movement Date. *Journal of Personality and Social Psychology, 52,* 554–564

Colby, A., & Damon, W. (1992). *Some do care: Contemporary lives of moral commitment.* New York: The Free Press

Cranach v., M. & Amman, A. (1999). Die Aufnahme der Willensfreiheit und ihre Konsequenzen für die Sozialwissenschaften, *Ethik und Sozialwissenschaften, 10*, 257–270

Dörner, D. (1979). *Problemlösen als Informationsverarbeitungsprozess*, 2. Aufl., Stuttgart et al.: Kohlhammer.

Esser, H. (2001). *Sinn und Kultur.* Frankfurt/Main, New York: Campus (Soziologie, Spezielle Grundlagen; Volume 6)

Esser, H. (1996). Die Definition der Situation. *Kölner Zeitschrift für Soziologie und Sozialpsychologie, 48*, 1–34

Euler, D. (1989). *Kommunikationsfähigkeit und computerunterstütztes Lernen*, Köln: Botermann & Botermann

Fazio, R.H. (1990). Multiple processes by which attitudes guide behavior: The MODE-Modell as an integrative framework. In M.P. Zana (Ed.), *Advances in experimental social psychology* (pp. 55–109). San Diego, London: Academic Press

Gollwitzer, P.M. (1996). Rubikonmodell der handlungsphasen. In J. Kuhl, & H. Heckhauen (Eds.) *Motivation, volition und handlung* (pp. 531–582). Göttingen et al.: Hogrefe (Enzyklopädie der Psychologie. Themenbereich C, Theorie und Forschung, Ser. 4, Motivation und Emotion; Volume 4)

Gollwitzer, P.M. & Malzacher, J. (1996) Absichten und vorsätze. In J. Kuhl, & H. Heckhauen (Eds.) *Motivation, volition und handlung* (pp. 209–240). Göttingen et al.: Hogrefe (Enzyklopädie der Psychologie. Themenbereich C, Theorie und Forschung, Ser. 4, Motivation und Emotion; Volume 4)

Gollwitzer, P.M. & Liu, C. (1996). Wiederaufnahme. In J. Kuhl, & H. Heckhauen (Eds.) *Motivation, volition und handlung* (pp. 209–240). Göttingen et al.: Hogrefe (Enzyklopädie der Psychologie. Themenbereich C, Theorie und Forschung, Ser. 4, Motivation und Emotion; Volume 4)

Haidt, J. (2001). The emotional dog and its rational tail: A social intuitionist approach to moral judgment. *Psychological Review, 108*(4), 814–834

Heckhausen, H. (1989). Motivation und handeln, 2. völlig überarb. u. erg. Aufl., Berlin et al.: Springer

Heckhausen, H. (1987). Perspektiven einer psychologie des wollens In H. Heckhausen, P.M. Gollwitzer, & F.E. Weinert (Eds.), *Jenseits des rubikon* (pp. 143–175). Berlin et al.: Springer.

Heckhausen, H. & Kuhl, J. (1985). From Wishes to Action: The Dead Ends and Short Cuts on the Long Way to Action. In M. Frese & J. Sabini (Hrsg.). *Goal Directed Behavior: The concept of Action in Psychology* (pp. 134–159). Hillsdale: Lawrence Earlbaum

Heinrichs, K. (2010). Urteilen und Handeln in der moralischen Entwicklung. In B. Latzko, & T. Malti (Eds.) *Moralentwicklung und Moralerziehung in Kindheit und Adoleszenz* (pp. 69–86). Göttingen: Hogrefe

Heinrichs, K. (2005). *Urteilen und Handeln. Ein Prozessmodell und seine moralpsychologische Spezifizierung.* Frankfurt/Main et al.: Peter Lang (Konzepte des Lehrens und Lernens; Volume 12)

Heinrichs, K., Minnameier, G., & Beck, K. (2013). Ethical and moral considerations on entrepreneurship education. In S. Weber, F. Oser, & F. Achtenhagen (Eds.), *Entrepreneurship education – Becoming an entrepreneur.* Rotterdam: Sense Publisher.

Hoffman, M.L. (2000). *Empathy and moral development: Implications for caring and justice.* New York: Cambridge University Press

Gollwitzer, P.M. (1996). Rubikonmodell der Handlungsphasen. In J. Kuhl & H. Heckhausen (Eds.). *Motivation, Volition und Handlung.* Enzyklopädie der Psychologie: Themenbereich C, Theorie und Forschung, Ser. 4, Motivation und Emotion, Volume 4 (pp. 531–582). Göttingen et al.: Hogrefe

Gollwitzer, P.M. & Liu, C. (1996). Wiederaufnahme. In J. Kuhl & H. Heckhausen (Eds.). *Motivation, Volition und Handlung.* Enzyklopädie der Psychologie: Themenbereich C, Theorie und Forschung, Ser. 4, Motivation und Emotion, Volume 4 (pp. 427–268). Göttingen et al.: Hogrefe

Gutzwiller-Helfenfinger, E., Gasser, L., & Malti, T. (2010). Moral emotions and moral judgments in children's narratives: Comparing real-life and hypothetical transgressions. In B. Latzko & T. Malti (Eds.), *Children's moral emotions and moral cognition: Developmental and educational perspectives. New Directions for Child and Adolescent Development, 129*, 11–31. San Francisco: Jossey-Bass.

Gutzwiller-Helfenfinger, E., Heinrichs, K., Latzko, B. & Minnameier, G. (2012, June). *Exploring moral motivation: Tracking the happy victimizer into adulthood.* Paper presented at the EARLI SIG13 Conference, Bergen.

Keller, M. (2007). Moralentwicklung und moralische Sozialisation. In Horster, D. (Ed.), *Moralentwicklung von Kindern und Jugendlichen* (pp. 17–49). Wiesbaden: VS Verlag für Sozialwissenschaften

Kohlberg, L. (1986). A current statement on some theoretical issues. In S. Modgil & C. Modgil (Eds.). *Lawrence Kohlberg – Consensus and controversy* (pp. 485–546), Philadelphia, London: Palmer Press

Kohlberg, L., & Candee, D. (1984a). Die Beziehung zwischen moralischem Urteilen und moralischem Handeln. In Kohlberg, L. (1996). *Die Psychologie der Moralentwicklung,* edited by W. Althof, G. Noam and F. Oser (pp. 373–493), Frankfurt/Main: Suhrkamp

Kohlberg, Lawrence/Candee, Daniel (1984b): Die Beziehung zwischen moralischem Urteilen und moralischem Handeln. In D. Garz,, F. Oser & W. Althof (Eds.) (1999). *Moralisches Urteil und Handeln* (pp. 13–46), Frankfurt/Main: Suhrkamp

Kohlberg, L., Levine, C., & Hewer, A. (1984). Zum gegenwärtigen Stand der Theorie der Moralstufen. In L. Kohlberg (1996). *Die Psychologie der Moralentwicklung*, W. Althof (Ed. , unter Mitarbeit von G. Noam, F. Oser) (pp. 217–372). Frankfurt/Main: Suhrkamp

Krapp, A. (1999). Intrinsische Lernmotivation und Interesse - Forschungsansätze und konzeptuelle Überlegungen, *Zeitschrift für Pädagogik, 45*, 387–406

Krebs, D.L., & Denton, K. (2005). Toward a more pragmatic approach to morality: A critical evaluation of Kohlberg's model. *Psychological Review, 112*, 629–649

Krebs, D.L., & Denton, K. (1999). Die Beziehung zwischen dem moralischem Urteilen und dem moralischen Handeln. In D. Garz, F. Oser, & W., Althof (Eds.) *Moralisches Urteilen und Handeln* (pp. 220–263). Frankfurt/Main: Suhrkamp

Krettenauer, T., Malti, T., & Sokol, B. (2008). The development of moral emotion expectancies and the happy victimizer phenomenon: A critical review of theory and application. *European Journal of Developmental Science, 2*, 221–235.

Kuhl, J. (1987). Motivation und Handllungskonttrolle. In H. Heckhausen, P.M. Gollwitzer, & F.E. Weinert (Eds.). *Jenseits des Rubikon* (pp. 101–120). Berlin et al.: Springer

Lapsley, D.K. & Narvaez, D. (2005). Moral psychology at the crossroads. In D.K. Lapsley & F.C. Power (Eds.), *Character psychology and character education* (pp. 18–35). Notre Dame, Louisiana: University of Notre Dame Press

Lakatos, I. (1982). *Die Methodologie der wissenschaftlichen Forschungsprogramme*, translated by A. Szabó, & H. Vetter. Braunschweig, Wiesbaden: Vieweg (Philosophische Schriften: Imre Lakatos, Bd. 1)

Malti, T., & Krettenauer, T. (2011). *The role of moral emotion attributions in children's and adolescents' pro- and antisocial behavior: A meta-analysis*

Malti, T., Gummerum, M., Keller, M., & Buchmann, M. (2009). Children's sympathy and prosocial behavior: The role of moral motivation. *Child Development, 80*, pp. 442–460

Maxwell, B. & Racine, E. (2011). Does research in affective neuroscience justify responsive early childcare ? Examining interwoven ethical and epistemological challenges. *Neuroethics, 4*(3) [DOI : 10.1007/s12152-011-9110-z]Minnameier, G. (2012). A cognitive approach to the "happy victimiser", *Journal of Moral Education* [Doi:10.1080/03057240.2012.700893]

Minnameier, G. (2010). The problem of moral motivation and the Happy Victimizer Phenomenon – Killing two birds with one stone. *New Directions for Child and Adolescent Development, 129*, 55–75.

Modgil, S./Modgil, C. (Hrsg.) (1986). *Lawrence Kohlberg - Consensus and Controversy*. Philadelphia, London: Falmer Press

Narvaez, D. (2009). Triune ethics theory and moral personality. In D. Narvaez & D.K. Lapsley (Eds.), *Personality, identity, and character: Explorations in moral psychology* (pp. 136–158). Cambridge:Cambridge University Press.

Narvaez, D. & Lapsley, D.K. (2005). The psychological foundations of everyday morality and moral expertise. In D.K. Lapsley & F.C. Power (Eds.), *Character psychology and character education* (pp. 140–165). Notre Dame, Louisiana: University of Notre Dame Press

Oser, F. (2005). Negatives Wissen und Moral. In D. Benner (Ed.). *Erziehung - Bildung – Negativität* (pp. 171–181). Weinheim et al.: Beltz

Popper, Karl R. (1994). Ausgangspunkte – Meine intellektuelle Entwicklung, 2. Aufl., Hamburg: Hoffmann und Campe

Rest, J.R. (1999). Die Rolle des moralischen Urteilens im moralischen Handeln. In D. Garz, F. Oser & W. Althof (Hrsg.). Moralisches Urteile und Handeln (pp. 82–116), Frankfurt/Main: Suhrkamp

Rest, J., Narvaez, D., Bebeau, M.J., & Thoma, S.J. (1999). *Postconventional moral thinking: A neo-Kohlbergian approach*. Mahwah, NJ: Lawrence Erlbaum Associates

Smetana, J.G. (2010). Social-Cognitive Domain-Theorie: Consistencies and variations in children's moral and social judgments. In M. Killen & J.G. Smetana (Eds.), *Handbook of moral development* (pp. 119–154). Mahwah, New Jersey: Psychological Press

Sokolowski, K. (1996). Wille und Bewußtsein. In J. Kuhl, & H. Heckhausen (Eds.) *Motivation, Volition und Handlung* (pp. 481–530). Göttingen et al.: Hogrefe (Enzyklopädie der Psychologie. Themenbereich C, Theorie und Forschung, Ser. 4, Motivation und Emotion; Volume 4)

Sokolowski, K. (1993). *Emotion und Volition – eine motivationspsychologische Standortbestimmung.* Göttingen et al.: Hogrefe (Motivationsforschung; Volume 14)

Turiel, E., (1983). *The development of social knowledge: Morality and convention.* Cambridge: Cambridge University Press

Ugazio, G., Lamm, C., & Singer, T. (2012). The role of emotions for moral judgments depends on the type of emotion and moral scenario. *Emotion, 12*(3), 579–590

Walker, L. (2004). Gus in the gap. In D.K. Lapsley, & D. Narvaez, (Eds.), (2004). *Moral development, self, and identity* (pp. 1–20). Mahwah, New Jersey: Lawrence Erlbaum Associates Publishers

AFFILIATION

Karin Heinrichs
Institute of Business Edcuation
Goethe-University,
Frankfurt/Main, Germany

INDEX

CPSIA information can be obtained at www.ICGtesting.com
Printed in the USA
BVOW021844300413

319525BV00004B/66/P